D0457262

RELIGION, MARRIAGE, AND FAMILY

Series Editors

Don S. Browning
John Wall

THE BOOK OF MARRIAGE

*The Wisest Answers
to the Toughest Questions*

Edited by

DANA MACK &
DAVID BLANKENHORN

WILLIAM B. EERDMANS PUBLISHING COMPANY
GRAND RAPIDS, MICHIGAN / CAMBRIDGE, U.K.

© 2001 Wm. B. Eerdmans Publishing Co.
All rights reserved

Wm. B. Eerdmans Publishing Co.
255 Jefferson Ave. S.E., Grand Rapids, Michigan 49503 /
P.O. Box 163, Cambridge CB3 9PU U.K.

Printed in the United States of America

06 05 04 03 02 01   7 6 5 4 3 2 1

Library of Congress Cataloging-in-Publication Data

The book of marriage: the wisest answers to the toughest questions /
    edited by Dana Mack and David Blankenhorn
       p.   cm.
    ISBN 0-8028-3896-0 (cloth: alk. paper)
    1. Marriage — Religious aspects — Christianity.
    I. Mack, Dana.   II. Blankenhorn, David.

    BV835.B65 2001
    306.81 — dc21

                         00-052152

www.eerdmans.com

Contents

CONTENTS

CONTENTS

Acknowledgments

In putting together this volume of readings, we have been lucky to have had the aid of a distinguished scholarly panel from across the academic disciplines. Every member of that panel made valuable suggestions, all of which we hope to have incorporated here. We are particularly indebted to Don Browning, whose University of Chicago research project exploring issues of religion and family has done much to stimulate rich discussion in this area, and we are pleased to include this volume in the Eerdmans series "Religion, Marriage, and Family," which he coedits with John Wall.

But besides these remarkable scholars, we have many people to thank for their contributions of time, energy, and financial support to this project. We are grateful to the Lilly Endowment for its generous support, and to the staff of the Institute for American Values for their time and energy — in particular Josephine Abbatiello, who worked indefatigably to produce a readable manuscript and to maintain the reproduction rights correspondence. We appreciate greatly Nadia Prinz's efforts in helping us track down reproduction rights addressees, as well as the many hours she spent at the copy machine. We are especially beholden to Jon Pott of Eerdmans Publishing for his faith in this book, and his wonderful suggestions for its improvement. And special thanks go to Jon Pott's assistant, Gwen Penning, and our editor, Jennifer Hoffman, for their patience and helpfulness. Finally, we are indebted to Lynne Swanson of the Wilton Library for her tireless help with interlibrary loans, and to Margaret Porter Gregory for her advice, help, and friendship.

We are especially obligated to several people who gave us much needed guidance with regard to the East Asian selections in this book, among them

ACKNOWLEDGMENTS

Maggie Gallagher Srivastov, Professor Charles Laughlin, Professor Scott Sunquist, Professor David Wei, and Professor Wei Shang. And we must not neglect to express our appreciation to the Maryland Society of Jesus and to the General Theological Seminary of New York for the biographical information on the authors J. E. Kerns and Derrick Sherwin Bailey, respectively.

It only remains for us to thank our respective spouses for their constancy, their love, their wisdom, and their faith in the institution of marriage.

DANA MACK
DAVID BLANKENHORN

Why This Book?

The idea for this anthology of source readings on the subject of marriage came up for the first time in 1997 at an Institute for American Values symposium marking the publication of a report entitled *Closed Hearts, Closed Minds: The Textbook Story of Marriage.* The report, authored by University of Texas sociology professor Norval Glenn, examined twenty leading college-level textbooks on marriage and family life, only to find that they were intellectually weak, noncommittal on the value of marriage in contemporary society, and even factually inaccurate.

Many scholars present at the release of the Glenn report pointed up the scarcity today of an intellectually engaging, morally serious, and ideologically balanced pedagogical literature on the subject of marriage and family life. Where, they asked, were books conveying the richness and profundity of human reflections on the institution of marriage? Where were educational materials that explored marriage themes not only through the sociological and psychological lens, but also through the entire variety of disciplines that touch on family life — from literature and history to cultural anthropology, sociology, religion, and the arts? Marriage, they contended, is a social institution of intrinsic intellectual interest. Yet, it wasn't only the academic literature that was unsatisfying. Even the literature produced by the burgeoning marriage preparation movement, it seemed, rarely addressed marriage in its cultural, historical, and spiritual dimensions.

Indeed, the pedagogical literature on marriage, whether for college or high school, for engaged or married couples, whether religious or secular, tends today to address marriage mainly in its psychological dimensions, and specifically in terms of managing the marital relationship. High school marriage skills courses in particular tend to focus on communications skill-building and therapeutic problem solving rather than on the deeper cultural meaning of the institution of marriage.

Worse, to date there is no single comprehensive book of source readings on marriage and family life for the general market — no text that celebrates the diversity and essential humanity of the marital experience in a way that is accessible, entertaining, and useful. The current "trade" literature on marriage can be roughly separated into two mutually exclusive categories: the aesthetic and the utilitarian. On the one side, there are the high-minded pleasure books, like the *Oxford Book of Marriage,* which offer delightful, even profound literary inspiration on the subject of marriage, but little reflection on the history of marriage as a universal social institution, and still less any marital problem-solving advice of value. Then there are the manifold self-help books, which in their narrow emphasis on communication scripts and psychotherapeutic catharsis offer scant literary gratification, and treat the institution of marriage as if it existed in a cultural and historical vacuum.

Aided by an advisory board of noted scholars in the fields of religion, political science, psychology, sociology, law, and classics, we have set out to produce an intellectually rigorous, morally rich, and politically balanced anthology of readings on marriage and family life. Directed to high school juniors and seniors, to college students, to engaged and married couples, as well as to educators, marriage counselors, therapists, pastors, religious leaders, and other family professionals, this book offers historical and contemporary observations on the importance of marriage as a social institution, as well as observations on the fundamentals of marital well-being.

A compendium of cultural wisdom on the subject of marriage, this book is not simply intended as a marriage skills or marriage preparation textbook. As a book of source readings which bridges the gap between the aesthetic and the utilitarian, between the scholarly and the popular, we would hope that it offers moral elevation and food for thought for newlywed couples, and even older married couples who have "been through it all."

Here is the simple organizing principle behind our book. The most vexing problems and challenges that face the marital union today are as old as the institution itself. The big questions of marriage — questions relating to the nature of marital love, to sexual fulfillment, to money management, gender roles, child rearing, mixed marriage, marital conflict, the death of a spouse, and even divorce, are questions that theologians, poets, philosophers, and playwrights have addressed from the beginning of history. They are questions that have been pondered for hundreds of years by literati, anthropologists, psychologists, jurists, and sociologists. In many areas, in fact, the widely accepted, so-called "modern" answers to the quandaries that face married couples day in and day out are not modern answers at all. They are as old as the beginnings of culture. Yet, some modern perspectives on married life did clearly evolve over time. In choosing readings for each chapter, what we have primarily sought to do is to represent several different spiritual and intellectual perspectives on a question across time and cultures — always with the object of enabling readers to better understand how contemporary perspectives of married life emerge from a cultural-historical tradition.

Our aim, then, has been to gather into one volume a cross-cultural selection of some of the deepest, wittiest, and most edifying and influential reflections on the great questions of marriage — questions every man or woman bent on marrying, as well as every husband and wife, are bound to ask themselves at one time or another. Yet, any anthology of source readings on the subject of marriage must focus on marriage not only as a set of personal challenges but also as a purposeful social institution. Thus, we have endeavored in each chapter to balance narratives delving into the interpersonal dynamics of the marital relationship with reflections on the marital ideal.

The core of our readings on marriage as an ideal explore the theology of marriage from the greatest Western scriptural writings (Bible, Talmud, and Qur'an) through the most prominent Western religious thinkers on marriage: Augustine, Aquinas, Maimonides, Luther, Milton, and D. S. Bailey. Why this interest in the theology of marriage? Until relatively recently, religion was the preeminent influence on the ideals governing marriage and the marital relationship in Western society. Only little more than a century ago, marriage was still viewed even in the widest reaches of society as a sacred covenant, a union of higher spiritual and moral purpose which could not be dissolved without serious justification.

Of course, in the past century our society's take on marriage as an institution has drastically altered. With the exception of a few religious thinkers, contemporary discourse tends to reflect the view that marriage is less a spiritual covenant than a simple legal and economic agreement — entered on for the good of society, perhaps, but less for spiritual purposes than for material and natural purposes.

While the secularization of marriage has created opportunities for higher marital satisfaction, as well as enabling easier release from unhappy unions, it has brought with it a serious problematic: the increasing absence of an important cultural support for marriage as a lifelong commitment. Indeed, in an age of secularization, individuation, and consequent shrinking social supports for marriage, how do couples meet the many challenges a marriage deals out?

What marital ideal can they grasp hold of when things are tough? This is a subject on which many great modern thinkers have reflected, and our anthology includes the work of such seminal twentieth-century thinkers on the future of the marital ideal as Isak Dinesen, G. B. Shaw, Edward Westermarck, and Bertrand Russell.

So much for the marital ideal. . . . Where the dynamics of the spousal relationship are concerned, we have found a number of wise old ruminations: from *Medea* to Chaucer's "The Wife of Bath"; from the *Odyssey* to *Othello*. And modern writers have also offered insights into the great personal challenges of even the best unions. Some very rich ruminations on the marital relationship included in our anthology come from contemporaries: among them, Bill Cosby, Molly Haskell, and John Bayley.

What we have tried to achieve with our collection of readings is a book that will provoke lively discussion in a counseling session or a family studies classroom, but will also stimulate thought in a reading chair. We hope readers find it interesting and challenging and that they derive from it a sense of the great historical, social, and cultural import of the marital bond. We hope it instills in them a sharper appreciation of the possibilities of marriage for personal fulfillment, as well as a sense of marriage as a pro-social, organic, and indispensable cultural instituion. Finally, we hope that readers come away with the feeling that in marrying, they are doing something very big; they are not only taking on the dignities of a noble institution but are assuming responsibility for another life as close to theirs as another life can be.

It is our firm belief that a successful marriage is in a real sense the finishing school of civic education. Through marriage, after all, we can learn the true meaning of community, of tolerance, of mutual understanding, of responsibility, and of spiritual cultivation — all of the things that make for the kind of society in which the good life is accessible to all.

DANA MACK
DAVID BLANKENHORN

What Is Marriage?
An Exploration   DON BROWNING

What is marriage? Modern society is having great difficulty in answering this question. Its inability to advance robust cultural and intellectual justifications for marriage has led to various efforts to enhance marriage on other grounds. These efforts are important and should be celebrated. But without deeper justifications that are accepted by the general public, they will have limited success in strengthening marriage. For instance, we have learned much about what constitutes good marital communication.[1] But this knowledge does not itself constitute a reason for marriage; it simply increases chances for achieving a good one for those already committed to that goal. More recently, we have gained strong evidence that marriage is good for one's mental and physical health, sex life, and bank account.[2] This too enhances the attractiveness of marriage, but it does not define what it is nor distinguish it from other healthy activities such as jogging, taking vitamins, or getting eight hours of sleep each night. The emerging marriage movement has new confidence that marriage is both good and achievable but has not confronted the truth that neither of these insights constitutes a definition of what marriage is.

The many justifications for marriage advanced through the ages can be organized along a continuum between its communal and personal dimensions. The march of history increasingly has subordinated the communal and elevated the personal. The idea of marriage as an institution has lost favor. More and more, marriage is viewed as an essentially private intersubjective agreement or "pure relationship" only incidentally sanctioned by state or church, if at all. In what follows, I will argue that marriage historically has consisted of five dimensions, all of which are essential for an adequate understanding of it as both an institution and a living human reality. Marriage has been understood as consisting of natural, contractual, social, religious, and communicative dimensions.[3] However important its personal dimensions, marriage in the past has been defined primarily as a social institution. Because of the important individual and social goods connected with marriage or marriage-like arrangements, the state is likely in the future to circumscribe such arrangements with institutional and legal stipulations. And this will be so with or without the personal consent of the persons involved.

The meaning of each of these five dimensions has varied over time. Which dimension was viewed as central and which as more peripheral also has shifted from period to period. It is difficult to ignore any one of these five elements without doing violence to the meaning of marriage.

Marriage as Organizing Natural Inclinations

To say that marriage has been perceived as a natural institution means it has been viewed as giving form to persistent yet sometimes conflicting natural inclinations and needs. Marriage is not a direct product of our instincts and needs, but it does organize a wide range of our natural human tendencies, elevating some and de-emphasizing others. A spectrum of natural inclinations are ordered by marriage — the desire for sexual union; the desire that Aristotle believed humans share with the animals "to leave behind them a copy of themselves";[4] and, following Aristotle again, the need to "supply" humans with their "everyday wants."[5] These perspectives on the natural purposes of marriage from Greek philosophy were absorbed into Christian commentary on Genesis 1 and 2, especially the writings of Thomas Aquinas. Genesis tells humans to "be fruitful and multiply" (Gen. 1:28). It also teaches that humans were made for companionship: "It is not good for man to be alone" (Gen. 2:18). For these reasons marriage was created: "Therefore a man leaves his father and his mother and clings to his wife, and they become one flesh" (Gen. 2:24).

At least from the time of Thomas Aquinas (1225-1274) — the great synthesizer of Aristotelian philosophy with the Judeo-Christian tradition — marriage often has been justified on two grounds, one drawn from the Jewish doctrine of creation and the other from the naturalism of Aristotle.[6] It is true that within the hands of Christian theologians, the Jewish and Christian theologies of creation provided the deeper context surrounding Aristotelian naturalism. But — and this is the point — Aquinas crystallized what had been gradually developing for centuries, i.e., a double language — one religious and one philosophical and naturalistic — used to justify marriage.

For purposes of developing a public philosophy, it is better to handle Genesis and the double language used to interpret it as "classics" rather than as divine revelation — a status for these texts that confessing religious groups, of course, have every right to assert.[7] These texts and the history of commentary on them are classics in that they have in fact decisively shaped Western marriage theory and because they have been perceived as containers of truths that have repeatedly enlightened and enriched the cultural consciousness.

In much of the Western tradition, the philosophical language used to justify marriage was considered vital for clarification of the religious language. One can see this in perspectives as disparate as those of Thomas Aquinas, John Locke, and the Roman Catholic marriage encyclicals of Pope Leo XIII.[8] All three developed an argument for the institution of marriage similar to one first put forth by Aquinas. Matrimony, he taught, is the joining of the father to the mother-infant relation because of the long period of dependency of the human infant and child — a dependency so extended as to require the material and educational labors over a long period of both of its procreators.[9] Locke wrote with special reference to humans that, "the Father, Who is bound to take care for those he hath begot, is under an Obligation to continue in Conjugal Society with the same Woman longer than other Creatures."[10]

The existence and importance of this double language about marriage is a point generally lost on fundamentalist Christians, much of the general public, and many leading intellectuals, all of whom seem to believe that marriage is a uniquely religious and even distinctively Christian practice. This is not true. Although I have illustrated its philosophical and naturalistic dimensions by referring to Aristotle and Locke, I could have done much the same by turning to Roman law. Buddhism, of course, is one of the purest examples of a nonreligious justification; marriage is practiced and respected by its adherents as natural and useful. But marriage has no religious meaning in Buddhism and is seen as secondary, and at best only transitional, to higher states of philosophical detachment.

Marriage as Contract

Because of the great natural goods — affective, sexual, procreative, and economic — involved in marriage, it has been seen for centuries in many cultures as requiring the regulation of contracts. But the parties involved in the contracts have varied over time. In ancient societies, the contracts were viewed as primarily between the families or clans of the husband and wife, with little if any reinforcement from king or prince. They involved agreements about such things as dowry and bride price, both generally seen according to Jack Goody as kinds of endowments for the wife.[11] When tribe and clan are the chief authorities in a society, redress for broken contracts takes the form of unmediated negotiations or revenge. In medieval Europe, marital contracts were activated by the free consent of husband and wife; they required no witness by either family, church, or state. The free consent alone, however, put into effect the stipulations of the codes of Roman Catholic canon law — an amalgamation of Christian teachings with Roman and German legal traditions.[12] These privately established contracts elevated the role of mutual consent between husband and wife, weakened the power of extended family, and strengthened the power of the church. They also gave rise to the phenomenon of "clandestine" or "secret" marriages — unwitnessed marriages that were either fraudulent or disputed.[13]

Marital contracts became fully public only in the Protestant Reformation when marriage became defined as first a social institution requiring registration and legitimation by the state and only later needing the blessing and confirmation of the church. The mutual consent of the couple, the confirmation by family and friends, the registration before the state, and the blessings of the church were viewed as an orchestrated whole, all of which were deemed important for the establishment of a valid and lasting marital contract. All of these witnesses and legitimating voices turned the marriage contract virtually into a covenant. But I will say more about this later. The establishment of marriage as a public contract in the countries influenced by the theological and legal scholars of the Reformation gradually brought to an end the practices and confusions of clandestine marriage.[14] And a view of the public nature of the marital contract held sway until the Enlightenment evolved an understanding of marriage as private agreement, a "pure relation" independent of either public contract or the constraints of nature.[15]

Marriage as a Social Good

Marriage has generally been seen as a social good. The health of marriage and family, especially in its child-rearing capacities, often has been seen as essential for the good of the larger society. Without marriage and strong families, Aristotle believed, children would grow up violent and the wider social fabric would be damaged. He taught that affection between children and invested natural parents inhibits the violent impulses of both adult and child. These restraining functions would decline, he predicted, with the weakening of families consisting of stable and committed parents.[16] The Lutheran Reformation, however, gave us the most emphatic statement of the social view of marriage. Marriage, Luther taught, was not a sacrament for salvation but an institution given by God at the foundations of creation for the good of couples, children, society, state, schools, and common social life.[17]

One of the clearest manifestations of the social view of marriage was in the Anglican commonwealth model that developed in England from the sixteenth to the late nineteenth century. John Witte tells us that this view absorbed the Reformation idea of the social good of marriage but extended it to include the ideal of an organic continuity and reinforcement between married couple, the wider family, church, and state — all for the common good.[18] This idea was first presented in hierarchical and patriarchal terms that emphasized a seamless line of authority flowing downward from king to priest, father, wife, and children. The commonwealth model of marriage gradually became more egalitarian, utilitarian, and secular in the thought of Locke and John Stuart Mill; but the idea that marriage was good for the social whole was constant throughout.[19] The belief that marriage is a social good and therefore a legitimate concern of the state lies behind the 1998 green paper on family and marriage issued by the Labor government in England,[20] the interest in marriage education in Australia,[21] and the moves into marriage preparation in Florida, Louisiana, and Arizona. The mass of legal codes governing marriage and family in the fifty states is also a sign of the long-standing belief that marriage deals with profound goods that must be monitored and ordered for the public good.

Marriage as Religious: Sacrament and Covenant

Although marriage has been seen as organizing natural yet conflicting desires, as requiring contracts, and as serving the public good, it also has been seen as a profoundly religious reality. Because of the dominance in the West of the religious view of marriage, this often blinds the faithful to its natural, contractual, and social dimensions. Nonetheless, it is true that the first two chapters of Genesis and their theologies of creation have been foundational for views of marriage in Judaism, Islam, and Christianity, as well as for the culture and law in the societies they have influenced. These texts establish marriage as an "order of creation" that expresses the will of God for all humankind. This order is preserved and enhanced through covenant promises between God and humans and between God and husband, wife, their families, and the wider community. As Leo Perdue points out, covenant in ancient Israel was simultaneously a religious, political, and familial concept.[22] The meaning of history, the rule of the king, and the order of marriage and household were all measured and given meaning by covenant faithfulness. The analogy between God's faithfulness to

Israel and Hosea's faithfulness to his wife Gomer has provided an archetypal pattern for marital commitment wherever Judaism, Islam, and Christianity have spread. It has elevated marriage to the status of recapitulating the dynamics of the divine life within the marital relation itself.

As an order of creation, marriage conceived as covenant was not itself viewed as a source of salvation, especially for Reformation Protestantism. On the other hand, marriage conceived as a sacrament in medieval Roman Catholicism *was* viewed as a source of supernatural grace and a vehicle for salvation.[23] Both covenantal and sacramental views drape marriage with a royal robe of divine seriousness and approval. Furthermore, they do not necessarily exclude each other or push aside the natural, contractual, or social views of marriage. Catholic sacramental views assume and build on covenantal views. In addition, Aquinas organically linked his appropriation of Aristotelian naturalism to his sacramental theory. For instance, since his naturalism suggested that infant dependency required a long period of commitment from both mother and father, Aquinas assured this commitment by making marriage an unbreakable sacrament. His view of infant and childhood dependency and his understanding of the fragility of male paternal investment led him to view marriage as permanent. His sacramentalism functioned to compensate for his naturalistic theory of the tentativeness of male commitment to their offspring.[24] Naturalistic understandings of the desires and needs organized and satisfied by marriage also appear in the thought of Luther and Calvin. And both covenant and sacrament went hand-in-hand with the idea of contract, strengthening and deepening the promises and agreements, both public and private, that marriage entails.

A public philosophy of marriage cannot be ruled directly by religious ideas of creation, covenant, and sacrament. But it must, nonetheless, understand our society's indebtedness to what these concepts did to form Western marriage. A public philosophy of marriage must take a generous and supportive attitude toward how these great ideas worked in communities of faith and shaped both secular law and wider cultural sensibilities. Furthermore, it should allow these ideas to sensitize public debate on how the deep experiences of marriage tend to call forth the kind of transcendent aspirations generally associated with religion. Whether it is the deep metaphors of covenant as in Judaism, Islam, and Reformed Protestantism; sacrament as in Roman Catholicism or Eastern Orthodoxy; the yin and yang of Confucianism; the quasi-sacramentalism of Hinduism; or the mysticism often associated with allegedly modern romantic love, humans tend to find values in marriage that call them beyond the mundane and everyday. Faith communities must cherish their religious perspectives on marriage, constantly reinterpret them, yet understand how they can fit with the naturalistic, contractual, and social perspectives outlined above. Religious perspectives will function most powerfully in our society when they serve to frame, not necessarily compete with, these other perspectives. The language of covenant and sacrament should not try to rule the entire field of social discourse about marriage and family, but it should inform them.

Marriage as Communicative Reality

There is a growing belief that marriage is a communicative reality between equals. But this idea has a history. The idea that marriage is for *mutual* comfort and assistance runs throughout the history of various discourses.[25] The canon law view of contract assumed the personhood and autonomy of the consenting husband and wife. In early Christianity the command to love your neighbor as yourself (what I have called a love ethic of equal regard) is taken directly into the inner dynamics of the husband-wife relationship; the famous marriage passages of Ephesians tell us that "husbands should love their wives as they do their own bodies" (Eph. 5:28). Aristotle saw marriage as a kind of friendship, although one in which the male had the higher honor.[26] Stoics such as Musonius Rufus took additional steps toward viewing marriage as a union of equals.[27] Early Christianity went further still. Judaism, Christianity, and Islam all depended on the Genesis accounts of creation that portrayed both male and female as made in the image of God (Gen. 1:27). But, for the most part, it is not until the mid-twentieth century that the social conditions necessary for the realization of this long history of the idea of marital mutuality began to fall into place.

Furthermore, in a variety of places as different as the writings of Pope John Paul II and those of some secular feminists, the theoretical grounds appeared for balancing the personal and unitive aspects of marriage *with* the procreative and material.[28] In much contemporary Protestant and Roman Catholic theology, the personal and unitive aspects of marriage are considered as fully important, in both theory and evolving practice, as the procreative and educational aspects of this institution — a significant shift from earlier formulations.

As marriage evolves toward higher levels of economic, educational, and political equality between husband and wife, the demands for communicative competence between equal partners accelerate. It is one thing to proclaim an ethic of equal regard between friends, neighbors, and strangers, as was done in the Golden Rule and stated philosophically by Kant and others. It is another step to bring this abstract principle into the inner precincts of marriage, as happened in early Christianity and Stoic philosophy. But it is another thing still to develop the communicative and intersubjective skills to implement this ethic in the countless small decisions of everyday life between husband and wife. This is the promise of marriage education. The skills of marriage education are real and profound. The founders of this movement — from Rogers and Buber to Hendrix, Markman, Stanley, Olson, and Gottman — have made real progress and major contributions.

But the marriage education movement is split between two alternative ethics that it has not clarified. One ethic follows the model of exchange typical of market economics; it sees marriage communication in analogy to a business negotiation. Knowing what you want, how to communicate it, and listening to the other is what it takes to strike a decent marital bargain. The alternative ethic is the ethic of equal regard, based on the principle of neighbor love and the Golden Rule, and grounded on respect for the other as an end and never as a means only.[29] If marriage education is built on this latter historic ethic, it will provide the communicative skills to implement intersubjectively the core ethical insights of the Western tradition. Marriage education should develop its guiding ethic and understanding of marriage in dialogue with the classic sources that have shaped marriage as an institution in the West. It should contribute to the continued enhancement of the personal and unitive aspects of marriage, but it should include as well the wider set of values I discussed under the natural, contractual, social, and religious dimensions of the institution of marriage. That is, it should continue to promote and serve marriage as a public institution.

The Use and Abuse of Marriage as a Public Institution

Marriage as a public institution, sanctioned by law, in service to the common good, and blessed by religion, must protect its private, personal, and intersubjective dimensions. Furthermore, we must never forget its procreative and educational functions. Not all persons will use marriage to balance the values of personal love, having and educating children, and the increase of the social good. Some couples — due to intention, inability, accident, age, or other interruptions — will not have children. But the cultural, legal, and religious definitions of marriage must retain procreation as one of its central values. In spite of the fact that some people who purchase automobiles seldom drive them, own them primarily for ostentation, or use them mainly on the back streets of small villages or for sightseeing in restricted venues, the cultural and statutory regulations of owning and operating a car are built on the necessary competence and safety required for its heavy use in busy traffic. So it must be with marriage. It is beyond the capacity of law or society to monitor all the ways people might use it. But its explicit cultural, legal, and religious responsibilities and entitlements must continue to honor all of its historic dimensions, including the task of bonding parents to their children and to each other. Among its many functions and dimensions, the procreation and education of children give marriage as an institution much of its special character.

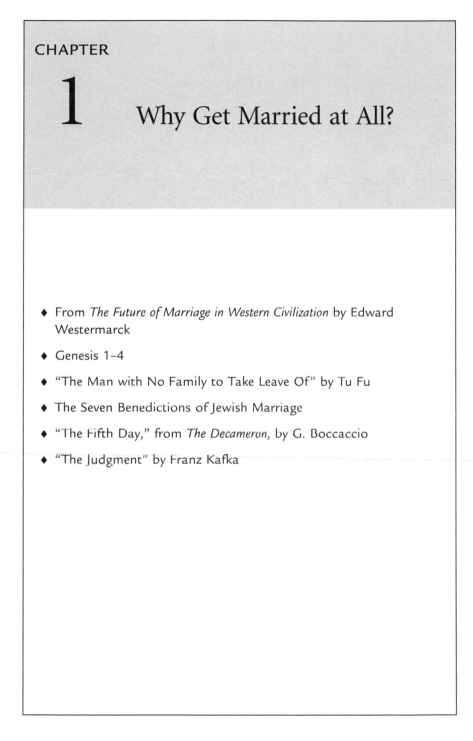

CHAPTER

1 Why Get Married at All?

- From *The Future of Marriage in Western Civilization* by Edward Westermarck

- Genesis 1–4

- "The Man with No Family to Take Leave Of" by Tu Fu

- The Seven Benedictions of Jewish Marriage

- "The Fifth Day," from *The Decameron,* by G. Boccaccio

- "The Judgment" by Franz Kafka

Being asked whether it was better to marry or not, [Socrates]
replied, "Whichever you do you will repent it."

— DIOGENES LAERTIUS, *Socrates*

Marriage has many pains, but celibacy has few pleasures.

— SAMUEL JOHNSON

Introduction

Fully a third of American children are born out of wedlock today. More and more young people choose not to marry. Is marriage going out of style? Hardly. Surveys show that approximately 90 percent of Americans marry at least once, and 85 percent of Europeans still marry. In technologically advanced societies, it is true, marriage is not as vital to survival as it once was. Yet, the yearning to marry is still strong. Indeed, it may be basic to human nature.

As the first selection of our book shows, marriage is a universal institution as old as culture itself. It has its roots in the mating patterns of primates. Among the apes, males typically remain with females after impregnation in order to help the females rear and protect the young. This nuclear family remains the basis for their larger social groupings.

Human mating patterns have, of course, differentiated themselves from the mating patterns of other primates in that, as Edward Westermarck observes, they involve not just "social habits" but "true customs" embedded in cultural ceremony. That is, mating assumes a formal institutional shape. That formal institutional shape — referred to as marriage — has been long recognized in literate societies by law. But even among preliterate peoples, the paternal duties associated with marriage — namely, the expectation that the male will care for his mate and provide for his offspring — have become consciously recognized social and moral obligations.

Westermarck asserts that from an anthropological standpoint "marriage is rooted in the family rather than the family in marriage." Yet, the marital union has come to satisfy social, cultural, and personal functions far beyond its original function with regard to the survival and propagation of the species. While marriage presupposes sexual union and procreation, and while it supports the human procreative endeavor, it is much more than merely a child-rearing bond. In certain cultures — particularly in the Judeo-Christian Western tradition — it remains the single sanctioned outlet for sexual desire, an institution formed for the purpose of disciplining the sexual passions. As Westermarck and the readings following his show, in many cultures marriage ideally involves romantic attachment and affection. It promises not only mutual care and provision throughout life, but true intellectual and spiritual companionship.

Westermarck's anthropological analysis of the origins and fundamental elements of marriage centers on the three major functions of marriage: sexual release, child rearing, and companionship. The last, which Westermarck aptly terms "community of life," is an especially important component of the Western marital ideal.

Perhaps there is no more powerful narrative of marital "community of life" than the creation narrative of the Bible, which reminds us that we are made for coupling ("Male and female He created them"). Adam and Eve, the first married couple, may very well have known community of life before they even knew sexual attraction to one another. The Bible story relates that God created Eve from Adam's rib because among "all the wild beasts . . . for Adam no fitting helper was found." Thus, Scripture stresses the similarities of men and women far more than their differences. Indeed, upon gazing on Eve for the first time, Adam is prompted to say, "This is now bone of my bones and flesh of my flesh." He identifies completely with her, not as an 'other' but as a creature almost exactly like himself. No doubt, of course, is cast on the ultimate meaning of Eve's sexual differences from Adam. But even these differences are hardly meant to separate Adam and Eve. Rather, it is clear from the Scriptures that Adam and Eve have been given different sexual equipment so that they will be drawn together in physical union. This union, it should be noted, is not something temporary, but permanent. As Scripture tells us, "Therefore shall a man leave his father and mother and shall cleave unto his wife, and they shall be one flesh."

Adam and Eve's community of life is from the beginning expressed in an unbroken longing for union of purpose. When Eve discovers that the forbidden fruit is a source of wisdom, she cannot wait to share it with Adam. Adam eats of it, presumably without much contemplation. Don't good husbands always do what their wives tell them to do? One must wonder whether the punishment for Adam and Eve's defiance of God's commandment does not seal their marital union in a far profounder way than ever before. Joined in sin, punished jointly, they are consigned to endure all the pleasures of married life in the knowledge that these pleasures will forever after be linked with suffering. Eve is made to bear children in pain, and is consigned to be ruled over by her husband. Adam is forced, as family provider, to toil the land by the sweat of his brow. Divided in their labors, individuated in a way they have not been before, they nevertheless continue to pursue a community of life. Together they will know both success and failure as parents. Their oldest child will turn murderer, their second child will be the murderer's victim. But through all this strife, Adam and Eve will remain together. More than that. Perhaps their strife brings them closer together. Out of their ever-renewed physical union, they will even replace a child they have lost.

The story of Adam and Eve is the seminal Western narrative of marriage. It touches on the fundamental importance of the institution to the course of each individual human life. Of course, Eastern literature has hardly been silent on the importance of marriage. The selection that follows the story of Adam and Eve is a poem by the great medieval Chinese poet, Tu Fu. Titled "The Man with No Family to Take Leave Of," it concerns a soldier-drummer who feels aimless and worthless because he hasn't yet found a wife. Left to "shoulder the hoe alone," he must go to war without so much as a loving good-bye from a wife and children to shore up his spirits. Because he has no family of his own, the "Man with No Family to Take Leave Of" is forced to question his very humanity.

While the sexual and companionate aspects of marriage are very important, marriage is more than pair bonding. Marriage is a formal social compact. What can that compact provide the individual that cannot be duplicated by a less formal pairing? Our last three readings, from the Jewish liturgy, from the Renaissance author Boccaccio, and from Franz Kafka, give us three distinct perspectives on the unique endowments of marriage. The first involves the spiritual meaning of marriage; the second involves the office of marriage in the preservation and enrichment of family and communal ties; the third involves the place of marriage in the larger scheme of life, as the psychological mark of adulthood.

Both the act of marriage and the special recognition society accords the institution of marriage enrich the individual's spiritual life, linking him to both the foundations and the future of all existence. Take the betrothal blessings and seven benedictions from the Jewish wedding ceremony: Recited at every Jewish wedding, these blessings affirm the joys of sexual union and childbearing, and link the formation of family inextricably with the miracle of creation. They reinforce the notion of conjugal love as a major source of spiritual fulfillment, celebrating it as an opportunity to participate in the holy act of creation. Finally, they exalt conjugal friendship as a model for the brotherhood of man — as an indispensable step toward the coming of the Messiah and the redemption of humanity.

Boccaccio's charming tale, one of impatient lovers caught in the act, touches on the importance of sound mate selection for the perpetuation of extended family and communal ties. A man may "leave his father and mother" to "cleave to his wife," but marriage involves much more than a union of two. It involves a union of families. Thus, in making a marriage, men and women must consider not only their own feelings, but also the desires of their families. Messer da Valbona seems the model of understanding when he finds his daughter in bed with her lover. But this all too generous posture toward sexual indiscretion has far more to do with the exalted social position of the boy and his eminent suitability as a husband than it has to do with any compassion da Valbona might feel for the urgencies of young love. Good marriage arrangements, Boccaccio seems to say, require more than simply an appreciation for the sexual drives of young people. Just because two people hear the call of "the nightingale" does not mean nature has heralded a decent marriage. Rather a good marriage is the product also of sound socio-economic considerations. A good marriage requires two people enough suited to each other in taste, education, and social class to establish a harmonious environment for the rearing of children and the fulfillment of the obligations they owe to their families and communities of origin.

Kafka's story "The Judgment" touches on some of the deepest psychological conflicts we face in the decision to marry. In becoming engaged, Georg is aware that he embarks on a joyous, life-affirming journey, a journey of love and begetting. But he is just as aware that this journey creates a rift between him and an old school friend, who has come upon hard times. Marriage likewise forces Georg's separation from his frail, elderly father. Georg, in short, is afraid to leave home. Consumed by guilt over the good fortune of his love, manipulated by his needy father, Georg ultimately ends up the victim of his own apprehensions. "The Judgment" points up questions all of us must face at one time or another: How long do we intend to wait for marriage? When and under what conditions must we separate from our parents? And what price might we pay for indulging too much our often-childish fears about the marital commitment? In Kafka's story, the price is life itself.

EDWARD WESTERMARCK

Moral philosopher and anthropologist Edward Alexander Westermarck (d. 1939) was born in Finland in 1862. His most important work was the ground-breaking three-volume *The History of Human Marriage,* a brilliant and exhaustive compilation and analysis of marriage customs and mores. In *The Future of Marriage in Western Civilization,* first published in 1936, Westermarck drew on his extensive knowledge of non-Western cultures, and incorporated the most recent social science findings on Western marriage to argue the survival of marriage as a primary sociocultural institution. The reader will undoubtedly notice that even in 1936, arguments for or against the "perpetuity" of marriage as an institution were politically charged. More conservative scholars defended marriage as fundamental to human culture. Many socialist thinkers, on the other hand, saw it as an artificial institution, which might, as society advanced, entirely disappear.

The Future of Marriage in Western Civilization

In my *History of Human Marriage* I laid down the rule that we can postulate the ancient prevalence of certain phenomena only if we find out their causes and may assume that the latter have operated in the past without being checked by other causes. So also we can predict future occurrences, with some hope of success, only if we may assume that the causes of such occurrences will operate without being checked by other causes.

This is the method which I am going to apply to my inquiry in this book. I shall deal with various aspects of marriage as they exist today, and by examining their causes try to find an answer to the question whether they are likely to survive or to undergo a change. Many of those causes cannot be properly understood without a knowledge of the past. Hence I shall repeatedly have to fall back upon my earlier researches in the history of marriage, when pondering over its future.

I. The Meaning and Origin of Marriage

In the earlier editions of my *History of Human Marriage* I defined marriage as "a more or less durable connection between male and female, lasting beyond the mere act of propagation till after the birth of the offspring." This definition has been much criticized, and not without reason. We do not say that a man and a woman are married simply because they live together, have a child together, and remain together after its birth; and on the other hand, there are married couples who get no children at all.

In the ordinary sense of the term, marriage is a social institution which may be defined as a relation of one or more men to one or more women that is recognized by custom or law, and involves certain rights and duties both in the case of the parties entering the union and in the case of the children born of it. These rights and duties vary among different peoples and cannot, therefore, all be included in a general definition; but there must, of course, be something that they have in common. Marriage always implies the right of sexual intercourse: society holds such intercourse allowable in the case of husband and wife, and, generally speaking, regards it as their duty to gratify in some measure the other partner's desire. But the right to sexual intercourse is not necessarily exclusive: there are polyandrous, polygynous, and group-marriages, and even where monogamy is the only legal form of marriage, adultery committed by the husband is not always recognized as a ground for dissolving the union.

The sexual side of marriage is nearly always combined with the living together of husband and wife; a mediaeval adage says, "Boire, manger, coucher ensemble est mariage, ce me semble."[1] Marriage is also an economic institution, which may in various ways affect the proprietary rights of the parties. Since ancient times it has been the husband's duty, so far as it is possible and necessary, to support his wife and children; but it may also be their duty to work for him. Even the Russian Soviet law, which does not compel either spouse to follow the other if the latter changes residence, recognizes the economic aspect of marriage by prescribing that the husband shall support his wife and the wife her husband in case the other party is necessitous and unable to work.[2]

As a rule, the husband has some power over his wife and children, although his power over the children is in most cases of limited duration. Very often marriage determines the place that a newly born individual is to take in the social structure of the community to which he or she belongs; but this can scarcely, as has sometimes been alleged,[3] be regarded as the chief and primary function of marriage, considering how frequently illegitimate children are treated exactly like legitimate ones with regard to descent, inheritance, and succession. It is, finally, necessary that the union, to be recognized as a marriage, should be concluded in accordance with the rules laid down by custom or law, whatever these rules may be. They may require the consent of the parties themselves or of their parents, or of both the parties and their parents. They may compel the man to give some consideration for his bride, or the parents of the latter to provide her with a dowry. They may prescribe the performance of a particular marriage ceremony of one kind or other. And no man and woman are regarded as husband and wife unless the conditions stipulated by custom or law are complied with.

In the present treatise I shall throughout use the term "marriage" in its conventional sense, as the name for a social institution sanctioned by custom or law. At the same time I maintain that my earlier definition had a deep biological foundation, as applying to a relation which exists among many species of animals as well as in mankind. I am of opinion that the institution of marriage has most probably developed out of a primeval habit: that even in primitive times it was the habit for a man and a woman, or several women, to live together, to have sexual relations with each other, and to rear their offspring in common, the man being the guardian of the family and the woman his helpmate and the nurse of their children. This habit was sanctioned by custom, and afterwards by law, and was thus transformed into a social institution.

Similar habits are found among many species of the animal kingdom, in which male and female remain together not only during the pairing season but till after the birth of the offspring. We may assume that the male is induced to stay with the female so long, even after the sexual relations have ceased, by an instinct which has been acquired through the process of natural selection, because it has a tendency to preserve the next generation and thereby the species. This is indicated by the fact that in such cases he not only stays with the female and young, but also takes care of them. Marital and paternal instincts, like maternal affection, seem to be necessary for the existence of certain species. This is the case with birds; among the large majority of them male and female keep together after the breeding season, and in very many species the parental instinct has reached a high degree of intensity on the father's side as well as on the mother's. Among mammals the young cannot do without their mother, who is consequently ardently concerned for their welfare, but in most of them the rela-

21

tions between the sexes are restricted to the pairing season. Yet there are also various species in which they are of a more durable character, and the male acts as a guardian of the family; indeed I have found that those species are considerably more numerous than I was aware of at the time when I first set forth my theory.[4] To them belong the apes. According to most earlier accounts of the orangutan only solitary old males, or females with young, or sometimes females and at other times males accompanied by half-grown young, had been met with; but more recently Volz[5] and Munnecke[6] have definitely proved the existence of family associations with that ape, whereas it apparently never, or scarcely ever, congregates in larger groups. The social unit of the chimpanzee[7] and gorilla[8] is the family; but several families may associate and then constitute a band or herd, in which a mature male acts as leader.[9] The family is asserted to be the nucleus of the society also among the smaller gregarious monkeys, never losing its identity within the herd; even the enormous herds of a species like the baboon consist of numerous families banded together.[10]

In the case of the apes there are some obvious facts that may account for the need of marital and paternal protection. One is the small number of young: the female brings forth but one at a time. Another is the long period of infancy: the gibbon is said to achieve sexual maturity at five to eight years of age, the orangutan and chimpanzee at eight to twelve, the gorilla at ten to fourteen.[11] Finally, none of these apes is permanently gregarious; even in the Cameroons, where the gorilla is particularly sociable, the herd scatters over a fairly wide district in search of food.[12] These considerations are of importance for a discussion of the origin of the family in mankind. The family consisting of parents and children prevails among the lowest savages as well as among the most civilized races of men; and we may suppose that the factors which made marital and paternal relations indispensable for the apes also made them so for our earliest human or half-human ancestors. If, as most authorities maintain, on the basis of morphological resemblances, man and apes have evolved from a common type, there is no doubt that in mankind, too, the number of children has always been comparatively very small, and that the period of infancy has always been comparatively very long; and it seems to me highly probable that with primitive man, as with the anthropoids, the large quantities of food which he required on account of his size were a hindrance to a permanently gregarious mode of life and therefore made family relations more useful for the preservation of the offspring. There are even now savages among whom the separate families often are compelled to give up the protection afforded them by living together, in order to find the food necessary for their subsistence, and may remain separated from the common group even for a considerable time; and this is the case not only in desolate regions where the supply of food is unusually scarce, but even in countries much more favored by nature.[13]

I have so far spoken of habits, not of institutions. But there is an intimate connection between them. Social habits have a strong tendency to become true customs, that is, rules of conduct in addition to their being habits. A habit may develop into a genuine custom simply because people are inclined to disapprove of anything which is unusual. But in the present case the transition from habit to custom has undoubtedly a deeper foundation. If, as I maintain, men are induced by instincts to remain with a woman with whom they have had sexual relations and to take care of her and of their common offspring, other members of the group, endowed with similar instincts, would feel moral resentment against a man who forsook his mate and children. And, as I have pointed out in another work, public or moral resentment or disapproval is at the bottom of the rules of custom and of all duties and rights.[14] That the functions of the husband and father are not merely of the sexual and procreative kind, but involve the duties of supporting and protecting the wife and children, is testified by an array of facts relating to peoples in all quarters of the world and in all stages of civilization.[15] Many savages do not allow a man to marry until he has given some proof of his ability to fulfill those duties.[16] Marriage and the family are thus most intimately connected with one another. Indeed, quite frequently true married life does not begin for persons who are formally married or betrothed, or a marriage does not become definite, until a child is born or there are signs of pregnancy; whilst in other cases sexual relations that happen to lead to pregnancy or the birth of a child are, as a rule, followed by marriage or make marriage compulsory.[17] We may truly say that marriage is rooted in the family rather than the family in marriage. . . .

In no case . . . could uninterrupted sexual stimulus, which Dr. Zuckerman regards as the sole source of the family with monkey and man, explain the male's relation to the offspring and the paternal instinct underlying it, which has been noticed both in the anthropoids and in other sub-human primates. Diard was told by the Malays, and found it afterwards to be true, that the young siamangs, when in their helpless state, are carried about by their parents, the males by the father and the females by the mother.[18] Von Oertzen states that among chimpanzees the father, as well as the mother, defends the young in case of danger.[19] The Duke of Mecklenburg tells us that one morning when he had shot down a young chimpanzee from a tree, an old male appeared with his mouth wide open, evidently inclined to attack him; he adds that old males "often accompany the families at a distance, but keep to themselves."[20] Livingstone says of the "sokos" in the Manuyema country, which would seem to be the common chimpanzee,[21] that "a male often carries a child, especially if they are passing from one patch of forest to another over a grassy space; he then gives it to the mother."[22] Forbes writes, perhaps on the authority of Von Koppenfels,[23] that chimpanzees build resting-places, not far from the ground, "in which the female and her young take refuge for the night, the male placing himself on guard beneath."[24] Von Koppenfels also says that the male gorilla in a similar manner protects the female and their young from the nocturnal attacks of leopards.[25] Burbridge mentions a case in which a great gorilla met death in a headlong charge to rescue his young.[26] Speaking of the gorilla of the Cameroons, Guthrie relates on native authority that in one instance, when a band was attacked by two men, "the old gorilla of the band first got his family out of danger, and then returned to the encounter."[27] Brehm mentions instances of the paternal instinct among some other monkeys.[28] It should finally be noticed, with reference to Dr. Zuckerman's hypothesis, that the lasting association of the sexes among the primates by no means presupposes an uninterrupted sexual capacity, since similar associations are found in many species whose sexual life is restricted to a certain season.

When I first set forth my theory of the origin of marriage I had to oppose a view which was then held by many eminent sociologists, namely, that the human race must originally have lived in a state of promiscuity, where individual marriage did not exist, where all the men in a horde or tribe had, indiscriminately, access to all the women, and where the children born of these unions belonged to the community at large. I do not know that this view nowadays is supported by any English writer, but it has, to some extent, survived in Germany. Iwan Bloch says that recent ethnological research has proved the untenability of my criticism, that there can be no doubt whatever that in the beginnings of human development a state of promiscuity actually prevailed, that it even seems incomprehensible how a dispute could ever have arisen in the matter; and he quotes with approval P. Näcke's dictum that an original state resembling promiscuity can, in fact, be assumed a priori. He argues that since even in our time, after the development of a sexual morality penetrating and influencing our entire social life, the human need for sexual variety continues to manifest itself in almost undiminished strength, "we can hardly regard it as necessary to prove that in primitive conditions sexual promiscuity was a more original, and, indeed, a more natural, state than marriage."[29] Now it is certainly true that the sexual instinct is stimulated by a change of its object, and that this taste for variety is a cause of much extra-matrimonial intercourse of a more or less promiscuous character. But the assumption that it dominated primitive man to such an extent as to exclude all unions of greater durability is warranted by nothing that is known either about anthropoid apes or savage men. When Dr. Bloch and some other authors speak of early marriage, they are too apt to overlook the fact that a wife is not only a cause of sexual pleasure but a help-mate, a food-provider, a cook, and a mother of children.

The main evidence adduced in support of the hypothesis of primitive promiscuity flows from two different sources. First, there are in books of ancient and modern writers notices of peoples who are alleged to live or to have lived promiscuously. Secondly, there are certain customs which have been interpreted as survivals of such a state in the past. As to the evidence of the former kind, I think it would be difficult to find a more untrustworthy collection of statements. Some of them are simply misrepresentations of theorists in which sexual laxity, frequency of separation, polyandry, group-marriage or something like it, or the absence of a marriage ceremony or of a word for "to marry" or of a marriage union similar to our own, is confounded with promiscuity. Others are based upon indefinite evidence which may be interpreted in one way or other, or on information proved to be inaccurate. And not a single statement can be said to be authoritative or even to make the existence of promiscuity as the regular form of the relations between the sexes at all probable in any case. That no known savage people nowadays is, or recently was, living in such a state is quite obvious; and this greatly discredits the supposition that promiscuity prevailed among any of the peoples mentioned by classical or medieval writers in their summary and vague accounts. Considering how uncertain the information is which people give about the sexual relations of their own neighbors, we must be careful not to accept as trustworthy evidence the statements made by Greek and Roman authors with reference to more or less distant tribes in Africa or Asia of whom they manifestly possessed very little knowledge.[30] Nor can I ascribe any evidentiary value at all to the supposed survivals of earlier promiscuity. After a detailed examination of them I arrived at the conclusion that none of them justifies the assumption that promiscuity has ever been the prevailing form of sexual relations among a single people, and far less that it has constituted a general stage in the social development of man.[31] But the hypothesis of promiscuity not only lacks all foundation to fact: it is positively opposed to the most probable inference we are able to make as regards the early condition of mankind. Darwin remarked that from what we know of the jealousy of all male quadrupeds, promiscuous intercourse is utterly unlikely to prevail in a state of nature.[32]

. . . Among modern savages living in the hunting and food-collecting stage, or at most acquainted with some primitive mode of agriculture, the family consisting of parents and children is a very well-marked social unit;[33] and it is so also among peoples who trace descent through the mother. Its world-wide prevalence has more recently been affirmed by Professor Malinowski, who has an intimate personal experience of matrilineal savages. He writes: "The typical family, a group consisting of mother, father, and their progeny, is found in all communities, savage, barbarous, and civilised; everywhere it plays an important rôle and influences the whole extent of social organisation and culture. . . . In no ethnographic area is the family absent as a domestic institution. . . . It is an undeniable fact that the family is universal and sociologically more important than the clan which, in the evolution of humanity, it preceded and outlasted."[34] If it exists universally both among monkeys and men, it would be a true marvel if primitive man had been the only primate who had been without it.

Theories concerning the earliest form of sexual relations in mankind have influenced speculations as to the future of marriage and the family. Socialist writers have tried to reinforce their social ideals by references to primeval sexual communism.[35] According to Dr. Briffault, "every inference that can be drawn from the facts of social history shows that the inevitable consequence must be a tendency for marriage to revert from patriarchal to so-called matriarchal forms; that is, to a very loose and unstable association."[36] I myself have been accused of attempting to justify the perpetuity of the family by representing it as the basic unit of primitive society.[37] But it never occurred to me to regard the existence of the family in primitive humanity as a sufficient reason for its preservation *ad infinitum*. It is, on the contrary, quite obvious that the general cause to which I have traced its origin, the need of the species, no longer operates: mankind would not succumb if women and children now and in the future had no husband or father to look after them. Yet I think that the origin of marriage and the family has had some bearing on their continuance by leaving behind deep-rooted instincts which will help to preserve them, even though no longer necessary for the survival of the race.

II. The Essential Elements in Marriage

There are three essential elements in every normal marriage: the gratification of the sexual impulse, the relation between husband and wife apart from it, and procreation. The comparative importance attached to these factors has varied considerably. The primary object of marriage has always been sexual union, as sexual desire is obviously the primary motive of relations between the sexes among animals, even when these relations last beyond the pairing season till after the birth of the offspring. But among existing savages the aspect of procreation also plays a very important role. The desire for offspring is very strong among them. A woman is valued not only as a wife but also as a mother; and the respect in which she is held is often proportionate to her fecundity, a barren wife being despised as an unnatural and useless being.[38] Pre-nuptial relations

26

frequently have the character of a trial by which the lover ascertains that the woman will gratify his desire for offspring, and in such a case marriage is not concluded before the birth of a child or until there are signs of pregnancy.[39] A very frequent cause of divorce among simple peoples is barrenness in the wife; and it is so not only where the husband may repudiate his wife at will, but also where his right of divorcing her is restricted.[40] A man without offspring is an unfortunate being under savage conditions of life, where individual safety and welfare depend upon family ties, and the old have to be supported by the young. The childless man may even have to suffer after his death for lack of off-spring, there being nobody to make offerings to his ghost.[41]

For a similar reason procreation has assumed an extraordinary impor-tance among the peoples of archaic civilization. According to Chinese ideas it is one of the greatest misfortunes that could befall a man, and at the same time an offense against the whole line of ancestors, to die without leaving a son to per-petuate the family cult; for it would doom father, mother, and all the ancestry in the Nether-world to a pitiable existence without descendants enough to serve them properly.[42] Among the Semites we meet with the idea that a dead man who has no children will miss something in Shĕol through not receiving that kind of worship which ancestors in early times appear to have received.[43] Among the Israelites procreation was the chief goal of marriages.[44] According to the Talmud "every Jew who does not occupy himself with generation is on a par with one who is guilty of bloodshed";[45] and all Jews desire to have a son who after his father's death can say the prayer on his behalf.[46] The ancient Indo-European nations believed that a man's happiness in the next world de-pended upon his having a continuous line of male descendants, whose duty it would be to make the periodical offerings for the repose of his soul.[47] The old idea still survives in India: "a Hindu man must marry and beget children to perform his funeral rites, lest his spirit wander uneasily in the waste places of the earth."[48] In the Zoroastrian books we likewise meet with the idea that a man should marry and get progeny;[49] the man without a son cannot enter par-adise because there is nobody to pay him the family worship.[50] Plato remarks that every individual is bound to provide for a continuance of representatives to succeed himself as ministers of the Divinity;[51] and Isaeus says: "All those who think their end approaching look forward with a prudent care that their houses may not become desolate, but that there may be some person to attend to their funeral rites and to perform the legal ceremonies at their tombs."[52] The ordi-nary Greek feeling on the object of marriage is no doubt expressed in the ora-tion against Neaera, ascribed to Demosthenes, where it is said: "We keep mis-tresses for our pleasures, concubines for constant attendance, and wives to bear us legitimate children and to be our faithful housekeepers."[53]

A very different view of marriage was introduced into Europe by Christianity. It was permitted to man as a restraint, however imperfect, on the sinful licentiousness of the sexual impulse. Said St. Paul: "It is good for a man not to touch a woman. Nevertheless, to avoid fornication, let each man have his own wife, and let each woman have her own husband."[54] He said nothing about procreation. But the Church also admitted marriage as a necessary expedient for the continuance of the human species, and at the same time pronounced this to be the only legitimate object of sexual intercourse even between husband and wife. The procreation of children was said to be the measure of a Christian's indulgence in appetite, just as the husbandman throwing the seed into the ground awaits the harvest, not sowing more upon it.[55] The Pope's encyclical of 31 December 1930 forbids the use of contraceptives on the ground that "the connubial act is naturally designed to evoke new life."[56]

Among orthodox Christians of other confessions we also find, to some extent, the theory that sexual intercourse is justifiable only as a means of generation; but it is certainly on the wane. Some interesting information on this point comes from America. Dr. Katharine B. Davis, who carried out a study on a thousand educated married women and about a thousand unmarried college women, put to them the question, "Are married people justified having intercourse except for the purpose of having children?" Only a small minority (15.3 percent) of those answering definitely this question replied negatively.[57] Dr. G. V. Hamilton put a similar question to one hundred married men and an equal number of married women, most of whom were well under forty years of age, residents of New York City, and classifiable as having attained a relatively high level of culture. He formulated it thus: "Do you believe that it is right to have the sex act for any other purpose than to bring children into the world?" Eighty-five men and 81 women replied, "Yes, it is right"; and 11 men and 12 women, "Formerly believed it to be wrong, now believe it to be right."[58] Again, the question whether it is right to use methods for preventing pregnancy was answered in the affirmative by 89.7 percent of more than 1000 women belonging to the Davis group, and in the negative only by 10.2 percent.[59] The enormous frequency of the use of contraceptives also bears testimony to people's feelings concerning it. The leader in the movement has been France, a largely Catholic country, where it started in the middle of the last century in the great cities and in the fertile districts of the south;[60] and the proportion of Catholic women who apply for advice at Margaret Sanger's clinic in New York is only one percentage lower than the proportion of Protestant women.[61] So far as England is concerned, Dr. A. W. Thomas wrote in 1906: "From my experience as a general practitioner, I have no hesitation in saying that 90 percent of young married couples of the comfortably-off classes use preventives";[62] and this rough estimate does not seem to be over the mark.[63] In Germany birth control was very prevalent before the War,[64] and has greatly increased afterwards.[65] In the United States 74.11 percent of the 985 married women who answered Dr. Davis' question referring to the use of contraceptives admitted it,[66] and 87 percent of the women belonging to the Hamilton group did the same.[67] At the same time contraception has still many opponents also in Protestant countries, and not only on political grounds as lowering the birth-rate; in Denmark there seems to be quite a widespread feeling against it.[68]

The use of contraceptives by a married couple does not, of course, mean that no children are wanted: it only implies a desire to control the appearance of children, their number, and the times when they are to be born. . . .

. . . According to Havelock Ellis, "most people, certainly most women, feel at moments, or at some period in their lives, a desire for children";[69] and in women the longing for a child "may become so urgent and imperative that we may regard it as scarcely less imperative than the sexual impulse."[70] Van de Velde writes: "To be a woman means to have the desire to become a mother both physically and mentally." He admits that "there are women, and presumably always have been women, although their number may be relatively very small, who feel such a strong antagonism to motherhood that they refuse to marry for this reason"; but he adds: "The absence of the maternal instinct in the modern woman is really nothing but a pose. The maternal instinct exists in spite of this, although there may be only one child. . . . Where it really is repressed, because some women think it fashionable, or because of decadence, or love of pleasure, it will also be seen that such repression has its revenge sooner or later. A more than temporary repression of the mother instinct is, practically speaking, impossible."[71] It may be that Bertrand Russell was deceived by that pose when he made the contrary suggestion that so long as women were in subjection they did not dare to be honest about their own emotions, but professed those which were pleasing to the male, and that consequently, until very recently, all decent women were supposed to desire children, because many men were shocked by those who frankly admitted that they did not desire any.[72] He thinks that the desire for children is commoner among men than among women, and that in a very large number of modern marriages the children are a concession on the part of the woman to the man's desires. He even writes: "It is for this reason, rather than for the sake of sex, that men marry, for it is not difficult to obtain sexual satisfaction without marriage."[73] He seems then to forget that marriage has other advantages to offer a man than the prospect of fatherhood and the gratification of the sexual impulse. But it is quite possible that though the desire for children does not play such an important part in the thoughts of men as it does with most women, nevertheless, as Popenoe observes, "the number of men to whom this aspect of marriage appeals strongly is far greater than is often realised."[74] Among European peasantry it is certainly a powerful motive. The so-called *Probeheiraten,* or trial marriages, in some districts of Bavaria and the *brutkoste* of the Dutch plainsmen have in a large measure the purpose of testifying the woman's capacity for bearing children.[75]

We now come to the third essential element in marriage: the relation between husband and wife apart from the gratification of the sexual impulse and procreation. If my theory of the origin of marriage is correct, this relation has from the beginning contained some degree of affection. In a species where the male remains with the female and takes care of her even after the pairing season has passed, it must be a feeling of this sort that accounts for it. We may assume that the tendency to feel some attachment to a being who has been the cause of pleasure, in this case sexual pleasure, is at the bottom of the marital instinct, and that the need of the species is the ultimate cause of the association between the sexual desire and affection, which is the essence of conjugal love. At the lower stages of human development conjugal affection seems to be considerably inferior to the tender feelings with which parents embrace their children,[76] but we must not be misled by statements to the effect that among some savages love between husband and wife is unknown. However different the love of a savage may be from that of a civilized man, we discover in it traces of the same ingredients. I have elsewhere given a long list of primitive peoples who are by no means strangers to conjugal love, and among these we find even the Australian aborigines, who generally have the reputation of being the greatest oppressors of women on earth; many authorities attest that married people among them are often much attached to each other, and continue to be so even when they grow old.[77]

Advancement in civilization has not at every step been favorable to the development of conjugal love. In a book containing the cream of the moral writings of the Chinese, and intended chiefly for children, we read: "A wife is like one's clothes; when clothes are worn out, we can substitute those that are new."[78] While the Vedic singers knew no more tender relation than that between the husband and his willing, loving wife, who was praised as "his home, the darling abode and bliss in his house,"[79] it is said that sincere mutual friendship is rarely met with in the families of the modern Hindus.[80] Among the Arabs, Burckhardt writes, "the passion of love is, indeed, much talked of by the inhabitants of towns; but I doubt whether anything is meant by them more than the grossest animal desire."[81] In Greece in the historic age the man recognized in the woman no other end than to minister to his pleasure or to become the mother of his children;[82] the love of women was only the offspring of the common Aphrodite, who "is of the body rather than the soul."[83] Both in the

East and in Greece progress in civilization widened the gulf between the sexes and tended to alienate husband and wife, because the higher culture became almost exclusively the prerogative of the men. Yet Europeans are apt to be somewhat mistaken when judging of the conjugal relations of Orientals. A factor which should be taken into account is their ideas of decency. In Morocco it is considered indecent to *show* any affection for one's wife; in the eyes of the outside world the husband should treat her with the greatest indifference. But this by no means implies that he is devoid of tender feelings towards her.[84]

Many students of the psychology of sex have emphasized the unity and transfusion of the spiritual and the bodily elements in sexual love among ourselves. Havelock Ellis writes: "Love, in the sexual sense, is, summarily considered, a synthesis of lust (in the primitive and uncoloured sense of sexual emotion) and friendship. . . . There can be no sexual love without lust; but, on the other hand, until the currents of lust in the organism have been so irradiated as to affect other parts of the psychic organism — at the least the affections and the social feelings — it is not yet sexual love. Lust, the specific sexual impulse, is indeed the primary and essential element in this synthesis, for it alone is adequate to the end of reproduction, not only in animals but in men. But it is not until lust is expanded and irradiated that it develops into the exquisite and enthralling flower of love."[85] "In human beings," says Dr. Beale, "the physical union of real lovers becomes the vehicle and symbol of a spiritual union which cannot in any other way be so completely effected or expressed. From the bodily coalescence of lover and beloved, from the thrill and ecstasy kindled and rekindled in that close embrace, the full mutual surrender and uttermost delight in one another, there spring emotions and sympathies that are quite unattainable save in this manner."[86] Bertrand Russell remarks that the sexual instinct "is not completely satisfied unless a man's whole being, mental quite as much as physical, enters into the relation. . . . Love should be a tree whose roots are deep in the earth, but whose branches extend into heaven."[87] Female writers also point out that the sex communion between husband and wife should be "a true union of souls, not merely a physical function for the momentary relief of the sexual organs,"[88] and that the complete act of union symbolizes and actually enhances the spiritual union.[89]

Dr. Loewenfeld observes that sexual love is a complex emotional state which in its well-developed or, as one may say, higher form is composed of three elements: first, such as appertain to the sexual instinct, or, at least, instinctive elements originating in the sexual sphere; secondly, feelings of affection and sympathy for some individual; and thirdly, feelings of esteem, ranging from simple esteem to veneration, admiration, or even idealizing. He adds that the feelings of the last-mentioned group, if very strongly developed, tend rather to diminish the sensual desire, and may easily lead to a feeling that the beloved object is debased by any attempt at satisfying the latter.[90] This takes us to the important fact that sexual love does not necessarily aim at the supreme satisfaction of the sexual impulse.[91] This impulse is an urge to sexual activity which has its seat and its irradiations in the whole body and the whole psychic personality, being largely dependent not only on the external secretions of the sex glands (sperm and egg cells), but especially on their internal secretions or hormones. And it may lead to tenderness, affection, admiration, or idealization in regard to the individual by whom it is aroused to such a degree that it is itself pushed into the background. In a young person's first love the desire for sexual intercourse is often completely absent, indeed the thought of it may fill him with reluctance; and if he has a desire for such an act, it is directed to another person than the beloved one. On the other hand, when the sensual attraction has ceased to be felt, its spiritual effect may still remain unabated, as is the case in long and happy marriages where husband and wife are united by lasting ties of mutual love and tenderness.

Though love is frequently considered the only justifiable basis for marriage, material aspects have always played a very prominent part in it. Marriage is a community of life with everything that is implied in it, with common interests bodily and mental; as the marriage service of the Church of England states, it exists for "the mutual society, help and comfort that the one ought to have of the other," as well as for the procreation of children. In early civilization a man will have a female companion who takes care of his house, who procures wood and water, lights and attends to the fire, prepares the food, dresses skins, makes clothes, gathers roots and berries, and among agricultural peoples very frequently cultivates the soil; and a woman wants to have a protector and supporter. The various occupations of life are divided between the sexes according to rules, the formation of which has no doubt been more or less influenced by the selfishness of the stronger sex, but which on the whole are in general conformity with the indications given by nature;[92] and so they have always, in a large measure, remained. Among ourselves, also, the desire to enhance one's own comfort and to have a home of one's own with a companion to look after one's interests, is an important motive for marriage. Love enthusiasts are apt to look down upon so prosaic a motive, and even declare that marriages should be continued only so long as love remains. But there is sufficient evidence that love offers no sufficient guarantee for a happy married life.

Economic considerations are certainly of great importance at the conclusion of a marriage. Poverty may cause much hardship to the couple, and may prevent them from having children, or if they have any, from giving them a proper education. Even some amount of wealth is not to be despised. It may increase the enjoyment of life in various ways; it may give the spouses leisure for some useful kind of work — scientific, literary, artistic, or social — which yields no pecuniary gain; and it may enable them to accomplish the education of their children. No wonder, then, that economic circumstances influence very largely the choice of a partner. . . .

The three essential elements in marriage are all sources of much happiness. The gratification of the sexual impulse not only gives intense momentary pleasure, but exercises also a wholesome influence on body and mind, and may lay the foundation of that exalted feeling of love which is the chief condition for a happy marriage. The community of life between husband and wife may in various ways be a blessing to both. It offers many advantages that are denied solitary men and women. It is a safeguard against loneliness; it is apt to be conducive not only to material comfort but to spiritual edification, to intensified life, to fulfillment of personality. Children increase the happiness of married life both as objects of parental affection and as binding links of love between husband and wife. Their presence may even induce the parents to carry on their marriage when personal feelings between them would not do so. Divorces are considerably more frequent in cases where there are no children or only one child. In England, during the period 1899-1930, never less than 60 percent of divorce petitions concerned families with no child or one only, while between 38 and 43 percent came from childless families.[93] In the United States almost two-thirds of the divorces are recruited from the 17 percent childless marriages, and an additional 20 percent of the divorces, or the majority of the remainder, come from that comparatively small category, the one-child marriage.[94] In Switzerland, two-fifths of the total number of divorces are said by Glasson to take place between married people who have no children, though the sterile marriages only amount to one-fifth of the number of marriages.[95]

But while those factors which we have now considered — the sexual impulse, the community of life, and the presence of children — may be conducive to much happiness in married life, they may also be quite the reverse. And it is the unhappy marriages that have in particular impressed those who nowadays speak of the decay of marriage and the disintegration of the family.

THE FIRST BOOK OF MOSES, CALLED GENESIS

Many volumes have been written about the biblical story of Adam and Eve. The origins of this story, according to the Anchor Bible, date back to "the oldest cultural stratum of Mesopotamia" (the word "Eden" is Sumerian). But while many themes here hearken back to such creation narratives as the Epic of Gilgamesh, no other ancient tale so concisely and effectively explained the mysterious life cycle of pair bonding, childbirth, and mortality. And no story, before or since, has so powerfully linked the human sexual impulse with spiritual aspiration.

Genesis 1–4

Chapter 1

1 In the beginning God created the heaven and the earth.
2 And the earth was without form, and void; and darkness was upon the face of the deep. And the Spirit of God moved upon the face of the waters.
3 And God said, Let there be light: and there was light.
4 And God saw the light, that it was good: and God divided the light from the darkness.
5 And God called the light Day, and the darkness he called Night. And the evening and the morning were the first day.
6 And God said, Let there be a firmament in the midst of the waters, and let it divide the waters from the waters.
7 And God made the firmament, and divided the waters which were under the firmament from the waters which were above the firmament: and it was so.

8 And God called the firmament Heaven. And the evening and the morning were the second day.

9 And God said, Let the waters under the heaven be gathered together unto one place, and let the dry land appear: and it was so.

10 And God called the dry land Earth; and the gathering together of the waters called he Seas: and God saw that it was good.

11 And God said, Let the earth bring forth grass, the herb yielding seed, and the fruit tree yielding fruit after his kind, whose seed is in itself, upon the earth: and it was so.

12 And the earth brought forth grass, and herb yielding seed after his kind, and the tree yielding fruit, whose seed was in itself, after his kind: and God saw that it was good.

13 And the evening and the morning were the third day.

14 And God said, Let there be lights in the firmament of the heaven to divide the day from the night; and let them be for signs, and for seasons, and for days, and years:

15 And let them be for lights in the firmament of the heaven to give light upon the earth: and it was so.

16 And God made two great lights; the greater light to rule the day, and the lesser light to rule the night: he made the stars also.

17 And God set them in the firmament of the heaven to give light upon the earth,

18 And to rule over the day and over the night, and to divide the light from the darkness: and God saw that it was good.

19 And the evening and the morning were the fourth day.

20 And God said, Let the waters bring forth abundantly the moving creature that hath life, and fowl that may fly above the earth in the open firmament of heaven.

21 And God created great whales, and every living creature that moveth, which the waters brought forth abundantly, after their kind, and every winged fowl after his kind: and God saw that it was good.

22 And God blessed them, saying, Be fruitful, and multiply, and fill the waters in the seas, and let fowl multiply in the earth.

23 And the evening and the morning were the fifth day.

24 And God said, Let the earth bring forth the living creature after his kind, cattle, and creeping thing, and beast of the earth after his kind: and it was so.

25 And God made the beast of the earth after his kind, and cattle after their kind, and every thing that creepeth upon the earth after his kind: and God saw that it was good.

26 And God said, Let us make man in our image, after our likeness: and let

them have dominion over the fish of the sea, and over the fowl of the air, and over the cattle, and over all the earth, and over every creeping thing that creepeth upon the earth.

27 So God created man in his own image, in the image of God created he him; male and female created he them.

28 And God blessed them, and God said unto them, Be fruitful, and multiply, and replenish the earth, and subdue it: and have dominion over the fish of the sea, and over the fowl of the air, and over every living thing that moveth upon the earth.

29 And God said, Behold, I have given you every herb bearing seed, which is upon the face of all the earth, and every tree, in which is the fruit of a tree yielding seed; to you it shall be for meat.

30 And to every beast of the earth, and to every fowl of the air, and to every thing that creepeth upon the earth, wherein there is life, I have given every green herb for meat: and it was so.

31 And God saw every thing that he had made, and, behold, it was very good. And the evening and the morning were the sixth day.

Chapter 2

1 Thus the heavens and the earth were finished, and all the host of them.

2 And on the seventh day God ended his work which he had made; and he rested on the seventh day from all his work which he had made.

3 And God blessed the seventh day, and sanctified it: because that in it he had rested from all his work which God created and made.

4 These are the generations of the heavens and of the earth when they were created, in the day that the Lord God made the earth and the heavens,

5 And every plant of the field before it was in the earth, and every herb of the field before it grew: for the Lord God had not caused it to rain upon the earth, and there was not a man to till the ground.

6 But there went up a mist from the earth, and watered the whole face of the ground.

7 And the Lord God formed man of the dust of the ground, and breathed into his nostrils the breath of life; and man became a living soul.

8 And the Lord God planted a garden eastward in Eden; and there he put the man whom he had formed.

9 And out of the ground made the Lord God to grow every tree that is pleasant to the sight, and good for food; the tree of life also in the midst of the garden, and the tree of knowledge of good and evil.

10 And a river went out of Eden to water the garden; and from thence it was parted, and became into four heads.

11 The name of the first is Pison: that is it which compasseth the whole land of Havilah, where there is gold;

12 And the gold of that land is good: there is bdellium and the onyx stone.

13 And the name of the second river is Gihon: the same is it that compasseth the whole land of Ethiopia.

14 And the name of the third river is Hiddekel: that is it which goeth toward the east of Assyria. And the fourth river is Euphrates.

15 And the LORD God took the man, and put him into the garden of Eden to dress it and to keep it.

16 And the LORD God commanded the man, saying, Of every tree of the garden thou mayest freely eat:

17 But of the tree of the knowledge of good and evil, thou shalt not eat of it: for in the day that thou eatest thereof thou shalt surely die.

18 And the LORD God said, It is not good that the man should be alone; I will make him an help meet for him.

19 And out of the ground the LORD God formed every beast of the field, and every fowl of the air; and brought them unto Adam to see what he would call them: and whatsoever Adam called every living creature, that was the name thereof.

20 And Adam gave names to all cattle, and to the fowl of the air, and to every beast of the field; but for Adam there was not found an help meet for him.

21 And the LORD God caused a deep sleep to fall upon Adam, and he slept: and he took one of his ribs, and closed up the flesh instead thereof;

22 And the rib, which the LORD God had taken from man, made he a woman, and brought her unto the man.

23 And Adam said, This is now bone of my bones, and flesh of my flesh: she shall be called Woman, because she was taken out of Man.

24 Therefore shall a man leave his father and his mother, and shall cleave unto his wife: and they shall be one flesh.

25 And they were both naked, the man and his wife, and were not ashamed.

Chapter 3

1 Now the serpent was more subtil than any beast of the field which the LORD God had made. And he said unto the woman, Yea, hath God said, Ye shall not eat of every tree of the garden?

2 And the woman said unto the serpent, We may eat of the fruit of the trees of the garden:

3 But of the fruit of the tree which is in the midst of the garden, God hath said, Ye shall not eat of it, neither shall ye touch it, lest ye die.

4 And the serpent said unto the woman, Ye shall not surely die:

5 For God doth know that in the day ye eat thereof, then your eyes shall be opened, and ye shall be as gods, knowing good and evil.

6 And when the woman saw that the tree was good for food, and that it was pleasant to the eyes, and a tree to be desired to make one wise, she took of the fruit thereof, and did eat, and gave also unto her husband with her; and he did eat.

7 And the eyes of them both were opened, and they knew that they were naked; and they sewed fig leaves together, and made themselves aprons.

8 And they heard the voice of the LORD God walking in the garden in the cool of the day: and Adam and his wife hid themselves from the presence of the LORD God amongst the trees of the garden.

9 And the LORD God called unto Adam, and said unto him, Where art thou?

10 And he said, I heard thy voice in the garden, and I was afraid, because I was naked; and I hid myself.

11 And he said, Who told thee that thou wast naked? Hast thou eaten of the tree, whereof I commanded thee that thou shouldest not eat?

12 And the man said, The woman whom thou gavest to be with me, she gave me of the tree, and I did eat.

13 And the LORD God said unto the woman, What is this that thou hast done? And the woman said, The serpent beguiled me, and I did eat.

14 And the LORD God said unto the serpent, Because thou hast done this, thou art cursed above all cattle, and above every beast of the field; upon thy belly shalt thou go, and dust shalt thou eat all the days of thy life:

15 And I will put enmity between thee and the woman, and between thy seed and her seed; it shall bruise thy head, and thou shalt bruise his heel.

16 Unto the woman he said, I will greatly multiply thy sorrow and thy conception; in sorrow thou shalt bring forth children; and thy desire shall be to thy husband, and he shall rule over thee.

17 And unto Adam he said, Because thou hast hearkened unto the voice of thy wife, and hast eaten of the tree, of which I commanded thee, saying, Thou shalt not eat of it: cursed is the ground for thy sake; in sorrow shalt thou eat of it all the days of thy life;

18 Thorns also and thistles shall it bring forth to thee; and thou shalt eat the herb of the field;

19 In the sweat of thy face shalt thou eat bread, till thou return unto the ground; for out of it wast thou taken: for dust thou art, and unto dust shalt thou return.

20 And Adam called his wife's name Eve; because she was the mother of all living.

21 Unto Adam also and to his wife did the LORD God make coats of skins, and clothed them.

22 And the LORD God said, Behold, the man is become as one of us, to know good and evil: and now, lest he put forth his hand, and take also of the tree of life, and eat, and live for ever:

23 Therefore the LORD God sent him forth from the garden of Eden, to till the ground from whence he was taken.

24 So he drove out the man; and he placed at the east of the garden of Eden Cherubims, and a flaming sword which turned every way, to keep the way of the tree of life.

Chapter 4

1 And Adam knew Eve his wife; and she conceived, and bare Cain, and said, I have gotten a man from the LORD.

2 And she again bare his brother Abel. And Abel was a keeper of sheep, but Cain was a tiller of the ground.

3 And in process of time it came to pass, that Cain brought of the fruit of the ground an offering unto the LORD.

4 And Abel, he also brought of the firstlings of his flock and of the fat thereof. And the LORD had respect unto Abel and to his offering:

5 But unto Cain and to his offering he had not respect. And Cain was very wroth, and his countenance fell.

6 And the LORD said unto Cain, Why art thou wroth? and why is thy countenance fallen?

7 If thou doest well, shalt thou not be accepted? and if thou doest not well, sin lieth at the door. And unto thee shall be his desire, and thou shalt rule over him.

8 And Cain talked with Abel his brother: and it came to pass, when they were in the field, that Cain rose up against Abel his brother, and slew him.

9 And the LORD said unto Cain, Where is Abel thy brother? And he said, I know not: Am I my brother's keeper?

10 And he said, What hast thou done? the voice of thy brother's blood crieth unto me from the ground.

11 And now art thou cursed from the earth, which hath opened her mouth to receive thy brother's blood from thy hand;

12 When thou tillest the ground, it shall not henceforth yield unto thee her strength; a fugitive and a vagabond shalt thou be in the earth.

13 And Cain said unto the LORD, My punishment is greater than I can bear.

14 Behold, thou hast driven me out this day from the face of the earth; and from thy face shall I be hid; and I shall be a fugitive and a vagabond in the earth; and it shall come to pass, that every one that findeth me shall slay me.

15 And the LORD said unto him, Therefore whosoever slayeth Cain, vengeance shall be taken on him sevenfold. And the LORD set a mark upon Cain, lest any finding him should kill him.

16 And Cain went out from the presence of the LORD, and dwelt in the land of Nod, on the east of Eden.

17 And Cain knew his wife; and she conceived, and bare Enoch: and he builded a city, and called the name of the city, after the name of his son, Enoch.

18 And unto Enoch was born Irad: and Irad begat Mehujael: and Mehujael begat Methusael: and Methusael begat Lamech.

19 And Lamech took unto him two wives: the name of the one was Adah, and the name of the other Zillah.

20 And Adah bare Jabal: he was the father of such as dwell in tents, and of such as have cattle.

21 And his brother's name was Jubal: he was the father of all such as handle the harp and organ.

22 And Zillah, she also bare Tubalcain, an instructer of every artificer in brass and iron: and the sister of Tubalcain was Naamah.

23 And Lamech said unto his wives, Adah and Zillah, Hear my voice; ye wives of Lamech, hearken unto my speech: for I have slain a man to my wounding, and a young man to my hurt.

24 If Cain shall be avenged sevenfold, truly Lamech seventy and sevenfold.

25 And Adam knew his wife again; and she bare a son, and called his name Seth: For God, said she, hath appointed me another seed instead of Abel, whom Cain slew.

26 And to Seth, to him also there was born a son; and he called his name Enos: then began men to call upon the name of the LORD.

TU FU

Tu Fu (712-770) was a painter as well as a poet, and is considered by many to be the finest Chinese poet who ever lived. Born into a privileged scholarly family, he was something of a literary prodigy, earning fame at the tender age of 15 for his essays as well as his poems. But his life, in a time of political turmoil, was marked by a seemingly endless series of professional humiliations, personal tragedies, and political exiles. After losing several of his children to starvation, he is said to have died of overeating, when after having endured several days without food during a flood, he was invited to a feast.

The Man with No Family to Take Leave Of

(T'ien-pao in the first line refers to the outbreak of the An Lu-shan rebellion in the 14th year of the T'ien-Pao era, 755.)

Ever since T'ien-pao, this silence and desolation,
fields and sheds mere masses of pigweed and bramble;
my village of a hundred households or more,
in these troubled times scattered, some east, some west;
not a word from those still living,
the dead ones all gone to dust and mire.
I was on the side that lost the battle,[1]
so I came home, looking for the old paths,
so long on the road, to find empty lanes,

41

the sun grown feeble, pain and sorrow in the air.
All I meet are foxes and raccoon dogs,
their fur on end, snarling at me in anger.
And for neighbors on four sides, who do I have?
One or two aging widows.
But the roosting bird loves his old branch;
how could he reject it, narrow perch though it is?
Now that spring's here I shoulder the hoe alone,
in the evening sun once more pour water on the fields.
The local officials know I'm back;
the call me in, order me to practice the big drum.[2]
Maybe they'll assign me to duty in my own province —
but still I've no wife, no one to take by hand.
Traveling to a post nearby, I'm one man all alone;
sent to a far-off assignment, I'll be more lost than ever.
But, since my house and village are a wilderness now,
near or far, it's all the same to me.
And always I grieve for my mother, sick so long;
five years I've left her buried in a mere ditch of a grave.
She bore me, but I hadn't the strength to help her;
to the end, both of us breathed bitter sighs.
A living man, but with no family to take leave of —
how can I be called a proper human being?

THE SEVEN BENEDICTIONS
OF JEWISH MARRIAGE

The Seven Benedictions of Jewish Marriage are called the "birchot chattanim," or the "groom's blessings." However, according to Jewish tradition, they should only be recited by the groom if there is no one else to recite them. While at most Jewish weddings today, it is the presiding Rabbi who gives the benedictions, it is also possible that honored guests participate in the readings. In *The Jewish Way in Love and Marriage*, Maurice Lamm remarks: "The Midrash records that God appointed angelic escorts for Adam and brought ornaments for Eve at their wedding, and that He arranged seven chuppot (Jewish wedding canopies) set up in Paradise, on which the Rabbis patterned the seven benedictions" (p. 224). Lamm also reminds the reader that the second benediction, praising God for creating "all things for His glory," is read only at weddings. Why would this very general blessing be read on no other occasion? Because the wedding "is the most important moment in life."

The Seven Benedictions (Sheva Brachot)

1. "Blessed art Thou, O Lord our God, King of the universe who hast created the fruit of the vine."
2. "Blessed art Thou, O Lord our God, King of the universe, who has created all things for His glory."
3. "Blessed art Thou, O Lord our God, King of the universe, creator of man."
4. "Blessed art Thou, O Lord our God, King of the universe who hast made

man in His image, after His likeness, and hast prepared for him out of his very self, a perpetual fabric. Blessed art Thou, O Lord, creator of man."

5. "May she who was barren be exceedingly glad and rejoice when her children are united in her midst in joy. Blessed art Thou, O Lord, who makes Zion joyful through her children."

6. "O make these beloved companions greatly rejoice even as Thou didst rejoice in Thy creation in the Garden of Eden as of old. Blessed art Thou, O Lord who makest bridegroom and bride to rejoice."

7. "Blessed art Thou, O Lord, King of the universe, who has created joy and gladness, bridegroom and bride, mirth and exultation, pleasure and delight, love, brotherhood, peace and fellowship. Soon may there be heard in the cities of Judah and in the streets of Jerusalem, the voice of joy and gladness, the voice of the bridegroom and the voice of the bride, the jubilant voice of bridegrooms from their canopies, and of youths from their feasts of song. Blessed art Thou, O Lord, who makest the bridegroom to rejoice with the bride."

GIOVANNI BOCCACCIO

One of the earliest prose works in the Italian language, the *Decameron* stands as a preeminent work of the Italian Renaissance. Giovanni Boccaccio (1313-1375) was the illegitimate son of a Florentine banker. His father wanted him to pursue a career in commerce, but the son loved letters. Sent to Naples to learn business, he drifted toward poetry and culture. Two events of his young manhood deeply affected his work: The first was his abortive love affair with Maria d'Aquino, daughter of Naples' King Robert the Wise. The second was the Black Death of 1348, which decimated more than half the population of Florence. One of the most remarkable things about the *Decameron* is its liveliness and comedy. Curiously, these life-affirming tales arise from a depressing premise: three young men and seven women seek refuge from the plague in a country villa, where they exchange stories to pass the time.

The Decameron

Fifth Day: Fourth Story

Ricciardo Manardi is discovered by Messer Lizio da Valbona with his daughter, whom he marries, and remains on good terms with her father.

Elissa, falling silent, listened as her companions lauded her tale, and the queen called upon Filostrato to tell his story. Laughing, he began as follows:

I have been teased so many times, and by so many of you, for obliging you to tell cruel stories and making you weep, that I feel obliged to make some slight amends for the sorrow I caused, and tell you something that will make you laugh a little. Hence I propose to tell you a very brief tale about a love which, apart from one or two sighs and a moment of fear not unmixed with embarrassment, ran a smooth course to its happy conclusion.

Not long ago then, excellent ladies, there lived in Romagna a most reputable and virtuous gentleman called Messer Lizio da Valbona, who, on the threshold of old age, had the good fortune to be presented by his wife, Madonna Giacomina, with a baby daughter. When she grew up, she outshone all the other girls in those parts for her charm and beauty, and since she was the only daughter left to her father and mother, they loved and cherished her with all their heart, and guarded her with extraordinary care, for they had high hopes of bestowing her in marriage on the son of some great nobleman.

Now, to the house of Messer Lizio there regularly came a handsome and sprightly youth called Ricciardo de' Manardi da Brettinoro with whom Messer Lizio spent a good deal of his time; and he and his wife would no more have thought of keeping him under surveillance than if he were their own son. Whenever he set eyes on the girl, Ricciardo was struck by her great beauty, her graceful bearing, her charming ways and impeccable manners, and, seeing that she was of marriageable age, he fell passionately in love with her. He took great pains to conceal his feelings, but the girl divined that he was in love with her, and far from being offended, to Ricciardo's great delight she began to love him with equal fervour. Though frequently seized with the longing to speak to her, he was always too timid to do so until one day, having chosen a suitable moment, he plucked up courage and said to her:

'Caterina, I implore you not to let me die of love for you.'

'Heaven grant,' she promptly replied, 'that you do not allow me to die first for love of you.'

Ricciardo was overjoyed by the girl's answer, and, feeling greatly encouraged, he said to her:

'Demand of me anything you please, and I shall do it. But you alone can devise the means of saving us both.'

Whereupon the girl said:

'Ricciardo, as you see, I am watched very closely, and for this reason I cannot think how you are to come to me. But if you are able to suggest anything I might do without bringing shame upon myself, tell me what it is, and I shall do it.'

Ricciardo turned over various schemes in his mind, then suddenly he said:

'My sweet Caterina, the only way I can suggest is for you to come to the balcony overlooking your father's garden, or better still, to sleep there. Although it is very high, if I knew that you were spending the night on the balcony, I would try without fail to climb up and reach you.'

'If you are daring enough to climb to the balcony,' Caterina replied, 'I am quite sure that I can arrange to sleep there.'

Ricciardo assured her that he was, whereupon they snatched a single kiss and went their separate ways.

It was already near the end of May, and on the morning after her conversation with Ricciardo, the girl began complaining to her mother that she had been unable to sleep on the previous night because of the heat.

'What are you talking about, child?' said her mother. 'It wasn't in the least hot.'

To which Caterina said:

'Mother, if you were to add "in my opinion", then perhaps you would be right. But you must remember that young girls feel the heat much more than older women.'

'That is so, my child,' said her mother, 'but what do you expect me to do about it? I can't make it hot or cold for you, just like that. You have to take the weather as it comes, according to the season. Perhaps tonight it will be cooler, and you will sleep better.'

'God grant that you are right,' said Caterina, 'but it is not usual for the nights to grow any cooler as the summer approaches.'

'Then what do you want us to do about it?' inquired the lady.

'If you and father were to consent,' replied Caterina, 'I should like to have a little bed made up for me on the balcony outside his room, overlooking the garden. I should have the nightingale to sing me off to sleep, it would be much cooler there, and I should be altogether better off than I am in your room.'

Whereupon her mother said:

'Cheer up, my child; I shall speak to your father about it, and we shall do whatever he decides.'

The lady reported their conversation to Messer Lizio, who, perhaps because of his age, was inclined to be short-tempered.

'What's all this about being lulled to sleep by the nightingale?' he exclaimed. 'She'll be sleeping to the song of the cicadas if I hear any more of her nonsense.'

Having heard what he had said, on the following night, more to spite her father than because she was feeling hot, Caterina not only stayed awake herself but, by complaining incessantly of the heat, also prevented her mother from sleeping.

So next morning, her mother went straight to Messer Lizio, and said:

'Sir, you cannot be very fond of this daughter of yours. What difference does it make to you whether she sleeps on the balcony or not? She didn't get a moment's rest all night because of the heat. Besides, what do you find so surprising about a young girl taking pleasure in the song of the nightingale? Young people are naturally drawn towards those things that reflect their own natures.'

'Oh, very well,' said Messer Lizio. 'Take whichever bed you please, and set it up for her on the balcony with some curtains round it. Then let her sleep there and hear the nightingale singing to her heart's content.'

On hearing that her father had given his permission, the girl promptly had a bed made up for her on the balcony; and since it was her intention to sleep there that same night, she waited for Ricciardo to come to the house, and gave him a signal, already agreed between them, by which he understood what was expected of him.

As soon as he had heard his daughter getting into bed, Messer Lizio locked the door leading from his own room to the balcony, and then he too retired for the night.

When there was no longer any sound to be heard, Ricciardo climbed over a wall with the aid of a ladder, then climbed up the side of the house by clinging with great difficulty to a series of stones projecting from the wall. At every moment of the ascent, he was in serious danger of falling, but in the end he reached the balcony unscathed, where he was silently received by the girl with very great rejoicing. After exchanging many kisses, they lay down together and for virtually the entire night they had delight and joy of one another, causing the nightingale to sing at frequent intervals.

Their pleasure was long, the night was brief, and though they were unaware of the fact, it was almost dawn when they eventually fell asleep without a stitch to cover them, exhausted as much by their merry sport as by the nocturnal heat. Caterina had tucked her right arm beneath Ricciardo's neck, whilst with her left hand she was holding that part of his person which in mixed company you ladies are too embarrassed to mention.

Dawn came, but failed to wake them, and they were still asleep in the same posture when Messer Lizio got up out of bed. Remembering that his daughter was sleeping on the balcony, he quietly opened the door, saying:

'I'll just go and see whether Caterina has slept any better with the help of the nightingale.'

Stepping out on to the terrace, he gently raised the curtain surrounding the bed and saw Ricciardo and Caterina, naked and uncovered, lying there asleep in one another's arms, in the posture just described.

Having clearly recognized Ricciardo, he left them there and made way to his wife's room, where he called to her and said:

'Be quick, woman, get up and come and see, for your daughter was so fascinated by the nightingale that she has succeeded in waylaying it, and is holding it in her hand.'

'What are you talking about?' said the lady.

'You'll see, if you come quickly,' said Messer Lizio.

The lady got dressed in a hurry, and quietly followed in Messer Lizio's footsteps until both of them were beside the bed. The curtain was then raised, and Madonna Giacomina saw for herself exactly how her daughter had taken and seized hold of the nightingale, whose song she had so much yearned to hear.

The lady, who considered that she had been seriously deceived in Ricciardo, was on the point of shouting and screaming abuse at him, but Messer Lizio restrained her, saying:

'Woman, if you value my love, hold your tongue! Now that she has taken him, she shall keep him. Ricciardo is a rich young man, and comes of noble stock. We could do a lot worse than have him as our son-in-law. If he wishes to leave this house unscathed, he will first have to marry our daughter, so that he will have put his nightingale into his own cage and into no other.'

The lady was reassured to see that her husband was not unduly perturbed by what had happened, and on reflecting that her daughter had enjoyed a good night, was well-rested, and had caught the nightingale, she held her peace.

Nor did they have long to wait before Ricciardo woke up, and on seeing that it was broad daylight, he almost died of fright and called to Caterina, saying:

'Alas, my treasure, the day has come and caught me unawares! What is to happen to us?'

At these words, Messer Lizio stepped forward, raised the curtain, and replied:

'What you deserve.'

On seeing Messer Lizio, Ricciardo nearly leapt out of his skin and sat bolt upright in bed, saying:

'My lord, in God's name have mercy on me. I know that I deserve to die, for I have been wicked and disloyal, and hence you must deal with me as you choose. But I beseech you to spare my life, if that is possible. I implore you not to kill me.'

'Ricciardo,' said Messer Lizio, 'this deed was quite unworthy of the love I bore you and the firm trust I placed in you. But what is done cannot be undone, and since it was your youth that carried you into so grievous an error, in order that you may preserve not only your life but also my honour, you must, before you do anything else, take Caterina as your lawful wedded wife. And thus, not only will she have been yours for this night, but she will remain yours for as long as she lives. By this means alone will you secure your freedom and my forgiveness; otherwise you can prepare to meet your Maker.'

Whilst this conversation was taking place, Caterina let go of the nightingale, and having covered herself up, she burst into tears and implored her father to forgive Ricciardo, at the same time beseeching Ricciardo to do as Messer Lizio wished, so that they might long continue to enjoy such nights as this together in perfect safety.

All this pleading was quite superfluous, however, for what with the shame of his transgression and his urge to atone on the one hand, and his desire to escape with his life on the other (to say nothing of his yearning to possess the object of his ardent love), Ricciardo readily consented, without a moment's hesitation, to do what Messer Lizio was asking.

Messer Lizio therefore borrowed one of Madonna Giacomina's rings, and Ricciardo married Caterina there and then without moving from the spot, her parents bearing witness to the event.

This done, Messer Lizio and his wife withdrew, saying:

'Now go back to sleep, for you doubtless stand in greater need of resting than of getting up.'

As soon as her parents had departed, the two young people fell once more into each other's arms, and since they had only passed half a dozen milestones in the course of the night, they added another two to the total before getting up. And for the first day they left it at that.

After they had risen, Ricciardo discussed the matter in greater detail with Messer Lizio, and a few days later he and Caterina took appropriate steps to renew their marriage vows in the presence of their friends and kinsfolk. Then, amid great rejoicing, he brought her to his house, where the nuptials were celebrated with dignity and splendour. And for many years thereafter he lived with her in peace and happiness, caging nightingales by the score, day and night, to his heart's content.

FRANZ KAFKA

Franz Kafka (1883-1924) is synonymous not only with the beginnings of literary modernism, but also with the emergence of the twentieth-century worldview. His influence on the way contemporary men and women view themselves in relation to society, in fact, is so great that we often refer to situations in which we feel dehumanized or alienated by the stresses of modernity as "Kafkaesque" moments. Kafka's literary world sometimes evokes the feeling of being trapped in a nightmare; other times we have the sense of being confined in an amusement park fun house. (Kafka was said to have howled with laughter when reading his writings for friends.) Despite the surface comedy and the absurdity of his images and plots, his writings are marked by spiritual longing, profound psychological insight, and, most of all, pathos. His main characters are always vulnerable human beings ensnared in a system that they can barely begin to comprehend. Born in Prague to a German-speaking Jewish family, Kafka studied law and worked in an Austrian government post. "The Judgment" was one of his first works to be published, appearing in 1913.

The Judgment

It was a Sunday morning in the very height of spring. Georg Bendemann, a young merchant, was sitting in his own room on the first floor of one of a long row of small, ramshackle houses stretching beside the river which were scarcely distinguishable from each other in height and coloring. He had just finished a letter to an old friend of his who was now living abroad, had put it into its envelope in a slow and dreamy fashion, and with his elbows propped on the writing table was gazing out of the window at the river, the bridge, and the hills on the farther bank with their tender green.

He was thinking about his friend, who had actually run away to Russia some years before, being dissatisfied with his prospects at home. Now he was carrying on a business in St. Petersburg, which had flourished to begin with but had long been going downhill, as he always complained on his increasingly rare visits. So he was wearing himself out to no purpose in a foreign country, the unfamiliar full beard he wore did not quite conceal the face Georg had known so well since childhood, and his skin was growing so yellow as to indicate some latent disease. By his own account he had no regular connection with the colony of his fellow countrymen out there and almost no social intercourse with Russian families, so that he was resigning himself to becoming a permanent bachelor.

What could one write to such a man, who had obviously run off the rails, a man one could be sorry for but could not help? Should one advise him to come home, to transplant himself and take up his old friendships again — there was nothing to hinder him — and in general to rely on the help of his friends? But that was as good as telling him, and the more kindly the more offensively, that all his efforts hitherto had miscarried, that he should finally give up, come back home, and be gaped at by everyone as a returned prodigal, that only his friends knew what was what and that he himself was just a big child who should do what his successful and home-keeping friends prescribed. And was it certain, besides, that all the pain one would have to inflict on him would achieve its object? Perhaps it would not even be possible to get him to come home at all — he said himself that he was now out of touch with commerce in his native country — and then he would still be left an alien in a foreign land embittered by his friends' advice and more than ever estranged from them. But if he did follow their advice and then didn't fit in at home — not out of malice, of course, but through force of circumstances — couldn't get on with his friends or without them, felt humiliated, couldn't be said to have either friends or a country of his own any longer, wouldn't it have been better for him to stay abroad just as he was? Taking all this into account, how could one be sure that he would make a success of life at home?

For such reasons, supposing one wanted to keep up correspondence with him, one could not send him any real news such as could frankly be told to the most distant acquaintance. It was more than three years since his last visit, and for this he offered the lame excuse that the political situation in Russia was too uncertain, which apparently would not permit even the briefest absence of a small businessman while it allowed hundreds of thousands of Russians to travel peacefully abroad. But during these three years Georg's own position in life had changed a lot. Two years ago his mother had died, since when he and his father had shared the household together, and his friend had of course been informed of that and had expressed his sympathy in a letter phrased so dryly that the grief caused by such an event, one had to conclude, could not be realized in a distant country. Since that time, however, Georg had applied himself with greater determination to the business as well as to everything else.

Perhaps during his mother's lifetime his father's insistence on having everything his own way in the business had hindered him from developing any real activity of his own, perhaps since her death his father had become less aggressive, although he was still active in the business, perhaps it was mostly due to an accidental run of good fortune — which was very probable indeed — but, at any rate during those two years, the business had developed in a most unexpected way, the staff had had to be doubled, the turnover was five times as great; no doubt about it, further progress lay just ahead.

But Georg's friend had no inkling of this improvement. In earlier years, perhaps for the last time in that letter of condolence, he had tried to persuade Georg to emigrate to Russia and had enlarged upon the prospects of success for precisely Georg's branch of trade. The figures quoted were microscopic by comparison with the range of Georg's present operations. Yet he shrank from letting his friend know about his business success, and if he were to do it now retrospectively that certainly would look peculiar.

So Georg confined himself to giving his friend unimportant items of gossip such as rise at random in the memory when one is idly thinking things over on a quiet Sunday. All he desired was to leave undisturbed the idea of the home town which his friend must have built up to his own content during the long interval. And so it happened to Georg that three times in three fairly widely separated letters he had told his friend about the engagement of an unimportant man to some equally unimportant girl, until, indeed, quite contrary to his intentions, his friend began to show some interest in this notable event.

Yet Georg preferred to write about things like these rather than to confess that he himself had got engaged a month ago to a Fräulein Frieda Brandenfeld, a girl from a well-to-do family. He often discussed this friend of his with his fiancée and the peculiar relationship that had developed between them in their correspondence. "So he won't be coming to our wedding," said she, "and yet I have a right to get to know all your friends." "I don't want to trouble him," answered Georg, "don't misunderstand me, he would probably come, at least I think so, but he would feel that his hand had been forced and he would be hurt, perhaps he would even envy me and certainly he'd be discontented, and without being able to do anything about his discontent he'd have to go away again alone. Alone — do you know what that means?" "Yes, but may he not hear about our marriage in some other fashion?" "I can't prevent that, of course, but it's unlikely, considering the way he lives." "Since your friends are like that, Georg, you shouldn't ever have got engaged at all." "Well, we're both to blame for that; but I wouldn't have it any other way now." And when, breathing quickly under his kisses, she still brought out, "All the same, I do feel upset," he thought it would not really involve him in trouble were he to send the news to his friend. "That's the kind of man I am and he'll just have to take me as I am," he said to himself. "I can't cut myself to another pattern that might make a more suitable friend for him."

And in fact he did inform his friend, in the long letter he had been writing that Sunday morning, about his engagement, with these words: "I have saved my best news to the end. I have got engaged to a Fräulein Frieda Brandenfeld, a girl from a well-to-do family, who only came to live here a long time after you went away, so that you're hardly likely to know her. There will be time to tell you more about her later, for today let me just say that I am very happy and as between you and me the only difference in our relationship is that instead of a quite ordinary kind of friend you will now have in me a happy friend. Besides that, you will acquire in my fiancée, who sends her warm greetings and will soon write you herself, a genuine friend of the opposite sex, which is not without importance to a bachelor. I know that there are many reasons why you can't come to see us, but would not my wedding be precisely the right occasion for giving all obstacles the go-by? Still, however that may be, do just as seems good to you without regarding any interests but your own."

With this letter in his hand Georg had been sitting a long time at the writing table, his face turned toward the window. He had barely acknowledged, with an absent smile, a greeting waved to him from the street by a passing acquaintance.

At last he put the letter in his pocket and went out of his room across a small lobby into his father's room, which he had not entered for months. There was in fact no need for him to enter it, since he saw his father daily at business and they took their mid-day meal together at an eating house; in the evening, it was true, each did as he pleased, yet even then, unless Georg — as mostly happened — went out with friends or, more recently, visited his fiancée, they always sat for a while, each with his newspaper, in their common sitting room.

It surprised Georg how dark his father's room was even on this sunny morning. So it was overshadowed as much as that by the high wall on the other side of the narrow courtyard. His father was sitting by the window in a corner hung with various mementos of Georg's dead mother, reading a newspaper which he held to one side before his eyes in an attempt to overcome a defect of vision. On the table stood the remains of his breakfast, not much of which seemed to have been eaten.

"Ah, Georg," said his father, rising at once to meet him. His heavy dressing gown swung open as he walked and the skirts of it fluttered around him. — "My father is still a giant of a man," said Georg to himself.

"It's unbearably dark here," he said aloud.

"Yes, it's dark enough," answered his father.

"And you've shut the window, too?"

"I prefer it like that."

"Well, it's quite warm outside," said Georg, as if continuing his previous remark, and sat down.

His father cleared away the breakfast dishes and set them on a chest.

"I really only wanted to tell you," went on Georg, who had been vacantly following the old man's movements, "that I am now sending the news of my engagement to St. Petersburg." He drew the letter a little way from his pocket and let it drop back again.

"To St. Petersburg?" asked his father.

"To my friend there," said Georg, trying to meet his father's eye. — In business hours he's quite different, he was thinking, how solidly he sits here with his arms crossed.

"Oh yes. To your friend," said his father, with peculiar emphasis.

"Well, you know, Father, that I wanted not to tell him about my engagement at first. Out of consideration for him, that was the only reason. You know yourself he's a difficult man. I said to myself that someone else might tell him about my engagement, although he's such a solitary creature that that was hardly likely — I couldn't prevent that — but I wasn't ever going to tell him myself."

"And now you've changed your mind?" asked his father, laying his enormous newspaper on the window sill and on top of it his spectacles, which he covered with one hand.

"Yes, I've been thinking it over. If he's a good friend of mine, I said to myself, my being happily engaged should make him happy too. And so I wouldn't put off telling him any longer. But before I posted the letter I wanted to let you know."

"Georg," said his father, lengthening his toothless mouth, "listen to me! You've come to me about this business, to talk it over with me. No doubt that does you honor. But it's nothing, it's worse than nothing, if you don't tell me the whole truth. I don't want to stir up matters that shouldn't be mentioned here. Since the death of our dear mother certain things have been done that aren't right. Maybe the time will come for mentioning them, and maybe sooner than we think. There's many a thing in the business I'm not aware of, maybe it's not done behind my back — I'm not going to say that it's done behind my back — I'm not equal to things any longer, my memory's failing, I haven't an eye for so many things any longer. That's the course of nature in the first place, and in the second place the death of our dear mother hit me harder than it did you. — But since we're talking about it, about this letter, I beg you, Georg, don't deceive me. It's a trivial affair, it's hardly worth mentioning, so don't deceive me. Do you really have this friend in St. Petersburg?"

Georg rose in embarrassment. "Never mind my friends. A thousand friends wouldn't make up to me for my father. Do you know what I think? You're not taking enough care of yourself. But old age must be taken care of. I can't do without you in the business, you know that very well, but if the business is going to undermine your health, I'm ready to close it down tomorrow forever. And that won't do. We'll have to make a change in your way of living. But a radical change. You sit here in the dark, and in the sitting room you would have plenty of light. You just take a bite of breakfast instead of properly keeping up your strength. You sit by a closed window, and the air would be so good for you. No, Father! I'll get the doctor to come, and we'll follow his orders. We'll change your room, you can move into the front room and I'll move in here. You won't notice the change, all your things will be moved with you. But there's time for all that later, I'll put you to bed now for a little, I'm sure you need to rest. Come, I'll help you to take off your things, you'll see I can do it. Or if you would rather go into the front room at once, you can lie down in my bed for the present. That would be the most sensible thing."

Georg stood close beside his father, who had let his head with its unkempt white hair sink on his chest.

"Georg," said his father in a low voice, without moving.

Georg knelt down at once beside his father, in the old man's weary face he saw the pupils, overlarge, fixedly looking at him from the corners of the eyes.

"You have no friend in St. Petersburg. You've always been a leg-puller and you haven't even shrunk from pulling my leg. How could you have a friend out there! I can't believe it."

"Just think back a bit, Father," said Georg, lifting his father from the chair and slipping off his dressing gown as he stood feebly enough, "it'll soon be three years since my friend came to see us last. I remember that you used not to like him very much. At least twice I kept you from seeing him, although he was actually sitting with me in my room. I could quite well understand your dislike of him, my friend has his peculiarities. But then, later, you got on with him very well. I was proud because you listened to him and nodded and asked him questions. If you think back you're bound to remember. He used to tell us the most incredible stories of the Russian Revolution. For instance, when he was on a business trip to Kiev and ran into a riot, and saw a priest on a balcony who cut a broad cross in blood on the palm of his hand and held the hand up and appealed to the mob. You've told that story yourself once or twice since."

Meanwhile Georg had succeeded in lowering his father down again and carefully taking off the woolen drawers he wore over his linen underpants and his socks. The not particularly clean appearance of his underwear made him reproach himself for having been neglectful. It should have certainly been his duty to see that his father had clean changes of underwear. He had not yet explicitly discussed with his bride-to-be what arrangements should be made for his father in the future, for they had both of them silently taken it for granted that the old man would go on living alone in the old house. But now he made a quick, firm decision to take him into his own future establishment. It almost looked, on closer inspection, as if the care he meant to lavish there on his father might come too late.

He carried his father to bed in his arms. It gave him a dreadful feeling to notice that while he took the few steps toward the bed the old man on his breast was playing with his watch chain. He could not lay him down on the bed for a moment, so firmly did he hang on to the watch chain.

But as soon as he was laid in bed, all seemed well. He covered himself up and even drew the blankets farther than usual over his shoulders. He looked up at Georg with a not unfriendly eye.

"You begin to remember my friend, don't you?" asked Georg, giving him an encouraging nod.

"Am I well covered up now?" asked his father, as if he were not able to see whether his feet were properly tucked in or not.

"So you find it snug in bed already," said Georg, and tucked the blankets more closely around him.

"Am I well covered up?" asked the father once more, seeming to be strangely intent upon the answer.

"Don't worry, you're well covered up."

"No!" cried his father, cutting short the answer, threw the blankets off with a strength that sent them all flying in a moment and sprang erect in bed. Only one hand lightly touched the ceiling to steady him.

"You wanted to cover me up, I know, my young sprig, but I'm far from being covered up yet. And even if this is the last strength I have, it's enough for you, too much for you. Of course I know your friend. He would have been a son after my own heart. That's why you've been playing him false all these years. Why else? Do you think I haven't been sorry for him? And that's why you had to lock yourself up in your office — the Chief is busy, mustn't be disturbed — just so that you could write your lying little letters to Russia. But thank goodness a father doesn't need to be taught how to see through his son. And now that you thought you'd got him down, so far down that you could set your bottom on him and sit on him and he wouldn't move, then my fine son makes up his mind to get married!"

Georg stared at the bogey conjured up by his father. His friend in St. Petersburg, whom his father suddenly knew too well, touched his imagination as never before. Lost in the vastness of Russia he saw him. At the door of an empty, plundered warehouse he saw him. Among the wreckage of his showcases, the slashed remnants of his wares, the falling gas brackets, he was just standing up. Why did he have to go so far away!

"But attend to me!" cried his father, and Georg, almost distracted, ran toward the bed to take everything in, yet came to a stop halfway.

"Because she lifted up her skirts," his father began to flute, "because she lifted her skirts like this, the nasty creature," and mimicking her he lifted his shirt so high that one could see the scar on his thigh from his war wound, "because she lifted her skirts like this and this you made up to her, and in order to make free with her undisturbed you have disgraced your mother's memory, betrayed your friend, and stuck your father into bed so that he can't move. But he can move, or can't he?"

And he stood up quite unsupported and kicked his legs out. His insight made him radiant.

Georg shrank into a corner, as far away from his father as possible. A long time ago he had firmly made up his mind to watch closely every least movement so that he should not be surprised by any indirect attack, a pounce from behind or above. At this moment he recalled this long-forgotten resolve and forgot it again, like a man drawing a short thread through the eye of a needle.

"But your friend hasn't been betrayed after all!" cried his father, emphasizing the point with stabs of his forefinger. "I've been representing him here on the spot."

"You comedian!" Georg could not resist the retort, realized at once the harm done and, his eyes starting in his head, bit his tongue back, only too late, till the pain made his knees give.

"Yes, of course I've been playing a comedy! A comedy! That's a good expression! What other comfort was left to a poor old widower? Tell me — and while you're answering me be you still my living son — what else was left to me, in my back room, plagued by a disloyal staff, old to the marrow of my bones? And my son strutting through the world, finishing off deals that I had prepared for him, bursting with triumphant glee, and stalking away from his father with the closed face of a respectable businessman! Do you think I didn't love you, I, from whom you are sprung?"

Now he'll lean forward, thought Georg, what if he topples and smashes himself! These words went hissing through his mind.

His father leaned forward but did not topple. Since Georg did not come any nearer, as he had expected, he straightened himself again.

"Stay where you are, I don't need you! You think you have strength enough to come over here and that you're only hanging back of your own accord. Don't be too sure! I am still much the stronger of us two. All by myself I might have had to give way, but your mother has given me so much of her strength that I've established a fine connection with your friend and I have your customers here in my pocket!"

"He has pockets even in his shirt!" said Georg to himself, and believed that with this remark he could make him an impossible figure for all the world. Only for a moment did he think so, since he kept on forgetting everything.

"Just take your bride on your arm and try getting in my way! I'll sweep her from your very side, you don't know how!"

Georg made a grimace of disbelief. His father only nodded, confirming the truth of his words, toward Georg's corner.

"How you amused me today, coming to ask me if you should tell your friend about your engagement. He knows it already, you stupid boy, he knows it all! I've been writing to him, for you forgot to take my writing things away from me. That's why he hasn't been here for years, he knows everything a hundred times better than you do yourself, in his left hand he crumples your letters unopened while in his right hand he holds up my letters to read through!"

In his enthusiasm he waved his arm over his head. "He knows everything a thousand times better!" he cried.

"Ten thousand times!" said Georg, to make fun of his father, but in his very mouth the words turned into deadly earnest.

"For years I've been waiting for you to come with some such question! Do you think I concern myself with anything else? Do you think I read my newspapers? Look!" and he threw Georg a newspaper sheet which he had somehow taken to bed with him. An old newspaper, with a name entirely unknown to Georg.

"How long a time you've taken to grow up! Your mother had to die, she couldn't see the happy day, your friend is going to pieces in Russia, even three years ago he was yellow enough to be thrown away, and as for me, you see what condition I'm in. You have eyes in your head for that!"

"So you've been lying in wait for me!" cried Georg.

His father said pityingly, in an offhand manner: "I suppose you wanted to say that sooner. But now it doesn't matter." And in a louder voice: "So now you know what else there was in the world besides yourself, till now you've known only about yourself! An innocent child, yes, that you were, truly, but still more truly have you been a devilish human being! — And therefore take note: I sentence you now to death by drowning!"

Georg felt himself urged from the room, the crash with which his father fell on the bed behind him was still in his ears as he fled. On the staircase, which he rushed down as if its steps were an inclined plane, he ran into his charwoman on her way up to do the morning cleaning of the room. "Jesus!" she cried, and covered her face with her apron, but he was already gone. Out of the front door he rushed, across the roadway, driven toward the water. Already he was grasping at the railings as a starving man clutches food. He swung himself over, like the distinguished gymnast he had once been in his youth, to his parents' pride. With weakening grip he was still holding on when he spied between the railings a motor-bus coming which would easily cover the noise of his fall, called in a low voice: "Dear parents, I have always loved you, all the same," and let himself drop.

At this moment an unending stream of traffic was just going over the bridge.

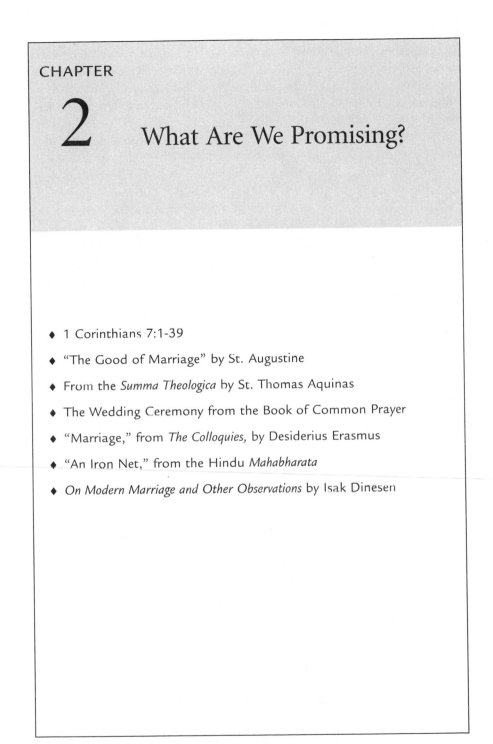

CHAPTER

2   What Are We Promising?

More things belong in marriage than four legs in bed.

— JOHN HEYWOOD

The sum which to married poeple owe to one another defies calculation. It is an infinite debt, which can only be discharged through all eternity.

— GOETHE

Introduction

In the first chapter of our anthology, we sought to penetrate the question of what the institution of marriage can do for the individual. Here, in this chapter, we tackle the question of what the individual is required to do for the institution of marriage. What do our wedding vows mean? What do we promise in taking them? What do we renounce in accepting them? What, finally, does the bride owe the groom according to her marriage oaths? What does the groom owe the bride? What, in effect, is the ideal we serve through marriage?

In the reading from 1 Corinthians 7, Saint Paul declares what many consider the core of Christian doctrine on marriage: "It is better to marry than to burn [with passion]." For Paul, marriage is a concession to carnal desires that should be made only by those men and women who find themselves unable to remain sexually continent. It follows, then, that sex is at the core of the marriage bond, and that the marriage vow is a vow of belonging to one another with the whole of the body. Paul sees marriage as the single legitimate outlet for sexual desire, and the nearest thing to celibacy. For him, it is a sexual relationship of permanence exclusive to one person, and one alone, as long as that person lives.

So sacred is the conjugal relationship that Paul enjoins husbands and wives they should never separate. If they do, they may not marry again as long as their former partner lives. Even marriage to an unbeliever, Paul insists, is an inviolable union, for the "unbelieving husband is sanctified by the [believing] wife, and the unbelieving wife is sanctified by the [believing] husband." Both husbands and wives have a mutual duty to one another to perform the sexual act, unless they mutually agree to abstain from sex temporarily for purposes of devotion to prayer. Underlying Paul's notions of sexual duty in marriage is the idea that the decision to marry is an active decision for things of this world. A married man, he says, cannot concern himself with the "Lord's affairs" and with the world to come, because he must think how he will "please his wife."

Pronouncing on the subject of marriage, St. Augustine reminds us again that the church offers Christians marriage as a concession, not as a commandment. (In this respect Christians distinguished themselves from the Jews, since Jews are commanded to marry.) Yet, while Paul was neutral on marriage, declaring it neither an evil nor a good, Augustine viewed the marital union as a "good." Marriage, Augustine wrote, is a good because it fosters the "natural companionship between the sexes" and provides for the continuance of the species. Like Paul, Augustine states that marriage is a permanent and unbreakable bond. Its two principal obligations involve fidelity and payment of the conjugal "debt" — i.e., intercourse. But Augustine emphasizes the importance of striving for as much sexual continence as possible within the marital union. In Augustine's view, married couples should ideally indulge in sexual relations purely for purposes of procreation. Sex for the purpose of pleasure alone is regarded as intemperance; it is a sin "pardonable" only as a safety valve in preventing adultery. For us moderns, it is interesting to note that the early Church Fathers considered it unseemly to demand sexual pleasure from a marriage partner for the mere sake of one's own satisfaction. Yet, they considered it one of the primary obligations of marriage to attend to one's *partner's* sexual demands, even at the cost of one's own aspirations to sexual continence. Indeed, the Christian tradition allows husbands and wives equal rights to sue for the conjugal debt, or to obtain an annulment of marriage in the event "payment" of that debt is "wrongfully" withheld.

Thomas Aquinas, the thirteenth-century philosopher, reasserted Augustine's three major "goods" of marriage: *proles* (procreation), *fides* (fidelity), and *sacramentum* (sacrament). While he restated that the Christian marital sacrament invested permanence on the union, he introduced the notion that the marriage of Christians also impresses holiness on the partners. Marriage, according to Aquinas, is more than a worldly arrangement. It offers a direct link to God. In elevating marriage to a spiritual union between the married couple and God, Aquinas and other theologians of his century elevated the obligations of marriage — sexual and otherwise — to means of salvation.

In fact, by the fourteenth century, the Church considered the sacrament of marriage to consist not in the completion of a public wedding ceremony or in the consummation of a marriage, but in the vows of intent made between the couple, even if those were made in secret, and even if the couple had not had intercourse. It is important to note that in taking upon themselves the vows of marriage, men and women are thought to mirror the relationship between Christ and the Church. But the intensity and sacredness of their private relationship must never override other obligations to Christian charity — to family and community. In fact, for Aquinas, marriage is something of an enlargement of the self, enabling a more conscientious fulfillment of those obligations of love and reverence for parents and community than remaining single would enable.

The most famous of wedding ceremonies, coming from the Book of Common Prayer, spells out obligations of marriage beyond procreation, fidelity, and sacrament. Here the husband and wife promise to love, to comfort, to honor, and to keep each other. They are exhorted to a community of life even in the most difficult of circumstances: "for richer or poorer, in sickness as in health." The sacramental nature of Episcopal marriage, in contrast to Catholic marriage, is expressed not as a mystical union, but as "signifying . . . the mystical union betwixt Christ and his Church." Here the Christian idea of the civic good of marriage is expressed. Marriage is described as an "honorable" estate with clear implications for the maintenance of social and moral order. In marrying, then, we promise to support that order.

Erasmus's Colloquy "Marriage" fleshes out in a humorous way the extent to which the marital promise involves obligations of good will, respect, and forbearance. The Colloquy is a dialogue between two wives, one wise, the other foolish. The first has smartly and painstakingly built a harmonious relationship with her husband; the second (though she claims she's living with the proverbial husband 'from hell') seems to have made no effort at a working marriage. When the foolish wife laments her husband's drinking, yelling, cavorting, and money-squandering, the wise wife counsels, "You bring reproach on yourself when you reproach your husband." She then proceeds to give her friend a few practical lessons in spouse management. Marriage, she reminds us, requires patience and work.

The East Indian tale that follows concerns a wealthy princess who searches far and wide for a kind and virtuous husband. Settling on a worthy but dispossessed prince, she is forced to live far from home in impoverished conditions. But her devotion to her chosen is perfect. When Death comes to take the prince away barely a year after their marriage, the princess manages, by way of cunning and sacrifice, to ransom him and save their future together. This rich story seems to beg the question as to whether we do not owe to marriage from the very beginning everything we can possibly give to it. Or at least it begs the question as to whether marriage will in any case *demand* everything we can give.

Having traced some of the key notions of marital obligation across time and culture, we come to Isak Dinesen's essay *On Modern Marriage and Other Observations*. In reviewing the small but increasingly unwilling personal sacrifices of modern husbands and wives (sacrifices of time, talent, independence, and whimsy), Dinesen confronts a terrible reality of the modern world, the decay of a sense of duty and obligation in marriage, a decay due to the weakening claims of church, family, and community on the modern individual. The great burden of marriage, Dinesen alleges, now rests entirely on the shoulders of married couples, for the ideals marriage once served — ideals of God, church, family, and community — are fading. Who will help married couples bear the burden of marriage? What ideal can marriage serve in the modern world? How can we restore the principle of marital duty? Where a marriage may no longer be contracted in the service of God, or in the service of the clan or community, or in the service of preserving the family title and properties, on what guiding ideal might it be contracted? Dinesen suggests that love is not enough, but that marriage still serves a crucial purpose in its child-rearing function. In this provocative defense of marriage as a form of eugenics, Dinesen argues that marital duty and marital fidelity are still keys to the healthy future of the human race.

THE FIRST LETTER
TO THE CORINTHIANS

First Corinthians was a letter written by St. Paul in the sixth decade of the first century A.D. It was addressed to the members of his fledgling Christian Church in Corinth, where he had spent eighteen months. After leaving Corinth, Paul went to Ephesus, where he kept himself informed of the activities of the Corinth Christian community, and resolved to advise its members on some pertinent issues of conduct, morals, religious observance, and theology. It should be remembered that Paul's words on marriage are written for men and women who lived in the pagan environment of ancient Greece. His judiciousness and tolerance with regard to matters of interrelations between heathens and members of the church may seem to us quite remarkable. But Paul understood and respected Greco-Roman culture.

1 Corinthians 7:1-39

1 Now concerning the things whereof ye wrote unto me: It is good for a man not to touch a woman.
2 Nevertheless, to avoid fornication, let every man have his own wife, and let every woman have her own husband.
3 Let the husband render unto the wife due benevolence; and likewise also the wife unto the husband.
4 The wife hath not power of her own body, but the husband; and likewise also the husband hath not power of his own body, but the wife.
5 Defraud ye not one the other, except it be with consent for a time, that ye

may give yourselves to fasting and prayer; and come together again, that Satan tempt you not for your incontinency.

6 But I speak this by permission, and not of commandment.

7 For I would that all men were even as I myself. But every man hath his proper gift of God, one after this manner, and another after that.

8 I say therefore to the unmarried and widows, it is good for them if they abide even as I.

9 But if they cannot contain, let them marry; for it is better to marry than to burn.

10 And unto the married I command, yet not I, but the Lord, Let not the wife depart from her husband:

11 But and if she depart, let her remain unmarried or be reconciled to her husband; and let not the husband put away his wife.

12 But to the rest speak I, not the Lord: If any brother hath a wife that believeth not, and she be pleased to dwell with him, let him not put her away.

13 And the woman which hath an husband that believeth not, and if he be pleased to dwell with her, let her not leave him.

14 For the unbelieving husband is sanctified by the wife, and the unbelieving wife is sanctified by the husband; else were your children unclean, but now are they holy.

15 But if the unbelieving depart, let him depart. A brother or a sister is not under bondage in such cases; but God hath called us to peace.

16 For what knowest thou, O wife, whether thou shalt save thy husband? or how knowest thou, O man, whether thou shalt save thy wife?

17 But as God hath distributed to every man, as the Lord hath called every one, so let him walk. And so ordain I in all churches.

18 Is any man called being circumcised? let him not become uncircumcised. Is any called in uncircumcision? let him not be circumcised.

19 Circumcision is nothing, and uncircumcision is nothing, but the keeping of the commandments of God.

20 Let every man abide in the same calling wherein he was called.

21 Art thou called being a servant? care not for it; but if thou mayest be made free, use it rather.

22 For he that is called in the Lord, being a servant, is the Lord's freeman; likewise also he that is called, being free, is Christ's servant.

23 Ye are bought with a price; be not ye the servants of men.

24 Brethren, let every man, wherein he is called, therein abide with God.

25 Now concerning virgins I have no commandment of the Lord; yet I give my judgment, as one that hath obtained mercy of the Lord to be faithful.

26 I suppose therefore that this is good for the present distress, I say, that it is good for a man so to be.

27 Art thou bound unto a wife? seek not to be loosed. Art thou loosed from a wife? seek not a wife.

28 But and if thou marry, thou hast not sinned; and if a virgin marry, she hath not sinned. Nevertheless such shall have trouble in the flesh; but I spare you.

29 But this I say, brethren, the time is short: it remaineth, that both they that have wives be as though they had none;

30 And they that weep, as though they wept not; and they that rejoice, as though they rejoiced not; and they that buy, as though they possessed not;

31 And they that use this world, as not abusing it; for the fashion of this world passeth away.

32 But I would have you without carefulness. He that is unmarried careth for the things that belong to the Lord, how he may please the Lord;

33 But he that is married careth for the things that are of the world, how he may please his wife.

34 There is difference also between a wife and a virgin. The unmarried woman careth for the things of the Lord, that she may be holy both in body and in spirit; but she that is married careth for the things of the world, how she may please her husband.

35 And this I speak for your own profit; not that I may cast a snare upon you, but for that which is comely, and that ye may attend upon the Lord without distraction.

36 But if any man think that he behaveth himself uncomely toward his virgin, if she pass the flower of her age, and need so require, let him do what he will, he sinneth not: let them marry.

37 Nevertheless he that standeth stedfast in his heart, having no necessity, but hath power over his own will, and hath so decreed in his heart that he will keep his virgin, doeth well.

38 So then he that giveth her in marriage doeth well; but he that giveth her not in marriage doeth better.

39 The wife is bound by the law as long as her husband liveth; but if her husband be dead, she is at liberty to be married to whom she will; only in the Lord.

ST. AUGUSTINE

St. Augustine, Bishop of Hippo (354-430), was born in North Africa of Roman parentage. A scholar and rhetorician, he lived for many years in Italy. His mother was a Christian, but Augustine himself was baptized only at the age of 33 years, after much philosophical rumination and spiritual torment. In his most famous work, the *Confessions,* he describes his conversion as an epiphany, a fit of despair suddenly tempered by reading St. Paul's exhortation in the Epistles, ". . . put ye on the Lord Jesus Christ, and make not provision for the flesh in the lusts thereof." Augustine never married, and his youth was spent in the throes of inner struggle between on the one hand his aspirations to sexual continence, and on the other his strong sexual desires. He sired a beloved natural son by a concubine whom his mother shipped back to Africa when she had, she thought, procured him a suitable bride. That son remained with his father when Augustine returned to North Africa a Christian. The boy, however, died at the age of 17.

The Good of Marriage

Chapter 1

Since every man is a part of the human race, and human nature is something social and possesses the capacity for friendship as a great and natural good, for this reason God wished to create all men from one, so that they might be held together in their society, not only by the similarity of race, but also by the bond of blood relationship. And so it is that the first natural tie of human society is man and wife. Even these God did not create separately and join them as if strangers, but He made the one from the other, indicating also the power of union in the side from where she was drawn and formed.[1] They are joined to each other side by side who walk together and observe together where they are walking. A consequence is the union of society in the children who are the only worthy fruit, not of the joining of male and female, but of sexual intercourse. For there could have been in both sexes, even without such intercourse, a kind of friendly and genuine union of the one ruling and the other obeying.

Chapter 2

(2) There is no need now for us to examine and put forth a final opinion on this question — how the progeny of the first parents might have come into being, whom God had blessed, saying, 'Be fruitful and multiply; fill the earth,'[2] if they had not sinned, since their bodies deserved the condition of death by sinning, and there could not be intercourse except of mortal bodies. Many different opinions have existed on this subject, and, if we must examine which of them agrees most with the truth of divine Scriptures, there is matter for an extended discussion:[3] Whether, for example, if our first parents had not sinned, they would have had children in some other way, without physical coition, out of the munificence of the almighty Creator, who was able to create them without parents, and who was able to form the body of Christ in a virgin's womb, and who, to speak now to the unbelievers themselves, was able to grant progeny to bees without intercourse; whether, in that passage, much was spoken in a mystical and figurative sense and the written words are to be understood differently: 'Till the earth and subdue it,' that is, that it should come to pass by the fullness and the perfection of life and power that the increasing and multiplying, where it is said: 'Be fruitful and multiply,' might be understood to be by the advancement of the mind and by the fullness of virtue, as it is expressed in the psalm: 'Thou shalt multiply me in my soul unto virtue,'[4] and that succession of offspring was not granted to man except that later, because of sin, there was to be a departure in death; whether, at first, the body of those men had been made spiritual but animal, so that afterwards by the merit of obedience it might become spiritual to grasp immortality, not after death, which came into the world through the envy of the Devil[5] and became the punishment for sin, but through that change which the Apostle indicates where he says: 'Then we who live, who survive, shall be caught up together with them in clouds to meet the Lord in the air,'[6] so that we may understand that the bodies of the first marriage were both mortal at the first formation and yet would not have died, if they had not sinned, as

73

God had threatened,[7] just as if He threatened a wound, because the body was vulnerable, which, however, would not have happened, unless that was done which He had forbidden.

Thus, then, even through sexual intercourse generations of such bodies could have come into existence, which would have had increase up to a certain point and yet would not have inclined to old age, or they would have inclined as far as old age and yet not to death, until the earth should be filled with that multiplication of the blessing. For, if God granted to the garments of the Israelites[8] their proper state without any damage for forty years, how much more would He have granted a very happy temperament of certain state to the bodies of those who obeyed His command, until they would be turned into something better, not by the death of man, by which the body is deserted by the soul, but by a blessed change from mortality to immortality, from an animal to a spiritual quality.

Chapter 3

It would be tedious to inquire and to discuss which of these opinions is true, or whether another or other opinions can still be extracted from these words.

(3) This is what we now say, that according to the present condition of birth and death, which we know and in which we were created, the marriage of male and female is something good. This union divine Scripture so commands that it is not permitted a woman who has been dismissed by her husband to marry again, as long as her husband lives, nor is it permitted a man who has been dismissed by his wife to marry again, unless she who left has died. Therefore, regarding the good of marriage, which even the Lord confirmed in the Gospel,[9] not only because He forbade the dismissal of a wife except for fornication, but also because He came to the marriage when invited,[10] there is merit in inquiring why it is a good.

This does not seem to me to be a good solely because of the procreation of children, but also because of the natural companionship between the two sexes. Otherwise, we could not speak of marriage in the case of old people, especially if they had either lost their children or had begotten none at all. But, in a good marriage, although one of many years, even if the ardor of youths has cooled between man and woman, the order of charity still flourishes between husband and wife. They are better in proportion as they begin the earlier to refrain by mutual consent from sexual intercourse, not that it would afterwards happen of necessity that they would not be able to do what they wished, but that it would be a matter of praise that they had refused beforehand what they were able to do. If, then, there is observed that promise of respect and of services due to each other by either sex, even though both members weaken in health and become almost corpse-like, the chastity of souls rightly joined together continues the purer, the more it has been proved, and the more secure, the more it has been calmed.

Marriage has also this good, that carnal or youthful incontinence, even if it is bad, is turned to the honorable task of begetting children, so that marital intercourse makes something good out of the evil of lust. Finally, the concupiscence of the flesh, which parental affection tempers, is repressed and becomes inflamed more modestly. For a kind of dignity prevails when, as husband and wife they unite in the marriage act, they think of themselves as mother and father.

Chapter 4

(4) There is the added fact that, in the very debt which married persons owe each other, even if they demand its payment somewhat intemperately and incontinently, they owe fidelity equally to each other. And to this fidelity the Apostle has attributed so much right that he called it power, when he said: 'The wife has not authority over her body, but the husband; the husband likewise has not authority over his body, but the wife.'[11] But the violation of this fidelity is called adultery, when, either by the instigation of one's own lust or by consent to the lust of another, there is intercourse with another contrary to the marriage compact. And so the fidelity is broken which even in material and base things is a great good of the soul; and so it is certain that it ought to be preferred even to the health of the body wherein his life is contained. For, although a small amount of straw as compared to much gold is as nothing, fidelity, when it is kept pure in a matter of straw, as in a matter of gold, is not of less importance on this account because it is kept in a matter of less value.

But, when fidelity is employed to commit sin, we wonder whether it ought to be called fidelity. However, whatever its nature may be, if even against this something is done, it has an added malice; except when this is abandoned with the view that there might be a return to the true and lawful fidelity, that is, that the sin might be amended by correcting the depravity of the will.

For example, if anyone, when he is unable to rob a man by himself, finds an accomplice for his crime and makes an agreement with him to perform the act together and share the loot, and, after the crime has been committed, he runs off with everything, the other naturally grieves and complains that fidelity had not been observed in his regard. In his very complaint he ought to consider that he should have observed his fidelity to human society by means of a good life, so that he would not rob a man unjustly, if he feels how wickedly fidelity was not kept with him in an association of sin. His partner, faithless on both counts, is certainly to be judged the more wicked. But, if he had been displeased with the wickedness which they had committed and so had refused to divide the spoils with his partner in crime on this account, that he could return them to the man from whom they were taken, not even the faithless man would call him faithless.

So, in the case of a woman who has broken her marriage fidelity but remains faithful to her adulterer, she is surely wicked, but, if she is not faithful even to her adulterer, she is worse. On the contrary, if she repents of her gross sin and returns to conjugal chastity and breaks off all adulterous unions and purposes, I cannot conceive of even the adulterer himself thinking of her as a violator of fidelity.

Chapter 5

(5) The question is also usually asked whether this case ought to be called a marriage: when a man and a woman (he not being the husband nor she the wife of another) because of incontinence have intercourse not for the purpose of procreating children but only for the sake of intercourse itself, with this pledge between them, that he will not perform this act with another woman, nor she with another man. Yet perhaps not without reason this can be called wedlock, if this has been agreed upon between them even until the death of one of them and if, although they do not have intercourse for the purpose of having children, they do not avoid it, so that they do not refuse to have children nor act in any evil way so that they will not be born. But, if both or either one of these conditions is lacking, I do not see how we can call this a marriage.

For, if a man lives with a woman for a time, until he finds another worthy either of his high station in life or his wealth, whom he can marry as his equal, in his very soul he is an adulterer, and not with the one whom he desires to find but with her with whom he now lives in such a way as not to be married to her. The same is true for the woman, who, knowing the situation and willing it, still has relations unchastely with him, with whom she has no compact as a wife. On the other hand, if she remains faithful to him and, after he has taken a wife, does not plan to marry and is prepared to refrain absolutely from such an act, surely I could not easily bring myself to call her an adulteress; yet who would say that she did not sin, when he knows that she had relations with a man though she was not his wife?

If from the union, as far as she is concerned, she wishes for nothing except children and whatever she endures beyond the cause of procreation she endures unwillingly, surely this woman is to be placed above many matrons, who, although they are not adulteresses, force their husbands, who often desire to be continent, to pay the debt of the flesh, not with any hope of progeny, but through an intemperate use of their right under the ardor of concupiscence, still, in the marriage of these women there is this good, that they are married. They are married for this purpose, that concupiscence may be brought under a lawful bond and may not waver disgracefully and loosely, having of itself a weakness of the flesh that cannot be curbed, but in marriage an association of fidelity that cannot be dissolved; of itself an increase of immoderate intercourse, in marriage a means of begetting chastely. For, although it is disgraceful to make use of a husband for purposes of lust, it is honorable to refuse to have intercourse except with a husband and not to give birth except from a husband.

Chapter 6

There also are men incontinent to such a degree that they do not spare their wives even when pregnant. Whatever immodest, shameful, and sordid acts the married commit with each other are the sins of the married persons themselves, not the fault of marriage.

(6) Furthermore, in the more immoderate demand of the carnal debt, which the Apostle enjoined on them not as a command but conceded as a favor, to have sexual intercourse even without the purpose of procreation, although evil habits impel them to such intercourse, marriage protects them from adultery and fornication. For this is not permitted because of the marriage, but because of the marriage it is pardoned. Therefore, married people owe each other not only the fidelity of sexual intercourse for the purpose of procreating children — and this is the first association of the human race in this mortal life — but also the mutual service, in a certain measure, of sustaining each other's weakness, for the avoidance of illicit intercourse, so that, even if perpetual continence is pleasing to one of them, he may not follow this urge except with the consent of the other. In this case, 'The wife has not authority over her body, but the husband; the husband likewise has not authority over his body, but the wife.' So, let them not deny either to each other, what the man seeks from matrimony and the woman from her husband, not for the sake of having children but because of weakness and incontinence, lest in this way they fall into damnable seductions through the temptations of Satan because of the incontinence of both or of one of them.

In marriage, intercourse for the purpose of generation has no fault attached to it, but for the purpose of satisfying concupiscence, provided with a spouse, because of the marriage fidelity, it is a venial sin; adultery or fornication, however, is a mortal sin. And so, continence from all intercourse is certainly better than marital intercourse itself which takes place for the sake of begetting children.

*   *   *

Chapter 10

(10) But I know what they murmur. 'What if,' they say, 'all men should be willing to restrain themselves from all intercourse, how would the human race survive?' Would that all men had this wish, if only in 'charity, from a pure heart and a good conscience and faith unfeigned.'[12] Much more quickly would the City of God be filled and the end of time be hastened. What else does it appear that the Apostle is encouraging when he says, in speaking of this: 'For I would that you all were as I am myself'?[13] Or, in another place: 'But this I say, brethren, the time is short; it remains that those who have wives be as if they had none; and those who weep, as though not weeping; and those who rejoice, as though not rejoicing; and those who buy, as though not buying; and those who use this world, as though not using it, for this world as we see it is passing away. I would have you free from care.' Then he adds: 'He who is unmarried thinks about the things of the Lord, how he may please the Lord. Whereas he who is married thinks about the things of the world, how he may please his wife, and he is divided. And the unmarried woman and the virgin, who is unmarried, is concerned about the things of the Lord, that she may be holy in body and in spirit. Whereas she who is married is concerned about the things of the world, how she may please her husband.'[14]

And so it seems to me that at this time only those who do not restrain themselves ought to be married in accord with this saying of the same Apostle: 'But if they do not have self-control, let them marry, for it is better to marry than to burn.'[15]

*   *   *

Chapter 15

Once, however, marriage is entered upon in the City [that is, Church] of our God, where also from the first union of the two human beings marriage bears a kind of sacred bond, it can be dissolved in no way except by the death of one of the parties. The bond of marriage remains, even if offspring, for which the marriage was entered upon, should not follow because of a clear case of sterility, so that it is not lawful for married people who know they will not have any children to separate and to unite with others even for the sake of having children. If they do unite, they commit adultery with the ones with whom they join themselves, for they remain married people.

It was indeed permissible among the ancients to have another woman with the consent of the wife, from whom common children might be born by the union and seed of the husband, by the privilege and authorization of the wife. Whether this is permissible now, as well, I would not care to say. There is not the need for procreation which there was then, when it was permissible for husbands who could have children to take other women for the sake of a more copious posterity, which certainly is not lawful now. The mysterious difference of times brings so great an opportunity of doing or of not doing something justly that, now, he does better who does not marry even one wife, unless he cannot control himself; then, however, they had without fault several wives, even they who could restrain themselves much more easily, except that piety in that time demanded something else. For, as the wise and just man, who for a long time was desiring to be dissolved and to be with Christ[16] and was delighted rather by this greatest good, not the desire of living here but the duty of caring for others, took food that he might remain in the flesh, which was necessary for the sake of others, so, too, for the men of those times it was not lust but duty to be joined with women by the law of marriage.

Chapter 16

(18) For, what food is to the health of man, intercourse is to the health of the race, and both are not without carnal pleasure, which, however, when modified and put to its natural use with a controlling temperance, cannot be a passion.[17] However, what unlawful food is in the sustaining of life, this is the intercourse of fornication or adultery in seeking a child; and what unlawful food is in the excessive indulgence of the stomach and palate, this is unlawful intercourse in a passion seeking no offspring; and what is immoderate appetite for some as regards lawful food, this is that pardonable intercourse in spouses. Therefore, just

as it is better to die of hunger than to eat food sacrificed to idols, so it is better to die childless than to seek progeny from an unlawful union.

However, from whatever source men are born, if they do not follow the vices of their parents and if they worship God rightly, they will be honest and safe. The seed of man, from any kind of man, is a creature of God and will prove bad for those who use it wrongly; of itself, it will not at any time be an evil. Yet, just as the good children of adulterers are no defense for adultery, so the bad children of married people do not constitute an accusation against marriage. Accordingly, just as the fathers of New Testament times, taking food because of the duty of caring for others, though they ate it with a natural delectation of the flesh — by no means, however, was their pleasure to be compared with the pleasure of those who were eating food sacrificed to idols or of those who, though they were consuming lawful foods, were doing so immoderately — so the fathers of Old Testament times had intercourse because of the duty of caring for others. That natural delight they derived was by no means given rein up to the point of unreasoning and wicked lust, nor is it to be compared to the debaucheries of lust or the intemperance of the married. Indeed, for the same fountainhead of charity, then carnally, now spiritually, were children to be propagated because of that great Mother Jerusalem; only the difference in times made the works of the fathers diverse. So, it was necessary that non-carnal Prophets copulate carnally, as it was necessary that non-carnal Apostles also eat carnally.

Chapter 17

(19) Therefore, as many women as there are now, to whom it is said: 'If they do not have self-control, let them marry,'[18] are not to be compared even to the holy women who married then. Marriage itself among all races is for the one purpose of procreating children, whatever will be their station and character afterwards; marriage was instituted for this purpose, so that children might be born properly and decently.

But the men who do not have self-control step up, as it were, into marriage by a step of honesty; those, however, who without a doubt would have practiced self-control, if the conditions of that time would have allowed this, step down, in a certain sense, into marriage by a step of piety. Therefore, the marriage of both, inasmuch as they are marriages because they exist for the sake of procreation, are equally good; yet, married men of our times are not to be compared to married men of those days. The former have something that is granted to them as a concession because of the dignity of marriage, although it does not pertain to marriage, that is, that departure which goes beyond the need for procreating, which the other men in question did not have. But neither can these, if any by chance are now to be found who do not seek or desire in marriage anything except that for which marriage was instituted, be put on the same footing with those men. For, in these the very desire for children is carnal; in those, however, it was spiritual, because it was in accord with the mystery of the time. In our day, it is true, no one perfect in piety seeks to have children except spiritually; in their day, however, the work of piety itself was to propagate children even carnally, because the generation of that people was a harbinger of future events and pertains to the prophetic dispensation.

*   *   *

Chapter 23

Therefore, if we compare the things themselves, in no way can it be doubted that the chastity of continence is better than the chastity of marriage. Although both, indeed, are a good, when we compare the men, the one who has the greater good than the other is the better. Moreover, he who has the greater good of the same kind has also that which is less; however, he who has only what is less certainly does not have what is greater. For, thirty is contained in sixty, but not sixty in thirty. The failure to act in accordance with one's full capacity to act depends upon the distribution of duties, not upon the lack of virtue, because he does not lack the good of mercy who does not come upon the unfortunate ones whom he could help in his mercy.

(29) We must take this into account, too, that it is not right to compare men with men in some one good. For, it can happen that one does not have something that the other has, but he has something that is to be valued more highly. Greater, indeed, is the good of obedience than the good of continence. Marriage is nowhere condemned by the authority of our Scriptures; disobedience, however, is nowhere condoned.

If, then, we have to choose between one who remains a virgin who is at the same time disobedient and a married woman who could not remain a virgin but who is nevertheless obedient — which of the two shall we say is the better? Is it the one who is less laudable than she would be if she were a virgin, or the one worthy of reproach although she is a virgin? So, if you compare a drunken virgin with a chaste spouse, who would hesitate to pass the same judgment? Marriage and virginity are, it is true, two goods; the second of them is the greater. So with sobriety and drunkenness, obedience and disobedience —

the former are goods; the latter, evils. However, it is better to have everything that is good in a lesser degree than to have a great good with a great evil, since even in the goods of the body it is better to have the stature of Zaccaeus[19] together with health than the height of Goliath[20] together with a fever.

(30) The right question is plainly not whether a virgin thoroughly disobedient should be compared with an obedient married woman, but a less obedient to a more obedient, for there is also nuptial chastity and it is indeed a good, but a lesser one than virginal chastity. Therefore, if the woman who is inferior in the good of obedience in proportion as she is greater in the good of chastity is compared with the other, then he who sees, when he compares chastity itself and obedience, that obedience in a certain way is the mother of all virtues, judges which woman is to be placed first. On this account, then, there can be obedience without virginity, because virginity is of counsel, not of precept. I am speaking of that obedience whereby precepts are obeyed. There can be obedience to precepts without virginity, but there cannot be this obedience without chastity. For it is of the essence of chastity not to commit fornication, not to commit adultery, not to be stained with any illicit intercourse. Whoever do not observe these precepts act against the commands of God and on this account are banished from the virtue of obedience. Virginity can exist by itself without obedience, since a woman can, although accepting the counsel of virginity and guarding her virginity, neglect the precepts; just as we know many sacred virgins who are garrulous, inquisitive, addicted to drink, contentious, greedy, proud. All these vices are against the precepts and destroy them through their sin of disobedience, like Eve herself. Therefore, not only is the obedient person to be preferred to the disobedient one, but the more obedient wife is to be preferred to the less obedient virgin.

(31) In accord with this, that patriarch who was not without a wife was prepared to be without his only son and one to be slain by his own hand.[21] Indeed, I may speak of 'his only son' not unfittingly, concerning whom he had heard from the Lord: 'Through Isaac shall your descendants be called.'[22] Therefore, how much more readily would he have obeyed if it were ordered that he was not to have a wife?

So it is that not in vain do we often wonder at some of both sexes, who, containing themselves from all intercourse, carelessly obey the commands, though they have so ardently embraced the idea of not using things that have been granted. Seeing this, who doubts that the men and women of our times, free from all intercourse but inferior in the virtue of obedience, are not rightly compared to the excellence of those holy patriarchs and mothers begetting children, even if the patriarchs had lacked the habit of mind that is manifest in the actions of the men of our day?

Therefore, let the young men singing a new canticle follow the Lamb, as it is written in the Apocalypse: 'Who have not defiled themselves with women,'[23] on no other account than that they remained virgins. Let them not think, then, that they are better than the early patriarchs, who used their marriage, if I may put it this way, nuptially. The use, indeed, of marriage is such that there is a defilement if anything is done in marriage through the union of the flesh that exceeds the need for generation, though this is pardonable. For, what does pardon expiate, if that departure does not defile entirely? It would be remarkable if the children following the Lamb would be free from this defilement unless they remained virgins.

Chapter 24

(32) The good, therefore, of marriage among all nations and all men is in the cause of generation and in the fidelity of chastity; in the case of the people of God, however, the good is also in the sanctity of the sacrament. Because of this sanctity it is wrong for a woman, leaving with a divorce, to marry another man while her husband still lives, even if she does this for the sake of having children. Although that is the sole reason why marriage takes place, even if this for which marriage takes place does not follow, the marriage bond is not loosed except by the death of a spouse. Just as if an ordination of the clergy is performed to gather the people, even if the congregation does not follow, there yet remains in those ordained the sacrament of orders. And if, because of any fault, anyone is removed from clerical office, he retains the sacrament of the Lord once it has been imposed, although it remains for judgment.

The Apostle is a witness to the fact that marriage exists for the sake of generation in this way: 'I desire,' he says, 'that the younger widows marry.'[24] And — as if it were said to him: for what reason? — he added immediately: 'to bear children, to rule their households.' But this pertains to the faithfulness of chastity: 'The wife has not authority over her body, but the husband; the husband likewise has not authority over his body, but the wife.'[25] As to the sanctity of the sacrament, this is pertinent: 'A wife is not to depart from her husband, and if she departs, that she is to remain unmarried or be reconciled to her husband,' and 'Let not a husband put away his wife.'[26] These are all goods on account of which marriage is a good: offspring, fidelity, sacrament. Yet, not to seek carnal offspring now at this time, and on this account to retain a certain perpetual freedom from all such practice and to be spiritually subject to one man, Christ, is better and indeed holier; especially if men use this freedom so acquired in such a way as it is written, to think about the things of the Lord, how they may please God,[27] that is, that continence unceasingly consider lest obedience fall short in any way. The holy patriarchs practiced this virtue as basic and, as it is customarily called, a source and clearly a universal one; but continence they possessed in the disposition of the soul. Even if they had been ordered to abstain from all intercourse, they certainly would have done so by means of the obedience by which they were just and holy and prepared for every good work. For, how much more easily were they able not to have intercourse at the command or bidding of God who could by being obedient immolate the offspring whose propagation alone they were making possible by having intercourse.

Chapter 25

(33) Since these things are so, I have answered enough and more than enough to the heretics, whether Manichaeans or whoever else calumniate the patriarchs for their many wives, alleging that this is an argument by which they prove their incontinence, if, however, they understand that what is not done contrary to nature is not a sin, since they made use of their wives, not for the sake of being wanton, but for procreation; nor against the customs, because at the time those things were being done; nor contrary to the precept, because they were not prohibited by any law. Those, indeed, who illicitly made use of women, either that divine dictum in the Scriptures convicts, or the text puts them before us as ones who are to be judged and avoided, not to be approved or imitated.

Chapter 26

(34) However, as much as we can, we advise our people who have spouses not to dare to judge those patriarchs according to their weakness, comparing, as the Apostle says, themselves with themselves,[28] and therefore not understanding what great powers the soul that serves justice has against the passions, so that it does not acquiesce in carnal impulses of this kind and does not allow them to fall into or to proceed to intercourse beyond the need for generation, that is, beyond what the order of nature, beyond what customs, beyond what laws permit.

Men indeed have this suspicion concerning these patriarchs because they themselves either have chosen marriage because of incontinence or they make use of their wives immoderately. But let continent people, either men whose wives have died, or women whose husbands have died, or both, who with equal consent have pledged their continence to God, know that a greater reward is due them than conjugal chastity demands. But, as to the marriage of the holy patriarchs, who were joined in a prophetic way, who neither in intercourse sought anything but progeny, nor anything in the progeny itself except what would profit Christ who was to come in the flesh, let them not only not despise it in comparison with their own resolution, but also in accordance with their own resolution; let them prefer it with hesitation.

(35) Most especially do we warn the young men and the virgins dedicating their virginity to God, so that they may know that they ought to guard the life they are living in the meantime upon earth with the greatest humility, since the greater life which they have vowed is of heaven. For it is written: 'The greater thou art, the more humble thyself in all things.'[29] Therefore, it is for us to say something of their greatness; it is theirs to think of great humility. Thus, with the exception of certain of the married patriarchs and married women of the Old Testament — for these, though they are not married, are not better than they, because if they were married they would not be equal — let them not doubt that all the other married people of this time, even the ones who are continent after experiencing marriage, are surpassed by them, not as much as Susanna is surpassed by Anna, but as much as both are surpassed by Mary. I am speaking of what pertains to the holy integrity of the flesh, for who is ignorant of the other merits that Mary had?

Therefore, let them add a fitting conduct to such a high resolve, so that they may have a certain security in respect to obtaining such a splendid reward, knowing, indeed, that to themselves and to all the faithful beloved and chosen members of Christ coming from the East and the West, though shining with a light different in each case, because of their merits, this great reward is given in common, to recline with Abraham and Isaac and Jacob in the kingdom of God,[30] who, not for the sake of this world but for the sake of Christ, were spouses, for the sake of Christ were parents.

ST. THOMAS AQUINAS

St. Thomas Aquinas, the most important Christian philosopher of the Middle Ages, was born near Naples in 1225. Pope Leo XIII, in his *Encyclical* of August 4, 1879, declared that Aquinas's writings form the very core of modern Catholic theology. The *Summa Theologica* represents the pinnacle of Aquinas's philosophical achievement. In this three-part work, he attempted to combine Christian creed with Aristotelian logic and ethics in a summation of both reasoned and revealed knowledge. Aquinas never completed the third volume of the *Summa Theologica*. He died in 1274 on his way to the General Council of Lyons where, invited by Pope Gregory X, he was to take part in an effort to unify the Greek and Latin churches.

Summa Theologica II-II, Q. 26, A. 11; III Supp. Q. 41, A. 4; Q. 42, AA. 1-3

Question 26: Of the Order of Charity

Eleventh Article: Whether a Man Ought to Love His Wife More Than His Father and Mother?

We proceed thus to the Eleventh Article: —

    Objection 1. It would seem that a man ought to love his wife more than his father and mother. For no man leaves a thing for another unless he love the latter more. Now it is written (Gen. ii.24) that *a man shall leave father and mother* on account of his wife. Therefore a man ought to love his wife more than his father and mother.

Obj. 2. Further, the Apostle says (Eph. v.33) that a husband should *love his wife as himself.* Now a man ought to love himself more than his parents. Therefore he ought to love his wife also more than his parents.

Obj. 2. Further, love should be greater where there are more reasons for loving. Now there are more reasons for love in the friendship of a man towards his wife. For the Philosopher says (*Ethic.* viii.12) that *in this friendship there are the motives of utility, pleasure, and also of virtue, if husband and wife are virtuous.* Therefore a man's love for his wife ought to be greater than his love for his parents.

On the contrary, According to Eph. 5:28, *men ought to love their wives as their own bodies.* Now a man ought to love his body less than his neighbor, as stated above (A. 5): and among his neighbors he should love his parents most. Therefore he ought to love his parents more than his wife.

I answer that, As stated above (A. 9), the degrees of love may be taken from the good (which is loved), or from the union between those who love. On the part of the good which is the object loved, a man should love his parents more than his wife, because he loves them as his principles and considered as a more exalted good.

But on the part of the union, the wife ought to be loved more, because she is united with her husband, as one flesh, according to Matth. xix.6: *Therefore now they are not two, but one flesh.* Consequently a man loves his wife more intensely, but his parents with greater reverence.

Reply Obj. 1. A man does not in all respects leave his father and mother for the sake of his wife: for in certain cases a man ought to succor his parents rather than his wife. He does however leave all his kinsfolk, and cleaves to his wife as regards the union of carnal connection and cohabitation.

Reply Obj. 2. The words of the Apostle do not mean that a man ought to love his wife equally with himself, but that a man's love for himself is the reason for his love of his wife, since she is one with him.

Reply Obj. 3. There are also several reasons for a man's love for his father; and these, in a certain respect, namely, as regards good, are more weighty than those for which a man loves his wife; although the latter outweigh the former as regards the closeness of the union.

As to the argument in the contrary sense, it must be observed that in the words quoted, the particle *as* denotes not equality of love but the motive of love. For the principal reason why a man loves his wife is her being united to him in the flesh.

Question 41: Of the Sacrament of Matrimony as Directed to an Office of Nature

Fourth Article: Whether the Marriage Act Is Meritorious?

We proceed thus to the Fourth Article: —

Objection. 1. It would seem that the marriage act is not meritorious. For Chrysostom[1] says in his commentary on Matthew: *Although marriage brings no punishment to those who use it, it affords them no meed* [i.e., honor]. Now merit bears a relation to meed. Therefore the marriage act is not meritorious.

Obj. 2. Further, to refrain from what is meritorious deserves not praise. Yet virginity whereby one refrains from marriage is praiseworthy. Therefore the marriage act is not meritorious.

Obj. 3. Further, he who avails himself of an indulgence granted him, avails himself of a favor received. But a man does not merit by receiving a favor. Therefore the marriage act is not meritorious.

Obj. 4. Further, merit like virtue, consists in difficulty. But the marriage act affords not difficulty but pleasure. Therefore it is not meritorious.

Obj. 5. Further, that which cannot be done without venial sin is never meritorious, for a man cannot both merit and demerit at the same time. Now there is always a venial sin in the marriage act, since even the first movement in such like pleasures is a venial sin. Therefore the aforesaid act cannot be meritorious.

On the contrary, Every act whereby a precept is fulfilled is meritorious if it be done from charity. Now such is the marriage act, for it is said (1 Cor. vii.3): *Let the husband render the debt to his wife.* Therefore, etc.

Further, every act of virtue is meritorious. Now the aforesaid act is an act of justice, for it is called the rendering of a debt. Therefore it is meritorious.

I answer that, Since no act proceeding from a deliberate will is indifferent, as stated in the Second Book (ii. *Sent.* D. 40, Q. 1, A. 3; I-II, Q. 18, A. 9), the marriage act is always either sinful or meritorious in one who is in a state of grace. For if the motive for the marriage act be a virtue, whether of justice that they may render the debt, or of religion, that they may beget children for the worship of God, it is meritorious. But if the motive be lust, yet not excluding the marriage blessings, namely that he would by no means be willing to go to another woman, it is a venial sin; while if he exclude the marriage blessings, so as to be disposed to act in like manner with any woman, it is a mortal sin. And nature cannot move without being either directed by reason, and thus it will be an act of virtue, or not so directed, and then it will be an act of lust.

Reply Obj. 1. The root of merit, as regards the essential reward, is charity itself; but as regards an accidental reward, the reason for merit consists in the difficulty of an act; and thus the marriage act is not meritorious except in the first way.

Reply Obj. 2. The difficulty required for merit of the accidental reward is a difficulty of labor, but the difficulty required for the essential reward is the difficulty of observing the mean, and this is the difficulty in the marriage act.

Reply Obj. 3. First movements in so far as they are venial sins are movements of the appetite to some inordinate object of pleasure. This is not the case in the marriage act, and consequently the argument does not prove.

Question 42: Of Matrimony as a Sacrament

We must next consider matrimony as a sacrament. Under this head there are four points of inquiry: (1) Whether matrimony is a sacrament? (2) Whether it ought to have been instituted before sin was committed? (3) Whether it confers grace? (4) Whether carnal intercourse belongs to the integrity of matrimony?

First Article: Whether Matrimony Is a Sacrament?

We proceed thus to the First Article: —

Objection 1. It would seem that matrimony is not a sacrament. For every sacrament of the New Law has a form that is essential to the sacrament. But the blessing given by the priest at a wedding is not essential to matrimony. Therefore it is not a sacrament.

Obj. 2. Further, a sacrament according to Hugh (*De Sacram*. i) is *a material element*. But matrimony has not a material element for its matter. Therefore it is not a sacrament.

Obj. 3. Further, the sacraments derive their efficacy from Christ's Passion. But matrimony, since it has pleasure annexed to it, does not conform man to Christ's Passion, which was painful. Therefore it is not a sacrament.

Obj. 4. Further, every sacrament of the New Law causes that which it signifies. Yet matrimony does not cause the union of Christ with the Church, which union it signifies. Therefore matrimony is not a sacrament.

Obj. 5. Further, in the other sacraments there is something which is reality and sacrament. But this is not to be found in matrimony, since it does not imprint a character, else it would not be repeated. Therefore it is not a sacrament.

On the contrary, It is written (Eph. v.32): *This is a great sacrament*. Therefore, etc.

Further, a sacrament is the sign of a sacred thing. But such is Matrimony. Therefore, etc.

I answer that, A sacrament denotes a sanctifying remedy against sin offered to man under sensible signs.[2] Wherefore since this is the case in matrimony, it is reckoned among the sacraments.

Reply Obj. 1. The words whereby the marriage consent is expressed are the form of this sacrament, and not the priest's blessing, which is a sacramental.

Reply Obj. 2. The sacrament of Matrimony, like that of Penance, is perfected by the act of the recipient. Wherefore just as Penance has no other matter than the sensible acts themselves, which take the place of the material element, so it is in Matrimony.

Reply Obj. 3. Although Matrimony is not conformed to Christ's Passion as regards pain, it is as regards charity, whereby He suffered for the Church who was to be united to Him as His spouse.

Reply Obj. 4. The union of Christ with the Church is not the reality contained in this sacrament, but is the reality signified and not contained, — and no sacrament causes a reality of that kind, — but it has another both contained and signified which it causes, as we shall state further on (*ad* 5). The Master, however (iv. *Sent.* D. 26), asserts that it is a non-contained reality, because he was of opinion that Matrimony has no reality contained therein.

Reply Obj. 5. In this sacrament also those three things[3] are to be found, for the acts externally apparent are the sacrament only; the bond between husband and wife resulting from those acts is reality and sacrament; and the ultimate reality contained is the effect of this sacrament, while the non-contained reality is that which the Master assigns *(loc. cit.)*.

Second Article: Whether This Sacrament Ought to Have Been Instituted before Sin Was Committed?

We proceed thus to the Second Article: —

Objection 1. It would seem that Matrimony ought not to have been instituted before sin. Because that which is of natural law needs not to be instituted. Now such is Matrimony, as stated above (Q. 41, A. 1). Therefore it ought not to have been instituted.

Obj. 2. Further, sacraments are medicines against the disease of sin. But a medicine is not made ready except for an actual disease. Therefore it should not have been instituted before sin.

Obj. 3. Further, one institution suffices for one thing. Now Matrimony was instituted also after sin, as stated in the text (iv. *Sent.* D. 26). Therefore it was not instituted before sin.

Obj. 4. Further, the institution of a sacrament must come from God. Now before sin, the words relating to Matrimony were not definitely said by God but by Adam; the words which God uttered (Gen. i.22), *Increase and multiply,* were addressed also to the brute creation where there is no marriage. Therefore Matrimony was not instituted before sin.

Obj. 5. Further, Matrimony is a sacrament of the New Law. But the sacraments of the New Law took their origin from Christ. Therefore it ought not to have been instituted before sin.

On the contrary, It is said (Matth. xix.4): *Have ye not read that He Who made man from the beginning "made them male and female"?*

Further, Matrimony was instituted for the begetting of children. But the begetting of children was necessary to man before sin. Therefore it behooved Matrimony to be instituted before sin.

I answer that, Nature inclines to marriage with a certain good in view, which good varies according to the different states of man, wherefore it was necessary for matrimony to be variously instituted in the various states of man in reference to that good. Consequently matrimony as directed to the begetting of children, which was necessary even when there was no sin, was instituted before sin; according as it affords a remedy for the wound of sin, it was instituted after sin at the time of the natural law; its institution belongs to the Mosaic Law as regards personal disqualifications; and it was instituted in the New Law in so far as it represents the mystery of Christ's union with the Church, and in this respect it is a sacrament of the New Law. As regards other advantages resulting from matrimony, such as the friendship and mutual services which husband and wife render one another, its institution belongs to the civil law. Since, however, a sacrament is essentially a sign and a remedy, it follows that the nature of sacrament applies to matrimony as regards the intermediate institution; that it is fittingly intended to fulfill an office of nature as regards the first institution; and, as regards the last-mentioned institution, that it is directed to fulfill an office of society.

Reply Obj. 1. Things which are of natural law in a general way, need to be instituted as regards their determination which is subject to variation according to various states; just as it is of natural law that evil-doers be punished, but that such and such a punishment be appointed for such and such a crime is determined by positive law.

Reply Obj. 2. Matrimony is not only for a remedy against sin, but is chiefly for an office of nature; and thus it was instituted before sin, not as intended for a remedy.

Reply Obj. 3. There is no reason why matrimony should not have had several institutions corresponding to the various things that had to be determined in connection with marriage. Hence these various institutions are not of the same thing in the same respect.

Reply Obj. 4. Before sin matrimony was instituted by God, when He fashioned a helpmate for man out of his rib, and said to them: *Increase and multiply.* And although this was said also to the other animals, it was not to be fulfilled by them in the same way as by men. As to Adam's words, he uttered them inspired by God to understand that the institution of marriage was from God.

Reply Obj. 5. As was clearly stated, matrimony was not instituted before Christ as a sacrament of the New Law.

Third Article: Whether Matrimony Confers Grace?

We proceed thus to the Third Article: —

Objection 1. It would seem that matrimony does not confer grace. For, according to Hugh (*De Sacram.* i) *the sacraments, by virtue of their sanctification, confer an invisible grace.* But matrimony has no sanctification essential to it. Therefore grace is not conferred therein.

Obj. 2. Further, every sacrament that confers grace confers it by virtue of its matter and form. Now the acts which are the matter in this sacrament are not the cause of grace (for it would be the heresy of Pelagius to assert that our acts cause grace); and the words expressive of consent are not the cause of grace, since no sanctification results from them. Therefore grace is by no means given in matrimony.

Obj. 3. Further, the grace that is directed against the wound of sin is necessary to all who have that wound. Now the wound of concupiscence is to be found in all. Therefore if grace were given in matrimony against the wound of concupiscence, all men ought to contract marriage, and it would be very stupid to refrain from matrimony.

Obj. 4. Further, sickness does not seek a remedy where it finds aggravation. Now concupiscence is aggravated by concupiscence, because, according to the Philosopher (*Ethic.* iii.12), *the desire of concupiscence is insatiable, and is increased by congenial actions.* Therefore it would seem that grace is not conferred in matrimony, as a remedy for concupiscence.

On the contrary, Definition and thing defined should be convertible. Now causality of grace is included in the definition of a sacrament. Since, then, matrimony is a sacrament, it is a cause of grace.

Further, Augustine says (*De Bono Viduit.* viii; *Gen. ad lit.* ix.7) that *matri-*

mony affords a remedy to the sick. But it is not a remedy except in so far as it has some efficacy. Therefore it has some efficacy for the repression of concupiscence. Now concupiscence is not repressed except by grace. Therefore grace is conferred therein.

I answer that, There have been three opinions on this point. For some[4] said that matrimony is nowise the cause of grace, but only a sign thereof. But this cannot be maintained, for in that case it would in no respect surpass the sacraments of the Old Law. Wherefore there would be no reason for reckoning it among the sacraments of the New Law; since even in the Old Law by the very nature of the act it was able to afford a remedy to concupiscence lest the latter run riot when held in too strict restraint.

Hence others[5] said that grace is conferred therein as regards the withdrawal from evil, because the act is excused from sin, for it would be a sin apart from matrimony. But this would be too little, since it had this also in the Old Law. And so they say that it makes man withdraw from evil, by restraining the concupiscence lest it tend to something outside the marriage blessings, but that this grace does not enable a man to do good works. But this cannot be maintained, since the same grace hinders sin and inclines to good, just as the same heat expels cold and gives heat.

Hence others[6] say that matrimony, inasmuch as it is contracted in the faith of Christ, is able to confer the grace which enables us to do those works which are required in matrimony, and this is more probable, since wherever God gives the faculty to do a thing, He gives also the helps whereby man is enabled to make becoming use of that faculty; thus it is clear that to all the soul's powers there correspond bodily members by which they can proceed to act. Therefore, since in matrimony man receives by Divine institution the faculty to use his wife for the begetting of children, he also receives the grace without which he cannot becomingly do so; just as we have said of the sacrament of orders (Q. 35, A. 1). And thus this grace which is given is the last thing contained in this sacrament.

Reply Obj. 1. Just as the baptismal water by virtue of its contact with Christ's body[7] is able to *touch the body and cleanse the heart,*[8] so is matrimony able to do so through Christ having represented it by His Passion, and not principally through any blessing of the priest.

Reply Obj. 2. Just as the water of Baptism together with the form of words results immediately not in the infusion of grace, but in the imprinting of the character, so the outward acts and the words expressive of consent directly effect a certain tie which is the sacrament of matrimony; and this tie by virtue of its Divine institution works dispositively,[9] to the infusion of grace.

Reply Obj. 3. This argument would hold if no more efficacious remedy could be employed against the disease of concupiscence; but a yet more powerful remedy is found in spiritual works and mortification of the flesh by those who make no use of matrimony.

Reply Obj. 4. A remedy can be employed against concupiscence in two ways. First, on the part of concupiscence by repressing it in its root, and thus matrimony affords a remedy by the grace given therein. Secondly, on the part of its act, and this in two ways: first, by depriving the act to which concupiscence inclines of its outward shamefulness, and this is done by the marriage blessings which justify carnal concupiscence; secondly, by hindering the shameful act, which is done by the very nature of the act, because concupiscence, being satisfied by the conjugal act, does not incline so much to other wickedness. For this reason the Apostle says (1 Cor. vii.9): *It is better to marry than to burn.* For though the works congenial to concupiscence are in themselves of a nature to increase concupiscence, yet in so far as they are directed according to reason they repress concupiscence, because like acts result in like dispositions and habits.

THE WEDDING CEREMONY FROM
THE BOOK OF COMMON PRAYER

The wedding ceremony printed here is the famous "Form of Solemnization of Matrimony" established by the Episcopal Church in 1928. These Episcopal vows remain the most well known in the English-speaking world. The reader will notice that the language is gender-role neutral, the promises egalitarian in spirit. It should be noted, however, that the Episcopal Church further modernized its wedding vows in 1979.

The Form of Solemnization of Matrimony (1928)

At the day and time appointed for Solemnization of Matrimony, the Persons to be married shall come into the body of the Church, or shall be ready in some proper house with their friends and neighbours; and there standing together, the Man on the right hand, and the Woman on the left, the Minister shall say,

Dearly beloved, we are gathered together here in the sight of God, and in the face of this company, to join together this Man and this Woman in holy Matrimony; which is an honourable estate, instituted of God, signifying unto us the mystical union that is betwixt Christ and his Church: which holy estate Christ adorned and beautified with his presence and first miracle that he wrought in Cana of Galilee, and is commended of Saint Paul to be honourable among all men: and therefore is not by any to be entered into unadvisedly or lightly; but reverently, discreetly, advisedly, soberly, and in the fear of God. Into this holy estate these two persons present come now to be joined. If any man can show just cause, why they may not lawfully be joined together, let him now speak, or else hereafter for ever hold his peace.

And also speaking unto the Persons who are to be married, he shall say,

I require and charge you both, as ye will answer at the dreadful day of judgment when the secrets of all hearts shall be disclosed, that if either of you know any impediment, why ye may not be lawfully joined together in Matrimony, ye do now confess it. For be ye well assured, that if any persons are joined together otherwise than as God's Word doth allow, their marriage is not lawful.

The Minister, if he shall have reason to doubt of the lawfulness of the proposed marriage, may demand sufficient surety for his indemnification; but if no impediment shall be alleged, or suspected, the Minister shall say to the Man,

N. [*name*] wilt thou have this Woman to thy wedded wife, to live together after God's ordinance in the holy estate of Matrimony? Wilt thou love her, comfort her, honour, and keep her in sickness and in health; and, forsaking all others, keep thee only unto her, so long as ye both shall live?

The Man shall answer,

I will.

Then shall the Minister say unto the Woman,

N. wilt thou have this Man to thy wedded husband, to live together after God's ordinance in the holy estate of Matrimony? Wilt thou love him, comfort him, honour, and keep him in sickness and in health; and, forsaking all others, keep thee only unto him, so long as ye both shall live?

The Woman shall answer,

I will.

Then shall the Minister say,

Who giveth this Woman to be married to this Man?

Then shall they give their troth to each other in this manner. The Minister, receiving the Woman at her father's or friend's hands, shall cause the Man with his right hand to take the Woman by her right hand, and to say after him as followeth.

I *N.* take thee *N.* to my wedded Wife, to have and to hold from this day forward, for better for worse, for richer for poorer, in sickness and in health, to love and to cherish, till death us do part, according to God's holy ordinance; and thereto I plight thee my troth.

Then shall they loose their hands; and the Woman with her right hand taking the Man by his right hand, shall likewise say after the Minister,

I *N.* take thee *N.* to my wedded Husband, to have and to hold from this day forward, for better for worse, for richer for poorer, in sickness and in health, to love and to cherish, till death us do part, according to God's holy ordinance; and thereto I give thee my troth.

Then shall they again loose their hands; and the man shall give unto the Woman a Ring on this wise: the Minister taking the Ring shall deliver it unto the Man, to put it upon the fourth finger of the Woman's left hand. And the Man holding the Ring there, and taught by the Minister, shall say,

With this Ring I thee wed: In the Name of the Father, and of the Son, and of the Holy Ghost. Amen.

And, before delivering the Ring to the Man, the Minister may say as followeth,

Bless, O Lord, this Ring, that he who gives it and she who wears it may abide in thy peace, and continue in thy favour, unto their life's end; through Jesus Christ our Lord. Amen.

Then, the Man leaving the Ring upon the fourth finger of the Woman's left hand, the Minister shall say,

Let us pray.

Then shall the Minister and the People, still standing, say the Lord's Prayer.

Our Father, who art in heaven, Hallowed be thy Name. Thy kingdom come. Thy will be done, On earth as it is in heaven. Give us this day our daily bread. And forgive us our trespasses, As we forgive those who trespass against us. And lead us not into temptation, But deliver us from evil. For thine is the kingdom, and the power, and the glory, for ever and ever. Amen.

Then shall the Minister add,

O eternal God, Creator and Preserver of all mankind, Giver of all spiritual grace, the Author of everlasting life; Send thy blessing upon these thy servants, this man and this woman, whom we bless in thy Name; that they, living faithfully together, may surely perform and keep the vow and covenant betwixt them made, (whereof this Ring given and received is a token and pledge,) and may ever remain in perfect love and peace together, and live according to thy laws; through Jesus Christ our Lord. *Amen.*

The Minister may add one or both of the following prayers.

O almighty God, Creator of mankind, who only art the well-spring of life; Bestow upon these thy servants, if it be thy will, the gift and heritage of children; and grant that they may see their children brought up in thy faith and fear, to the honour and glory of thy Name; through Jesus Christ our Lord. *Amen.*

O God, who hast so consecrated the state of Matrimony that in it is represented the spiritual marriage and unity betwixt Christ and his Church; Look mercifully upon these thy servants, that they may love, honour, and cherish each other, and so live together in faithfulness and patience, in wisdom and true godliness, that their home may be a haven of blessing and of peace; through the same Jesus Christ our Lord, who liveth and reigneth with thee and the Holy Spirit ever, one God, world without end. *Amen.*

Then shall the Minister join their right hands together, and say,

Those whom God hath joined together let no man put asunder.

DESIDERIUS ERASMUS

Desiderius Erasmus (d. 1536) was born in Rotterdam to unwed parents. He himself seems to have been uncertain about the year of his birth. The leading humanist of the Renaissance and a copious man of letters, he was still a teenager when he was orphaned and left in the care of guardians who wished to educate him for the monastic life. His love of learning, his wit, and his generous mindedness earned him the patronage of many influential men of church and state. Well traveled and cultivated in the classics, Erasmus was not simply a theologian and moralist, but a brilliant satirist. (Afflicted with delicate health, Erasmus liked to tease about his fussy eating habits, saying that his "heart was Catholic," but his "stomach Lutheran.") As the Colloquy "Marriage" attests, Erasmus's temperament was not very spiritual; rather, he was a man of solid religious faith, of common sense, and of razor-sharp intellect.

"Marriage," from *The Colloquies*

EULALIA   Greetings, Xanthippe! I've been dying to see you.

XANTHIPPE   Same to you, my dearest Eulalia. You look lovelier than ever.

EUL.   So you greet me by making fun of me right away?

XAN.   Not at all: I mean it.

EUL.   Maybe this new dress flatters my figure.

XAN.   Of course it does. I haven't seen anything prettier for a long time. British cloth, I suppose?

EUL.   British wool with Venetian dye.

XAN. Softer than satin. What a charming shade of purple! Where did you get such a marvelous gift?

EUL. Where should honest wives get them except from their husbands?

XAN. Lucky you to have such a husband! As for me — I might as well have married a mushroom when I married my Nicholas.

EUL. Why so, if you please? Are you falling out so soon?

XAN. I'll never fall in with the likes of him. You see I'm in rags: that's how *he* allows his wife to appear. Damned if often I'm not ashamed to go out in public when I see how well dressed other women are who married husbands much worse off than mine.

EUL. Feminine finery, as St. Peter the apostle teaches (for I heard this in a sermon recently), consists not of clothes or any other adornment of the person but of chaste and modest sentiments and embellishments of the mind. Harlots are decked out for vulgar eyes. We're sufficiently well dressed if we please one husband.

XAN. But meanwhile that fine gentleman, so stingy toward his wife, squanders the dowry he got from me — no slight one — as fast as he can.

EUL. On what?

XAN. On whatever he pleases: wine — whores — dice.

EUL. That's no way to talk.

XAN. But it's the truth. Besides, when he comes home drunk in the middle of the night, after being long awaited, he snores all night and sometimes vomits in bed — to say no worse.

EUL. Hush! You bring reproach on yourself when you reproach your husband.

XAN. Hope to die if I wouldn't rather sleep with a brood sow than with such a husband!

EUL. Don't you welcome him with abuse then?

XAN. Yes — as he deserves. He finds I'm no mute!

EUL. What does he do to counter you?

XAN. At first he used to talk back most ferociously, thinking he'd drive me away with harsh words.

EUL. The bickering never came to actual blows?

XAN. Once, at least, the argument grew so hot on both sides that it very nearly ended in a fight.

EUL. You don't say so!

XAN. He was swinging a club, yelling savagely all the while and threatening terrible deeds.

EUL. Weren't you scared at that?

XAN. Oh, no. When it came my turn, I grabbed a stool. Had he laid a finger on me, he'd have found I didn't lack arms. . . . If he won't treat me as a wife, I won't treat him as a husband.

EUL. But Paul teaches that wives should be obedient to their husbands in all subjection. And Peter sets before us the example of Sarah, who would call her husband Abraham "lord."

XAN. So I've heard. But this same Paul teaches that husbands should cherish their wives as Christ has cherished his spouse the Church. Let him remember his duty and I'll remember mine.

EUL. All the same, when things have come to such a pass that one person must yield to the other, the wife should give way to the husband.

XAN. Provided he deserves to be called husband. He treats me like a servant.

EUL. But tell me, my dear Xanthippe, did he stop threatening to beat you after that?

XAN. Yes — and he was wise to do so or he'd have got a cudgeling.

EUL. But haven't you stopped brawling with him?

XAN. No, and I won't stop.

EUL. What does he do all this time?

XAN. Do? Sometimes he sleeps, the lazy loafer. Occasionally he just laughs; and at other times grabs his guitar, which has hardly three strings, and plays it as loud as he can to drown out my screaming.

EUL. That infuriates you?

XAN. More than I could say. At times I can hardly keep my hands off him.

EUL. Xanthippe, my dear, may I speak rather frankly with you?

XAN. You may.

EUL. You may do the same with me. Our intimacy — which goes back almost to the cradle — surely demands this.

XAN. That's true. You've always been my dearest friend.

EUL. Whatever your husband's like, bear in mind that there's no exchanging him for another. Once upon a time divorce was a final remedy for irreconcilable differences. Nowadays this has been entirely abolished; you must be husband and wife till the day you die.

XAN. May heaven punish whoever robbed us of this right!

EUL. Mind what you're saying. Christ so willed.

XAN. I can scarcely believe it.

EUL. It's the truth. There's nothing left now but to try to live in harmony by adjusting yourselves to each other's habits and personalities.

XAN. Can I reform him?

EUL. What sort of men husbands are depends not a little on their wives.

XAN. Do you get along well with your husband?

EUL. Everything's peaceful now.

XAN. There was some turmoil at first, then?

EUL. Never a storm, but slight clouds appeared occasionally: the usual human experience. They could have caused a storm had they not been met with forbearance. Each of us has his own ways and opinions, and — to tell the truth — his own peculiar faults. If there's any place where one has a duty to recognize these, not resent them, surely it's in marriage.

XAN. Good advice.

EUL. It frequently happens, however, that good will between husband and wife breaks down before they know each other well enough. This above all is to be avoided, for once contention arises love is not easily recovered, especially if the affair reaches the point of harsh abuse. Things glued together are easily separated if you shake them immediately, but once the glue has dried they stick together as firmly as anything. Hence at the very outset no pains should be spared to establish and cement good will between husband and wife. This is accomplished mainly by submissiveness and courtesy, for good will won merely by beauty of person is usually short-lived.

XAN. But tell me, please, by what arts you draw your husband to your ways.

EUL. I'll tell you in order that you may imitate them. . . . My first concern was to be agreeable to my husband in every respect, so as not to cause him any annoyance. I noted his mood and feeling; I noted the circumstances too, and what soothed and irritated him. . . . When he's at leisure and not disturbed, worried, or tipsy, . . . admonish him politely, or rather entreat him — in private — to take better care of his property, reputation, or health in one respect or another. And this very admonition should be seasoned with wit and pleasantries. Sometimes I'd make my husband promise in advance not to be angry if I, a foolish woman, reproved him about something that seemed to concern his honor, health, or welfare. After reproving him as I intended, I'd break off that talk and turn to other, more cheerful topics. For as a rule, my dear Xanthippe, our mistake is that once we've started to talk we can't stop.

XAN. So they say.

EUL. Above all I was careful not to scold my husband in the presence of others or to carry any complaint farther than the front door. Trouble's sooner mended if it's limited to two. But if something of this sort does prove intolerable, or can't be cured by the wife's reproof, it's more polite for her to take her complaint to her husband's parents and relatives than to her own, and to state her case with such restraint that she won't seem to hate her husband but his fault instead. She should refrain from blurting out everything, though, so that her husband may tacitly acknowledge and admire his wife's courtesy.

XAN. Whoever could do all this must be a philosopher.

EUL. Oh, no; by such practices we'll entice our husbands to similar courtesy.

XAN. There are some no courtesy would improve.

EUL. Well, I don't think so, but suppose there are. In the first place, remember you must put up with your husband, whatever he's like. Better, therefore, to put up with one who behaves himself or is made a little more accommodating by our politeness than with one who's made worse from day to day by our harshness. What if I were to cite examples of husbands who improved their wives by courtesy of this kind? How much more fitting for us to do the same for our husbands! . . . If you don't mind, I'll tell you something about a husband reformed by his wife's kindness: something that happened recently in this very city. . . . There's a certain man of no mean rank who, like most of his class, used to hunt a good deal. In the country he came across some girl, the daughter of a poor peasant woman, with whom he — a man already fairly well along in years — fell passionately in love. On her account he'd often spend the night away from home, his excuse being his hunting. His wife, a woman of exceptional goodness, suspected something, investigated her husband's secret doings, and, after discovering the facts (I don't know how), went to their rude cottage. She found out everything: where he slept, what he drank out of, what dinnerware he had. No furniture there — just sheer poverty. The wife went home but soon came back, bringing with her a comfortable bed and furnishings and some silver vessels. She added money, too, advising the girl to treat him more handsomely on his next visit — all the while concealing the fact that she herself was his wife and pretending to be his sister. Some days later the husband returns there secretly. Noticing the new furniture and the more expensive household utensils, he asks where this uncommon luxury comes from. Some good lady (he's told), a relative of his, had brought it and had left orders to entertain him more properly thereafter. He suspected at once that his wife had done this. Back home, he asks her; she doesn't deny it. And why, he asks finally, had she sent the furniture to him? "My dear husband," she replies, "you're used to a pretty comfortable life. I saw you were shabbily treated there. I thought that since you're so fond of the place, I ought to see that you're entertained more elegantly."

XAN. Too good a wife! I'd sooner have made him a bed of nettles and thistles.

EUL. But hear the conclusion. In view of so much gentleness and kindness on the part of his wife, the husband never again engaged in secret amours but enjoyed himself at home with his own wife. — I know you're acquainted with Gilbert the Dutchman.

103

XAN. I know him.

EUL. As you're aware, when he was in the prime of life he married a woman already in her declining years.

XAN. Perhaps he married the dowry, not the wife.

EUL. Yes. Despising his wife, he doted on a mistress with whom he would often enjoy himself away from home. He seldom lunched or dined at home. What would you have done in this situation?

XAN. What? I'd have flown at his sweetheart's hair; and when my husband was going to her I'd have emptied the chamber pot on him, so he'd be perfumed for his party.

EUL. But how much more sensible this woman was! She invited the girl to her own home and received her cordially. Thus she enticed her husband home too, without sorcery. And whenever he went out to dinner at the girl's, she sent over some fancy dish, bidding them have a good time.

XAN. I'd rather die than be bawd to my husband.

EUL. But consider the case. Wasn't this far better than if she had simply alienated her husband by her fury and spent her whole time in brawling?

XAN. It's the lesser evil, I admit — but I couldn't do it.

EUL. I'll add one more example; and this will be the last. One day a neighbor of ours, a good, honest man but a little short-tempered, beat his wife, a most worthy woman. She withdrew to her room, and there, weeping and sobbing, she cried out her grief. Sometime later her husband happened to go into that room and found her weeping. "Why are you crying and sobbing here like a child?" he said. "What?" she answered discreetly, "Isn't it better to bewail my misfortune here than to scream in the street as other women usually do?" The man's heart was so touched, so overcome by such wifely speech, that he solemnly promised her he would never lay a hand on her again; and he didn't.

XAN. I got the same promise from my husband by a different method.

EUL. But meanwhile there's constant warfare between you.

XAN. What would you have me do, then?

EUL. First of all, keep to yourself any wrong your husband does you and win him over gradually by favors, cheerfulness, gentleness. Either you'll triumph at last or certainly you'll find him much more affable than you do now.

XAN. He's too savage to soften under any favors.

EUL. Oh, don't say that. No creature's so fierce that he can't be tamed. Don't despair of the man. Try for several months; blame me if you don't find this advice has helped you. There are even some failings you ought to wink at. Above all, in my judgment, you must be careful not to start an argument in the bedroom or in bed, but try to see that everything there is pleasant and agreeable. If that place, which is dedicated to dispelling grudges and renewing love, is profaned by any contention or bitterness, every means of recovering good will is clean gone. Some women are so peevish that they even quarrel and complain during sexual intercourse and by their tactlessness render disagreeable that pleasure which ordinarily rids men's minds of whatever vexation may be therein — spoiling the very medicine that could have cured their ills.

XAN. That's often happened to me.

EUL. Yet, even though a wife should always be careful not to offend her husband on any occasion, she should take special pains to show herself wholly complaisant and agreeable to him in that union.

XAN. Husband! My business is with a monster.

EUL. Do stop talking in that horrid fashion. Usually it's our fault that husbands are bad. But to return to the subject. Those well read in ancient poetry say that Venus, whom they make the patroness of married love, has a girdle fashioned by Vulcan. Woven in it is some drug to arouse love. She puts on this girdle whenever she's going to sleep with her husband.

XAN. That's a mere story.

EUL. A story, yes, but hear what the story signifies.

XAN. Tell me.

EUL. It teaches that a wife must take every precaution to be pleasing to her husband in sexual relations, in order that married love may be rekindled and renewed and any annoyance or boredom driven out of mind.

XAN. But where shall I get that girdle?

EUL. You don't need sorcery or charms. No charm is more effective than good behavior joined with good humor.

XAN. I can't humor such a husband.

EUL. Yet it's important to you that he stop being such. If by Circe's arts you could turn your husband into a swine or a bear, would you do it?

XAN. I don't know.

EUL. Don't know? Would you rather have a swine than a man for a husband?

XAN. I'd prefer a man, of course.

EUL. Well, now, what if by Circe's arts you could change him from drunk to sober, spendthrift to thrifty, idler to worker? Wouldn't you do it?

XAN. Indeed I would, but where can I find those arts?

EUL. But you've those very arts in yourself if only you're willing to make use of them. He's yours whether you like it or not; that's settled. The better you make him, the better off you'll be. You have eyes only for his failings. These intensify your disgust, and with this handle you're simply catching him where he can't be held. Mark the good in him, rather, and by this means take him where he can be held. The time to weigh his faults was before you married him, since a husband should be chosen not only with eyes, but with ears too. Now's the time for improving him, not blaming him.

XAN. What woman ever picked a husband by ear?

EUL. The one who sees nothing but good looks chooses him with her eyes. The woman who chooses by ear is the one who considers his reputation carefully.

XAN. Good advice — but too late!

EUL. But it's not too late to try to improve your husband. If you present your husband with a child, that will help.

XAN. I've already had one.

EUL. When?

XAN. Long ago.

EUL. How many months ago?

XAN. Almost seven.

EUL. What do I hear? Are you reviving the old joke about the three-month baby?

XAN. Not at all.

EUL. You must be if you count the time from your wedding day.

XAN. Oh, no, we had some conversation before marriage.

EUL. Are children born from conversation?

XAN. Chancing to find me alone, he began to play, tickling me under the arms and in the sides to make me laugh. I couldn't stand the tickling, so I fell back on the bed. He leaned over and kissed me — I'm not sure what else he did. I am sure my belly began to swell soon afterward.

EUL. Go on! Belittle a husband who begot children in sport? What will he do when he goes to work in earnest?

XAN. I suspect I'm pregnant now, too.

EUL. Fine! A good plowman's found a good field.

XAN. He's better at this than I would like.

EUL. Few wives join you in that complaint. But were you engaged?

XAN. Engaged, yes.

EUL. Then your sin was the lighter. Is the child a boy?

XAN. Yes.

EUL. That will reconcile you two if you meet him halfway. What do others — his friends and business associates — have to say about your husband?

XAN. They say he's very easy to get along with, cheerful, generous; a trusty friend.

EUL. And this makes me confident he'll be the way we want him.

XAN. But to me alone is he different.

EUL. Now behave toward him as I've told you, and call me Pseudolalia instead of Eulalia if he doesn't begin to be such to you too. And just remember this: he's still a young man; not over twenty-four, I believe. He doesn't know yet what it's like to be head of a family. You must not even think of divorce.

XAN. But I've often thought of it.

EUL. Whenever the notion comes into your head, consider with yourself, first of all, what a paltry thing a woman is if separated from her husband. A woman's highest praise is to be obedient to her husband. It's the order of Nature, the will of God, that woman be entirely dependent on man. Only think what the situation is: he's your husband; you can't get a different one. In the second place, think about the little boy you two have. What will you do about him? Take him with you? You'll rob your husband of his possession. Leave him with your husband? You'll deprive yourself of the one dearest to you. Tell me, finally: have you any enemies?

XAN. I have a stepmother — the genuine article — and a mother-in-law just like her.

EUL. Do they hate you so very much?

XAN. They'd like me to drop dead.

EUL. Have a thought for them, too. How could you give them greater pleasure than by letting them see you parted from your husband, living like a widow, nay worse than a widow? For widows may at least remarry.

XAN. Well, I like your advice, but a long-drawn-out job I don't like.

EUL. But consider how much work it took before you taught this parrot here to talk.

XAN. Plenty, to be sure.

EUL. And do you shrink from working hard to reform your husband, with whom you might spend your life pleasantly? How much labor men put into training a horse! And shall we be hesitant about laboring to make our husbands more tractable?

XAN. What should I do?

EUL. I've already told you. See that everything at home is neat and clean and there's no trouble that will drive him out of doors. Show yourself affable to him, always mindful of the respect owed by wife to husband. Avoid gloominess and irritability. Don't be disgusting or wanton. Keep the house spick and span. You know your husband's taste; cook what he likes best. Be cordial and courteous to his favorite friends, too. Invite them to dinner frequently, and see that everything is cheerful and gay there.

Finally, if he strums his guitar when he's a bit tipsy, accompany him with your singing. Thus you'll get your husband used to staying at home and you'll reduce expenses. At long last he'll think, "I'm a damned fool to waste my money and reputation away from home on a drab when I have at home a wife much nicer and much fonder of me, from whom I can get a more elegant and more sumptuous welcome."

XAN. Do you think I'll succeed if I try?

EUL. Look at me. I'll vouch for it, and meantime I'll approach your husband and remind him too of his duty.

XAN. I approve of the plan, but watch out he doesn't suspect this plot; he'd raise hell.

EUL. Don't fear. I'll speak to him in such a roundabout way that he'll tell me himself what the trouble is between you. After that I'll draw him on very innocently, in my usual fashion and — I hope — make him more considerate of you. When I get a chance, I'll tell him a fib about you — how lovingly you spoke of him.

XAN. May Christ favor our effort!

EUL. He will — if only you do your part.

FROM THE HINDU *MAHABHARATA*

(retold by William Buck)

The *Mahabharata,* one of the two national epics of India, is supposed to have been written somewhere between the third century B.C. and 200 A.D. A recounting of the civil war in the region of Delhi almost 3,000 years ago, it is reputed to be the longest verse in world literature, consisting of over 90,000 couplets. Tradition has it that this poem was written by the Indian sage Vyasa. But scholars of Sanskrit attribute it to a number of Hindu poets and priests.

William Buck (1943-1970) devoted his entire adult life to the study and retelling of the *Mahabharata* and *Ramayana* after finding a nineteenth-century version of *The Sacred Song of the Lord, the Bhagavad Gita of Lord Krishna* in a Carson City, Nevada, library. His goal was to capture the original narrative and poetry of the Indian epics while eliminating the superimposed "treatises" and theological pronouncements he believed "only slow the story." Tragically, Buck died only a few months after completing his modern version of these epics.

An Iron Net

Listen —

Savitri, the daughter of the Madra king Aswapati, was young and very beautiful. Many men came to her father's court to marry her, but she desired none of them, for they were every one graceless and idle and vain, and puffed up with pride, and stiff with empty conceit. Then Savitri told her father, "I will myself go out in my golden war chariot, and I will not return until I have found my husband."

She went to the towns and villages, but they were afraid of her, so she turned into the forests to find her mate. Her chariot broke its way through the trees, and the birds flew away in fear, while of the animals, some stood their ground and watched her, while others ran behind rocks, or into caves, or dug into the Earth, and still others hid themselves in the trees and closed their eyes.

Savitri went to the forest retreats of Brahmanas and Kshatriyas who had retired from the world, and sometime later she returned to Aswapati and said: *"I have found him."*

"Who?" asked the king,

"He is Satyavan," answered Savitri. "Because Time took away King Dyumatsena's sight, so that be became blind, an enemy drove him from the throne of Salwa, and Dyumatsena went to live in the forest with his wife and their only son, Satyavan."

"Ah, I am content," said the king. "I will make arrangements; we will go to him together." When Savitri left him, Aswapati called his minister and asked, "What of Satyavan?"

"Majesty," replied the minister, "he was born in his father's city, but as a babe in arms he was taken into the forest and has lived there since. He is loyal and kind, and is handsome as the moon, and has the power and energy of the sun. He is generous and brave and patient as the Earth. He has only one defect and no other — a year from this day Satyavan will die."

Aswapati told Savitri what be had heard and he said, "Change your mind. Do not marry into unhappiness."

Savitri replied, "Twice I will not choose. Whether his life be short or long, I have taken him as my husband in my heart."

Aswapati saw that her heart did not falter. "It will be as you say. Tomorrow we will go to Dyumatsena in the forest."

Then on foot the king took Savitri to Dyumatsena's hermitage, where he sat beside the blind king on grass mats under a tree, and asked him to accept Savitri for his daughter.

"How will she bear living in the forest?" asked Dyumatsena.

Aswapati said, "She and I both know that happiness and sorrow come and go their ways wherever we may be. I bow to you in friendship. Do not disregard me; do not destroy my hope."

"You are welcome," said Dyumatsena. "Blessed be you both."

*   *   *

The two kings made the marriage between Savitri and Satyavan, and Aswapati returned to his city. With love and a happy marriage the year of Satyavan's life passed quickly by, and Savitri counted off the days till but one remained. The night before he was to die she watched Satyavan sleep by her side until the dawn. She cooked for him but did not eat, expecting the hour and the moment, and thinking: *"Today is that day."*

When the sun was two hands high, Satyavan set his axe on his shoulder and went into the forest with Savitri to gather some wood. Softly she followed him in seeming smiles, watching all his moods.

Soon they came to a fallen tree. Satyavan started to cut away its branches, but he was trembling and wet with perspiration. When he stopped to dry himself his head began to ache, and the light hurt his eyes. He put down the axe and lay down with his head on Savitri's lap to rest.

When he shut his eyes his face was for a moment pale and drawn. Then the color returned, and he was asleep on her thigh, peacefully. Savitri ran her fingers through his wet hair. But she felt someone watching her, and looked up.

A large man was looking at Satyavan with dark, quiet eyes. His skin was dark green, and he wore red robes and a red flower in his loose black hair. He stood but a bow's length from Satyavan, holding a small noose of silver thread in his left hand, gazing steadily at Savitri's husband with a look of great patience and kindness.

Savitri gently placed Satyavan's head on the Earth. The god looked at her, turning his head, but never his dark eyes, and she said, "Lord Yama, I am Savitri."

Yama spoke softly, "The days of Satyavan's life are full, and I have come for him."

The Death Lord reached into Satyavan's breast, on the left side, somewhere near the heart, and drew forth his soul, a person no larger than a thumb, and bound the soul in his noose. And when the soul was taken and held, Satyavan's body no longer breathed and was cold.

Yama withdrew into the forest, but Savitri followed and walked beside him. He stopped and said, "Return, and make his funeral."

Savitri said, "I have heard that you were the first man to die, to make your way to the home that cannot be taken away."

"It is so," said Yama. "Now go back. You cannot follow any farther. You are free of every tie to Satyavan, and every trust."

"All who are born must one day follow you. Let me only go a little farther, as your friend."

Yama stopped, and slowly turned and looked at Savitri. "It is true. You have no fear of me. I take you for my friend, and do you take in return a gift from me, whatever I can give. But I cannot give his life again to Satyavan."

111

"Friendship may come after only seven steps taken together," said Savitri. "Let Dyumatsena's blindness fall from him."

"It falls. Now return, for you are tired."

"But I am not," said Savitri. "I am with Satyavan for the last time. Give me leave to walk on a while."

"I give. Always I take away, and again take away. It is good to be giving. Follow then if you will, and take another gift from me, except only as before."

"Let Dyumatsena regain his kingdom," said Savitri.

"He will," said Yama. He and Savitri walked on, to the south, and the branches and hanging vines parted for them to pass and closed behind. They came to a stream and the Death Lord held water in his hands for Savitri to drink.

"It is not hard to give," said Yama, "for when life is finished, and all must be given up, it is not difficult. There is pain in life, but none in death. What is very hard is to find one worthy of giving anything to. No one escapes me. I have seen them all." He looked at Savitri. "Yet . . . this water is not clearer than your heart. You seek what you want, you choose and it is done, you do not wish to be anyone else. For long I have not seen this. Ask another gift, anything but the life of Satyavan."

"Let my father have one hundred sons."

"He shall have them," said Yama. "But ask of me something more, for yourself, anything but Satyavan's life."

Savitri answered, "Then may I too have one hundred sons by my husband."

Yama sat down on the riverbank and watched the water flow by like a silver serpent. "With no thought you answered me. You told the truth. How can you have sons if Satyavan is dead? But you did not think of that."

"No."

"I know you didn't. But he has no more life. It is all gone."

"That is why I asked nothing for myself, for I am one half dead, and I do not wish even for heaven."

Yama sighed. "I am forever equal towards every man, and I more than anyone — I know what are truth and justice. I know that all the past and all the future are held fast by truth. Danger flees from it. How much is your life worth without Satyavan?"

"Nothing, Lord."

"Will you give me half your days on Earth?"

"Yes, you may have them," said Savitri.

Again Yama's unblinking, unmoving eyes rested long on Savitri. At last he said, "It is done. I have taken your days and given them to your husband as his own. Shall I tell you the number of those days?"

"No. Will we go back now?"

The Death Lord held up his silver noose, and it was empty. "His soul rests with you. You will carry it back yourself."

Yama stood up and walked on alone, to the Land of the Dead, with an empty noose. As Savitri turned back, a lightning bolt fell striking a tree near her home.

*   *   *

It was night when Savitri returned, and Satyavan's corpse lay chill in the moonlight. She sat beside him, with his head in her lap, and felt his skin grow warm against her body.

Satyavan looked up at her, as one returned from a long journey will look at his home when he sees it again. Then he sat up and said, "I have slept all day. I had a dream, of being carried away."

"That one has gone," said Savitri.

"It was not a dream?"

"It's late. There burns a tree to guide us back." She helped Satyavan to his feet, and steadied him, with his arm over her shoulder and her arm round his waist. "I will carry the axe," she said, "and we will talk when we are at home."

In the hermitage, Dyumatsena was feeding wood to the fire and telling his wife stories of the kings of time gone past. He looked at Savitri and Satyavan when they arrived, and said, "There are stars in your hair to my new eyes, and gold from the firelight on your skin. Today I have recovered my sight."

They sat down and Savitri said, "Yama came to carry off your son, but he left without him. And from kindness he gave your sight, and soon your kingdom, and also sons for Aswapati and for us. Now stay, and I shall make our supper."

But Dyumatsena put his hand on her shoulder and would not let her rise, but brought the food to her himself. When they had finished, a messenger came from Salwa, and Dyumatsena said, "If it be no secret, tell us why you have come."

"There is no secret to keep," said the man. "I come from the king's minister, who says: *Majesty, with a new knife I have taken away the life of the unlawful king, and his friends have fled the city and dare not look at me. I hold the kingdom for you in those same hands. Now do what is best.*"

*   *   *

"That is all my story, Princess," said Vyasa. "Savitri made misfortune into happiness, and here you do the same for your husbands, for though they are banished and in exile, they do not lose heart with you to love."

113

ISAK DINESEN

Danish author Isak Dinesen's (1885-1962) best-known work is *Out of Africa* (1937). *On Modern Marriage* was a very early effort, published for the first time posthumously in 1977 by the Karen Blixen Society. (Karen von Blixen was Dinesen's married name.) The occasion for this twelve-chapter essay, written shortly after Dinesen's 1921 divorce from the Baron von Blixen, was an ongoing conversation on sexual morality between Dinesen and her brother, who stayed with her for two and a half years on her coffee farm in Kenya, helping her manage business affairs there. Although the reader will not likely ascertain this from the selection below, Dinesen's work in general is known for its unusual preoccupation with the supernatural.

The references in this text to St. Christopher, the patron saint of travel, deserve some explanation. Tradition has it that St. Christopher, while carrying a small boy across a river, suddenly felt a great weight upon him. The boy turned out to be Jesus, who bore in his arms the entire world.

On Modern Marriage and Other Observations

IX. . . . [St. Christopher] Sets Out on His Wanderings

In the course of its development, humanity imperceptibly discards a great many ideals as not merely objectionable but inapplicable.

A discussion arose during a party regarding how many of the ten commandments could be said to be necessary for the highest ideal of modern times — the perfect gentleman — to keep.

Although there was a certain amount of discussion, on the whole opinions were fairly uniform and would probably be much the same wherever this problem came to be debated.

The commandment that the perfect gentleman could not evade was the eighth. Also, the general opinion was that violation of the ninth and tenth commandments should not be a characteristic of the perfect gentleman, although a single case of this probably would not do him much harm. Where the seventh commandment was concerned, everything depended on circumstances. The view was that there are presumably many professional thieves in the world who can be called true gentlemen, and the present day has after all created a kind of ideal in the gentleman-thief Raffles.

As it is generally taken for granted that the perfect gentleman is in a position to be able to ignore the difference between the Sabbath and the days of the week, a scrupulous observation of the third commandment might perhaps cast a shadow of doubt over his perfection; but still in itself this cannot be said to have anything to do with the understanding of the perfect gentleman.

But the ten commandments were once given in thunder and lightning from Sinai, and we have no justification for believing any of them to have been incised on the tablets of stone just as padding. On the contrary, we must assume that to take the Lord's name in vain must lower a man's esteem among the moral elite of his time, at least as much as, for example, to have enlarged upon one's conquests in love would have done fifty years ago, or lack of generosity toward subordinates, or the attempt to force or persuade a wife to intercourse that was distasteful to her, or the suspicion of cheating at cards would do today.

This thought of how moral evaluations are thus radically transformed must prepare us to expect that in the future the moral code of our day will seem utterly incomprehensible.

Is it then true that the great concept of the family — which for so many centuries held its place as one of the highest and most incontestable ideals, and for which so much blood, so much strength, so many personal feelings and sufferings have been sacrificed — has now been struck out of the human dictionary? And is it the idea of the family that has taken marriage with it into the grave?

If St. Christopher came to me personally and questioned me on these observations, I would answer yes.

Marriage is built on the family, the clan, the nation, and when the course of development, when the spirit of modern times did what they could to abolish these concepts and all their works and being, and in time tricked them out of what they had appropriated of esteem and property right down to the ground under their feet, they tore away the very foundation of marriage. Then it could not be long before it fell, and its fall was great.

There is no longer any really active material left alive by which to examine the concept of the family. No one can expect that by dealing with it, they will find material that will have a direct influence on or aid for the present time. The whole enterprise would be more like visiting a museum, where it is true that we can sometimes hope that by immersing ourselves in the essence of former times we can find something that will assist the understanding of or can indirectly be used in the present.

Let us then, in order to see to what extent a noble family connection realized the demands made on marriage, stop by . . . a tomb. By the tomb of the duchesse de Rohan, who, when she was expecting a child, demanded higher marks of honor because she was pregnant with a Rohan.

Now it must be thought that the concept of Rohan became rooted in the consciousness — in the consciousness of the whole nation as well as in that of the two young people who entered into a marriage for the sake of this family. It represents here certain definite qualities: courage, loyalty to the crown, liberality, chivalrousness; and perhaps, too, some that are not usually regarded as meritorious: hardness, indulgence, or red hair and small eyes. Yet this is of no account. The family is a concept that as such has a part in the history of the country; a Rohan is more (or less) than a human being: he is a Rohan.

Nor is there any doubt in his own soul that it is this quality that is the highest and most significant in his personality; indeed, his whole personality serves it, and gains stature thereby. Whatever personal advantages he may have — good looks, talents, valor — are of value because they can be of use to or cast luster on the Rohan family. The Rohan who believes that through his personal beauty, talents, valor he is something different or more than a Rohan has degenerated from the idea of his family.

Therefore the young duc de Rohan who is about to wed may have met and loved many women from every nation, faith and cast of mind . . . yet there always remains not only a difference of degree but a deeply essential difference between these relationships and their role in his life, and his relationship to a wife. For he has loved, conquered, suffered as a young, handsome, talented, valorous, passionate man, but he becomes a married man in the attribute of a Rohan, the highest idea his life can realize.

The contract that is entered into through his marriage is not a personal concern; what is essential here is that "the woman (and man) of noble birth marries as the man of noble birth fights, on political and family grounds not on personal ones."

His bride's personality will be judged in the same way as his own, according to its value to the family. Her beauty, wit and efficiency are of importance: it is she who is to wear the Rohan jewels, to do the honors in their house, to keep up the family name in difficult times. Provided that she is useful to the Rohan family or sheds luster on it, she can be casual about the yardstick by which the rest of the world judges her. The young mademoiselle de Rohan who became the wife of the duc de Guise's son, the duc de Chevreuse, was renowned for her adventures and intrigues, but her gifts and charm were still pearls that were quite satisfactory enough to be added to the thread on which hung the rest of the family's precious collection. Brought up and singled out for the service of an idea, she was an acquisition of tremendously great value for the Rohan family; at her wedding she kneeled to receive a task and a name that rested on her brow like a diadem.

The relationship between the spouses was no personal one, and strictly speaking they could not personally or directly bring happiness to or disappoint each other, but must mutually provide the greatest significance to each other through the relationship they occupied and the importance they had for their mutual task in life. For the duc de Rohan, there could never be any real comparison between his wife and other women: no matter how much more beautiful and gifted and attractive they might be, she still remained the only woman in the world who could give birth to a duc de Rohan. The receptions she held were receptions for the Rohans, the poor she supported were the Rohans' peasants and poor.

Even the style of their personal feelings had to be judged in the light of the same idea, so that an intense devotion was of great value to the family and safeguarded its happiness, while a violent personal passion might put it in danger . . . even their intimate life together was carried out, so to speak, in the service of an idea.

On principle, both spouses were probably obliged to close their eyes amiably to that aspect of their partner's nature that was ruled by the heart and what were known as "feelings" — provided that there was no betrayal of the idea that for both of them represented what was most important and ideally elevated in their life. But it is probable that this impersonal element in the relationship would often, between decent people, have led to "that sweet friendship, that tender confidence, which, joined to esteem, form, so it seems to me, the true and solid happiness of marriage" (as the hypocrite Madame de Merteuil, in an age that had lost respect for the idea of the family and that cultivated personal passion, with smooth-tongued falsity describes marriage). In any case, both would have realized that their relationship was indissoluble, just as their relationship to the king and country was in those times when feeling for these institutions was deep-rooted; indeed, it continued beyond the grave. They were united in coming generations of Rohans, or in the history of the family. Perhaps some of them might dream of being reunited with a more beloved spirit in Paradise, but in their tomb in the Rohan chapel they remained together in eternal rest within the imperishable marble.

Of course it can be said that all this applies to only a very limited number of families. But the presence of an elite is felt throughout the nation. The luster that shone from the relations between great families always illuminated the celebration of the marriage ceremony.

Nor was it any less sincere, even though less pompous, when a young clergyman married the young daughter of the vicarage, and two families were united who had been the guardians of Christianity in the country for centuries, or when an old yeoman family that had devotedly worked the beloved land for many generations acquired an excellent and decorous mistress for the people and animals on the farm, and a mother and grandmother for those who would take up their work there with renewed faithfulness . . . the highest feminine position that they were able to conceive of. Never mind that such concepts as feminine position and the sanctity of marriage may lose some of their luster when one is from Morbihan [i.e., the provinces]. There is no doubt that the farmer at Hill Farm — as long as respect for the family and the idea of property was deep and unquestioned — went to bed with his wife at Hill Farm with more solemnity and reverence than he could have shown any royal princess who had done him that honor.

Indeed, it may well be thought that in a country like Germany before the war, for instance, some of this luster could shine upon a whole nation's marriages and their task: to provide new Germans and raise them in the true faith. Or that in former days, when the human family represented the consciousness of being the children of God in the battle against natural forces and evil, the same luster might fall upon that task, of peopling the earth, and thus would make, so to speak, every love affair into a marriage.

But is it not asking too much of Candidate Petersen to expect him to feel something of her personality and of their personal love relationship symbolized abstractly in his young Mrs. Petersen, who went along with him one morning to the registry office, and with whom he shares a succession of different apartments and summer cottages, troubles with successive "maids" and tradesmen, a certain amount of unnecessary and tiresome socializing and utterly impersonal good works? Isn't it asking too much, not so much of his moral stamina as of his imagination, to expect him to see a radical difference between the child born to him and a pretty office girl before his marriage and his three legitimate children, the third of whom he and his wife hoped and tried to avoid?

Young Mrs. Petersen gave up her youth and vigor, as well as the time and talents that she previously (and as she now sometimes thinks with more appreciation) gave to her work, for the pleasure of living with Mr. Petersen and having a couple of dear little babies, whom she hopes will be able to make their way in life somehow or other. If the pleasure is now and again mixed, the whole enterprise may begin to seem somewhat dubious.

As a financial speculation — a viewpoint from which she has probably never considered it — it was dubious from the outset, for she had in fact felt freer and in a better position as a stenographer, and if she had had a free relationship with consequently only one child and the father's obligatory maintenance, she would have managed really well.

It is true that her children took his name, but she had herself been born a Petersen.

No wonder that this young married couple look back on their engagement as the most satisfactory period of their relationship, while for the duc and duchesse de Rohan this time held nothing at all apart from its promises.

The charm factor in Mr. and Mrs. Petersen's marriage is that of a free relationship, and it has not been raised to any higher plane, but has only been allotted some of the significance that a free love relationship, a purely personal relationship, finds it hard to uphold.

On that evening of May 1 when, as a young engaged couple, they rode out to Grib Lake on a motorcycle and smoked a cigarette by the shore while a nightingale started to sing in the beech forest behind them, while for once they felt they were quite alone in the whole world, and life seemed to have neither past nor future . . . then they felt themselves to be something real and their relationship something real.

Could not this quality and this reality have been more cherished, and were they not justified in sadly and reproachfully asking family and society, and themselves: "What actually is it, and what good does it do, that they have sacrificed themselves for?"

But the time of the family is past, and cannot be recalled. Nor would it be recalled even if this were possible. Many generations have given their thought and strength in order to annihilate it. We read of the values that its concept may have contained with a certain wistfulness, just as at the Chateau de Chambord "the Voitures de Gala which were prepared in 1873 for the royal entrance of the comte de Chambord in Paris may be seen for 1 franc extra per person."

St. Christopher must turn away from the past and look to the present or the future.

X. . . . Continues His Wanderings

People in general have a somewhat confused understanding of the idea of truth.

Many people interpret truth in a negative sense: the person who does not lie tells the truth. So they go to their grave without ever having told a lie and without any idea at all of what truth is.

Others think that truth is best practiced as a kind of mental and emotional communism. The person who wishes to be truthful in relation to another must keep nothing to himself, but must reveal everything as well as demand to know everything. Truth cannot be fully achieved before people know all about each other's childhood love affairs and toothaches in detail. The true friend, son, husband has not a single corner of his soul that he can call his own, no possession that he has not shared out among the commune, and he feels that a secret is not a sweetness in the soul but a weight on his conscience.

This type of search for truth is practiced particularly in the home, and Danish art, which on the whole has paid homage to such a form of truth, has glorified it in many hundreds of interiors: the husband reading, with his pipe or his glass of toddy beside him, the elder children at their lessons, drinking milk and tea and eating their bread and butter, the wife nursing the youngest child, all gathered around the same lamp, while the dog, stretched out on the carpet, contributes to the intimate atmosphere of the home.

When our homes still surround themselves with an aura of ideality, indeed, regard themselves as the nation's greatest treasure, it is perhaps because they feel themselves to be the upholders of this particular type of truth . . . related to the type of love of truth and real intimacy that in the old days furnished "the smallest room" snugly enough with a row of seats, one beside the other, where a gathering of good friends might sit and discuss their mutual affairs in peace and quiet.

They plead this love of truth as one of their worthiest qualities, and maintain that one of the corrupting aspects of free love affairs is that a mistress makes use of her wiles and her attraction to hold on to her lover out of necessity (oh dear, oh dear, these poor old aging mistresses — *quote*), instead of appearing before him truthfully as she would be able to do if she were a legitimate wife with the law on her side, and so had no need to fear being weighed and found wanting. Many wedded wives bring to mind this creed, because in their homes one cannot help thinking what an almost divine change it would be for their husbands if they were suddenly caused to realize that their position was not at all as secure as they had thought, and that they would have to make some effort to keep it.

In reality, long unbroken cohabitation is probably a dangerous situation in which to practice such truth and intimacy, and there is something to be said for the old rule that "the nightdress is taken off for the lover, but kept on for the husband."

A pair of lovers can and must discard the last garment because their meetings are purely beautiful, in the mood for love. But even the most enamored couple, who intend to continue their relationship for the rest of their lives, ought to consider that sooner or later in the course of so long a time circumstances will arise that will make it preferable to retain a minimum of covering, and that it is not an especially attractive moment when they are obliged to dress again. It is easier to add to the truth and frankness within a relationship than to curtail it once it has been introduced, and the old habit of spouses using the formal manner of addressing each other probably had the same effect sometimes as the sort of cool atmosphere in which goods keep well without much deterioration.

It is not easy to accommodate oneself to cold comfort, and no doubt in the homes of former times they found, as King Frederik VI experienced, that "pillows were hard right from the cradle." But looked at from the viewpoint of mental hygiene, perhaps both these aspects had their good sides. The homes in which the young people of today are prepared for life, and which are completely devoid of any underlying idea at all (apart from the dogma of the sanctity of the home in itself), can often be compared to a nice soft bed. It cannot be denied, of course, that there is much to be said for this, for it gives rest to the weary, and is a solace for the sick and the overburdened. But it is not something to idealize; rather, it may be said that the briefer time one can with impunity stay in it the better. Neither is the nostalgia for it to be idealized, even though one can sympathize with it, but the homesickness that children who have been poisoned with self-pity feel and suffer can often be compared with a spoiled person's longing for his nice soft bed. Least of all is there anything to idealize in the custom of keeping fit people, who feel like getting up, in bed against their will . . . and yet how frequently that is the practice and is even idealized in homes where there are children and young people.

How often when one goes into one of these idealized homes does one get the same feeling, morally and intellectually, that strikes one physically in a crowded carriage or waiting room, where the windows are closed: the air is stale.

What one breathes in is the harmonically blended breath exhaled from the assembly, right down to the jokes now turned to dust that were new when the paterfamilias was a boy, and the taste of his favorite books that are stuffed into the younger generation like infinitely ancient cakes that it is no longer possible to digest or make use of as nourishment.

This is where many proud men have been boiled down into bread and milk, and many lovely young women have ended up with their whole family in a mutual mental cannibalism that has left them all with nothing but their bones; or parents and children have similarly suffered as would be the case where a mother kept her children at the breast until they were quite big, tearfully confronting anyone who tried to save either mother or child from being worn out or undernourished with the sanctity of mother's milk.

Where self-righteous people live together in a home that is not borne up by any idea at all except the dogma of the sanctity of that home, their self-righteousness will not only be increased but multiplied. Then they will end up by "becoming persuaded even unto unconsciousness that no one can even dwell under their roof without deep cause for thankfulness. Their children, their servants, must be fortunate ipso facto that they are theirs. . . ." In such a setting, the moral evaluation of other people will be decided solely in relation to their own evaluation of this holy home and the blessed society dwelling in it: that is to say that they, who know that Mama is wonderful and Papa unique, and Beech Grove the loveliest place in the world, are nice people, whereas the others are either stupid or nasty, or one does not reckon with them as people at all, and takes no interest in their existence. As a preparation for life these blessed homes resemble the dancing school in *Emmeline*, where the girls learned the steps of the minuet like this: "three chassés forward to the mirror, a pas de basque in front of the console table . . ."

. . . For most past generations of men — whose understanding of these things was not completely controlled by their women — it was their work, war, ideas, the family that they took seriously, while love to them was pleasure and play.

But there has been some inequality here, and women were not in a position where they could play, even when they had a predisposition to do so. It might still have been possible in those societies and periods in which marriage was the concern of the clan, the family or society, and was arranged by them — in the same way that the family, the home and work represented life in earnest to the woman, and love in itself had no place there — as is still the case in old-fashioned society in the Latin nations, or among the Arabs, for instance, from whom the crusader knights are said to have taken their first ideas of love as a game and an art.

But in a situation where the whole future, position, indeed life of women was entirely dependent on their love relationships in a completely different way from that of their men — as for instance for the last century in England and the whole of northern Europe — then one could hardly expect them to have a sense of play. Zarathustra might well point out to them that "in every man there hides a child who wants to play. Come then, you women, and find the child in man." This would seem a risky idea to someone who knew that the whole life, welfare and property of herself and her children were utterly dependent on that child.

And throughout all ages and societies, woman's physical contribution to a love relationship — whether, so to speak, she would or no — made it an extremely serious matter for her.

Many, many love affairs and marriages all through the ages have deteriorated and become embittered through this unequal situation.

From the purely practical point of view it might be arranged that men divided themselves among two sides of the feminine personality, and "had wedded wives to run our houses and bear us legitimate children, and hetairai to teach us the joys of love."

This was probably quite a workable arrangement, for the women as well, who after all could generally choose according to their taste whether they would be ladies of pleasure or nannies. And you might say that if the men had had a spark of good sense, they would have made every effort to maintain this state of things.

But almost all the slavery in the world has been — albeit not always consciously — abolished from above. For the slaveowner is unsatisfied and demands slaves with a sense of responsibility, or wives who can sing for him and entertain his friends, or mistresses with whom he can discuss his business affairs. Apart from those with the most primitive natures, perhaps average men would have found that their house was not run as they might have wished, or that the joys of love in which they were instructed did not bring them long-lasting happiness, or that their children's beauty or talents were not what they had hoped for. And hereby there developed, quite slowly, the phenomenon that took shape and outraged the world in the last century, which was called the emancipated woman.

She came at a serious time, and was therefore obliged to behave seriously in order to be taken seriously. Perhaps, too, an instinct that has taken centuries to develop is the hardest thing of all for the liberated to liberate themselves from. Young liberated women were prepared to give as good as they got, for now was the moment when the world was to feel the effect of woman's hard-tried moral sense. Men's ideals of love had in the past done her much harm and little good, and now, when she was no longer the plaything of love but a comrade in work and striving, now most of all love, whether it be free or bound, was to be taken seriously.

But force of circumstances brought a change in her, even before she had changed her program. In the softer air of freedom she herself, after a couple of generations, came to take everything more easily. Now her grand-daughters, mentally and physically independent, are their young men's playmates in these postwar years.

They do not seem to be quite sure of the game yet. There is still to this day a certain amount of hissing and scratching in protest at the rule applying to all games, that no one must "lose their temper," but the loser and the winner must shake hands without rancor. To educate the next generation, we might need a court and school of love like that of the comtesse de Provence of old, where young people learned discipline in affairs of the heart and were taught courtesy, boldness and sophistication in love.

Much is demanded of those who are to be really proficient at play. Courage and imagination, humor and intelligence, but in particular that blend of unselfishness, generosity, self-control and courtesy that is called *gentilezza*. Alas, there has been so little demand and exercise of this in love affairs. So many excellent men and women have demanded it of themselves in relation to their circles of acquaintances and subordinates, but in their marriages have thought that they had every possible right to be egoistic, uncontrolled, jealous . . . for where love was concerned, it was not really an ideal.

And yet it is play's own spirit, true *gentilezza*, that there is most need of in human love affairs, and that has most power, the minute it appears, to idealize them — whether they are to last for a day or for all eternity.

Those who love to play are constantly being criticized for being superficial . . . and not least where love is concerned.

"Yes," they can reply, "we are superficial in the same way as a ship sailing across the sea. We do not consider it any advantage to reach the bottom, for at best that is what is known as going aground."

Those violent passions that take themselves so "seriously" cannot run a smooth course. The life they create is like that of the pendulum and they result in reactions, indeed, in total impotence.

But it is easy to imagine a game going on throughout eternity, like the games of the Aesir on the plains of Ida, as Shelley imagines it in *Prometheus Unbound*. When the fearful sufferings of humanity are at an end and the forces of tyranny have been cast into the abyss by the Demogorgon, then will all human passions

> . . . in life's green grove
> sport like tame beasts, none knew how gentle
> they could be!

XII. The Heavy Child: A Fantasy

King Louis XVI wrote in his diary: "14/7 1789: Nothing."[1] And it is very possible that if Pilate had kept a diary, he would have written in it on the night of Good Friday: "Nothing. Slight earthquake just before dinner." Yes, God help us, this is how we all keep diaries, for it requires unusual superiority to take in what is right in front of our noses.

Perhaps this is how the historians of humanity will record the first twenty-five years of the twentieth century and will note: "Airplanes, the Great War, revolutions and Bolshevism," ignorant of the fact that an idea has seen the light of day from which quite different revolutions will grow, a new religion has been established or practiced, and not write down in their history: "It was during these years that the idea of birth-control and eugenics was first mooted and consolidated."

It is disturbing to think that many times this really is what happens; it is disturbing to think of good-natured King Louis seating himself in his bedroom at Versailles, taking thought and writing his few words, and think that from that day on the ground trembled beneath his feet and shook the fat powdered head on his shoulders. It is disturbing to think that now we take part in small arguments as to whether the discussion of "birth-control" is decent or indecent, and that the idea of it is present in the consciousness and way of thinking of young people here, there, and everywhere, and is accepted by families with a sigh of relief, as a gift, a mercy, quite simply, to smooth the rough path of life, while perhaps it really means that now a tremendous demand is being made on humanity from which it can never again release itself, a great burden has been placed on our shoulders.

After St. Christopher had searched for a long time for someone stronger than himself whom he might serve, he finally settled down to the job of carrying travelers across a river. One day a small child came and asked to be carried across, and Reprobus set him on his shoulders. But as they went deeper out into the water, the child grew heavier and heavier, and when they were halfway across he staggered under the weight and turned to reproach the child for putting his life in danger. Then the child began to speak and said: "Be not afraid of my weight, Reprobus, for on your shoulders you bear him who made the world and sustains it."

Now, we cannot tell whether this really reassured Reprobus. One would think that he could not possibly have been told anything that would have terrified him more, just at the moment when he was staggering about in the middle of the river. But at least now his search was over and he had found one who was strong enough for him and whom he could serve with all his heart.

To return to the problem of love and of ideality in love and love relationships, and to sum up all these observations: the considered opinion must be that a love affair is ideal to the degree that the individuals feel that they are in contact with and are influenced by their highest ideals.

Thus, when the clan and the family were the highest things in life, the ideal love relationships were those that served the clan and the family, that is to say, the lawful marriages, in which a wife bore her husband many children.

Thus, at the time when the practice of a certain religion, the Church, and the future life in Paradise were the highest ideals in life, then (although all earthly circumstances were in themselves open to doubt) the love affair that enjoyed the blessing of the Church, that was perfectly in accordance with the spirit and discipline of the Church, was the most ideal.

But it is hypocritical, superficial and immoral, it is altogether wrong and unreasonable to attempt to idealize a love relationship with rules and formulae from those ideals that no longer are ideal and no longer have any real life. They are salt that has lost its power, and no matter how much of that kind of salt orthodoxy uses, it will not stop the rot.

Therefore, to an artist, for whom his art is the highest thing, that love relationship and the mistress who gives him inspiration are great and noble; but the things under whose influence his art declines in quality are the opposite of ideal.

Therefore, to the present young generation, who prize individualism above all else, who see love as the highest thing in human life, and whose ideals, when they have any, are freedom and beauty, every love affair that can be conducted freely and beautifully and in which the personalities can understand, help, give joy to each other has every possibility of existing ideally in itself, without any external enlightenment.

Therefore, when people take up eugenics in earnest, the love that collaborates in this will be judged as the ideal.

Then it will really have discovered something stronger than itself that it can serve with enthusiasm and that does not, like the ruler of Canaan, fear the Devil, or, like the Devil himself, fear the Cross. In the middle of the river it will acquire the strength to bear its burden in the consciousness of its enormous importance and extent.

Throughout the ages human beings have constantly striven to widen their horizons, the area of their interdependence and interest. It spread from the home, the family and the clan to the class and the nation. Now, while the concept of patriotism is still not a century old, humanity surely has courage and imagination enough to take the huge step of encompassing the race itself, the whole of humanity, with the same feeling of responsibility, the same burning desire to serve.

And people will widen their horizon, as far as time is concerned. They must come to reckon with a completely new yardstick for temporality and eternity.

Both past and future are, to an unlimited extent in the family and the race, present in the individual and the present. A thousand families have blended their blood in the single individual, and he can, in coming generations, extend his influence over the life of the race for a thousand years into the future.

It is reasonable to suppose that when the sense of interdependence, of unity as a race, has penetrated human consciousness, a person will be evaluated far more for his extraction and his "blood" than at present, just as is the case with individual specimens of purebred animals.

Now, it is sometimes said that it takes three generations to produce a "gentleman," and against this very modest demand other opinions maintain that ten or twenty years of educating the individual will suffice. Coming generations will probably work with quite different periods of time, with gentlemen of ten, twenty, fifty generations, and people in general will be assessed according to events that have taken place, circumstances that have occurred, many generations before their birth. What Samuel Butler wrote fifty years ago will be generally acknowledged: "If a man is to enter the Kingdom of Heaven he must do so, not only as a little child, but as a little embryo, or rather as a little zoosperm — and not only this, but as one that has come of zoosperms which have entered into the Kingdom of Heaven before him for many generations . . . postnatal accidents are not, as a rule, so permanent in their effect. . . ." Or, to cite another English author, that humanity has made a great error in "seizing on a certain moment, no more intrinsically notable than any other moment, and [has] called it Birth. The habit of honouring one single instant of the universal process to the disadvantage of all other instants has done more, perhaps, than anything to obfuscate the crystal clearness of the fundamental flux."

It requires no laws and rules to practice such a philosophy of life. They will be innate in the consciousness in the same way as are present-day moral laws, and no decent person will be able to avoid them. . . .

In its constant striving for growth, for the ability to grasp as much as possible, humanity can surely reach further, find something greater than itself.

For those nations that were — or still are, as in the case of the Somalis — divided up into mutually hostile tribes, it seems unreasonable and unnatural to this day that they should ever be able to be united under one national banner. And to the burning patriots of the last generation it seemed quite impossible that they should feel anything for humanity in general, or fraternity for any other than a countryman.

And yet love of clan has undoubtedly grown out of love of family and home, love of country out of love for clan, and the idea of the brotherhood of all humanity has arisen the stronger from the fearful flames the love of country burst out into.

The human beings of the future, who will not have the slightest difficulty in comprehending the fourth dimension — and this will undoubtedly not take long if we start on it straightaway — and who have consciously taken the work of development out of the hands of nature and said to it: "My will be done, not thine," will then perhaps be able enthusiastically to merge into an even higher unity and embrace a larger brotherhood with the same enthusiasm as that with which Habr Yunis meets Habr Yunis, and with which the patriots of the forties sang to and embraced the children of their beloved common fatherland.

So with these fantasies must these observations, begun in all modesty, end.

No one can know what he is in for when he embarks on a search for the strongest . . . nor where he may end up when he begins to talk about it.

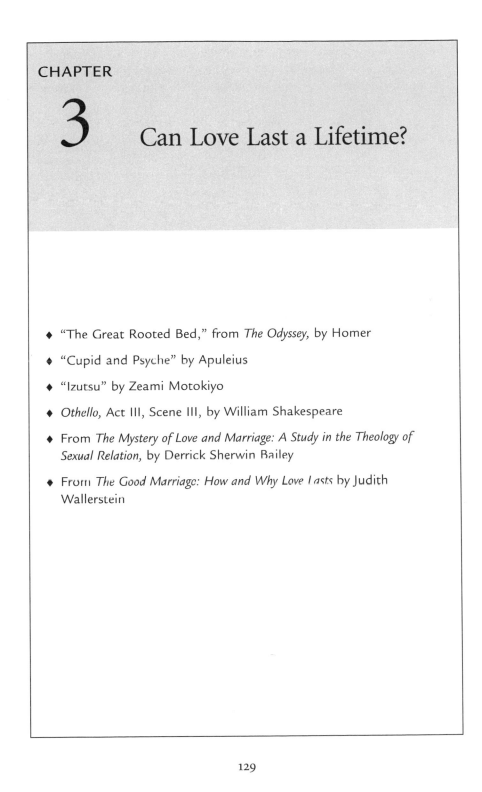

CHAPTER

3   Can Love Last a Lifetime?

I may commit many follies in life, but I never intend to marry for love.

— BENJAMIN DISRAELI

Let me not to the marriage of true minds
Admit impediments. Love is not love
Which alters when it alteration finds.

— WILLIAM SHAKESPEARE

A happy marriage is a thing of slow growth.

— GRAHAM GREENE

Introduction

Many men and women enter marriage deeply in love, but with a nagging worry: Will I feel like this forever? The readings in this chapter explore the dynamics of several marriages in which love lasts and grows — and one marriage that the intensity of love destroys. The first selection, from Robert Fagles's new translation of the *Odyssey*, reveals three elements in marriage that are essential to lasting marital love: fidelity, friendship, and sexual interest. In this magnificent chapter of the Homeric epic, the warrior Odysseus has returned home after two decades of wanderings and struggle, only to find his house invaded by his wife's suitors. Though Penelope despairs of his return, she has stubbornly resisted them. In one brief bloody battle, Odysseus overcomes the intruders; yet his wife Penelope will not believe her redeemer to be her husband. Even on her first meeting with Odysseus, Penelope remains unmoved, refusing to sleep with Odysseus until he has proven his identity. She resolves to test him, ordering her maid to move the bedstead from their bridal chamber. His response, that the bedstead (which he crafted with his own hands) is too sturdy for any mortal to move, proves to her that he is indeed the man he claims he is. She falls into his arms. Their reunion is a night of renewed love and recounting, made sweeter by the efforts of Athena, who blesses them by "reining in Dawn of the golden throne at Ocean's banks."

Apuleius' story of Cupid and Psyche explores the theme of marital love as mystery and revelation. Psyche is not permitted to look upon her husband Cupid, the god of love. But the urgings of her sisters and her own curiosity about the source of her nightly pleasures compel her to sneak a peek at her spouse while he is sleeping. For this indiscretion she is gravely punished, and must endure a number of trials that — in putting the love relationship of husband and wife on a very different footing — prove her worthy of being the wife of an immortal. This story shows us not only that prolonged intimacy changes the very nature of love, but also that the trials of marriage deepen us and strengthen our marriage bond.

In Zeami Motokiyo's fourteenth-century Japanese Noh play, "Izutsu," marital love lasts even beyond the grave. This play concerns a roving husband who is ultimately tamed by his wife's unswerving devotion to him. Playmate of her husband's childhood, lover of his youth, the virtuous wife is the very model of selflessness. She fairly wills marital love to last, despite her husband's betrayals. In fact, her devotion to her spouse is so profound that it moves her to complete identification with his person. Even her ghost, in its wandering, occasionally takes on his features.

Of course, husbands and wives can love "not wisely, but too well." In the tragedy *Othello,* Shakespeare paints the portrait of an insecure husband whose love of his wife far exceeds his trust in her. Thus, he allows himself to be tricked by an ambitious courtier into believing that his wife is unfaithful. His deep love turned to desperate hatred; he takes his wife's life.

What is healthy marital love, and what is its relationship to Eros? Derrick Sherwin Bailey asserts that this is a theme the churches have not properly tackled. Taking his philosophical cue from Buber's "I-thou" theory of relationships, and applying that theory to the Judeo-Christian ideal of the marital relationship, "one-flesh," Bailey's ruminations on the nature of romantic love become a meditation on the experience and nature of God. "Through the encounter of lovers," he writes, "the mystery of God's will and the destiny of man in Christ are proclaimed."

Finally, psychologist Judith Wallerstein weighs in on the subject of lasting love in a selection from her 1995 book, *The Good Marriage.* In a "surprising number" of good marriages, Wallerstein asserts, love was not very passionate at first, but "grew in the rich soil of the marriage, nourished by emotional and physical intimacy, appreciation, and fond memories." People who build lasting love, Wallerstein found in her interviews with hundreds of married couples, are people for whom marriage and children are regarded as their principal pastime and achievement. These are people who, despite even serious differences with their spouses, are in for "the long haul." Yes, love *can* last a lifetime, but in order to last, our marriages have to be first on our list of priorities.

HOMER

Nothing is really known about the life of Homer, who is said to have composed *The Iliad* and *The Odyssey* sometime in the late eighth or early seventh century B.C. What is known, however, is that we can trace ceremonial recitations of Homer back to the sixth century B.C. and we recognize Homeric influences on Greek poets and pottery makers back as far as the seventh century B.C. Modern scholars have come to believe that Homer was a bard who used the brand-new technique of script to record and refine epic narratives familiar to him from an oral tradition. Incidentally, the "book" numbers of *The Odyssey* refer to the papyrus rolls on which the 12,000-line poem was preserved and handed down over hundreds of years.

"The Great Rooted Bed," Book 23 in The Odyssey

Up to the rooms the old nurse clambered, chuckling all the way,
to tell the queen her husband was here now, home at last.
Her knees bustling, feet shuffling over each other,
till hovering at her mistress' head she spoke:
"Penelope — child — wake up and see for yourself,
with your own eyes, all you dreamed of, all your days!
He's here — Odysseus — he's come home, at long last!
He's killed the suitors, swaggering young brutes
who plagued his house, wolfed his cattle down,
rode roughshod over his son!"

"Dear old nurse," wary Penelope replied,
"the gods have made you mad. They have that power,
putting lunacy into the clearest head around
or setting a half-wit on the path to sense.
They've unhinged you, and you were once so sane.
Why do you mock me? — haven't I wept enough? —
telling such wild stories, interrupting my sleep,
sweet sleep that held me, sealed my eyes just now.
Not once have I slept so soundly since the day
Odysseus sailed away to see that cursed city. . . .
Destroy,[1] I call it — I hate to say its name!
Now down you go. Back to your own quarters.
If any other woman of mine had come to me,
rousing me out of sleep with such a tale,
I'd have her bundled back to her room in pain.
It's only your old gray head that spares you that!"

"Never" — the fond old nurse kept pressing on —
"dear child, I'd never mock you! No, it's all true,
he's here — Odysseus — he's come home, just as I tell you!
He's the stranger they all manhandled in the hall.
Telemachus knew he was here, for days and days,
but he knew enough to hide his father's plans
so *he* could pay those vipers back in kind!"

Penelope's heart burst in joy, she leapt from bed,
her eyes streaming tears, she hugged the old nurse
and cried out with an eager, winging word,
"Please, dear one, give me the whole story.
If he's really home again, just as you tell me,
how did he get those shameless suitors in his clutches? —
single-handed, braving an army always camped inside."

"I have no idea," the devoted nurse replied.
"I didn't see it, I didn't ask — all I heard
was the choking groans of men cut down in blood.
We crouched in terror — a dark nook of our quarters —
all of us locked tight behind those snug doors
till your boy Telemachus came and called me out —
his father rushed him there to do just that. Then

I found Odysseus in the thick of slaughtered corpses;
there he stood and all around him, over the beaten floor,
the bodies sprawled in heaps, lying one on another. . . .
How it would have thrilled your heart to see him —
splattered with bloody filth, a lion with his kill!
And now they're all stacked at the courtyard gates —
he's lit a roaring fire,
he's purifying the house with cleansing fumes
and he's sent me here to bring you back to him.
Follow me down! So now, after all the years of grief,
you two can embark, loving hearts, along the road to joy.
Look, your dreams, put off so long, come true at last —
he's back alive, home at his hearth, and found you,
found his son still here. And all those suitors
who did him wrong, he's paid them back, he has,
right in his own house!"
                              "Hush, dear woman,"
guarded Penelope cautioned her at once.
"Don't laugh, don't cry in triumph — not yet.
You know how welcome the sight of him would be
to all in the house, and to me most of all
and the son we bore together.
But the story can't be true, not as you tell it,
no, it must be a god who's killed our brazen friends —
up in arms at their outrage, heartbreaking crimes.
They'd no regard for any man on earth —
good or bad — who chanced to come their way. So,
thanks to their reckless work they die their deaths.
Odysseus? Far from Achaea now, he's lost all hope
of coming home . . . he's lost and gone himself."

    "Child," the devoted old nurse protested,
"what nonsense you let slip through your teeth.
Here's your husband, warming his hands at his own hearth,
here — and you, you say he'll never come home again,
always the soul of trust! All right, this too —
I'll give you a sign, a proof that's plain as day.
That scar, made years ago by a boar's white tusk —
I spotted the scar myself, when I washed his feet,
and I tried to tell you, ah, but he, the crafty rascal,

clamped his hand on my mouth — I couldn't say a word.
Follow me down now. I'll stake my life on it:
if I am lying to *you* —
kill me with a thousand knives of pain!"

"Dear old nurse," composed Penelope responded,
"deep as you are, my friend, you'll find it hard
to plumb the plans of the everlasting gods.
All the same, let's go and join my son
so I can see the suitors lying dead
and see . . . the one who killed them."

                                With that thought
Penelope started down from her lofty room, her heart
in turmoil, torn . . . should she keep her distance,
probe her husband? Or rush up to the man at once
and kiss his head and cling to both his hands?
As soon as she stepped across the stone threshold,
slipping in, she took a seat at the closest wall
and radiant in the firelight, faced Odysseus now.
There he sat, leaning against the great central column,
eyes fixed on the ground, waiting, poised for whatever words
his hardy wife might say when she caught sight of him.
A long while she sat in silence . . . numbing wonder
filled her heart as her eyes explored his face.
One moment he seemed . . . Odysseus, to the life —
the next, no, he was not the man she knew,
a huddled mass of rags was all she saw.

"Oh mother," Telemachus reproached her,
"cruel mother, you with your hard heart!
Why do you spurn my father so — why don't you
sit beside him, engage him, ask him questions?
What other wife could have a spirit so unbending?
Holding back from her husband, home at last for *her*
after bearing twenty years of brutal struggle —
your heart was always harder than a rock!"

                                "My child,"
Penelope, well-aware, explained, "I'm stunned with wonder,
powerless. Cannot speak to him, ask him questions,
look him in the eyes. . . . But if he is truly

Odysseus, home at last, make no mistake:
we two will know each other, even better —
we two have secret signs,
known to us both but hidden from the world."

    Odysseus, long-enduring, broke into a smile
and turned to his son with pointed, winging words:
"Leave your mother here in the hall to test me
as she will. She soon will know me better.
Now because I am filthy, wear such grimy rags,
she spurns me — your mother still can't bring herself
to believe I am her husband.
                  But you and I,
put heads together. What's our best defense?
When someone kills a lone man in the realm
who leaves behind him no great band of avengers,
still the killer flees, good-bye to kin and country.
But we brought down the best of the island's princes,
the pillars of Ithaca. Weigh it well, I urge you."

    "Look to it all yourself now, father," his son
deferred at once. "You are the best on earth,
they say, when it comes to mapping tactics.
No one, no mortal man, can touch you there.
But we're behind you, hearts intent on battle,
nor do I think you'll find us short on courage,
long as our strength will last."
                    "Then here's our plan,"
the master of tactics said. "I think it's best.
First go and wash, and pull fresh tunics on,
and tell the maids in the hall to dress well too.
And let the inspired bard take up his ringing lyre
and lead off for us all a dance so full of heart
that whoever hears the strains outside the gates —
a passerby on the road, a neighbor round about —
will think it's a wedding-feast that's under way.
No news of the suitors' death must spread through town
till we have slipped away to our own estates,
our orchard green with trees. There we'll see
what winning strategy Zeus will hand us then."

They hung on his words and moved to orders smartly.
First they washed and pulled fresh tunics on,
the women arrayed themselves — the inspired bard
struck up his resounding lyre and stirred in all
a desire for dance and song, the lovely lilting beat,
till the great house echoed round to the measured tread
of dancing men in motion, women sashed and lithe.
And whoever heard the strains outside would say,
"A miracle — someone's married the queen at last!"

   "One of her hundred suitors."
                   "That callous woman,
too faithless to keep her lord and master's house
to the bitter end — "
            "Till he came sailing home."

   So they'd say, blind to what had happened:
the great-hearted Odysseus was home again at last.
The maid Eurynome bathed him, rubbed him down with oil
and drew around him a royal cape and choice tunic too.
And Athena crowned the man with beauty, head to foot,
made him taller to all eyes, his build more massive,
yes, and down from his brow the great goddess
ran his curls like thick hyacinth clusters
full of blooms. As a master craftsman washes
gold over beaten silver — a man the god of fire
and Queen Athena trained in every fine technique —
and finishes off his latest effort, handsome work . . .
so she lavished splendor over his head and shoulders now.
He stepped from his bath, glistening like a god,
and back he went to the seat that he had left
and facing his wife, declared,
"Strange woman! So hard — the gods of Olympus
made you harder than any other woman in the world!
What other wife could have a spirit so unbending?
Holding back from her husband, home at last for *her*
after bearing twenty years of brutal struggle.
Come, nurse, make me a bed, I'll sleep alone.
She has a heart of iron in her breast."
                "Strange *man*,"

wary Penelope said. "I'm not so proud, so scornful,
nor am I overwhelmed by your quick change. . . .
You look — how well I know — the way he looked,
setting sail from Ithaca years ago
aboard the long-oared ship.

                Come, Eurycleia,
move the sturdy bedstead out of our bridal chamber —
that room the master built with his own hands.
Take it out now, sturdy bed that it is,
and spread it deep with fleece,
blankets and lustrous throws to keep him warm."

   Putting her husband to the proof — but Odysseus
blazed up in fury, lashing out at his loyal wife:
"Woman — your words, they cut me to the core!
Who could move my bed? Impossible task,
even for some skilled craftsman — unless a god
came down in person, quick to lend a hand,
lifted it out with ease and moved it elsewhere.
Not a man on earth, not even at peak strength,
would find it easy to prise it up and shift it, no,
a great sign, a hallmark lies in its construction.
I know, I built it myself — no one else. . . .
There was a branching olive-tree inside our court,
grown to its full prime, the bole like a column, thickset.
Around it I built my bedroom, finished off the walls
with good tight stonework, roofed it over soundly
and added doors, hung well and snugly wedged.
Then I lopped the leafy crown of the olive,
clean-cutting the stump bare from roots up,
planing it round with a bronze smoothing-adze —
I had the skill — I shaped it plumb to the line to make
my bedpost, bored the holes it needed with an auger.
Working from there I built my bed, start to finish,
I gave it ivory inlays, gold and silver fittings,
wove the straps across it, oxhide gleaming red.
There's our secret sign, I tell you, our life story!
Does the bed, my lady, still stand planted firm? —
I don't know — or has someone chopped away
that olive-trunk and hauled our bedstead off?"

        Living proof —
Penelope felt her knees go slack, her heart surrender,
recognizing the strong clear signs Odysseus offered.
She dissolved in tears, rushed to Odysseus, flung her arms
around his neck and kissed his head and cried out,
"*Odysseus* — don't flare up at me now, not you,
always the most understanding man alive!
The gods, it was the gods who sent us sorrow —
they grudged us both a life in each other's arms
from the heady zest of youth to the stoop of old age.
But don't fault me, angry with me now because I failed,
at the first glimpse, to greet you, hold you, so. . . .
In my heart of hearts I always cringed with fear
some fraud might come, beguile me with his talk;
the world is full of the sort,
cunning ones who plot their own dark ends.
Remember Helen of Argos, Zeus's daughter —
would *she* have sported so in a stranger's bed
if she had dreamed that Achaea's sons were doomed
to fight and die to bring her home again?
Some god spurred her to do her shameless work.
Not till then did her mind conceive that madness,
blinding madness that caused her anguish, ours as well.
But now, since you have revealed such overwhelming proof —
the secret sign of our bed, which no one's ever seen
but you and I and a single handmaid, Actoris,
the servant my father gave me when I came,
who kept the doors of our room you built so well . . .
you've conquered my heart, my hard heart, at last!"

    The more she spoke, the more a deep desire for tears
welled up inside his breast — he wept as he held the wife
he loved, the soul of loyalty, in his arms at last.
Joy, warm as the joy that shipwrecked sailors feel
when they catch sight of land — Poseidon has struck
their well-rigged ship on the open sea with gale winds
and crushing walls of waves, and only a few escape, swimming,
struggling out of the frothing surf to reach the shore,
their bodies crusted with salt but buoyed up with joy
as they plant their feet on solid ground again,

spared a deadly fate. So joyous now to her
the sight of her husband, vivid in her gaze,
that her white arms, embracing his neck
would never for a moment let him go. . . .
Dawn with her rose-red fingers might have shone
upon their tears, if with her glinting eyes
Athena had not thought of one more thing.
She held back the night, and night lingered long
at the western edge of the earth, while in the east
she reined in Dawn of the golden throne at Ocean's banks,
commanding her not to yoke the windswift team that brings men light,
Blaze and Aurora, the young colts that race the Morning on.
Yet now Odysseus, seasoned veteran, said to his wife,
"Dear woman . . . we have still not reached the end
of all our trials. One more labor lies in store —
boundless, laden with danger, great and long,
and I must brave it out from start to finish.
So the ghost of Tiresias prophesied to me,
the day that I went down to the House of Death
to learn our best route home, my comrades' and my own.
But come, let's go to bed, dear woman — at long last
delight in sleep, delight in each other, come!"

"If it's bed you want," reserved Penelope replied,
"it's bed you'll have, whenever the spirit moves,
now that the gods have brought you home again
to native land, your grand and gracious house.
But since you've alluded to it,
since a god has put it in your mind,
please, tell me about this trial still to come.
I'm bound to learn of it later, I am sure —
what's the harm if I hear of it tonight?"

                                        "Still so strange,"
Odysseus, the old master of stories, answered.
"Why again, why force me to tell you all?
Well, tell I shall. I'll hide nothing now.
But little joy it will bring you, I'm afraid,
as little joy for me.

                        The prophet said
that I must rove through towns on towns of men,

that I must carry a well-planed oar until
I come to a people who know nothing of the sea,
whose food is never seasoned with salt, strangers all
to ships with their crimson prows and long slim oars,
wings that make ships fly. And here is my sign,
he told me, clear, so clear I cannot miss it,
and I will share it with you now. . . .
When another traveler falls in with me and calls
that weight across my shoulder a fan to winnow grain,
then, he told me, I must plant my oar in the earth
and sacrifice fine beasts to the lord god of the sea,
Poseidon — a ram, a bull and a ramping wild boar —
then journey home and render noble offerings up
to the deathless gods who rule the vaulting skies,
to all the gods in order.
And at last my own death will steal upon me . . .
a gentle, painless death, far from the sea it comes
to take me down, borne down with the years in ripe old age
with all my people here in blessed peace around me.
All this, the prophet said, will come to pass."

   "And so," Penelope said, in her great wisdom,
"if the gods will really grant a happier old age,
there's hope that we'll escape our trials at last."

   So husband and wife confided in each other,
while nurse and Eurynome, under the flaring brands,
were making up the bed with coverings deep and soft.
And working briskly, soon as they'd made it snug,
back to her room the old nurse went to sleep
as Eurynome, their attendant, torch in hand,
lighted the royal couple's way to bed and,
leading them to their chamber, slipped away.
Rejoicing in each other, they returned to their bed,
the old familiar place they loved so well.

   Now Telemachus, the cowherd and the swineherd
rested their dancing feet and had the women do the same,
and across the shadowed hall the men lay down to sleep.

But the royal couple, once they'd reveled in all
the longed-for joys of love, reveled in each other's stories,
the radiant woman telling of all she'd borne at home,
watching them there, the infernal crowd of suitors
slaughtering herds of cattle and good fat sheep —
while keen to win her hand —
draining the broached vats dry of vintage wine.
And great Odysseus told his wife of all the pains
he had dealt out to other men and all the hardships
he'd endured himself — his story first to last —
and she listened on, enchanted. . . .
Sleep never sealed her eyes till all was told.

He launched in with how he fought the Cicones down,
then how he came to the Lotus-eaters' lush green land.
Then all the crimes of the Cyclops and how he paid him back
for the gallant men the monster ate without a qualm —
then how he visited Aeolus, who gave him a hero's welcome
then he sent him off, but the homeward run was not his fate,
not yet — some sudden squalls snatched him away once more
and drove him over the swarming sea, groaning in despair.
Then how he moored at Telepylus, where Laestrygonians
wrecked his fleet and killed his men-at-arms.
He told her of Circe's cunning magic wiles
and how he voyaged down in his long benched ship
to the moldering House of Death, to consult Tiresias,
ghostly seer of Thebes, and he saw old comrades there
and he saw his mother, who bore and reared him as a child.
He told how he caught the Sirens' voices throbbing in the wind
and how he had scudded past the Clashing Rocks, past grim Charybdis,
past Scylla — whom no rover had ever coasted by, home free —
and how his shipmates slaughtered the cattle of the Sun
and Zeus the king of thunder split his racing ship
with a reeking bolt and killed his hardy comrades,
all his fighting men at a stroke, but he alone
escaped their death at sea. He told how he reached
Ogygia's shores and the nymph Calypso held him back,
deep in her arching caverns, craving him for a husband —
cherished him, vowed to make him immortal, ageless, all his days,
yes, but she never won the heart inside him, never . . .

then how he reached the Phaeacians — heavy sailing there —
who with all their hearts had prized him like a god
and sent him off in a ship to his own beloved land,
giving him bronze and hoards of gold and robes . . .
and that was the last he told her, just as sleep
overcame him . . . sleep loosing his limbs,
slipping the toils of anguish from his mind.

    Athena, her eyes afire, had fresh plans.
Once she thought he'd had his heart's content
of love and sleep at his wife's side, straightaway
she roused young Dawn from Ocean's banks to her golden throne
to bring men light and roused Odysseus too, who rose
from his soft bed and advised his wife in parting,
"Dear woman, we both have had our fill of trials.
You in our house, weeping over my journey home,
fraught with storms and torment, true, and I,
pinned down in pain by Zeus and other gods,
for all my desire, blocked from reaching home.
But now that we've arrived at our bed together —
the reunion that we yearned for all those years —
look after the things still left me in our house.
But as for the flocks those strutting suitors plundered,
much I'll recoup myself, making many raids;
the rest our fellow-Ithacans will supply
till all my folds are full of sheep again.
But now I must be off to the upland farm,
our orchard green with trees, to see my father,
good old man weighed down with so much grief for me.
And you, dear woman, sensible as you are,
I would advise you, still . . .
quick as the rising sun the news will spread
of the suitors that I killed inside the house.
So climb to your lofty chamber with your women.
Sit tight there. See no one. Question no one."

    He strapped his burnished armor round his shoulders,
roused Telemachus, the cowherd and the swineherd,
and told them to take up weapons honed for battle.
They snapped to commands, harnessed up in bronze,

opened the doors and strode out, Odysseus in the lead.
By now the daylight covered the land, but Pallas,
shrouding them all in darkness,
quickly led the four men out of town.

APULEIUS

The tale of Cupid and Psyche stems from a collection of stories, often fantastic, compiled by Lucius Apuleius in the second century A.D. and entitled, after other works featuring the same narratives, *Metamorphoses*. Apuleius, a Roman philosopher and rhetorician born in North Africa, differentiated his *Metamorphoses* by setting them in the context of a larger romance with pagan mystical elements. He influenced such later authors as Boccaccio and Cervantes. It should be noted that this is the only myth with ancient roots that Apuleius narrates as a myth.

Cupid and Psyche

Psyche was the youngest daughter of a king and queen. She had two elder sisters both of whom were remarkably beautiful. Their beauty, however, might be described in words. But the beauty of Psyche herself was past all description, as was the majesty of her bearing and her sweet and gracious disposition. So from all over the world people came to the country where she lived merely to look at her. They looked at her with wonder and adoration, believing her to be either the goddess Venus herself, who was born from the foam of the sea, or else a new Venus, no less divine than the goddess of beauty and love.

Thus the temples and ceremonies of Venus were neglected. People no longer offered sacrifices and prayed to her. Instead, they thronged to visit Psyche, worshiping her as soon as she left her home in the morning, and laying garlands before her feet.

The true Venus was greatly angered by the neglect shown to her by men.

"It is I," she said to herself, "to whom, on Mount Ida, Paris gave the prize of beauty. And am I to share my honours with a mere mortal girl? She will soon be sorry for being more beautiful than is allowed."

Then Venus called for her winged son, Cupid, the god of love, who with his arrows can conquer the gods themselves, who ranges over the earth like a bee, the brilliant and mischievous youth. "Now, my dear son," she said to him, "you must revenge the injury done to your mother. Mortals are worshiping this girl Psyche instead of me. I want you to make her fall in love with some wretched creature, poor and abject, the ugliest in the world. You with your bow and arrows can do this."

She took him then to the city where Psyche lived and pointed her out to him. Then she herself, after kissing her son, went to the shore nearby, planted her rosy feet on the sea-water, making it calm, and took her way over the sea to her sacred island of Cyprus. Around her played the dolphins and sea gods rose from the waves to make music for her on their horns of shell; nymphs of the sea came to shade her from the sun with their veils of silk or to hold before her eyes her golden mirror.

Meanwhile Psyche received no advantages from the adoration which was given everywhere to her extraordinary beauty. She was praised and worshiped, but no king or noble or even any common person came to woo her to be his wife. All wondered at her, but only as one might wonder at a picture or exquisite statue. Her two sisters, though less beautiful than she, had married kings. Psyche sat alone at home, hating the beauty which delighted everyone except herself.

In the end her father, suspecting that the gods must be envious of his youngest daughter, sent messengers to the oracle of Apollo to inquire what he should do. The reply of the oracle was: "Let Psyche be dressed in black, as for a funeral, and let her be placed on the top of the mountain that rises above your city. Her husband is no mortal being. He is like a dragon that flies in the night. The gods of heaven and earth, even the darkness of Styx, fear his powers."

Psyche's father and mother, who had been so proud of their daughter's beauty, now wept and lamented the sad fate that was in store for her. What the oracle commanded seemed more like death than a wedding. As they prepared to carry out the will of the oracle not only they, but all the people, wept continuously in mourning for the unhappy event. But Psyche said: "You should have wept before, in the time when everyone worshiped me and gave me the name of Venus on earth. Now you see what has come of my beauty. I am overtaken by the jealousy of the gods. Come now, lead me to the dreaded place. I myself long for this marriage I have been promised. At least it will end my unhappiness."

Then, in a great procession, most unlike a wedding procession, they took her to the wild rocky summit of the mountain. There were no glad songs or bright lights. Tears put out the torches. The people went back to their houses with bowed heads, and Psyche's wretched parents shut themselves for days in their palace, mourning for her fate.

Meanwhile Psyche was left alone, trembling and weeping, on the high rock. But there came a mild gentle breeze which softly lifted her from the ground and carried her, with her clothes lightly fluttering, gradually past the precipices and forests till it brought her to a deep and sheltered valley where she was laid down on a bed of grassy turf among the most beautiful and sweet-smelling flowers. This soft bed and the fragrance of the flowers calmed Psyche's restless and astonished mind. Soon she rose to her feet and saw in front of her a fine and pleasant wood with, in the middle of it, a running river as bright as crystal. And there among the trees stood a palace so beautiful that you would think it to be a mansion for one of the gods. The roof was made of citron and ivory. It was supported by pillars of gold. The pavements were of precious stones arranged by some great artist in the form of splendid pictures of animals, birds and flowers. The walls were built of great blocks of gold, and each door and porchway seemed to give out its own light.

The wonder of the place so enchanted Psyche that she boldly went inside and here again found everything magnificent and looked lovingly at everything. There were fine store rooms full of rich dresses and all kinds of wealth. What greatly surprised her was that in all the palace nothing was barred or bolted, nor was there anyone there to guard all these immense riches. While she stood still, half in amazement and half in delight at what she saw, she heard a voice, though no body was to be seen. "Why do you wonder, my lady, at all this wealth? It is yours to command. We, whose voices you hear, are your servants and are ready to do anything you desire. Go therefore to your room and rest on your bed. Then tell us which kind of bath you wish to have prepared for you. Then, when you have refreshed your body, a royal dinner will be served."

Psyche, wondering still more, went to her room and rested. After a perfumed bath, she found the table all set for her convenience. Invisible hands brought her rare wines and delicious dishes of food. After dinner, another unseen servant came and sang; yet another played on the harp. Then it seemed that she was in the middle of a great choir of voices singing most perfectly to the sound of all kinds of instruments. Yet singers and instruments alike were invisible.

As night approached the concert of music ended and Psyche went to bed. Now she became frightened at the thought of the terrible husband promised her by the oracle; but again invisible voices assured her that her husband was one to be loved and not feared. When it was dark, he came and lay down beside her. Though she never saw his face, she heard his voice and felt his body. In the morning he left before dawn, after telling her of his love and promising to return to her each night. So, though she was lonely in the day, she passed each day in great pleasure, being most pleased with the beautiful singing voices that surrounded her; and each night she spent with her husband whom she loved more and more.

Meanwhile her father and mother did nothing but weep and lament for their daughter whom they thought must certainly be lost forever, either devoured by wild beasts or by the terrible dragon. The news of her fate spread far and wide, and Psyche's two sisters came to visit their parents and to mourn with them. That night Psyche's husband spoke to her. He said: "My sweet love and dear wife, a cruel fortune is bringing you into terrible danger, and I wish you to be greatly careful. Your sisters, thinking that you are dead, will come to the mountain in order to mourn for you. If you hear their voices, do not answer them, for, if you do, you will bring me great sorrow and bring yourself absolute ruin."

Psyche listened to him and promised that she would do as he said; but, when he went away next day, she passed all her time in weeping, and began to think that her fine house was really no better than a prison, if she was allowed to see no one and not even able to console her dear sisters who were mourning for her. She ate nothing that day and took no pleasure in her music. Red-eyed with crying, she went to bed early. Her husband also returned earlier than usual and at once he said to her: "Is this the way you keep your promise, my sweet wife? Crying all day and not even now comforted in your husband's arms? Do what you want to do. You may remember my words too late, if you bring on yourself your own ruin."

Then Psyche begged him more and more urgently to give her what she wanted, that she might see her sisters and speak with them. In the end he was won over by her entreaties and told her that she should give her sisters all the gold and jewels that she wished, but he earnestly entreated her never to be led by her sisters' advice into a longing to see his own face. If she did so, he said, she would lose the good life she had now, and would never feel his arms about her again.

Psyche was now full of gratitude and love for him. "I would die a hundred times," she said, "rather than be separated from you, my sweet husband. Whoever you are, I love you and keep you in my heart as though you were my own life. I could not love you more if you were Cupid himself. Now I beg you to let your servant the West Wind bring my sisters down to me here tomorrow, as he brought me." Then she kissed him and called him her sweet soul, her husband and her darling. He, such was the power of her love, agreed to do as she desired.

Next day her sisters came to the rock where Psyche had been seen last, and there they cried and lamented for her, so that the rock rang with their cries. The sound came to Psyche's ears and she called back to them, "I whom you weep for am here, alive and happy." Then she called to the West Wind who gently carried her two sisters down to the valley where she lived. For long there was nothing but embracing and tears of joy. Then Psyche showed her sisters her gorgeous house with its store of treasure. She ordered the unseen musicians to sing; she feasted them with fine food and wine, and they (shameful creatures that they were) became filled with envy of her and determined in some way to ruin her happiness. Often they asked her about her husband, and Psyche, remembering the warning that she had had, pretended that she knew him by sight. He was a handsome young man, she said, with the down just growing on his chin, and his chief pleasure in the day was to go hunting in the mountains. Then, since she feared that she might make some mistake in her speech, she gave them all the gold and jewels that they could carry and ordered the West Wind to take them back to the mountain.

No sooner were they alone together than they each began bitterly and enviously to complain of Psyche's good fortune. "She is the youngest one of us three," said the older sister. "Why should she have a palace and stores of wealth? Why should she have those miraculous servants and be able to give orders to the West Wind? Indeed her husband may end by making her into a goddess. Even now she has every happiness. As for me, my husband is old enough to be my father. He is as bald as a coot and he keeps all his riches under lock and key."

The second sister was just as jealous as the first. "My husband," she said, "is always ill and I have to waste my time nursing him as though I were a doctor's assistant. I certainly cannot bear to see my younger sister so happy. Let us therefore tell no one of what we have seen; and let us try to think of some way in which we can do her harm."

So these unnatural sisters hid the gold and jewels which Psyche had given them. Instead of consoling their parents with the news of her safety and happiness, they pretended that they had searched the mountains for her in vain and that they were, with their sad faces, still mourning for her loss. Afterwards, they went back to their own homes, and there began to think out plans by which they could somehow injure the sister whom they pretended to love.

Meanwhile Psyche's husband again spoke to her in the night. "My sweet wife," he said to her, "those wicked sisters of yours are threatening you with great evil. I think that they will come to see you again. Now I beg you either not to talk with them at all (which would be the best thing) or at least not to talk to them about me. If you obey me, we shall still be happy. Already you have in your body a child of yours and mine. If you conceal my secret, the child, when it is born, will be a god; if you do not, then it will be a mortal."

Psyche was very glad to know that she would have a divine child and was more pleased with her husband than ever. But her sisters hastened on with their wicked plots and, as they had arranged, came once more to the country where Psyche was. Once again her husband warned her: "Now is the last and final day," he said. "Now I beg you, sweet Psyche, to have pity on yourself, on me and on our unborn child. Do not see these wicked women who do not deserve to be called your sisters."

But Psyche said, "Dear husband, you know that you can trust me. Did I not keep silent before? Let me at least see my sisters, since I cannot see you. Not that I blame you for this, and indeed darkness is like day to me when I hold you, who are my light, within my arms."

With such words she persuaded him once more to order the West Wind to carry her sisters to her. Before dawn he left her, and early in the day her sisters were brought to the soft and fragrant valley and to her palace. They were gladly welcomed as before by Psyche, who told them proudly that before many months she would become a mother. This made the sisters more jealous than ever, but they hid their feelings beneath smiling faces and began to ask her once more about her husband. Psyche, forgetting that before she had told them that he was a young man, now said that he was a great merchant from a nearby province, and that among his brown hair he had a few hairs of grey. Instantly the two sisters, when Psyche had left them for a moment alone, began to say she must be lying. "Perhaps," said one of them, "she has never seen her husband. If so, then he must be one of the gods and she will have a child who will be more than mortal. How can we bear this, that our youngest sister should have everything? Let us at once think out some lies by which we may destroy her."

So they spoke together, and when Psyche returned to them she found that they were both weeping. Not knowing that their tears were pretended, she asked them in surprise what had happened. "Poor Psyche," they said, "you who do not know the face of your husband, it is terrible for us to tell you the truth, but we must do so to save your life and the life of the child who will be born to you. The real shape of your husband is not what you think at all. No, it is a great and savage snake that comes to you every night. Remember the oracle that said you would be married to a fierce dragon. The country people have often seen him, swimming through the rivers as he returns at evening. They say that he will wait a little longer and then eat both you and your child. We have done our sad duty in telling you of this. If you are wise, you will take our loving advice and escape from your danger while you still may."

Poor Psyche in her simplicity believed in the false story and in her sisters' love. "It is true," she said, "that I have never seen my husband's face, and he tells me that something dreadful will happen to me if I try to see it. Oh, what am I to do?"

Then her sisters began to work still more upon her fears. "We will help you in this, as in everything," they said. "What you must do is to take a knife as sharp as a razor and hide it under your pillow. You must have hidden also in your bedroom a lamp with oil ready for burning. When he comes to bed and his limbs are all relaxed in sleep, you must get up quietly, on your bare feet, light the lamp, and holding the knife firmly, cut off the head of that poisonous serpent just where it joins the neck. If you do this, we will come back to you next day. We will take all the riches out of his house and marry you to some real man who is not a monster."

Then these wicked women left her, and Psyche, trembling and shrinking from the thought of it, still prepared to do what her sisters had advised. Night came, and her husband, after he had kissed her and taken her in his arms, soon fell asleep. Psyche, made bold by fear, yet still scarcely able to believe that what her sisters had told her was true, slipped from the bed, grasped the knife firmly in her right hand and took the lamp, hardly daring to wonder what she would see when the lamp was lit. What she saw was no monster, but the sweetest of all things, Cupid himself, at whose sight even the lamp burned more brightly. His hair was gold and seemed itself to shine; his neck was whiter than milk; the tender down on the feathers of his wings trembled with the light movement of his breathing and of the air. For long Psyche gazed in love and wonder at the beauty of his divine face, his smooth and soft body. In shame at what she had thought of doing she turned the knife against herself, but the knife shrunk from such a dreadful act and slipped from her hands. At the foot of the bed were Cupid's bow and arrows, small weapons for so great a god. Psyche took them up and, as she tried the sharpness of an arrow on her finger, she pricked herself. Then of her own accord she fell in love with Love and she bent over the bed, kissing him with joy and thankfulness as he slept.

As she was doing so a drop of burning oil fell on the white shoulder of the sleeping god. He woke and saw that she had broken her promise and her faith. Without uttering a word he fled away from her kisses and her embraces; but she clung to him, following him out of the great palace and crying to him.

Then he alighted on the top of a cypress-tree and spoke angrily to her: "Oh foolish Psyche, think how I disobeyed the orders of my mother, who told me that you should be married to some base and worthless man, and instead of this I came myself to be your husband. Did I seem a monster to you that you should try to cut off my head with its eyes that love you so much? Did I not warn you often of this? Your sisters will suffer for what they have done. You too will suffer from not having me with you."

He fled away through the air and Psyche, as long as she could see him, kept her eyes fixed on him as he went, weeping and crying for him. When he had gone beyond her sight, in her despair she threw herself into the running river; but the gentle stream would not take her life; instead it set her on the bank, where again she lamented what she had lost.

The sun rose in the sky and Psyche, weary and wretched, turned away from the palace where she had lived, and wandered through forests and rocky ways aimlessly, except that her aim was to find somehow, if it might be possible, her husband. In her wanderings she came to the city where the husband of her eldest sister was king. She could not forgive her sister's treachery, and now she pretended to be more simple than she really was. To her sister's questions she replied, "I took your advice, my dear sister, but when I raised the lamp, I saw no monster but Cupid himself. Because of my disobedience he has left me, and he said that instead of me he would have you as his wife."

No sooner had Psyche spoken these words than her sister, without offering Psyche herself any help in her distress, hurried away from her home and came to the mountain as she had done before. There was no West Wind blowing, but in spite of this the greedy and deceitful creature threw herself down, crying out: "Now Cupid, I come to you. Take me to yourself as a more worthy wife." Instead of the gentle passage through the air which she had expected, her body was torn and broken on the rocks. Wild beasts and birds tore it limb from limb and devoured it. The other sister suffered the same fate, for Psyche in her wanderings came also to her city and told her the same story that she had told to the elder of the two. Her greed and folly were the same, and she had the punishment that she deserved.

So Psyche went through country after country looking for her husband Cupid. He, however, was resting in his mother's house, ill and suffering from the wound in his shoulder which had been made by the burning oil. Nor did his mother Venus yet know anything of what had happened. But a talkative white gull came to her as she was bathing on the sea-shore and told her of how Cupid was wounded and how he had lived in marriage with her enemy Psyche. At this news the anger of Venus grew greater than ever it had been. "Will he," she said, "not only disobey his own mother, but actually fall in love with this wicked girl whose beauty was said to be equal to mine? I shall lock him in the house and make him suffer for it. As for the girl, I shall find her and make her wish she had never set eyes upon my son."

Then she mounted her glorious chariot of gold, thick set with precious stones. Four white doves drew the chariot lightly through the air; sparrows chirped merrily around it, and there followed flocks of all kinds of singing birds, who, being in the choir of Venus, had no fear of hawks, eagles or other fierce birds of prey. So, as the clouds yielded before her, Venus went on her way to heaven and there she complained to all the gods and goddesses of her son Cupid and of his love for Psyche. The others, and especially Juno and Ceres, tried to soothe her anger, partly because they were afraid of Cupid themselves; but Venus refused to be comforted, and ordered her servants to search for Psyche throughout the world.

Meanwhile Psyche, tired out with her wandering and with the weight of her child that had not yet been born, visited the temples of all the gods, asking them for their help. Juno and Ceres indeed would have wished to help her, but they did not dare to offend Venus. Though all pitied her, none would give her rest and sanctuary, so that in the end Psyche decided, in her despair, that she would go to the house of Venus herself. "Perhaps," she thought, "my mother-in-law will forgive me and have pity on me. Perhaps I shall see my husband. Then at least I shall die happy. And in any case my life is now unbearable."

Venus, when she saw the girl for whom she had been so long searching, laughed cruelly at her. "So you have at last decided to come and call on me, have you?" she said. "I suppose you are thinking that, just because you are going to have a baby, I shall be glad to be called a grandmother! You wicked immoral girl, I shall soon show you what I think of you."

Then she leapt on Psyche, tearing her clothes and pulling her hair and knocking her head upon the ground. Afterwards, with her fierce cruel anger satisfied, she put in front of her a great pile of wheat, barley, millet, poppyseed, peas, lentils and beans. She said, "You are so ugly that no one could want you for your face. Possibly you might find a husband by being a good housewife. Let me see what you can do. I order you to separate all these different grains from each other, before I come back from dinner." Then Venus, putting garlands on her bright gold hair, went away to a great banquet and Psyche sat in front of the heap of grain, weeping to herself since she knew that her task was impossible.

But a little ant took pity on her. He went out and spoke to all the other ants, saying, "My friends, let us help this poor girl who is the wife of Cupid and in great danger of her life." So the ants came and with their quick careful labour soon neatly separated the grains each in its own pile.

At midnight Venus returned, all fragrant with perfumes and well warmed with wine. When she saw how the work was done, she said: "This is not your doing, you vile wicked thing. It must be the work of he who loves you." Then she threw Psyche a crust of brown bread and she saw that Cupid was locked in the most secure room of the house. So these two, who loved each other, spent separate and sad hours in the same house.

In the morning Venus came to Psyche and said, "You see that river over there, with reeds and bushes along the banks? By the river is a flock of sheep which have fleeces gleaming with gold. Go and bring me back some of their wool."

Psyche rose from the hard floor and went out. Her real wish now was to throw herself in the river and die; but when she reached the river a tall green reed, by divine inspiration, spoke to her and said, "Poor innocent Psyche, do not stain my holy water by your death. But do not go near those terrible wild sheep until after the middle of the day. Till noon they are fierce and will kill anyone who comes near them. Afterwards they will rest in the shade and you may easily go up to them and take the wool you will find hanging on the briars."

Warned by this gentle reed, Psyche did as she was advised and in the afternoon came back to Venus with her apron full of the wool from the golden fleeces. Venus still frowned at her in anger. "This again," she said, "is no work of your own. Now I will prove whether you have the courage that you pretend to have. Do you see that overhanging rock at the top of the great mountain over there? From that rock gushes out a stream of black and freezing water that feeds the rivers of Hell, Styx and Cocytus. Go to the very summit and bring me a bottle of water from the middle of the source of the stream."

Psyche climbed the mountain, but when she drew near the summit she thought indeed that it would be better to hurl herself down on the rocks than to proceed any further with her task. The black stream ran in great foaming cataracts, and slid over slippery stones. Even the force of water and the rugged steep slopes were enough to make her journey impossible. Then on each side of the stream she saw great dragons creeping over the hollow rocks and stretching out their long necks. Their sleepless eyes never ceased to watch the sacred water, and the water itself foamed and bubbled with voices all saying, "Go away! Go away! Fly or you will die."

Psyche therefore stood still, weeping at the hopelessness of what lay before her. But Jupiter's royal eagle saw her and wished to do good to the wife of Cupid. He flew past her face and said to her, "Poor simple girl, do you think that you can even approach these terrible waters that are feared even by the gods? Give me your bottle." Then, taking her bottle in his beak, he flew past the darting tongues and flashing teeth of the dragons, plunged the bottle in the stream and brought it back filled with the water of Styx. Psyche took it back to Venus who again looked angrily at her and spoke harshly. "You must be," she said, "some sort of witch or enchantress to carry out my orders so quickly. Well, there is one more thing that I want you to do. Take this box and go down to hell, to the dwellings of the dead. There you are to ask Proserpine, the Queen of Hell, to send me a little of her beauty, just enough to last for a day. Tell her that I have lost some of mine in looking after my son who is wounded. But you must return quickly, as I have to go to the theatre of the gods."

Now poor Psyche felt that all pretense was over and she was surely doomed to die. She knew of no way of going to the House of the Dead except by killing herself, and so she climbed in a high tower, resolved to throw herself down from the top. But the tower spoke to her and said: "Do not yield, Psyche, to this last and final danger. If you kill yourself, you will indeed visit the world of the dead, but you will never come back to this world. Listen to my words and do as I say. Not far from here is Taenarum where you will find a great hole in the ground. Go down the path bravely and it will lead you to the very palace of Pluto. But you must not go empty-handed. In your hands you must carry two cakes of barley and honey mixed. In your mouth you must have two halfpennies. When you have gone some way on your journey you will see a lame donkey carrying wood and a lame man driving him. The man will ask you to help him pick up some of the sticks that have fallen, but you must go on without a word, and do no such thing. Then you will come to the river of the dead where the foul old man Charon with his leaking boat ferries the souls between the banks. He will do nothing unless he is paid, and you must let him take from your mouth one of your two halfpennies. When you are on the black and deathly river you will see an old man swimming there who will beg and pray you to help him into the boat. You must not listen to him, since this is not allowed. When you have crossed the river you will pass by some old women weaving. They will ask you to help them, but you must not listen to them. These are all traps which Venus will set for you so as to make you drop one of the cakes from your hands. Yet without these cakes you can never make the journey or return again; for you will come to the great three-headed watchdog Cerberus, whose barking rings for ever through this desolate plain. He will never let you pass till you have given him one of your cakes to eat. Once you have passed him you will come into the presence of Proserpine and she will offer you a fine chair on which to sit and fine food to eat. But you must sit upon the ground and ask only for a crust of bread. Above all, do not look inside the box that Proserpine will give you. There is no need for you to have any curiosity about the treasure of heavenly beauty."

So the tower advised Psyche, and she took the two halfpennies and the two cakes and then made her way to Taenarum. She descended the dreadful path to Hell, passed by the lame donkey in silence, paid her halfpenny to Charon, gave no attention either to the man swimming in the river or to the women weaving, gave one of her cakes to the terrible watchdog and came finally into the presence of Proserpine. Here she refused the fine food that was set before her and sat humbly on the ground, asking only for a crust of bread. Then she gave Venus' message and received the secret gift in the closed box. On her way back she gave the cake to Cerberus and her last halfpenny to Charon. So she reached the upper air in safety, but then she said to herself, "What a fool I am to be carrying in this box the divine beauty and not to take a little of it for myself. If I take some I may please my husband in the end."

She opened the box but could see no beauty in it at all. Instead a deadly sleep came over her like a cloud and she fell fainting to the ground, lying where she fell like a dead body.

But Cupid was now cured of his wound, and, in longing for his wife, had climbed out of an upper window. He flew straight to her and, when he had wiped away the deadly sleep from her face and put it back in the box, he woke her by gently pricking her hand with one of his arrows. "Poor creature," he said, "again you were nearly ruined by your excess curiosity. Now go back to my mother and leave me to arrange the rest." Then he flew into the air and Psyche brought the box to Venus. Cupid meanwhile flew up to heaven and begged Jupiter, the father of the gods, to help him in his faithful love. Jupiter called all the gods and goddesses to council and said to them, "It is not good that Cupid should always be loose and wandering about the earth. He has chosen a wife and it is right that he should enjoy her company and her love. In order that the marriage shall not be an unequal one I shall make Psyche immortal, and she and Cupid will live together in happiness for ever. This is my will and, since Psyche will be a real goddess, even Venus must be glad of the marriage."

Then he sent Mercury to bring Psyche up to heaven and, when she had come there, he said, "Take this cup of immortality, Psyche, and drink it to the end, so that you may live forever and that Cupid may never leave you again, but be your everlasting husband."

Then the great feast and wedding banquet was prepared. Cupid and Psyche sat in the places of honour and by them were Jupiter and Juno and all the gods in order. Bacchus filled their glasses with nectar, the wine of the gods. Vulcan prepared the supper. The Hours and Graces adorned the house with roses and other sweet smelling flowers. Apollo and the Muses sang together and Venus danced with divine grace to the music. So Psyche was married to Cupid and in time she bore a child whom we call Pleasure.

ZEAMI MOTOKIYO

Zeami Motokiyo (1363-1443) was the greatest of the Noh playwrights and the son of the man (Kanami Kiyotsugu) who is said to have invented the Noh drama. Interestingly, the play *Izutsu* concerns the life of another famous literary figure, Ariwara-no-Narihira, who lived during the Early Heian Period of the ninth and early tenth centuries. It would be appropriate here to say a few words about the Japanese Noh play, a highly stylized genre combining poetry, music, masks, mime, and dance, always written on a serious, classical theme, and in extremely concise and pregnant language. While they contend with the emotions, the Noh dramas are philosophical and reflective works, styled so as to minimize pathos. The idea of the Noh drama, then, is not to bring the audience to identify with the characters on stage, but rather to bring them to contemplate the poetry, the music, and the images on stage. The editors have taken the liberty of translating the musical directions.

Izutsu

Introduction

Izutsu ["well-curb"] is a *kazura-mono* or 'female-wig' play in which the *jo-no-mai* [slow] dance is accompanied by a large and a small hand-drum.

About a thousand years ago there lived two famous lovers: Ariwara-no-Narihira, one of the Six Major Poets[1] of the Early Heian Period (794-930), and the daughter of Ki-no-Aritsune. Narihira, who came of a princely family and

160

was known not less for his gallantry than for his poetry, has since become a legendary figure. In this play, however, the Narihira legend is greatly modified. As children, hero and heroine were neighbours. Outside the gate of one of their houses was a well, and the children used to lean over its wooden curb *(izutsu)* and peer down at their smiling faces and flowing hair reflected in its waters. As they grew older, they became self-conscious and shy of each other. In spite of this, their mutual attachment was growing stronger, and later they married. Their married life, however, was not happy. For Narihira, who was by nature passionate and fickle, soon fell in love with another woman living over the hills in Kawachi Province, to whom he paid nightly visits. . . .

In Part One a travelling priest visits a temple which, according to tradition, was built on the site of the house occupied by Narihira and his wife. The sight of an old wooden well-curb half-hidden by *susuki* grass and of an ancient tombstone, recalls to his mind their famous love-story.

In Part Two the heroine, dressed in her husband's princely robe and headgear, performs an *utsuri-mai* (impersonation dance) — in this case a type of *jo-no-mai* accompanied by a large and a small hand-drum. The climax is reached when the wife in her intense longing for the past identifies herself, as it were, with her husband and reclining on the well-curb sees his image in place of her own reflected in the still waters below her. All this, however, is but a vision. Day dawns, the vision fades, and nothing remains but dreary reality which fills the priest with sadness and regret.

Izutsu

Persons

Travelling Priest	*Waki* [Supporting Role]
Maiden	*Shite* [Main Role] in Part One
Man of the Place	*Kyōgen*
Ghost of Ki-no-Aritsune's Daughter	*Shite* [Main Role] in Part Two

Place

Ariwara Temple, Isonokami, Yamato Province

Season

Autumn

Part One

Stage-attendants place on the front of the stage a framework square well-curb with a sheaf of susuki *grass at one corner.*

1

While the entrance music nanoribue *is being played, the* Priest, *wearing a pointed hood, plain kimono and broad-sleeved robe, appears and advances to the* Shite Seat.

Priest: I am a priest on pilgrimage from province to province. Of late I have visited the Seven Great Temples of Nara,³ and now am on my way to Hatsuse.⁴

When I enquired from someone about this temple, I was told it was the Ariwara Temple. I will enter the grounds and see what it is like.
Advances to the centre of the stage and faces the well-curb.

Surely in bygone days the Ariwara Temple
Was the Isonokami home
Where Narihira and Ki-no-Aritsune's daughter
Once lived as man and wife.
Surely here too was written
"Over Tatsuta's mountain pass⁵
Perilous as storm-tossed seas . . ."

sage-uta   As I stand on the site of this ancient tale,
[low-pitched   I feel the transitoriness of life.
singing]   Now, for the sake of those twin souls,
Will I perform religious rites,
Will I perform religious rites.
Joins his hands in prayer and moves to the Waki *Seat.*

2

While the entrance music shidai *is being played, the* Maiden, *wearing a 'young woman' mask, wig, painted gold-patterned under-kimono and brocade outer-kimono, appears carrying a spray of leaves⁶ and stands at the* Shite *Seat.*

Maiden:	Gazing into the crystal water I draw each morning,
shidai	Gazing into the crystal water I draw each morning,
	The moon, too, seems to cleanse her heart.
Chorus:	Gazing into the crystal water I draw each morning,
jidori	The moon, too, seems to cleanse her heart.
Maiden:	Autumn nights are lonely anywhere,
sashi	Yet even lonelier
[recitative]	Is this old temple rarely visited,
	When the autumn winds sough through the garden pines.
	The moon sinking westward,
	The drooping eaves o'ergrown with waving ferns —
	All reminds me of the past.
	Alas! how long must I still live
	And naught to hope for in the future!
	Each thing that happens leaves its mark upon the mind;
	Such is our mortal world.
sage-uta	Buddha, I cast myself on thee
	With all my heart, praying continually
	That with the unseen thread held in thy hand[7]
	Thou wilt at last lead me to Paradise!
age-uta	Thy vow is to enlighten those in darkness,
[high-pitched	Thy vow is to enlighten those in darkness.
singing]	Although the moon at dawn
	Does surely hasten towards the western hills
	Where lies the Land of Bliss,
	Yet between here and there
	Stretches the vast and empty autumn sky
	As far as eye can reach.
	We hear the winds soughing through the pines,
	But know not whence they blow nor whither.[8]
	In this world more fleeting than the wind,
	Vain dreams deceive our minds.
	What call will have the power to waken us,
	What call will have the power to waken us!

Comes to the front of the stage, sits down, places the spray of leaves before her and joins her hands in prayer, then returns to the Shite Seat.

3

Priest:	While meditating in the temple grounds I see an attractive woman draw water from a well with a

163

| | wooden curb and, having poured it into a wooden vessel containing flowers, offer it reverently to a grass-covered mound. Pray, who are you? | *Turns to the Maiden.* |

Maiden: I am a woman of this neighbourhood. The pious benefactor of this temple, Ariwara-no-Narihira, was a famous man and the tombstone by this mound is supposed to be his. Therefore I offer flowers to it and pray for his salvation.

Priest: Yes, Narihira has left an undying name behind him. This place may indeed have been the site of his home, but since his story goes back to ancient times, I am filled with wonder that any one, especially a woman, should thus be praying for him.

Perchance you are related to him?

Maiden: You ask whether I am related to him? But even in his day he was called the 'Ancient.'9 Now, after this long lapse of time, he belongs to the remote past. How can there still live any one related to him?

Priest: You speak truth,

Yet this was once his home.

Maiden: Though he is long since dead,

Priest: This place remains as it was once,

Maiden: And tales that keep his fame alive

Priest: Are handed down to us.

Maiden: So the 'Ancient'

Chorus: Is still remembered,

age-uta Though time-worn is the Ariwara Temple,

Though time-worn is the Ariwara Temple.

Grass covers this mound

Shadowed by ancient pines,

And only this one bush

Of flowering *susuki*

Marks where he sleeps for evermore,

And might, indeed, unfold a tale

Of bygone days.

The sight of this old mound,

Hidden under lush grass

Drenched with weary dew,

Is precious to the lonely heart,

is precious to the lonely heart!

The Maiden sits down and weeps.

4

Priest:	I wish you would tell me more about Narihira.	*The* Maiden
Chorus:	Once Narihira, captain of the Imperial Body-guard,	*rises and, coming to the*
kuri	Enjoyed for many years spring flowers and autumn	*centre of the stage, sits down.*
[lively piece	moons	
with varying	Here at Isonokami, then fallen into decay.	
rhythms]		

Priest: I wish you would tell me more about Narihira.

Priest: I wish you would tell me more about Narihira.
Chorus: Once Narihira, captain of the Imperial Body-guard,
kuri   Enjoyed for many years spring flowers and autumn
[lively piece   moons
with varying   Here at Isonokami, then fallen into decay.
rhythms]

The Maiden *rises and, coming to the centre of the stage, sits down.*

Maiden: 'Twas when he lived in wedlock
sushi   With Ki-no-Aritsune's daughter,
            Bound each to other by strong love!
Chorus: Later bewitched by a new love
            At Takayasu[10] in Kawachi Province,
            And loth to give up either,
            Secretly he visited her of nights.
Maiden: "Over Tatsuta's mountain pass,
Chorus: Perilous as storm-tossed seas,
            He speeds at midnight all alone!"
            Thus sang his wife
            Fearing that treacherous pass.
            Moved by her selfless love,
            His new love withered.
Maiden: Since poetry alone can tell our deepest feelings,
Chorus: Well might her selfless love inspire such a moving poem.
kuse   Here in this province long ago
            Two households once lived side by side,
            The children, boy and girl, were playmates;
            Leaning over the well-curb beyond the gate,
            They peered together down the well
            Where mirrored lay their faces cheek to cheek,
            Their sleeves hanging o'er each other's shoulder.
            Thus used those bosom friends to play.
            In time they grew reserved and shy,
            Till the faithful-hearted youth
            Sent her a letter with a poem
            Telling his flower-like love
            In words like sparkling dew-drops:
Maiden: "Standing against the well-curb,
            As children we compared our heights,
Chorus: But I have grown much taller

Since last I saw you."[11]
Answering the maiden wrote:
"The hair I parted
When by the well-curb we compared our heights,
Now loose flows down my back.
For whom but you should it again be tied?"[12]
For this exchange of poems
They called her the 'Lady of the Well-Curb.'

5

Chorus:	Listening to this ancient lovers' tale,
rongi	I am filled with wonder at your charm.
["debate	Please disclose your name!
song"]	
Maiden:	If you would know the truth,
	Taking the shape of Aritsune's daughter,
	By yearning moved, I have come back to my old home,
	Treading under the veil of night
	A road perilous as the Tatsuta Pass.
Chorus:	How wonderful!
	Then you are the lady of the Tatsuta Pass?
Maiden:	"Daughter of Ki-no-Aritsune" am I
Chorus:	And "Lady of the Well-Curb" too.
Maiden:	With shame I own to both those names.
Chorus:	Scarce has she revealed the name
	Of her who tied the nuptial knot
	When but nineteen
	And made her vow before the gods, *The* Maiden *rises.*
	Then she fades away behind the well-curb,
	Then she fades away behind the well-curb. *The* Maiden *goes out.*

Interlude

The Man of the Place *enters the stage, wearing a striped kimono, sleeveless robe and trailing divided skirt, and short sword. In reply to the* Priest's *request, he tells him the tale of* Ki-no-Aritsune's Daughter.

Part Two

1

Priest:	The night is growing old!
machi-utai	Above the temple hangs the moon,
[waiting	Above the temple hangs the moon.
song]	Wishing to dream of times gone by,
	I turn my robe inside out,[13]
	And lay me down upon this bed of moss,
	And lay me down upon this bed of moss.

2

While the entrance music issei *is being played, the
Ghost of Ki-no-Aritsune's Daughter, wearing a 'young
woman' mask, wig, man's ceremonial headgear, painted
gold-patterned under-kimono, dancing* chōken *robe and
embroidered* koshimaki *outer-kimono, appears and
stands at the* Shite *Seat.*

Daughter:	"Though people call them shifty,
sashi	Yet the cherry-blossoms never fail
	Him who seeks my garden once a year
	Less for my sake than for theirs."[14]
	This poem gained for me
	The name of 'Friend-Awaiting Woman.'
	Many a year has passed with varying fortunes
	Since Narihira and I played by the well-curb;
	Now bereft of him, though ill-becoming,
	I don this robe he gave me
	And dance as he was wont to do.
Chorus:	Graceful as whirling flakes of snow,
	The dancer waves her flowery sleeves.
	The Daughter *performs a* jo-no-mai *dance.*

Daughter:	Hither returned I call back time past
	And on the ancient well

Of the Ariwara Temple
The moon shines brightly as of old,
The moon shines brightly as of old.

3

Daughter:	"Is not the moon in heaven the same?
	Is not the springtime as it was?"[15]
	Thus did he sing, long, long ago.
	"Standing against the well-curb,
Chorus:	Standing against the well-curb,
	As children we compared our heights.
Daughter:	But I
Chorus:	Have grown much taller."
Daughter:	And much older.
Chorus:	Wearing this robe and headgear
	As Narihira did,
	It does not look like a woman,
	But a man — the living image of Narihira.
Daughter:	How dear the face I see!
Chorus:	How dear the face, though it be mine!
	See! The ghost of the dead lady fades
	Like the lingering scent of fading flowers.
	The sky is turning grey;
	The Ariwara Temple's bell starts to toll,
	Ushering in the morn.
	The garden pines awaken with the breeze;
	And like the torn leaves of the *bashō*-tree
	The priest's dream is shattered and day dawns,
	The priest's dream is shattered and day dawns.

*Dances while the
following lines are
chanted.*

*Approaching the well,
the Daughter pushes
aside the* susuki *grass
and peers down into
it.*

*The Daughter moves
away.*

*She wraps the left
sleeve round her arm
and covers her face
with the open fan and
bends forward.
She stands still as if
listening to the bell.*

*She stamps twice on
the* Shite *Seat.*

WILLIAM SHAKESPEARE

Othello is one of Shakespeare's greatest dramas. It was written in the most productive era of Shakespeare's career (the years 1600-1607), when the bard was at the height of his artistic powers. Curiously, the plot was borrowed from the *Ecatommiti* [One Hundred Tales], a work by the Italian writer Giraldi Cinthio that was published in 1565 and later translated into English. Shakespeare (1564-1616) was born at Stratford-on-Avon in England, the son of a businessman. There he grew up, married, and remained until the early 1590s, when he began to write plays. By 1594 he had emerged in London as an actor and playwright for the Lord Chamberlain's Men, a troupe that performed at court. Part owner of both the Globe and Blackfriars Theatres in London, Shakespeare lived there until 1610, when he returned to Stratford.

Likely, the dramatis personae here need no introduction, but in case the reader is not yet familiar with this play, Desdemona is the loving wife of Othello, a Moor in the "the service of the Venetian state." Cassio is his loyal lieutenant. Iago, the villain of the piece, is his ensign, determined to convince Othello that Desdemona and Cassio are lovers. Finally, Emilia is Iago's wife and an intimate of Desdemona.

Othello, Act III, Scene III

> *Enter Othello and Iago, at a distance.*
> EMILIA   Madam, here comes my lord.
> CASSIO   Madam, I'll take my leave.

DESDEMONA   Nay, stay, and hear me speak.
CAS.   Madam, not now: I am very ill at ease,
     Unfit for mine own purposes.
DES.   Well, do your discretion.   *[Exit Cassio.*
IAGO   Ha! I like not that.
OTHELLO   What dost thou say?
IAGO   Nothing, my lord: or if — I know not what.
OTH.   Was not that Cassio parted from my wife?
IAGO   Cassio, my lord! No, sure, I cannot think it,
     That he would steal away so guilty-like,
     Seeing you coming.
OTH.   I do believe 'twas he.
DES.   How now, my lord!
     I have been talking with a suitor here,
     A man that languishes in your displeasure.
OTH.   Who is 't you mean?
DES.   Why, your lieutenant, Cassio. Good my lord,
     If I have any grace or power to move you,
     His present reconciliation take;
     For if he be not one that truly loves you,
     That errs in ignorance and not in cunning,
     I have no judgement in an honest face:
     I prithee, call him back.
OTH.   Went he hence now?
DES.   Ay, sooth; so humbled
     That he hath left part of his grief with me,
     To suffer with him. Good love, call him back.
OTH.   Not now, sweet Desdemona; some other time.
DES.   But shall 't be shortly?
OTH.   The sooner, sweet, for you.
DES.   Shall 't be to-night at supper?
OTH.   No, not to-night.
DES.   To-morrow dinner, then?
OTH.   I shall not dine at home;
     I meet the captains at the citadel.
DES.   Why then to-morrow night; or Tuesday morn;
     On Tuesday noon, or night; on Wednesday morn:
     I prithee, name the time; but let it not
     Exceed three days: in faith, he's penitent;
     And yet his trespass, in our common reason —

Save that, they say, the wars must make examples
Out of their best — is not almost a fault
To incur a private check. When shall he come?
Tell me, Othello: I wonder in my soul,
What you would ask me, that I should deny,
Or stand so mammering on. What! Michael Cassio,
That came a-wooing with you, and so many a time,
When I have spoke of you dispraisingly,
Hath ta'en your part; to have so much to do
To bring him in! Trust me, I could do much, —

OTH. Prithee, no more: let him come when he will:
I will deny thee nothing.

DES.   Why, this is not a boon;
'Tis as I should entreat you wear your gloves,
Or feed on nourishing dishes, or keep you warm,
Or sue to you to do a peculiar profit
To your own person: nay, when I have a suit
Wherein I mean to touch your love indeed,
It shall be full of poise and difficult weight,
And fearful to be granted.

OTH.   I will deny thee nothing:
Whereon, I do beseech thee, grant me this,
To leave me but a little to myself.

DES. Shall I deny you? no: farewell, my lord.

OTH. Farewell, my Desdemona: I'll come to thee straight.

DES. Emilia, come. Be as your fancies teach you;
Whate'er you be, I am obedient.
[Exeunt Desdemona, and Emilia.

OTH. Excellent wretch! Perdition catch my soul,
But I do love thee! and when I love thee not,
Chaos is come again.

IAGO My noble lord, —

OTH.   What dost thou say, Iago?

IAGO Did Michael Cassio, when you woo'd my lady,
Know of your love?

OTH. He did, from first to last: why dost thou ask?

IAGO But for a satisfaction of my thought;
No further harm.

OTH.   Why of thy thought, Iago?

IAGO I did not think he had been acquainted with her.

171

OTH. O, yes; and went between us very oft.

IAGO Indeed!

OTH. Indeed! ay, indeed: discern'st thou aught in that?
Is he not honest?

IAGO Honest, my lord!

OTH. Honest! ay, honest.

IAGO My lord, for aught I know.

OTH. What dost thou think?

IAGO   Think, my lord!

OTH. Think, my lord!
      By heaven, he echoes me,
As if there were some monster in his thought
Too hideous to be shown. Thou dost mean something:
I heard thee say even now, thou likedst not that,
When Cassio left my wife: what didst not like?
And when I told thee he was of my counsel
In my whole course of wooing, thou criedst 'Indeed!'
And didst contract and purse thy brow together,
As if thou then hadst shut up in thy brain
Some horrible conceit: if thou dost love me,
Show me thy thought.

IAGO My lord, you know I love you.

OTH.   I think thou dost;
And, for I know thou'rt full of love and honesty,
And weigh'st thy words before thou givest them breath,
Therefore these stops of thine fright me the more:
For such things in a false disloyal knave
Are tricks of custom, but in a man that's just
They are close relations, working from the heart
That passion cannot rule.

IAGO   For Michael Cassio,
I dare be sworn I think that he is honest.

OTH. I think so too.

IAGO   Men should be what they seem;
Or those that be not, would they might seem none!

OTH. Certain, men should be what they seem.

IAGO Why then I think Cassio's an honest man.

OTH. Nay, yet there's more in this:
I prithee, speak to me as to thy thinkings. . . .
Thou dost conspire against thy friend, Iago,

If thou but think'st him wrong'd and makest his ear
A stranger to thy thoughts. . . .
By heaven, I'll know thy thoughts.

Iago You cannot, if my heart were in your hand;
    Nor shall not, whilst 'tis in my custody.

Oth. Ha!

Iago   O, beware, my lord, of jealousy;
    It is the green-eyed monster which doth mock
    The meat it feeds on: that cuckold lives in bliss
    Who, certain of his fate, loves not his wronger;
    But, O, what damned minutes tells he o'er
    Who dotes, yet doubts, suspects, yet strongly loves!

Oth. O misery!

Iago Poor and content is rich, and rich enough,
    But riches fineless is as poor as winter
    To him that ever fears he shall be poor.
    Good heaven, the souls of all my tribe defend
    From jealousy!

Oth.   Why, why is this?
    Think'st thou I'ld make a life of jealousy,
    To follow still the changes of the moon
    With fresh suspicions? No; to be once in doubt
    Is once to be resolved: exchange me for a goat,
    When I shall turn the business of my soul
    To such exsufflicate and blown surmises,
    Matching thy inference. 'Tis not to make me jealous
    To say my wife is fair, feeds well, loves company,
    Is free of speech, sings, plays and dances well;
    Where virtue is, these are more virtuous:
    Nor from mine own weak merits will I draw
    The smallest fear or doubt of her revolt;
    For she had eyes, and chose me. No, Iago;
    I'll see before I doubt; when I doubt, prove;
    And on the proof, there is no more but this,
    Away at once with love or jealousy!

Iago I am glad of it; for now I shall have reason
    To show the love and duty that I bear you
    With franker spirit: therefore, as I am bound,
    Receive it from me. I speak not yet of proof.
    Look to your wife; observe her well with Cassio;

Wear your eye thus, not jealous nor secure:
I would not have your free and noble nature,
Out of self-bounty, be abused; look to 't:
I know our country disposition well;
In Venice they do let heaven see the pranks
They dare not show their husbands; their best conscience
Is not to leave 't undone, but keep 't unknown.

OTH. Dost thou say so?

IAGO She did deceive her father, marrying you;
And when she seem'd to shake and fear your looks,
She lov'd them most.

OTH.   And so she did.

IAGO   Why, go to, then;
She that so young could give out such a seeming,
To seel her father's eyes up close as oak —
He thought 'twas witchcraft; — but I am much to blame —
I humbly do beseech you of your pardon
For too much loving you.

OTH.   I am bound to thee for ever.

IAGO I see this hath a little dash'd your spirits.

OTH. Not a jot, not a jot.

IAGO   I' faith, I fear it has.
I hope you will consider what is spoke
Comes from my love. But I do see you're moved
I am to pray you not to strain my speech
To grosser issues nor to larger reach
Than to suspicion.

OTH. I will not.

IAGO   Should you do so, my lord,
My speech should fall into such vile success
As my thoughts aim not at. Cassio's my worthy friend —
My lord, I see you're moved.

OTH.   No, not much moved:
I do not think but Desdemona's honest.

IAGO Long live she so! and long live you to think so!

OTH. And yet, how nature erring from itself, —

IAGO Ay, there's the point: as — to be bold with you —
Not to affect many proposed matches
Of her own clime, complexion, and degree,
Whereto we see in all things nature tends —

Foh! one may smell in such, a will most rank,
Foul disproportions, thoughts unnatural.
But pardon me; I do not in position
Distinctly speak of her; though I may fear
Her will, recoiling to her better judgement,
May fall to match you with her country forms
And happily repent.

OTH.   Farewell, farewell:
If more thou dost perceive, let me know more;
Set on thy wife to observe: leave me, Iago.

IAGO [*Going*] My lord, I take my leave.

OTH. Why did I marry? This honest creature doubtless
Sees and knows more, much more, than he unfolds. . . .
If I do prove her haggard,
Though that her jesses were my dear heart-strings,
I'ld whistle her off and let her down the wind,
To prey at fortune. Haply, for I am black
And have not those soft parts of conversation
That chamberers have, or for I am declined
Into the vale of years, — yet that's not much —
She's gone. I am abused; and my relief
Must be to loathe her. O curse of marriage,
That we can call these delicate creatures ours,
And not their appetites! I had rather be a toad,
And live upon the vapour of a dungeon,
Than keep a corner in the thing I love
For others' uses. Yet, 'tis the plague of great ones;
Prerogativ'd are they less than the base;
'Tis destiny unshunnable, like death:
Even then this forked plague is fated to us
When we do quicken. Desdemona comes:
Re-enter Desdemona and Emilia.
If she be false, O, then heaven mocks itself!
I'll not believe 't.

DES.   How now, my dear Othello!
Your dinner, and the generous islanders
By you invited, do attend your presence.

OTH. I am to blame.

DES.   Why do you speak so faintly?
Are you not well?

OTH. I have a pain upon my forehead here.
DES. 'Faith, that's with watching; 'twill away again:
    Let me but bind it hard, within this hour
    It will be well.
OTH.   Your napkin is too little:
    [He puts the handkerchief from him; and it drops.
    Let it alone. Come, I'll go in with you.
DES. I am very sorry that you are not well.
    [Exeunt Othello and Desdemona.
EMIL. I am glad I have found this napkin:
    This was her first remembrance from the Moor:
    My wayward husband hath a hundred times
    Woo'd me to steal it; but she so loves the token,
    For he conjured her she should ever keep it,
    That she reserves it evermore about her
    To kiss and talk to. I'll have the work ta'en out,
    And give 't Iago; what he will do with it
    Heaven knows, not I;
    I nothing but to please his fantasy.
    Re-enter Iago.
IAGO How now! what do you here alone?
EMIL. Do not you chide; I have a thing for you.
IAGO A thing for me? it is a common thing —
EMIL. Ha!
IAGO To have a foolish wife.
EMIL. O, is that all? What will you give me now
    For that same handkerchief?
IAGO   What handkerchief?
EMIL. What handkerchief!
    Why, that the Moor first gave to Desdemona;
    That which so often you did bid me steal.
IAGO Hast stol'n it from her?
EMIL. No, 'faith; she let it drop by negligence,
    And, to the advantage, I, being here, took 't up.
    Look, here it is.
IAGO.   A good wench; give it me.
EMIL. What will you do with 't, that you have been so earnest
    To have me filch it?
IAGO *[Snatching it]* Why, what's that to you?
EMIL. If 't be not for some purpose of import

Give 't me again; poor lady, she'll run mad
When she shall lack it.

IAGO   Be not acknown on 't; I have use for it.
Go, leave me.   *[Exit Emilia.*
I will in Cassio's lodging lose this napkin,
And let him find it. Trifles light as air
Are to the jealous confirmations strong
As proofs of holy writ; this may do something.
The Moor already changes with my poison:
Dangerous conceits are in their natures poisons,
Which at the first are scarce found to distaste,
But with a little act upon the blood,
Burn like the mines of sulphur. I did say so:
Look, where he comes!
Re-enter Othello.
                  Not poppy, nor mandragora,
Nor all the drowsy syrups of the world,
Shall ever medicine thee to that sweet sleep
Which thou owedst yesterday.

OTH.   Ha! ha! false to me?

IAGO   Why, how now, general! no more of that.

OTH.   Avaunt! be gone! thou hast set me on the rack:
I swear 'tis better to be much abused
Than but to know 't a little.

IAGO   How now, my lord?

OTH.   What sense had I in her stol'n hours of lust?
I saw 't not, thought it not, it harm'd not me:
I slept the next night well, was free and merry;
I found not Cassio's kisses on her lips:
He that is robb'd, not wanting what is stol'n,
Let him not know 't, and he's not robb'd at all.

IAGO   I am sorry to hear this.

OTH.   I had been happy, if the general camp,
Pioners and all, had tasted her sweet body,
So I had nothing known. O, now for ever
Farewell the tranquil mind! farewell content!
Farewell the plumed troops and the big wars
That make ambition virtue! O, farewell!
Farewell the neighing steed and the shrill trump,
The spirit-stirring drum, th' ear-piercing fife,

      The royal banner, and all quality,
      Pride, pomp, and circumstance of glorious war!
      And O you mortal engines, whose rude throats
      Th' immortal Jove's dread clamours counterfeit,
      Farewell! Othello's occupation's gone!

IAGO Is 't possible, my lord?

OTH. Villain, be sure thou prove my love a whore,
      Be sure of it; give me the ocular proof;
      Or, by the worth of man's eternal soul,
      Thou hadst been better have been born a dog
      Than answer my waked wrath!

IAGO   Is 't come to this?

Oth. Make me to see 't; or, at the least, so prove it,
      That the probation bear no hinge nor loop
      To hang a doubt on; or woe upon thy life!

IAGO My noble lord, —

OTH. If thou dost slander her and torture me,
      Never pray more; abandon all remorse;
      On horror's head horrors accumulate;
      Do deeds to make heaven weep, all earth amazed;
      For nothing canst thou to damnation add
      Greater than that.

IAGO   O grace! O heaven forgive me!
      Are you a man? have you a soul or sense?
      God be wi' you; take mine office. O wretched fool,
      That livest to make thine honesty a vice!
      O monstrous world! Take note, take note, O world,
      To be direct and honest is not safe.
      I thank you for this profit, and from hence
      I'll love no friend, sith love breeds such offence.

OTH. Nay, stay: thou shouldst be honest.

IAGO I should be wise, for honesty's a fool
      And loses that it works for.

OTH.   By the world,
      I think my wife be honest, and think she is not;
      I think that thou art just, and think thou art not.
      I'll have some proof. Her name, that was as fresh
      As Dian's visage, is now begrimed and black
      As mine own face. If there be cords, or knives,

Poison, or fire, or suffocating streams,
I'll not endure it. Would I were satisfied!

IAGO I see, sir, you are eaten up with passion:
I do repent me that I put it to you.
You would be satisfied?

OTH.   Would! nay, I will.

IAGO And may: but, how? how satisfied, my lord?
Would you, the supervisor, grossly gape on —
Behold her topp'd?

OTH.   Death and damnation! O!

IAGO . . . It is impossible you should see this,
Where they as prime as goats, as hot as monkeys,
As salt as wolves in pride, and fools as gross
As ignorance made drunk. But yet, I say,
If imputation and strong circumstances,
Which lead directly to the door of truth,
Will give you satisfaction, you might have 't.

OTH. Give me a living reason she's disloyal.

IAGO I do not like the office:
But, sith I am enter'd in this cause so far,
Prick'd to 't by foolish honesty and love,
I will go on. I lay with Cassio lately;
And, being troubled with a raging tooth,
I could not sleep.
There are a kind of men so loose of soul,
That in their sleeps will mutter their affairs:
One of this kind is Cassio:
In sleep I heard him say 'Sweet Desdemona,
Let us be wary, let us hide our loves';
And then, sir, would he gripe and wring my hand,
Cry 'O sweet creature!' and then kiss me hard,
As if he pluck'd up kisses by the roots,
That grew upon my lips: then laid his leg
Over my thigh, and sigh'd, and kiss'd; and then
Cried 'Cursed fate that gave thee to the Moor!'

OTH. O monstrous! monstrous!

IAGO   Nay, this was but his dream.

OTH. But this denoted a foregone conclusion:
'Tis a shrewd doubt, though it be but a dream.

IAGO   And this may help to thicken other proofs
         That do demonstrate thinly.
OTH.   I'll tear her all to pieces.
IAGO   Nay, but be wise: yet we see nothing done;
         She may be honest yet. Tell me but this,
         Have you not sometimes seen a handkerchief
         Spotted with strawberries in your wife's hand?
OTH.   I gave her such a one; 'twas my first gift.
IAGO   I know not that: but such a handkerchief —
         I am sure it was your wife's — did I to-day
         See Cassio wipe his beard with.
OTH.   If it be that, —
IAGO   If it be that, or any that was hers,
         It speaks against her with the other proofs.
OTH.   O, that the slave had forty thousand lives!
         One is too poor, too weak for my revenge.
         Now do I see 'tis true. Look here, Iago;
         All my fond love thus do I blow to heaven:
         'Tis gone.
         Arise, black vengeance, from thy hollow cell!
         Yield up, O love, thy crown and hearted throne
         To tyrannous hate! Swell, bosom, with thy fraught,
         For 'tis of aspics' tongues!
IAGO   Yet be content.
OTH.   O, blood, blood, blood!
IAGO   Patience, I say; your mind perhaps may change.
OTH.   Never, Iago. Like to the Pontic sea,
         Whose icy current and compulsive course
         Ne'er feels retiring ebb, but keeps due on
         To the Propontic and the Hellespont,
         Even so my bloody thoughts, with violent pace,
         Shall ne'er look back, ne'er ebb to humble love
         Till that a capable and wide revenge
         Swallow them up.

DERRICK SHERWIN BAILEY

Derrick Sherwin Bailey (1910-1983?) graduated from Lincoln Theological College in 1940 and received his Ph.D. in literature from the University of Edinburgh in 1947. He was ordained an Anglican priest in 1943 and held many offices in the Church of England, including those of Prebendary, Chancellor, and Precentor of Wells Cathedral. Between 1951 and 1955 he was Central Lecturer to the Church of England Moral Welfare Council. The majority of his published work is on the subject of sexual ethics.

The Mystery of Love and Marriage: A Study in the Theology of Sexual Relation, "Love" II-VII

II

If confusion is to be avoided, the character and meaning of the love which is 'the ontological basis of the marriage union' must be clearly indicated. . . .

. . . No definition could embody at once its complexity and its distinctive character. Only by analysing the total experience, so far as that is possible, and then considering in turn its constituent elements, can love be understood, and this is the method adopted in the pages which follow. An analysis of this kind cannot, of course, pretend to be complete, but at least the principal features of sexual love can be isolated and described. But the order in which they are examined here is not that of importance, and no single element can be said to confer upon the whole experience its evident *sui generis* character; nor do all the features mentioned relate exclusively to the sexual love which is the basis of the 'one flesh' union.

III

Love may first be considered in terms of personal relation, as a metaphysical experience which can best be described in Martin Buber's now familiar categories of *I* and *Thou*. Marriage, he says, springs from the

> . . . revealing by two people of the *Thou* to one another. Out of this a marriage is built up by the *Thou* that is neither of the *I*'s. This is the metaphysical and metapsychical factor of love, to which feelings of love are mere accompaniments [1]

For Buber, the *Thou* is a subject which can be *met* (that is, with whom it is possible to enter into personal relation) but not *experienced*, whereas the *It* is an object which can be experienced, but with which it is impossible to enter into direct personal relation. The *I* likewise is a subject, and the 'world of *Thou*' is the sphere in which personal confrontation and relation occur between the *I* and the *Thou*. The 'world of *It*,' on the other hand, is the sphere in which the *I* stands over against the *It* as subject to object, experiencing and appropriating, but never meeting in direct personal relation.

The meeting of two *I*'s is no irrational, impulsive coming together; in the encounter of lovers it has no connexion at all with the fatalism of passion. However rarely it may appear to be deliberate, it is always in fact an act of choice:

> The *Thou* confronts me. But I step into direct relation with it. Hence the relation means being chosen and choosing, suffering and action in one . . .[2]

This is of great significance if the love of man and woman is to be properly understood.[3]

What Buber calls the 'eternal' character of love is due, not to a pseudo-romantic escapism which would repudiate the 'vanity,' the contingency of our temporal state, but to the entry of man and woman into the world of *Thou* which is 'not set in the context of either [space or time].'[4] In the unique relational event of falling in love the woman[5] whom a man loves (objectively *She,* someone to be experienced and evaluated) becomes *Thou;* and in this *I-Thou* meeting both enter into the eternity of the world of *Thou.* But this experience of love's eternity is only for a moment, when 'time stands still,' though the moment may recur again and again.

> Love itself cannot persist in direct relation. It endures, but in interchange of actual and potential being.[6]

> The particular *Thou,* after the relational event has run its course, is bound to become an *It.*[7]

Herein lies one distinction between Divine and human love; for God, the *Thou* is eternally present; for man, the *Thou* tends always to lapse into *He* or *She.* Thus there is in love a continual alternation between the states of *I-Thou* and *I-It,* and the intensity of the experience, and especially of certain moments in it, bears a direct relation to the frequency of alternation. This is a necessity, not a defect of the relation. Because love has a proper concern with objective value, the beloved must become *She:* only so can she be compared, evaluated, and experienced, and therefore known as desirable — as more to be desired than all others. It is during her relapse from *Thou* to *She* that the lover becomes aware of the beloved's qualities, that he sees her as 'fairest among women'; in the recurrent *I-Thou* relation all objective particularity is swallowed up in the experience of meeting in personal encounter.

This explains the difference between the lover and the onlooker, a difference to which reference will be made again later. To the onlooker the beloved is always a *She* who may for one moment become for him a *Thou;* to the lover, she is a *Thou* who, though continually relapsing into objectivity, into the state of *She,* as continually becomes *Thou* again — for her relation with him is a relation grounded in the world of *Thou.* This alternation in relation is of great significance in the life of lovers and of husband and wife as 'one flesh'; it is inevitable, being a consequence of man's temporality, but upon its frequency the quality and duration of love largely depend. There can be no love without the experience of meeting in personal relation, and that is impossible where the other is merely an object, part of the world of *It,* and is allowed to remain so. And with the loss of true personal relation goes all participation in the *Thou* of eternity. Buber's quotation, '"When a man is together with his wife the longing of the eternal hills blows round about them,"'[8] is only true, therefore, if 'together' means united in a relation which is rooted in, and continually recurs to the basic *I-Thou* which belongs to eternity, and is not set in the context of space and time.

IV

Through the relational event in which the beloved first becomes *Thou* instead of *She* there is mediated a 'vision of perfection.' This vision is no rare experience, but accompanies every genuine and complete falling in love, and may even follow, in a different way, from the relational meeting between man and man or woman and woman — though with the latter we are not concerned here. It has been described with great authority and insight by the poets, but has not escaped degeneration into the conventional artificialities of the dance 'lyric' and sentimental song. Even there, however, the attribution to the beloved of a sort of perfection (regardless of the standards by which it is determined) bears witness to a common and authentic experience. Often it is only through such amatory banalities that the great mass of the wholly or partly inarticulate can express at second hand what is for them, as for others, something intensely moving and significant. In a more sensitive and polished way the highest levels of poetry sometimes exhibit no less a reliance upon conventional imagery. . . . Nowhere has the vision been recorded and analysed more completely than in the writings of Dante. . . . It is inevitable therefore that any consideration of this experience should begin with Dante's meeting with Beatrice and her 'blessed' salutation, as they are described in the *Vita Nuova*. For a commentary in detail upon this significant encounter the reader must turn to Mr. Charles Williams, to whose work my debt will be obvious.[9]

For Dante 'a kind of dreadful perfection has appeared in the streets of Florence; something like the glory of God is walking down the street towards him.'[10] Though others might have expressed it differently, his experience so far was normal and not uncommon. But Dante proceeded from experience to analysis and exposition; the full significance of the everyday event was set forth with unique precision and insight. Nothing calls for comment in this, except that it was possible without diminishing in any way the wonder or 'romance' of falling in love. The vision has its intellectual aspect, which must not be neglected if the significance of love is to be fully appreciated.

It is important to understand the sense in which 'perfection' is attributed to the beloved. It is essentially a perfection known only in the vision and for the purpose of the revelation mediated through the vision. Obviously the beloved is not, and cannot be perfect in the strict meaning of the term. The perfection which the lover sees, therefore,

> . . . involves no folly of denial of the girl's faults or sins. The vision of perfection arises independently of the imperfection; it shines through her body whatever she makes of her body. Thus chastity is exhibited in the

lecherous, and industry in the lazy, and humility in the proud, and truth in the false.[11]

Apart from the vision the beloved is known objectively, as she is — that is, one *She* among others, perhaps better, perhaps worse than they. But in the vision she is seen no longer as part of that world in which evaluations and comparisons are made, because the vision itself belongs to the sphere where relative values are obliterated in the meeting of *I* and *Thou*.

Although, therefore, it is neither absolute nor strictly objective, the perfection disclosed in the vision is no romantic illusion. It is a potential perfection — a perfection to which the beloved has not attained, but to which, by the grace of God, she may be brought. The vision reveals the possibility of a new life, and is accompanied by a momentary but none the less real experience of a restoration of nature. It

> . . . flashes for a moment into the lover the life he was meant to possess instead of his own by the exposition in [the beloved] of the life she was meant to possess instead of her own.[12]

God's mysterious purpose in Christ is made known in terms of the individual life, and His will for lover and beloved is declared, though it still remains to be done, in and by them both. There is no restoration apart from grace and faith and persistent endeavour, but if they have seen the vision and have understood, they know at least that restoration is possible. Thus, through the encounter of lovers, the mystery of God's will and the destiny of man in Christ are proclaimed. The perfection seen in the vision is the perfection of man recreated after the pattern of the Second Adam.

The vision and the revelation are exclusive, and concern none but the lover and the beloved; that is why love is often quite incomprehensible to the onlooker. Sometimes it seems the most natural thing in the world that a man and a woman should fall in love, but not infrequently there is to be heard the comment: What can he see in her? — the onlooker being incapable of seeing anything to explain the relationship. The comment, of course, is meaningless: the onlooker cannot expect to *see* anything, for seeing is the vision, and that cannot be for him. To the onlooker, the beloved belongs to the world of *It*, and she is accordingly assessed by conventional standards at her 'face value.' But to the lover she is *Thou*: through the relational event of falling in love, with its vision of perfection, he has seen her, not as she is, but as she may become by the grace of God — and he cannot forget what he has seen. She has been revealed as God made her to be and wills her to become, and she is loved both as she is and as grace may remake her. Love is not blind, but exceptionally clear of sight; only the lover regards the beloved's faults and sins from a standpoint which the spectator does not and cannot share. In de Rougement's saying: 'To choose a woman for wife is to say to Miss So-and-so, "I want to live with you just as you are,"'[13] there is profound truth, once it is realized that because of the vision the lover's 'just as you are' takes account of potentialities which have been hidden from all but him. To the spectator, however, 'just as you are' can imply only a subjective judgement passed upon one who by predetermined standards, personal or conventional, has been evaluated as *She*.

In this vision the lover also sees reflected in the beloved something of the perfection of God, who according to their limited capacity reveals Himself and can be known in His creatures, and specially in man, His image and likeness. Because of the particularity of love, however, the beloved appears to the lover, not as one image of God among many, but uniquely for him as *the* image of God. Man has so been created that it is normally his nature to fall in love, and through that experience to see his Creator's perfection mirrored in the beloved through whom God reveals himself to the lover. When the falling in love is mutual, the lovers communicate to each other a vision of God who is the end of their love and their life.

> Every particular *Thou* is a glimpse through to the eternal *Thou*: by means of every particular *Thou* the primary word addresses the eternal *Thou*.[14]

> He who loves a woman, and brings her life to present realization in his, is able to look in the *Thou* of her eyes into a beam of the eternal *Thou*.[15]

Falling in love and the recurring encounters of love become moments in which the eternal *Thou* is revealed, since true relation between an *I* and a *Thou* means being brought, not only into a mutual relation, but into a common relation with the living, Divine Centre. The context of the world of *Thou* is not space or time, but

> . . . in the Centre, where the extended lines of relations meet — in the eternal *Thou*.[16]

Not only is the vision a revelation, through the beloved to the lover, of the perfection of God; it is also a means whereby both experience God, for their love is rooted in their relation with him.

The perfection made known in the vision is not only a potential moral perfection; it foreshadows also the integration of lover and beloved in their perfect union as 'one flesh' which is the end of their love. One purpose of the *henosis* is the establishment of a balanced and fruitful androgyniety in place of the disruptive androgyniety of the solitary and unintegrated man or woman. In the completing of each lover by the other the tension of strife between the androgynous elements in the personality of each is resolved and converted into a tension of repose. Both become fully integrated in themselves, and also integrated together in the 'one flesh' where the full meaning of love is realized.

The lover feels that through this vision of the beloved's perfection he has been given an ineffable perception of the meaning of things. The very sight of her

> . . . arouses a sense of intense significance, a sense that an explanation of the whole universe is being offered, and indeed in some sense understood, only it cannot yet be defined. Even when the intellect seems to apprehend, it cannot express its purpose: 'the tongue cannot follow that which the intellect sees.'[17]

In terms of relation the beloved, the *She*, has become *Thou*; she 'fills the heavens' and 'all else lives in [her] light.'[18]

Not only is the beloved the means of a significant illumination of the intellect, but she appears also as

> '. . . the pattern of man's essence existing in thought within the divine mind . . . she is as completely perfect as the essence of man can possibly be.' She is, that is, the perfect centre and norm of humanity; others exist, it seems, because and in so far as they resemble her virtue. The extraordinary vision is that of the ordinary thing *in excelsis*.[19]

The beloved represents an ideal of creaturely perfection; she even seems to be 'unaffected by time.' This quality in her springs from the 'metaphysical association of the visible light' — the 'light that lightens every man that comes into the world' is made 'visible through her, by the will of grace. . . .'[20]

Finally, the beloved is revealed in the vision as

> . . . the Mother of Love — of *caritas*, and even of a *caritas* beyond any *caritas* we can imagine; she is the chosen Mother of the goodwill of God.[21]

So she awakens charity in the lover; he feels a sense of well-disposition towards everyone, so that even forgiveness is a necessity. This experience of possession by *caritas* is in some degree or other common to all lovers, and often finds expression in an increase of courtesy and refinement.[22] Sometimes, admittedly, the experience may not last long, yet even so, it may serve to awaken the realization that a new life and a new basis of relation are possible.

The love which gives inward validity to the 'one flesh' *henosis* demands a mutual, though not necessarily simultaneous, vision of perfection, but it is important not to dogmatize concerning the occurrence of the vision. There is 'love at first sight' and there is mutual 'love at first sight,' though such experiences are not so common as amatory convention insists. In most cases the vision happens, not at the first encounter, but after a period of more or less intimate friendship, and the man and the woman rarely experience it together. But where the vision is wanting there is no true love and therefore no inwardly valid 'one flesh' union. The vision cannot be organized, and may occur at any time — even after marriage — though it would be wrong in the extreme to marry in anticipation of it. To establish by sexual intercourse a state of 'one flesh' with someone through whom the Divine glory had never shone is comparable to prostitution; subsequently the vision may ratify and procure pardon for the union, but to contract it on that assumption is indefensible. The vision alone can justify the act by which the *henosis* is set up.[23] . . .

But the problem of the disappearance of the vision has to be faced. At the time it will seem to the lover impossible that it should be transient, yet so it proves to be. Although it is seen in and through a relational event (falling in love) it is not integral to the relational meeting of lover and beloved; it may recur, and recur often, or it may not. Its withdrawal, therefore, cannot affect the 'systolic-diastolic' alternation of relation in which *I-Thou* and *I-It* for ever succeed one another. To expect or to demand the continuation of the vision is unrealistic. It has its purpose and fulfils it, and it serves a purpose even in being withdrawn, whether for a time or for ever.

V

This brings us to the question of fidelity in love. Brunner says that the stability of marriage is based 'not on love but on fidelity. Fidelity is the ethical element which enhances natural love.'[24] This dichotomy between love and fidelity is, of course, due to the sense in which Brunner understands love, and upon this I have already commented. If love is ontologically both the basis of the 'one flesh' *henosis* and a permanent element therein, fidelity, the guarantee of its permanence, must be an integral feature of love; in fact, it is indispensable to the monism, the single-mindedness, which Brunner himself claims to be characteristic of 'genuine natural love.' Otherwise there can be no sincerity or even meaning in the words which love implies: 'it is with this particular person that I wish to live alone and for always.'[25] Once fidelity has been accepted as essential to love, even the withdrawal of the vision and the fading of the glory with which it had invested the beloved are seen to have their significance. They are a necessary stage in the progress of love, since they create the occasion and the need for the development and exercise of this essential fidelity.

But fidelity to the vision during the time of its withdrawal — and therefore to the beloved through whom it came and in whom the glory was seen, and to God, its ultimate source — is not required only of those who have consummated their love and have become 'one flesh.' It is demanded from all lovers from the very moment they accept their vocation and know that thenceforth their lives are bound together in a single destiny. Even in the case of a unilateral love-experience an obligation to remain faithful to the mediator or mediatrix of the vision *may* be regarded as absolute and life-long. The essence of fidelity may be said to consist in treating as unconditional *in its own sphere* the claim which (under God) lovers are entitled to make one upon the other, and in the ordering of their lives with constant reference to the single centre around which (under God) their individual, personal lives revolve — the idea of love which they have built up, which enshrines all that is most precious in their relational experience, and to which they are bound in allegiance.

VI

To the relational event in which the vision is seen no sexual implication is necessarily attached. But the whole love-experience initiated in that meeting tends towards and looks for fulfilment in the physical, sexual act by which the 'one flesh' *henosis* is established, and the physical sexual element is always important in the relation between lovers. They are always aware — sometimes acutely aware — of each other's sexuality, for an instinctive sexual attraction is the primary and most powerful feature of love. When allowed free course this attraction generally ensures the mating of those who are sexually compatible, although sexual compatibility, important as it is in conjunction with other factors, is quite insufficient by itself to ensure a true and fruitful love or a successful marriage. God's vocation of man and woman to union as 'one flesh' is partly indicated by the mystery of sexual correspondence; in love a principle of selection generally operates to secure the union of those who are physically compatible, and there is a real sense in which they can be said to have been 'made for one another.' But the false romanticism which asserts that for each there is one destined partner and one alone must be repudiated; it is one of the

189

dangerous illusions which have contributed to the contemporary sexual disorder.

Almost from the first it is normal for lovers to seek expression through the intimacies of physical contact. This is natural and inevitable, for they find that their deepest feelings and assurances demand a medium of communication more flexible and delicate than speech. These instinctive intimacies are certainly sexual, and have their origin in the sexual attraction which is a basic element in love. But though they may often resemble to some extent the sequence of acts which generally precede and culminate in sexual intercourse, they are done in a different context, and within the limits proper to erotic expression between the unmarried are not to be deprecated or condemned. It is right and natural for lovers to take pleasure in their physical natures, and any constraint, coldness, or distaste for the normal and innocuous endearments of courtship may indicate a degree of sexual incompatibility which would prove disastrous in marriage. But nothing said here must be misconstrued; only too easily can one thing lead to another, and limits must be set and strictly observed. There is a world of difference between premarital sexual licence and the reverent, restrained, yet natural physical intimacies of the lovers who understand the meaning of responsibility and detachment, who know the power of the sexual impulse, and for whom the physical is only one element in the love by which they are united.[26]

VII

The vocational aspect of love has already been mentioned; various factors combine to emphasize that all true lovers receive each other at the hand of God. In the vision of perfection, in sexual selection, and in relational experience, the Divine calling is made known, as well as in those many circumstances in which the Christian will see the purpose of God, and the non-Christian unaccountable coincidences or strokes of good fortune. But this Divine vocation is often misunderstood as the operation of some fate or destiny in obedience to which lovers are thrown together, and this fatalism is encouraged by the irresistible, sometimes almost demonic power of sexual attraction and emotion. Men and women feel that control has passed out of their hands, and that they act under the compulsion of an inexorable destiny against which they are powerless to assert their own wills and exercise the responsibility demanded by true love. Insistence that love is Divine vocation and not fatal destiny can alone dispose of this dangerous and barren fatalism which has been extensively exploited in literature.

In this connexion it must not be forgotten that love is fundamentally the result of the extensive activity of the life-giving and unifying Spirit of God, who draws lovers together and unites them in a unique and mysterious relation. Consequently it is invested with a real natural sanctity.

Since love is a Divine vocation and the work of the Holy Spirit, it demands of lovers a great responsibility to and for one another; it is 'the responsibility of an *I* for a *Thou*,'[27] and is received direct from God, to whom they are ultimately answerable for what they have made of their love.

JUDITH WALLERSTEIN

Psychologist Judith Wallerstein is perhaps best known as the author of the groundbreaking longitudinal study *Second Chances: Men, Women and Children a Decade After Divorce* (1989). Educated at Columbia University and the Topeka Institute for Psychoanalysis, Wallerstein earned her Ph.D. in Psychology from Lund University in Sweden in 1978. A children's therapist by training (she worked for 17 years at the famous Menningers Clinic), her first clinical work involved the resettlement in the United States of Jewish children who had been orphaned by the Holocaust. Dr. Wallerstein's professional interest in marriage began in the late sixties. Soon after the first no-fault divorce law was passed, she was asked to consult for a clinic treating troubled children. Several years later she founded the Judith Wallerstein Center for the Family in Transition, a clinic located in Marin County, California. The Wallerstein Center provides counseling for divorcing parents and children, and training in issues of divorce for family law attorneys, judges, teachers, ministers, pediatricians, and mental health professionals. *The Good Marriage* was published in 1995.

The Good Marriage: How and Why Love Lasts, excerpt from *"Conclusion"*

As I come to the end of writing this book, I think about my own marriage, as I have so often in the course of the study. I am aware of the physical changes of aging in my body: my right knee is getting stiff with arthritis, and I walk more slowly than before. When my husband and I walk together, as we do daily, I notice that he has slowed his pace because of my infirmity. Of course he is aware that he is getting less exercise, but that thought is not at the center of his consciousness, and he does not expect me to express my gratitude. It goes without saying that he will accommodate to my need and we will both walk more slowly.

When we return home, he usually has some tasks he urgently wants to attend to, and that is fine with me; I know that if he doesn't do them he will be unhappy. I am also aware that he, too, is less flexible than he used to be. So I postpone conversation until he has finished his work. I expect no appreciative comment from him. This is the give-and-take of life, and this is what marriage is about: keeping up, not getting too far ahead and not falling behind.

Marriage is made up of little things, and it is the little things that count, both the good and the bad. The little changes, too, add to the important rhythms of life. The changing interactions between my husband and me are part of this major chapter in our married life. We are building a marriage now just as surely as when we were younger, as surely as when we returned from our honeymoon and started out on our life together. The thousand and one changes in our relationship, in observing each other and adjusting to each other, are no different today. Except that we are better at it — we have had a lot of practice. Strangely enough, it is these little things, the ebb and flow of the relationship, that so many couples cannot manage.

I bring this book to a close with mixed feelings of exhilaration and sadness. From my encounters with the couples in the study I have learned a great deal about building a happy marriage, even beyond my own high expectations. I have also learned about the rigors of maintaining one's adulthood and of being a parent amid the pressures of contemporary society. It has been a wonderful experience to spend time with couples who are thriving, who have held on to friendship and love for each other and for their children in a society in which divorce has become commonplace.

The people in these good marriages did not all start off with advantages. They came from a wide range of backgrounds: a few rich, most modest, some dirt-poor. A lucky few had parents who loved each other, but more came from marriages they perceived as unhappy. Most were eager to create a marriage that would be different from and happier than the one in which they were raised. In this they succeeded. Each couple created an emotionally rich, enduring relationship that was designed to their liking. They were frank with me about the pleasures of the marriage and also about the areas in which they felt pinched or disappointed. Their generosity has led me to new knowledge that can be put to immediate use by other married couples. I take leave of them with affection and deep gratitude.

I will miss having almost everyone I meet at social gatherings ask me anxiously, "What have you found out?" — and then wait for a one-line answer. It is truly distressing to hear over and over again how worried most of us are and how eager we all are for a message that will give us some control over the most intimate aspects of our lives.

I shall also miss the wonderfully condensed responses I received when I turned the question back to the asker. My all-time favorite: "Do I know what makes a happy marriage?" said a woman, laughing. "A bad memory." She had a point. Surely, being able to forget the day-to-day disappointments and keep one's eyes on the big issues is what is needed to make a marriage go. And in fact separating the trivial from the important is one of the great gifts of a sense of humor. No one would gainsay the usefulness of humor in sweetening the stresses of marriage and raising children. But in truth there are no one-line answers to the question of what makes a marriage happy.

What then are the secrets? How do a man and a woman who meet as strangers create a relationship that will satisfy them both throughout their lives?

First, the answer to the question I started with — what do people define as happy in their marriage? — turned out to be straightforward. For everyone, happiness in marriage meant feeling respected and cherished. Without exception, these couples mentioned the importance of liking and respecting each other and the pleasure and comfort they took in each other's company. Some spoke of the passionate love that began their relationship, but for a surprising number love grew in the rich soil of the marriage, nourished by emotional and physical intimacy, appreciation, and fond memories. Some spoke of feeling well cared for, others of feeling safe, and still others of friendship and trust. Many talked about the family they had created together. But all felt that they were central to their partner's world and believed that creating the marriage and the family was the major commitment of their adult life. For most, marriage and children were the achievements in which they took the greatest pride.

For these couples, respect was based on integrity; a partner was admired and loved for his or her honesty, compassion, generosity of spirit, decency, loyalty to the family, and fairness. An important aspect of respect was admiration of the partner as a sensitive, conscientious parent. The value these couples placed on the partner's moral qualities was an unexpected finding. It helps explain why many divorcing people speak so vehemently of losing respect for their former partner. The love that people feel in a good marriage goes with the conviction that the person is worthy of being loved.

These people were realists. No one denied that there were serious differences — conflict, anger, even some infidelity — along the way. No one envisioned marriage as a rose garden, but all viewed its satisfactions as far out-weighing the frustrations over the long haul. Most regarded frustrations, big and small, as an inevitable aspect of life that would follow them no matter whom they married. Everyone had occasional fantasies about the roads not taken, but their commitment to the marriage withstood the impulse to break out.

Above all, they shared the view that their partner was special in some important regard and that the marriage enhanced each of them as individuals. They felt that the fit between their own needs and their partner's responses was unique and probably irreplaceable. In this they considered themselves very lucky, not entitled.

Their marriages had benefited from the new emphasis in our society on equality in relationships between men and women. However they divided up the chores of the household and of raising the children, the couples agreed that men and women had equal rights and responsibilities within the family. Women have taken many casualties in the long fight to achieve equality, and many good men have felt beleaguered, confused, and angry about this contest. But important goals have been achieved: marriages today allow for greater flexibility and greater choice. Relationships are more mature on both sides and more mutually respectful. A couple's sex life can be freer and more pleasurable. Today's men and women meet on a playing field that is more level than ever before.

Unlike many unhappy families, these couples provided no evidence for the popular notion that there is a "his" marriage and a "her" marriage. On the contrary, the men and women were very much in accord. I did not see significant differences between husbands and wives in their goals for the marriage, in their capacity for love and friendship, in their interest in sex, in their desire to have children, or in their love and commitment to the children. They fully shared the credit for the success of the marriage and the family. Both men and women said, "Everything we have we did together."

Although some men were inhibited in their expression of feelings at the beginning of the marriage, as compared with their wives, I did not find much difference between the sexes in their ability to express emotions over the course of their relationship. Both spoke easily of their love for their partner. In response to my questioning, both men and women cried when they contemplated losing the other.

The children were central, both as individuals and as symbols of a shared vision, giving pleasure and sometimes unexpected meaning to the parents' lives and to the marriage. As the couples reported to me in detail, the children reflected their love and pride. And this powerful bond did not diminish when the children left home.

As I compared the happily married couples with the thousands of divorc-ing couples I have seen in the past twenty-five years, it was clear that these men and women had early on created a firm basis for their relationship and had continued to build it together. Many of the couples that divorced failed to lay such a foundation and did not understand the need to reinforce it over the years. Many marriages broke because the structure was too weak to hold in the face of life's vicissitudes. The happy couples regarded their marriage as a work in progress that needed continued attention lest it fall into disrepair. Even in re-tirement they did not take each other for granted. Far too many divorcing cou-ples fail to understand that a marriage does not just spring into being after the ceremony. Neither the legal nor the religious ceremony makes the marriage. People do, throughout their lives.

What is the work that builds a happy marriage? What should people know about and what should they do? On the basis of the study I proposed nine psy-chological tasks that challenge men and women throughout their life together. These tasks, the building blocks of the marriage, are not imposed on the couple from the outside; they are inherent in a relationship in today's world. If the is-sues represented by each psychological task are not addressed, the marriage is likely to fail whether the couple divorces or remains legally married. The tasks begin at the start of the marital journey and are continually renegotiated. A good marriage is always being reshaped so that the couple can stay in step with each other and satisfy their changing needs and wishes.

The first task is to detach emotionally from the families of childhood, commit to the relationship, and build new connections with the extended fami-lies. Husband and wife help each other complete the transition into adulthood or, in a second marriage, detach from a prior relationship and commit emo-tionally to the new partner.

The second task is to build togetherness through intimacy and to expand the sense of self to include the other, while each individual carves out an area of autonomy. The overarching identification with the other provides the basis for bonding. As one man put it succinctly, "In a good marriage, it can't be Me-Me-Me, it's gotta be Us-Us-Us." Exactly! But within the new unity, there must be room for autonomy, otherwise there is no true equality. These two early tasks launch the marriage.

The third task is to expand the circle to include children, taking on the daunting roles of parenthood from infancy to the time when the child leaves home, while maintaining the emotional richness of the marriage. The challenge of this task is to maintain a balance between raising the children and nurturing the couple's relationship.

The fourth task is to confront the inevitable developmental challenges and the unpredictable adversities of life, including illness, death, and natural disasters, in ways that enhance the relationship despite suffering. Every crisis carries within it the seeds of destruction as well as the possibility of renewed strength. Managing stress is the key to having a marriage that can reinvent itself at each turning rather than one that becomes a shadow of its former self.

The fifth task is to make the relationship safe for expressing difference, anger, and conflict, which are inevitable in any marriage. All close relationships involve love and anger, connectedness and disruption. The task is to find ways to resolve the differences without exploiting each other, being violent, or giving away one's heart's desire. Conflict ran high among several couples in this group, but I saw no evidence that conflict by itself wrecks a marriage.

The sixth task is to establish an imaginative and pleasurable sex life. Creating a sexual relationship that meets the needs and fantasies of both people requires time and love and sensitivity. Because a couple's sex life is vulnerable to interference by the stresses of work and by family life, and because sexual desire changes, often unpredictably, over the life course, this aspect of the marriage requires special protection in order to flourish.

The seventh task is to share laughter and humor and to keep interest alive in the relationship. A good marriage is alternately playful and serious, sometimes flirtatious, sometimes difficult and cranky, but always full of life.

The eighth task is to provide the emotional nurturance and encouragement that all adults need throughout their lives, especially in today's isolating urban communities and high-pressure workplaces.

Finally, the ninth task is the one that sustains the innermost core of the relationship by drawing sustenance and renewal from the images and fantasies of courtship and early marriage and maintaining that joyful glow over a lifetime. But these images, nourished by the partners' imaginations, must be combined with a realistic view of the changes wrought by time. It is this double image that keeps love alive in the real world.

I have learned from these happily married couples that marriages come in different shapes and sizes. Under today's looser rules a marriage can be custom-made by the couple to an extent their grandparents never dreamed possible. I have therefore suggested a typology of marriage to capture what I have observed in this study. This typology includes romantic, rescue, companionate, and traditional marriages. Second marriages can belong to any of these groups. I suspect that more types will emerge in the future as marriage continues to reflect people's changing emotional needs and values.

No marriage provides for all the wishes and needs that people bring to it.

Although every good marriage provides many satisfactions, each type maximizes different rewards and exacts a different price. In each type the psychological tasks are resolved differently. The kind and degree of togetherness and autonomy vary, as does the importance of children, work, and sexual passion. The values on which the marriage is built differ among the types, although they overlap. Children growing up in each kind of marriage have quite different experiences.

Moreover, the various types of marriages require different kinds of support from society. For traditional marriages to succeed, society must offer jobs that pay enough money for one parent to support the family while the other raises the children. Society also must provide economic and educational opportunities for the child-rearing parent when the children have grown up. Similarly, for companionate marriages to flourish, society must ensure that workplace demands are not allowed to overwhelm the marriage and the family. Companionate couples also need good-quality child care and enlightened personnel policies so that they do not have to make anguished choices between the demands of work and of family, especially at times of crisis.

I have tried to show the importance of the fit between the couple and the kind of marriage they create. The idea that different people seek different kinds of marriages has important practical implications. If couples understand in advance that each kind of marriage poses different hazards and requires different tending, they can anticipate where problems are likely to develop and take steps to resolve them. The deepest satisfaction of the romantic marriage is that it gratifies the desire for passionate love, which in some cases is reinforced by the powerful wish to restore a beloved figure lost in childhood. By their nature, romantic marriages absorb most of a couple's emotional investment, and one hazard is that the children may feel peripheral to the couple's relationship.

The rescue marriage is often less emotionally intense than the romantic marriage; its great contribution is in allowing people to revise their sorrowful expectations of life. People who have suffered severe traumas are freed to pursue their lives, because the marriage gives them strength. But there is danger that the old problems will reemerge, either in the couple's relationship or between parent and child. Romantic and rescue marriages are not subject to voluntary choice, but in each type the tasks can be resolved and the marriage shaped to avoid the most likely hazards.

Companionate marriage does represent a choice, based on the couple's commitment to two careers or economic necessity or both. At its best, companionate marriage provides the gratifications of family life and the rewards of a successful career for both partners. But each individual's separate path may supersede the togetherness that happy marriage requires, leading to the loss of intimacy and emotional connectedness. Or child care may be delegated to others to the point that neither parent is primary in the child's upbringing.

Traditional marriage can meet people's needs for a home and a stable family life and provide comfort and nurturance for both adults and children. But the danger in a traditional marriage is that the partners' lives may become increasingly separate. And at midlife, when the all-absorbing tasks of child rearing are over and the tasks of the marriage need to be negotiated anew, the partners may feel estranged from each other.

A good marriage, I have come to understand, is transformative. The prevailing psychological view has been that the central dimensions of personality are fully established in childhood. But from my observations, men and women come to adulthood unfinished, and over the course of a marriage they change each other profoundly. The very act of living closely together for a long time brings about inner change, not just conscious accommodation. The physical closeness of sex and marriage has its counterpart in psychological closeness and mutual identification.

As the men and women in good marriages respond to their partner's emotional and sexual needs and wishes, they grow and influence each other. The needs of one's partner and children become as important as one's own needs. Ways of thinking, self-image, self-esteem, and values all have the potential for change. The second marriages show clearly that the capacity of men and women to love each other passionately revives in their relationship despite early disappointments. The power of marriage to bring about change is especially evident in rescue marriages. As I have described, people who have been severely traumatized during childhood are able, with the help of a loving relationship, to restore their self-esteem.

A willingness to reshape the marriage in response to new circumstances and a partner's changing needs and desires is an important key to success. All of the couples in the study understood that unless they renegotiated the tasks of the relationship at key points, one or both partners would be unhappy. There are shaky times in every marriage. Many life-course changes, such as the birth of a baby or a child's adolescence, can be anticipated, but others, such as major illness or job loss, cannot. At all of these times, emotional changes in the individual coincide with external changes. If the couple does not take steps to protect it, the marriage may be in peril. These couples succeeded in reshaping their relationship at each major crossroads so that it continued to fit their needs. All mentioned that they had experienced many different marriages within their one enduring relationship.

I have learned a great deal about the intimate connectedness of a good marriage. It became clear to me early on that popular notions about marital communication failed to capture the subtlety of the daily interactions between these men and women. They had learned that a little tact goes a long way, that sometimes silence is golden, and that timing is everything. They listened carefully to each other and tried to speak both honestly and tactfully. But they recognized intuitively that true communication in marriage extends far beyond words. It involves paying attention to changing moods, facial expressions, body language, and the many other cues that reveal inner states of mind. It means knowing each other's history and catching the echoes and behaviors that reverberate from the past. It includes knowing enough about the other so that at critical times one can take an imaginative leap inside the other's skin. That is what empathy in a marriage is about.

These were not talents that came naturally to all of these people, nor were these individuals necessarily empathic in other domains of their lives. They learned to listen and to be sensitive to their partner's cues because they wanted the marriage to work; they had learned that by anticipating a partner's distress, they could protect themselves and the marriage.

These couples also understood that symbolically a marriage is always much greater than the sum of its parts. It is enriched by the continued presence of fantasy. When the marriage is successful, it represents a dream come true, the achievement of full adulthood. Tragically, when it fails, the symbolic loss may cause enormous suffering. The home these couples created gave them both real and symbolic pleasure because they felt strongly that it was their own creation. Their pleasure in each other, especially during times of leisure and reflection, represented more than current satisfaction; it represented the fulfillment of wishes extending way back to the dreams of early childhood.

Finally, I learned again, as I have learned many times over from the divorced couples I have worked with, the extraordinary threats that contemporary society poses to marriage. The stresses of the workplace and its fierce impact on the couple are writ large in the lives of these families, no matter what their economic level. Their stories told and retold how few supports newly married couples have to keep them together and how many powerful forces pull them apart. As the younger couples made clear, the whole world seems to invade the couple's private time together. . . .

Because of societal pressures and the essential loneliness of modern life, marriage serves many purposes in today's world. It is our only refuge. The couples in the study were realistically aware that they had to fulfill many needs for each other; there are not many opportunities at work or elsewhere in society for gratifying our desires for friendship, comfort, love, reassurance, and self-expression. These couples wanted a marriage that could respond to all these complex needs without breaking. They discovered anew each day the many ways in which they helped each other and how pleased and proud they were of the marriage they had created. . . .

As I write these final paragraphs, my thoughts turn to my grandmother and to Nikki, my youngest grandchild. My grandmother, who brought her three young children to the new land in the hold of a ship and raised them by herself, knew exactly what she wanted for me. When I was growing up, she used to sing Yiddish folk songs about love and marriage, about mysterious suitors from distant lands. Whom will you marry? the songs asked. Her hopes for me were built on her own tears. My future happy marriage and my unborn healthy children made her sacrifice worthwhile.

Nikki has just turned four. She has recently demoted her twenty or so stuffed bears, puppies, kittens, even her beloved tiger, to the foot of her bed. They who were her special joy hardly have her attention now. She has entered a new phase. I am to address her as "Princess" when I call. (The great advantage of grandmothers, I have discovered, is that they follow instructions, whereas mothers issue instructions.) She is Princess Jasmine, and she awaits Aladdin. She is practicing at being a grown-up young lady, preparing for the future with all the energy and devotion that she brought to caring for her animals. No one works harder or with greater purpose than a child at play.

What do I want for Nikki? The roads that were so clear to my grandmother have become harder to follow. They fork often and sometimes lead to a dead end. Some directions, however, are still visible. I, too, want my granddaughter to be strong and brave and virtuous. I want her to love and be loved passionately and gently and proudly by a man worth loving. I want her to experience the joys and terrors of raising children. But far beyond what my grandmother envisioned for me, I want Nikki to have the choices in life that I and many others had to fight for, real choices that the community will respect and support. And I want her to know how to choose wisely and understand how to make it all work. I hope that Nikki finds the Aladdin that she has started to look for. If he comes flying into her life on a magic carpet, so much the better. This book contains her legacy, a set of annotated maps for their journey.

4 Should I Marry One of My Own?

- From *Medea* by Euripides

- Judges 14–15

- The Book of Ruth

- "The Thirteenth Night" by Higuchi Ichiyo

- From *Love* by Elizabeth von Arnim

- "A Jew Discovered," from *The Color of Water: A Black Man's Tribute to His White Mother* by James McBride

How I do hate those words, "an excellent marriage." In them is contained more of wicked worldliness than any other words one ever hears spoken.

— ANTHONY TROLLOPE

Like blood, like good, and like age make the happiest marriages.

— PROVERB

Introduction

In our culturally diverse society, racially and religiously mixed marriages occur ever more frequently. Even the former social barriers to May-September unions are falling, as are old prejudices against unions between people of different social class. But neither marrying "down," exogamy, nor May-September marriages are a recent phenomenon; since the beginning of time such unconventional unions have presented their own particular set of problems for the married couple, and have excited their own particular social prejudices.

Indeed, received wisdom has it that the more homogamous the couple in terms of racial, religious, and social background the more stable the marriage is likely to be. Social scientists are now beginning to test this theory. They have found that religiously mixed marriages *are* more vulnerable to breakup except in cases where one spouse has prior to marriage converted to the other's religion.[1] Where a marriage between two people of differing social status is concerned, it seems that where the man is of higher social status, less marital problems ensue than when the woman is of higher social status.

There is no story of exogamy in Western culture more powerful, more filled with pathos and horror than the story of Medea. Medea, who by means of her magic skills has helped Jason procure the Golden Fleece, leaves her home in Colchis and returns with Jason to Corinth, were she bears him two children. Jason, however, cruelly casts her off, deciding it would be politic to divorce Medea and to marry Crusea, princess of Corinth. Betrayed by her husband, banished from her adopted country, suspect to all around her as a foreigner and a sorceress, Medea exacts revenge. This desperate woman resolves to hurt her husband in the most vicious way possible. Not only does she murder her husband's future wife, but she takes the lives of her own two children.

The two Bible stories that form the core of this chapter's readings reflect two very different takes on the viability of mixed marriages. The first, the story of Samson and the manipulative Philistine woman of Timnath with whom he falls helplessly in love, touches upon the problems of deep distrust and misunderstanding that can haunt some cross-cultural marriages. In brief, Samson's marriage with the woman of Timnath is both a personal and a political disaster, inciting a war between Israel and the Philistines.

The second Bible story, the famous story of Ruth, is a positive look at mixed marriage. Ruth, a Moabite, and the childless widow of a Hebrew, will not leave her mother-in-law, Naomi, when that woman decides to return to her people in Judah. Rather, Ruth casts her lot with her husband's nation, returning also to Judah where, in accordance with the Law of Moses, she marries a relative of her deceased husband. Ruth's identification with her husband's faith and Naomi's acceptance of the girl as a full-fledged member of her family will pay off in a big way for the Jewish people. Ruth and her second husband, Boaz, will be ancestors of the greatest hero of the Jewish nation: King David.

Higuchi Ichiyo's poignant story, "The Thirteenth Night," explores a common scenario with uncommon sensitivity. Oseki, a beautiful girl from a modest background, marries Isamu, a man of means and position. The marriage brings the material advantage of connection to her family of origin; but it estranges them from her socially. Moreover, the longer Oseki is married, the more ashamed Isamu is of her lack of breeding. Oseki tries in every way to please her husband. But instead of educating her to her new position, Isamu treats her as a lost cause, verbally abusing her. In the end, Oseki comes to realize that she must accept her destiny with Isamu, for ill as well as for good. Isamu loved her once; she married him, however, only for material advantage, abandoning her real love, a boy of her own social class.

Our next selection is from Elizabeth von Arnim's novel, *Love*. Here is the tale of the middle-aged English widow, Catherine, who, when pursued by a young man, discovers a passion she has never known before. In defying convention and resolving to marry, she and the young man will endure some painful disapproval and skepticism — from children, friends, and even servants. Most painful of all, her son-in-law, no "spring chicken" himself, seems to have gotten away with marrying a young woman without suffering the least bit of censure. Indeed, despite their committed love, Catherine and her bridegroom Christopher will be forced to face some unpleasant facts. Because of their very different stages of life, there will forever be discrepancies in their respective hopes for the future, their energy levels, and their social expectations.

In James McBride's touching memoir of self-discovery, *The Color of Water*, a black man discovers a part of his background he has never before fully encountered when he revisits the Jewish community in which his white mother grew up. This uplifting memoir on the gifts and handicaps of a mixed heritage, both racial and religious, is a reflection on the challenges of living cross-cultural lives in a Balkanized society. A testament to hope and universal brotherhood, it explores some of the psychological needs that can drive us out of the community in which we are raised. And it explores both the feelings of homelessness and the opportunities for emancipation from convention that mark the children of exogamous unions.

EURIPIDES

The Greek playwright Euripides (c. 485–c. 406 B.C.) is considered by many to be the father of modern theater. Although he employed many of the same plots and themes as his more classical contemporaries Aeschylus and Sophocles, his language was not so high flown as theirs, and his characters were more down to earth. In fact, in his time he was thought rather vulgar. But today one sees in his plays (of which only nineteen of ninety-two have survived) things one does not see in the plays of the more high minded of his contemporaries: social criticism, and authentic identification with the struggles of the weak. Euripides was something of a social casualty himself. His origins were humble, his marriages apparently unhappy, his literary success meager, and his personality unruly and ill adapted to the attainment of the secure social position his ample literary talents might have predicted. In ancient Greece, theater had very specific ritual functions, with specific aesthetic and moral aims. Euripides' plays subtly tend to subvert the beliefs, lessons, and assumptions they were ostensibly supposed to support. Thus, Euripides' rueful lack of artistic acclaim during his lifetime.

Medea

History has much to tell of the relations of men with women.

You, Medea, in the mad passion of your heart sailed away from your father's home, threading your way through the twin rocks of the Euxine, to settle in a foreign land. Now, your bed empty, your lover lost, unhappy woman, you are being driven forth in dishonor into exile.

Gone is respect for oaths. Nowhere in all the breadth of Hellas is honor any more to be found; it has vanished into the clouds. Hapless one, you have no father's house to which you might fly for shelter from the gales of misfortune; and another woman, a princess, has charmed your husband away and stepped into your place.

[*Enter Jason.*]

JASON   Often and often ere now I have observed that an intractable nature is a curse almost impossible to deal with. So with you. When you might have stayed on in this land and in this house by submitting quietly to the wishes of your superiors, your forward tongue has got you expelled from the country. Not that your abuse troubles *me* at all. Keep on saying that Jason is a villain of the deepest dye. But for your insolence to royalty consider yourself more than fortunate that you are only being punished by exile. I was constantly mollifying the angry monarch and expressing the wish that you be allowed to stay. But in unabated folly you keep on reviling the king. That is why you are to be expelled.

But still, despite everything, I come here now with unwearied goodwill, to contrive on your behalf, Madam, that you and the children will not leave this country lacking money or anything else. Exile brings many hardships in its wake. And even if you do hate me, I could never think cruelly of you.

MEDEA   Rotten, heart-rotten, that is the word for you. Words, words, magnificent words. In reality a craven. You come to me, you come, my worst enemy! This isn't bravery, you know, this isn't valor, to come and face your victims. No! it's the ugliest sore on the face of humanity, Shamelessness. But I thank you for coming. It will lighten the weight on my heart to tell your wickedness, and it will hurt you to hear it. I shall begin my tale at the very beginning.

I saved your life, as all know who embarked with you on the Argo, when you were sent to master with the yoke the fire-breathing bulls and to sow with dragon's teeth that acre of death. The dragon, too, with wreathed coils, that kept safe watch over the Golden Fleece and never slept — I slew it and raised for you the light of life again. Then, forsaking my father and my own dear ones, I came to Iolcus where Pelias reigned, came with you, more than fond and less than wise. On Pelias too I brought death, the most painful death there is, at the hands of his own children. Thus I have removed every danger from your path.

And after all those benefits at my hands, you basest of men, you have betrayed me and made a new marriage, though I have borne you children. If you were still childless, I could have understood this love of yours for a new wife. Gone now is all reliance on pledges. You puzzle me. Do you believe that the gods of the old days are no longer in office? Do you think that men are now living under a new dispensation? For surely you know that you have broken all your oaths to me. Ah my hand, which you so often grasped, and oh my knees, how all for nothing have we been defiled by this false man, who has disappointed all our hopes.

But come, I shall confide in you as though you were my friend, not that I expect to receive any benefit from you. But let that go. My questions will serve to underline your infamy. As things are now, where am I to turn? Home to my father? But when I came here with you, I betrayed my home and my country. To the wretched daughters of Pelias! They would surely give me a royal welcome to their home; I only murdered their father. For it is how it is. My loved ones at home have learned to hate me; the others, whom I need not have harmed, I have made my enemies to oblige you. And so in return for these services you have made me envied among the women of Hellas! A wonderful, faithful husband I have in you, if I must be expelled from the country into exile, deserted by my friends, alone with my friendless children! A fine story to tell of the new bridegroom, that his children and the woman who saved his life are wandering about in aimless beggary! O Zeus, why O why have you given to mortals sure means of knowing gold from tinsel, yet men's exteriors show no mark by which to descry the rotten heart?

LEADER Horrible and hard to heal is the anger of friend at strife with friend.

JASON It looks as if I need no small skill in speech if, like a skillful steersman, riding the storm with close-reefed sheets, I am to escape the howling gale of your verbosity, woman. Well, since you are making a mountain out of the favors you have done me, I'll tell *you* what *I* think. It was the goddess of Love and none other, mortal or immortal, who delivered me from the dangers of my quest. You have indeed much subtlety of wit, but it would be an invidious story to go into, how the inescapable shafts of Love compelled you to save my life. Still, I shall not put too fine a point on it. If you helped me in some way or other, good and well. But as I shall demonstrate, in the matter of my rescue you got more than you gave.

In the first place, you have your home in Greece, instead of in a barbarian land. You have learned the blessings of Law and Justice, instead of the Caprice of the Strong. And all the Greeks have realized

211

your wisdom, and you have won great fame. If you had been living on the edges of the earth, nobody would ever have heard of you. May I have neither gold in my house nor skill to sing a sweeter song than Orpheus if my fortune is to be hid from the eyes of men. That, then, is my position in the matter of the fetching of the Fleece. (It was you who proposed the debate.)

There remains my wedding with the Princess, which you have cast in my teeth. In this connection I shall demonstrate, one, my wisdom; two, my rightness; three, my great service of love to you and my children. (Be quiet, please.) When I emigrated here from the land of Iolcus, dragging behind me an unmanageable chain of troubles, what greater windfall could I have hit upon, I an exile, than a marriage with the king's daughter? Not that I was weary of your charms (that's the thought that galls you) or that I was smitten with longing for a fresh bride; still less that I wanted to outdo my neighbors in begetting numerous children. Those I have are enough, there I have no criticism to make. No! what I wanted, first and foremost, was a good home where we would lack for nothing (well I knew that the poor man is shamed and avoided by all his friends); and secondly, I wanted to bring up the children in a style worthy of my house, and, begetting other children to be brothers to the children born of you, to bring them all together and unite the families. Then my happiness would be complete. What do *you* want with more children? As for me, it will pay me to advance the children I have by means of those I intend to beget.[1] Surely that is no bad plan? You yourself would admit it, if jealousy were not pricking you.

You women have actually come to believe that, lucky in love, you are lucky in all things, but let some mischance befall that love, and you will think the best of all possible worlds a most loathsome place. There ought to have been some other way for men to beget their children, dispensing with the assistance of women. Then there would be no trouble in the world.

LEADER Jason, you arrange your arguments very skillfully. And yet in my opinion, like it or not, you have acted unjustly in betraying your wife.

MEDEA Yes! I do hold many opinions that are not shared by the majority of people. In my opinion, for example, the plausible scoundrel is the worst type of scoundrel. Confident in his ability to trick out his wickedness with fair phrases he shrinks from no depth of villainy. But there is a limit to his cleverness. As there is also to yours. You may as well drop that fine front with me, and all that rhetoric. One word will floor you. If you had been an honorable man, you would have sought my consent to the new match and not kept your plans secret from your own family.

JASON   And if I had announced to you my intention to marry I am sure I would have found you a most enthusiastic accomplice. Why! even now you cannot bring yourself to master your heart's deep resentment.

MEDEA   That's not what griped you. No! your foreign wife was passing into an old age that did you little credit.

JASON   Accept my assurance, it was not for the sake of a woman that I made the match I have made. As I told you once already, I wanted to save you and to beget princes to be brothers to my own sons, thereby establishing our family.

MEDEA   May it never be mine . . . a happiness that hurts, blessedness that frets my soul.

JASON   Do you know how to change your prayer to show better sense? "May I regard nothing useful as grievous, no good fortune as ill."

MEDEA   Insult me. *You* have a refuge, but I am helpless, faced with exile.

JASON   It was your own choice. Don't blame anyone else.

MEDEA   What did I do? Did I betray you and marry somebody else?

JASON   You heaped foul curses on the king.

MEDEA   And to your house also I shall prove a curse.

JASON   Look here, I do not intend to continue this discussion any further. If you want anything of mine to assist you or the children in your exile, just tell me. I am ready to give it with an ungrudging hand and to send letters of introduction to my foreign friends who will treat you well. If you reject this offer, woman, you will be a great fool. Forget your anger, and you will find it greatly to your advantage.

MEDEA   I would not use your friends on any terms or accept anything of yours. Do not offer it. The gifts of the wicked bring no profit.

JASON   At any rate, heaven be my witness that I am willing to render every assistance to you and the children. But you do not like what is good for you. Your obstinacy repulses your friends; it will only aggravate your suffering.

MEDEA   Be off with you. As you loiter outside here, you are burning with longing for the girl who has just been made your wife. Make the most of the union. Perhaps, god willing, you are making the kind of marriage you will some day wish unmade.

[*Exit Jason.*]

CHORUS *Love may go too far and involve men in dishonor and disgrace. But if the goddess comes in just measure, there is none so rich in blessing. May you never launch at me, O Lady of Cyprus, your golden bow's passion-poisoned arrows, which no man can avoid.*

May Moderation content me, the fairest gift of Heaven. Never may the Cyprian pierce my heart with longing for another's love and bring on me angry quarrelings and never-ending recriminations. May she have respect for harmonious unions and with discernment assort the matings of women.

O Home and Fatherland, never, never, I pray, may I be cityless. It is an intolerable existence, hopeless, piteous, grievous. Let me die first, die and bring this life to a close. There is no sorrow that surpasses the loss of country.

My eyes have seen it; not from hearsay do I speak. You have neither city nor friend to pity you in your most terrible trials. Perish, abhorred, the man who never brings himself to unbolt his heart in frankness to some honored friends! Never shall such a man be a friend of mine.

[*Enter Aegeus (king of Athens), in traveler's dress.*]

AEGEUS Medea, good health to you. A better prelude than that in addressing one's friends, no man knows.

MEDEA Good health be yours also, wise Pandion's son, Aegeus. Where do you come from to visit this land?

AEGEUS I have just left the ancient oracle of Phoebus.

MEDEA What sent you to the earth's oracular hub?

AEGEUS I was enquiring how I might get children.

MEDEA In the name of Heaven, have you come thus far in life still childless?

AEGEUS By some supernatural influence I am still without children.

MEDEA Have you a wife or are you still unmarried?

AEGEUS I have a wedded wife to share my bed.

MEDEA Tell me, what did Phoebus tell you about offspring?

AEGEUS His words were too cunning for a mere man to interpret.

MEDEA Is it lawful to tell me the answer of the god?

AEGEUS Surely. For, believe me, it requires a cunning mind to understand.

MEDEA What then was the oracle? Tell me, if I may hear it.

AEGEUS I am not to open the cock that projects from the skin. . . .

MEDEA Till you do what? Till you reach what land?

AEGEUS Till I return to my ancestral hearth.

MEDEA Then what errand brings your ship to this land?

AEGEUS There is one Pittheus, king of Troezen. . . .

MEDEA The child of Pelops, as they say, and a most pious man.

AEGEUS To him I will communicate the oracle of the god.

MEDEA Yes, he is a cunning man and well-versed in such matters.

AEGEUS. Yes, and of all my comrades in arms the one I love most.

MEDEA Well, good luck to you, and may you win your heart's desire.

AEGEUS Why, what's the reason for those sad eyes, that wasted complexion?

MEDEA Aegeus, I've got the basest husband in all the world.

AEGEUS What do you mean? Tell me the reason of your despondency, tell me plainly.

MEDEA Jason is wronging me; I never did him wrong.

AEGEUS What has he done? Speak more bluntly.

MEDEA He has another wife, to lord it over me in our home.

AEGEUS You don't mean that he has done so callous, so shameful a deed!

MEDEA Indeed he did. Me that used to be his darling he now despises.

AEGEUS Has he fallen in love? Does he hate your embraces?

MEDEA Yes, it's a grand passion! He was born to betray his loved ones.

AEGEUS Let him go, then, since he is so base, as you say.

MEDEA He became enamored of getting a king for a father-in-law.

AEGEUS Who gave him the bride? Please finish your story.

MEDEA Creon, the ruler of this Corinth.

AEGEUS In that case, Madam, I can sympathize with your resentment.

MEDEA My life is ruined. What is more, I am being expelled from the land.

AEGEUS By whom? This new trouble is hard.

MEDEA Creon is driving me out of Corinth into exile.

AEGEUS And does Jason allow this? I don't like that either.

MEDEA He says he does not, but he'll stand it. Oh! I beseech you by this beard, by these knees, a suppliant I entreat you, show pity, show pity for my misery. Do not stand by and see me driven forth to a lonely exile. Receive me into your land, into your home and the shelter of your hearth. So may the gods grant you the children you desire, to throw joy round your deathbed. You do not know what a lucky path you have taken to me. I shall put an end to your childlessness. I shall make you beget heirs of your blood. I know the magic potions that will do it.

AEGEUS Many things make me eager to do this favor for you, Madam. Firstly, the gods, and secondly, the children that you promise will be born to me. In that matter I am quite at my wits' end. But here is how I stand. If you yourself come to Athens, I shall try to be your champion, as in duty bound. This warning, however, I must give you! I shall not consent to take you with me out of Corinth. If you yourself come to my palace, you will find a home and a sanctuary. Never will I surrender you to anybody. But your own efforts must get you away from this place. I wish to be free from blame in the eyes of my hosts also.

MEDEA And so you shall. But just let me have a pledge for these services, and I shall have all I could desire of you.

AEGEUS Do you not trust me? What is your difficulty?

MEDEA I do trust you. But both the house of Pelias and Creon are my enemies. Bound by oaths, you would never hand me over to them if they tried to extradite me. But with an agreement of mere words, unfettered by any sacred pledge, you might be won over by their diplomatic advances to become *their* friend. For I have no influence or power, whereas they have the wealth of a royal palace.

AEGEUS You take great precautions, Madam. Still, if you wish, I will not refuse to do your bidding. For me too it will be safer that way, if I have some excuse to offer to your enemies, and *you* will have more security. Dictate the oath.

MEDEA Swear by the Floor of Earth, by the Sun my father's father, by the whole family of the gods, one and all ———

AEGEUS To do or not do what? Say on.

MEDEA Never yourself to cast me out of your country and never, willingly, during your lifetime, to surrender me to any of my foes that desire to seize me.

AEGEUS I swear by the Earth, by the holy majesty of the Sun, and by all the gods, to abide by the terms you propose.

MEDEA Enough! And if you abide not by your oath, what punishment do you pray to receive?

AEGEUS The doom of sacrilegious mortals.

MEDEA Go and fare well. All is well. I shall arrive at your city as soon as possible, when I have done what I intend to do, and obtained my desire.

LEADER [*as Aegeus departs*] May Maia's son, the Lord of Journeys, bring you safe to Athens, and may you achieve the desire that hurries you homeward; for you are a generous man in my esteem.

MEDEA O Zeus and his Justice, O Light of the Sun! The time has come, my friends, when I shall sing songs of triumph over my enemies. I am on my way. Now I can hope that my foes will pay the penalty. Just as my plans were most storm-tossed at sea, this man has appeared, a veritable harbor, where I shall fix my moorings, when I get to the town and citadel of Pallas.

Now I shall tell you all my plans; what you hear will not be said in fun. I shall send one of my servants to ask Jason to come and see me. When he comes, I shall make my language submissive, tell him I approve of everything else and am quite contented [with his royal marriage and his betrayal of me, that I agree it is all for the best]; I shall only ask him to allow my children to remain. Not that I wish to leave them in a hostile land [for my enemies to insult]. No! I have a cunning plan to kill the princess. I shall send them with gifts to offer to the bride, to allow them to stay in the land — a dainty robe and a head-dress of beaten gold. If she takes the finery and puts it on her, she will die in agony. She and anyone who touches her. So deadly are the poisons in which I shall steep my gifts.

But now I change my tone. It grieves me sorely, the horrible deed I must do next. I shall murder my children, these children of mine. No man shall take them away from me. Then when I have accomplished the utter overthrow of the house of Jason, I shall flee from the land, to escape the consequences of my own dear children's murder and my other accursed crimes. My friends, I cannot bear being laughed at by my enemies.

So be it. Tell me, what has life to offer them. They have no father, no home, no refuge from danger.

My mistake was in leaving my father's house, won over by the words of a Greek. But, as god is my ally, he shall pay for his crime. Never, if I can help it, shall he behold his sons again in this life. Never shall he beget children by his new bride. She must die by my poisons, die the death she deserves. Nobody shall despise *me* or think me weak or passive. Quite the contrary. I am a good friend, but a dangerous enemy. For that is the type the world delights to honor.

LEADER You have confided your plan in me, and I should like to help you, but since I also would support the laws of mankind, I entreat you not to do this deed.

MEDEA It is the only way. But I can sympathize with your sentiments. You have not been wronged like me.

LEADER Surely you will not have the heart to destroy your own flesh and blood?

MEDEA I shall. It will hurt my husband most that way.

LEADER But it will make you the unhappiest woman in the world.

MEDEA Let it. From now on all words are superfluous. [*To the nurse.*] Go now, please, and fetch Jason. Whenever loyalty is wanted, I turn to you. Tell him nothing of my intentions, as you are a woman and a loyal servant of your mistress.

[*Exit Nurse.*]

CHORUS *The people of Erechtheus have been favored of Heaven from the beginning. Children of the blessed gods are they, sprung from a hallowed land that no foeman's foot has trodden. Their food is glorious Wisdom. There*

217

the skies are always clear, and lightly do they walk in that land where once on a time blonde Harmony bore nine chaste daughters, the Muses of Pieria.

Such is the tale, which tells also how Aphrodite sprinkled the land with water from the fair streams of Cephissus and breathed over it breezes soft and fragrant. Ever on her hair she wears a garland of sweet-smelling roses, and ever she sends the Loves to assist in the court of Wisdom. No good thing is wrought without their help.

How then shall that land of sacred rivers, that hospitable land receive you the slayer of your children? It would be sacrilege for you to live with them. Think. You are stabbing your children. Think. You are earning the name of murderess. By your knees we entreat you, by all the world holds sacred, do not murder your children.

Whence got you the hardihood to conceive such a plan? And in the horrible act, as you bring death on your own children, how will you steel your heart and hand? When you cast your eyes on them, your own children, will you not weep that you should be their murderess? When your own children fall at your feet and beg for mercy, you will never be able to dye your hands with their blood. Your heart will not stand it.

THE BOOK OF JUDGES

The Book of Judges weaves the political history of the ancient Hebrews and their religious development during the period between Joshua's occupation of the Promised Land and the establishment of the monarchy. It is not quite clear how the story of Samson fits into the book's larger narrative. Bible scholars assume that the adventures of Samson were added to Judges as an afterthought. If this is true, the addition would have been a remarkable tribute to a popular military hero, a warrior of legendary physical strength and — where women were concerned — conspicuous weakness of character. Indeed, Samson's religious significance is almost inconsequential, but his hot-blood romantic exploits are among the most famous stories of the Bible.

Judges 14, 15: The Story of Samson and the Woman of Timnath

Chapter 14

1 And Samson went down to Timnath, and saw a woman in Timnath of the daughters of the Philistines.

2 And he came up, and told his father and his mother, and said, I have seen a woman in Timnath of the daughters of the Philistines: now therefore get her for me to wife.

3 Then his father and his mother said unto him, Is there never a woman among the daughters of thy brethren, or among all my people, that thou

goest to take a wife of the uncircumcised Philistines? And Samson said unto his father, Get her for me; for she pleaseth me well.

4 But his father and his mother knew not that it was of the LORD, that he sought an occasion against the Philistines: for at that time the Philistines had dominion over Israel.

5 Then went Samson down, and his father and his mother, to Timnath, and came to the vineyards of Timnath: and, behold, a young lion roared against him.

6 And the spirit of the LORD came mightily upon him, and he rent him as he would have rent a kid, and he had nothing in his hand: but he told not his father or his mother what he had done.

7 And he went down, and talked with the woman; and she pleased Samson well.

8 And after a time he returned to take her, and he turned aside to see the carcase of the lion: and, behold, there was a swarm of bees and honey in the carcase of the lion.

9 And he took thereof in his hands, and went on eating, and came to his father and mother, and he gave them, and they did eat: but he told not them that he had taken the honey out of the carcase of the lion.

10 So his father went down unto the woman: and Samson made there a feast; for so used the young men to do.

11 And it came to pass, when they saw him, that they brought thirty companions to be with him.

12 And Samson said unto them, I will now put forth a riddle unto you: if ye can certainly declare it me within the seven days of the feast, and find it out, then I will give you thirty sheets and thirty change of garments:

13 But if ye cannot declare it me, then shall ye give me thirty sheets and thirty change of garments. And they said unto him, Put forth thy riddle, that we may hear it.

14 And he said unto them, Out of the eater came forth meat, and out of the strong came forth sweetness. And they could not in three days expound the riddle.

15 And it came to pass on the seventh day, that they said unto Samson's wife, Entice thy husband, that he may declare unto us the riddle, lest we burn thee and thy father's house with fire: have ye called us to take that we have? is it not so?

16 And Samson's wife wept before him, and said, Thou dost but hate me, and lovest me not: thou hast put forth a riddle unto the children of my people, and hast not told it me. And he said unto her, Behold, I have not told it my father nor my mother, and shall I tell it thee?

17 And she wept before him the seven days, while their feast lasted: and it came to pass on the seventh day, that he told her, because she lay sore upon him: and she told the riddle to the children of her people.

18 And the men of the city said unto him on the seventh day before the sun went down, What is sweeter than honey? and what is stronger than a lion? And he said unto them, If ye had not plowed with my heifer, ye had not found out my riddle.

19 And the spirit of the Lord came upon him, and he went down to Ashkelon, and slew thirty men of them, and took their spoil, and gave change of garments unto them which expounded the riddle. And his anger was kindled, and he went up to his father's house.

20 But Samson's wife was given to his companion, whom he had used as his friend.

Chapter 15

1 But it came to pass within a while after, in the time of wheat harvest, that Samson visited his wife with a kid; and he said, I will go in to my wife into the chamber. But her father would not suffer him to go in.

2 And her father said, I verily thought that thou hadst utterly hated her; therefore I gave her to thy companion: is not her younger sister fairer than she? take her, I pray thee, instead of her.

3 And Samson said concerning them, Now shall I be more blameless than the Philistines, though I do them a displeasure.

4 And Samson went and caught three hundred foxes, and took firebrands, and turned tail to tail, and put a firebrand in the midst between two tails.

5 And when he had set the brands on fire, he let them go into the standing corn of the Philistines, and burnt up both the shocks, and also the standing corn, with the vineyards and olives.

6 Then the Philistines said, Who hath done this? And they answered, Samson, the son in law of the Timnite, because he had taken his wife, and given her to his companion. And the Philistines came up, and burnt her and her father with fire.

7 And Samson said unto them, Though ye have done this, yet will I be avenged of you, and after that I will cease.

8 And he smote them hip and thigh with a great slaughter: and he went down and dwelt in the top of the rock Etam.

9 Then the Philistines went up, and pitched in Judah, and spread themselves in Lehi.

10 And the men of Judah said, Why are ye come up against us? And they answered, To bind Samson are we come up, to do to him as he hath done to us.

11 Then three thousand men of Judah went to the top of the rock Etam, and said to Samson, Knowest thou not that the Philistines are rulers over us? what is this that thou hast done unto us? And he said unto them, As they did unto me, so have I done unto them.

12 And they said unto him, We are come down to bind thee, that we may deliver thee into the hand of the Philistines. And Samson said unto them, Swear unto me, that ye will not fall upon me yourselves.

13 And they spake unto him, saying, No; but we will bind thee fast, and deliver thee into their hand: but surely we will not kill thee. And they bound him with two new cords, and brought him up from the rock.

14 And when he came unto Lehi, the Philistines shouted against him: and the spirit of the LORD came mightily upon him, and the cords that were upon his arms became as flax that was burnt with fire, and his bands loosed from off his hands.

15 And he found a new jawbone of an ass, and put forth his hand, and took it, and slew a thousand men therewith.

16 And Samson said, With the jawbone of an ass, heaps upon heaps, with the jaw of an ass have I slain a thousand men.

17 And it came to pass, when he had made an end of speaking, that he cast away the jawbone out of his hand, and called that place Ramathlehi.

18 And he was sore athirst, and called on the LORD, and said, Thou hast given this great deliverance into the hand of thy servant: and now shall I die for thirst, and fall into the hand of the uncircumcised?

19 But God clave an hollow place that was in the jaw, and there came water thereout; and when he had drunk, his spirit came again, and he revived: wherefore he called the name thereof Enhakkore, which is in Lehi unto this day.

20 And he judged Israel in the days of the Philistines twenty years.

THE BOOK OF RUTH

The story of Ruth ostensibly takes place around the time of the Judges (about the twelfth century B.C.). But it is attributed by Bible scholars to a later period than the completion of the Book of Judges, somewhere between the fifth and third centuries B.C. In fact, some scholars have considered it to be a rejoinder to the harsh edicts of Ezra, the prophet who, following the first Babylonian exile, ordered the returned Jews to purge themselves of foreign influences by casting out their Babylonian wives and children.

The Book of Ruth

Chapter 1

1 Now it came to pass in the days when the judges ruled, that there was a famine in the land. And a certain man of Bethlehem-judah went to sojourn in the country of Moab, he, and his wife, and his two sons.

2 And the name of the man was Elimelech, and the name of his wife Naomi, and the name of his two sons Mahlon and Chilion, Ephrathites of Bethlehem-judah. And they came into the country of Moab, and continued there.

3 And Elimelech Naomi's husband died; and she was left, and her two sons.

4 And they took them wives of the women of Moab; the name of the one was Orpah, and the name of the other Ruth: and they dwelled there about ten years.

5 And Mahlon and Chilion died also both of them; and the woman was left of her two sons and her husband.

6 Then she arose with her daughters in law, that she might return from the country of Moab: for she had heard in the country of Moab how that the LORD had visited his people in giving them bread.

7 Wherefore she went forth out of the place where she was, and her two daughters in law with her; and they went on the way to return unto the land of Judah.

8 And Naomi said unto her two daughters in law, Go, return each to her mother's house: the LORD deal kindly with you, as ye have dealt with the dead, and with me.

9 The LORD grant you that ye may find rest, each of you in the house of her husband. Then she kissed them; and they lifted up their voice, and wept.

10 And they said unto her, Surely we will return with thee unto thy people.

11 And Naomi said, Turn again, my daughters: why will ye go with me? are there yet any more sons in my womb, that they may be your husbands?

12 Turn again, my daughters, go your way; for I am too old to have an husband. If I should say, I have hope, if I should have an husband also to night, and should also bear sons;

13 Would ye tarry for them till they were grown? would ye stay for them from having husbands? nay, my daughters; for it grieveth me much for your sakes that the hand of the LORD is gone out against me.

14 And they lifted up their voice, and wept again: and Orpah kissed her mother in law; but Ruth clave unto her.

15 And she said, Behold, thy sister in law is gone back unto her people, and unto her gods: return thou after thy sister in law.

16 And Ruth said, Entreat me not to leave thee, or to return from following after thee: for whither thou goest, I will go; and where thou lodgest, I will lodge: thy people shall be my people, and thy God my God:

17 Where thou diest, will I die, and there will I be buried: the LORD do so to me, and more also, if ought but death part thee and me.

18 When she saw that she was stedfastly minded to go with her, then she left speaking unto her.

19 So they two went until they came to Bethlehem. And it came to pass, when they were come to Bethlehem, that all the city was moved about them, and they said, Is this Naomi?

20 And she said unto them, Call me not Naomi, call me Mara[1]: for the Almighty hath dealt very bitterly with me.

21 I went out full, and the LORD hath brought me home again empty: why

then call ye me Naomi, seeing the LORD hath testified against me, and the Almighty hath afflicted me?

22 So Naomi returned, and Ruth the Moabitess, her daughter in law, with her, which returned out of the country of Moab: and they came to Bethlehem in the beginning of barley harvest.

Chapter 2

1 And Naomi had a kinsman of her husband's, a mighty man of wealth, of the family of Elimelech; and his name was Boaz.

2 And Ruth the Moabitess said unto Naomi, Let me now go to the field, and glean ears of corn after him in whose sight I shall find grace. And she said unto her, Go, my daughter.

3 And she went, and came, and gleaned in the field after the reapers: and her hap was to light on a part of the field belonging unto Boaz, who was of the kindred of Elimelech.

4 And, behold, Boaz came from Bethlehem, and said unto the reapers, The LORD be with you. And they answered him, The LORD bless thee.

5 Then said Boaz unto his servant that was set over the reapers, Whose damsel is this?

6 And the servant that was set over the reapers answered and said, It is the Moabitish damsel that came back with Naomi out of the country of Moab:

7 And she said, I pray you, let me glean and gather after the reapers among the sheaves: so she came, and hath continued even from the morning until now, that she tarried a little in the house.

8 Then said Boaz unto Ruth, Hearest thou not, my daughter? Go not to glean in another field, neither go from hence, but abide here fast by my maidens:

9 Let thine eyes be on the field that they do reap, and go thou after them: have I not charged the young men that they shall not touch thee? and when thou art athirst, go unto the vessels, and drink of that which the young men have drawn.

10 Then she fell on her face, and bowed herself to the ground, and said unto him, Why have I found grace in thine eyes, that thou shouldest take knowledge of me, seeing I am a stranger?

11 And Boaz answered and said unto her, It hath fully been showed me, all that thou hast done unto thy mother in law since the death of thine husband: and how thou hast left thy father and thy mother, and the land of

thy nativity, and art come unto a people which thou knewest not heretofore.

12 The LORD recompense thy work, and a full reward be given thee of the LORD God of Israel, under whose wings thou art come to trust.

13 Then she said, Let me find favour in thy sight, my lord; for that thou hast comforted me, and for that thou hast spoken friendly unto thine handmaid, though I be not like unto one of thine handmaidens.

14 And Boaz said unto her, At mealtime come thou hither, and eat of the bread, and dip thy morsel in the vinegar. And she sat beside the reapers: and he reached her parched corn, and she did eat, and was sufficed, and left.

15 And when she was risen up to glean, Boaz commanded his young men, saying, Let her glean even among the sheaves, and reproach her not:

16 And let fall also some of the handfuls of purpose for her, and leave them, that she may glean them, and rebuke her not.

17 So she gleaned in the field until even, and beat out that she had gleaned: and it was about an ephah of barley.

18 And she took it up, and went into the city: and her mother in law saw what she had gleaned: and she brought forth, and gave to her that she had reserved after she was sufficed.

19 And her mother in law said unto her, Where hast thou gleaned to day? and where wroughtest thou? blessed be he that did take knowledge of thee. And she showed her mother in law with whom she had wrought, and said, The man's name with whom I wrought to day is Boaz.

20 And Naomi said unto her daughter in law, Blessed be he of the LORD, who hath not left off his kindness to the living and to the dead. And Naomi said unto her, The man is near of kin unto us, one of our next kinsmen.

21 And Ruth the Moabitess said, He said unto me also, Thou shalt keep fast by my young men, until they have ended all my harvest.

22 And Naomi said unto Ruth her daughter in law, It is good, my daughter, that thou go out with his maidens, that they meet thee not in any other field.

23 So she kept fast by the maidens of Boaz to glean unto the end of barley harvest and of wheat harvest; and dwelt with her mother in law.

Chapter 3

1 Then Naomi her mother in law said unto her, My daughter, shall I not seek rest for thee, that it may be well with thee?

2 And now is not Boaz of our kindred, with whose maidens thou wast? Behold, he winnoweth barley to night in the threshingfloor.

3 Wash thy self therefore, and anoint thee, and put thy raiment upon thee, and get thee down to the floor: but make not thyself known unto the man, until he shall have done eating and drinking.

4 And it shall be, when he lieth down, that thou shalt mark the place where he shall lie, and thou shalt go in, and uncover his feet, and lay thee down; and he will tell thee what thou shalt do.

5 And she said unto her, All that thou sayest unto me I will do.

6 And she went down unto the floor, and did according to all that her mother in law bade her.

7 And when Boaz had eaten and drunk, and his heart was merry, he went to lie down at the end of the heap of corn: and she came softly, and uncovered his feet, and laid her down.

8 And it came to pass at midnight, that the man was afraid, and turned himself: and, behold, a woman lay at his feet.

9 And he said, Who art thou? And she answered, I am Ruth thine handmaid: spread therefore thy skirt over thine handmaid; for thou art a near kinsman.

10 And he said, Blessed be thou of the Lord, my daughter: for thou hast showed more kindness in the latter end than at the beginning, inasmuch as thou followedst not young men, whether poor or rich.

11 And now, my daughter, fear not; I will do to thee all that thou requirest: for all the city of my people doth know that thou art a virtuous woman.

12 And now it is true that I am thy near kinsman: howbeit there is a kinsman nearer than I.

13 Tarry this night, and it shall be in the morning, that if he will perform unto thee the part of a kinsman, well; let him do the kinsman's part: but if he will not do the part of a kinsman to thee, then will I do the part of a kinsman to thee, as the Lord liveth: lie down until the morning.[2]

14 And she lay at his feet until the morning: and she rose up before one could know another. And he said, Let it not be known that a woman came into the floor.

15 Also he said, Bring the veil that thou hast upon thee, and hold it. And when she held it, he measured six measures of barley, and laid it on her: and she went into the city.

16 And when she came to her mother in law, she said, Who art thou, my daughter? And she told her all that the man had done to her.

17 And she said, These six measures of barley gave he me; for he said to me, Go not empty unto thy mother in law.

18 Then said she, Sit still, my daughter, until thou know how the matter will fall: for the man will not be in rest, until he have finished the thing this day.

Chapter 4

1 Then went Boaz up to the gate, and sat him down there: and, behold, the kinsman of whom Boaz spake came by; unto whom he said, Ho, such a one! turn aside, sit down here. And he turned aside, and sat down.

2 And he took ten men of the elders of the city, and said, Sit ye down here. And they sat down.

3 And he said unto the kinsman, Naomi, that is come again out of the country of Moab, selleth a parcel of land, which was our brother Elimelech's:

4 And I thought to advertise thee, saying, Buy it before the inhabitants, and before the elders of my people. If thou wilt redeem it, redeem it: but if thou wilt not redeem it, then tell me, that I may know: for there is none to redeem it beside thee; and I am after thee. And he said, I will redeem it.

5 Then said Boaz, What day thou buyest the field of the hand of Naomi, thou must buy it also of Ruth the Moabitess, the wife of the dead, to raise up the name of the dead upon his inheritance.

6 And the kinsman said, I cannot redeem it for myself, lest I mar mine own inheritance: redeem thou my right to thyself; for I cannot redeem it.

7 Now this was the manner in former time in Israel concerning redeeming and concerning changing, for to confirm all things; a man plucked off his shoe, and gave it to his neighbour: and this was a testimony in Israel.

8 Therefore the kinsman said unto Boaz, Buy it for thee. So he drew off his shoe.

9 And Boaz said unto the elders, and unto all the people, Ye are witnesses this day, that I have bought all that was Elimelech's, and all that was Chilion's and Mahlon's, of the hand of Naomi.

10 Moreover Ruth the Moabitess, the wife of Mahlon, have I purchased to be my wife, to raise up the name of the dead upon his inheritance, that the name of the dead be not cut off from among his brethren, and from the gate of his place: ye are witnesses this day.

11 And all the people that were in the gate, and the elders, said, We are witnesses. The LORD make the woman that is come into thine house like Rachel and like Leah, which two did build the house of Israel: and do thou worthily in Ephrathah, and be famous in Bethlehem:

12 And let thy house be like the house of Pharez, whom Tamar bare unto Judah, of the seed which the LORD shall give thee of this young woman.

13 So Boaz took Ruth, and she was his wife: and when he went in unto her, the LORD gave her conception, and she bare a son.

14 And the women said unto Naomi, Blessed be the LORD, which hath not left thee this day without a kinsman, that his name may be famous in Israel.

15 And he shall be unto thee a restorer of thy life, and a nourisher of thine old age: for thy daughter in law, which loveth thee, which is better to thee than seven sons, hath borne him.

16 And Naomi took the child, and laid it in her bosom, and became nurse unto it.

17 And the women her neighbours gave it a name, saying, There is a son born to Naomi; and they called his name Obed: he is the father of Jesse, the father of David.

18 Now these are the generations of Pharez: Pharez begat Hezron,

19 And Hezron begat Ram, and Ram begat Amminadab,

20 And Amminadab begat Nahshon, and Nahshon begat Salmon,

21 And Salmon begat Boaz, and Boaz begat Obed,

22 And Obed begat Jesse, and Jesse begat David.

HIGUCHI ICHIYO

Higuchi Ichiyo (b. 1872) is considered to be one of Japan's greatest woman writers. In a country that has produced some remarkable female literary talent over time, this is no mean honor. She was largely self-taught, and incredibly prolific, producing in her short twenty-four years of life almost 4000 classical poems, twenty-one short stories, an enormous diary, and many essays. One of the marks of her work was her capacity to depict the anguish of her characters with almost clinical perspicacity. More than many other writers of her era, she was able in her work to mix traditional literary style with forward-looking psychological and social understanding. Haunted all her life by poverty, she died in 1896 of tuberculosis. "The Thirteenth Night" was written in 1895.

The Thirteenth Night (Jūsan'ya, 1895)

Ordinarily, Oseki rode in a handsome black rickshaw, and, when her parents heard the sound of it approaching their gate, they would run out to greet her. Tonight, however, she had hired a rickshaw on the street corner. She paid the driver, sent him away, and stood dejectedly at the door to her parents' house.

Inside, she could hear her father talking in the same loud voice as always. "You could say I'm one of the lucky ones. We have good children. Never a speck of trouble when they were growing up. People are always praising them. And we've never wanted for a thing, have we? Don't think I'm not thankful."

He would be talking to her mother, then. It gave Oseki pause. How was she going to broach the question of divorce when they were so happy, so unaware of things? What a sermon there would be! She was a mother herself, and it wasn't easy, God knows, leaving little Tarō behind. It was a bit late now to be bringing her parents such startling news. The last thing she wanted was to destroy their happiness, as if it were so many bubbles on a stream. For a moment, she felt the urge to go back without saying anything. She could go on just as before — mother to Tarō, wife to Isamu — and her parents could go on boasting of a son-in-law with an imperial appointment. So long as she was careful, nothing would have to change. The little gifts of food they liked, the spending money now and then, all the filial courtesies would continue. But if she had her way and went through with the divorce, it would be the end of everything. Tarō would be miserable with a stepmother. In a single instant, her parents would lose the only reason they had to hold their heads high. There was no telling what people would think of her. And her brother's future — any basis for his success in life — would be swept away by her selfishness and her caprice. Perhaps she *should* go back home to her husband. No! She couldn't. He was inhuman, and she trembled at the thought of him and reeled against the lattice at the gate.

Inside they heard the noise. "Who's there?" her father called out. "Some urchin at the wrong house, I suppose."

But the sound outside turned to laughter. "Papa, it's me." It was a lovely voice.

"Who is it?" Her father pushed back the sliding door. "Oseki! What are you doing here? And without a rickshaw, or your maid? Hurry up — come in. What a surprise! No, we certainly weren't expecting you. Don't bother about the door, I'll get it. Let's go into the other room. We can see the moon from there. Here, use a cushion. No, no, use a cushion, the mats are dirty. I told the landlord, but he says we have to wait till the matting people can get around to making new ones. Don't be so polite with us — you'll get dirty if you don't take a cushion. Well, well, it's awfully late for you to be visiting. Is everyone all right?"

Her father treated her with the usual courtesy, and it made Oseki feel uncomfortable. She disliked it when they deferred to her as the wife of someone important.

"Yes, everyone's fine, in spite of the weather." There, she had managed to bring her emotions under control. "I'm sorry for not coming sooner. How are you?"

"I've been fine. Not so much as a sneeze. Your mother has one of her fainting spells now and then, but it's nothing to speak of. If she lies down for a few hours, it goes away." From his hearty laugh, she could tell he was in good health.

"I don't see Inosuke. Has he gone out somewhere? Still studying hard?"

"He's just left for night school. He's had a promotion, Oseki, thanks to you," her mother said ebulliently as she served the tea. "His supervisor is quite fond of him. Everything seems to be going well. It's thanks to our having Harada Isamu for a son-in-law, of course. Not a day goes by we don't acknowledge it. Ino isn't very good with words, and I know that when he sees Isamu, he probably doesn't express his gratitude as fully as he might. You know about these things, Oseki. I hope you'll let Isamu know how grateful we are to him, and always do your best to make him happy. See to it that he keeps on taking an interest in Ino. How is Tarō in this weather? This change in the seasons! I could do without it. Is he still up to his old tricks? You should have brought him with you tonight. Grandpa and I would have liked to see him."

"I thought I would, but he goes to bed so early. He was already asleep when I left. He really is full of the dickens, and he never listens to reason. When I go out, he wants to go too. He follows me around the house and keeps a good eye on me. He's a handful, all right! I don't know what makes him that way."

She felt overcome with remorse at the thought of the little son she had abandoned. In her resolve to find a new life, she had left him sleeping in his bed. He would probably be awake by now, and calling for her, giving the maids no end of trouble. No treats would placate him tonight. His nursemaid and the housekeeper would end up threatening to wash their hands of him and feed him to the devil if he didn't behave himself. "The poor thing!" she wanted to cry out. But seeing her parents in such a happy mood, she held her tongue. Instead, she took several puffs on her pipe, coughing into her sleeve to hide her tears.

"By the old calendar, it's the thirteenth night. You may think I'm old-fashioned," her mother said, "but I made some dumplings to offer to the moon, like the old moon-viewing parties. I know you like them. I thought I'd have Inosuke bring you some. But you know how self-conscious he is, he didn't want to have any part of it. So I didn't send you any on the fifteenth, and then I didn't think I ought to start in now. Still, I did want you to have some — it's like a dream, that you've come tonight. It's as if you read my mind! You must have all kinds of good things to eat at home, Oseki, but it's not often you can have your mother's cooking, is it? Let's see you eat some beans and chestnuts — you used to like them so when you were little. Tonight you can forget you're a married woman. Be your old self, don't worry about your manners.

"You know, your father and I are always talking about your success. What an extraordinary match you've made, how wonderful it is, the circles you move in, how impressive you are. But I'm sure it's not easy being the wife of someone as important as Isamu. Why, it's hard just to have people under you — maids to manage, guests to entertain. Not to mention the problem of coming from a poor family like ours. I'll bet you have to be on your toes all the time to make a good impression. Your father and I are well aware of all this. That's why we don't want to make a nuisance of ourselves, much as we would like to see more of you and little Tarō. Sometimes, you know, we pass in front of your gate, in our cotton clothes and carrying our old umbrellas, and we look up at the bamboo blinds on the second floor and wonder to ourselves what you're doing. Then we walk on by. If only your own family were a little better off, you wouldn't have to be so ashamed of us. With all your other problems, if your father and mother were from a higher station, it would be one less thing for you to worry about . . . But what good does it do to talk like this? I can't even send over any dumplings for moon-viewing without being ashamed of the box. I know how you must feel."

Delighted as she was with her daughter's visit, all too quickly the woman had recalled anew how seldom these occasions were, how little freedom she had to see her own daughter.

"I really am an undutiful child," Oseki said, as if to allay her mother's regrets about their humble station. "I may look grand dressed up in soft silks and riding in a private rickshaw, but I can't even help my own parents. I've only helped myself: I'd be much happier doing piecework and living at home with you."

"Don't be a fool!" her father said. "You should never talk that way. What married woman supports her parents? When you were here, you were our daughter. But you're married now, you're the wife of Harada Isamu. Your only responsibility is to Isamu — to make him happy and to manage his household. It's a big job, to be sure, but it was your fate to marry a man who's somebody, Oseki. You have to take the bad with the good. Women are always complaining. Your mother is the same way. What a nuisance it is. She's been irritable all day, just because she couldn't give you any of her dumplings. She's made such a fuss over those dumplings, you'd better eat them up and put her mind at ease . . . Good, aren't they?"

When her father made a joke of things, how could Oseki introduce what she had come to talk about? Dutifully, she began to eat the chestnuts and soybeans her mother had prepared.

In the seven years she had been married, Oseki had never called on them at night. For her to come alone and without a gift was completely unprecedented. Somehow, too, she did not seem quite as well dressed as usual. In their joy at seeing her, at first her parents failed to detect any difference. But she had brought not one word of greeting from their son-in-law, her smile seemed forced. It appeared that something was troubling her.

Her father glanced at the clock on the desk. "Say, it's almost ten. Is it all right for you to stay the night? If you're going back, you'd better be off pretty soon." As he watched Oseki, he tried to fathom what was on his daughter's mind.

There was no more time for pleasantries, and she looked him in the eye. "Papa, actually, I've come to ask you something. Please hear me out." Stiffly, she bowed before him. A tear trickled down her cheek. She was about to reveal now the layers of sorrow she had been keeping to herself.

Disconcerted, her father leaned forward. "What is it?"

"I came here tonight vowing never to return to Isamu. He knows nothing about it. When I put Tarō to bed, I knew I would never see him again. He won't let anyone else take care of him, but I tricked him. I waited for him to fall asleep, and then, as he dreamt, I crept away like an evil spirit. Papa! Mama! Please put yourself in my place! Until today, I've never mentioned our relations to anyone. I've had second thoughts a hundred times, a thousand times, but now my mind's made up, for once and for all. I can't go on another day like this. I must leave Isamu. Please help me. I'll take on any kind of work. I'll do anything to help Inosuke. I just want to live life alone." She burst into sobs and bit her sleeve to try to hold them back. It seemed as if the black bamboo pattern on her robe would turn purple from her tears.

"What happened?" her mother and father asked, drawing closer to Oseki.

"I haven't said anything until now, but if you could see us together for half a day, you'd understand. The only time Isamu talks to me is when he has something for me to do. And even then, he's always hostile. In the morning when he wakes up and I ask him how he slept, he turns the other way and makes a point of showing his indifference. 'The garden is doing well,' he'll say, or something like that. This alone would suffice to make me angry, but he is my husband, so I hold my temper. I've never argued with him. He starts in at me at the breakfast table, and it never stops. In front of the maids even he complains how I can't do anything right, how ill-bred I am. If that were all, I could endure it, but he never lets up. He slights me for my lack of learning. You should hear him dismiss me as 'a woman without any education.' Nobody ever said I went to school with the nobility. I admit I can't hold my own in a discussion of flower arranging or the tea ceremony or poetry or art with the wives of his friends. But if it embarrasses him so much, why doesn't he let me take some proper lessons? He doesn't have to announce publicly how lowborn I am, so that my own maids stare at me!

"You know, for the first six months or so after we were married, he was always at my side, doing everything he could for me. But as soon as Tarō was born — it's frightening how much a man can change! After that, I felt as if I'd been thrown into a dark valley, and I haven't seen the sunlight since. At first I thought he must be teasing. But then I began to understand: he had tired of me, and that was that. He bullies and bullies me in the hope that eventually I'll run away or ask for a divorce.

"Even if he were making a fool of himself over some geisha or keeping a mistress, I would control my jealousy . . . I hear rumors from the maids, but that's the way men are. When a man works as hard as Isamu, you have to expect he'll want to play sometimes. When he goes out, I lay out his clothes carefully, to please him. But no matter how hard I try, nothing I do satisfies him. The reason he doesn't spend more time at home, he says, is because I do everything so badly. I can't even seem to hold my chopsticks to suit him. If he would just tell me what it is he doesn't like, it wouldn't be so bad, but all he ever says is how boring I am, how worthless. He sneers and says he can never have a conversation with me because I don't understand anything, and that, as far as he's concerned, I'm just a wet nurse for Tarō! He's a monster, not a husband. He doesn't come right out and tell me to go away. I'm such a coward, and so attached to Tarō, that I listen to his complaints and never speak up. Then he calls me a slug and says how can he care for anyone with so little spirit or self-respect? On the other hand, if I do stand up for myself in the slightest, then he *will* tell me to go. Mama, it means nothing to me to leave him. He's a great man in name only, and I won't have a moment's regret at being divorced.

"But when I think of Tarō, who can't possibly understand any of this, left with only one parent, that's when my resolve weakens, and I go on apologizing for myself and trying to humor Isamu, and trembling at the least little thing. That's how I've lived until today — quietly enduring everything. How unlucky I've been!" In pouring out her sorrows to them, Oseki had already said much more than she had intended.

Her parents looked at each other in amazement. "We never dreamt things were like this between you."

For a while no one spoke.

Like any mother, she was partial to her children, and, the more she had listened to Oseki, the more distressed her mother felt. "I don't know what your father thinks but, in the first place, we didn't ask Isamu to marry you. What gall he has, complaining about your schooling, or your family's position! Perhaps he's already forgotten how things were, but I haven't. You were seventeen and it was New Year's when he first saw you. It was the seventh day of January, in the morning. I remember it very clearly. The pine boughs were still up on the gate. We lived in the old house then, in Sarugakuchō. You were playing badminton out in front with the little girl next door. She hit the shuttlecock into Isamu's carriage as it was passing by, and you went running after him to fetch it. Oh, he was taken with you the minute he saw you. Those go-betweens of his began arriving fast and furious. He had his heart set on you. I don't know how many times we refused. Why, we told him over and over again that our social standing was no match for his, that you were still a child, that you hadn't had the proper training yet — that, given our circumstances, we could hardly arrange for a big wedding. But he wouldn't hear of it. No, no. He had no parents, he said, so there wouldn't be any in-laws making demands to worry about. It was his choice alone, and, as far as he was concerned, no need to fret about social status or anything of the kind. As for training in the polite accomplishments, he said you could take lessons after you were married. He was so persuasive in his arguments. What care he said he'd lavish on you! We never asked him for it, but he even provided funds for your trousseau. You really were the girl of his dreams.

"The reason we don't visit you more often," her mother went on, "is certainly not because we're intimidated by Isamu's standing. You're not his mistress, after all. You're his lawful wife. He begged us for your hand. We have nothing to be embarrassed about on that account. Still, he is so successful. We live a simpler life. We're not about to start hanging onto the coattails of our son-in-law. I couldn't stand to have people think of us that way. It's not out of false pride that we want to be correct in our relations with Isamu. That's why we haven't called on you as often as we would have liked.

"How stupid of us! When he treats you like some foundling! How arrogant he is! He has no right to grumble that you're not cultivated. Oseki, if you don't protest when he criticizes you, it will only get worse. It will become a habit, this abuse of his. First of all, he shouldn't say such things in front of the maids. When a wife's authority is questioned, before you know it, none of the servants will even listen to her. And in front of Tarō! What will happen if he starts to lose respect for you? I think you should speak your mind. If Isamu won't listen, walk out. Tell him you have a family of your own to turn to. I think you've made a terrible mistake in keeping quiet until now. You're too well-mannered. He's taken advantage of that. It makes me sick, just hearing about this. There's no reason to take any more from him. I don't care what our 'status' is — you *do* have a father and mother, and a brother, even if he is still young. Why should you have to suffer like this? Isn't that so, Papa? I'd like to see Isamu once and tell him a thing or two!" In her wrath the woman had lost all perspective.

For some time, Oseki's father had been listening with arms folded and eyes closed. "Now, Mother, don't say anything rash. Hearing all this for the first time, I've been trying to think what we should do. I know Oseki wouldn't say these things without a good reason. It's plain how you've suffered. Does Isamu know you're here tonight? Was there a new flare-up?" He spoke to his daughter in measured tones. "Has he mentioned a divorce yet?"

"Isamu hasn't been home since the day before yesterday," Oseki said. "But that doesn't mean anything. Sometimes he stays away for five or six days. Before he left, he got angry with me for the way I'd laid out his clothes. I apologized profusely, but he wouldn't listen. He ripped the kimono off and flung it on the floor and changed into a suit, one he took out himself. He yelled at me as he went out. 'There couldn't be another man as unhappy as I am,' he said, 'with a woman like you for a wife!' Why is he like this to me? Three hundred and sixty-five days a year, he says almost nothing. Then, on the rare occasions when he does speak, it's to heap abuse upon me. In the face of all this, do you think I want to go on being the wife of Harada Isamu? How can I go on being Tarō's mother? How can I go on wiping the tears away year after year in secret? I don't understand why I should have to suffer so. I've finally made up my mind to forget him, and my child, too.

"You know, when I think back to the days before I was married, I have no unpleasant memories. But the way I feel now, miserable enough to abandon innocent little Tarō as he lies sleeping, I know I can't go on living with Isamu. 'A child grows up even without his parents,' they say. He might be better off without such an unfortunate mother. A stepmother or a mistress — someone who gets along with Isamu — might do Tarō more good than I can. His father might grow to like the boy. In the long run, it's for his own benefit. After tonight, I'll never set foot in Isamu's house again." She spoke bravely, but her voice quavered. It was not so easy to cast off the affection she had for her child.

"Well, no one can say you're being unreasonable," her father sighed. "I'm sure it's been hard on you. It sounds like a dreadful marriage." For a long time he studied Oseki's appearance. Almost without the father's recognizing it, his daughter had become the perfect matron: the proper hairdo fastened with a gold circlet, the black crepe jacket, it was all very tasteful. How could he watch her throw these things away? How could he let her change into a work coat, with her sleeves tied up and her hair pulled back, the better to take in washing or to tackle the scrubbing? And there was Tarō to think of. A moment's anger could dismantle a hundred years of good fortune, and she would then be the butt of ridicule. Once she went back to being the daughter of Saitō Kazue, all the laughter and tears in the world could never reinstate her as the mother of Harada Tarō. She might well have no fondness for her husband, but forgetting her child would not be so easy. After they were separated, she would find herself yearning for him more and more. She would come to long for those days when she endured the ordeal for the sake of being with Tarō. It was Oseki's misfortune to have been born so beautiful, and to have married above herself.

When he thought about her hardships, the man's pity for his daughter doubled. "Oseki, you may think I'm heartless, that I don't understand your situation. But I'm not saying any of this to scold you: when people come from different backgrounds, it's only natural their ways of thinking aren't always going to be the same. I'm sure you're doing your best to please Isamu. But that doesn't mean everything is fine and dandy — not in his eyes, anyway. Isamu is a smart man. He knows what's what. I don't think he means to be unreasonable with you. It's often the case, though: men who are hardworking and admired by the world can sometimes be very selfish. Away from home they hide their swollen heads. With their families they let their hair down; they take out all the discontent they bring home from the office. It must be terribly hard on you to be the target of all Isamu's grievances.

"On the other hand, your responsibilities as the wife of a man like Isamu are of another kind altogether. You're not married to someone in the ward office, you know — some fellow who lights the fire underneath the kettle for you and goes off to work every day with a lunch box tied to his waist. You can't compare Isamu's place in society with an ordinary office worker's. Even if he is fussy and a little difficult sometimes, it's still a wife's duty to humor her husband. You can never tell, but I'd be surprised if there are many wives who enjoy completely happy relations with their husbands. If you think you're the only one in a bind like this, Oseki, it'll only embitter you. Fact is, it's a burden many people have to bear. What with the difference in your backgrounds, it's natural you'd meet with more suffering than a wife whose husband comes from the same class.

"Your mother talks big, but remember: the fine salary your brother is making is all thanks to Isamu. They say the light a parent sheds on his child is sevenfold. In that case, the benefits we've received from Isamu must be tenfold! His way of helping out is to do things behind the scenes, but we're indebted to him nonetheless. It's trying for you, Oseki, I know. Think what your marriage means to us, though, and to Inosuke, and to Tarō. If you've been able to put up with things this long, surely you can continue. And how do you know a divorce is the answer? Isamu would have custody of Tarō, and you'd be my daughter again. Once the bonds are cut, there's no going back — even for a glimpse of little Tarō. If you're going to cry over spilt milk, you might as well do your crying as the wife of Harada. All right? Wouldn't that be better, Oseki? Get hold of yourself and go home tonight as if nothing had happened. Go on being just as careful as you have been. Even if you don't tell us anything more after this, we'll know now, we'll all understand how you feel. We'll share your tears with you." As he urged his daughter to bow to the inevitable, he too wiped a tear from his eyes.

Sobbing, Oseki gave in to his advice. "It was selfish of me to think of a divorce. You're right. If I couldn't see Tarō, there'd be no point in living. I might flee my present sorrows, but what kind of future would I have? If I could think of myself as already dead, that would solve everything . . . Then Tarō would have both his parents with him. It was a foolish idea I had, and I've troubled you with the whole unpleasant business. From tonight I will consider myself dead — a spirit who watches over Tarō. That way I can bear Isamu's cruelty for a hundred years to come. You've convinced me, Papa. Don't worry. I won't mention any of this again." No sooner had she wiped her eyes than fresh tears came.

"Poor child!" her mother sobbed.

At that moment even the bright moon looked disconsolate. Even the wild grasses in the vase, picked by her brother Inosuke from the thicket along the back bank, swayed as if to offer their sympathy.

Her parents' house was at the foot of Shinzaka in Ueno, on the road toward Surugadai. It was a shady, secluded spot. But tonight the moon shone brilliantly, and on the main street it was as light as midday. Her parents were not patrons of any of the rickshaw stations; from their window they hailed a rickshawman as he went by.

"Well, then, if you agree, Oseki, I think you'd better be off. Going out without permission while your husband's away, you'll have a lot of explaining to do. It's getting late. It won't take long by rickshaw, though. We'll come soon and talk about things. But tonight you'd best get back." Her father led her by the hand as if to drag her out. The pity he felt for Oseki did not preclude his desire to see the matter settled quietly.

Oseki was resigned to her fate. "That's the end of it, this talk. I'm going home. I'm still Harada's wife. Isamu mustn't know about tonight. Inosuke still has the backing of an important man. Don't worry. As long as you are all happy, I won't have any regrets. I won't do anything rash, so please, you mustn't worry. From now on, I'll consider myself Isamu's property. I'll do whatever he says. Well, I'd better go. Say hello to Inosuke when he comes home. Take care of yourselves. The next time, I'll come with happy news." It was apparent in the way she rose to leave that Oseki had no choice in all of this.

Taking her purse, with what little money she had, Oseki's mother went out to the rickshaw driver. "How much is it to Surugadai?"

"No, Mother. I'll pay. Thank you anyway." Her voice was subdued as she touched her sleeve to her face to brush a tear. Quietly, she passed through the front door and stepped into the rickshaw.

Inside the house, her father coughed to clear his voice, and, from the sound of it, he too was crying.

The faint cry of crickets sounded mournful in the moonglow and the autumn wind. No sooner had they reached Ueno than Oseki was given a start.

"I'm sorry," the man said, abruptly putting down the poles of the rickshaw. "I can't take you any farther. I won't charge you anything."

Oseki was astonished. "What? What am I supposed to do? I'm in a hurry. I'll pay you extra, please try. I'm not going to find another rickshaw in a lonely place like this, now, am I? Come on, do stop grumbling and take me home." She trembled slightly as she implored him.

"I'm not asking you to pay double. I'm asking you to let me stop. Please get out. I can't take you any farther. I'm too tired."

"Are you sick? What's the matter?" She began to raise her voice. "You can't just drop me here and say you're tired."

"Forgive me. I'm too tired, really." He held the lantern in his hand and stepped aside from the poles of the rickshaw.

"What a selfish man you are! All right, I won't ask you to take me all the way, just to where I can find another rickshaw. I'll pay you — at least go as far as Hirokōji." She spoke in a soft voice to cajole him.

"Well, you are a young lady. I suppose it wouldn't be very nice of me to leave you here, in this forsaken spot. It was wrong of me. All right, let's go. I'll take you there. I must have scared you."

When he picked up the lantern to be off, he did not seem so rough, and Oseki breathed a sigh of relief. Feeling safe in his charge, she looked into the man's face. He was twenty-five or -six, of dark complexion and a wiry build. He was not very tall. Wait — that face now turned away from her in the moonlight! She knew it! His name was on the tip of her tongue, but she hesitated to utter it.

"Is it you?" she asked before she knew what she was saying.

"Hm?" Surprised, he turned around to look at her.

"Goodness! It *is* you. Surely you haven't forgotten me, have you?" She slipped down from the rickshaw, never taking her eyes from him.

"Saitō Oseki? I'm ashamed for you to see me like this. How could I have known it was you — without eyes in the back of my head? I should have recognized you from your voice. I guess I've gotten pretty stupid," he said, avoiding her look.

Oseki studied him from head to toe. "No, no. If we had met walking in the street, I wouldn't have recognized you. Until just now I thought you were a stranger, only a rickshawman. Why should you have recognized me? Forgive *me*. How long have you been doing this? You're not overworking yourself, are you? You look frail. I heard somewhere that your aunt closed the shop in Ogawamachi and moved to the countryside. I'm not the person I used to be, either. Things get in the way of what we want," she sighed. "I haven't been able to visit you or even write you a letter. Where are you living now? How is your wife? Do you have children? Now and then I go to see the shops in Ogawamachi. The old store looks the same as always. It's the same tobacco shop, only it's called the Notoya now. Whenever I go by, I look at it and think to myself, 'That's where Kōsaka Roku lived when we were children.' Remember how we used to sneak a smoke on the way to school? What little know-it-alls we were! I've always wondered where you'd gone, what you were doing now. Anyone as gentle as you would be having a hard time of it. I worried about you. When I go home to see my parents, I ask if anyone's heard what became of you. It's been five years since I moved away from Sarugakuchō, and all that time I've never heard a thing. How I've missed you!" She seemed to have forgotten that she was a married woman as she deluged him with her questions.

"I'm ashamed how low I've fallen," he said as he took his towel and wiped the sweat from his forehead. "I don't even have a place I can call home any more. I sleep upstairs in a cheap inn in Asakusa run by a man named Murata. Some days I spend the whole day there, doing nothing. Some days, like tonight, I work until late pulling the rickshaw. Then when I get tired of it, I loaf again: my life's just going up in smoke. I heard that you were still as beautiful as ever, Oseki, and that you were someone's wife now. I always hoped that, by some slim chance, I'd see you again and we'd be able to talk once more. My life isn't worth anything, I didn't think it mattered what happened to me — but if I hadn't gone on living, I couldn't have met you tonight. Gosh, I'm glad you recognized me! Thank you, Oseki." He looked down at the ground.

There were tears in her eyes as Oseki tried to console him. "You're not the only one to suffer in this sad world . . . Tell me something about your wife."

"You probably knew her. She was the daughter of the Sugitas, kitty-corner from us. The one people were always complimenting for her fair skin and her pretty figure. Well, I was leading a bad life — out carousing, never coming home — which one of my pig-headed relatives mistook for proof that I ought to get married. Mother put her glasses on and began looking for candidates and soon settled on the Sugita girl. She kept pestering me, so I finally gave in. We were married just about the time I heard that you were expecting. And then, a year later, people were congratulating us. But you don't think a few baby's toys were enough to make me change my ways, do you? People think that with a pretty wife a man will stop playing around, and with a child he'll become more serious. But it wouldn't have mattered what beauty of a wife I had. Ono no Komachi, Lady Hsi Shih, Princess Sotoori herself dancing before my eyes — my bad habits wouldn't have changed. Why should a little thing that reeks of its mother's milk inspire some sort of religious awakening in a man? I fooled around to my heart's content and drank myself silly. I neglected my family, I had no use for work. It got to the point where I didn't have a chopstick to my name. That was three years ago. My mother went to live with my sister, who had

241

gone to the provinces to marry. My wife took the baby and returned to her folks. We haven't had a thing to do with each other since. The baby was a girl, anyway, so I never missed her much. I heard she died late last year of typhoid. Girls are precocious, though — I bet she didn't die without remembering her papa. If she'd lived, she would have been five this year. I don't know why I'm telling you all this, it's not really very interesting."

A smile played across his somber face. "If I'd known it was you, Oseki, I wouldn't have been so gruff tonight. Come on, get in and I'll take you home. I must have given you a good scare. You know, I'm not much of a rickshawman, even. I don't get any thrill out of clutching these poles, I'll tell you that. What does a fellow like me have to look forward to? Making a living like a horse, like some ox! You think I'm happy when I get a few coins? You think a little wine's going to drive my sorrows away? I'm really fed up with it. Who cares if I have a passenger? When I'm tired, that's it! I don't go any farther. Pretty selfish and disgusting, aren't I? Well, come on, get in."

"What! Do you think I could ride now that I know who you are? It was different when I didn't know it was you. But I will ask you to walk with me as far as Hirokōji. *Please.* I'm afraid to stay here alone. We can talk along the way." Oseki held up the bottom of her kimono as she walked. The clatter of her lacquered sandals rang despondently against the cobblestones.

Of all her friends, he was the one she had never quite forgotten: Kōsaka's boy at the tobacco stall in Ogawamachi, where everything was always ship-shape. Now his skin was dark and he looked pretty shabby, but in the old days he had cut a different figure, in his fine matched cottons and his snappy apron. What a charmer he was then! So friendly and grown-up. He was just a boy, but the store did better under him than it had when his father was alive. Everyone thought so highly of him, he was so intelligent. He had certainly changed . . . After her engagement was announced, as she remembered it, he had become another person, wild and dissipated. The decline was so extraordinary, it seemed as if some evil spirit had taken hold of him. That's what people said. And tonight he looked it. It was pitiful . . . She would never have dreamt that Kōsaka Roku would end up living in a cheap rooming house.

He had been in love with her once, and, from the time she was twelve until she was seventeen, they saw each other every day. She used to imagine what it would be like to sit behind the counter of the tobacco shop, reading the paper and waiting on customers. But then a stranger came along and asked her to marry him. Her parents pressed her, how could she defy them? She had always hoped to marry Roku, though he had never made any overtures, it was true. In the end, her parents persuaded her, and she told herself that her dreams of helping Roku run the shop were only that — the dreams of a schoolgirl, puppy love. She put him out of her mind and resigned herself to marrying Harada. It had not been easy; until the last moment, there were tears in Oseki's eyes for Kōsaka Roku. He must have yearned for her, too. Perhaps she was even the cause of his ruin. How repellent he must find it to see her tonight, looking smug and matronly. She was not as happy and contented as she might look, she wanted to tell him. She turned to him, wondering what he was thinking, but his face was blank, and he did not appear to be rejoicing in this rare encounter.

They came out into Hirokōji. Here Oseki would be able to find a rickshaw. She took some money from her purse and gently wrapped it in chrysanthemum paper. "Forgive me, Roku, for being rude," she said, offering it to him. "Please buy yourself some paper handkerchiefs or something. I haven't seen you in so long — there are so many things I'd like to say. It's hard to put them into words . . . Take good care of yourself, Roku, so your mother doesn't worry. I'll pray for you. I want to see the old Roku I used to know, with that fine shop again. Good-bye."

He took the paper from her. "I shouldn't accept this. But since it's from you, I will. As a keepsake. I hate to say good-bye to you, Oseki. It's been like a dream, seeing you again. Well, I'll be going too, then. It's lonely on the road late at night, isn't it?"

He started off with the empty rickshaw behind him, and when he had gone a little way he turned back to look at her. He was heading east; she would be going south. The branches of the willow trees trailed beside her in the moonlight as she walked, dispirited, along the main road. One living on the second floor of Murata's boardinghouse; the other, the wife of the great Harada: each knew his share of sadness in life.

ELIZABETH von ARNIM

Elizabeth von Arnim (1866-1941) was born in Australia and educated in England. A gifted pianist and organist, she initially attracted her first husband, the Prussian Count Henning August von Arnim-Schlagenthin with her elegant playing of Bach. She began her writing career with the publication in 1898 of the now famous *Elizabeth and Her German Garden,* a light and breezy picture of her life at Nassenheide, her husband's country estate in Pomerania. Elizabeth bore the Count, to whom she was devoted, five children. In 1910 he died, leaving her by her own admission in a state of inconsolable grief. But she soon rediscovered men, the most 'fatal' of her many attractions being to Francis, the second Earl Russell, whom she married in 1916 and who made her so miserable, she was compelled to run away. The plot of *Love* is based on von Arnim's own affair, at the age of 54, with a man in his mid-twenties.

Love

. . . Mrs. Mitcham, not expecting her mistress back till Monday, went on that Saturday to visit a friend in Camden Town, and when she came back soon after nine was surprised to find Miss Virginia's husband on the mat outside the door of the flat ringing the bell. He, of all people, should know her mistress wasn't there, thought Mrs. Mitcham, seeing that it was in Miss Virginia's house she was staying.

The carpet on the stairs was thick, and Mrs. Mitcham arrived at Stephen's side unnoticed. He was absorbed in ringing. He rang and rang.

"I beg your pardon, sir," said Mrs. Mitcham respectfully.

He turned quickly. "Where is your mistress?" he inquired.

"My mistress, sir?" said Mrs. Mitcham, much surprised. "I understood she was coming back on Monday, sir."

"She left the Manor this afternoon on her way home. She ought to have been here long ago. Have you had no telegram announcing her arrival?"

"No, sir."

"Well, I have," he said, looking quite upset, Mrs. Mitcham noticed, and pulling a telegram out of his overcoat pocket. "My wife telegraphed her mother had started, and asked me to see if she got here safely."

"Safely, sir?" echoed Mrs. Mitcham, surprised at the word.

"Mrs. Cumfrit was — motoring up. As you know, my wife should not be worried and made anxious just now," said Stephen frowning. "It is most undesirable — most undesirable."

"Yes, sir," said Mrs. Mitcham. "But I'm sure there is no cause. Mrs. Cumfrit will be here presently. It's not more than nine o'clock, sir."

"She left at half-past two."

"Allowing for punctures, sir — " suggested Mrs. Mitcham respectfully. "Will you come in, sir?" she added, unlocking the door and holding it open for him.

"Yes — and wait," said Stephen in a determined voice.

He went straight into the drawing-room without taking off his overcoat. That Miss Virginia's husband was upset was plain to Mrs. Mitcham. He hardly seemed like the same gentleman who had on his last visit so nicely called her and her mistress little children and told them to love one another. She was quite glad to get away from him into her calm kitchen.

Stephen was very much upset. He had received Virginia's telegram at six o'clock, just as he was quietly sitting in his hotel bedroom going over his sermons and giving them the last important touches. These were valuable hours, these afternoon and evening hours of the Saturdays before he preached, and to be taken away from them for any reason was most annoying. To be taken away from them for this one was more than annoying, it was gravely disturbing. Again that side-car; again that young man; as if a whole morning in it and with him were not sufficiently deplorable. No wonder his poor little darling at home was anxious. She said so in the telegram. It ran: *Mother left for Hertford Street in Mr. Monckton's side-car 2:30. Do see if arrived safely. Anxious.*

Two-thirty; and it was then six. He went round at once. He didn't know much about motor-cycles, but at the pace he had seen them going he judged that Monckton, not less swift than his confreres in upsetting the peace of God's countryside, would have had time to get to London.

No one, however, was in the flat, not even Mrs. Mitcham, who was bound to it by duty. He rang in vain. As he went away he inquired of the hall porter why no one was there, and learned that Mrs. Mitcham had gone out at three o'clock and had not yet returned, and that Mrs. Cumfrit had been away for the last week in the country — which he already only too well knew.

At half-past seven he called again — his sermons would suffer, he was painfully aware — but with the same result. It was dark then, and he too began to feel anxious; not on his mother-in-law's account, for whatever happened to her would be entirely her own fault, but on Virginia's. She would be in a terrible state if she knew her mother had not reached home yet. That Mrs. Mitcham should still be absent from her duties he regarded as not only reprehensible and another proof of Mrs. Cumfrit's laxness, but as a sign that she was unaware of her mistress's impending return, which was strange.

Immediately after dinner — a bad one, but if it had been good he could not have appreciated it in his then condition of mind — he went back to Hertford Street, and unable to believe, in spite of the hall porter's assurances, that the flat was still empty, rang and rang, and was found by Mrs. Mitcham ringing. His mother-in-law must be there by now. She was inside. He felt she was inside, and had gone to bed tired.

But directly he got in he knew she was not. There was a chill, a silence about the flat, such as only places abandoned by their inhabitants have. The drawing-room was as cold and tidy as a corpse. He kept his coat on. The idea of taking it off in such bleakness would not have occurred to him. He would have liked to keep his hat on too, for he had gone bald early, but the teaching of his youth on the subject of ladies' drawing-rooms and what to do in them prevented him.

Mrs. Mitcham, coming in to light the fire, found him staring out of the window in the dark. The room was only lit by the shining in of the street lamps. She was quite sorry for him. She had not supposed him so much attached to Mrs. Cumfrit. Mrs. Mitcham was herself feeling rather worried by now, and as she made Catherine's bed and got her room ready she had only kept cheerful by recollecting that a car had four tyres, all of which might puncture, besides innumerable other parts, no doubt equally able to have things the matter with them.

"I'll light the fire, if you please, sir," she said.

"Not for me," said Stephen, without moving.

She lit it nevertheless, and also turned on the light by the sofa. She didn't like to draw the curtains, because he continued to stand at the window staring into the street. Watching, thought Mrs. Mitcham; watching anxiously. She was quite touched.

"Is there anything you would like, sir?" she inquired.

"Nothing," said Stephen, his gaze riveted on the street.

Throughout that dreadful night Stephen watched at the window, and Mrs. Mitcham came in at intervals to see what she could do for him. She made coffee at eleven o'clock, and brought it to him and fetched it away again at midnight cold and untouched. She carried in an armful of blankets at one o'clock, and arranged a bed for him on the sofa, into which he did not go. At five she brought him tea, which he did not drink. At eight she began to get breakfast ready. Throughout the night he stood at the window, or walked up and down the room, and each time she saw him he seemed to have grown thinner. Certainly his face looked sharper than it had the night before. Mrs. Mitcham could not but be infected by such agitation, though being naturally optimistic she felt somehow that her mistress was delayed rather than hurt. Still, it was impossible to see a gentleman like Mr. Colquhoun, a gentleman of great learning, she had heard, who must know everything about everything and had preached in St. Paul's Cathedral — it was impossible to see such a gentleman grow thinner with anxiety before one's eyes without becoming, in spite of one's secret faith, anxious too. And the hard fact that her mistress's bed had not been slept in stared her in the face.

"I must wash," said Stephen hoarsely, when she told him breakfast was ready and would do him good.

She conducted him to the bathroom.

"I must shave," he said, looking at her with hollow eyes. "I have to preach this morning. I must go back to my hotel and shave."

"Oh no, sir," said Mrs. Mitcham; and brought him George's razors — a little blunt, but yet razors.

He stared at them. His eyes seemed to become more hollow.

"Razors?" he said. "Here?"

That there should be razors in the apartment of a widow —

"The late Mr. Cumfrit's, sir," said Mrs. Mitcham.

Of course. Really his control was gone; he was no longer apparently able to keep his thoughts from plunging into the most incredible places.

He stropped the razors, thinking of the probable last time they had been stropped by his father-in-law before being folded away by him who would never strop again, and shaved in front of the glass in the bathroom before which the excellent man must so often have stood. *Pulvis et umbra sumum* [sic], said Stephen to himself in his profound dejection, forgetting for a moment the glorious resurrection he so carefully believed in. At what point did one, he wondered, his mind returning to his troubles — at what point did one, in the circumstances in which he found himself, inform the police?

He forced himself to eat some breakfast for fear he might otherwise collapse in the pulpit, and he drank a cup of strong coffee with the same idea of being kept up. The thought that it was his own mother-in-law who had brought all this trouble on him had a peculiar sting. Quite evidently there had been an accident, and God knew how he would get through his sermon, with the fear crushing him of the effect such terrible news would have on the beloved mother of his child to be. There was no blessing, he told himself, outside the single straight path of one's duty. If his mother-in-law had continued in that path as she used to continue in it, instead of suddenly taking to giving way to every impulse — that she should still have impulses was in itself indecent — this misery for Virginia, and accordingly for himself, would have been avoided. To go rushing about the country with a young man — why, how scandalous at her age. And the punishment for this, the accident that had so evidently happened, fell most heavily, as punishments so mysteriously often did — only one must not question God's wisdom — on the innocent. What living thing in the whole world could be more innocent than his wife? Except the child; except the little soul of love she bore about with her beneath her heart; and that too would suffer through her suffering.

Stephen prayed. He couldn't bear the thought of what Virginia was going to suffer. He bowed his head on his arms and prayed. Mrs. Mitcham found him like this when she came to clear away the breakfast. She was deeply sorry for him; he seemed to have been so much more attached to her mistress than one would have ever guessed.

"You'll feel better, sir," she consoled him, "when your breakfast has had more time." And she ventured to ask, "Was it Miss Virginia's car bringing Mrs. Cumfrit up? I beg pardon, sir — I mean, your car? Because if so, I'll be bound she'll be safe with Smithers."

Stephen shook his head. He could bear no questions. He could not go into the story of the motor-cycle with Mrs. Mitcham. He felt ill after his night walking about the drawing-room; his head seemed to be bursting. He got up and left the room.

He had to go to the hotel on his way to St. Jude's to fetch his sermon. He waited till the last possible minute, still hoping that some news might come; and then, when he dared wait no longer, and Mrs. Mitcham was helping him into his coat, he told her he would come back immediately after morning service and consider what steps should be taken as to informing the police.

"The police?" repeated Mrs. Mitcham, much shocked. The police and her mistress. Out of her heart disappeared the last ray of optimism.

"We must somehow find out what has happened," said Stephen sharply.

"Yes, sir," said Mrs. Mitcham, opening the door for him.

The police and her mistress. She had a feeling that the mere putting the police on to search would make them find something dreadful — that if nothing had happened, the moment they began to look something would have happened.

Feeling profoundly conscious of being only a weak woman in a world full of headstrong men, she opened the door for Stephen, and he, going through it without further speech, met Catherine coming out of the lift — Catherine perfectly sound and unharmed — and with her was Christopher.

They all three stopped dead.

"You, Stephen?" said Catherine after a moment, very faintly. "Why, how — ?"

"I have," said Stephen, "been waiting all night. Waiting and watching for you."

"I — we — broke down."

He made a sign to the lift boy that he was coming down with him.

"Enough — enough," he said, with a queer gesture of pushing her and everything connected with her out of his sight; and hurried into the lift and disappeared.

Catherine and Christopher looked at each other.

That was an awful day for Stephen.

Men have found out, with terrible pangs, that their wives, whom they regarded as models of blamelessness, were secretly betraying their homes and families, but Stephen could not recall any instance of a man's finding this out about his wife's mother. It was not, he supposed, quite so personally awful as if it were one's wife, but on the other hand it had a peculiar awfulness of its own. A young woman might descend declivities, impelled by the sheer momentum of youth; but for women of riper years, for the matrons, for the dowager, for those whose calm remaining business in life is to hold aloft the lantern of example, whose pride it should be to be quiet, to be immobile, to be looked-up to and venerated — for these to indulge in conduct that disgraced their families and ruined themselves was, in a way, even more horrible. In any woman of riper years it was horrible and terrible. In this one — what it was to this one was hardly to be uttered, for she — ah, ten times horrible and terrible — was his own mother-in-law.

He preached his sermon mechanically, with no sense of what he was reading, never lifting his eyes from his manuscript. The dilapidated pair — they had looked extraordinarily dilapidated as they stood there, guilty and caught, in the unsparing light of Sunday morning — floated constantly before him, and made it impossible for him to attend to a word he was saying.

What was he to do next? How could he ever face Virginia, and answer her anxious, loving questions about her mother's safety? It must be kept from her, the appalling, the simply unutterable truth; at all costs it must be kept from her in her present condition, or it well might kill her. He felt he must tell his mother, for he could not bear this burden alone, but no one else must ever know what he knew. It would be the first secret between him and Virginia, and what a secret!

His thoughts whirled this way and that, anywhere but where he was, while his lips read out what he had written in those days last week of innocent peace, that now seemed so far away, about Love. Love! What sins, thought Stephen, were committed in its name. Incredible as it was, almost impossible to imagine at their different ages, and shocking to every feeling of decency and propriety, the word had probably frequented the conversations of those two.

He shuddered away. There were some things one simply could not think of. And yet he did think of them; they haunted him, "We broke down," she had said. Persons in her position always said that. He was man of the world enough to know what that meant. And then their faces — their startled, guilty faces, when they found him so unexpectedly confronting them.

"*Love,*" read out Stephen from his manuscript, quoting part of his text and with mechanically uplifted hand and emphasis impressing it on his congregation, "*thinketh no evil. . . .*"

After the service he went straight back to Hertford Street. Useless to flinch from his duty. His first impulse that morning, and he had followed it, was to remove himself at once from contact with his mother-in-law. But he was a priest; he was her nearest living male relative; he was bound to do something.

He went straight back to Hertford Street, and found her in the dining-room quietly eating mutton.

It had always seemed grievous to Stephen, and deeply to be regretted, that no traces of sin should be physically visible on the persons of the sinners, that a little washing and tidying should be enough to make them indistinguishable from those who had not sinned. Here was this one, looking much the same as usual, very like any other respectable quiet lady at her Sunday luncheon, eating mutton as though nothing had happened. At such a crisis, he felt, at such an overwhelming moment of all their lives, of his, of hers, of his dear love's, whitely unconscious at home, whatever his mother-in-law did it ought anyhow not to have been that.

She looked up when he came in, walking in unannounced, putting Mrs. Mitcham aside when she tried to open the door for him.

"I'm glad you've come back. Stephen," she said, leaning forward and pushing out the chair on her right hand for him to sit on — as though he would dream of sitting! — "I want to tell you what happened."

He took no notice of the chair, and stood facing her at the end of the table, leaning on it with both hands, their thin knuckles white with his heavy pressure.

"Won't you sit down?" she said.

"No."

"Have you had lunch?"

"No."

"Will you have some?"

"No."

There was nothing for it, Catherine knew, but to face whatever music Stephen should make, but she did think he might have said "No, thank you." Still, her position was very weak, so she accepted his monosyllables without comment. Besides — poor Stephen — he did look wretchedly upset; he must have had a dreadful night.

She was very sorry for him, and began to tell him what had happened, how the petrol had run out just when they were in that bare stretch of country between Salisbury and Andover —

Stephen raised his hand. "Spare me all this," he said. "Spare me and yourself."

"There's nothing to spare," said Catherine. "I assure you I don't mind telling you what happened."

"You should *blush*," said Stephen, leaning forward on his knuckles. "You should *blush*."

"Blush?" she repeated.

"Do you not know that you are fatally compromised?"

"My dear Stephen — "

He longed to forbid her to call him by that name.

"Fatally," he said.

"My dear Stephen, don't be ridiculous. I know it was most unfortunate that I shouldn't get back till this morning — "

"Unfortunate!"

"But who will ever hear about it? And I couldn't help it. You don't suppose I *liked* it?"

Then, as she said the words, the remembrance of herself being kept warm in Christopher's arms, and of him softly kissing her eyes, came back to her. Yes; she had liked that. Yes; she knew she had liked that, and been happy.

A deep red flooded her face even as she said the words, and she lowered her eyes.

Stephen saw; and any faint hope he had had that her story might be true went out. His soul seemed to drop into a pit of blackness. She was guilty. She had done something unthinkable. Virginia's mother. It was horror to be in the same room with her.

"This thing," he said in a low voice, his eyes wide open and blazing, as though he indeed beheld horror, "must be made good somehow. There is only one way. It is a shame, a shame to have to utter it in connection with a boy of his age and a woman of yours, but the only thing left for you to do is to marry him."

"Marry him?"

She stared at him, her mouth open in her amazement.

"Nothing else will save you, either from man's condemnation or God's punishment."

"Stephen," she said, "are you mad?" — that *he* should be urging her to marry Christopher! — "Why should I do anything of the sort?"

"Why? You ask me why? Am I to suffer the uttermost shame, and be forced to put into words what you have done?"

"You are certainly mad, Stephen," said Catherine, trying to keep her head up, but terribly handicapped, she being of so blameless a life that the least speck on it was conspicuous and looked to her enormous, by the memory of those dimly felt kisses.

If only she had trudged all night in the mud, trudged on, however much exhausted she had been, she could have faced Stephen with the proper indignation of virtue unjustly suspected; but there were those hours asleep, folded warm in Christopher's arms, and through her sleep the consciousness of his kisses. She would probably have been very ill if she had trudged all night, but she could have held up her head and ordered Stephen out of her presence. As it was, her head wouldn't hold up, and Stephen was as certain as if he had seen the pair in some hotel that there had been no breakdown, and his mother-in-law was lying.

Hideous, he thought; too hideous. So hideous that one couldn't even pray about it, for to speak about such matters to God . . .

"I have nothing more to say," he said slowly, his face as cold and hard as frozen rock, "except that unless you marry him you will never be allowed to see my wife again. But the *disgrace* of such a marriage — the *disgrace* — "

She stared at him, pale now.

"But Stephen — " she began.

She stared at him, across the absurd mutton, the mutton he had felt was so incongruous, gone cold and congealed on its dish. This silliness, this madness, this determination to insist on sin! She might have laughed if she had not been so angry; she might have laughed, too, if it had not been for the awkward, the mortifying memory of those kisses; she might, even so, have laughed, if he had not had the power to cut her off from Virginia. But he had the power — he, the stranger she had let in to her gates when she could so easily have been ungenerous and shut him out. Why, it wouldn't even have been ungenerous, but merely prudent. Three years more of freedom she would have gained, of freedom from him and possession of her child, by just saying one word. And she hadn't said it. She had let him in. And here he was with power to destroy her.

She looked at him, very pale. "It's at least a mercy, then," she said, her eyes full of bright tears of indignation at the injustice, the cruelty of the man she had made so happy, "that I love Christopher."

"You love him!" repeated Stephen, appalled by the shamelessness of such a confession.

"Yes," said Catherine. "I love him very much. He loves me so much, and I find it impossible — I find it impossible — "

Her voice faltered, but with a great effort she got it steady again, and went on, "I find it impossible not to love people who are good, if they love me."

"You dare," said Stephen, "to mention love? You dare to use that word in connection with this boy and yourself?"

"But would you have me marry him and not love him?"

"It is shameful," said Stephen, beside himself at what seemed to him her ghastly effrontery, "that some one so much older should even think of love in connection with some one so much younger."

"But what, then," said Catherine, "about you and Virginia?"

It was the first time she had ever alluded to it. The instant she had said it she was sorry. Always she had rather be hurt than hurt, rather be insulted than insult.

He looked at her a moment, his thin face white with this last outrage. Then he turned, and went away without a word. . . .

JAMES C. McBRIDE

James C. McBride was born in 1957. His father was a Baptist minister, his mother the daughter of an Eastern European rabbi who had settled in the South. McBride was raised in Brooklyn and Queens by his mother and stepfather. (His father died before he was born.) Beyond his career in journalism (writing freelance, and for the *Washington Post* and the *Boston Globe*), he has also worked as a professional musician, playing jazz saxophone and composing. *The Color of Water* was published in 1996.

The Color of Water: A Black Man's Tribute to His White Mother

A Jew Discovered

It was afternoon, August 1992, and I was standing in front of the only synagogue in downtown Suffolk, a collection of old storefronts, dimly lit buildings, and old railroad tracks that tell of better, more populous times. It's a small, old, white building with four tall columns and a row of stairs leading to a tall doorway. This is the synagogue that young Rachel Shilsky walked to with her family and where Rabbi Shilsky led the congregation during the Jewish holidays Rosh Hashana, the Jewish New Year, and Yom Kippur, the day of atonement and fasting. When I was a boy, Jewish holidays meant a day off from school for me and that was it. I certainly had no idea they had anything to do with me.

I felt like an oddball standing in front of the quiet, empty building, and looked up and down the street every couple of minutes lest the cops come by and wonder why a black man was loitering in front of a white man's building in the middle of the day in Suffolk, Virginia. This is, after all, the nineties, and any black man who loiters in front of a building for a long time looking it over is bound to draw suspicion from cops and others who probably think he's looking for an open entrance so he can climb in and steal something. Black males are closely associated with crime in America, not with white Jewish mothers, and I could not imagine a police officer buying my story as I stood in front of the Jewish temple saying, "Uh, yeah, my grandfather was the rabbi here, you know . . ." The sun was baking the sidewalk and it was so hot I sat down on the steps, placing my tape recorder and notebook next to me. . . .

I wanted to see the inside of the synagogue. I wanted to see it, then later tell my black wife and my two children about it — because some of my blood runs through there, because my family has a history there, because there's a part of me in there whether I, or those that run the synagogue, like it or not. In truth, I had never been inside an actual synagogue before, the closest being the time I was working as a reporter and did a story about a Jewish school in Queens that had a synagogue attached to it. In the course of interviewing the headmaster, a woman, I mentioned that my mother was Jewish and she exclaimed, "Well, according to Jewish law that means you're Jewish too! We have a black Jew who works in our school!" She hit the intercom button on her desk phone and said, "Sam, can you come up here a minute?" Minutes later the black janitor walked in, holding a mop, smiling. I'd pay good money for a picture of my face at that moment. Ol' Sam smiled and said hello and I gurgled out a polite response, though I wanted to choke myself for opening up my big mouth.

When I called the rabbi of my mother's old synagogue he spoke to me with neither nostalgia nor surprise, only grudging recognition. He had heard I was in town from other Jews whom I had met. He knew I was black and he knew who my mother was. "I remember your mother," he said. I explained to him that I was writing a book about my family and asked if I might see some of the synagogue records. "There's nothing in them that would help you," he said curtly. I asked if I could see the inside of the synagogue itself. He said, "I'll have to check with some other board members to see who would have time to open it up to let you see it," and hung up. I knew the deal. Given the photo of the board members on the synagogue's anniversary pamphlet I'd obtained, I doubted if half the old geezers on the board were still drawing air. I hung up, muttering to myself, "I didn't want to see your silly old synagogue anyway."

By then I had seen enough anyway. The smell of azaleas and the creeping loneliness that climbed over me as I poked around Suffolk had begun to suffocate me. The isolation my family had felt, the heartbreak they had suffered, seemed to ooze out of the trees, curling through the stately old brick buildings and rising like steam off the Civil War statue that seemed to point its cannon directly at me as I wandered through the town graveyard. I wanted to leave right at that moment, but instead sat on the synagogue steps as if glued, as my mind reeled back to a previous trip in 1982, when fate and luck led me deep into the bowels of a state office building where Aubrey Rubenstein was working for the highway department right-of-way office. Rubenstein was in his early sixties then, a heavyset man with dark hair, a deep southern accent, and a very clear and concise manner. His father had taken over my grandfather's store around 1942 after the old man left town. When I walked into his office and explained who I was, he looked at me a long, long time. He didn't smile. He didn't frown. Finally he spoke: "What a surprise," he said softly. He offered me a seat and a cup of coffee. I accepted. "Don't move from there," he said.

He got on the phone. "Jaffe," he said, "I have incredible news. Fishel Shilsky's grandson is here. Sitting in my office. No kidding. . . . Uh-huh. And you won't believe it. He's black. No. I'm not lying. He's a reporter writing a book about his family. . . . Yep." When he hung up the phone, he said, "When we're done, go around to the slaughterhouse on Main and see Gerry Jaffe and his family. They'd like to see you in person." I knew the name Jaffe. Mommy had spoken of them several times. *The Jaffes had a slaughterhouse down the road. Tateh would take us there to slaughter the cows in the kosher faith. . . .* I made it a point to go see them. Like most of the Jews in Suffolk they treated me very kindly, truly warm and welcoming, as if I were one of them, which in an odd way I suppose I was. I found it odd and amazing when white people treated me that way, as if there were no barriers between us. It said a lot about this religion — Judaism — that some of its followers, old southern crackers who talked with southern twangs and wore straw hats, seemed to believe that its covenants went beyond the color of one's skin. The Sheffers, Helen Weintraub, the Jaffes, they talked to me in person and by letter in a manner and tone that, in essence, said "Don't forget us. We have survived here. Your mother was part of this. . . ."

Sitting in his office, Aubrey Rubenstein talked easily, as a black colleague sat nearby eavesdropping with awe at the macabre conversation that unfolded between this elderly white man and myself. "There are not that many of us left," Aubrey said. "We had maybe twenty-five or thirty Jewish families here at one time, back when your grandfather was around. The older ones died, the younger ones left. Some went to California, some to Virginia Beach, or just moved. The only ones who stayed had businesses with their fathers that dropped down to them."

"Why did they all leave?" I asked.

"Why stay?" he said. "It was not that easy a place for a Jew to live. It was a tiny population of Jews. Most were merchants of one type or another. I suppose some found it easier to make a living elsewhere." Wandering Jews, I thought.

We spoke easily for quite a while. "It's an interesting thing that you've come down to check on your granddaddy," he said. "It's quite a story, I must say."

I asked him about my family. "Well, it was kind of a tragedy, really. Shilsky wasn't the man he could have been. He was a good rabbi — by that I mean he knew what he was teaching. In fact, he taught me a little as a boy. But he went into business full-time, which didn't please a lot of Jews here, and he was seeing another woman for years. I'm not sure whether he was divorced when he left here or not, but I ran into him in New York after the war, maybe '46. Me and another fella went to see him about buying the piece of property next door to his store. He was up in Brooklyn."

"What was he doing there?"

"I don't know. But I believe Mrs. Shilsky had died by then. The whole thing was very tragic." Seeing the expression on my face, he added, "Your grandmother was a fine lady. I still remember her coming to temple, lighting the candles, and standing up to say her prayers. I remember her clearly. She was crippled in the leg. She was a very fine lady."

I asked him if anyone knew how Rabbi Shilsky treated his family, and Rubenstein shrugged.

"There are things that you hear, but no one asked. He was tight with his money and they could have been doing better than they looked. The Shilskys kept to themselves. Your Uncle Sam, he joined the air force and got killed in a plane crash in Alaska. They didn't find his body or that of the other pilot for a long time, if they ever did find them. I heard this and don't know it to be true or not. Your Aunt Gladys, you don't know her, do you? She was a very bright girl. Your mother . . . well, she was a fine girl. Of course we had heard rumors, and I'm being frank, that she had run off and married a black man, but I never knew it to be true or not. My daddy at one time said it, but my parents never gave it any further comment. My father and mother were like liberals in their days. I never heard them knock anybody for being white or black or green or Christian or Jew or Catholic."

I said nothing, listening in silence. I imagined that the news of Mommy's marriage crashed through the Jewish community like an earthquake.

"How is your mother?" he asked.

"Fine."

"You know," he said, fingering the papers on his desk, "you look a little bit like your mother. The smile. Do you attend temple, being part Jewish?"

"No. She didn't raise us Jewish."

"Well, maybe that was for the best," he said.

I was surprised by his candidness and said so.

We talked for a while longer before I rose to go. "Next time you come back I'll see if I can dig up a picture of that old store," he said. "Make sure to tell your mother Aubrey Rubenstein said hello."

I pointed to my tape player on his desk. "The tape is running," I said. "You can say it yourself."

He leaned over to the tape and spoke into it softly. When he was done, he leaned back in his chair, and looked at the ceiling thoughtfully. "She picked that life for herself and she lived it, that's all. What her reasons for it were I don't know. But she did a good job. She raised twelve children. She led a good life."

I told him I'd be back in a few months. "I'll have a picture of that store for you," he promised. But I waited ten years to come back, and when I called on him again he had died. I kept the tape with his greeting to Mommy on it for years, and while I never played it for her, thinking it might be too emotional for her to hear it, I played it for myself many times, thinking, wishing, hoping that the world would be this open-minded, knowing that God is: *Ruth, this is Aubrey Rubenstein. I don't know if you remember me or not, but if you do, I'm glad to meet your son and I see you've accomplished a great deal in your life. If you're ever down this way stop on by and say hello to us. We all remember you. We wish you the best.*

As I sat on the steps of the synagogue in the hot August sun, his words sliced through my memory like raindrops. I watched as two little black girls strode by, waved, and walked on. One was eating a bag of potato chips. I said to myself, "Whatever I'm looking for, I've found it." I got in my car and drove back to the McDonald's where the store had been. I walked around the grounds once again, as if the earth would speak to me. But it did not. It was just a cement parking lot. They ought to take the whole kit and caboodle of these cement parking lots and heave them into the sea, I thought. The Shilskys were gone. Long gone.

That night I slept in a motel just down the road from the McDonald's, and at about four in the morning I sat straight up. Something just drew me awake. I tossed and turned for an hour, then got dressed and went outside, walking down the road toward the nearby wharf. As I walked along the wharf and looked over the Nansemond River, which was colored an odd purple by the light of the moon, I said to myself, "What am I doing here? This place is so lonely. I gotta get out of here." It suddenly occurred to me that my grandmother had walked around here and gazed upon this water many times, and the loneliness and agony that Hudis Shilsky felt as a Jew in this lonely southern town — far from her mother and sisters in New York, unable to speak English, a disabled Polish immigrant whose husband had no love for her and whose dreams of seeing her children grow up in America vanished as her life drained out of her at the age of forty-six — suddenly rose up in my blood and washed over me in waves. A penetrating loneliness covered me, lay on me so heavily I had to sit down and cover my face. I had no tears to shed. They were done long ago, but a new pain and a new awareness were born inside me. The uncertainty that lived inside me began to dissipate; the ache that the little boy who stared in the mirror felt was gone. My own humanity was awakened, rising up to greet me with a handshake as I watched the first glimmers of sunlight peek over the horizon. There's such a big difference between being dead and alive, I told myself, and the greatest gift that anyone can give anyone else is life. And the greatest sin a person can do to another is to take away that life. Next to that, all the rules and religions in the world are secondary; mere words and beliefs that people choose to believe and kill and hate by. My life won't be lived that way, and neither, I hope, will my children's. I left for New York happy in the knowledge that my grandmother had not suffered and died for nothing.

5 How Do We Handle Money?

Remember it's as easy to marry a rich woman as a poor woman.

— WILLIAM THACKERAY

Be sure, before you marry, of a house wherein to tarry.

— PROVERB

Introduction

Building up households and bank accounts is an important part of marriage. But economic prosperity, while nice to boast, is certainly not the be-all and end-all of marital success. In fact, two economists — David Blanchower of Dartmouth College and Andrew Oswald of Warwick University in Britain, have managed to put a price on marital satisfaction which challenges the idea that money brings happiness in and of itself. If happiness can be measured in dollars, being happily married, they say, is as good as having an extra $100,000 a year in your bank account. This means that in order to be as happy as the poorest happily married man or woman (someone with $0 in yearly income), a single person would theoretically have to earn a salary of $100,000.

Many married people believe that they can avoid disagreements over money by keeping finances separate. But though prenuptial agreements and separate bank accounts are becoming ever more common, marriage in Western society presumes the management of a common household. Thereby it also presumes a great deal of cooperation in money matters. Wise management of finances in marriage does not only bolster one's marital stability; it protects children, and benefits society at large. Nobody, as yet, has calculated the enormous economic costs of divorce and single childbearing, comparing them with the economic value of stable families. We do know, however, that a stably married man or woman tends to accumulate far more wealth over a lifetime than a man or woman who has remained single or who has divorced. This, despite the fact that children today are no longer, as they were in pre-industrial society, an economic boon to the married couple, but rather a substantial economic burden.[1]

Perhaps the healthiest way married couples can handle money is to look beyond the play of finances in their own relationship, and beyond the financial cares of everyday life. Marriage has a larger economic function in society than simply the material welfare of the nuclear family. Aristotle, for example, looks to the household economy as the ultimate source of societal health and to competent household management as a model of virtue in government. In fact, the word "economy" stems from the word for household — *oikonomia*. For the Greeks, the family and its household were a microcosm for the larger community. Where households were productive, prosperous, and happy, household leadership was bound to be just. In the first selection of this chapter, from the *Politics*, Aristotle subtly argues the dignity and humanity of every member of the household, even the slave. He elucidates the importance of virtuous household government in the proper employment and preservation of both animate and inanimate resources. It should be noted that in his patriarchal world, there was no real notion of equality between husband and wife. Rather, each had rights and obligations that were proportionate to their position of honor and respect, with the husband clearly the head of the household. But while Aristotle's household comprises ruler and ruled, each "subordinate," or "instrument" of the household economy is intrinsically valued; that is, it is employed respectfully and judiciously for the benefit of all.

We find another ode to the household economy as the basis of civic health in the Bible's famous Proverb of the "virtuous woman." Here the mistress of the house is praised as the bulwark of society because of her profound contributions to the family in both business and the domestic arts. "The heart of her husband doth safely trust in her," the Proverb says. Does managing the affairs of the household while her husband sits "with the elders of the land" mean that the good wife is a second-class citizen — silently laboring while her husband grandstands? No. She, too, "openeth her mouth with wisdom." Her labor is "praised in the gates," her opinions taken as seriously as her husband's.

The fifth-century poem by Hsü Chün-Ch'ien that follows the excerpt from Proverbs concerns a husband who proudly admires his wife's fashionable raiment, both as a reflection of her deeper attractions, and as a reflection of the prosperity they enjoy together. Here, one has the feeling that prosperity *is* directly related to marital fulfillment. And why shouldn't it be? Should not couples who achieve financial security rejoice in it?

In fact, money may not be everything in a marriage, but married couples must live on something besides love. In her great novels of courtship, Jane Austen often waxed facetious about marriages of convenience. But she also appreciated their occasional necessity. The reading from *Pride and Prejudice* here concerns a woman who accepts a proposal of marriage solely on considerations of material comfort. Charlotte Lucas is not a fortune hunter. But she resolves to marry the boring and pompous Mr. Collins because he can provide her much needed financial security, and because at the age of twenty-seven, she is unlikely to get a better offer. Can such a marriage succeed? Chances are it will, because Charlotte is entering it with a generous will and open eyes. Indeed, her pragmatic criteria for mate-selection have lowered her expectations of the married state to a degree where she may ultimately be more content with her lot than many a girl who has been swept off her feet into an economically imprudent union.

The next reading, from John Milton's classic poem, *Paradise Lost,* touches on the ultimate meaning of the household economy. When husbands and wives work as a team to build and tend their fortunes, they fortify themselves against innumerable dangerous temptations — both material and moral. When they work at cross-purposes, however, they leave themselves open to temptation.

This excerpt finds Eve insisting that there is no reason she and Adam must always pursue their labors in the Garden of Eden together. She wishes to work alone; he should also pursue his chores independently. Adam, on the other hand, urges his wife to remain at his side. Eve chides Adam for his lack of faith in her intelligence and fortitude. Though she's his wife, their lives a unity, Adam cannot refuse her. She has, after all, free will. We know the end of the story. It is, of course, in the very moment of separation that Eve is approached by the serpent. Perhaps husbands and wives *do* need to plan and manage their wealth together, just as they should manage all other aspects of their lives together. For without unity of purpose, they may end up squandering their blessings.

Finally, a selection from cultural anthropologist Bronislaw Malinowski, who reminds us that while marriage in most societies involves the establishment of a common household, a common household is not a central feature of the institution of marriage in every culture. If we were to define marriage across cultures, we could presume the institution to carry no other universal purpose than the establishment of legitimacy of birth. In fact, in some matrilineal societies, not only is there no common marital home, but husbands are economically "superfluous." While Malinowski allows that in all cultures, marriages help tie communities together in ways that foster economic production and prosperity, his observations remind us that whatever the tie of marriage to the household economy in Western society, the institution of marriage performs a universal social function well beyond the economic.

ARISTOTLE

The Greek philosopher Aristotle (384-322 B.C.) was a student of Plato and tutor to Alexander the Great. His surviving work is mostly composed of notes his students took on the lectures he gave in the Lyceum of Athens between 335 and 323 B.C. Aristotle's interests were sweeping, comprising the fields of natural science, metaphysics, ethics, politics, and the arts. He is considered the founder of the scientific method in that he stated that any knowledge or theory about nature must derive from observation. *The Politics* reflects Aristotle's attempt to establish reason as the basis of human governance. Aristotle believed that the greatest human virtue lay in the use of man's rational faculties.

The Politics, Book I

Chapter 3

(1) Since it is evident out of what parts the city is constituted, it is necessary first to speak of household management; for every city is composed of households. The parts of household management correspond to the parts out of which the household itself is constituted. Now the complete household is made up of slaves and free persons. Since everything is to be sought for first in its smallest elements, and the first and smallest parts of the household are master, slave, husband, wife, father, and children, three things must be investigated to determine what each is and what sort of thing it ought to be. (2) These are expertise in mastery, in marital [rule] (there is no term for the union of man and

268

woman), and thirdly in parental [rule] (this too has not been assigned a term of its own). (3) So much, then, for the three we spoke of. There is a certain part of it, however, which some hold to be [identical with] household management, and others its greatest part; how the matter really stands has to be studied. I am speaking of what is called business expertise.

Let us speak first about master and slave, so that we may see at the same time what relates to necessary needs and whether we cannot acquire something in the way of knowledge about these things that is better than current conceptions. (4) For some hold that mastery is a kind of science, and that managing the household, mastery, and expertise in political and kingly [rule] are the same, as we said at the beginning. Others hold that exercising mastery is against nature; for [as they believe] it is by law that one person is slave and another free, there being no difference by nature, and hence it is not just, since it rests on force.

Chapter 4

(1) Now possessions are a part of the household, and expertise in acquiring possessions a part of household management (for without the necessary things it is impossible either to live or to live well); and just as the specialized arts must of necessity have their proper instruments if their work is to be performed, so too must the expert household manager. (2) Now of instruments some are inanimate and others animate — the pilot's rudder, for example, is an inanimate one, but his lookout an animate one; for the subordinate is a kind of instrument for the arts. A possession too, then, is an instrument for life, and one's possessions are the multitude of such instruments; and the slave is a possession of the animate sort. Every subordinate, moreover, is an instrument that wields many instruments, (3) for if each of the instruments were able to perform its work on command or by anticipation, as they assert those of Daedalus did, or the tripods of Hephaestus (which the poet says "of their own accord came to the gods' gathering"), so that shuttles would weave themselves and picks play the lyre, master craftsmen would no longer have a need for subordinates, or masters for slaves. . . .

A possession is spoken of in the same way as a part. A part is not only part of something else, but belongs wholly to something else; similarly with a possession. Accordingly, while the master is only master of the slave and does not belong to him, the slave is not only slave to the master but belongs wholly to him.

(6) What the nature of the slave is and what his capacity, then, is clear from these things. For one who does not belong to himself by nature but is an-

269

other's, though a human being, is by nature a slave; a human being is another's who, though a human being, is a possession; and a possession is an instrument of action and separable [from its owner].

Chapter 12

(1) Since there are three parts of expertise in household management — expertise in mastery, which was spoken of earlier, expertise in paternal [rule], and expertise in marital [rule] — [the latter two must now be taken up. These differ fundamentally from the former, since one ought] to rule a wife and children as free persons, though it is not the same mode of rule in each case, the wife being ruled in political, the children in kingly fashion. For the male, unless constituted in some respect contrary to nature, is by nature more expert at leading than the female, and the elder and complete than the younger and incomplete. (2) In most political offices, it is true, there is an alternation of ruler and ruled, since they tend by their nature to be on an equal footing and to differ in nothing; all the same, when one rules and the other is ruled, [the ruler] seeks to establish differences in external appearance, forms of address, and prerogatives. . . . The male always stands thus in relation to the female. (3) But rule over the children is kingly. For the one who generates is ruler on the basis of both affection and age, which is the very mark of kingly rule. Homer thus spoke rightly of Zeus when he addressed as "father of men and gods" the king of them all. For by nature the king should be different, but he should be of the same stock; and this is the case of the elder in relation to the younger and the one who generates to the child.

Chapter 13

(1) It is evident, then, that household management gives more serious attention to human beings than to inanimate possessions, to the virtue of these than that of possessions (which we call wealth), and to the virtue of free persons rather than that of slaves. (2) First, then, one might raise a question concerning slaves: whether there is a certain virtue belonging to a slave besides the virtues of an instrument and a servant and more honorable than these, such as moderation and courage and justice and the other dispositions of this sort, or whether there is none besides the bodily services. (3) Questions arise either way, for if there is [such a virtue], how will they differ from free persons? But if there is not, though they are human beings and participate in reason, it is odd. Nearly the

same question arises concerning a woman and a child, whether there are virtues belonging to these as well — whether the woman should be moderate and courageous and just, and whether a child is [capable of being] licentious and moderate or not. (4) And in general, then, this must be investigated concerning the ruled by nature and the ruler, whether virtue is the same or different. For if both should share in gentlemanliness, why should the one rule and the other be ruled once and for all? For it is not possible for them to differ by greater and less, since being ruled and ruling differ in kind, not by greater and less; (5) but that one should [have such virtue] and the other not would be surprising. For unless the ruler is moderate and just, how will he rule finely? And unless the ruled is, how will he be ruled finely? For if he is licentious and cowardly he will perform none of his duties. It is evident, then, that both must of necessity share in virtue, but that there are differences in their virtue, as there are in [that of] those who are by nature ruled. (6) Consideration of the soul guides us straightway [to this conclusion]. For in this there is by nature a ruling and a ruled element, and we assert there is a different virtue of each — that is, of the element having reason and of the irrational element. It is clear, then, that the same thing holds in the other cases as well. Thus by nature most things are ruling and ruled. (7) For the free person rules the slave, the male the female, and the man the child in different ways. The parts of the soul are present in all, but they are present in a different way. The slave is wholly lacking the deliberative element; the female has it but it lacks authority; the child has it but it is incomplete. (8) It is to be supposed that the same necessarily holds concerning the virtues of character: all must share in them, but not in the same way, but to each in relation to his own work. Hence the ruler must have complete virtue of character (for a work belongs in an absolute sense to the master craftsman, and reason is a master craftsman); while each of the others must have as much as falls to him. (9) It is thus evident that there is a virtue of character that belongs to all these mentioned, and that the moderation of a woman and a man is not the same, nor their courage or justice, as Socrates supposed, but that there is a ruling and a serving courage, and similarly with the other virtues.

PROVERBS

Traditionally the Proverbs have been attributed to King Solomon. But scholars think this broad collection of Biblical wise sayings was compiled over a long period of time, some of the Proverbs dating back as far as the tenth century B.C.

Proverbs 31

1 The words of king Lemuel, the prophecy that his mother taught him.
2 What, my son? and what, the son of my womb? and what, the son of my vows?
3 Give not thy strength unto women, nor thy ways to that which destroyeth kings.
4 It is not for kings, O Lemuel, it is not for kings to drink wine; nor for princes strong drink:
5 Lest they drink, and forget the law, and pervert the judgment of any of the afflicted.
6 Give strong drink unto him that is ready to perish, and wine unto those that be of heavy hearts.
7 Let him drink, and forget his poverty, and remember his misery no more.
8 Open thy mouth for the dumb in the cause of all such as are appointed to destruction.
9 Open thy mouth, judge righteously, and plead the cause of the poor and needy.
10 Who can find a virtuous woman? for her price is far above rubies.

11 The heart of her husband doth safely trust in her, so that he shall have no need of spoil.

12 She will do him good and not evil all the days of her life.

13 She seeketh wool, and flax, and worketh willingly with her hands.

14 She is like the merchants' ships; she bringeth her food from afar.

15 She riseth also while it is yet night, and giveth meat to her household, and a portion to her maidens.

16 She considereth a field, and buyeth it: with the fruit of her hands she planteth a vineyard.

17 She girdeth her loins with strength, and strengtheneth her arms.

18 She perceiveth that her merchandise is good: her candle goeth not out by night.

19 She layeth her hands to the spindle, and her hands hold the distaff.

20 She stretcheth out her hand to the poor; yea, she reacheth forth her hands to the needy.

21 She is not afraid of the snow for her household: for all her household are clothed with scarlet.

22 She maketh herself coverings of tapestry; her clothing is silk and purple.

23 Her husband is known in the gates, when he sitteth among the elders of the land.

24 She maketh fine linen, and selleth it; and delivereth girdles unto the merchant.

25 Strength and honour are her clothing; and she shall rejoice in time to come.

26 She openeth her mouth with wisdom; and in her tongue is the law of kindness.

27 She looketh well to the ways of her household, and eateth not the bread of idleness.

28 Her children arise up, and call her blessed; her husband also, and he praiseth her.

29 Many daughters have done virtuously, but thou excellest them all.

30 Favour is deceitful, and beauty is vain: but a woman that feareth the LORD, she shall be praised.

31 Give her of the fruit of her hands; and let her own works praise her in the gates.

HSÜ CHÜN CH'IEN

Hsü Chün Ch'ien was a poet of sixth-century China, a century whose end was marked by a restoration of political unity after more than 350 years of instability. It should be noted that certain poetic themes, namely themes of love and the pleasures of domestic life, are more passionately developed in the Chinese poetry of this era than in earlier or later periods.

Beginning of Spring — A Stroll with My Wife

Hairdo and ornaments all the latest fashion,
your outfit strictly in the newest style;
the grass still short enough to poke through sandals,
the plums so fragrant their perfume rubs off!
Trees slant down to pluck at your brocade shawl,
breezes sidle up and get under your crimson kerchief —
Fill the cups with orchid blossom wine![1]
These are sights to make the spirit sing.

JANE AUSTEN

Jane Austen, as sharp an observer of the rituals, follies, and triumphs of court-ship as ever lived, was engaged for a short time, but never married. Born in 1775, the daughter of a clergyman, she spent her entire life in the intimate domestic circle into which she was born, living in adulthood with her mother and sister in Hampshire, England. Though the conventions of her times were very different from the those of our own, her work remains wildly popular. Her keen delinea-tion of character, her sarcastic wit, her subtle moral compass and the realism with which she portrayed human relationships have made her one of the most beloved writers of all time. Austen had the rare gift as a novelist of being very ro-mantic without degenerating into sentimentality. She died in 1817.

Pride and Prejudice

Chapter 22

The Bennets were engaged to dine with the Lucases and again during the chief of the day was Miss Lucas so kind as to listen to Mr. Collins. Elizabeth took an opportunity of thanking her. "It keeps him in good humour," said she, "and I am more obliged to you than I can express." Charlotte assured her friend of her satisfaction in being useful, and that it amply repaid her for the little sacrifice of her time. This was very amiable, but Charlotte's kindness extended farther than Elizabeth had any conception of; its object was nothing else than to secure her from any return of Mr. Collins's addresses, by engaging them towards herself.

Such was Miss Lucas's scheme; and appearances were so favourable, that when they parted at night, she would have felt almost sure of success if he had not been to leave Hertfordshire so very soon. But here she did injustice to the fire and independence of his character, for it led him to escape out of Longbourn House the next morning with admirable slyness, and hasten to Lucas Lodge to throw himself at her feet. He was anxious to avoid the notice of his cousins, from a conviction that if they saw him depart, they could not fail to conjecture his design, and he was not willing to have the attempt known till its success could be known likewise; for though feeling almost secure, and with reason, for Charlotte had been tolerably encouraging, he was comparatively diffident since the adventure of Wednesday. His reception, however, was of the most flattering kind. Miss Lucas perceived him from an upper window as he walked towards the house, and instantly set out to meet him accidentally in the lane. But little had she dared to hope that so much love and eloquence awaited her there.

In as short a time as Mr. Collins's long speeches would allow, everything was settled between them to the satisfaction of both; and as they entered the house he earnestly entreated her to name the day that was to make him the happiest of men; and though such a solicitation must be waived for the present, the lady felt no inclination to trifle with his happiness. The stupidity with which he was favoured by nature must guard his courtship from any charm that could make a woman wish for its continuance; and Miss Lucas, who accepted him solely from the pure and disinterested desire of an establishment, cared not how soon that establishment were gained.

Sir William and Lady Lucas were speedily applied to for their consent; and it was bestowed with a most joyful alacrity. Mr. Collins's present circumstances made it a most eligible match for their daughter, to whom they could give little fortune; and his prospects of future wealth were exceedingly fair. Lady Lucas began directly to calculate, with more interest than the matter had ever excited before, how many years longer Mr. Bennet was likely to live; and Sir William gave it as his decided opinion, that whenever Mr. Collins should be in possession of the Longbourn estate, it would be highly expedient that both he and his wife should make their appearance at St. James's. The whole family, in short, were properly overjoyed on the occasion. The younger girls formed hopes of *coming out* a year or two sooner than they might otherwise have done; and the boys were relieved from their apprehension of Charlotte's dying an old maid. Charlotte herself was tolerably composed. She had gained her point, and had time to consider of it. Her reflections were in general satisfactory. Mr. Collins, to be sure, was neither sensible nor agreeable; his society was irksome, and his attachment to her must be imaginary. But still he would be her husband. Without thinking highly either of men or of matrimony, marriage had always been her object; it was the only honourable provision for well-educated young women of small fortune, and however uncertain of giving happiness, must be their pleasantest preservative from want. This preservative she had now obtained; and at the age of twenty-seven, without having ever been handsome, she felt all the good luck of it. The least agreeable circumstance in the business was the surprise it must occasion to Elizabeth Bennet, whose friendship she valued beyond that of any other person. Elizabeth would wonder, and probably would blame her; and though her resolution was not to be shaken, her feelings must be hurt by such a disapprobation. She resolved to give her the information herself, and therefore charged Mr. Collins, when he returned to Longbourn to dinner, to drop no hint of what had passed before any of the family. A promise of secrecy was of course very dutifully given, but it could not be kept without difficulty; for the curiosity excited by his long absence burst forth in such very direct questions on his return as required some ingenuity to evade, and he was at the same time exercising great self-denial, for he was longing to publish his prosperous love.

As he was to begin his journey too early on the morrow to see any of the family, the ceremony of leave-taking was performed when the ladies moved for the night; and Mrs. Bennet, with great politeness and cordiality, said how happy they should be to see him at Longbourn again, whenever his other engagements might allow him to visit them.

"My dear madam," he replied, "this invitation is particularly gratifying, because it is what I have been hoping to receive; and you may be very certain that I shall avail myself of it as soon as possible."

They were all astonished; and Mr. Bennet, who could by no means wish for so speedy a return, immediately said:

"But is there not danger of Lady Catherine's disapprobation here, my good sir? You had better neglect your relations than run the risk of offending your patroness."

"My dear sir," replied Mr. Collins, "I am particularly obliged to you for this friendly caution, and you may depend upon my not taking so material a step without her ladyship's concurrence."

"You cannot be too much on your guard. Risk anything rather than her displeasure; and if you find it likely to be raised by your coming to us again, which I should think exceedingly probable, stay quietly at home, and be satisfied that *we* shall take no offence."

"Believe me, my dear sir, my gratitude is warmly excited, by such affectionate attention; and depend upon it, you will speedily receive from me a letter of thanks for this, as for every other mark of your regard during my stay in Hertfordshire. As for my fair cousins, though my absence may not be long enough to render it necessary, I shall now take the liberty of wishing them health and happiness, not excepting my cousin Elizabeth."

With proper civilities the ladies then withdrew; all of them equally surprised to find that he meditated a quick return. Mrs. Bennet wished to understand by it that he thought of paying his addresses to one of her younger girls, and Mary might have been prevailed on to accept him. She rated his abilities much higher than any of the others; there was a solidity in his reflections which often struck her, and though by no means so clever as herself, she thought that if encouraged to read and improve himself by such an example as hers, he might become a very agreeable companion. But on the following morning, every hope of this kind was done away. Miss Lucas called soon after breakfast, and in a private conference with Elizabeth related the event of the day before.

The possibility of Mr. Collins's fancying himself in love with her friend had once occurred to Elizabeth within the last day or two; but that Charlotte could encourage him seemed almost as far from possibility as she could encourage him herself, and her astonishment was consequently so great as to overcome at first the bounds of decorum, and she could not help crying out:

"Engaged to Mr. Collins! My dear Charlotte — impossible!"

The steady countenance which Miss Lucas had commanded in telling her story, gave way to a momentary confusion here on receiving so direct a reproach; though, as it was no more than she expected, she soon regained her composure, and calmly replied:

"Why should you be surprised, my dear Eliza? Do you think it incredible that Mr. Collins should be able to procure any woman's good opinion, because he was not so happy as to succeed with you?"

But Elizabeth had now recollected herself, and making a strong effort for it, was able to assure her with tolerable firmness that the prospect of their relationship was highly grateful to her, and that she wished her all imaginable happiness.

"I see what you are feeling," replied Charlotte. "You must be surprised, very much surprised — so lately as Mr. Collins was wishing to marry you. But when you have had time to think it all over, I hope you will be satisfied with what I have done. I am not romantic, you know; I never was. I ask only a comfortable home — and considering Mr. Collins's character, connections, and situation in life, I am convinced that my chance of happiness with him is as fair as most people can boast on entering the marriage state."

Elizabeth quietly answered "Undoubtedly"; and after an awkward pause, they returned to the rest of the family. Charlotte did not stay much longer, and Elizabeth was then left to reflect on what she had heard. It was a long time before she became at all reconciled to the idea of so unsuitable a match. The strangeness of Mr. Collins's making two offers of marriage within three days was nothing in comparison of his being now accepted. She had always felt that Charlotte's opinion of matrimony was not exactly like her own, but she could not have supposed it possible that, when called into action, she would have sacrificed every better feeling to worldly advantage. Charlotte the wife of Mr. Collins was a most humiliating picture! And to the pang of a friend disgracing herself and sunk in her esteem, was added the distressing conviction that it was impossible for that friend to be tolerably happy in the lot she had chosen.

JOHN MILTON

John Milton (1608-74) was the greatest epic poet of the English language. But he was also an important political figure and pamphleteer in his time, agitating for freedom of the press and serving in and defending Oliver Cromwell's Puritan government (1649-60). His unhappy first marriage in 1643 with Mary Powell, a woman much younger than himself, led him to pen four well-known essays arguing for the legal right to divorce on the grounds of irreconcilable differences. Two years later, John Milton and Mary Powell did reconcile. But she died in 1652, after giving him three children. (Milton married two more times; his third wife survived him.) *Paradise Lost,* which took Milton five years to complete, was a work written quite consciously for posterity. Milton had long planned to write a grand epic poem meant to instruct his nation in the moral virtues. Indeed, his aims were even higher: He hoped that his art would serve the purpose of encouraging faith in God by capturing through language something of the nature of God.

The following excerpt was annotated by Christopher Ricks of the University of Cambridge.

Paradise Lost

Book IX, lines 192-407

Now when as sacred Light began to dawn
In Eden on the humid Flow'rs, that breath'd
Their morning Incense, when all things that breathe,

From th'Earth's great Altar send up silent praise
To the Creator, and his Nostrils fill
With grateful[1] Smell, forth came the human pair
And join'd their vocal Worship to the Choir
Of Creatures wanting voice, that done, partake
The season, prime for sweetest Scents and Airs:
Then cómmune how that day they best may ply
Their growing work: for much their work outgrew
The hands' dispatch of two Gard'ning so wide.
And Eve first to her Husband thus began.

   "Adam, well may we labour still to dress
This Garden, still to tend Plant, Herb and Flow'r,
Our pleasant task enjoin'd, but till more hands
Aid us, the work under our labour grows,
Luxurious by restraint; what we by day
Lop overgrown, or prune, or prop, or bind,
One night or two with wanton growth derides
Tending to wild. Thou therefore now advise
Or hear what to my mind first thoughts present,
Let us divide our labours, thou where choice
Leads thee, or where most needs, whether to wind
The Woodbine round this Arbour, or direct
The clasping Ivy where to climb, while I
In yonder Spring of Roses intermixt
With Myrtle, find what to redress till Noon:
For while so near each other thus all day
Our task we choose, what wonder if so near
Looks intervene and smiles, or object new
Casual discourse draw on, which intermits
Our day's work brought to little, though begun
Early, and th'hour of Supper comes unearn'd."

   To whom mild answer Adam thus return'd.
"Sole Eve, Associate sole, to me beyond
Compare above all living Creatures dear,
Well hast thou motion'd, well thy thoughts employ'd
How we might best fulfill the work which here
God hath assign'd us, nor of me shalt pass
Unprais'd: for nothing lovelier can be found
In woman, than to study household good,
And good works in her Husband to promote.

Yet not so strictly hath our Lord impos'd
Labour, as to debar us when we need
Refreshment, whether food, or talk between,
Food of the mind, or this sweet intercourse
Of looks and smiles, for smiles from Reason flow,
To brute deni'd, and are of Love the food,
Love not the lowest end of human life.
For not to irksome toil, but to delight
He made us, and delight to Reason join'd.
These paths and Bow'rs doubt not but our joint hands
Will keep from Wilderness with ease, as wide
As we need walk, till younger hands erelong
Assist us: But if much convérse perhaps
Thee satiate, to short absence I could yield.
For Solitude sometimes is best society,
And short retirement urges sweet return.
But other doubt possesses me, lest harm
Befall thee sever'd from me; for thou know'st
What hath been warn'd us, what malicious Foe
Envying our happiness, and of his own
Despairing, seeks to work us woe and shame
By sly assault; and somewhere nigh at hand
Watches, no doubt, with greedy hope to find
His wish and best advantage, us asunder,
Hopeless to circumvent us join'd, where each
To other speedy aid might lend at need;
Whether his first design be to withdraw
Our fealty from God, or to disturb
Conjugal Love, than which perhaps no bliss
Enjoy'd by us excites his envy more;
Or this, or worse, leave not the faithful side
That gave thee being, still shades thee and protects.
The Wife, where danger or dishonour lurks,
Safest and seemliest by her Husband stays,
Who guards her, or with her the worst endures."
　To whom the Virgin Majesty of Eve,
As one who loves, and some unkindness meets,
With sweet austere composure thus repli'd.
　"Offspring of Heav'n and Earth, and all Earth's Lord,
That such an Enemy we have, who seeks

Our ruin, both by thee inform'd I learn,
And from the parting Angel overheard
As in a shady nook I stood behind,
Just then return'd at shut of Evening Flow'rs.
But that thou shouldst my firmness therefore doubt
To God or thee, because we have a foe
May tempt it, I expected not to hear.
His violence thou fear'st not, being such,
As wee, not capable of death or pain,
Can either not receive, or can repel.
His fraud is then thy fear, which plain infers
Thy equal fear that my firm Faith and Love
Can by his fraud be shak'n or seduc't;
Thoughts, which how found they harbour in thy breast,
Adam, misthought of her to thee so dear?"
    To whom with healing words Adam repli'd.
"Daughter of God and Man, immortal Eve,
For such thou art, from sin and blame entire:
Not diffident[2] of thee do I dissuade
Thy absence from my sight, but to avoid
Th'attempt itself, intended by our Foe.
For hee who tempts, though in vain, at least asperses
The tempted with dishonour foul, suppos'd
Not incorruptible of Faith, not proof
Against temptation: thou thyself with scorn
And anger wouldst resent the offer'd wrong,
Though ineffectual found: misdeem not then,
If such affront I labour to avert
From thee alone, which on us both at once
The Enemy, though bold, will hardly dare,
Or daring, first on mee th'assault shall 'light.
Nor thou his malice and false guile contemn;
Subtle he needs must be, who could seduce
Angels, nor think superfluous others' aid.
I from the influence of thy looks receive
Access[3] in every Virtue, in thy sight
More wise, more watchful, stronger, if need were
Of outward strength; while shame, thou looking on,
Shame to be overcome or over-reacht
Would utmost vigour raise, and rais'd unite.

Why shouldst not thou like sense within thee feel
When I am present, and thy trial choose
With me, best witness of thy Virtue tri'd."
   So spoke domestic Adam in his care
And Matrimonial Love, but Eve, who thought
Less áttribúted to her Faith sincere,
Thus her reply with accent sweet renew'd.
   "If this be our condition, thus to dwell
In narrow circuit strait'n'd by a Foe,
Subtle or violent, we not endu'd
Single with like defence, wherever met,
How are we happy, still[4] in fear of harm?
But harm precedes not sin: only our Foe
Tempting affronts us with his foul esteem
Of our integrity: his foul esteem
Sticks no dishonour on our Front, but turns
Foul on himself; then wherefore shunn'd or fear'd
By us? who rather double honour gain
From his surmise prov'd false, find peace within,
Favour from Heav'n, our witness from th'event.[5]
And what is Faith, Love, Virtue unassay'd
Alone, without exterior help sustain'd?
Let us not then suspect our happy State
Left so imperfect by the Maker wise,
As not secure to single or combin'd.
Frail is our happiness, if this be so,
And Eden were no Eden thus expos'd."
   To whom thus Adam fervently repli'd.
"O Woman, best are all things as the will
Of God ordained them, his creating hand
Nothing imperfect or deficient left
Of all that he Created, much less Man,
Or aught that might his happy State secure,
Secure from outward force; within himself
The danger lies, yet lies within his power:
Against his will he can receive no harm.
But God left free the Will, for what obeys
Reason, is free, and Reason he made right,
But bid her well beware, and still erect,[6]
Lest by some fair appearing good surpris'd

She dictate false, and misinform the Will
To do what God expressly hath forbid.
Not then mistrust, but tender love enjoins,
That I should mind[7] thee oft, and mind thou me.
Firm we subsist, yet possible to swerve,
Since Reason not impossibly may meet
Some specious object by the Foe suborn'd,
And fall into deception unaware,
Not keeping strictest watch, as she was warn'd.
Seek not temptation then; which to avoid
Were better, and most likely if from mee
Thou sever not: Trial will come unsought.
Wouldst thou approve thy constancy, approve
First thy obedience; th'other who can know,
Not seeing thee attempted, who attest?
But if thou think, trial unsought may find
Us both securer[8] than thus warn'd thou seem'st,
Go; for thy stay, not free, absents thee more;
Go in thy native innocence, rely
On what thou hast of virtue, summon all,
For God towards thee hath done his part, do thine."
    So spake the Patriarch of Mankind, but Eve
Persisted, yet submiss, though last, repli'd.
    "With thy permission then, and thus forewarn'd
Chiefly by what thy own last reasoning words
Touch'd only, that our trial, when least sought,
May find us both perhaps for less prepar'd.
The willinger I go, nor much expect
A Foe so proud will first the weaker seek;
So bent, the more shall shame him his repulse."
Thus saying, from her Husband's hand her hand
Soft she withdrew, and like a Wood-Nymph light
Oread or Dryad,[9] or of Delia's[10] Train,
Betook her to the Groves, but Delia's self
In gait surpass'd and Goddess-like deport,
Though not as shee with Bow and Quiver arm'd,
But with such Gard'ning Tools as Art yet rude,
Guiltless of[11] fire had form'd, or Angels brought.
To Pales,[12] or Pomona,[13] thus adorn'd,
Likest she seem'd, Pomona when she fled

Vertumnus[14] or to Ceres[15] in her Prime,
Yet Virgin of Proserpina from Jove.
Her long with ardent look his Eye pursu'd
Delighted, but desiring more her stay.
Oft he to her his charge of quick return
Repeated, shee to him as oft engag'd
To be return'd by Noon amid the Bow'r,
And all things in best order to invite
Noontide repast, or Afternoon's repose.
O much deceiv'd, much failing, hapless Eve,
Of thy presum'd return! event perverse!
Thou never from that hour in Paradise
Found'st either sweet repast, or sound repose.

BRONISLAW MALINOWSKI

Anthropologist Bronislaw Malinowski (1884-1942) was born in Poland and educated at the University of Krakow. His first studies involved the Trobriand Islanders, but his work in cultural anthropology carried him to many other parts of the world. He was the first advocate of the theory of "functionalism," by which he meant "every custom, material object, idea and belief fulfills some vital function, has some task to accomplish . . . within a [society's] working whole."[1] Because he was committed to analyzing primitive cultures on their own terms, he was a cautious analyst of the common drives, common ends, and common institutions that linked human societies. One of his greatest and most elegant synthetic works of cultural anthropology was the essay, *Sex and Repression in Savage Cultures,* a brilliant empirical critique of Freud's Oedipal theories.

Marriage

8. The Economics of the Household and Family. — We are thus led at all stages of our argument to the conclusion that the institution of marriage is primarily determined by the needs of the offspring, by the dependence of the children upon their parents. More specially, the mother since she is handicapped at pregnancy and for some time after birth, needs the assistance of a male partner. The rôle of male associate and helpmate is almost universally played by the husband exclusively, though in some extremely matrilineal societies the wife's brother shares with the husband in some of the responsibilities and burdens of the household. The economic as well as the biological norm of a family is thus mother, child and husband — or exceptionally both the husband and the wife's brother.

In the vast majority of human societies the individual family, based on monogamous marriage and consisting of mother, father and children, forms a self-contained group, not necessarily however cut off from society. Within the household there is a typical scheme of division in functions, again almost universal. By virtue of natural endowment the wife has not only to give birth to and nourish the children, but she is also destined to give them most of the early tender cares: to keep them warm and clean, to lull them to sleep and soothe their infantile troubles. Even in this the husband often helps to a considerable degree, prompted by natural inclination as well as by custom. This latter often imposes upon him duties and ritual manifestations such as taboos during the pregnancy of his wife and at childbirth, and performances at the time of confinement. . . . All such obligations emphasize the father's responsibility and his devotion to the child. Later on in the education of offspring both parents have to take part, performing their respective duties, which vary with the society and with the sex of the children.

Apart from the special task of producing and rearing the children, the wife normally looks after the preparation of the food, she almost invariably provides the fuel and the water, is the actual attendant at the hearth or fireplace, manufactures, tends and owns the cooking-vessels, and she is also the main carrier of burdens. In the very simplest cultures the woman also erects the hut or shelter and looks after camp arrangements (Australians, Bushmen, Andaman Islanders). The husband is the protector and defender of the family, and he also performs all the work which requires greater strength, courage and decision, such as hunting game, fishing, heavy building of houses and craft, and clearing the timber.

The division of labour between husband and wife outside the household follows the line of men's and women's occupations which differ with the community, but on the whole make fighting, hunting, sailing, metal work purely male occupations; collecting, agriculture, pottery, weaving predominantly female; while fishing, cattle-tending, making of clothing and utensils are done by one sex or the other according to culture.

The division of labour outside the household does not mean merely that husband and wife collect food and manufacture goods for their family each in a different manner. It means also as a rule that each has to collaborate with other members of the community of the same sex in some wider collective enterprise, from which the family benefits only partially and indirectly. In spite of repeated theoretical assertions as to the existence of the "closed household economy" or even of individual search for food among primitive peoples, we find in every community, however simple, a wider economic collaboration embracing all members and welding the various families into larger co-operative units. . . .

The fuller our knowledge of relevant facts, the better we see on the one hand the dependence of the family upon the rest of the community, and on the other hand the duty of each individual to contribute not only to his own household but to those of others as well. Thus in Australia a great part of a man's yield in hunting has to be divided according to fixed rules among his relatives, own and classificatory. Throughout Oceania a network of obligations unites the members of the community and overrules the economic autonomy of the household. In the Trobriand Islands a man has to offer about half of his garden produce to his sister and another part to various relatives, only the remainder being kept for his own household, which in turn is supported substantially by the wife's brother and other relatives. Economic obligations of such a nature cutting across the closed unity of the household could be quoted from every single tribe of which we have adequate information.

The most important examples however come from the communities organised on extreme mother-right, where husband and wife are in most matters members of different households, and their mutual economic contributions show the character of gifts rather than of mutual maintenance.

9. **The Split Household Under Matrilocal Mother-right.** — Most of what has been said so far refers to the marriage based on a united household and associated as a rule both under father-right and mother-right with *patrilocal* residence. This means that the bride moves to the husband's community, when she either joins his family house or camp, or else inhabits a house built for the new couple and owned in the husband's name. Patrilocal marriages are by far the most prevalent all over the world.

Matrilocal marriage consists in the husband's joining the wife's community, taking up residence in her parents' house and often having to do some services for them. Matrilocal residence may be permanent; or it may be temporary, the husband having to remain for a year or two with his parents-in-law, and having also possibly to work for them. (Eskimo, Kwakiutl, Guaycuru, Fuegians of America; Bushmen, Hottentots, Bapedi, Bakumbi, Nuer of Africa; negrites of Philippines; Ainu of Japan.) . . .

In a few cases which might be regarded as the extreme development of mother-right combined with matrilocal conditions, the wife remains at her mother's residence and the husband does not even take up a permanent abode there, but simply joins her as a frequent and regular but still temporary visitor (Menangkabau Malays of Sumatra, Pueblo and Seri Indians of N. America, Nairs of Malabar). Such extreme cases of mother-right are an exception. They are the product of special conditions found as a rule at a high level of culture and should never be taken as the prototype of "primitive marriage." . . .

The most important fact about such extreme matriarchal conditions is that even there the principle of social legitimacy holds good; that though the father is domestically and economically almost superfluous, he is legally indispensable and the main bond of union between such matrilineal and matrilocal consorts is parenthood. We see also that the economic side can have a symbolic, ritual significance — the gift-exchange functions as token of affection — it marks thus a sociological interdependence, while it has hardly any utilitarian importance.

10. **Marriage as an Economic Contract.** — This last point, together with the foregoing analysis of the household and family economics, allows us to frame the conclusion that while marriage embraces a certain amount of economic co-operation as well as of sexual connubium, it is not primarily an economic partnership any more than a merely sexual appropriation. It is as necessary to guard against the exclusively economic definition of marriage as against the over-emphasis of sex. This materialistic view of marriage, to be found already in older writers such as Lippert, E. Grosse, Dargun, appears again in some recent important works. Criticising the exaggeration of sex, Briffault says about marriage: "The institution, its origin and development, have been almost exclusively viewed and discussed by social historians in terms of the operation of the sexual instincts and of the sentiments connected with those instincts, such as the exercise of personal choice, the effects of jealousy, the manifestations of romantic love. The origin, like the biological foundation, of *individual marriage being essentially economic,* those psychological factors are the products of the association rather than the causes or conditions which have given rise to it." And again: "Individual marriage has its *foundation* in *economic* relations. In the vast majority of uncultured societies marriage is regarded almost *exclusively* in the light of *economic* considerations, and throughout by far the greater part of the history of the institution the various changes which it has undergone have been *conditioned by economic causes.*" (*The Mothers*, vol. II, p. 1; the italics are those of the present writer.)

This is a distortion of a legitimate view. Marriage is not entered upon for economic considerations, exclusively or even mainly; nor is the primary bond between the two parties established by the mutual economic benefits derived from each other. This is best shown by the importance of matrimonial bonds even where there is neither community of goods nor co-operation nor even full domesticity. Economics are, like sex, a means to an end, which is the rearing, education and dual parental influence over the offspring. Economic co-operation is one of the obligations of marriage and like sexual cohabitation, mutual assistance in legal and moral matters it is prescribed to the married by law and enjoined by religion in most cultures. But it certainly is not either the principal end or the unique cause of marriage.

11. **"Marriage by Purchase."** — As erroneous as the overemphasis on economics and its hypostasis as the *vera causa* and essence of marriage is also the tearing out of some one economic trait and giving it a special name and thus an artificial entity. This has been done notably with regard to the initial gifts at marriage, especially when given by the husband. More or less considerable gifts from the husband to his wife's family at marriage occur very widely (*see* the comprehensive list of references in Westermarck, *History of Human Marriage,* vol. II, chap. xxiii). The term "marriage by purchase" applied to such gifts usually serves to isolate them from their legal and economic context, to introduce the concept of a commercial transaction, which is nowhere to be found in primitive culture as a part of marriage, and to serve as one more starting point for fallacious speculations about the origin of marriage.

The presents given at marriage should always be considered as a link — sometimes very important, sometimes insignificant — in the series of services and gifts which invariably run throughout marriage. The exchange of obligations embraces not only the husband and the wife, but also the children, who under mother-right are counted as one with the mother while under father-right they take over the father's obligations. The family and clan of the wife, and more rarely of the husband, also become part of the scheme of reciprocities. The presents offered at marriage by the husband are often made up of contributions, given him towards this end by his relatives and clansmen (Banaka, Bapuka, Thonga, Zulu, Xosa, Bechwana, Madi of Africa; Toradjas, Bogos of Indonesia; Buin, Mekeo, Roro, Trobrianders of Melanesia), and are not all retained by the girl's parents but shared among her relatives and even clansmen (Achomawi, Delaware, Osage, Araucanians of America; S.E. Bantu, Swahili, Pokomo, Turkana, Bavili, Ewhe, Baganda, Masai, Lotuko of Africa; Ossetes, Samoyeds, Aleut, Yakut, Yukaghir of Siberia; Koita, Mekeo, S. Massim, Buin of Melanesia). The giving of presents is thus a transaction binding two groups rather than two individuals, a fact which is reflected in such institutions as the inheritance of wives, sororate, levirate, etc. A correct understanding of the initial marriage gift can be obtained only against the background of the wider economic mutuality of husband and wife, parents and children, maternal and paternal families and clans.

Another type of marriage gift is the *lobola* found among the patrilineal and patrilocal communities of the S.E. Bantu, who live by combined agriculture and cattle-raising. The wife and children are here regarded as a definite economic and sociological asset. The wife is the main agricultural and domestic worker, while the children are valuable because the boys continue the line and the girls bring in wealth at marriage. Marriage is concluded by the payment of cattle, the amount varying greatly according to tribe, rank and other considerations from a couple of head to a few score. These cattle are known as *lobola*, or "bride-price," as is the current but incorrect anthropological expression. The *lobola* in fact is not the motive for the transaction, nor is there any bidding on any market, nor can the cattle be disposed of at will by the receiver, *i.e.*, the girl's father. Some of them have to be distributed by him according to fixed tribal custom among particular relatives of the girl; the rest he has to use for the provision of a wife for his son, *i.e.*, the girl's brother, or else, if he has no male heir, he contracts another wife for himself, in order to obtain the desired male descendants. In case of divorce the marriage gift has to be returned as the identical cattle given and not merely in an equivalent form. The *lobola* is thus rather a symbolic equivalent representing the wife's economic efficiency, and it has to be treated as a deposit to be spent on another marriage.

In Melanesia the husband's initial gift at marriage is a ritual act, and is always reciprocated by the wife's family. This is the case also among certain American tribes (Tshimshian, Coast Salish, Bellacoola, Delaware, Ojibway, Navaho, Miwok), in Siberia (Mordwin, Ainu, Buryat, Samoyed, Koryak), and in Polynesia (Samoa). This return gift may take the form of a dowry given to the bride by her father or parents or other relatives but also directly or indirectly benefiting her husband (Greenlanders, Brazilian aborigines, Yahgans of America; Ibo, Ovambo, S.E. Bantu, Banyoro, Masai of Africa; Buryat, Yukaghir, Samoyed of Siberia; Toda of India; Banks Islanders, Buin, Maori of Oceania). In some communities the balance of gifts is so much in favour of the husband that instead of wife purchase we could speak of buying a husband for the girl (N. Massim; coast tribes of British Columbia; Tehuelches of Patagonia; Yakut). Both concepts, however, that of "wife purchase" and "husband purchase" are obviously inadmissible.

12. **Property and Inheritance Within Marriage.** — As a rule, whatever the manner of economic inauguration of marriage and whatever the mutual services exchanged between the partners, the latter have not only their own sphere of activity but their own possessions. The wife usually claims the title and right of disposing of her articles of apparel, of the domestic utensils and often of the special implements and fruits of her pursuit. The importance of woman's work in agriculture, her social influence due to this and her specific claims to the agricultural produce — not the ownership of the land, which is generally vested in man — have given rise to the economic theory of mother right. . . .

Very often the possessions of the husband and wife are inherited by their respective kindred, and not by the surviving partner. The inheritance of the wife by the husband's brother (the custom of levirate *q.v.*), which is known from the Old Testament, but has a fairly wide range of distribution . . . is not to be regarded as an economic transaction. Like the inheritance of a widow under mother-right and like the custom of killing the widows and the *suttee* of India, it is the expression of the matrimonial bonds outlasting death, and defining the widow's behaviour afterwards.

6 Who's the Head of the Family?

- ◆ Ephesians 5:22-33

- ◆ "The Wife of Bath," from *The Canterbury Tales,* by Geoffrey Chaucer

- ◆ "The Man Makes and the Woman Takes," an African-American folktale

- ◆ From *The Taming of the Shrew* by William Shakespeare

- ◆ From *On the Subjection of Women* by John Stuart Mill

- ◆ From *Getting Married* by George Bernard Shaw

- ◆ "Gender Politics: Love and Power in the Private and Public Spheres" by Francesca M. Cancian

Marriage: a community consisting of a master, a mistress, and two slaves, making in all, two.

— AMBROSE BIERCE

Man and woman may only enter Paradise hand in hand. Together . . . they left it, and together they must return.

— RICHARD GARNETT

Introduction

Who's the head of the family? In traditional societies, it is the male. But among Christians, even in ancient days, male headship did not mean simple domination. While in our passage from Ephesians, Paul exhorts Christian wives to "submit" to their husbands "in everything," he also warns husbands never to arbitrarily exert their authority. "Husbands," he says, "must love their wives as Christ loved the church," and must care for their wives as they would care for themselves. Thus, the physical superiority of the male, along with his primal protective function in the family, is recognized in Christian scripture. But so also are the profound responsibilities of household headship. It would be important to say that within the context of the honor-shame culture of the ancient Greco-Roman world, the Christian notion of male family headship represented a significant step forward with regard to respect for what we now consider the self-evident rights of women and children. In the "chastened patriarchy" of the early Christian world, the notion of male service to the family was every bit as important as the notion of male authority.

Many of us think that only modern minds have challenged the traditional notion of male headship in marriage. Not so. One of the reasons that Chaucer's Wife of Bath has exerted so much charm over the centuries is that she quite convincingly argues the opposite. Many a wise man, she reminds us, allows himself to be ruled by the woman in his life. The Wife of Bath is no neophyte in matters of marital power relations. She has had five husbands. And not one has pushed her around — not, at least, and gotten away with it. The prayer she lives by: "Jesu Christ send us husbands who are meek, young, and lively in bed, and grace to outlive those that we marry . . . [and] shorten the lives of those that won't be governed by their wives."

The African-American folktale that follows the tale of the Wife of Bath seems also to suggest that in the struggle for power in marriage, women more often than not come out on top. In this amusing "just-so" story, we find out how that came to be. Men might possess the brute strength they need to dominate women, but women have acquired unassailable weapons of their own. They have the "keys" to the kitchen, the bedroom, and the cradle, and can force their husbands to "mortgage" their strength for the sake of domestic fulfillment and children.

Of course, there must be a limit even to a woman's sovereignty in the household. In Shakespeare's comedy, *The Taming of the Shrew*, Katharina, an aggressive, stubborn, and ill-tempered girl, is matched with Petruchio, a man too contentious to be true. He addresses her in public as "my goods, my chattels, . . . my ox, my ass, my anything," rips her away from her own nuptial feast, and gives her a lecture in sexual continence — this on her wedding night! The husband from hell? Not really. Petruchio has a plan. . . . He's convinced that if his new wife can just get a healthy taste of her own medicine she'll become a woman he can reasonably live with.

Returning to more serious reflections on gender roles and power, our next reading is from John Stuart Mill's seminal work, *On the Subjection of Women*. Mill asserts that assuming modern marriage to be a voluntary tie, it is "not true that in all voluntary associations between two people one of them must be absolute master: still less that the law must determine which of them it shall be." *On the Subjection of Women* was an appeal for the establishment of property and decision making rights for women in marriage. Mill's ruminations marked a milestone in the history of thought on women's rights. It would be important to emphasize, however, that although Mill viewed men and women essentially as equals in the marital relationship, he considered they had different roles to play in the labor force. Mill was not in favor of married women working outside the home; indeed, he viewed such work as unconscionable exploitation of women.

In *Getting Married,* Bernard Shaw provocatively suggested that marriage in the capitalist society of the early twentieth century was nothing other than female economic slavery. Mastery of the household and everyone in it belonged to men, because men controlled the material resources. The only cure for the subjection of women in marriage? In Shaw's view: independent employment outside the home. Seeing many unhappy marriages, Shaw also wanted to advance an argument in favor of unilateral, no-fault divorce. He cleverly foresaw that the economic liberation of women would force a loosening of restrictions on divorce. Needless to say, Shaw's arguments had enormous influence on feminism and on the views regarding marriage of the twentieth-century political left. Ironically, while the growth in this century of economic opportunities for women outside the home may have led to a more equitable distribution of power within marriage, women with children who divorce remain economically extremely vulnerable.

Finally, contemporary sociologist Francesca Cancian meditates on power in marriage. In this thoughtful and sensitive essay, Cancian argues that the power advantages modern males may still enjoy within marriage are likely based on an errant assumption that men are more independent of women than women are of men. This is a cultural myth, Cancian asserts. Rather men and women express their dependence upon each other in different ways. Males are more apt to show love instrumentally, through actions and deeds; females demonstrate love expressively, through words and affection. The final achievement of equality in marriage, Cancian suggests, may rest in clarifying the separate interrelational styles of men and women, and in reassuring women that men are just as emotionally attached in marriage as women, if not more attached. Acknowledging the "interdependence" of the sexes, and working to create social conditions that encourage more expressive love in men and more instrumental love from women will, in Cancian's view, also go far toward equalizing power relations within marriage.

EPHESIANS

The book Ephesians of the New Testament, written in the early second century, offers one of the clearest and most concise elucidations of early Christian thought on marriage. Here, Paul places marriage firmly in the new ethical and theological universe of Christianity which, while offering the privileges and rewards of eternal life in the world to come, required specific sacrifices and responsibilities in this world. It should be noted that Paul's command to wives to "submit" themselves to their husbands follows directly on his exhortation to Christians in general to submit "one to another in the fear of God." Thus, the word "submission" carries more the connotation of informed spiritual reverence than blind obedience to temporal authority. Paul's goal was for the same harmonious community of life between spouses as among members of the church. Indeed, Paul compares the marital union of flesh to the union of Christ and his church.

Ephesians 5:22-33

22 Wives, submit yourselves unto your own husbands, as unto the Lord.
23 For the husband is the head of the wife, even as Christ is the head of the church: and he is the saviour of the body.
24 Therefore as the church is subject unto Christ, so let the wives be to their own husbands in every thing.
25 Husbands, love your wives, even as Christ also loved the church, and gave himself for it;

26 That he might sanctify and cleanse it with the washing of water by the word,

27 That he might present it to himself a glorious church, not having spot, or wrinkle, or any such thing; but that it should be holy and without blemish.

28 So ought men to love their wives as their own bodies. He that loveth his wife loveth himself.

29 For no man ever yet hated his own flesh; but nourisheth and cherisheth it, even as the Lord the church:

30 For we are members of his body, of his flesh, and of his bones.

31 For this cause shall a man leave his father and mother, and shall be joined unto his wife, and they two shall be one flesh.

32 This is a great mystery: but I speak concerning Christ and the church.

33 Nevertheless let every one of you in particular so love his wife even as himself; and the wife see that she reverence her husband.

GEOFFREY CHAUCER

Geoffrey Chaucer was an English court poet and administrator of the fourteenth century. The son of a wine merchant, his origins would probably not in themselves have predicted the close connections he later established with kings Edward III, Richard II, and later Henry IV. A cultivated and well-traveled man, Chaucer was a skillful and successful courtier and emissary. Though he is mainly known for his brilliant, unfinished *Tales of Canterbury* — the plot of which concerns a group of traveling pilgrims who, having met at an inn, entertain each other with stories — Chaucer wrote many other works. Of those other works that survive, the best known today is probably the romance *Troilus and Criseyde*.

The Wife of Bath

Certainly, my feelings all come
from Venus, and my heart from Mars:
Venus gave me my lust, my lecherousness,
and Mars gave me my sturdy hardiness,
because Taurus was in the ascendant when I was born, and
Mars was in that sign. Alas, alas, that ever love was sin!
I always followed my inclination
according to the stellar influences at my birth;
I was so made that I could not withhold
my chamber of Venus from a good fellow.
I still have the mark of Mars on my face,

and also in another private place.
For as surely as God is my salvation,
I never had any discrimination in love,
but always followed my appetite,
be he short or tall, dark or fair;
I didn't care, so long as he pleased me,
how poor he was, nor of what rank.

What should I say, except that at the end of the month
this gay clerk Jankin, that was so pleasant,
wedded me with great ceremony,
and to him I gave all the lands and property
that had ever been given to me before;
but afterward I repented this sorely:
he would not allow anything I wanted.
By God, he hit me once on the ear
because I had torn a leaf out of his book;
as a result of that stroke, my ear became totally deaf.
I was stubborn as a lioness,
and as for my tongue, an absolute ranter;
and I'd walk, as I'd done before,
from house to house, although he'd sworn I wouldn't;
because of this he would often preach
and teach me of the deeds of ancient Romans:
how Simplicius Gallus left his wife
and forsook her for the rest of his life
just because he saw her looking out
of his door bareheaded one day.

He told me by name of another Roman
who also, because his wife was at a summer game
without his knowledge, forsook her.
And then he would seek in his Bible
for that proverb of Ecclesiasticus
where he makes a command strictly forbidding
a man to allow his wife to go roaming about;
then you could be sure he would say this:
'Whoever builds his house of willows,
and rides his blind horse over plowed land,
and allows his wife to visit shrines,

305

is worthy to be hanged on the gallows.'
But all for naught; I didn't care a berry
for his proverbs and old saw,
nor would I be corrected by him.
I hate that man who tells me my vices,
and so, God knows, do more of us than I.
This made him utterly furious with me;
I wouldn't give in to him in any case.

Now I'll tell you truly, by Saint Thomas,
why I tore a leaf out of his book,
for which he hit me so that I became deaf.
He had a book that he always loved to read
in night and day to amuse himself.
He called it Valerius and Theophrastus;
at which book he was always laughing heartily;
and also there was at some time a clerk at Rome,
a cardinal, that was called St. Jerome,
who wrote a book against Jovinian;
in this book there was also . . . the parables of Solomon,
Ovid's Art of Love, and many other books,
and all these were bound in one volume.
And every day and night it was his custom,
when he had leisure and could rest
from other worldly occupation,
to read in this book about wicked wives.
He knew more legends and lives of them
than there are of good wives in the Bible.
For believe me, it is an impossibility
for any clerk to speak good of wives —
unless it be of the lives of holy saints,
but never of any other woman . . .
By God, if women had written stories, as clerks have in their oratories,
they would have written more of men's wickedness
than all of the sex of Adam can redress.
The children of Mercury and of Venus
are quite contrary in their ways;
Mercury loves wisdom and learning,
and Venus loves revelry and expenditure.
And because of their diverse dispositions,

each loses power when the other is dominant;
and thus, God knows, Mercury is powerless
in the Sign of the Fish, where Venus is dominant,
and Venus falls when Mercury ascends;
and therefore no woman is praised by any clerk.
The clerk, when he is old, and unable to do
any of Venus' work worth his old shoe,
then sits down and writes in his dotage
that women cannot keep their marriage vows!

. . . Behold the words between the Summoner and the Friar

The Friar laughed, when he had heard all this:
"Now dame," said he, "as I may have joy or bliss,
this is a long preamble to a tale!"
And when the summoner heard the Friar exclaim,
"Lo!" said the Summoner, "By God's two arms!
A friar will always be butting in."

. . . Our Host cried "Peace! And that at once!"
And said, "Let the woman tell her tale.
You behave like people who have got drunk on ale.
Tell your tale, dame; that is best."

"Already sir," said she, "just as you wish,
if I have the permission of this worthy Friar. . . ."

. . . In the old days of King Arthur,
of whom Britons speak great honor,
this land was all filled with fairies.
The elf queen with her jolly company
danced often in many a green meadow —
this was the old belief, as I have read;
I speak of many hundred years ago.
But now no one can see elves any more,
for now the great charity and prayers
of limiters and other holy friars,
who search every field and stream
as thick as specks of dust in a sunbeam,
blessing halls, chambers, kitchens, bedrooms,

307

cities, towns, castles, high towers,
villages, barns, stables, dairies:
this is the reason that there are no fairies.
For where an elf was wont to walk,
there now walks the limiter himself,
in afternoons and in mornings,
and says his Matins and his holy things,
as he goes about within his limits.
Women may go up and down safely;
in every bush or under every tree
there is no other incubus but he —
and he won't do anything but dishonor to them.

It so happened that this King Arthur
had in his house a lusty bachelor,
who one day came riding from the river;
and it happened that he saw a maiden
walking before him, alone as she was born.
And from this maiden then, against her will,
and by pure force, he took her maidenhood.
Because of this violation, there was such a clamor
and such a petitioning to King Arthur
that this knight was condemned to die
according to law, and should have lost his head —
it happened that such was the statute then —
except that the Queen and various other ladies
prayed to the king for grace so long
that he granted him his life on the spot,
and gave him to the queen, completely at her will,
to choose whether she would save or destroy him.

The queen thanked the king heartily,
and then spoke thus to the knight,
one day, when she saw a fitting time,
"You are still in such a position," said she,
"that you have no guarantee of your life as yet.
I will grant you life if you can tell me
what thing it is that women most desire.
Be wary, and keep your neck from the ax.
And if you cannot tell it to me now,

I will still give you leave to go
a year and a day to seek and learn
a sufficient answer in this matter.
And I want a guarantee, before you go,
that you will yield up your person in this place."

The knight was woeful, and he sighed sorrowfully;
but then, he could not do as he pleased.
And in the end he decided to go off,
and to come back again just at the end of the year,
with such an answer as God would provide for him;
he took his leave and went forth on his way.

He sought in every house and every place
where he hoped to find favor,
in order to learn what thing women most love;
but he reached no land where he could find
two people who were in agreement
with each other on this matter.

Some said women love riches best;
some said honor; some said amusement;
some, rich apparel; some said pleasure in bed,
and often to be widowed and remarried.
Some said that our hearts are most soothed
when we are flattered and pampered:
he came near the truth, I will not lie;
a man can win us best with flattery,
and with constant attendance and assiduity
we are ensnared, both high and low.

And some said that we love best
to be free, and do just as we please,
and to have no man reprove us for our vice,
but say that we are wise and not at all foolish.
For truly, if anyone will scratch us
on a sore spot, there is not one of us
who will not kick for being told the truth;
try it, and he who does shall find this out.

No matter how full of vice we are within,
we wish to be thought wise and clean from sin.

And some said that we take delight
in being thought reliable and able to keep a secret
and hold steadfast to a purpose
and not betray anything that people tell us.
But that idea isn't worth a rake handle;
by heaven, we women can't conceal a thing. . . .

. . . When this knight whom my tale specially concerns
saw that he couldn't come by it —
that is to say, what women love most —
his spirit was very sorrowful within his breast;
but home he went, he might not linger:
the day was come when he must turn homeward.
And on his way, burdened with care, he happened
to ride by the edge of the forest,
when he saw more than twenty-four
ladies moving in a dance;
he drew eagerly toward that dance
in the hope that he might learn something.
But indeed, before he quite got there,
the dancers vanished, he knew not where.
He saw no living creature,
except a woman sitting on the green;
no one could imagine an uglier creature.
This old woman rose before the knight
and said, "Sir knight, no road lies this way.
Tell me, by your faith, what you seek for.
Perhaps it may be the better;
these old folks know many things," said she.

"Dear mother," said this knight, "certainly
I am as good as dead unless I can say
what thing it is that women most desire.
If you could tell me, I would repay your trouble well."

"Give me your promise, here upon my hand," said she,
"that you will do the next thing I require

310

of you, if it lies in your power,
and I will tell it to you before nightfall."
"Here is my promise," said the knight. "I grant it."

"Then," said she, "I dare to boast
that your life is safe, for I'll swear
upon my life that the queen will say as I do.
Let's see whether the proudest of all those
that wear coverchief or headdress
dares deny what I shall teach you;
let's go on without any more talk."
Then she whispered a message in his ear,
and told him to be glad and not afraid.

When they had come to the court, this knight
said he had kept his day as he had promised,
and his answer, he said, was ready.
Many a noble wife and many a maiden,
and many a widow (since widows are so wise),
were assembled to hear his answer
with the queen herself sitting as judge;
and then the knight was ordered to appear.

Everyone was commanded to keep silence,
and the knight was commanded to tell in open assembly
what thing it is that secular women love best.
This knight did not stand in beastlike silence,
but answered to his question at once
with a manly voice, so that all the court heard it:

"My liege lady," he said, "generally
women desire to have dominion
over their husbands as well as their lovers,
and to be above them in mastery.
This is your greatest desire, though you may kill me;
do as you please, I am at your will here."

In all the court there was neither wife nor maiden
nor widow who contradicted what he said,
but all said he deserved to have his life.

And at that word up jumped the old woman
whom the knight had seen sitting on the green:
"Mercy," said she, "my sovereign lady queen!
Before your court depart, do right by me.
I taught this answer to the knight;
for this he gave me his promise there
that he would do the first thing
I required of him, if it lay in his power.
Before the court, then, I pray you, sir knight,"
said she, "to take me as your wife;
for well you know that I have saved your life.
If I say false, deny me, on your faith."

The knight answered, "Alas and woe is me!
I know quite well that such was my promise.
For the love of God ask for something else;
take all my property and let my body go."

"No then," said she. "Curse the two of us!
For though I am ugly and old and poor,
I wouldn't want all the metal or ore
that is buried under the earth or lies above
unless I were your wife and your love as well."

"My love?" said he; "No, my damnation!
Alas, that any of my birth
should ever be so foully disgraced!"
But it was all for nothing; the end was this, that he
was forced to accept the fact that he must needs wed her;
and he took his old wife and went to bed.

Now some people might say, perhaps,
that out of negligence I am not bothering
to tell you about the joy and the pomp
at the feast that day,
to which objection I shall answer briefly:
I am telling you that there was no joy or feast at all,
there was nothing but gloom and much sorrow;
for he married her privately in the morning

and afterward hid himself like an owl all day —
he was so dejected because his wife looked so ugly.

Great was the woe in the knight's mind
when he was brought with his wife to bed:
he tossed and he turned to and fro.
His old wife lay smiling all the time,
and said, "O dear husband, bless my soul!
Does every knight behave with his wife as you do?
Is this the law of King Arthur's house?
Is every one of his knights so cold?
I am your own love and your wife;
I am she who saved your life;
And certainly I never yet did wrong to you.
Why do you act thus with me the first night?
You act like a man who has lost his mind.
What am I guilty of? For God's sake, tell me
and it shall be corrected, if I can manage it."

"Corrected?" said this knight, "Alas, no, no!
It will never be corrected!
You are so loathsome and so old,
and what is more, of such low birth,
that it is little wonder if I toss and turn.
I wish to God my heart would break!"

"Is this," said she, "the cause of your unrest?"
"Yes certainly," said he, "it's no wonder."
"Now, sir," said she, "I could rectify all this,
if I wanted to, before three days were up,
if you behaved yourself to me well.

But in the matter of your speaking of such nobility
as descends from ancient wealth,
claiming that because of it you are supposed to be
noblemen — such arrogance is not worth a hen.
Find who is always the most virtuous,
privately and publicly, and who always tries hardest
to do what noble deeds he can,
and consider him the greatest nobleman.

313

GEOFFREY CHAUCER

Christ wants us to claim our nobility from him,
not from our ancestors because of their ancient wealth:
for though they give us all their heritage,
on the strength of which we claim to be of noble descent,
yet they cannot bequeath by any means
or to any of us their virtuous manner of life
which made them be called noblemen;
and which summoned us to follow them at the same level. . . .

. . . Take fire, and bear it into the darkest house
from here to the Mount of Caucasus,
and let men shut the doors and go away;
yet the fire will blaze and burn as well
as if twenty thousand men were looking at it;
it will maintain its natural function always
until it dies, I'll stake my life.

By this you can easily see that nobility
is not tied to possession,
since people do not perform their function
without variation as does the fire, according to its nature.
For, God knows, men may very often find
a lord's son committing shameful and vile deeds;
and he who wishes to have credit for his nobility
because he was born of a noble house,
and because his elders were noble and virtuous,
but will not himself do any noble deeds
or follow the example of his late noble ancestor,
he is not noble, be he duke or earl,
for villainous, sinful deeds make him a churl.
This kind of nobility is only the renown
of your ancestors, earned by their great goodness,
which is a thing apart from yourself.
Your nobility comes from God alone;
then our true nobility comes of grace,
it was in no way bequeathed to us with our station in life. . . .

. . . And there, dear husband, I thus conclude
that even if my ancestors were low
yet God on high may — and so I hope —

grant me grace to live virtuously;
then I am noble, from the time when I begin
to live virtuously and avoid sin.

And as for the poverty you reprove me for,
high God in whom we believe
chose to live his life in willing poverty;
and certainly every man, maiden, or wife
can understand that Jesus, heaven's king,
would not choose a vicious way of life.
Contented poverty is an honorable thing, indeed;
that is said by Seneca and other learned men.
Whoever is content with his poverty
I hold to be rich, even if he hasn't a shirt.
He who covets anything is a poor man,
for he wants to have something which is not in his power.
But he who has nothing and desires nothing is rich . . .
although you may consider him nothing but a lowly man.

True poverty sings of its own accord.
Juvenal says of poverty, 'Merrily can
the poor man sing and joke before the
thieves when he goes by the road.'
Poverty is a good that is hated, and, I guess,
a great expeller of cares;
a great amender of knowledge, too,
to him that takes it in patience.
Poverty is this, although it seem unhealthy:
possession of that which no man will challenge.
Poverty will often, when a man is low,
make him know his God and himself as well.
Poverty is a glass, it seems to me,
through which he can see his true friends.
And therefore, sir, since I do not harm you by it,
do not reprove me for my poverty any more.

Now, sir, you reprove me for age;
but certainly, sir, aside from bookish
authority, you nobles who are honorable
say that one should honor an old person,

and call him father, for the sake of your nobility;
and I can find authors to that effect, I imagine.

Now as to the point that I am ugly and old —
then you need not dread being a cuckold;
for ugliness and age, as I may thrive,
are great wardens of chastity.
But, nevertheless, since I know what pleases you,
I shall fulfill your fleshly appetite.

"Choose now," said she, "one of these two things:
to have me ugly and old until I die,
and be a faithful, humble wife to you,
and never displease you in all my life,
or else to have me young and fair,
and take your chances on the flocking
of people to your house because of me —
or to some other place, it may well be.
Now choose yourself, whichever you like."

The knight considered and sighed sorely,
but at last he spoke in this manner,
"My lady and my love, and wife so dear,
I put myself under your wise control;
you yourself choose which may be most pleasurable
and most honorable to you and to me also.
I don't care which of the two I get;
for whatever pleases you suffices for me."

"Then have I got mastery over you," said she,
"since I may choose and rule as I please?"

"Yes, certainly, wife," said he, "I consider that best."

"Kiss me," said she, "we won't be angry any more;
for I swear I will be both these things to you;
that is to say, both fair indeed and good.
I pray to God that I may die of madness
if I am not just as good and true to you
as ever was wife since the world began.

And, if I am not tomorrow as fair to see
as any lady, empress, or queen
between the east and the west,
do with the question of my life and death just as you wish.
Raise the curtain, and see how it is."

And when the knight actually saw all this —
that she was so fair and so young, too,
he seized her in his two arms for joy;
his heart was bathed in bliss;
he kissed her a thousand times in a row.
And she obeyed him in everything
that might give him pleasure or joy.

And thus they lived to the end of their lives
in perfect joy; and Jesu Christ send us
husbands who are meek, young, and lively in bed,
and grace to outlive those that we marry.
And also I pray Jesu to shorten the lives
of those that won't be governed by their wives;
and as for old and angry niggards of their money,
God send them soon a very pestilence.

THE MAN MAKES AND THE WOMAN TAKES

"The Man Makes and the Woman Takes" is a tale from Florida. It was originally recorded by the distinguished folklorist Zora Neale Hurston, and published in her 1935 collection of African-American tales, *Mules and Men*.

The Man Makes and the Woman Takes

You see, in the very first days, God made a man and a woman and put them in a house together to live. Back in those days the women were just as strong as the men, and both of them did the same things. They used to get to fussing about who was going to do this and that; and sometimes they'd fight. But they were even balanced and neither one could get the better of the other.

One day the man said to himself, "I believe I'm going to go see God and ask him for a little more strength so I can make this woman obey me. I'm tired of the way things are." So he went on up to God. "Good morning, Old Father."

"Howdy, man. What are you doing around my throne so early this morning?"

The man said: "I'm troubled in my mind, and nobody can ease my spirit except you." God said: "Put your plea in the right form and I'll hear it and answer."

"Old Maker, with the morning stars glittering in your shining crown, with the dust from your footsteps making worlds upon worlds, with the blazing bird we call the sun flying out of your right hand in the morning and consuming all day the flesh and blood of stump-black darkness, and flying home every evening to rest on your left hand, and never once in all your eternal years mistook the left hand for the right, I ask you please to give me more strength than that woman you give me, so I can make her obey me. I know you don't want to be coming down way past the moon and stars to be straightening her out all the time. So give me a little more strength, Old Maker, and I'll do it."

"All right, man, I'll give you more strength than the woman."

So the man ran all the way down the stairs from Heaven until he reached home. He was so anxious to try his new strength on the woman that he couldn't take his time. As soon as he got in the house he hollered, "Woman! Here's your Boss. God told me to handle you in whatever way I please. So look at me good and listen well, for from now on I'm your boss."

The woman started fighting him right away. She fought him hard, but he beat her. She got her second wind and tried him again, but again he beat her. She got herself together and made the third try on him vigorously, but he beat her every time. He was so proud that he could whip her at last that he just crowed over her and made her do a lot of things she didn't like. He told her, "As long as you obey me, I'll be good to you, but every time you disobey, I'm going to put plenty of wood on your back and plenty of water in your eyes."

The woman was so mad she went straight to Heaven and stood before the Lord. She didn't waste any words either. She said, "Lord, I come before you mighty mad today. I want back the strength and power I used to have."

"Woman, you got the same power you had since the beginning."

"Why is it that the man can beat me now and he used to not be able to do it?"

"He's got more strength than he used to have. He came and asked me for it and I gave it to him. I give to them that ask, and you haven't ever asked me for more power."

"Please, sir, God, I'm asking you for it now. Just give me the same as you gave him."

God shook his head. "It's too late now, woman. What I give, I never take back. I gave him more strength than you, and no matter how much I give you, he'll always have more."

The woman was so mad she wheeled around and went on off straight to the Devil and told him what had happened. He said, "Don't be discouraged, woman. Just listen to me and take those frowns out of your face. Turn around and go right on back to Heaven and ask God to give you that bunch of keys hanging by the mantelpiece. Then you bring them to me and I'll show you what to do with them."

So the woman climbed back up to Heaven again. She was mighty tired, but she was more mad than she was tired. So she climbed all night long and got back up to Heaven again. When she got before the throne, butter wouldn't melt in her mouth.

"O Lord and Master of the rainbow, I know your power. You never make two mountains without putting a valley in between. I know you can hit a straight lick with a crooked stick."

"Ask for what you want, woman," God said.

"God, please give me that bunch of keys hanging by your mantelpiece, and I won't ask for anything more."

He laughed and said, "Take them."

So the woman took the keys and hurried on back to the Devil with them. There were three keys. The Devil said, "You see these three keys? They have more power in them than all the strength the man can ever get if you handle them right. Now this first big key is to the door of the kitchen, and you know a man always favors his stomach. This second one is the key to the bedroom, and he doesn't like to be shut out from that either. And this last key is the key to the cradle, and he doesn't want to be cut off from his generations at all. So now you take these keys and go lock up everything and wait until he comes to you. Then don't unlock anything until he uses his strength for your benefit and your desires."

The woman thanked him and told him, "If it wasn't for you, Lord knows what us poor women would do."

So she started off, but the Devil stopped her. "Just one more thing: Don't go home bragging about your keys. Just lock up everything and say nothing until you get asked. And then don't talk too much."

The woman went on home and did like the Devil told her. When the man came home from work she was sitting on the porch singing some song about "Peck on the wood make the bed go good." And when the man found those doors fastened that used to stand wide open, he swelled up like pine lumber after a rain. First thing he tried to break in because he figured his strength would overcome all obstacles. When he saw he couldn't do it, he asked the woman, "Who locked this door?"

She told him, "Me."

"Where did you get the key from?"

"God gave it to me."

He ran up to God and said, "God, woman has me locked away from my food, my bed, and my generations, and she said you gave her the keys." God said, "I did, man, I gave her the keys, but the Devil showed her how to use them."

"Well, Old Maker, please give me some keys just like them so she can't get full control."

"No, man, what I give, I give. Woman has the keys."

"How can I know about my generations?"

"Ask the woman."

So the man came on back and had to give his respect to the woman. And when he did, she opened the doors. Man is proud, so it took a lot out of him, but he did what he needed to do, and the woman opened the doors.

After a while he said to the woman, "Let's divide up. I'll give you half of my strength if you let me hold the keys in my hands."

The woman was thinking that over when the Devil popped up and told her, "Tell him no. Let him keep his strength, and you keep your keys."

So the woman wouldn't trade with him, and the man had to mortgage his strength to her to live. And that's why the man makes and the woman takes. You men is still bragging about your strength and the women is sitting on the keys and letting you blow off till she ready to put the bridle on you.

Stepped on a pin, the pin bent,
And that's the way the story went.

WILLIAM SHAKESPEARE

The Taming of the Shrew is one of Shakespeare's most beloved works. But one senses that this comedy was less a reflection on a woman's "place" in the household than simply a vehicle for some boisterous fun on a popular theme. In fact, Shakespeare's comedies feature a number of assertive female characters (one thinks immediately of Portia in *The Merchant of Venice* and of Beatrice in *As You Like It*) whose wit, wisdom, and grace earn them the reverence of their suitors. Scholars trace the play to several contemporary sources. It is thought that the bard threw bits of these works together in fashioning his comedy. In any case, nobody has contended that Shakespeare's personal life was in any way reflected here.

Shakespeare's own marriage, to Anne Hathaway, seems to have been an unsatisfactory union. His wife did not follow him to London, so that they were separated for a long period of time. And Shakespeare confounded later generations by leaving her his "second best bed" in his will.

The Taming of the Shrew

Act III, Scene II

Before Baptista's House
[Reenter Petruchio, Katharina, Bianca, Baptista, Hortensio, Grumio, and Tranio.]
PETRUCHIO Gentlemen and friends, I thank you for your pains:

      I know you think to dine with me today,
      And have prepared great store of wedding cheer;
      But so it is, my haste doth call me hence,
      And therefore here I mean to take my leave.
BAPTISTA Is't possible you will away tonight?
PET.   I must away today, before night come:
      Make it no wonder; if you knew my business,
      You would entreat me rather go than stay.
      And, honest company, I thank you all,
      That have beheld me give away myself
      To this most sweet and virtuous wife:
      Dine with my father, drink a health to me;
      For I must hence; and farewell to you all.
TRANIO   Let us entreat you stay till after dinner.
PET.   It may not be.
GREMIO   Let me entreat you.
PET.   It cannot be.
KATHARINA   Let me entreat you.
PET.   I am content.
KATH. Are you content to stay?
PET.   I am content you shall entreat me stay;
      But yet, not stay, entreat me how you can.
KATH. Now, if you love me, stay.
PET.   Grumio, my horse.
GRUMIO   Ay, sir, they be ready: the oats have eaten the horses.
KATH. Nay, then,
      Do what thou canst, I will not go today;
      No, nor tomorrow, not till I please myself.
      The door is open, sir; there lies your way;
      You may be jogging whiles your boots are green;
      For me, I'll not be gone till I please myself:
      'Tis like you'll prove a jolly surly groom,
      That take it on you at the first so roundly.
PET.   O Kate, content thee; prithee, be not angry.
KATH. I will be angry: what hast thou to do?
      Father, be quiet: he shall stay my leisure.
GRE. Ay, marry, sir, now it begins to work.
KATH. Gentlemen, forward to the bridal dinner:
      I see a woman may be made a fool,
      If she had not a spirit to resist.

PET.   They shall go forward, Kate, at thy command.
        Obey the bride, you that attend on her;
        Go to the feast, revel and domineer,
        Carouse full measure to her maidenhead,
        Be mad and merry, or go hang yourselves:
        But for my bonny Kate, she must with me.
        Nay, look not big, nor stamp, nor stare, nor fret;
        I will be master of what is mine own:
        She is my goods, my chattels; she is my house,
        My household stuff, my field, my barn,
        My horse, my ox, my ass, my any thing;
        And here she stands, touch her whoever dare;
        I'll bring mine action on the proudest he
        That stops my way in Padua. Grumio,
        Draw forth thy weapon, we are beset with thieves;
        Rescue thy mistress, if thou be a man.
        Fear not, sweet wench, they shall not touch thee, Kate:
        I'll buckler thee against a million.
        [Exeunt Petruchio, Katharina, and Grumio.]
BAP.   Nay, let them go, a couple of quiet ones.
GRE.   Went they not quickly I should die with laughing.
TRA.   Of all mad matches never was the like.
LUCENTIO Mistress, what's your opinion of your sister?
BIANCA   That, being mad herself, she's madly mated.
GRE.   I warrant him, Petruchio is Kated.
BAP.   Neighbors and friends, though bride and bridegroom wants
        For to supply the places at the table,
        You know there wants no junkets at the feast.
        Lucentio, you shall supply the bridegroom's place;
        And let Bianca take her sister's room.
TRA.   Shall sweet Bianca practise how to bride it?
BAP.   She shall, Lucentio. Come, gentlemen,
        let's go. *[Exeunt.]*

Act IV, Scene I

Petruchio's Country House
[Enter Curtis.]
CURT. Who is it that calls so coldly?

GRU. A piece of ice: if thou doubt it, thou mayst slide from my shoulder to
my heel with no greater a run but my head and my neck. A fire, good
Curtis.

CURT. Is my master and his wife coming, Grumio?

GRU. Oh, ay, Curtis, ay: and therefore fire, fire; cast on no water.

CURT. Is she so hot a shrew as she's reported?

GRU. She was, good Curtis, before this frost:
but, thou knowest, winter tames man, woman
and beast; for it hath tamed my old master and
my new mistress and myself, fellow Curtis. . . .
Where's the cook? is supper ready,
the house trimmed, rushes strewed, cobwebs swept;
the serving men in their new fustian,
their white stockings, and every officer his
wedding-garment on? Be the jacks fair within,
the jills fair without, the carpets laid, and every
thing in order?

CURT. All ready; and therefore, I pray thee,
news.

GRU. First, know, my horse is tired; my
master and mistress fallen out.

CURT. How?

GRU. Out of their saddles into the dirt; and
thereby hangs a tale.

CURT. Let's ha't, good Grumio.

GRU. Lend thine ear.

CURT. Here.

GRU. There. [*Strikes him.*]

CURT. That is to feel a tale, not to hear a tale.

GRU. And therefore 'tis called a sensible tale:
and this cuff was but to knock at your ear, and
beseech listening. Now I begin; Imprimis, we
came down a foul hill, my master riding behind
my mistress, —

CURT. Both of one horse?

GRU. What's that to thee?

CURT. Why, a horse.

GRU. Tell thou the tale: but hadst thou not
crossed me, thou shouldst have heard how her
horse fell and she under her horse; thou shouldst

325

have heard in how miry a place, how she was
bemoiled, how he left her with the horse upon her,
how he beat me because her horse stumbled,
how she waded through the dirt to pluck him off
me, how he swore, how she prayed, that never
prayed before, how I cried, how the horses ran
away, how her bridle was burst, how I lost my
crupper, with many things of worthy memory,
which now shall die in oblivion and thou return
unexperienced to thy grave.

CURT. By this reckoning he is more shrew
than she.

GRU. Ay; and that thou and the proudest of
you shall find when he comes home. But what
talk I of this? Call forth Nathaniel, Joseph,
Nicholas, Philip, Walter, Sugarsop and the rest:
let their heads be sleekly combed, their blue
coats brushed and their garters of an indifferent
knit: let them curtsy with their left legs and not
presume to touch a hair of my master's
horsetail till they kiss their hands. Are they all ready?

CURT. They are.
[Enter four or five Serving-men.]

NATH. Welcome home, Grumio!

PHIL. How now, Grumio!

JOS. What, Grumio!

NICH. Fellow Grumio!

NATH. How now, old lad?

GRU. Welcome, you; — how now, you; — what,
you; — fellow, you; — and thus much for greeting.
Now, my spruce companions, is all ready, and
all things neat?

NATH. All things is ready. How near is our master?

GRU. E'en at hand, alighted by this;
and therefore be not — Cock's passion, silence! I hear
my master.
[Enter Petruchio and Katharina.]

PET. Where be these knaves? What, no man at door
To hold my stirrup nor to take my horse!
Where is Nathaniel, Gregory, Philip?

326

ALL SERV. Here, here, sir; here, sir.

PET.   Here, sir! here, sir! here sir! here, sir!
    You logger-headed and unpolish'd grooms!
    What, no attendance? no regard? no duty?
    Where is the foolish knave I sent before?

GRU.   Here, sir; as foolish as I was before.

PET.   You peasant swain! You whoreson malthouse drudge!
    Did I not bid thee meet me in the park,
    And bring along these rascal knaves with thee?

GRU.   Nathaniel's coat, sir, was not fully made,
    And Gabriel's pumps were all unpink'd i' the heel;
    There was no link to colour Peter's hat,
    And Walter's dagger was not come from sheathing:
    There were none fine but Adam, Ralph, and Gregory;
    The rest were ragged, old, and beggarly;
    Yet, as they are, here are they come to meet you.

PET.   Go, rascals, go, and fetch my supper in.
    [Exeunt Servants.]
    [Singing]
    Where is the life that late I led —
    Where are those — Sit down, Kate, and welcome. —
    Soud, soud, soud, soud!
    [Reenter Servants with supper.]
    Why, when, I say? Nay, good sweet Kate, be merry.
    Off with my boots, you rogues! you villains, when
    [Sings]
    It was the friar of orders gray,
    As he forth walked on his way: —
    Out, you rogue! you pluck my foot awry:
    Take that, and mend the plucking off the other.
    [Strikes him.]
    Be merry, Kate. Some water, here; what, ho!
    Where's my spaniel Troilus? Sirrah, get you hence,
    And bid my cousin Ferdinand come hither:
    One, Kate, that you must kiss, and be acquainted with.
    Where are my slippers? Shall I have some water?
    [Enter one with water.]
    Come, Kate, and wash, and welcome heartily.
    You whoreson villain! will you let it fall?
    [Strikes him.]

KATH. Patience, I pray you; 'twas a fault unwilling.

PET.   A whoreson bettle-headed, flap-ear'd knave!
     Come, Kate, sit down; I know you have a stomach.
     Will you give thanks, sweet Kate; or else shall I?
     What's this? mutton?

FIRST SERV. Ay.

PET.   Who brought it?

PETER I.

PET.   'Tis burnt; and so is all the meat.
     What dogs are these! Where is the rascal cook?
     How durst you, villains, bring it from the dresser,
     And serve it thus to me that love it not?
     There, take it to you, trenchers, cups, and all:
     [Throws the meat, etc., about the stage.]
     You heedless joltheads and unmanner'd slaves!
     What, do you grumble? I'll be with you straight.

KATH. I pray you, husband, be not so disquiet:
     The meat was well, if you were so contented.

PET.   I tell thee, Kate, 'twas burnt and dried away;
     And I expressly am forbid to touch it,
     For it engenders choler, planteth anger;
     And better 'twere that both of us did fast,
     Since, of ourselves, ourselves are choleric,
     Than feed it with such over-roasted flesh.
     Be patient; tomorrow't shall be mended,
     And for this night, we'll fast for company:
     Come, I will bring thee to thy bridal chamber.
     [Exeunt.]
     [Reenter Servants severally.]

NATH. Peter, didst ever see the like?
     Peter. He kills her in her own humour.
     [Reenter Curtis.]

GRU. Where is he?

CURT. In her chamber, making a sermon of continency to her;
     And rails, and swears, and rates, that she, poor soul,
     Knows not which way to stand, to look, to speak,
     And sits as one new-risen from a dream.
     Away, away! for he is coming hither.
     [Exeunt.]
     [Reenter Petruchio.]

PET.   Thus have I politicly begun my reign,
And 'tis my hope to end successfully.
My falcon now is harp and passing empty;
And till she stoop she must not be full-gorged,
For then she never looks upon her lure.
Another way I have to man my haggard,
To make her come and know her keeper's call,
That is, to watch her, as we watch these kites
That bate and beat and will not be obedient.
She eat no meat today, nor none shall eat;
Last night she slept not, nor tonight she shall not;
As with the meat, some undeserved fault
I'll find about the making of the bed;
And here I'll fling the pillow, there the bolster,
This way the coverlet, another way the sheets:
Ay, and amid this hurly I intend
That all is done in reverend care of her;
And in conclusion she shall watch all night:
And if she chance to nod I'll rail and brawl
And with the clamour keep her still awake.
This is a way to kill a wife with kindness;
And thus I'll curb her mad and headstrong humour.
He that knows better how to tame a shrew,
Now let him speak: 'tis charity to show.
[Exit]

JOHN STUART MILL

John Stuart Mill (1806-1873) was one of the most important and influential thinkers of the nineteenth-century English-speaking world. A British philosopher and political economist, he was a great advocate of democratic reform, and viewed marriage as a principal institution in need of such reform. *On the Subjection of Women* was published for the first time in 1869, more than ten years after the death of Mill's wife, Harriet Taylor Mill. But the work was very much influenced by her ideas and advice. Indeed, Mill viewed his wife as a collaborator in the planning of this and three other works: On *Liberty, Utilitarianism,* and *Thoughts on Parliamentary Reform.*

On the Subjection of Women

. . . But how, it will be asked, can any society exist without government? In a family, as in a state, some one person must be the ultimate ruler. Who shall decide when married people differ in opinion? Both cannot have their way, yet a decision one way or the other must be come to.

It is not true that in all voluntary association between two people, one of them must be absolute master: still less that the law must determine which of them it shall be. The most frequent case of voluntary association, next to marriage, is partnership in business: and it is not found or thought necessary to enact that in every partnership, one partner shall have entire control over the concern, and the others shall be bound to obey his order. No one would enter into partnership on terms which would subject him to the responsibilities of a principal, with only the powers and privileges of a clerk or agent. If the law dealt with other contracts as it does with marriage, it would ordain that one partner should administer the common business as if it was his private concern; that the others should have only delegated powers; and that this one should be designated by some general presumption of law, for example as being the eldest. The law never does this: nor does experience show it to be necessary that any theoretical inequality of power should exist between the partners, or that the partnership should have any other conditions than what they may themselves appoint by their articles of agreement. Yet it might seem that the exclusive power might be conceded with less danger to the rights and interests of the inferior, in the case of partnership, than in that of marriage, since he is free to cancel the power by withdrawing from the connexion. The wife has no such power,[1] and even if she had, it is almost always desirable that she should try all measures before resorting to it.

It is quite true that things which have to be decided every day, and cannot adjust themselves gradually, or wait for a compromise, ought to depend on one will; one person must have their sole control. But it does not follow that this should always be the same person. The natural arrangement is a division of powers between the two; each being absolute in the executive branch of their own department, and any change of system and principle requiring the consent of both. The division neither can nor should be pre-established by the law, since it must depend on individual capacities and suitabilities. If the two persons chose, they might pre-appoint it by the marriage contract, as pecuniary arrangements are now often pre-appointed. There would seldom be any difficulty in deciding such things by mutual consent, unless the marriage was one of those unhappy ones in which all other things, as well as this, become subjects of bickering and dispute. The divisions of rights would naturally follow the division of duties and functions; and that is already made by consent, or at all events not by law, but by general custom, modified and modifiable at the pleasure of the persons concerned.

The real practical decision of affairs, to whichever may be given the legal authority, will greatly depend, as it even now does, upon comparative qualifications. The mere fact that he is usually the eldest, will in most cases give the preponderance to the man; at least until they both attain a time of life at which the difference in their years is of no importance. There will naturally also be a more potential voice on the side, whichever it is, that brings the means of support. Inequality from this source does not depend on the law of marriage, but on the general conditions of human society, as now constituted. The influence of mental superiority, either general or special, and of superior decision of character, will necessarily tell for much. It always does so at present. And this fact shows how little foundation there is for the apprehension that the powers and responsibilities of partners in life (as of partners in business), cannot be satisfactorily apportioned by agreement between themselves. They always are so apportioned, except in cases in which the marriage institution is a failure. Things never come to an issue of downright power on one side, and obedience in the other, except where the connexion altogether has been a mistake, and it would be a blessing to both parties to be relieved from it. Some may say that the very thing by which an amicable settlement of differences becomes possible is the power of legal compulsion known to be in reserve; as people submit to an arbitration because there is a court of law in the background, which they know that they can be forced to obey. But to make the cases parallel, we must suppose that the rule of the court of law was, not to try the cause, but to give judgment always for the same side, suppose the defendant. If so, the amenability to it would be a motive with the plaintiff to agree to almost any arbitration, but it would be just the reverse with the defendant. The despotic power which the law gives to the husband may be a reason to make the wife assent to any compromise by which power is practically shared between the two, but it cannot be the reason why the husband does. That there is always among decently conducted people a practical compromise, though one of them at least is under no physical or moral necessity of making it, shows that the natural motives which lead to a voluntary adjustment of the united life of two persons in a manner acceptable to both, do on the whole, except in unfavourable cases, prevail. The matter is certainly not improved by laying down as an ordinance of law, that the superstructure of free government shall be raised upon a legal basis of despotism on one side and subjection on the other, and that every concession which the despot makes may, at his mere pleasure, and without any warning, be recalled. Besides that no freedom is worth much when held on so precarious a tenure, its conditions are not likely to be the most equitable when the law throws so prodigious a weight into one scale; when the adjustment rests between two persons one of whom is declared to be entitled to everything, the other not only entitled to nothing except during the good pleasure of the first, but under the strongest moral and religious obligation not to rebel under any excess of oppression.

A pertinacious adversary, pushed to extremities, may say, that husbands indeed are willing to be reasonable, and to make fair concessions to their partners without being compelled to it, but that wives are not: that if allowed any rights of their own, they will acknowledge no rights at all in anyone else, and never will yield in anything, unless they can be compelled, by the man's mere authority, to yield in everything. This would have been said by many persons some generations ago, when satires on women were in vogue, and men thought it a clever thing to insult women for being what men made them. But it will be said by no one now who is worth replying to. It is not the doctrine of the present day that women are less susceptible of good feeling, and consideration for those with whom they are united by the strongest ties, than men are. On the contrary, we are perpetually told that women are better than men, by those who are totally opposed to treating them as if they were as good; so that the saying has passed into a piece of tiresome cant, intended to put a complimentary face upon an injury, and resembling those celebrations of royal clemency which, according to Gulliver, the king of Lilliput always prefixed to his most sanguinary decrees. If women are better than men in anything, it surely is in individual self-sacrifice for those of their own family. But I lay little stress on this, so long as they are universally taught that they are born and created for self-sacrifice. I believe that equality of rights would abate the exaggerated self-abnegation which is the present artificial ideal of feminine character, and that a good woman would not be more self-sacrificing than the best man: but on the other hand, men would be much more unselfish and self-sacrificing than at present, because they would no longer be taught to worship their own will as such a grand thing that it is actually the law for another rational being. There is nothing which men so easily learn as this self-worship; all privileged persons, and all privileged classes, have had it. The more we descend in the scale of humanity, the intenser it is; and most of all in those who are not, and can never expect to be, raised above anyone except an unfortunate wife and children. The honourable exceptions are proportionally fewer than in the case of almost any other human infirmity. Philosophy and religion, instead of keeping it in check, are generally suborned to defend it; and nothing controls it but that practical feeling of the equality of human beings, which is the theory of Christianity, but which Christianity will never practically teach, while it sanctions institutions grounded on an arbitrary preference of one human being over another.

There are, no doubt, women, as there are men, whom equality of consideration will not satisfy; with whom there is no peace while any will or wish is regarded but their own. Such persons are a proper subject for the law of divorce. They are only fit to live alone, and no human beings ought to be compelled to associate their lives with them. But the legal subordination tends to make such characters among women more, rather than less, frequent. If the man exerts his whole power, the woman is of course crushed: but if she is treated with indulgence, and permitted to assume power, there is no rule to set limits to her encroachments. The law, not determining her rights, but theoretically allowing her none at all, practically declares that the measure of what she has a right to, is what she can contrive to get.

The equality of married persons before the law, is not only the sole mode in which that particular relation can be made consistent with justice to both sides, and conducive to the happiness of both, but it is the only means of rendering the daily life of mankind, in any high sense, a school of moral cultivation. Though the truth may not be felt or generally acknowledged for generations to come, the only school of genuine moral sentiment is society between equals. The moral education of mankind has hitherto emanated chiefly from the law of force, and is adapted almost solely to the relations which force creates. In the less advanced states of society, people hardly recognise any relation with their equals. To be an equal is to be an enemy. Society, from its highest place to its lowest, is one long chain, or rather ladder, where every individual is either above or below his nearest neighbour, and wherever he does not command he must obey. Existing moralities, accordingly, are mainly fitted to a relation of command and obedience. Yet command and obedience are but unfortunate necessities of human life: society in equality is its normal state. Already in modern life, and more and more as it progressively improves, command and obedience become exceptional facts in life, equal association its general rule. The morality of the first ages rested on the obligation to submit to power; that of the ages next following, on the right of the weak to the forbearance and protection of the strong. How much longer is one form of society and life to content itself with the morality made for another? We have had the morality of submission, and the morality of chivalry and generosity; the time is now come for the morality of justice. Whenever, in former ages, any approach has been made to society in equality, Justice has asserted its claims as the foundation of virtue. It was thus in the free republics of antiquity. But even in the best of these, the equals were limited to the free male citizens; slaves, women, and the unenfranchised residents were under the law of force. The joint influence of Roman civilisation and of Christianity obliterated these distinctions, and in theory (if only partially in practice) declared the claims of the human being, as such, to be paramount to those of sex, class, or social position. The barriers which had begun to be leveled were raised again by the northern conquests; and the whole of modern history consists of the slow process by which they have since been wearing away. We are entering into an order of things in which justice will again be the primary virtue; grounded as before on equal, but now also on sympathetic association; having its root no longer in the instinct of equals for self-protection, but in a cultivated sympathy between them; and no one being now left out, but an equal measure being extended to all. It is no novelty that mankind do not distinctly foresee their own changes, but that their sentiments are adapted to past, not to coming ages. To see the futurity of the species has always been the privilege of the intellectual elite, or of those who have learnt from them; to have the feelings of that futurity has been the distinction, and usually the martyrdom, of a still rarer elite. Institutions, books, education, society, all go on training human beings for the old, long after the new has come; much more when it is only coming. But the true virtue of human beings is fitness to live together as equals; claiming nothing for themselves but what they as freely conceded to everyone else; regarding command of any kind as an exceptional necessity, and in all cases a temporary one; and preferring, when ever possible, the society of those with whom leading and following can be alternate and reciprocal. To these virtues, nothing in life as at present constituted gives cultivation by exercise. The family is a school of despotism, in which the virtues of despotism, but also its vices, are largely nourished. Citizenship, in free countries, is partly a school of society in equality; but citizenship fills only a small place in modern life, and does not come near the daily habits or inmost sentiments. The family, justly constituted, would be the real school of the virtues of freedom. It is sure to be a sufficient one of everything else. It will always be a school of obedience for the children, of command for the parents. What is needed is, that it should be a school of sympathy in equality, of living together in love, without power on one side or obedience on the other. This it ought to be between the parents. It would then be an exercise of those virtues which each requires to fit them for all other association, and a model to the children of the feelings and conduct which their temporary training by means of obedience is designed to render habitual, and therefore natural, to them. The moral training of mankind will never be adapted to the conditions of the life for which all other human progress is a preparation, until they practise in the family the same moral rule which is adapted to the normal constitution of human society. Any sentiment of freedom which can exist in a man whose nearest and dearest intimacies are with those of whom he is absolute master, is not the genuine or Christian love of freedom, but, what the love of freedom generally was in the ancients and in the middle ages — an intense feeling of the dignity and importance of his own personality; making him disdain a yoke for himself, of which he has no abhorrence whatever in the abstract, but which he is abundantly ready to impose on others for his own interest or glorification.

I readily admit (and it is the very foundation of my hopes) that numbers of married people even under the present law (in the higher classes of England probably a great majority), live in the spirit of a just law of equality. Laws never would be improved, if there were not numerous persons whose moral sentiments are better than the existing laws. Such persons ought to support the principles here advocated; of which the only object is to make all other married couples similar to what these are now. But persons even of considerable moral worth, unless they are also thinkers, are very ready to believe that laws or practices, the evils of which they have not personally experienced, do not produce any evils, but (if seen to be generally approved of) probably do good, and that it is wrong to object to them. It would, however, be a great mistake in such married people to suppose, because the legal conditions of the tie which unites them do not occur to their thoughts once in a twelvemonth, and because they live and feel in all respects as if they were legally equals, that the same is the case with all other married couples, wherever the husband is not a notorious ruffian. To suppose this, would be to show equal ignorance of human nature and of fact. The less fit a man is for the possession of power — the less likely to be allowed to exercise it over any person with that person's voluntary consent — the more does he hug himself in the consciousness of the power the law gives him, exact its legal rights to the utmost point which custom (the custom of men like himself) will tolerate, and take pleasure in using the power, merely to enliven the agreeable sense of possessing it. What is more; in the most naturally brutal and morally uneducated part of the lower classes, the legal slavery of the woman, and something in the merely physical subjection to their will as an instrument, causes them to feel a sort of disrespect and contempt towards their own wife which they do not feel towards any other woman, or any other human being, with whom they come in contact; and which makes her seem to them an appropriate subject of any kind of indignity. Let an acute observer of the signs of feeling, who has the requisite opportunities, judge for himself whether this is not the case: and if he finds that it is, let him not wonder at any amount of disgust and indignation that can be felt against institutions which lead naturally to this depraved state of the human mind.

We shall be told, perhaps, that religion imposes the duty of obedience; as every established fact which is too bad to admit of any other defense, is always presented to us as an injunction of religion. The Church, it is very true, enjoins it in her formularies, but it would be difficult to derive any such injunction from Christianity. We are told that St. Paul said, "Wives, obey your husbands": but he also said, "Slaves, obey your masters." It was not St. Paul's business, nor was it consistent with his object, the propagation of Christianity, to incite anyone to rebellion against existing laws. The Apostle's acceptance of all social institutions as he found them, is no more to be construed as a disapproval of attempts to improve them at the proper time, than his declaration, "The powers that be are ordained of God," gives his sanction to military despotism, and to that alone, as the Christian form of political government, or commands passive obedience to it. To pretend that Christianity was intended to stereotype existing forms of government and society, and protect them against change, is to reduce it to the level of Islamism or Brahminism. It is precisely because Christianity has not done this, that it has been the religion of the progressive portion of mankind, and Islamism, Brahminism, etc. have been those of the stationary portions; or rather (for there is no such thing as a really stationary society) of the declining portions. There have been abundance of people, in all ages of Christianity, who tried to make it something of the same kind; to convert us into a sort of Christian Mussulmans, with the Bible for a Koran, prohibiting all improvement: and great has been their power, and many have had to sacrifice their lives in resisting them. But they have been resisted, and the resistance has made us what we are, and will yet make us what we are to be.

After what has been said respecting the obligation of obedience, it is almost superfluous to say anything concerning the more special point included in the general one — a woman's right to her own property; for I need not hope that this treatise can make any impression upon those who need anything to convince them that a woman's inheritance or gains ought to be as much her own after marriage as before. The rule is simple: whatever would be the husband's or wife's if they were not married, should be under their exclusive control during marriage; which need not interfere with the power to tie up property by settlement, in order to preserve it for children. Some people are sentimentally shocked at the idea of a separate interest in money matters, as inconsistent with the ideal fusion of two lives into one. For my own part, I am one of the strongest supporters of community of goods, when resulting from an entire unity of feeling in the owners, which makes all things common between them. But I have no relish for a community of goods resting on the doctrine, that what is mine is yours, but what is yours is not mine; and I should prefer to decline entering into such a compact with anyone, though I were myself the person to profit by it.

This particular injustice and oppression to women, which is, to common apprehensions, more obvious than all the rest, admits of remedy without interfering with any other mischiefs: and there can be little doubt that it will be one of the earliest remedied. . . .

GEORGE BERNARD SHAW

Playwright, philosopher, essayist, economist, music critic, and social reformer George Bernard Shaw (1856-1950) was interested in the subject of marriage from the very beginning of his career as a writer. Shaw regarded a critique of the institution of marriage as a key to the puzzle of women's cultural adaptation. And he saw the reform of marriage as a means toward a socialist future, as evidenced in this work and his famous *The Intelligent Woman's Guide to Socialism* (1928). Despite the typically Shavian tinge of sarcasm in this selection, Shaw was a deadly serious proponent of the economic and legal reform of marriage, as well as the equality of women and men within matrimony.

Getting Married

Economic Slavery Again the Root Difficulty

. . . Until the economic independence of women is achieved, we shall have to . . . maintain marriage as a slavery. And here let me ask the Government of the day (1910) a question with regard to the Labor Exchanges it has very wisely established throughout the country. What do these Exchanges do when a woman enters and states that her occupation is that of a wife and mother; that she is out of a job; and that she wants an employer? If the Exchange refuses to entertain her application, they are clearly excluding nearly the whole female sex from the benefit of the Act. If not, they must become matrimonial agencies, unless, indeed, they are prepared to become something worse by putting the woman down as a housekeeper and introducing her to an employer without making marriage a condition of the hiring.

Labor Exchanges and the White Slavery

Suppose, again, a woman present herself at the Labor Exchange, and states her trade as that of a White Slave, meaning the unmentionable trade pursued by thousands of women in all civilized cities. Will the Labor Exchange find employers for her? If not, what will it do with her? If it throws her back destitute and unhelped on the streets to starve, it might as well not exist as far as she is concerned; and the problem of unemployment remains unsolved at its most painful point. Yet if it find honest employment for her and for all the unemployed wives and mothers, it must find new places in the world for women; and in so doing it must achieve for them economic independence of men. And when this is done, can we feel sure that any woman will consent to be a wife and mother (not to mention the less respectable alternative) unless her position is made as eligible as that of the women for whom the Labor Exchanges are finding independent work? Will not many women now engaged in domestic work under circumstances which make it repugnant to them, abandon it and seek employment under other circumstances? As unhappiness in marriage is almost the only discomfort sufficiently irksome to induce a woman to break up her home, and economic dependence the only compulsion sufficiently stringent to force her to endure such unhappiness, the solution of the problem of finding independent employment for women may cause a great number of childless unhappy marriages to break up spontaneously, whether the marriage laws are altered or not. And here we must extend the term childless marriages to cover households in which the children have grown up and gone their own way, leaving the parents alone together: a point at which many worthy couples discover for the first time that they have long since lost interest in one another, and have been united only by a common interest in their children. We may expect, then, that marriages which are maintained by economic pressure alone will dissolve when that pressure is removed; and as all the parties to them will certainly not accept a celibate life, the law must sanction the dissolution in order to prevent a recurrence of the scandal which has moved the government to appoint the Commission now sitting to investigate the marriage question: the scandal, that is, of a great number of persons, condemned to celibacy by magisterial separation orders,[1] and, of course, refusing to submit to the condemnation, forming illicit connections to an extent which threatens to familiarize the working classes with an open disuse of marriage. In short, once set women free from

339

their economic slavery, and you will find that unless divorce is made as easy as the dissolution of a business partnership, the practice of dispensing with marriage will presently become so common that conventional couples will be ashamed to get married.

FRANCESCA CANCIAN

Francesca Cancian is a Professor of Sociology on the faculty of the University of California at Irvine. Currently, her major areas of research are intimate relationships and gender roles. In borrowing from the fields of history, economics, psychology, and even anthropology in her analysis of family life, her scholarly work is indicative of the eclectic approach of much sociological research on the family today. Cancian downplays the idea of biological determinacy in men's and women's different styles of love. Her notion is that many of our individual expectations of love and intimacy may actually be socially programmed.

Gender Politics: Love and Power in the Private and Public Spheres

Love has been a feminine specialty and preoccupation since the nineteenth century, a central part of women's sphere. Women's dependency on men's love has been attacked by feminists as a mystification that gives men power over women (Flax, 1982). And their argument makes sense in terms of an exchange theory of power — if women need men more than men need women, then men will have the power advantage in marriage and couple relationships.

This . . . [essay] . . . presents a perspective on the social organization of love that clarifies the links between love, dependency, and power. My perspective is based, first of all, on the empirical generalization that women and men prefer different styles of love that are consistent with their gender role. Women prefer emotional closeness and verbal expression; men prefer giving instrumental help and sex, forms of love that permit men to deny their dependency on women. Second, I argue that love is feminized in our society: that is, only women's style of love is recognized, and women are assumed to be more skilled at love and more in need of it.

My perspective clarifies how the social organization of love bolsters the power of men over women in close relationships, but it also suggests that men's power advantage in the private sphere is quite limited. It is primarily in the public sphere that feminized love promotes inequality in power. The feminization of love implies that men are independent individuals and by so doing obscures relations of dependency and exploitation in the work place and the community.

. . . Two styles of love emerged clearly in a study of seven couples by Wills, Weiss and Patterson (1974). The couples recorded their own interactions for several days. They noted how pleasant their relations were and also counted how often their spouse did a helpful chore, like cooking a good meal or repairing a faucet, and how often the spouse expressed acceptance or affection. The social scientists followed traditional usage and labeled practical help as "instrumental behavior" and expressing acceptance as "affectionate behavior," thereby denying the affectionate aspect of practical help. The wives seemed to be using the same scheme: they thought their marital relations were pleasant that day if their husband had directed a lot of affectionate behavior to them, regardless of his positive instrumental behavior. But the husbands' enjoyment of their marital relations depended on their wife's instrumental actions, not her affection (Wills et al., 1974). One husband, when told by the researchers to increase his affectionate behavior toward his wife, decided to wash her car, and was surprised when neither his wife nor the researchers accepted that as an "affectionate" act.

Other studies of married couples and friends report similar findings. Margaret Reedy (1977) surveyed 102 married couples and asked them how well a series of statements described their marriage. The men emphasized practical help and spending time together and gave higher ratings to statements like: "When she needs help I help her," and "She would rather spend her time with me than with anyone else." Men also described themselves as more sexually attracted. The women emphasized emotional security and were more likely to describe the relationship as secure, safe, and comforting. Another study of the ideal and actual relationship of several hundred young couples found that the husbands gave greater emphasis to feeling responsible for the partner's well-being and putting the spouse's needs first, as well as to spending time together. The wives gave greater importance to emotional involvement and verbal self-disclosure (Perlman, 1980). In friendships also, men value sharing activities, while women emphasize confiding their troubles and establishing a supportive emotional attachment (Dickens & Perlman, 1981).

There is also a large body of research showing that women are more skilled and more interested in love than men. Women are closer to their relatives and are more likely to have intimate friends (Adams, 1968; Dickens & Perlman, 1981). Women are more skilled in verbal self-disclosure and emotional expression (Henley, 1977; Komarovsky, 1962). When asked about what is most important in their lives, women usually put family relations first, while men are more likely to put work first.

. . . Bert Adams found that women were much more likely than men to say that their parents and relatives were very important to their lives (58% of women and 37% of men). However, when he looked at actual contact with relatives, he found much smaller differences (88% of women and 81% of men whose parents lived in the city saw their parents weekly). He concludes that "differences between males and females in relations with parents are discernible primarily in the subjective sphere: contact frequencies are quite similar" (Adams, 1968, p. 169).

In sum, women and men have different styles of love, but love is feminized. It is identified with qualities that are stereotypically feminine and with styles of love that women prefer.

Social historians help us identify the causes of this social organization of love. They describe how love became feminized in the nineteenth century as economic production became separated from the home and from personal relationships (see Degler, 1980; Ryan, 1979, 1981; Welter, 1966). They have shown how the increasing divergence of men's and women's daily activities produced a polarization of gender roles. Wives became economically dependent on their husbands, and an ideology of separate spheres developed that exaggerated the differences between women and men and between the loving home and the ruthless work place.

Building on this historical research, I interpret the feminization of love and gender differences in styles of love as caused primarily by: (1) the sexual division of labor that makes wives economically dependent on their husbands and makes women responsible for childrearing; (2) the separation of the public and private spheres; and (3) beliefs about gender roles. Thus, there are both socioeconomic and cultural causes of our social organization of love.

Love and the Power of Men over Women

In the private sphere of marriage and close relationships, the social organization of love bolsters men's power over women in two ways. First, it exaggerates women's dependency on men. If most people believe that women need heterosexual love more than men, then women will be at a power disadvantage, as many feminists have pointed out (Flax, 1982).

In fact, there is strong medical and sociological evidence that men depend on marriage as much as, or more than, women. For example, the mortality rate of unmarried men is much higher than married men, while marriage has a weaker effect on the mortality of women (Gove, 1973). The fact that men's health benefits from marriage more than women's health suggests that men depend more on marriage, whether or not they acknowledge this need. Men's dependency on marriage is also suggested by the tendency for women to have closer ties with friends and relatives than men. Thus, men are more dependent on their spouses for social support (Cancian, n.d. [a]. chap. 3). Men also remarry at higher rates than women (Stein, 1981, p. 358) and when they are asked about their major goals in life, a happy marriage is usually first or second on their list (Campbell, Converse, & Rodgers, 1976). But the centrality of independence to the masculine role seems to make us forget these facts. A dominant picture of gender politics in our culture is still a woman trying to entrap a man into an enduring love relationship, while all he wants is temporary sex.

Because of the social organization of love, men's dependency on close relationships remains covert and repressed, whereas women's dependency is overt and exaggerated. And it is overt dependency that affects power, according to social exchange theory. Thus, a woman gains power over her husband if he clearly places a high value on her company or if he expresses a high demand or need for what she supplies (Blau, 1964; Homans, 1967). If his need for her and high evaluation of her remain covert and unexpressed, her power will be low.

The denial of dependency is also evident in the styles of love that men prefer. Insofar as men admit that they are loving, their styles of love involve fulfilling women's needs and not on being dependent and needy themselves. Providing practical help, protection, and money, implies superiority over the one who receives these things. Sex also expresses male dominance insofar as the man takes the initiative and intercourse is defined either as him "taking" his pleasure or being skilled at "giving" her pleasure, in either case defining her as passive. The man's power advantage will also be strengthened if the couple assumes that his need for sex can be filled by any attractive woman, while her sexual needs can only be filled by the man she loves.

In contrast, women's preferred ways of loving involve admitting dependency and sharing or losing power. The intimate talk about personal troubles that appeals to women requires a mutual vulnerability, an ability to see oneself as weak and in need of support. Women's love is also associated with being responsive to the needs of others; this leads to giving up control, in the sense of being "on call" to provide care whenever it is requested.

In addition to affecting the balance of dependency between women and men, the feminization of love bolsters men's power by devaluing women's sphere of activities. Defining love as expressive devalues love, since our society tends to glorify instrumental achievement and to disparage emotional expression as sentimental and foolish (Fiedler, 1966; Inkeles, 1979). In fact, much of women's love consists of instrumental acts like preparing meals, washing clothes, or providing care during illness, but this is obscured by focusing on the expressive side of love. In our culture, a woman washing her husband's shirt tends to be seen as expressing loving feelings, while a man washing his wife's car tends to be seen as doing a job.

The well-known study of gender stereotypes among mental health workers by Broverman, Broverman, Clarkson, Rosenkrantz and Vogel (1970) vividly demonstrates how defining love as expressive is connected to decreasing women's status and power. In the study, therapists were asked to describe mentally healthy adults, femininity, and masculinity. They associated both mental health and masculinity with being independent, unemotional, dominant, and businesslike, qualities the researchers labeled as "competence." In contrast, "expressive" qualities like being tactful, gentle, or aware of the feelings of others were associated with femininity and not with mental health. These results document a devaluation of femininity and show how the dominant concept of mental health is biased against women and against love and attachment (see Gilligan, 1982).

In sum, the power of men over women in close relationships is strengthened by the feminization of love and by men's and women's different styles of love.

But Men Are Not That Powerful

Men clearly dominate women in close relationships. Husbands tend to have more power in making decisions, a situation that has not changed in recent decades (Blood & Wolfe, 1960; Duncan, Schuman, & Duncan, 1973). The evidence on the superior mental and physical health of married men vs. women has led some researchers, like Jessie Bernard (1972), to conclude that the institution of marriage is controlled by men for men's benefit.

However, given that power means the ability to get what one wants from another, men's power over women in intimate relationships is severely limited by the social organization of love. First, the legitimacy of men's style of love is denied. He will probably fail to persuade her that his practical help is a sign of love and that his sexual advances are a request for intimacy. As one of the working-class husbands interviewed by Lillian Rubin said, "She complains that all I want from her is sex, and I try to make her understand that it's an expression of love": and a wife commented, "he keeps saying he wants to make love, but it just doesn't feel like love to me" (1976, p. 146). In contrast, the legitimacy of her desire for intimate communication is supported by the mass media and by therapists. Thus, there is probably more social pressure for him to express his feelings than for her to enjoy sex.

Moreover, because of the avoidance of dependency associated with the male role, he may not even know what he wants or needs from her and, therefore, may be unable to try to get it. Thus, the covert nature of a man's dependency may increase his power by hiding his neediness from women. But it may also decrease his power by hiding his needs from himself.

Women's responsibility for love and their overt dependence can also leave both partners feeling controlled by the other. Insofar as love is defined as the woman's "turf," an area where she sets the rules and expectations, a man is likely to feel threatened and controlled when she seeks more intimacy. Talking about the relation, like she wants, feels like taking a test that she made up and he will fail. The husband is likely to react with withdrawal and passive aggression. He is blocked from straightforward counterattack insofar as he believes that intimacy is good.

From a woman's perspective, since love is in her sphere and she is responsible for success, she is very highly motivated to have a successful relationship. When there are problems in the relationship, she typically wants to take steps to make things better. She is likely to propose solutions such as discussing their problem or taking a vacation: and he is likely to respond with passive resistance and act as if she were pushy, demanding, and unfeminine. His withdrawal and veiled accusations will probably make her feel helpless and controlled.

Thus, a woman's control of the sphere of love ends up making her feel less powerful, not more, because she can succeed in her sphere only by getting the right response from him. Women's separate sphere of love and the family probably produced much more power for women in Victorian times, when a woman could succeed in love through her relations with her children and women friends and through sacrificing herself for her husband: in those times, being a loving woman was less dependent on the behavior of men (Ryan, 1979).

In these times, one of the most frequent marital conflicts reported by therapists is the conflict between a woman who wants more intimacy, more love, something more from her husband, and the man who withdraws and feels pressured (Raush, Barry, Hertel, & Swain, 1974; Rubin, 1983). The same pattern showed up in a survey of middle-class couples that asked how people wanted their spouse to change. The major sex difference was that husbands wanted their spouse to be less emotional and create less stress, while wives wanted the spouse to be more responsive and receptive (Burke, Weir, & Harrison, 1976). . . .

Power in the Public Sphere

Love may have a more important effect on power relations in the public sphere than in the private sphere. Feminized love covers up the material dependency of women on men and the interdependence of all people. It is part of a worldview that explains people's life situation by their inherent nature and not by the relations of exchange, sharing, or exploitation between them.

The way feminized love mystified social relations of dependency and exploitation was especially clear in the nineteenth century, when wives were totally dependent economically on their husbands and the ideology of woman's special sphere of love was emerging. A central argument in this ideology was that women were powerless and dependent because they were naturally submissive and affectionate. An article by an antislavery writer in the mid-nineteenth century illustrates this perspective:

> The comparison between women and the colored race is striking. Both are characterized by affection more than by intellect; both have a strong development of the religious sentiment; both are exceedingly adhesive in their attachments; both, comparatively speaking, have a tendency to submission, and hence, both have been kept in subjection by physical force, and considered rather in the light of property, than as individuals. (Rose, 1982, p. 45)

This perspective denies the material basis of women's dependency. It also defines religious morality and the need for affection as qualities peculiar to women.

The other side of defining women as naturally dependent, moral, and affectionate is defining men as naturally independent, amoral, and isolated. As Marxist scholars have pointed out, the ideology of the isolated individual accompanied and justified the rise of capitalism (Zaretsky, 1976). Men were encouraged to see themselves as independent, competitive, and self-made. If they were rich or poor, it was the result of their own individual merit, not relations of dependency with other people. And if they were real men, they would thrive on the impersonal, competitive relationships that prevailed at work.

Contemporary views of human nature often perpetuate the ideology of separate spheres and the self-made man. They assume that independence is the central human virtue, and dependency and attachments are feminine qualities associated with weakness. As Carol Gilligan has documented (1982), current psychological theories of human development assert that a healthy person develops from a dependent child into an independent, autonomous adult. For example, Daniel Levinson's conception of development for men centers on the "Dream" of glorious achievement in his occupation. Attachments are subservient to the goals of becoming an autonomous person and attaining the "Dream": a man who has not progressed toward his "Dream" by mid-life should break out of his established way of life by "leaving his wife, quitting his job, or moving to another region" (1978, p. 206). This concept of a healthy man condemns men without challenging careers, which includes most middle- and working-class men. It also ignores the fact that "successful" men depend on others: on wives and mothers who raised them and their children, on men and women who worked with them and for them. In many ways, Levinson's position is a restatement of the ideology of the self-made man, an excellent justification of meritocracy and inequality.

Thus, defining affection and dependency as feminine supports inequality in the public sphere in addition to maintaining men's power over women at home. It also motivates men to work hard at impersonal jobs and to blame themselves for their poverty or failure.

. . . There are other ways that the social organization of love contributes to economic and political inequality (see Skoloff, 1980). In particular, it strengthens the power of men over women at the work place not only by encouraging women to devote themselves to love the family but also by supporting the belief that money and dreams of achievement are not very important to women.

The consequences of love would be more positive if love were the responsibility of men as well as women and if love were defined more broadly to include instrumental help as well as emotional expression. Our current social organization of love maintains a situation where at home, women and men are in conflict. . . .

Conclusion

I have focused on how love affects power relations. In conclusion, I want to return to the causes of our current social organization of love. The foregoing analysis suggests that one reason for the persistence of the feminization of love and the accompanying emphasis on the independence of men is that these patterns serve the interests of the ruling classes. This functional explanation is weak until we can specify the mechanisms by which ruling groups manage to establish beliefs and social practices that benefit them. The historical research on the origins of the feminization of love in the nineteenth century suggest that the major causes were the differentiation of the harsh public sphere and the loving private sphere and also the sexual division of labor, especially the economic dependency of women on men.

This explanation suggests that our conceptions of love will change now that women are less economically dependent. It also suggests that in societies where the public sphere is seen as cooperative and helpful, love will be identified with men as well as women and with instrumental as well as expressive activity. . . . These issues should be explored in future research. We also need to focus on the masculine gender role and clarify how men's identification with the marketplace affects gender roles and love relationships. By clarifying the causes of our patterns of love, hopefully we can also clarify the social conditions that would encourage a more androgynous kind of love that combined emotional expression and practical help and acknowledged the interdependence of men and women.

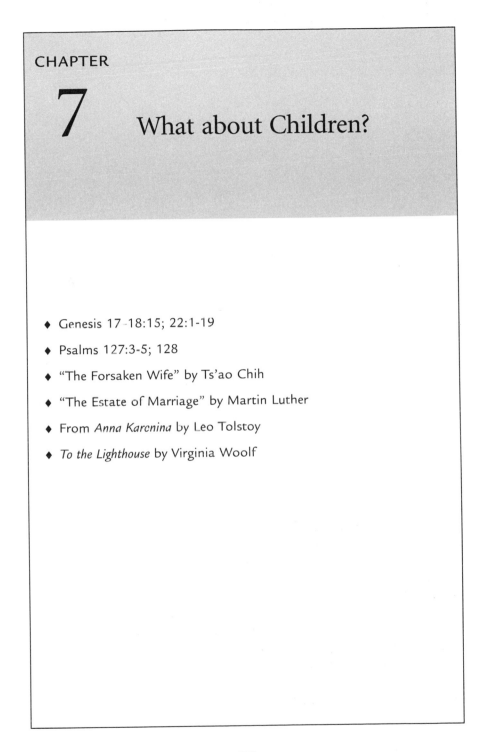

CHAPTER

7   What about Children?

- Genesis 17–18:15; 22:1-19

- Psalms 127:3-5; 128

- "The Forsaken Wife" by Ts'ao Chih

- "The Estate of Marriage" by Martin Luther

- From *Anna Karenina* by Leo Tolstoy

- *To the Lighthouse* by Virginia Woolf

Men and women everywhere would have a lot more chance of acquiring recreation and fame and financial independence if they didn't have to spend most of their time and money tending and supporting two or three unattractive descendants.

— OGDEN NASH

Whoever considers the length and feebleness of human infancy, with the concern which both sexes naturally have for their offspring, will easily perceive, that there must be an union of male and female for the education of the young, and that this union must be of considerable duration.

— DAVID HUME

Introduction

The biological foundations of the institution of marriage are obvious to us all. Bronislaw Malinowski wrote that "love and marriage are closely associated in day-dreams and in fiction, in folk-lore and in poetry, in the manners, morals and institutions of every human community — but marriage is more than the happy ending of a successful courtship. Marriage as an ideal is the end of a romance; it is also the beginning of a sterner task . . . the production and maintenance of children."

Our two readings from the Bible touch upon many of the most important themes of childbearing and child rearing as they relate to the institution of marriage. Most of us expect children from marriage, and when children arrive, we view them as the greatest of life's blessings — indeed, as our only hope for immortality. How easy, then, it is to appreciate the story of Abraham and Sarah, a devoted but childless couple blessed in old age with a son. The result: the birth of a boy who is heralded as the progenitor of a nation. Yet, when that son, Isaac, grows up, God puts Abraham to the test, ordering the child sacrificed. Abraham must acknowledge that this gift from God, his beloved son, ultimately belongs to God. With great trepidation, he binds the young man on a mountain top, and lifts the knife. An angel intercedes. . . . Abraham has passed the test, having demonstrated obedience to God even at the risk of losing what is most precious to him. Though we love our children more than life itself, we must never forget that ultimately, they belong to God.

The next selection, from Psalms, reinforces the lessons of the story of Abraham. Scripture tells us that children are our joy, our comfort, our future, and ultimately even our armor — "as arrows in the hand of a mighty man." They are also our reward if we "fear the Lord, [and] walk in His ways."

In many primitive cultures, the single highest value placed on a woman was her ability to bear children. Indeed, in the very first selection of our book, from *The Future of Marriage in Western Civilization*, E. Westermarck observes that in many societies, "true married life does not begin for persons who are formally married or betrothed, or marriage does not become definite, until a child is born or there are signs of pregnancy." So fundamental is childbearing to the notion of a successful union even in highly developed societies that the unfulfilled wish and expectation of a child still puts enormous strain on many marriages. The third reading in this chapter, "The Forsaken Wife," is a touching Chinese poem of the early third century A.D. It concerns the ruminations of a young woman who knows her husband's patience has worn thin with longing for a child. "She with children is a moon that sails the sky; the childless one, a falling star," the young wife reflects. Yet, understanding the workings of nature as she does, she trusts in "the gods." She'll "dry" her "tears" and "sigh again." If her husband would "only wait with trusting heart!"

Martin Luther's straightforward take on childbearing can be summarized in his exhortation to husbands and wives that as the hardest work of marriage, children are also its greatest gift and purpose, their rearing the "noblest" task of a God-pleasing "estate." Why? Because to God there "can be nothing dearer than the salvation of souls." "What does Christian faith say . . . [of child-rearing]?" Luther asks. "It opens its eyes, looks upon all these insignificant, distasteful, and despised duties in the Spirit, and is aware that they are all adorned with divine approval as with the costliest gold and jewels. It says, 'O God, because I am certain that thou hast created me as a man and hast from my body begotten this child, I also know for a certainty that it meets with thy perfect pleasure. I confess to thee I am not worthy to rock the little babe or wash its diapers, or to be entrusted with the care of the child and its mother. [But] how gladly will I do so, though the duties be even more insignificant and despised.'"

Perhaps nowhere in all of literature do we encounter such a powerful birth scene — and from the perspective of a father — as in Leo Tolstoy's great novel, *Anna Karenina*. The reading included here explores the wide range and jumble of feelings a devoted husband experiences as his wife endures labor. From guilt to pity to terror, despair, and awe, Levin undergoes a myriad of emotional transformations awaiting the birth of his son. In the end he is overcome by a heady sense of responsibility. He even resents a bit the "howling creature" who appears, it seems, "out of nowhere" — a creature who has "no consideration for anything," and who by its mere existence has changed his life forever.

In the last reading of this chapter, an excerpt from Virginia Woolf's novel *To the Lighthouse*, we experience the blessings and burdens of a very fruitful marriage — a marriage that has produced eight children. The very real encounter depicted in these pages, an encounter between a husband of contemplative disposition and a down-to-earth wife, is a literary distillation of the many joys, regrets, preoccupations, licenses, and taboos of parenthood. The Ramsays have a good marriage. They retain a certain freshness of attraction to one another, and it is clear that their intimacy as a couple has been cultivated with great care. Their children — for good and for ill — occupy the very center of their existence, and very often intrude on their relationship. Mr. and Mrs. Ramsay are both well aware that whatever the hassles of family life, if they are left alone without the double anchors of marriage and children, their spirits might very well drift to sea.

THE FIRST BOOK OF MOSES, CALLED GENESIS

The story of Abraham, the father of the Jewish nation, and Isaac, inheritor to the covenant, might well be considered the very centerpiece of the book of Genesis. It is perhaps the greatest metaphor of religious devotion in the entire Old Testament. I have inserted it here as a complete story. But the reader should be aware that this remarkable narrative is actually interrupted in the biblical text — first by the story of Abraham's intercession for Sodom (chapter 18:16-33), and then by a peculiar recounting of Abraham's trying to pass off his wife as his sister (chapter 20). Genesis 20 is actually the second such story that involves Abraham offering his wife to the hosts of the lands he visits in return for protection. And it is not, I think, too far-fetched to put forward the idea that Abraham takes advantage of his wife's childlessness in ways that will later come to pain him. Between the heralding of Isaac's birth and the shattering story of his binding (that terrible "test" of faith to which Abraham is finally subjected) there is also the sad story of Hagar and Ishmael, expelled from their home by Sarah, a woman for whom the boon of a legitimate heir has enabled a cruel assertion of power.

Genesis 17–18:15; 22:1-19

Chapter 17

1 And when Abram was ninety years old and nine, the LORD appeared to Abram, and said unto him, I am the Almighty God; walk before me, and be thou perfect.

2 And I will make my covenant between me and thee, and will multiply thee exceedingly.

3 And Abram fell on his face; and God talked with him, saying,

4 As for me, behold, my covenant is with thee, and thou shalt be a father of many nations.

5 Neither shall thy name any more be called Abram, but thy name shall be Abraham; for a father of many nations have I made thee.

6 And I will make thee exceeding fruitful, and I will make nations of thee, and kings shall come out of thee.

7 And I will establish my covenant between me and thee and thy seed after thee in their generations for an everlasting covenant, to be a God unto thee, and to thy seed after thee.

8 And I will give unto thee, and to thy seed after thee, the land wherein thou art a stranger, all the land of Canaan, for an everlasting possession; and I will be their God.

9 And God said unto Abraham, Thou shalt keep my covenant therefore, thou, and thy seed after thee in their generations.

10 This is my covenant, which ye shall keep, between me and you and thy seed after thee; Every man child among you shall be circumcised.

11 And ye shall circumcise the flesh of your foreskin; and it shall be a token of the covenant betwixt me and you.

12 And he that is eight days old shall be circumcised among you, every man child in your generations, he that is born in the house, or bought with money of any stranger, which is not of thy seed.

13 He that is born in thy house, and he that is bought with thy money, must needs be circumcised: and my covenant shall be in your flesh for an everlasting covenant.

14 And the uncircumcised man child whose flesh of his foreskin is not circumcised, that soul shall be cut off from his people; he hath broken my covenant.

15 And God said unto Abraham, As for Sarai thy wife, thou shalt not call her name Sarai, but Sarah shall her name be.

16 And I will bless her, and give thee a son also of her: yea, I will bless her, and she shall be a mother of nations; kings of people shall be of her.

17 Then Abraham fell upon his face, and laughed, and said in his heart, Shall a child be born unto him that is an hundred years old? and shall Sarah, that is ninety years old, bear?

18 And Abraham said unto God, O that Ishmael might live before thee!

19 And God said, Sarah thy wife shall bear thee a son indeed; and thou shalt

call his name Isaac: and I will establish my covenant with him for an everlasting covenant, and with his seed after him.

20 And as for Ishmael, I have heard thee: Behold, I have blessed him, and will make him fruitful, and will multiply him exceedingly; twelve princes shall he beget, and I will make him a great nation.

21 But my covenant will I establish with Isaac, which Sarah shall bear unto thee at this set time in the next year.

22 And he left off talking with him, and God went up from Abraham.

23 And Abraham took Ishmael his son, and all that were born in his house, and all that were bought with his money, every male among the men of Abraham's house; and circumcised the flesh of their foreskin in the selfsame day, as God had said unto him.

24 And Abraham was ninety years old and nine, when he was circumcised in the flesh of his foreskin.

25 And Ishmael his son was thirteen years old, when he was circumcised in the flesh of his foreskin.

26 In the selfsame day was Abraham circumcised, and Ishmael his son.

27 And all the men of his house, born in the house, and bought with money of the stranger, were circumcised with him.

Chapter 18

1 And the Lord appeared unto him in the plains of Mamre: and he sat in the tent door in the heat of the day;

2 And he lift up his eyes and looked, and, lo, three men stood by him: and when he saw them, he ran to meet them from the tent door, and bowed himself toward the ground,

3 And said, My Lord, if now I have found favour in thy sight, pass not away, I pray thee, from thy servant:

4 Let a little water, I pray you, be fetched, and wash your feet, and rest yourselves under the tree;

5 And I will fetch a morsel of bread, and comfort ye your hearts; after that ye shall pass on; for therefore are ye come to your servant. And they said, So do, as thou hast said.

6 And Abraham hastened into the tent unto Sarah, and said, Make ready quickly three measures of fine meal, knead it, and make cakes upon the hearth.

7 And Abraham ran unto the herd, and fetched a calf tender and good, and gave it unto a young man; and he hasted to dress it.

8 And he took butter, and milk, and the calf which he had dressed, and set it before them; and he stood by them under the tree, and they did eat.

9 And they said unto him, Where is Sarah thy wife? And he said, Behold, in the tent.

10 And he said, I will certainly return unto thee according to the time of life; and, lo, Sarah thy wife shall have a son. And Sarah heard it in the tent door, which was behind him.

11 Now Abraham and Sarah were old and well stricken in age; and it ceased to be with Sarah after the manner of women.

12 Therefore Sarah laughed within herself, saying, After I am waxed old shall I have pleasure, my lord being old also?

13 And the LORD said unto Abraham, Wherefore did Sarah laugh, saying, Shall I of a surety bear a child, which am old?

14 Is any thing too hard for the LORD? At the time appointed I will return unto thee, according to the time of life, and Sarah shall have a son.

15 Then Sarah denied, saying, I laughed not; for she was afraid. And he said, Nay; but thou didst laugh.

Chapter 22

1 And it came to pass after these things, that God did tempt Abraham, and said unto him, Abraham: and he said, Behold, here I am.

2 And he said, Take now thy son, thine only son Isaac, whom thou lovest, and get thee into the land of Moriah; and offer him there for a burnt offering upon one of the mountains which I will tell thee of.

3 And Abraham rose up early in the morning, and saddled his ass, and took two of his young men with him, and Isaac his son, and clave the wood for the burnt offering, and rose up, and went unto the place of which God had told him.

4 Then on the third day Abraham lifted up his eyes, and saw the place afar off.

5 And Abraham said unto his young men, Abide ye here with the ass; and I and the lad will go yonder and worship, and come again to you.

6 And Abraham took the wood of the burnt offering, and laid it upon Isaac his son; and he took the fire in his hand, and a knife; and they went both of them together.

7 And Isaac spake unto Abraham his father, and said, My father: and he said, Here am I, my son. And he said, Behold the fire and the wood: but where is the lamb for a burnt offering?

8 And Abraham said, My son, God will provide himself a lamb for a burnt offering: so they went both of them together.

9 And they came to the place which God had told him of; and Abraham built an altar there, and laid the wood in order, and bound Isaac his son, and laid him on the altar upon the wood.

10 And Abraham stretched forth his hand, and took the knife to slay his son.

11 And the angel of the LORD called unto him out of heaven, and said, Abraham, Abraham: and he said, Here am I.

12 And he said, Lay not thine hand upon the lad, neither do thou any thing unto him: for now I know that thou fearest God, seeing thou hast not withheld thy son, thine only son from me.

13 And Abraham lifted up his eyes, and looked, and behold behind him a ram caught in a thicket by his horns: and Abraham went and took the ram, and offered him up for a burnt offering in the stead of his son.

14 And Abraham called the name of that place Jehovah-jireh: as it is said to this day, In the mount of the LORD it shall be seen.

15 And the angel of the LORD called unto Abraham out of heaven the second time,

16 And said, By myself have I sworn, saith the LORD, for because thou hast done this thing, and hast not withheld thy son, thine only son:

17 That in blessing I will bless thee, and in multiplying I will multiply thy seed as the stars of the heaven, and as the sand which is upon the sea shore; and thy seed shall possess the gate of his enemies;

18 And in thy seed shall all the nations of the earth be blessed; because thou hast obeyed my voice.

19 So Abraham returned unto his young men, and they rose up and went together to Beer-sheba; and Abraham dwelt at Beer-sheba.

THE BOOK OF PSALMS

The Psalms, of which there are 150, are religious hymns that have been central to both the Jewish and Christian liturgy for two thousand years. Their subjects range from prophetic vision to adoration to wisdom on worldly matters. They are attributed to a number of leaders of ancient Israel, among them Moses, David, and Solomon. It is doubtful whether any date back to the time of Moses, but many are believed to date back to the time of King David, around 1000 B.C.

Psalms 127:3-5; 128

Psalm 127

3 Lo, children are an heritage of the LORD; and the fruit of the womb is his reward.
4 As arrows are in the hand of a mighty man; so are children of the youth.
5 Happy is the man that hath his quiver full of them: they shall not be ashamed, but they shall speak with the enemies in the gate.

Psalm 128

1 Blessed is every one that feareth the LORD; that walketh in his ways.
2 For thou shalt eat the labour of thine hands; happy shalt thou be, and it shall be well with thee.

3 Thy wife shall be as a fruitful vine by the sides of thine house; thy children like olive plants round about thy table.

4 Behold, that thus shall the man be blessed that feareth the LORD.

5 The LORD shall bless thee out of Zion; and thou shalt see the good of Jerusalem all the days of thy life.

6 Yea, thou shalt see thy children's children, and peace upon Israel.

TS'AO CHIH

Ts'ao Chih (191-232) was a younger son of Ts'ao Ts'ao, a military adventurer who used his powerful volunteer army to defeat the warlords who threatened the Han dynasty. By political cunning, Ts'ao Ts'ao was able to secure his eldest son's good fortune; that son, Ts'ao Pi (also a poet), became emperor of the Wei king-dom, ruling the north of China after the fall of the Han dynasty. Ts'ao Chih lived at court, but apparently not very happily, as he seems to have been distrusted by his elder brother. At any rate he was a prodigious talent, and is said to have im-provised so well that once, on a dare from his brother, he authored an entire stanza while walking seven steps.

The Forsaken Wife

The pomegranate grows in the garden front,
pale green leaves that tremble and turn,
vermilion flowers, flame on flame,
a shimmering glory of light and hue;
light that flares like the ten-colored turquoise,
fit for holy creatures to sport with.
Birds fly down and gather there;
Beating their wings, they make sad cries.
Sad cries — what are they for?
Vermilion blossoms bear no fruit.
I beat my breast and sigh long sighs;
the childless one will be sent home.

She with children is a moon that sails the sky;
the childless one, a falling star.
Sky and moon have end and beginning,
but the falling star sinks in spiritless death.
She whose sojourn fails of its rightful goal
falls among tiles and stones.
Dark thoughts well up;
I sigh till the dawn cocks crow,
toss from side to side, sleepless,
rise and wander in the courtyard outside.
I pause and turn to my room again;
chamber curtains swish and sigh;
I lift them and bind my girdle tighter,
stroke the strings of a white wood lute;
fierce and pleading, the tone lingers on,
soft and subtle, plaintive and clear.
I will dry my tears and sigh again;
how could I turn my back on the gods?
The star Chao-yao waits for frost and dew;[1]
why should spring and summer alone be fertile?
Late harvests gather good fruit —
if my lord will only wait with trusting heart!

MARTIN LUTHER

Martin Luther, 1483-1546, was the son of a Saxon iron smelter. His parents wanted him to study law, but he resolved to become a monk when, one May day in 1505, he was seized with terror during a thunderstorm on the road from Erfurt to Mansfeld. Despite his devotion to the monastic life, Luther found it hard to attain the peace of mind he desperately sought. By 1513 and eight years in his order, he had decided that perhaps the road to his own salvation lay not in fulfillment of a thoroughly regulated ascetic existence, but simply in faith alone. Thus was born his doctrine of "justification by faith alone," which taught that communion with God could only be achieved through God's grace, not through man's actions. Luther did not set out to create an alternative church, but in wrestling with the Catholic faith he came to loggerheads with its authorities for criticizing certain practices he viewed as corrupt. He also came to support a de-mocratized form of worship that denied any intercessionary spiritual powers of the priesthood and provided all members of the community direct access to scripture. At the time Luther wrote "The Estate of Marriage," he was not yet mar-ried to Katharina von Bora, who bore him five children and was his devoted wife for the last twenty years of his life. But in this work, two of the more remarkable qualities of Luther's personality are amply evident: first, his ability, despite great erudition, to communicate in the simplest of language; second, his appreciation for the dignities of the most ordinary of life's experiences.

The Estate of Marriage

Part Three

In the third part, in order that we may say something about the estate of marriage which will be conducive toward the soul's salvation, we shall now consider how to live a Christian and godly life in that estate. I will pass over in silence the matter of the conjugal duty, the granting and the withholding of it, since some filth-preachers have been shameless enough in this matter to rouse our disgust. Some of them designate special times for this, and exclude holy nights and women who are pregnant. I will leave this as St. Paul left it when he said in 1 Corinthians 7 [:9], "It is better to marry than to burn"; and again [in v. 2], "To avoid immorality, each man should have his own wife, and each woman her own husband." Although Christian married folk should not permit themselves to be governed by their bodies in the passion of lust, as Paul writes to the Thessalonians [1 Thess. 4:5], nevertheless each one must examine himself so that by his abstention he does not expose himself to the danger of fornication and other sins. Neither should he pay any attention to holy days or work days, or other physical considerations.

What we would speak most of is the fact that the estate of marriage has universally fallen into such awful disrepute. There are many pagan books which treat of nothing but the depravity of womankind and the unhappiness of the estate of marriage, such that some have thought that even if Wisdom itself were a woman one should not marry. A Roman official was once supposed to encourage young men to take wives (because the country was in need of a large population on account of its incessant wars). Among other things he said to them, "My dear young men, if we could only live without women we would be spared a great deal of annoyance; but since we cannot do without them, take to ourselves wives," etc. He was criticized by some on the ground that his words were ill-considered and would only serve to discourage the young men. Others, on the contrary, said that because Metellus was a brave man he had spoken rightly, for an honorable man should speak the truth without fear or hypocrisy.[1]

So they concluded that woman is a necessary evil, and that no household can be without such an evil. These are the words of blind heathen, who are ignorant of the fact that man and woman are God's creation. They blaspheme his work, as if man and woman just came into being spontaneously! I imagine that if women were to write books they would say exactly the same thing about men.

What they have failed to set down in writing, however, they express with their grumbling and complaining whenever they get together.

Every day one encounters parents who forget their former misery because, like the mouse, they have now had their fill.[2] They deter their children from marriage but entice them into priesthood and nunnery, citing the trials and troubles of married life. Thus do they bring their own children home to the devil, as we daily observe; they provide them with ease for the body and hell for the soul.

Since God had to suffer such disdain of his work from the pagans, he therefore also gave them their reward, of which Paul writes in Romans 1 [:24-28], and allowed them to fall into immorality and a stream of uncleanness until they henceforth carnally abused not women but boys and dumb beasts. Even their women carnally abused themselves and each other. Because they blasphemed the work of God, he gave them up to a base mind, of which the books of the pagans are full, most shamelessly crammed full.

In order that we may not proceed as blindly, but rather conduct ourselves in a Christian manner, hold fast first of all to this, that man and woman are the work of God. Keep a tight rein on your heart and your lips; do not criticize his work, or call that evil which he himself has called good. He knows better than you yourself what is good and to your benefit, as he says in Genesis 1 [2:18], "It is not good that the man should be alone; I will make him a helper fit for him." There you see that he calls the woman good, a helper. If you deem it otherwise, it is certainly your own fault; you neither understand nor believe God's word and work. See, with this statement of God one stops the mouths of all those who criticize and censure marriage.

For this reason young men should be on their guard when they read pagan books and hear the common complaints about marriage, lest they inhale poison. For the estate of marriage does not set well with the devil, because it is God's good will and work. This is why the devil has contrived to have so much shouted and written in the world against the institution of marriage, to frighten men away from this godly life and entangle them in a web of fornication and secret sins. Indeed, it seems to me that even Solomon, although he amply censures evil women, was speaking against just such blasphemers when he said in Proverbs 18 [:22], "He who finds a wife finds a good thing, and obtains favor from the Lord." What is this good thing and this favor? Let us see.

The world says of marriage, "Brief is the joy, lasting the bitterness."[3] Let them say what they please; what God wills and creates is bound to be a laughing-stock to them. The kind of joy and pleasure they have outside of wedlock they will be most acutely aware of, I suspect, in their consciences. To recognize the estate of marriage is something quite different from merely being married. He who is married but does not recognize the estate of marriage cannot continue in wedlock without bitterness, drudgery, and anguish; he will inevitably complain and blaspheme like the pagans and blind, irrational men. But he who recognizes the estate of marriage will find therein delight, love, and joy without end; as Solomon says, "He who finds a wife finds a good thing," etc. [Prov. 18:22].

Now the ones who recognize the estate of marriage are those who firmly believe that God himself instituted it, brought husband and wife together, and ordained that they should beget children and care for them. For this they have God's word, Genesis 1 [:28], and they can be certain that he does not lie. They can therefore also be certain that the estate of marriage and everything that goes with it in the way of conduct, works, and suffering is pleasing to God. Now tell me, how can the heart have greater good, joy, and delight than in God, when one is certain that his estate, conduct, and work is pleasing to God?

That is what it means to find a wife. Many *have* wives, but few *find* wives. Why? They are blind; they fail to see that their life and conduct with their wives is the work of God and pleasing in his sight. Could they but find that, then no wife would be so hateful, so ill-tempered, so ill-mannered, so poor, so sick that they would fail to find in her their heart's delight and would always be reproaching God for his work, creation, and will. And because they see that it is the good pleasure of their beloved Lord, they would be able to have peace in grief, joy in the midst of bitterness, happiness in the midst of tribulations, as the martyrs have in suffering.

We err in that we judge the work of God according to our own feelings, and regard not his will but our own desire. This is why we are unable to recognize his works and persist in making evil that which is good, and regarding as bitter that which is pleasant. Nothing is so bad, not even death itself, but what it becomes sweet and tolerable if only I know and am certain that it is pleasing to God. Then there follows immediately that of which Solomon speaks, "He obtains favor from the Lord" [Prov. 18:22].

Now observe that when that clever harlot, our natural reason (which the pagans followed in trying to be most clever), takes a look at married life, she turns up her nose and says, "Alas, must I rock the baby, wash its diapers, make its bed, smell its stench, stay up nights with it, take care of it when it cries, heal its rashes and sores, and on top of that care for my wife, provide for her, labor at my trade, take care of this and take care of that, do this and do that, endure this and endure that, and whatever else of bitterness and drudgery married life involves? What, should I make such a prisoner of myself? O you poor, wretched fellow, have you taken a wife? Fie, fie upon such wretchedness and bitterness! It is better to remain free and lead a peaceful, carefree life; I will become a priest or a nun and compel my children to do likewise."

What then does Christian faith say to this? It opens its eyes, looks upon all these insignificant, distasteful, and despised duties in the Spirit, and is aware that they are all adorned with divine approval as with the costliest gold and jewels. It says, "O God, because I am certain that thou hast created me as a man and hast from my body begotten this child, I also know for a certainty that it meets with thy perfect pleasure. I confess to thee that I am not worthy to rock the little babe or wash its diapers, or to be entrusted with the care of the child and its mother. How is it that I, without any merit, have come to this distinction of being certain that I am serving thy creature and thy most precious will? O how gladly will I do so, though the duties should be even more insignificant and despised. Neither frost nor heat, neither drudgery nor labor, will distress or dissuade me, for I am certain that it is thus pleasing in thy sight."

A wife too should regard her duties in the same light, as she suckles the child, rocks and bathes it, and cares for it in other ways; and as she busies herself with other duties and renders help and obedience to her husband. These are truly golden and noble works. This is also how to comfort and encourage a woman in the pangs of childbirth, not by repeating St. Margaret[4] legends and other silly old wives' tales but by speaking thus, "Dear Grete, remember that you are a woman, and that this work of God in you is pleasing to him. Trust joyfully in his will, and let him have his way with you. Work with all your might to bring forth the child. Should it mean your death, then depart happily, for you will die in a noble deed and in subservience to God. If you were not a woman you should now wish to be one for the sake of this very work alone, that you might thus gloriously suffer and even die in the performance of God's work and will. For here you have the word of God, who so created you and implanted within you this extremity." Tell me, is not this indeed (as Solomon says [Prov. 18:22]) "to obtain favor from the Lord," even in the midst of such extremity?

Now you tell me, when a father goes ahead and washes diapers or performs some other mean task for his child, and someone ridicules him as an effeminate fool — though that father is acting in the spirit just described and in Christian faith — my dear fellow you tell me, which of the two is most keenly ridiculing the other? God, with all his angels and creatures, is smiling — not because that father is washing diapers, but because he is doing so in Christian faith. Those who sneer at him and see only the task but not the faith are ridiculing God with all his creatures, as the biggest fool on earth. Indeed, they are only ridiculing themselves; with all their cleverness they are nothing but devil's fools.

St. Cyprian, that great and admirable man and holy martyr, wrote that one should kiss the newborn infant, even before it is baptized, in honor of the hands of God here engaged in a brand new deed.[5] What do you suppose he would have said about a baptized infant? There was a true Christian, who correctly recognized and regarded God's work and creature. Therefore, I say that all nuns and monks who lack faith, and who trust in their own chastity and in their order, are not worthy of rocking a baptized child or preparing its pap, even if it were the child of a harlot. This is because their order and manner of life has no word of God as its warrant. They cannot boast that what they do is pleasing in God's sight, as can the woman in childbirth, even if her child is born out of wedlock.

I say these things in order that we may learn how honorable a thing it is to live in that estate which God has ordained. In it we find God's word and good pleasure, by which all the works, conduct, and sufferings of that estate become holy, godly, and precious so that Solomon even congratulates such a man and says in Proverbs 5 [:18], "Rejoice in the wife of your youth," and again in Ecclesiastes 11 [9:9], "Enjoy life with the wife whom you love all the days of your vain life." Doubtless, Solomon is not speaking here of carnal pleasure, since it is the Holy Spirit who speaks through him. He is rather offering godly comfort to those who find much drudgery in married life. This he does by way of defense against those who scoff at the divine ordinance and, like the pagans, seek but fail to find in marriage anything beyond a carnal and fleeting, sensual pleasure. . . .

. . . It is no slight boon that in wedlock fornication and unchastity are checked and eliminated. This in itself is so great a good that it alone should be enough to induce men to marry forthwith, and for many reasons.

The first reason is that fornication destroys not only the soul but also body, property, honor, and family as well. For we see how a licentious and wicked life not only brings great disgrace but is also a spendthrift[6] life, more costly than wedlock, and that illicit partners necessarily occasion greater suffering for one another than do married folk.[7] Beyond that it consumes the body, corrupts flesh and blood, nature, and physical constitution. Through such a variety of evil consequences God takes a rigid position, as though he would actually drive people away from fornication and into marriage. However, few are thereby convinced or converted.

Some, however, have given the matter thought and so learned from their own experience that they have coined an excellent proverb, "Early to rise and early to wed; that should no one ever regret."[8] Why? Well, because from that there come people who retain a sound body, a good conscience, property, and honor and family, all of which are so ruined and dissipated by fornication, that, once lost, it is well-nigh impossible to regain them — scarcely one in a hundred succeeds. This was the benefit cited by Paul in 1 Corinthians 7 [:2], "To avoid immorality, each man should have his own wife, and each woman her own husband."

The estate of marriage, however, redounds to the benefit not alone of the body, property, honor, and soul of an individual, but also to the benefit of whole cities and countries, in that they remain exempt from the plagues imposed by God. We know only too well that the most terrible plagues have befallen lands and people because of fornication. This was the sin cited as the reason why the world was drowned in the Deluge, Genesis 6 [:1-13], and Sodom and Gomorrah were buried in flames, Genesis 19 [:1-24]. Scripture also cites many other plagues, even in the case of holy men such as David [2 Samuel 11–12], Solomon (1 Kings 11:1-13], and Samson [Judg. 16:1-21]. We see before our very eyes that God even now sends more new plagues.[9]

Many think they can evade marriage by having their fling [*auss bubenn*] for a time, and then becoming righteous. My dear fellow, if one in a thousand succeeds in this, that would be doing very well. He who intends to lead a chaste life had better begin early, and attain it not with but without fornication, either by the grace of God or through marriage. We see only too well how they make out every day. It might well be called plunging into immorality rather than growing to maturity.[10] It is the devil who has brought this about, and coined such damnable sayings as, "One has to play the fool at least once";[11] or, "He who does it not in his youth does it in his old age";[12] or, "A young saint, an old devil."[13] Such are the sentiments of the poet Terence[14] and other pagans. This is heathenish; they speak like heathens, yea, like devils.

It is certainly a fact that he who refuses to marry must fall into immorality. How could it be otherwise, since God has created man and woman to produce seed and to multiply? Why should one not forestall immorality by means of marriage? For if special grace does not exempt a person, his nature must and will compel him to produce seed and to multiply. If this does not occur within marriage, how else can it occur except in fornication or secret sins? But, they say, suppose I am neither married nor immoral, and force myself to remain continent? Do you not hear that restraint is impossible without the special grace? For God's word does not admit of restraint; neither does it lie when it says, "Be fruitful and multiply" [Gen. 1:28]. You can neither escape nor restrain yourself from being fruitful and multiplying; it is God's ordinance and takes its course.

Physicians are not amiss when they say: If this natural function is forcibly restrained it necessarily strikes into the flesh and blood and becomes a poison, whence the body becomes unhealthy, enervated, sweaty, and foul-smelling. That which should have issued in fruitfulness and propagation has to be absorbed within the body itself. Unless there is terrific hunger or immense labor or the supreme grace, the body cannot take it; it necessarily becomes unhealthy and sickly. Hence, we see how weak and sickly barren women are. Those who are fruitful, however, are healthier, cleanlier, and happier. And even if they bear themselves weary — or ultimately bear themselves out — that does not hurt. Let them bear themselves out. This is the purpose for which they exist. It is better to have a brief life with good health than a long life in ill health.[15]

But the greatest good in married life, that which makes all suffering and labor worthwhile, is that God grants offspring and commands that they be brought up to worship and serve him. In all the world this is the noblest and most precious work, because to God there can be nothing dearer than the salvation of souls. Now since we are all duty bound to suffer death, if need be, that we might bring a single soul to God, you can see how rich the estate of marriage is in good works. God has entrusted to its bosom souls begotten of its own body, on whom it can lavish all manner of Christian works. Most certainly father and mother are apostles, bishops, and priests to their children, for it is they who make them acquainted with the gospel. In short, there is no greater or nobler authority on earth than that of parents over their children, for this authority is both spiritual and temporal. Whoever teaches the gospel to another is truly his apostle and bishop. Mitre and staff and great estates indeed produce idols, but teaching the gospel produces apostles and bishops. See therefore how good and great is God's work and ordinance!

Here I will let the matter rest and leave to others the task of searching out further benefits and advantages of the estate of marriage.

LEO TOLSTOY

Leo Tolstoy (1828-1910) was born into a Russian noble family. As a young man, he led something of a degenerate existence, but he soon relented. After a brief stint in the army, at which time he began to write, he became a judge of land disputes. Tolstoy's literary works concern themselves with Christian love and the possibilities of the moral life, which ideally would govern the way we seek to fill our basic human needs, the way we treat our fellow human beings, and the way we respond to our emotions. His compassion for the weaknesses of his characters and his ability to get inside them are the secret of his lasting power as a writer; nobody can read *War and Peace* or *Anna Karenina* and come away without the characters in these novels indelibly etched on the consciousness. As evidenced in *Anna Karenina,* Tolstoy had a remarkable gift for drawing realistic portraits of both bad and good marriages. His own marriage was blissfully happy and fruitful. He fathered nine children.

Anna Karenina

Book VII, Chapter 13

There are no conditions to which a man cannot get accustomed, especially if he sees that everyone around him lives in the same way. Levin would not have believed it possible three months earlier that he could go quietly to sleep in the circumstances in which he now found himself; that while living an aimless, senseless life, a life, moreover, that was above his means; and after his hard drinking (he could find no other words for what he had been doing at the club), after his clumsy attempt to be friendly with a man with whom his wife had once been in love and the even more inappropriate call on a woman who could aptly be called a fallen woman; and after having almost fallen in love with that woman and grieved his wife — that after all this he could fall asleep so peacefully. But under the influence of his weariness, of a late night, and the wine he'd had to drink, he slept soundly and peacefully.

At five o'clock he was wakened by the creaking of an opening door. He sat up and looked round. Kitty was not in bed beside him. But behind the partition a light was moving about and he heard her steps.

"What is it? What?" he asked, half awake. "Kitty, what is it?"

"Nothing," she said, coming from behind the partition with a lighted candle in her hand. "I didn't feel well," she added with a particularly sweet and meaning smile.

"What? Has it begun? Has it?" he asked in a frightened voice. "We must send . . ." He began dressing hurriedly.

"No, no," she said, smiling and holding him back with her hand. "It's probably nothing. I only felt a little unwell. But it's over now."

She went up to the bed, put out the candle, lay down, and was quiet. Though her quietness, just as though she were holding her breath, seemed suspicious to him, and especially the particular tenderness and excitement with which, coming out from behind the partition, she had said, "Nothing," he was so drowsy that he fell asleep at once. It was only afterward that he remembered that bated breath and realized what was going on in her dear, sweet soul when, while lying motionless at his side, she was awaiting the greatest event in a woman's life. At seven o'clock he was awakened by the touch of her hand on his shoulder and a faint whisper. She seemed to be torn between regret at waking him and a desire to speak to him.

"Darling, don't be frightened. . . . It's all right. . . . Only I think . . . I think we'd better send for Lizaveta Petrovna."

She had lit the candle again. She was sitting on the bed, holding in her hand some knitting she had been doing during the last few days.

"Please, don't be frightened. It's all right. I'm not a bit afraid," she said, seeing his alarmed face, and she pressed his hand to her bosom and then to her lips.

He jumped out of bed, hardly conscious of himself, and without taking his eyes off her for a moment, put on his dressing gown, and stood still, gazing at her. He had to go, but he was unable to move, so struck was he by the look on her face. He, who loved her face and knew every expression and look on it, had never seen it like this. . . . Her flushed face, with the soft hair escaping from under her nightcap, was radiant with joy and resolution.

Little as there was of artificiality and conventionality in Kitty's character, Levin was still astonished at what was laid bare to him now when every veil had been removed and the very kernel of her soul shone through her eyes. And in this simplicity and in this baring of her soul he could see her, the woman he loved, more clearly than ever. She looked and smiled at him; but suddenly her brow contracted, she raised her head, and going up quickly to him took his hand and clung close to him, her hot breath engulfing him. She was in pain and seemed to be complaining to him of her suffering. For a moment he felt, from force of habit, that he really was to blame for it. But the tenderness in her eyes told him that far from blaming him, she loved him for her suffering. "If I am not to blame for it, then who is?" he could not help thinking, looking for someone responsible for those sufferings so as to punish him. She suffered, complained, triumphed, and rejoiced in the suffering and loved it. He saw that something beautiful was taking place in her soul — but what? That he could not understand. That was beyond his comprehension.

"I've sent for Mother, and you go quickly for Lizaveta Petrovna. . . . Oh, darling! . . . It's nothing, it's passed."

She moved away from him and rang the bell.

"Well, go along now. Pasha's coming. I'm all right."

And Levin was amazed to see her taking up the knitting she had fetched in the night and starting work on it again.

As Levin was going out of one door he heard the maid coming in at the other. He stopped at the door and heard Kitty give detailed instructions to the maid to help her move the bed.

He dressed and, while his carriage was being made ready (it was too early for a cab), he ran back to the bedroom not on tiptoe but, as it seemed to him, on wings. Two maids were busy moving something in the bedroom. Kitty was walking up and down and knitting, quickly throwing the wool over the needle, and giving orders.

"I'm going to fetch the doctor now. They've already gone for Lizaveta Petrovna, but I'll go around there too. Anything else? Oh yes, shall I go and fetch Dolly too?"

She looked up at him, apparently not hearing what he was saying.

"Yes, yes. Go, go!" she said quickly, frowning and motioning him away with her hand.

He was entering the drawing room when he suddenly heard a pitiful moan coming from the bedroom and lasting only a moment. He stopped and for a long time could not understand.

"Of course, it was Kitty," he said to himself and, clutching his head, ran downstairs.

"Lord, have mercy on us! Pardon and help us!" He kept repeating the words that suddenly and unexpectedly sprang to his lips. And, unbeliever that he was, he kept repeating those words not with his lips only. Now, at this moment, he knew that not only all his doubts, but, as he realized so well, the very impossibility of believing with his reason, did not prevent him in the least from appealing to God. All that fell away, like dust, from his soul. To whom else was he to appeal, if not to Him in whose hands he felt himself, his soul, and his love to be?

The carriage was not ready yet, but in feeling a tremendous access of physical strength and alertness and anxious not to lose a single moment, he did not wait, but started off on foot, telling Kuzma to catch him up.

At the corner of the street he saw a night cabman hurrying along. In the little sledge sat Lizaveta Petrovna in a velvet cloak with a shawl over her head. "Thank God, thank God!" he murmured, overjoyed to recognize the fair-haired woman with her little face, which now wore a particularly serious, even stern expression. Without telling the driver to stop, he ran along beside her.

"Two hours ago, not longer?" she asked. "You'll find the doctor, only don't hurry him. And get some opium at the chemist's."

"So you think it will be all right? Lord, have mercy on us and help us!" said Levin, seeing his horse coming out of the gate. Jumping into the sledge beside Kuzma, he told him to drive to the doctor's.

Chapter 14

The doctor was not up yet, and his servant said that he had gone late to bed and given orders that he was not to be called, but that he would be up soon. The servant was cleaning the lamp glasses and seemed very absorbed in his work. His attention to the glasses and complete indifference to what was taking place at Levin's astonished Levin at first, but on thinking it over he at once realized that no one knew or was obliged to know his feelings and that it was therefore all the more necessary to act calmly, deliberately, and firmly to break through this wall of indifference and attain his end. "Do not hurry and do not let anything go by default," Levin said to himself, feeling an ever-increasing access of physical strength and alertness.

Having learned that the doctor was not up yet, Levin decided, out of the many plans that occurred to him, on the following: Kuzma was to go with a note to another doctor, while he himself would go to the chemist's for opium and if, on his return, the doctor had not got up yet, he would either bribe the footman or, if need be, force his way into the bedroom and wake him.

At the chemist's a lean dispenser was sealing up a packet of powders for a coachman, who was waiting for it, with the same indifference with which the doctor's servant was cleaning the lamp glasses, and refused to let him have any opium. Levin, trying not to hurry and not to get flustered, gave the names of the doctor and the midwife and explained why the opium was needed. The dispenser asked in German whether he should let him have it and, receiving an affirmative reply from behind the partition, took down a bottle and a funnel, slowly poured some of the drug into a smaller bottle, stuck on a label, though Levin begged him not to do it, and was about to wrap it up. But this was more than Levin could stand: he determinedly snatched the bottle from the dispenser's hands and rushed out of the big glass doors. The doctor had not got up yet and his valet, who was now busy putting down a carpet, refused to wake him. Levin quietly took out a ten-ruble note and, speaking slowly but without losing time, handed him the note and explained that the doctor (how great and important this doctor, so insignificant before, seemed to him now!) had promised to come at any time and that he would most certainly not be angry and must therefore be wakened at once.

The servant consented, went upstairs, and asked Levin to wait in the waiting room.

Levin could hear the doctor behind the door coughing, walking about, washing, and saying something. Three minutes passed; to Levin it seemed more than an hour. He could not wait any longer.

"Doctor, Doctor!" he called in a beseeching voice through the open door. "I'm terribly sorry, Doctor, but, please, for God's sake see me as you are. It's over two hours. . . ."

"Coming, coming. . . ."

"Just for one minute! . . ."

"Coming. . . ."

Two more minutes passed while the doctor was putting on his boots and another two minutes while he was putting on his coat and combing his hair.

"Doctor!" Levin began again in a piteous voice, but at that moment the doctor came out, dressed and his hair brushed. "These people have no conscience," thought Levin. "Brushing his hair while we are about to die!"

"Good morning!" said the doctor to him, holding out his hand and almost teasing him by his composure. "There's no need for you to be in a hurry. Well, sir?"

Trying to be as circumstantial as possible, Levin began to tell the doctor all the unnecessary details about his wife's condition, continually interrupting his account with requests that the doctor should come with him at once.

"Don't be in such a hurry. You don't know whether I shall be needed at all. However, I promised and I suppose I'd better come. But there is no hurry. Sit down, please. Would you like some coffee?"

Levin looked at him as though he did not know whether the doctor was laughing at him or not. But the doctor never thought of laughing.

"I know, my dear sir, I know," he said with a smile. "I'm a married man myself. We husbands are the most pathetic creatures at a time like this. I have a patient whose husband always runs away to the stables on such occasions."

"But what do you think, Doctor? Do you think it will be all right?"

"Everything seems to point to a favorable result."

"Then you will come at once?" said Levin, staring furiously at the servant bringing in coffee.

"In about an hour."

"An hour? For heaven's sake, Doctor. . . ."

"Very well, let me have a cup of coffee first."

The doctor began drinking his coffee. Both were silent.

"The Turks seem to be getting a real good beating," said the doctor, munching a roll. "Did you read yesterday's *Telegram*?"

"I'm sorry, I can't stand it!" said Levin, jumping up. "So you'll come in a quarter of an hour, won't you?"

"Half an hour."

"On your word of honor?"

Levin returned home as the old princess arrived, and they went up to the bedroom together. The princess had tears in her eyes and her hands shook. When she saw Levin, she embraced him and burst out crying.

"Well, Lizaveta Petrovna, my dear?" she said, seizing the midwife's hand as she came out of the bedroom with a beaming, but preoccupied face.

"It's going on all right," she said. "Please, persuade her to lie down. It will be easier for her."

From the very moment Levin woke up that morning and realized what the situation was, he had been bracing himself to endure what was before him without reflection and without any unnecessary anticipation, firmly suppressing all his thoughts and feelings, resolved not to upset his wife, but on the contrary to calm her and keep up her spirits. Not allowing himself even to think of what was going to happen or how it would all end and finding out how long a confinement usually lasted, he mentally prepared himself to endure and steel his heart for five hours, which seemed not impossible to him. But when he came back from the doctor's and again saw Kitty's sufferings, he began repeating more and more often: "Lord have mercy on us and help us," sighing and raising his head toward heaven; and he was overcome by a feeling of fear that he might not be able to bear the strain and would either run away or burst into tears. So terrible did he feel. And only one hour had passed.

But after that hour, another passed, a second, a third, and all the five hours that he had imposed on himself as the limit of his endurance, and the situation was still unchanged. He went on enduring because there was nothing else he could do, imagining every moment that he had reached the limit of his endurance and that any moment his heart would burst with pity.

But minutes passed and hours, and more hours, and his suffering and horror and strain grew more and more intense.

All the ordinary conditions of life, without which one can have no idea of anything, no longer existed for Levin. He had lost the sense of time. The minutes — those minutes when she called him to her and he held her perspiring hand, now squeezing his with extraordinary strength and now pushing him away — seemed like hours to him, and hours seemed like minutes. He was surprised when Lizaveta Petrovna asked him to light a candle behind the partition and he learned that it was five o'clock in the afternoon. Had he been told that it was only ten o'clock, he would have been no less surprised. He was as little aware of where he had been all the time as he had of when and where it had been happening. He saw her burning face, sometimes bewildered and suffering and sometimes smiling and trying to calm him. He saw the old princess, red-faced and tense, the curls of her gray hair undone, in tears, which she did her best to keep back, and biting her lips; he saw Dolly, and the doctor smoking fat cigars, and Lizaveta Petrovna with a firm, determined, and reassuring expression on her face, and the old prince pacing up and down the ballroom and frowning. But how they came and went, and where they were, he did not know. The old princess was one moment in the bedroom with the doctor and the next in the study, where a table laid for a meal made its appearance; and then it was not the princess but Dolly. Then Levin remembered that he had been sent somewhere. Once he was sent to move a table and a sofa to another room. He did it with a will, thinking that it was necessary for Kitty, and only afterward did he find out that he had been preparing a bed for himself. Then he was sent to the study to ask the doctor something. The doctor had answered and then began talking about the disorderly scenes in the town council. After that he had been sent to fetch an icon in a silver-gilt case from the old princess' bedroom, and he and the princess' old maid had climbed onto a small cupboard to get it down and had broken the little lamp, and the princess' maid had tried to comfort him about his wife and the lamp, and he had brought the icon back with him and put it at Kitty's head, carefully pushing it behind the pillows. But where, when, and why all this was done he did not know. Nor did he understand why the old princess took his hand and, looking mournfully at him, begged him to calm himself, and Dolly tried to persuade him to eat something and led him out of the room, and even the doctor looked at him gravely and with sympathy, offering him some drops.

He only knew and felt that what was happening was similar to what had happened in the hotel of the provincial town a year ago on the deathbed of his brother Nikolai. Only that had been sorrow and this was joy. But both that sorrow and this joy were equally beyond the ordinary conditions of life. In this ordinary life they were like openings through which something higher became visible. And what was happening now was equally hard and agonizing to bear and equally incomprehensible, and one's soul, when contemplating it, soared to a height such as one did not think possible before and where reason could not keep up with it.

"Lord have mercy on us and help us," he kept repeating incessantly to himself, in spite of his long and seemingly complete alienation from religion, feeling that he was turning to God as trustingly and as simply as in the days of his childhood and early youth.

All this time he was in two distinctly separate moods. One when he was away from her, with the doctor, who smoked one fat cigarette after another and stubbed them out on the rim of the overflowing ashtray, with Dolly and the old prince, where they talked about dinner and politics or Mary Petrovna's illness and where Levin suddenly forgot what was going on in the house and felt as though he were waking up; and the other mood, at her bedside, by her pillow, where his heart was about to burst with pity, and yet did not burst, and where he prayed without stopping to God. And every time that a scream, reaching him from the bedroom, roused him from his momentary forgetfulness, he succumbed to the same strange delusion that possessed him at the very first — every time he heard the scream he jumped up, ran to justify himself, remembered on the way that he was not to blame, and was overcome by a desire to protect and help her. But when he looked at her he again realized that he could not help and was horrified and murmured, "Lord have mercy on us and help us!" And the longer it lasted, the more intense those two moods grew: the calmer he became when away from her, almost indeed forgetting her, the more and more poignantly did he react to her suffering and his own helplessness. He would jump up, wishing to run away somewhere, but ran to her room instead.

Sometimes, when she called him again and again, he reproached her. But seeing her meek, smiling face and hearing the words, "I've worn you out," he reproached God, but the thought of God made him at once pray for forgiveness and mercy.

Chapter 15

He did not know whether it was late or early. The candles had all burned low. Dolly had just been in the study and suggested that the doctor should lie down. Levin sat listening to the doctor's story about a quack magnetizer and looking at the ash of his cigarette. It was a period of rest and he was only half awake. He had completely forgotten what was going on. He listened to the doctor's story and took it in. Suddenly there was a terrible scream. It was so terrible that Levin did not even jump up, but looked questioningly at the doctor with bated breath, too terrified to speak. The doctor bent his head on one side as he listened and smiled approvingly. Everything was so extraordinary that nothing surprised Levin any more. "I suppose that's all right," he thought and went on sitting where he was. But who was screaming? He jumped up, ran on tiptoe into the bedroom, walked round the midwife and the old princess and took up his old position at the head of the bed. The screaming had stopped, but something was different now. What it was he neither saw nor understood and did not want to see or understand. But he read it in the midwife's face, which was stern and pale, but still as resolute, though her jaw trembled a little and her eyes were fixed intently on Kitty. Kitty's flushed, worn-out face, a strand of hair clinging to her perspiring forehead, was turned to him, seeking his eyes. Her raised hands were asking for his hands. Seizing his cold hands with her perspiring ones, she began pressing them to her face. "Don't go, don't go! I'm not afraid, I'm not afraid!" she said rapidly. "Mother, take off my earrings. They are in the way. You're not frightened, are you? Soon, soon, Lizaveta Petrovna. . . ."

She was speaking very rapidly and she tried to smile. But suddenly her face became distorted and she pushed him away.

"Oh, this is terrible! I'm dying, dying! Go, go!" And again he heard that terrible scream.

Levin clasped his head in his hands and ran out of the room.

"It's nothing, nothing, everything's all right," Dolly called after him.

But whatever they said, he knew that now it was all over. Leaning his head against the jamb of the door, he stood in the next room and heard someone shrieking and howling in a way he had never heard before and he knew that these screams came from what had once been Kitty. He had long ceased wishing for a child. He hated this child now. He did not even wish her to live now. All he wished was that these terrible sufferings should end.

"Doctor, what is it? What is it? Oh, my God!" he said, seizing the doctor's hand as he entered.

"It's the end," said the doctor.

The doctor's face was so grave as he said it that Levin understood him to mean that Kitty was dying.

Beside himself, he rushed into her room. The first thing he saw was the midwife's face. It looked more frowning and more severe than ever. Kitty's face was not there. In its place was something horrible both because of the strained expression and the frightful sounds that issued from it. He pressed his head to the wood of the bedstead, feeling that his heart was breaking. The terrible screaming did not cease; it grew more terrible and, as though reaching the utmost limit of horror, it suddenly ceased. Levin could not believe his ears, but there was no doubt about it: the screaming stopped and all he heard was a soft bustling, a rustling, and the sound of hurried breathing, and her voice, her live, tender, happy voice, saying: "It's over!"

He raised his head. Her arms drooping helplessly on the blanket and looking extraordinarily gentle and beautiful, she gazed silently at him, trying to smile but unable to do so.

And suddenly Levin felt himself transported in a flash from the mysterious, terrible, and strange world in which he had been living for the last twenty-two hours into his old everyday world, now radiant with the light of such new happiness that he could hardly bear it. The taut cords snapped. The sobs and tears of joy he had not foreseen rose with such force within him that his whole body shook and for a long time prevented him from speaking.

Falling on his knees by her bed, he held his wife's hand to his lips and kissed it, and her hand responded to his kisses with a weak movement of fingers. Meanwhile, at the foot of the bed, in the midwife's expert hands, like the flame of a lamp, flickered the life of a human being who had never existed before and who, with the same rights and importance to itself, would live and beget others like himself.

"Alive! Alive! And it's a boy! Nothing to worry about!" Levin heard the midwife's voice saying as she slapped the baby's back with a trembling hand.

"Is it true, Mother?"

The old princess' quiet sobbing was the only reply she got.

And amid the silence, as an unmistakable answer to his mother's question, there came a voice quite unlike the other subdued voices in the room. It was a bold, insolent cry of a human being that had no consideration for anything and that seemed to have appeared out of nowhere.

Had Levin been told before that Kitty was dead, that he had died with her, and that their children were angels, and that God was present before them — he would not have been surprised at anything. But now, having returned to the world of reality, he had to make a great effort to realize that she was alive and well and that the desperately howling creature was his son. Kitty was alive and her sufferings were at an end. And he was ineffably happy. That he understood and it filled him with joy. But the child? Whence and why had he come? And who was he? He just could not understand, he could not accustom himself to the idea. It seemed something superfluous, something too much, something which it would take him a long time to get used to.

Chapter 16

About ten o'clock the old prince, Koznyshev, and Oblonsky were sitting at Levin's and, after talking about the young mother, they began discussing other matters. Levin listened to them, and as they talked, involuntarily thought of what had been happening before that morning and remembered himself as he had been the previous day before the birth of his child. A hundred years seemed to have elapsed since then. He felt as if he were on some inaccessible height from which he was carefully descending so as not to hurt the feelings of those he was talking to. He talked and never for a moment ceased thinking of his wife, of her present condition, and of his son, to the idea of whose existence he was trying to accustom himself. The whole world of woman, which after his marriage had assumed a new, hitherto unsuspected significance for him, now rose so high in his estimation that his imagination could not grasp it. He listened to the conversation about yesterday's dinner at the club and thought, "What is happening to her now? How is she? What is she thinking of? Is our son Dmitry crying?" And in the middle of the conversation, in the middle of a sentence, jumped up and left the room.

"Send someone to let me know if I can see her," said the old prince.

"All right," replied Levin and, without stopping, went to her room.

She was not asleep, but was talking quietly with her mother, making arrangements for the christening.

Tidied and her hair brushed, a smart cap trimmed with something blue on her head, her hands on the counterpane, she lay on her back and, meeting his glance, drew him to her with a look. Her look, already bright, grew still brighter, the nearer he approached her. Her face showed the same change from the earthly to the unearthly as is seen on the faces of the dead; but there it was a farewell, while here it was a welcome. His heart was again gripped by agitation as at the moment of the child's birth. She took his hand and asked whether he had slept. He could not bring himself to answer and turned away, conscious of his own weakness.

"I've had a good sleep, darling," she said, "and I feel so good now."

She gazed at him and suddenly her expression changed.

"Let me have him," she said, hearing the baby's weak cry. "Let me have him, Lizaveta Petrovna, and let his father see him too."

"Why, yes, let his father have a look at him," said the midwife, lifting something strange, red, and wriggling. "But wait, let's first make him tidy," and she put the wriggling red object on the bed, began unwrapping and wrapping it up again, raising and turning him over with one finger and powdering him with something.

Looking at this tiny, pathetic little creature, Levin tried in vain to discover in his heart anything in the least resembling paternal feeling. He felt nothing for the baby but aversion. But when it was stripped and he caught sight of such thin little hands and feet, saffron-colored, with little fingers and toes, and the big toe even looking quite different from the others, and when he saw the midwife bending the little, sticking-out arms as though they were springs and encasing them in little garments, he was filled with such pity for the little creature and such fear that she might hurt them that he tried to restrain her hand.

Lizaveta Petrovna laughed.

"Don't be afraid, don't be afraid!"

When the baby had been swaddled and transformed into a hard cocoon, the midwife lifted it in her arms, as though proud of her work, and drew back so that Levin could see his son in all his beauty.

Without taking her eyes off the baby, Kitty, glancing around, looked in the same direction.

"Let me have him! Let me have him!" Kitty said and was even going to sit up.

"What are you doing?" the midwife said to her. "You mustn't move like that! Wait, I'll give him to you. Let's first show Daddy what a fine lad we are!"

And Lizaveta Petrovna held out to Levin on one hand (with the other she merely supported the nape of the wobbly head) this strange, wriggly red creature that tried to hide its head in the swaddling clothes. But there was also a nose, a pair of squinting eyes, and smacking lips.

"A beautiful baby!" said Lizaveta Petrovna.

Levin sighed with disappointment. This beautiful baby only inspired him with a feeling of disgust and pity. It was not at all the sort of feeling he had expected.

He turned away while the midwife got the baby to take the unaccustomed breast.

A sudden laugh made him raise his head. It was Kitty who laughed. The baby had taken the breast.

"Well, that's enough, that's enough!" said Lizaveta Petrovna, but Kitty would not give up the baby. He fell asleep in her arms.

"Have a look at him now," said Kitty, turning the baby so that Levin could see him. The old man's face wrinkled up still more and the baby sneezed.

Smiling and scarcely able to keep back tears of tenderness, Levin kissed his wife and left the darkened room.

What he felt about the little creature was not at all what he had expected. There was nothing happy or cheerful about it; on the contrary, there was a new distressful feeling of fear. It was the consciousness of another sphere of vulnerability. And this consciousness was so painful at first, his fear that that helpless creature might suffer was so strong, that it completely submerged the strange feeling of unreasoning joy and even pride he had felt when the baby sneezed.

VIRGINIA WOOLF

Virginia Woolf (b. 1882), one of the most famous writers of the twentieth century, was at the center of the Bloomsbury Group, a circle of influential artists and writers which became synonymous with British intellectual life between the World Wars. Woolf was among the first writers to employ the stream-of-consciousness technique. Curiously, despite her ability to open up and lay bare the internal world of her characters to the very depths of their personalities, her own internal world could never be so conquered. Throughout her life she struggled with mental illness. In 1941, dreading yet another mental breakdown, she drowned herself.

To the Lighthouse

10

For Cam grazed the easel by an inch; she would not stop for Mr Bankes and Lily Briscoe; though Mr Bankes, who would have liked a daughter of his own, held out his hand; she would not stop for her father, whom she grazed also by an inch; nor for her mother, who called 'Cam! I want you a moment!' as she dashed past. She was off like a bird, bullet, or arrow, impelled by what desire, shot by whom, at what directed, who could say? What, what? Mrs Ramsay pondered, watching her. It might be a vision — of a shell, of a wheelbarrow, of a fairy kingdom on the far side of the hedge; or it might be the glory of speed; no one knew. But when Mrs Ramsay called 'Cam!' a second time, the projectile dropped in mid career, and Cam came lagging back, pulling a leaf by the way, to her mother.

What was she dreaming about, Mrs Ramsay wondered, seeing her engrossed, as she stood there, with some thought of her own, so that she had to repeat the message twice — ask Mildred if Andrew, Miss Doyle, and Mr Rayley have come back? — The words seemed to be dropped into a well, where, if the waters were clear, they were also so extraordinarily distorting that, even as they descended, one saw them twisting about to make Heaven knows what pattern on the floor of the child's mind. What message would Cam give the cook? Mrs Ramsay wondered. And indeed it was only by waiting patiently, and hearing that there was an old woman in the kitchen with very red cheeks, drinking soup out of a basin, that Mrs Ramsay at last prompted that parrot-like instinct which had picked up Mildred's words quite accurately and could now produce them, if one waited, in a colourless singsong. Shifting from foot to foot, Cam repeated the words, 'No, they haven't, and I've told Ellen to clear away tea.'

Minta Doyle and Paul Rayley had not come back then. That could only mean, Mrs Ramsay thought, one thing. She must accept him, or she must refuse him. This going off after luncheon for a walk, even though Andrew was with them — what could it mean? except that she had decided, rightly, Mrs Ramsay thought (and she was very, very fond of Minta), to accept that good fellow, who might not be brilliant, but then, thought Mrs Ramsay, realizing that James was tugging at her to make her go on reading aloud the Fisherman and his Wife, she did in her own heart infinitely prefer boobies to clever men who wrote dissertations; Charles Tansley for instance. Anyhow it must have happened, one way or the other, by now.

But she read, 'Next morning the wife awoke first, and it was just daybreak, and from her bed she saw the beautiful country lying before her. Her husband was still stretching himself . . .'

But how could Minta say now that she would not have him? Not if she agreed to spend whole afternoons traipsing about the country, alone — for Andrew would be off after his crabs — but possibly Nancy was with them. She tried to recall the sight of them standing at the hall door after lunch. There they stood, looking at the sky, wondering about the weather, and she had said, thinking partly to cover their shyness, partly to encourage them to be off (for her sympathies were with Paul),

'There isn't a cloud anywhere within miles,' at which she could feel little Charles Tansley, who had followed them out, snigger. But she did it on purpose. Whether Nancy was there or not, she could not be certain, looking from one to the other in her mind's eye.

She read on: 'Ah, wife,' said the man, 'why should we be king? I do not want to be King.' 'Well,' said the wife, 'if you won't be King, I will; go to the Flounder, for I will be King.'

'Come in or go out, Cam,' she said, knowing that Cam was attracted only by the word 'Flounder' and that in a moment she would fidget and fight with James as usual. Cam shot off. Mrs Ramsay went on reading, relieved, for she and James shared the same tastes and were comfortable together.

'And when he came to the sea, it was quite dark grey, and the water heaved up from below, and smelt putrid. Then he went and stood by it and said,

"Flounder, flounder, in the sea,
Come, I pray thee, here to me;
For my wife, good Ilsabil,
Wills not as I'd have her will."

"Well, what does she want then?" said the Flounder.' And where were they now? Mrs Ramsay wondered, reading and thinking, quite easily, both at the same time; for the story of the Fisherman and his Wife was like the bass gently accompanying a tune, which now and then ran up unexpectedly into the melody. And when should she be told? If nothing happened, she would have to speak seriously to Minta. For she could not go traipsing about all over the country, even if Nancy were with them (she tried again, unsuccessfully, to visualize their backs going down the path, and to count them). She was responsible to Minta's parents — the Owl and the Poker. Her nicknames for them shot into her mind as she read. The Owl and the Poker — yes, they would be annoyed if they heard — and they were certain to hear — that Minta, staying with the Ramsays, had been seen etcetera, etcetera, etcetera. 'He wore a wig in the House of Commons and she ably assisted him at the head of the stairs,' she repeated, fishing them up out of her mind by a phrase which, coming back from some party, she had made to amuse her husband. Dear, dear, Mrs Ramsay said to herself, how did they produce this incongruous daughter? this tomboy Minta, with a hole in her stocking? How did she exist in that portentous atmosphere where the maid was always removing in a dust-pan the sand that the parrot had scattered, and conversation was almost entirely reduced to the exploits — interesting perhaps, but limited after all — of that bird? Naturally, one had asked her to lunch, tea, dinner, finally to stay with them up at Finlay, which had resulted in some friction with the Owl, her mother, and more calling, and more conversation, and more sand, and really at the end of it, she had told enough lies about parrots to last her a lifetime (so she had said to her husband that night, coming back from the party). However, Minta came . . . Yes, she came, Mrs Ramsay thought, suspecting some thorn in the tangle of this thought; and disengaging it found it to be this: a woman had once accused her of 'robbing her of her daughter's affections'; something Mrs Doyle had said made her remember that charge again. Wishing to dominate, wishing to interfere, making people do what she wished — that was the charge against her, and she thought it most unjust. How could she help being 'like that' to look at? No one could accuse her of taking pains to impress. She was often ashamed of her own shabbiness. Nor was she domineering, nor was she tyrannical. It was more true about hospitals and drains and the dairy. About things like that she did feel passionately, and would, if she had had the chance, have liked to take people by the scruff of their necks and make them see. No hospital on the whole island. It was a disgrace. Milk delivered at your door in London positively brown with dirt. It should be made illegal. A model dairy and a hospital up here — those two things she would have liked to do, herself. But how? With all these children? When they were older, then perhaps she would have time; when they were all at school.

Oh, but she never wanted James to grow a day older or Cam either. These two she would have liked to keep forever just as they were, demons of wickedness, angels of delight, never to see them grow up into long-legged monsters. Nothing made up for the loss. When she read just now to James, 'and there were numbers of soldiers with kettle-drums and trumpets,' and his eyes darkened, she thought, why should they grow up, and lose all that? He was the most gifted, the most sensitive of her children. But all, she thought, were full of promise. Prue, a perfect angel with the others, and sometimes now, at night especially, she took one's breath away with her beauty. Andrew — even her husband admitted that his gift for mathematics was extraordinary. And Nancy and Roger, they were both wild creatures now, scampering about over the country all day long. As for Rose, her mouth was too big, but she had a wonderful gift with her hands. If they had charades, Rose made the dresses; made everything; liked best arranging tables, flowers, anything. She did not like it that Jasper should shoot birds; but it was only a stage; they all went through stages. Why, she asked, pressing her chin on James's head, should they grow up so fast? Why should they go to school? She would have liked always to have had a baby. She was happiest carrying one in her arms. Then people might say she was tyrannical, domineering, masterful, if they chose; she did not mind. And, touching his hair with her lips, she thought, he will never be so happy again, but stopped herself, remembering how it angered her husband that she should say that. Still, it was true. They were happier now than they would ever be again. A tenpenny tea set made Cam happy for days. She heard them stamping and crowing on the floor above her head the moment they woke. They came bustling along the passage. Then the door sprang open and in they came, fresh as roses, staring, wide awake, as if this coming into the dining-room after breakfast, which they did every day of their lives was a positive event to them; and so on, with one thing after another, all day long, until she went up to say good-night to them, and found them netted in their cots like birds among cherries and raspberries still making up stories about some little bit of rubbish — something they had heard, something they had picked up in the garden. They had all their little treasures . . . And so she went down and said to her husband, Why must they grow up and lose it all? Never will they be so happy again. And he was angry. Why take such a gloomy view of life? he said. It is not sensible. For it was odd; and she believed it to be true; that with all his gloom and desperation he was happier, more hopeful on the whole, than she was. Less exposed to human worries — perhaps that was it. He had always his work to fall back on. Not that she herself was 'pessimistic,' as he accused her of being. Only she thought life — and a little strip of time presented itself to her eyes, her fifty years. There it was before her — life. Life: she thought but she did not finish her thought. She took a look at life, for she had a clear sense of it there, something real, something private, which she shared neither with her children nor with her husband. A sort of transaction went on between them, in which she was on one side, and life was on another, and she was always trying to get the better of it, as it was of her; and sometimes they parleyed (when she sat alone); there were, she remembered, great reconciliation scenes; but for the most part, oddly enough, she must admit that she felt this thing that she called life terrible, hostile, and quick to pounce on you if you gave it a chance. There were the eternal problems: suffering; death; the poor. There was always a woman dying of cancer even here. And yet she had said to all these children, You shall go through with it. To eight people she had said relentlessly that (and the bill for the greenhouse would be fifty pounds). For that reason, knowing what was before them — love and ambition and being wretched alone in dreary places — she had often the feeling, Why must they grow up and lose it all? And then she said to herself, brandishing her sword at life, nonsense. They will be perfectly happy. And here she was, she reflected, feeling life rather sinister again, making Minta marry Paul Rayley; because whatever she might feel about her own transaction and she had had experiences which need not happen to everyone (she did not name them to herself); she was driven on, too quickly she knew, almost as if it were an escape for her too, to say that people must marry; people must have children.

Was she wrong in this, she asked herself, reviewing her conduct for the past week or two, and wondering if she had indeed put any pressure upon Minta, who was only twenty-four, to make up her mind. She was uneasy. Had she not laughed about it? Was she not forgetting again how strongly she influenced people? Marriage needed — oh all sorts of qualities (the bill for the greenhouse would be fifty pounds); one — she need not name it — *that* was essential; the thing she had with her husband. Had they that?

'Then he put on his trousers and ran away like a madman,' she read. 'But outside a great storm was raging and blowing so hard that he could scarcely keep his feet; houses and trees toppled over, the mountains trembled, rocks rolled into the sea, the sky was pitch black, and it thundered and lightened, and the sea came in with black waves as high as church towers and mountains, and all with white foam at the top.'

She turned the page; there were only a few lines more, so that she would finish the story, though it was past bedtime. It was getting late. The light in the garden told her that; and the whitening of the flowers and something grey in the leaves conspired together to rouse in her a feeling of anxiety. What it was about she could not think at first. Then she remembered; Paul and Minta and Andrew had not come back. She summoned before her again the little group on the terrace in front of the hall door, standing looking up into the sky. Andrew had his net and basket. That meant he was going to catch crabs and things. That meant he would climb out on to a rock; he would be cut off. Or coming back single file on one of those little paths above the cliff one of them might slip. He would roll and then crash. It was growing quite dark.

But she did not let her voice change in the least as she finished the story, and added, shutting the book, and speaking the last words as if she had made them up herself, looking into James's eyes: 'And there they are living still at this very time.'

'And that's the end,' she said, and she saw in his eyes, as the interest of the story died away in them, something else take its place; something wondering, pale, like the reflection of a light, which at once made him gaze and marvel. Turning, she looked across the bay, and there, sure enough, coming regularly across the waves first two quick strokes and then one long steady stroke, was the light of the lighthouse. It had been lit.

In a moment he would ask her, 'Are we going to the Lighthouse?' And she would have to say, 'No: not tomorrow; your father says not.' Happily, Mildred came in to fetch them, and the bustle distracted them. But he kept looking back over his shoulder as Mildred carried him out, and she was certain that he was thinking, we are not going to the Lighthouse tomorrow, and she thought, he will remember that all his life.

11

No, she thought, putting together some of the pictures he had cut out — a refrigerator, a mowing machine, a gentleman in evening dress — children never forget. For this reason, it was so important what one said, and what one did, and it was a relief when they went to bed. For now she need not think about anybody. She could be herself, by herself. And that was what now she often felt the need of — to think; well not even to think. To be silent; to be alone. All the being and the doing, expansive, glittering, vocal, evaporated; and one shrunk, with a sense of solemnity, to being oneself, a wedge-shaped core of darkness, something invisible to others. Although she continued to knit, and sat upright, it was thus that she felt herself; and this self having shed its attachments was free for the strangest adventures. When life sank down for a moment, the range of experience seemed limitless. And to everybody there was always this sense of unlimited resources, she supposed; one after another, she, Lily, Augustus Carmichael, must feel, our apparitions, the things you know us by, are simply childish. Beneath it is all dark, it is all spreading, it is unfathomably deep; but now and again we rise to the surface and that is what you see us by. Her horizon seemed to her limitless. There were all the places she had not seen; the Indian plains; she felt herself pushing aside the thick leather curtain of a church in Rome. This core of darkness could go anywhere, for no one saw it. They could not stop it, she thought, exulting. There was freedom, there was peace, there was, most welcome of all, a summoning together, a resting on a platform of stability. Not as oneself did one find rest ever, in her experience (she accomplished here something dexterous with her needles), but as a wedge of darkness. Losing personality, one lost the fret, the hurry, the stir; and there rose to her lips always some exclamation of triumph over life when things came together in this peace, this rest, this eternity; and pausing there she looked out to meet that stroke of the Lighthouse, the long steady stroke, the last of the three, which was her stroke, for watching them in this mood always at this hour one could not help attaching oneself to one thing especially of the things one saw; and this thing, the long steady stroke, was her stroke. Often she found herself sitting and looking, sitting and looking, with her work in her hands until she became the thing she looked at — that light for example. And it would lift up on it some little phrase or other which had been lying in her mind like that — 'Children don't forget, children don't forget' — which she would repeat and begin adding to it, It will end, It will end, she said. It will come, it will come, when suddenly she added, We are in the hands of the Lord.

But instantly she was annoyed with herself for saying that. Who had said it? not she; she had been trapped into saying something she did not mean. She looked up over her knitting and met the third stroke and it seemed to her like her own eyes meeting her own eyes, searching as she alone could search into her mind and her heart, purifying out of existence that lie, any lie. She praised herself in praising the light, without vanity, for she was stern, she was searching, she was beautiful like that light. It was odd, she thought, how if one was alone,

one leant to things, inanimate things; trees, streams, flowers; felt they expressed one; felt they became one; felt they knew one, in a sense were one; felt an irrational tenderness thus (she looked at that long steady light) as for oneself. There rose, and she looked and looked with her needles suspended, there curled up off the floor of the mind, rose from the lake of one's being, a mist, a bride to meet her lover.

What brought her to say that: 'We are in the hands the Lord?' she wondered. The insincerity slipping in among the truths roused her, annoyed her. She returned to her knitting again. How could any Lord have made this world? she asked. With her mind she had always seized the fact that there is no reason, order, justice: but suffering, death, the poor. There was no treachery too base for the world to commit; she knew that. No happiness lasted; she knew that. She knitted with firm composure, slightly pursing her lips and, without being aware of it, so stiffened and composed the lines of her face in a habit of sternness that when her husband passed, though he was chuckling at the thought that Hume, the philosopher, grown enormously fat, had stuck in a bog, he could not help noting, as he passed, the sternness at the heart of her beauty. It saddened him, and her remoteness pained him, and he felt, as he passed, that he could not protect her, and, when he reached the hedge, he was sad. He could do nothing to help her. He must stand by and watch her. Indeed, the infernal truth was, he made things worse for her. He was irritable — he was touchy. He had lost his temper over the Lighthouse. He looked into the hedge, into its intricacy, its darkness.

Always, Mrs Ramsay felt, one helped oneself out of solitude reluctantly by laying hold of some little odd or end, some sound, some sight. She listened, but it was all very still; cricket was over; the children were in their baths; there was only the sound of the sea. She stopped knitting; she held the long reddish-brown stocking dangling in her hands a moment. She saw the light again. With some irony in her interrogation, for when one woke at all, one's relations changed, she looked at the steady light, the pitiless, the remorseless, which was so much her, yet so little her, which had her at its beck and call (she woke in the night and saw it bent across their bed, stroking the floor), but for all that she thought, watching it with fascination, hypnotized, as if it were stroking with its silver fingers some sealed vessel in her brain whose bursting would flood her with delight, she had known happiness, exquisite happiness, intense happiness, and it silvered the rough waves a little more brightly, as daylight faded, and the blue went out of the sea and it rolled in waves of pure lemon which curved and swelled and broke upon the beach and the ecstasy burst in her eyes and waves of pure delight raced over the floor of her mind and she felt, It is enough! It is enough!

He turned and saw her. Ah! She was lovely, lovelier now than ever he thought. But he could not speak to her. He could not interrupt her. He wanted urgently to speak to her now that James was gone and she was alone at last. But he resolved, no; he would not interrupt her. She was aloof from him now in her beauty, in her sadness. He would let her be, and he passed her without a word, though it hurt him that she should look so distant, and he could not reach her, he could do nothing to help her. And again he would have passed her without a word had she not, at that very moment, given him of her own free will what she knew he would never ask, and called to him and taken the green shawl off the picture frame, and gone to him. For he wished, she knew, to protect her.

12

She folded the green shawl about her shoulders. She took his arm. His beauty was so great, she said, beginning to speak of Kennedy the gardener at once; he was so awfully handsome, that she couldn't dismiss him. There was a ladder against the greenhouse, and little lumps of putty stuck about, for they were beginning to mend the greenhouse roof. Yes, but as she strolled along with her husband, she felt that that particular source of worry had been placed. She had it on the tip of her tongue to say, as they strolled, 'It'll cost fifty pounds,' but instead, for her heart failed her about money, she talked about Jasper shooting birds, and he said, at once, soothing her instantly, that it was natural in a boy, and he trusted he would find better ways of amusing himself before long. Her husband was so sensible, so just. And so she said, 'Yes; all children go through stages,' and began considering the dahlias in the big bed, and wondering what about next year's flowers, and had he heard the children's nickname for Charles Tansley, she asked. The atheist, they called him, the little atheist. 'He's not a polished specimen,' said Mr Ramsay. 'Far from it,' said Mrs Ramsay.

She supposed it was all right leaving him to his own devices, Mrs Ramsay said, wondering whether it was any use sending down bulbs; did they plant them? 'Oh, he has his dissertation to write,' said Mr Ramsay. She knew all about *that,* said Mrs Ramsay. He talked of nothing else. It was about the influence of somebody upon something. 'Well, it's all he has to count on,' said Mr Ramsay. 'Pray Heaven he won't fall in love with Prue,' said Mrs Ramsay. He'd disinherit her if she married him, said Mr Ramsay. He did not look at the flowers, which his wife was considering, but at a spot about a foot or so above them. There was no harm in him, he added, and was just about to say that anyhow he was the only young man in England who admired his — when he choked it back. He would not bother her again about his books. These flowers seemed creditable, Mr Ramsay said, lowering his gaze and noticing something red, something brown. Yes, but then these she had put in with her own hands, said Mrs Ramsay.

The question was, what happened if she sent bulbs down; did Kennedy plant them? It was his incurable laziness, she added, moving on. If she stood over him all day long with a spade in her hand, he did sometimes do a stroke of work. So they strolled along, towards the red-hot pokers. 'You're teaching your daughters to exaggerate,' said Mr Ramsay, reproving her. Her Aunt Camilla was far worse than she was, Mrs Ramsay remarked. 'Nobody ever held up your Aunt Camilla as a model of virtue that I'm aware of,' said Mr Ramsay. 'She was the most beautiful woman I ever saw,' said Mrs Ramsay. 'Somebody else was that,' said Mr Ramsay. Prue was going to be far more beautiful than she was, said Mrs Ramsay. He saw no trace of it, said Mr Ramsay. 'Well, then, look to-night,' said Mrs Ramsay. They paused. He wished Andrew could be induced to work harder. He would lose every chance of a scholarship if he didn't. 'Oh scholarships!' she said. Mr Ramsay thought her foolish for saying that, about a serious thing, like a scholarship. He should be very proud of Andrew if he got a scholarship, he said. She would be just as proud of him if he didn't, she answered. They disagreed always about this, but it did not matter. She liked him to believe in scholarships, and he liked her to be proud of Andrew whatever he did. Suddenly she remembered those little paths on the edge of the cliffs.

Wasn't it late? she asked. They hadn't come home yet. He flicked his watch carelessly open. But it was only just past seven. He held his watch open for a moment, deciding that he would tell her what he had felt on the terrace. To begin with, it was not reasonable to be so nervous. Andrew could look after himself. Then, he wanted to tell her that when he was walking on the terrace just now — here he became uncomfortable, as if he were breaking into that solitude, that aloofness, that remoteness of hers . . . But she pressed him. What had he wanted to tell her, she asked, thinking it was about going to the Lighthouse; and that he was sorry he had said 'Damn you.' But no. He did not like to see her look so sad, he said. Only wool gathering, she protested, flushing a little. They both felt uncomfortable, as if they did not know whether to go on or go back. She had been reading fairy tales to James, she said. No, they could not share that; they could not say that.

They had reached the gap between the two clumps of red-hot pokers, and there was the Lighthouse again, but she would not let herself look at it. Had she known that he was looking at her, she thought, she would not have let herself sit there, thinking. She disliked anything that reminded her that she had been seen sitting thinking. So she looked over her shoulder, at the town. The lights were rippling and running as if they were drops of silver water held firm in a wind. And all the poverty, all the suffering had turned to that, Mrs Ramsay thought. The lights of the town and of the harbour and of the boats seemed like a phantom net floating there to mark something which had sunk. Well, if he could not share her thoughts, Mr Ramsay said to himself, he would be off, then, on his own. He wanted to go on thinking, telling himself the story how Hume was stuck in a bog; he wanted to laugh. But first it was nonsense to be anxious about Andrew. When he was Andrew's age he used to walk about the country all day long, with nothing but a biscuit in his pocket and nobody bothered about him, or thought that he had fallen over a cliff. He said aloud he thought he would be off for a day's walk if the weather held! He had had about enough of Bankes and of Carmichael. He would like a little solitude. Yes, she said. It annoyed him that she did not protest. She knew that he would never do it. He was too old now to walk all day long with a biscuit in his pocket. She worried about the boys, but not about him. Years ago, before he had married, he thought, looking across the bay, as they stood between the clumps of red-hot pokers, he had walked all day. He had made a meal off bread and cheese in a public house. He had worked ten hours at a stretch; an old woman just popped her head in now and again and saw to the fire. That was the country he liked best, over there; those sandhills dwindling away into darkness. One could walk all day without meeting a soul. There was not a house scarcely, not a single village for miles on end. One could worry things out alone. There were little sandy beaches where no one had been since the beginning of time. The seals sat up and looked at you. It sometimes seemed to him that in a little house out there, alone — he broke off, sighing. He had no right. The father of eight children — he reminded himself. And he would have been a beast and a cur to wish a single thing altered. Andrew would be a better man than he had been. Prue would be a beauty, her mother said. They would stem the flood a bit. That was a good bit of work on the whole — his eight children. They showed he did not damn the poor little universe entirely, for on an evening like this, he thought, looking at the land dwindling away, the little island seemed pathetically small, half swallowed up in the sea.

'Poor little place,' he murmured with a sigh.

She heard him. He said the most melancholy things, but she noticed that directly he had said them he always seemed more cheerful than usual. All this phrase-making was a game, she thought, for if she had said half what he said, she would have blown her brains out by now.

It annoyed her, this phrase-making, and she said to him, in a matter-of-fact way, that it was a perfectly lovely evening. And what was he groaning about, she asked, half laughing, half complaining, for she guessed what he was thinking — he would have written better books if he had not married.

He was not complaining, he said. She knew that he did not complain. She knew that he had nothing whatever to complain of. And he seized her hand and raised it to his lips and kissed it with an intensity that brought the tears to her eyes, and quickly he dropped it.

They turned away from the view and began to walk up the path where the silver-green spear-like plants grew, arm in arm. His arm was almost like a young man's arm, Mrs Ramsay thought, thin and hard, and she thought with delight how strong he still was, though he was over sixty, and how untamed and optimistic, and how strange it was that being convinced, as he was, of all sorts of horrors, seemed not to depress him, but to cheer him. Was it not odd, she reflected? Indeed he seemed to her sometimes made differently from other people, born blind, deaf, and dumb, to the ordinary things, but to the extraordinary things, with an eye like an eagle's. His understanding often astonished her. But did he notice the flowers? No. Did he notice the view? No. Did he even notice his own daughter's beauty, or whether there was pudding on his plate or roast beef? He would sit at table with them like a person in a dream. And his habit of talking aloud, or saying poetry aloud, was growing on him, she was afraid; for sometimes it was awkward —

Best and brightest, come away!

poor Miss Giddings, when he shouted that at her, almost jumped out of her skin. But then, Mrs Ramsay, though instantly taking his side against all the silly Giddingses in the world, then, she thought, intimating by a little pressure on his arm that he walked up hill too fast for her, and she must stop for a moment to see whether those were fresh mole-hills on the bank, then, she thought, stooping down to look, a great mind like his must be different in every way from ours. All the great men she had ever known, she thought, deciding that a rabbit must have got in, were like that, and it was good for young men (though the atmosphere of lecture-rooms was stuffy and depressing to her beyond endurance almost) simply to bear him, simply to look at him. But without shooting rabbits, how was one to keep them down? she wondered. It might be a rabbit; it might be a mole. Some creature anyhow was ruining her Evening Primroses. And looking up, she saw above the thin trees the first pulse of the full-throbbing star, and wanted to make her husband look at it; for the sight gave her such keen pleasure. But she stopped herself. He never looked at things. If he did, all he would say would be, Poor little world, with one of his sighs.

At that moment, he said, 'Very fine,' to please her, and pretended to admire the flowers. But she knew quite well that he did not admire them, or even realize that they were there. It was only to please her . . . Ah, but was that not Lily Briscoe strolling along with William Bankes? She focussed her short-sighted eyes upon the backs of a retreating couple. Yes, indeed it was. Did that not mean that they would marry? Yes, it must! What an admirable idea! They must marry!

8   What about When We Fight?

Marriage with peace is the world's paradise: with strife, this life's purgatory.

— PROVERB

The test of a man's and woman's breeding is how they behave in a quarrel.

— GEORGE BERNARD SHAW

Introduction

St. Jerome wrote, "He who is not arguing is not married." In our first selection, from Joseph Kerns's fine compendium of Catholic wisdom on the subject of marriage, the overriding message is that marriage is tough. To be subject to the will, plans, and opinions of another, to lose one's autonomy, to live with a spouse in the kind of everyday intimacy that prevents one from concealing one's own weaknesses of personality and character, to devote oneself entirely to the welfare and comfort of another — this is to live a life of real trial.

In this chapter we explore healthy and unhealthy examples of marital conflict. Our readings begin with Martin Luther's advice to a henpecked husband: "Act the man!" No wife, Luther asserts, should be allowed to mistake good will and generosity for submissiveness. For in undermining a woman's respect, a man "dishonors the glory of God" and does evil to his marriage.

But just as men should not submit to abuse from a woman, so no woman should submit to abuse from a man. The selection that follows, from George Eliot, offers us a tragic glimpse of a marriage that has become nothing less than a desperate game of cat and mouse. Gwendolen Grandcourt, the heroine of George Eliot's novel, *Daniel Deronda,* has married for money. In her anxiousness to appease her guilt and to preserve the dignity of her position vis-à-vis the outside world, she encourages her spoiled and cruel husband to dominate and abuse her. Eventually she will succumb to her own deep hatred and contempt for him. Indeed, eventually Gwendolyn will become an agent in her husband's demise.

The mire of marital conflict in Edward Albee's famous play, *Who's Afraid of Virginia Woolf?,* is far different from that in Eliot's work. It is open conflict, not repressed. And it is engaged in by two people whose love and need for one another is at least as powerful as their contempt for one another. What George and Martha have together is a relationship that could be described as clinically pathological, a *follée à deux.* They have brought marital strife to a level of intricacy that defies unraveling; but their closeness also defies undoing. They alternate between tearing at each other and tearing at the world outside. There may be some small dynamic of this type of relationship in every marriage.

A more upbeat reflection on marital conflict comes next, authored by one of America's favorite comedians, Bill Cosby. Every married couple, and many engaged ones, too, will recognize themselves in Cosby's amusing and loving portrait of that eternal battle of the sexes, love. Every day on the stage of married life two worldviews collide. Being married, Cosby reminds us, means having to cultivate a healthy dose of tolerance and a good sense of humor.

Finally, a work of modern psychology on marital conflict. In all mar-

403

riages, psychologist John Gottman observes, there will be differences. Some of these are bound to mean irreconcilable, lifelong disagreements. Marital longevity and happiness, he discovered in twenty years of studying married couples, does not depend on curbing the amount of conflict in a marriage, but rather on handling conflict in healthy ways. Indeed, people who divorce do not fight any more often than those who stay married. Rather, people who stay married and who register high marital satisfaction tend to display more equanimity with regard to the inevitability of conflict, and tend to diffuse the harmful physiological effects of conflict with humor, laughter, affection, and other signals of friendship, commitment, and shared private meaning. Most importantly, happily married couples don't allow their negative feelings — however justified and powerful — to overtake their relationship. They make sure their interactions with their spouses are marked by far more positive than negative moments.

JOSEPH E. KERNS

Joseph E. Kerns, S.J. (d. 1999), was born in Philadelphia in 1924. He entered the Society of Jesus at the age of 18, in 1942, and was ordained as a priest in 1955 in Woodstock, Maryland. After receiving a degree in theology at Gregorian University in Rome, he taught at Wheeling College. In 1969, he left the Jesuit Order to marry.

The Theology of Marriage: The Historical Development of Christian Attitudes toward Sex and Sanctity in Marriage

Chapter 11, "For Better, for Worse . . ."

In Matthew's Gospel Our Lord tells the Pharisees that the man who takes a wife acquires a relationship with her which no human authority can sever. The impact of this statement may be judged from the comment it evoked — and not from the Pharisees.

> 'If that is the predicament of a married man,' the disciples said to Him, 'then one had better not get married!'[1]

The man who marries loses the autonomy that he has always known. His life has now been joined with that of another person and will continually feel the pull of that other life. To the disciples, at least, this is not an attractive prospect.

Nor does it seem any more appealing to Christians of the Middle East during the late 300's. Chrysostom, in fact, goes so far as to say that Paul, when speaking against divorce, is really persuading his readers not to marry.

> For anyone who hears that, after marriage, he will no longer be his own but will be subject to the will of his wife, will try to free himself without delay from that most bitter slavery — or rather, will not even take the yoke upon himself, since once he has done so, he must be a slave as long as it pleases his wife.[2]

The mind of the Western Church at this time is evident from Ambrose's remark about the bridal dowry.

> The girl who is married is sold into slavery with her own money.[3]

> The chain of love is indeed good, but it is still a chain. A wife cannot release herself from it when she likes. She cannot have free disposal of herself. . . .
> If the one who is stronger does not have power over himself, how much less the weaker? The wife is not exempted from this mutual slavery. In fact, she is the one more closely bound.[4]

Since both Jerome and Augustine speak in the same vein,[5] it is not hard to predict the statements of writers in the West during the decline of Rome and the first stirring of medieval culture.

> Jerome understands that this is the slavery which the Apostle has in mind when he says: 'Have you been called as a slave? Let that not disturb you.'
> For the man who, after being married for some time, is converted to the faith of Christ is, by God's inspiration, called and drawn as a slave.
> What should be called a greater slavery than the fact that husband and wife do not have power over their own body and may not abstain from the use of the flesh or devote themselves to prayer except by agreement?[6]

Alain de Lille, though so many of his lectures at Paris during the late 1100's assail the Cathars who are claiming that marriage is sinful, still declares,

> In that state a wife is placed under the power of her husband, even a violent husband . . .[7]

During the 1400's Denis the Carthusian concludes,

The wise young girl does not consent to a husband without great fear.[8]

St. Antoninus looks at it from the man's side.

What is the dominion of women like? Listen to Cicero in his paradoxes.

'Is a man free when he is under a woman's orders? She imposes laws, prescribes, commands, forbids whatever seems good to her; and as for refusing when she gives a command, he cannot or dare not.

'In my opinion he should be called, not a slave but the most wretched of slaves, though he be born of the noblest family.'[9]

Theologians of the Counter-Reformation agree. In fact, a celebrated commentary on Genesis has Adam refer to marriage as a trap.[10] Bourdaloue asks the Parisians who flock to hear him during the late 1600's,

Is not a state which makes you subject without really knowing the one to whom you are giving yourself and takes from you all freedom to change, the state of a slave? . . . By the priesthood I have been bound only to God and myself. . . . By marriage you transfer that dominion which you have over yourself to someone else.[11]

These warnings may seem to be pointing to nothing more than the irritation that arises, partly from selfishness, at never being able to act without giving thought to the feelings of another. But by the time of the Greek Fathers it is evident that this "slavery" is something more serious. Chrysostom, for example, explains why Our Lord's disciples felt that, without divorce, it is better not to marry.

It seemed really burdensome to have a wife full of every wickedness whom you must endure and to be harboring an untamed beast in your home.[12]

The difficulty is not just being bound, but being bound to someone hard to live with. As Jerome puts it,

He who is not arguing is not married.[13]

He describes the problem as it appears to him.

407

We may cite that golden book of Theophrastus, *Marriage,* in which he asks whether a wise man takes a wife. When he has carefully stated the conditions, . . . he adds at once, 'It is rare that all these things are found in a single marriage. Therefore, a wise man should not take a wife.

'First of all, his study of philosophy would be hindered. No one can dedicate himself at the same time to books and a wife. There are many things which are necessary to the daily life of women: expensive clothes, gold, jewelry, purchases, slave girls, a dress for each occasion. . . .

'Then throughout entire nights the long-winded complaints: "That woman has nicer things to wear outside. . . . This one is looked up to by everybody. . . . Poor little me. When the girls get together, they laugh at me. . . . Why were you looking at that woman next door? . . . What were you saying to the smart young slave girl? . . . What did you bring back with you from the forum?"

'No friend may we have, no companion. She suspects that love of the other is hatred for her. . . .

'Then too, there is no chance to try a wife out. You take her as she is. If she is hot-tempered, lazy, deformed, conceited, ugly — whatever defect there is, you learn after the wedding. A horse, a donkey, a cow, a dog . . . are tried out first and then paid for. A wife is the only thing that isn't demonstrated. They're afraid that she'll displease you before she's taken home.

'You have to keep noticing her face all the time and praising her and telling her how pretty she is for fear that, if you look at another woman, she'll think she's unattractive. . . .

'If you entrust the entire house to her to be managed, you have to be her servant. If you reserve anything to your own judgment, she doesn't think you trust her. Then she turns to hatred and quarrels; and if you don't look out at once, she'll get some poison ready.'[14]

Jerome has never been accused of understating his case; and of course, he is merely quoting a pagan author. Still, his own conviction is clear.

During the Middle Ages some writers quote him. Others take the side of the wife. But all agree,

That contract is of itself difficult to keep faithfully, because of the many miseries of the contracting parties and the infirmities, physical and moral, of two people who are bound to come to each other's aid until death.[15]

Scotus thinks it is harder to live in a home than in a monastery, where a hundred people are taking care of one and helping him in his infirmities.[16]

One of the most widely published books of the 1300's, Ludolph of Saxony's *Life of Christ the Lord,* quotes both Chrysostom and Jerome on the trials of having a spouse.[17] A century later Denis the Carthusian observes,

> It also turns out on many occasions that they do not get along well together and frequently quarrel and, little by little, conceive a great distaste for each other, until finally an amazing and very deep-rooted hatred arises between them.
>
> Then side by side they lead a bitter life. The more they are together every day, at home, at table, in bed, in conversation, in work that they do, the harder it is to bear.[18]

Writers after the Council of Trent continue the warnings.[19] After quoting Theophrastus on the trials of a husband, Lessius adds those of a wife.

> Subject to her husband in everything, she must put up with his moodiness, contrariness, nights of eating too much and drinking too much, jealousy, suspicions, incontinence, adulteries, quarrels, blows. She must follow him, be with him everywhere, obey and serve him like a slave. . . . He uses up the money they have on dice, card games, drink, dinners, lavish gifts, ruinous contracts, ill-advised lawsuits and other ways, and the wife can apply no remedy.[20]

The great French preachers of the late 1600's point to the more subtle conflicts that arise between every husband and wife. Bossuet takes the case of an ideal couple:

> Both of them are equally reasonable, if you like — something amazingly rare and not to be hoped for. Even then each has moods, prejudices, habits, associations. Whatever be the things they have in common, people's dispositions are always different enough to cause a frequent chafing in so long a life together. They see each other so near at hand, so often, with so many defects on either side, in the most natural situations and ones so unexpected that it is impossible to be prepared.
>
> They get tired. The thrill is gone. The other's imperfection is irritating. Human nature makes itself felt more and more. . . . They love their cross, I am happy to say, but what they are carrying is the cross.[21]

Fénelon agrees that,

> They get tired of each other in this need of being almost always together and acting in unison on every occasion. It requires a great grace and great fidelity to the grace received to bear this yoke patiently. . . . A person must prepare for it in a spirit of penance when he believes he is called to it by God.[22]

Bourdaloue summarizes the problem.

> In religious life I do not find myself bound to one person in particular. It is not exclusively and forever to this one or that but now to the one and now to the other, and this tends to make the yoke infinitely easier to bear. In marriage, however, your pledge is perpetual to this man or this woman. . . .
>
> May I add one more difference between our two states of life that is new, my friends, but very notable? For the religious state there is a noviceship and a time of testing. There is none for marriage. . . .
>
> Now that this young man is courting you, he has only words of agreement with you, only tokens of kindness, moderation, virtue. But once the knot is tied, you will soon learn what he is like. . . .
>
> Now while this girl is not yet settled in life and you strike her as an agreeable choice, she knows how to calm herself and hide her feelings. But once she no longer has so many tactics to adopt or so many things to gain by pleasing you, you will soon experience her caprices, her oddities, her fits of stubbornness, her expressions of conceit. . . .
>
> Bear well in mind then, my friends, what such a pledge is, or such a slavery for the rest of your life and without remission. There is no vow so solemn that the Church cannot dispense it; but when it comes to marriage, she has her hands tied. . . . What I say is in no way meant to give you a horror of it. It is to make you realize how much you need God's help in marriage.[23]

Though the rhetoric of authors like Jerome is not the word of God, we cannot ignore this persistent reaction of men who have looked at marriage in the light of faith. Besides the distracting cares and a distaste for things of the spirit, revelation seems to have shown them another problem. To marry is to lose a basic autonomy. Time and work and even prayer will now depend on another, and this can be painful.

A sermon by Ephrem the Deacon during the late 300's points to something still more serious. A husband is deeply sensitive to the wishes of his wife, and this often leads a man off to punishment.[24]

The Greek Fathers a few years later also see married life not just as a trial but as a danger.

He who has a wife will find it easier to be pure, since he has a great comfort. But in other things the matter is not so clear. And what is more, even in that area we see more married people falling than monks. There are not as many leaving the monasteries for marriage as the marriage bed for impurity.

Now, if they fall so frequently in contests that are easy for them, what are they likely to do in the face of other affections of soul by which they are more tried than monks? . . . If anyone has reason to be afraid, surely it is not those who flee the storms or those who hurry to port but those who are tossed by squall and tempest. In their case there is more reason to fear a shipwreck since there is more disturbance and those who should be resisting are more sluggish . . . This is why we draw them into the desert, not just to put on sack-cloth, not just to spread ashes to sleep on, but first of all to flee vices and elect virtue.

What then? Will all married people perish? I certainly do not say that. But I do say that they are faced with greater labors if they wish to achieve salvation, and this because of the 'imminent necessity.' The man who is unhampered runs more easily than the one who is bound with chains.[25]

The mind of the Latin Fathers at this time is summarized by Ambrose.

If a good marriage is slavery, what is a bad one in which they cannot sanctify each other but cause each other to perish?[26]

Two centuries later Pope St. Gregory the Great describes the problem in words which will often be quoted.

Some things are harmful in themselves such as sins and crimes. Others, such as temporal power or marital relations, hurt us because of the things that surround them. For marriage is good, but the things which grow up around it due to concern for this world are evil. . . . Thus, while a person has something which does not hurt him, because of the things nearby he very often does what will hurt him. We are often travelling a straight and clear road, and yet our clothes are caught and we are held back by thorn bushes that have grown beside the roadbed.[27]

Writers around the year 800 agree that,

> A wife is a heavy burden, since husbands are not permitted to dismiss them
> nor may women dismiss their husbands no matter how they may be toward
> each other. . . . Each then must realize his or her danger.[28]

The most influential voice of the 1100's, St. Bernard of Clairvaux, will
brook no talk from Cathars about marriage being a sin, but he admits,

> It is clear that the road is dangerous. We find ourselves grieving that so
> many perish on it and seeing so few travel it in the right way.[29]

The Schoolmen a century later feel that this is why marriage demands
special grace from God.[30] Bonaventure asks,

> How many annoyances do you think married women who are religious and
> anxious to give time to God endure when they are forbidden by their hus-
> band to whom they must be subject? This is a great burden in marriage
> when wives are joined to such men as disagree with their good habits and
> devout way of life. How many married women do you think there are who
> would be willing to buy even at the price of death the ability to pay the Lord
> free homage, released from the power of evil men?[31]

During the 1400's Denis the Carthusian describes the dangers of married
life,[32] and a century later Salmeron calls attention to the self-control that a husband needs to avoid offending God "as Adam did to keep from saddening
Eve."[33]

Writing to a Frenchwoman during the early 1600's, St. Francis de Sales is
kind but no less forthright.

> Ah, my daughter, how pleasing the virtues of a married woman are to God!
> For they have to be strong and of extremely high quality to survive in that
> vocation.[34]

Toward the end of the century Claude de la Columbière explains why this
is so.

> You must join the use of legitimate pleasures with a complete removal from
> those that are not allowed, a very minute care of temporal goods with a per-
> fect detachment of heart from these same goods, a great readiness to assent

to the wishes of the person to whom God has bound you with an inviolable fidelity to the desires of God, not to take any part in his passions.[35]

He goes on to point out "the dangers in which the love of a husband involves you if he is given to sin."[36] Bourdaloue, though aware of this danger,[37] sees a greater one if there is no love.

> The one thing really deplorable is that these household trials only serve to remove you farther from God and make you more guilty before God. You look for compensation outside. You turn your inclinations toward others. To what disorders do you not allow yourself to be borne?[38]

This complete oneness of life with another has thus appeared to Christians as a cause of real concern. It involves more than a certain loss of freedom, more than the chafing of two personalities so different and so imperfect. There is also a definite risk.

The restrictions and irritations can lead to sins of anger or impatience or contempt. If the pain grows too serious and constant, escape can be so attractive a thought that moral considerations are put aside. And on the other hand, love has its problems. The terrible choice can present itself between God and this human being.

To run such a risk day in, day out, to fall at times, to see no hope of a change — this wearying existence can lead to more chronic illnesses: discouragement, disillusionment with life. If such dangers are too extreme to be likely for most married couples, there is another that is common: the continual drag of sharing life with someone whose ideals are not as high as your own. . . .

MARTIN LUTHER

On questions of marriage and many other issues, Luther was a social reformer, but certainly no social revolutionary. Social order and authority were extremely important to him; he refused to sacrifice these principles in his political allegiances, and was just as unwilling to sacrifice them in his pastoral work. Luther regarded the family as the very basis of societal stability. Husbands, as heads of the household, were for him the final arbiters of all matters pertaining to the family, from the seat of the household to the approval of marriage partners for children. The "letter of spiritual counsel" below was written to a notary whose wife refused to move with him to a new city.

Letters of Spiritual Counsel

"On Questions of Marriage and Sex: To Stephen Roth," April 12, 1528

Stephen Roth had married Ursula Krüger in Wittenberg on May 11, 1524. When Roth entered upon his duties as notary in Zwickau on February 15, 1528, his wife refused to go with him. It is not clear whether she was unwilling to leave her relatives and native town, was dissatisfied with her husband's new position, or was concerned about her health. Whatever the case may have been, Luther was convinced that she had no adequate reason for not moving to Zwickau. She was willful and perverse, he thought, because her husband had spoiled her. Roth was naturally troubled by his wife's refusal and asked her to consult Luther. When she failed to do

414

this, Luther wrote the following letter and had John Bugenhagen cosign it. Roth's wife moved to Zwickau shortly afterward.

Grace and peace in Christ, and authority over your wife!

My dear Stephen:

Your lord and mistress has not yet come to see me, and this her disobedience to you displeases me greatly. Indeed, I am beginning to be somewhat put out with you too, for by your softheartedness you have turned into tyranny that Christian service[1] which you owe her, and you have hitherto so encouraged her that it would seem to be your own fault that she now ventures to defy you in everything. Certainly when you saw that the fodder was making the ass insolent[2] (that is, that your wife was becoming unmanageable as a result of your indulgence and submissiveness), you should have remembered that you ought to obey God rather than your wife, and so you should not have allowed her to despise and trample underfoot that authority of the husband which is the glory of God,[3] as Saint Paul teaches. It is enough that you yield this glory of God to such an extent that you take on the form of a servant,[4] but when it is done away, wiped out, and reduced to nothing, this is going too far.

See to it, therefore, that you act the man. So bear with your wife's infirmity that you do not encourage her malice and that by your excessive submissiveness you do not give a dangerous example and dishonor the glory of God that is in you. It is easy to tell whether hers is infirmity or malice. Infirmity is to be borne; malice is to be counteracted. Infirmity carries with it a readiness to learn and to listen, at least once in twelve hours; malice is marked by obstinate resistance and persistence. When she observes that you mistake her malice for infirmity, there is no wonder that she gets worse. By your own fault you are now opening a window in this weaker vessel through which Satan can enter at will and laugh at you, irritate you and vex you in every way.

You are an intelligent man, and the Lord will enable you to understand what I write. At the same time you will recognize how sincerely I wish you to come to an agreement and Satan to be driven off. Farewell in Christ.

Martin Luther
Easter, 1528
John Bugenhagen of Pomerania.

GEORGE ELIOT

George Eliot was born Mary Ann Evans in 1819. She began her literary career as a translator, editor, and essayist. It was only at the age of 35, after she had met George Henry Lewes, who became her muse and consort for twenty-four years, that she started to write novels. (Lewes was separated from his wife, and because of the British laws of the time, could not obtain a divorce.) Eliot's psychologically astute characterizations and encyclopedic learning lent her novels — mostly stories of English provincial life — a very special mark. *Daniel Deronda* was her last novel, published in 1878, only two years before her death.

Daniel Deronda

Book VI, Chapter 48

One instance in which Grandcourt stimulated a feeling in Gwendolen that he would have liked to suppress without seeming to care about it, had relation to Mirah. Gwendolen's inclination lingered over the project of the singing lessons as a sort of obedience to Deronda's advice, but day followed day with that want of perceived leisure which belongs to lives where there is no work to mark off intervals; and the continual liability to Grandcourt's presence and surveillance seemed to flatten every effort to the level of the boredom which his manner expressed: his negative mind was as diffusive as fog, clinging to all objects, and spoiling all contact.

But one morning when they were breakfasting, Gwendolen, in a recurrent fit of determination to exercise her old spirit, said, dallying prettily over her prawns without eating them —

'I think of making myself accomplished while we are in town, and having singing lessons.'

'Why?' said Grandcourt, languidly.

'Why?' echoed Gwendolen, playing at sauciness, 'because I can't eat *pâté de foie gras* to make me sleepy, and I can't smoke, and I can't go to the club to make me like to come away again — I want a variety of *ennui*. What would be the most convenient time, when you are busy with your lawyers and people, for me to have lessons from that little Jewess, whose singing is getting all the rage?'

'Whenever you like,' said Grandcourt, pushing away his plate, and leaning back in his chair while he looked at her with his most lizard-like expression, and played with the ears of the tiny spaniel on his lap (Gwendolen had taken a dislike to the dogs because they fawned on him).

Then he said, languidly, 'I don't see why a lady should sing. Amateurs make fools of themselves. A lady can't risk herself in that way in company. And one doesn't want to hear squalling in private.'

'I like frankness: that seems to me a husband's great charm,' said Gwendolen, with her little upward movement of her chin, as she turned her eyes away from his, and lifting a prawn before her, looked at the boiled ingenuousness of its eyes as preferable to the lizard's. 'But,' she added, having devoured her mortification, 'I suppose you don't object to Miss Lapidoth's singing at our party on the 4th? I thought of engaging her. Lady Brackenshaw had her, you know; and the Raymonds, who are very particular about their music. And Mr Deronda, who is a musician himself, and a first-rate judge, says that there is no singing in such good taste as hers for a drawing-room. I think his opinion is an authority.'

She meant to sling a small stone at her husband in that way.

'It's very indecent of Deronda to go about praising that girl,' said Grandcourt, in a tone of indifference.

'Indecent!' exclaimed Gwendolen, reddening and looking at him again, overcome by startled wonder, and unable to reflect on the probable falsity of the phrase — 'to go about praising.'

'Yes; and especially when she is patronised by Lady Mallinger. He ought to hold his tongue about her. Men can see what is his relation to her.'

'Men who judge of others by themselves,' said Gwendolen, turning white after her redness, and immediately smitten with a dread of her own words.

'Of course. And a woman should take their judgment — else she is likely to run her head into the wrong place,' said Grandcourt, conscious of using pincers on that white creature. 'I suppose you take Deronda for a saint.'

'Oh dear no!' said Gwendolen, summoning desperately her almost miraculous power of self-control, and speaking in a high hard tone. 'Only a little less of a monster.'

She rose, pushed her chair away without hurry, and walked out of the room with something like the care of a man who is afraid of showing that he has taken more wine than usual. She turned the keys inside her dressing-room doors, and sat down for some time looking as pale and quiet as when she was leaving the breakfast-room. Even in the moments after reading the poisonous letter she had hardly had more cruel sensations than now; for emotion was at the acute point, where it is not distinguishable from sensation. Deronda unlike what she had believed him to be, was an image which affected her as a hideous apparition would have done, quite apart from the way in which it was produced. It had taken hold of her as pain before she could consider whether it were fiction or truth; and further to hinder her power of resistance came the sudden perception, how very slight were the grounds of her faith in Deronda — how little she knew of his life — how childish she had been in her confidence. His rebukes and his severity to her began to seem odious, along with all the poetry and lofty doctrine in the world, whatever it might be; and the grave beauty of his face seemed the most unpleasant mask that the common habits of men could put on.

All this went on in her with the rapidity of a sick dream; and her start into resistance was very much like a waking. Suddenly from out the grey sombre morning there came a stream of sunshine, wrapping her in warmth and light where she sat in stony stillness. She moved gently and looked round her — there was a world outside this bad dream, and the dream proved nothing; she rose, stretching her arms upward and clasping her hands with her habitual attitude when she was seeking relief from oppressive feeling, and walked about the room in this flood of sunbeams.

'It is not true! What does it matter whether *he* believes it or not?' This was what she repeated to herself — but this was not her faith come back again; it was only the desperate cry of faith, finding suffocation intolerable. And how could she go on through the day in this state? With one of her impetuous alternations, her imagination flew to wild actions by which she would convince herself of what she wished: she would go to Lady Mallinger and question her about Mirah; she would write to Deronda and upbraid him with making the world all false and wicked and hopeless to her — to him she dared pour out all the bitter indignation of her heart. No; she would go to Mirah. This last form taken by her need was more definitely practicable, and quickly became imperious. No matter what came of it. She had the pretext of asking Mirah to sing at her party on the 4th. What was she going to say besides? How satisfy herself? She did not foresee — she could not wait to foresee. If that idea which was maddening her had been a living thing, she would have wanted to throttle it without waiting to foresee what would come of the act. She rang her bell and asked if Mr Grandcourt were gone out: finding that he was, she ordered the carriage, and began to dress for the drive; then she went down, and walked about the large drawing-room like an imprisoned dumb creature, not recognising herself in the glass panels, not noting any object around her in the painted gilded prison. Her husband would probably find out where she had been, and punish her in some way or other — no matter — she could neither desire nor fear anything just now but the assurance that she had not been deluding herself in her trust.

She was provided with Mirah's address. Soon she was on the way with all the fine equipage necessary to carry about her poor uneasy heart, depending in its palpitations on some answer or other to questioning which she did not know how she should put. She was as heedless of what happened before she found that Miss Lapidoth was at home, as one is of lobbies and passages on the way to a court of justice — heedless of everything till she was in a room where there were folding-doors, and she heard Deronda's voice behind it. Doubtless the identification was helped by forecast, but she was as certain of it as if she had seen him. She was frightened at her own agitation, and began to unbutton her gloves that she might button them again, and bite her lips over the pretended difficulty, while the door opened, and Mirah presented herself with perfect quietude and a sweet smile of recognition. There was relief in the sight of her face, and Gwendolen was able to smile in return, while she put out her hand in silence; and as she seated herself, all the while hearing the voice, she felt some reflux of energy in the confused sense that the truth could not be anything that she dreaded. Mirah drew her chair very near, as if she felt that the sound of the conversation should be subdued, and looked at her visitor with placid expectation, while Gwendolen began in a low tone, with something that seemed like bashfulness —

'Perhaps you wonder to see me — perhaps I ought to have written — but I wished to make a particular request.'

'I am glad to see you instead of having a letter,' said Mirah, wondering at the changed expression and manner of the 'Vandyke duchess,' as Hans had taught her to call Gwendolen. The rich colour and the calmness of her own face were in strong contrast with the pale agitated beauty under the plumed hat.

'I thought,' Gwendolen went on — 'at least, I hoped you would not object to sing at our house on the 4th — in the evening — at a party like Lady Brackenshaw's. I should be so much obliged.'

'I shall be very happy to sing for you. At ten?' said Mirah, while Gwendolen seemed to get more instead of less embarrassed.

'At ten, please,' she answered; then paused, and felt that she had nothing more to say. She could not go. It was impossible to rise and say good-bye. Deronda's voice was in her ears. She must say it — she could contrive no other sentence —

'Mr Deronda is in the next room.'

'Yes,' said Mirah, in her former tone. 'He is . . . with my brother.'

'You have a brother?' said Gwendolen, who had heard this from Lady Mallinger, but had not minded it then.

'Yes, a dear brother who is ill — consumptive, and Mr Deronda is the best of friends to him, as he has been to me,' said Mirah, with the impulse that will not let us pass the mention of a precious person indifferently.

'Tell me,' said Gwendolen, putting her hand on Mirah's, and speaking hardly above a whisper — 'tell me — tell me the truth. You are sure he is quite good. You know no evil of him. Any evil that people say of him is false.'

Could the proud-spirited woman have behaved more like a child? But the strange words penetrated Mirah with nothing but a sense of solemnity and indignation. With a sudden light in her eyes and a tremor in her voice, she said —

'Who are the people that say evil of him? I would not believe any evil of him, if an angel came to tell it me. He found me when I was so miserable — I was going to drown myself — I looked so poor and forsaken — you would have thought I was a beggar by the wayside. And he treated me as if I had been a king's daughter. He took me to the best of women. He found my brother for me. And he honours my brother — though he too was poor — oh, almost as poor as he could be. And my brother honours him. That is no light thing to say' — here Mirah's tone changed to one of proud emphasis, and she shook her head backward — 'for my brother is very learned and great-minded. And Mr Deronda says there are few men equal to him.' Some Jewish defiance had flamed into her indignant gratitude, and her anger could not help including Gwendolen, since she seemed to have doubted Deronda's goodness.

But Gwendolen was like one parched with thirst, drinking the fresh water that spreads through the frame as a sufficient bliss. She did not notice that Mirah was angry with her; she was not distinctly conscious of anything but of the penetrating sense that Deronda and his life were no more like her husband's conception than the morning in the horizon was like the morning mixed with street gas: even Mirah's words seemed to melt into the indefiniteness of her relief. She could hardly have repeated them, or said how her whole state of feeling was changed. She pressed Mirah's hands, and said, 'Thank you, thank you,' in a hurried whisper — then rose, and added, with only a hazy consciousness, 'I must go, I shall see you — on the 4th — I am so much obliged' — bowing herself out automatically; while Mirah, opening the door for her, wondered at what seemed a sudden retreat into chill loftiness.

Gwendolen, indeed, had no feeling to spare in any effusiveness towards the creature who had brought her relief. The passionate need of contradiction to Grandcourt's estimate of Deronda, a need which had blunted her sensibility to everything else, was no sooner satisfied than she wanted to be gone: she began to be aware that she was out of place, and to dread Deronda's seeing her. And once in the carriage again, she had the vision of what awaited her at home. When she drew up before the door in Grosvenor Square, her husband was arriving with a cigar between his fingers. He threw it away and handed her out, accompanying her up-stairs. She turned into the drawing-room, lest he should follow her farther and give her no place to retreat to; then sat down with a weary air, taking off her gloves, rubbing her hand over her forehead, and making his presence as much of a cipher as possible. But he sat too, and not far from her — just in front, where to avoid looking at him must have the emphasis of effort.

'May I ask where you have been at this extraordinary hour?' said Grandcourt.

'Oh yes; I have been to Miss Lapidoth's to ask her to come and sing for us,' said Gwendolen, laying her gloves on the little table beside her, and looking down at them.

'And to ask her about her relations with Deronda?' said Grandcourt, with the coldest possible sneer in his low voice, which in poor Gwendolen's ear was diabolical.

For the first time since their marriage she flashed out upon him without inward check. Turning her eyes full on his she said, in a biting tone —

'Yes; and what you said is false — a low, wicked falsehood.'

'She told you so — did she?' returned Grandcourt, with a more thoroughly distilled sneer.

Gwendolen was mute. The daring anger within her was turned into the rage of dumbness. What reasons for her belief could she give? All the reasons that seemed so strong and living within her — she saw them suffocated and shrivelled up under her husband's breath. There was no proof to give, but her own impression, which would seem to him her own folly. She turned her head quickly away from him and looked angrily towards the end of the room: she would have risen, but he was in her way.

Grandcourt saw his advantage. 'It's of no consequence so far as her singing goes,' he said, in his superficial drawl. 'You can have her to sing, if you like.' Then, after a pause, he added in his lowest imperious tone, 'But you will please to observe that you are not to go near that house again. As my wife, you must take my word about what is proper for you. When you undertook to be Mrs Grandcourt, you undertook not to make a fool of yourself. You have been making a fool of yourself this morning; and if you were to go on as you have begun, you might soon get yourself talked of at the clubs in a way you would not like. What do *you* know about the world? You have married *me*, and must be guided by my opinion.'

Every slow sentence of that speech had a terrific mastery in it for Gwendolen's nature. If the low tones had come from a physician telling her that her symptoms were those of a fatal disease, and prognosticating its course, she could not have been more helpless against the argument that lay in it. But she was permitted to move now, and her husband never again made any reference to what had occurred this morning. He knew the force of his own words. If this white-handed man with the perpendicular profile had been sent to govern a difficult colony, he might have won reputation among his contemporaries. He had certainly ability, would have understood that it was safer to exterminate than to cajole superseded proprietors, and would not have flinched from making things safe in that way.

Gwendolen did not, for all this, part with her recovered faith. . . .

But the issue of that visit, as it regarded her husband, took a strongly active part in the process which made an habitual conflict within her, and was the cause of some external change perhaps not observed by any one except Deronda. As the weeks went on bringing occasional transient interviews with her, he thought that he perceived in her an intensifying of her superficial hardness and resolute display, which made her abrupt betrayals of agitation the more marked and disturbing to him.

In fact, she was undergoing a sort of discipline for the refractory which, as little as possible like conversion, bends half the self with a terrible strain, and exasperates the unwillingness of the other half. Grandcourt had an active divination rather than discernment of refractoriness in her, and what had happened about Mirah quickened his suspicion that there was an increase of it dependent on the occasions when she happened to see Deronda: there was some 'confounded nonsense' between them: he did not imagine it exactly as flirtation, and his imagination in other branches was rather restricted; but it was nonsense that evidently kept up a kind of simmering in her mind — an inward action which might become disagreeably outward. Husbands in the old time are known to have suffered from a threatening devoutness in their wives, presenting itself first indistinctly as oddity, and ending in that mild form of lunatic asylum, a nunnery: Grandcourt had a vague perception of threatening moods in Gwendolen which the unity between them in his views of marriage required him peremptorily to check. Among the means he chose, one was peculiar, and was less ably calculated than the speeches we have just heard.

He determined that she should know the main purport of the will he was making, but he could not communicate this himself, because it involved the fact of his relation to Mrs Glasher and her children; and that there should be any overt recognition of this between Gwendolen and himself was supremely repugnant to him. Like all proud, closely-wrapped natures, he shrank from explicitness and detail, even on trivialities, if they were personal: a valet must maintain a strict reserve with him on the subject of shoes and stockings. And clashing was intolerable to him: his habitual want was to put collision out of the question by the quiet massive pressure of his rule. But he wished Gwendolen to know that before he made her an offer it was no secret to him that she was aware of his relations with Lydia, her previous knowledge being the apology for bringing the subject before her now. Some men in his place might have thought of writing what he wanted her to know, in the form of a letter. But Grandcourt hated writing: even writing a note was a bore to him, and he had long been accustomed to have all his writing done by Lush. We know that there are persons who will forego their own obvious interest rather than do anything so disagreeable as to write letters; and it is not probable that these imperfect utilitarians would rush into manuscript and syntax on a difficult subject in order to save another's feelings. To Grandcourt it did not even occur that he should, would, or could write to Gwendolen the information in question; and the only medium of communication he could use was Lush, who, to his mind, was as much of an implement as pen and paper. But here too Grandcourt had his reserves, and would not have uttered a word likely to encourage Lush in an impudent sympathy with any supposed grievance in a marriage which had been discommended by him. Who that has a confidant escapes believing too little in his penetration, and too much in his discretion? Grandcourt had always allowed Lush to know his external affairs indiscriminately, irregularities, debts, want of ready money; he had only used discrimination about what he would allow his confidant to say to him; and he had been so accustomed to this human tool, that the having him at call in London was a recovery of lost ease. It followed that Lush knew all the provisions of the will more exactly than they were known to the testator himself.

Grandcourt did not doubt that Gwendolen, since she was a woman who could put two and two together, knew or suspected Lush to be the contriver of her interview with Lydia, and that this was the reason why her first request was for his banishment. But the bent of a woman's inferences on mixed subjects which excite mixed passions is not determined by her capacity for simple addition; and here Grandcourt lacked the only organ of thinking that could have saved him from mistake — namely, some experience of the mixed passions concerned. He had correctly divined one half of Gwendolen's dread — all that related to her personal pride, and her perception that his will must conquer hers; but the remorseful half, even if he had known of her broken promise, was as much out of his imagination as the other side of the moon. What he believed her to feel about Lydia was solely a tongue-tied jealousy, and what he believed Lydia to have written with the jewels was the fact that she had once been used to wearing them, with other amenities such as he imputed to the intercourse of jealous women. He had the triumphant certainty that he could aggravate the jealousy and yet smite it with a more absolute dumbness. His object was to engage all his wife's egoism on the same side as his own, and in his employment of Lush he did not intend an insult to her: she ought to understand that he was the only possible envoy. Grandcourt's view of things was considerably fenced in by his general sense, that what suited him, others must put up with. There is no escaping the fact that want of sympathy condemns us to a corresponding stupidity. Mephistopheles thrown upon real life, and obliged to manage his own plots, would inevitably make blunders.

One morning he went to Gwendolen in the boudoir beyond the back drawing-room, hat and gloves in hand, and said with his best-tempered, most persuasive drawl, standing before her and looking down on her as she sat with a book on her lap —

'A — Gwendolen, there's some business about property to be explained. I have told Lush to come and explain it to you. He knows all about these things. I am going out. He can come up now. He's the only person who can explain. I suppose you'll not mind.'

'You know that I do mind,' said Gwendolen, angrily, starting up. 'I shall not see him.' She showed the intention to dart away to the door. Grandcourt was before her, with his back towards it. He was prepared for her anger, and showed none in return, saying, with the same sort of remonstrant tone that he might have used about an objection to dining out —

'It's no use making a fuss. There are plenty of brutes in the world that one has to talk to. People with any *savoir vivre* don't make a fuss about such things. Some business must be done. You don't expect agreeable people to do it. If I employ Lush, the proper thing for you is to take it as a matter of course. Not to make a fuss about it. Not to toss your head and bite your lips about people of that sort.'

The drawling and the pauses with which this speech was uttered gave time for crowding reflections in Gwendolen, quelling her resistance. What was there to be told her about property? This word had certain dominant associations for her, first with her mother, then with Mrs Glasher and her children. What would be the use if she refused to see Lush? Could she ask Grandcourt to tell her himself? That might be intolerable, even if he consented, which it was certain he would not, if he had made up his mind to the contrary. The humiliation of standing an obvious prisoner, with her husband barring the door, was not to be borne any longer, and she turned away to lean against a cabinet, while Grandcourt again moved towards her.

'I have arranged with Lush to come up now, while I am out,' he said, after a long organ stop, during which Gwendolen made no sign. 'Shall I tell him he may come?'

Yet another pause before she could say 'Yes' — her face turned obliquely and her eyes cast down.

'I shall come back in time to ride, if you like to get ready,' said Grandcourt. No answer. 'She is in a desperate rage,' thought he. But the rage was silent, and therefore not disagreeable to him. It followed that he turned her chin and kissed her, while she still kept her eyelids down, and she did not move them until he was on the other side of the door.

What was she to do? Search where she would in her consciousness, she found no plea to justify a plaint. Any romantic illusions she had had in marrying this man had turned on her power of using him as she liked. He was using her as he liked.

She sat awaiting the announcement of Lush as a sort of searing operation that she had to go through. The facts that galled her gathered a burning power when she thought of their lying in his mind. It was all a part of that new gambling in which the losing was not simply a *minus,* but a terrible *plus* that had never entered into her reckoning.

Lush was neither quite pleased nor quite displeased with his task. Grandcourt had said to him by way of conclusion, 'Don't make yourself more disagreeable than nature obliges you.'

'That depends,' thought Lush. But he said, 'I will write a brief abstract for Mrs Grandcourt to read.' He did not suggest that he should make the whole communication in writing, which was a proof that the interview did not wholly displease him.

Some provision was being made for himself in the will, and he had no reason to be in a bad humour, even if a bad humour had been common with him. He was perfectly convinced that he had penetrated all the secrets of the situation; but he had no diabolic delight in it. He had only the small movements of gratified self-loving resentment in discerning that this marriage fulfilled his own foresight in not being as satisfactory as the supercilious young lady had expected it to be, and as Grandcourt wished to feign that it was. He had no persistent spite much stronger than what gives the seasoning of ordinary scandal to those who repeat it and exaggerate it by their conjectures. With no active compassion or goodwill, he had just as little active malevolence, being chiefly occupied in liking his particular pleasures, and not disliking anything but what hindered those pleasures — everything else ranking with the last murder and the last *opera buffa*, under the head of things to talk about. Nevertheless, he was not indifferent to the prospect of being treated uncivilly by a beautiful woman, or to the counter-balancing fact that his present commission put into his hands an official power of humiliating her. He did not mean to use it needlessly; but there are some persons so gifted in relation to us that their 'How do you do?' seems charged with offence.

By the time that Mr Lush was announced, Gwendolen had braced herself to a bitter resolve that he should not witness the slightest betrayal of her feeling, whatever he might have to tell. She invited him to sit down with stately quietude. After all, what was this man to her? He was not in the least like her husband. Her power of hating a coarse, familiar-mannered man, with clumsy hands, was now relaxed by the intensity with which she hated his contrast.

He held a small paper folded in his hand while he spoke.

'I need hardly say that I should not have presented myself if Mr Grandcourt had not expressed a strong wish to that effect — as no doubt he has mentioned to you.'

From some voices that speech might have sounded entirely reverential, and even timidly apologetic. Lush had no intention to the contrary, but to Gwendolen's ear his words had as much insolence in them as his prominent eyes, and the pronoun 'you' was too familiar. He ought to have addressed the folding-screen, and spoken of her as Mrs Grandcourt. She gave the smallest sign of a bow, and Lush went on, with a little awkwardness, getting entangled in what is elegantly called tautology.

'My having been in Mr Grandcourt's confidence for fifteen years or more — since he was a youth, in fact — of course gives me a peculiar position. He can speak to me of affairs that he could not mention to any one else; and, in fact, he could not have employed any one else in this affair. I have accepted the task out of friendship for him. Which is my apology for accepting the task — if you would have preferred some one else.'

He paused, but she made no sign, and Lush, to give himself a countenance in an apology which met no acceptance, opened the folded paper, and looked at it vaguely before he began to speak again.

'This paper contains some information about Mr Grandcourt's will, an abstract of a part he wished you to know — if you'll be good enough to cast your eyes over it. But there is something I had to say by way of introduction — which I hope you'll pardon me for, if it's not quite agreeable.' Lush found that he was behaving better than he had expected, and had no idea how insulting he made himself with his 'not quite agreeable.'

'Say what you have to say without apologising, please,' said Gwendolen, with the air she might have bestowed on a dog-stealer come to claim a reward for finding the dog he had stolen.

'I have only to remind you of something that occurred before your engagement to Mr Grandcourt,' said Lush, not without the rise of some willing insolence in exchange for her scorn. 'You met a lady in Cardell Chase, if you remember, who spoke to you of her position with regard to Mr Grandcourt. She had children with her — one a very fine boy.'

Gwendolen's lips were almost as pale as her cheeks: her passion had no weapons — words were no better than chips. This man's speech was like a sharp knife-edge drawn across her skin; but even her indignation at the employment of Lush was getting merged in a crowd of other feelings, dim and alarming as a crowd of ghosts.

'Mr Grandcourt was aware that you were acquainted with this unfortunate affair beforehand, and he thinks it only right that his position and intentions should be made quite clear to you. It is an affair of property and prospects; and if there were any objection you had to make, if you would mention it to me — it is a subject which of course he would rather not speak about himself — if you will be good enough just to read this.' With the last words Lush rose and presented the paper to her.

When Gwendolen resolved that she would betray no feeling in the presence of this man, she had not prepared herself to hear that her husband knew the silent consciousness, the silently accepted terms on which she had married him. She dared not raise her hand to take the paper, lest it should visibly tremble. For a moment Lush stood holding it towards her, and she felt his gaze on her as ignominy, before she could say even with low-toned haughtiness —

'Lay it on the table. And go into the next room, please.'

Lush obeyed, thinking as he took an easy-chair in the back drawing-room, 'My lady winces considerably. She didn't know what would be the charge for that superfine article, Henleigh Grandcourt.' But it seemed to him that a penniless girl had done better than she had any right to expect, and that she had been uncommonly knowing for her years and opportunities: her words to Lydia meant nothing, and her running away had probably been part of her adroitness. It had turned out a master-stroke.

Meanwhile Gwendolen was rallying her nerves to the reading of the paper. She must read it. Her whole being — pride, longing for rebellion, dreams of freedom, remorseful conscience, dread of fresh visitation — all made one need to know what the paper contained. But at first it was not easy to take in the meaning of the words. When she had succeeded, she found that in the case of there being no son an issue of her marriage, Grandcourt had made the small Henleigh his heir; — that was all she cared to extract from the paper with any distinctness. The other statements as to what provision would be made for her in the same case, she hurried over, getting only a confused perception of thousands and Gadsmere. It was enough. She could dismiss the man in the next room with the defiant energy which had revived in her at the idea that this question of property and inheritance was meant as a finish to her humiliations and her thraldom.

She thrust the paper between the leaves of her book, which she took in her hand, and walked with her stateliest air into the next room, where Lush immediately rose, awaiting her approach. When she was four yards from him, it was hardly an instant that she paused to say in a high tone, while she swept him with her eyelashes —

'Tell Mr Grandcourt that his arrangements are just what I desired' — passing on without haste, and leaving Lush time to mingle some admiration of her graceful back with that half-amused sense of her spirit and impertinence, which he expressed by raising his eyebrows and just thrusting his tongue between his teeth. He really did not want her to be worse punished, and he was glad to think that it was time to go and lunch at the club, where he meant to have a lobster salad.

What did Gwendolen look forward to? When her husband returned he found her equipped in her riding-dress, ready to ride out with him. She was not again going to be hysterical, or take to her bed and say she was ill. That was the implicit resolve adjusting her muscles before she could have framed it in words, as she walked out of the room, leaving Lush behind her. She was going to act in the spirit of her message, and not to give herself time to reflect. She rang the bell for her maid, and went with the usual care through her change of toilet. Doubtless her husband had meant to produce a great effect on her: by-and-by perhaps she would let him see an effect the very opposite of what he intended; but at present all that she could show was a defiant satisfaction in what had been presumed to be disagreeable. It came as an instinct rather than a thought, that to show any sign which could be interpreted as jealousy, when she had just been insultingly reminded that the conditions were what she had accepted with her eyes open, would be the worst self-humiliation. She said to herself that she had not time to-day to be clear about her future actions; all she could be clear about was that she would match her husband in ignoring any ground for excitement. She not only rode, but went out with him to dine, contributing nothing to alter their mutual manner, which was never that of rapid interchange in discourse; and curiously enough she rejected a handkerchief on which her maid had by mistake put the wrong scent — a scent that Grandcourt had once objected to. Gwendolen would not have liked to be an object of disgust to this husband whom she hated: she liked all disgust to be on her side.

But to defer thought in this way was something like trying to talk down the singing in her own ears. The thought that is bound up with our passion is as penetrative as air — everything is porous to it; bows, smiles, conversation, repartee, are mere honeycombs where such thought rushes freely, not always with a taste of Honey. And without shutting herself up in any solitude, Gwendolen seemed at the end of nine or ten hours to have gone through a labyrinth of reflection, in which already the same succession of prospects had been repeated, the same fallacious outlets rejected, the same shrinking from the necessities of every course. Already she was undergoing some hardening effect from feeling that she was under eyes which saw her past actions solely in the light of her lowest motives. She lived back in the scenes of her courtship, with the new bitter consciousness of what had been in Grandcourt's mind — certain now, with her present experience of him, that he had had a peculiar triumph in conquering her dumb repugnance, and that ever since their marriage he had had a cold exultation in knowing her fancied secret. Her imagination exaggerated every tyrannical impulse he was capable of. 'I will insist on being separated from him' — was her first darting determination: then, 'I will leave him, whether he consents or not. If this boy becomes his heir, I have made an atonement.' But neither in darkness nor in daylight could she imagine the scenes which must carry out those determinations with the courage to feel them endurable. How could she run away to her own family — carry distress among them, and render herself an object of scandal in the society she had left behind her? What future lay before her as Mrs Grandcourt gone back to her mother, who would be made destitute again by the rupture of the marriage for which one chief excuse had been that it had brought that mother a maintenance? She had lately been seeing her uncle and Anna in London, and though she had been saved from any difficulty about inviting them to stay in Grosvenor Square by their wish to be with Rex, who would not risk a meeting with her, the transient visits she had had from them helped now in giving stronger colour to the picture of what it would be for her to take refuge in her own family. What could she say to justify her flight? Her uncle would tell her to go back. Her mother would cry. Her aunt and Anna would look at her with wondering alarm. Her husband would have power to compel her. She had absolutely nothing that she could allege against him in judicious or judicial ears. And to 'insist on separation!' That was an easy combination of words; but considered as an action to be executed against Grandcourt, it would be about as practicable as to give him a pliant disposition and a dread of other people's unwillingness. How was she to begin? What was she to say that would not be a condemnation of herself? 'If I am to have misery anyhow,' was the bitter refrain of her rebellious dreams, 'I had better have the misery that I can keep to myself.' Moreover, her capability of rectitude told her again and again that she had no right to complain of her contract, or to withdraw from it.

And always among the images that drove her back to submission was Deronda. The idea of herself separated from her husband, gave Deronda a changed, perturbing, painful place in her consciousness: instinctively she felt that the separation would be from him too, and in the prospective vision of herself as a solitary, dubiously regarded woman, she felt some tingling bashfulness at the remembrance of her behaviour towards him. The association of Deronda with a dubious position for herself was intolerable. And what would he say if he knew everything? Probably that she ought to bear what she had brought on herself, unless she were sure that she could make herself a better woman by taking any other course. And what sort of woman was she to be — solitary, sickened of life, looked at with a suspicious kind of pity? — even if she could dream of success in getting that dreary freedom. Mrs Grandcourt 'run away' would be a more pitiable creature than Gwendolen Harleth condemned to teach the bishop's daughters, and to be inspected by Mrs Mompert.

One characteristic trait in her conduct is worth mentioning. She would not look a second time at the paper Lush had given her; and before ringing for her maid she locked it up in a travelling-desk which was at hand, proudly resolved against curiosity about what was allotted to herself in connection with Gadsmere — feeling herself branded in the minds of her husband and his confidant with the meanness that would accept marriage and wealth on any conditions, however dishonourable and humiliating.

Day after day the same pattern of thinking was repeated. There came nothing to change the situation — no new elements in the sketch — only a recurrence which engraved it. The May weeks went on into June, and still Mrs Grandcourt was outwardly in the same place, presenting herself as she was expected to do in the accustomed scenes, with the accustomed grace, beauty, and costume; from church at one end of the week, through all the scale of desirable receptions, to opera at the other. Church was not markedly distinguished in her mind from the other forms of self-presentation, for marriage had included no instruction that enabled her to connect liturgy and sermon with any larger order of the world than that of unexplained and perhaps inexplicable social fashions. While a laudable zeal was labouring to carry the light of spiritual law up the alleys where law is chiefly known as the policeman, the brilliant Mrs Grandcourt, condescending a little to a fashionable Rector and conscious of a feminine advantage over a learned Dean, was, so far as pastoral care and religious fellowship were concerned, in as complete a solitude as a man in a lighthouse.

EDWARD ALBEE

Edward Albee (b. 1928) is undoubtedly one of the most important of America's many innovative twentieth-century playwrights. Despite the intellectual demands of his plays, his identification with the "theater of the absurd," and his rancorous send-ups of American life and values, his works have been remarkably popular. *Who's Afraid of Virginia Woolf?* was written in 1962. The themes of tortuous family intimacy it explores are familiar in most of his work. As a playwright, Albee has always been haunted by certain specific marital problems: sexual dysfunction, anger, and the confusion of the all-American happy family 'image' with the substance of happy family life.

Who's Afraid of Virginia Woolf?

Act One: Fun and Games

> *Set in darkness. Crash against front door. Martha's laughter heard. Front door opens, lights are switched on. Martha enters, followed by George.*

MARTHA Jesus . . .

GEORGE . . . Shhhhhhh . . .

MARTHA . . . H. Christ . . .

GEORGE For God's sake, Martha, it's two o'clock in the . . .

MARTHA Oh, George!

GEORGE Well, I'm sorry, but . . .

MARTHA What a cluck! What a cluck you are.

GEORGE It's late, you know? Late.

MARTHA *(Looks about the room. Imitates Bette Davis.)* What a dump. Hey, what's that from? "What a dump!"

GEORGE How would I know what . . .

MARTHA Aw, come on! What's it from? *You* know. . . .

GEORGE . . . Martha . . .

MARTHA WHAT'S IT FROM, FOR CHRIST'S SAKE?

GEORGE *(Wearily.)* What's what from?

MARTHA I just told you; I just did it. "What a dump!" Hunh? What's that from?

GEORGE I haven't the faintest idea what. . . .

MARTHA Dumbbell! It's from some goddamn Bette Davis picture . . . some goddamn Warner Brothers epic. . . .

GEORGE I can't remember all the pictures that . . .

MARTHA Nobody's asking you to remember every single goddamn Warner Brothers epic . . . just one! One single little epic! Bette Davis gets peritonitis in the end . . . she's got this big black fright wig she wears all through the picture and she gets peritonitis, and she's married to Joseph Cotten or something. . . .

GEORGE . . . Some*body* . . .

MARTHA . . . some*body* . . . and she wants to go to Chicago all the time, 'cause she's in love with that actor with the scar. . . . But she gets sick, and she sits down in front of her dressing table. . . .

GEORGE What actor? What scar?

MARTHA *I* can't remember his name, for God's sake. What's the name of the *picture?* I want to know what the name of the picture is. She sits down in front of her dressing table . . . and she's got this peritonitis . . . and she tries to put her lipstick on, but she can't . . . and she gets it all over her face . . . but she decides to go to Chicago anyway, and . . .

GEORGE *Chicago!* It's called *Chicago.*

MARTHA Hunh? What . . . what is?

GEORGE The picture . . . it's called *Chicago.* . . .

MARTHA Good grief! Don't you know *anything? Chicago* was a 'thirties musical, starring little Miss Alice *Faye.* Don't you know *anything?*

GEORGE Well, that was probably before my *time,* but . . .

MARTHA Can it! Just cut that out! This picture . . . Bette Davis comes home from a hard day at the grocery store . . .

GEORGE She works in a grocery store?

MARTHA   She's a housewife; she buys things . . . and she comes home with
the groceries, and she walks into the modest living room of the
modest cottage modest Joseph Cotten has set her up in. . . .

GEORGE   Are they married?

MARTHA   *(Impatiently.)* Yes. They're married. To each other. Cluck! And she
comes in, and she looks around, and she puts her groceries down,
and she says, "What a dump!"

GEORGE   *(Pause.)* Oh.

MARTHA   *(Pause.)* She's discontent.

GEORGE   *(Pause.)* Oh.

MARTHA   *(Pause.)* Well, what's the name of the picture?

GEORGE   I really don't know, Martha. . . .

MARTHA   Well, think!

GEORGE   I'm tired, dear . . . it's late . . . and besides . . .

MARTHA   I don't know what you're so tired about . . . you haven't *done* anything all day; you didn't have any classes, or anything. . . .

GEORGE   Well, I'm tired. . . . If your father didn't set up these goddamn Saturday night orgies all the time . . .

MARTHA   Well, that's too bad about you, George. . . .

GEORGE   *(Grumbling.)* Well, that's how it is, anyway.

MARTHA   You didn't *do* anything; you never *do* anything; you never mix. You
just sit around and *talk*.

GEORGE   What do you want me to do? Do you want me to act like you? Do
you want me to go around all night *braying* at everybody, the way
you do?

MARTHA   *(Braying.)* I DON'T BRAY!

GEORGE   *(Softly.)* All right . . . you don't bray.

MARTHA   *(Hurt.)* I do not *bray*.

GEORGE   All right. I said you didn't bray.

MARTHA   *(Pouting.)* Make me a drink.

GEORGE   What?

MARTHA   *(Still softly.)* I said, make me a drink.

GEORGE   *(Moving to the portable bar.)* Well, I don't suppose a nightcap'd kill
either one of us. . . .

MARTHA   A nightcap! Are you kidding? We've got guests.

GEORGE   *(Disbelieving.)* We've got what?

MARTHA   Guests. GUESTS.

GEORGE   GUESTS!

MARTHA   Yes . . . guests . . . people. . . . We've got guests coming over.

GEORGE   When?

MARTHA   NOW!

GEORGE   Good Lord, Martha . . . do you know what time it . . . *Who's* coming over?

MARTHA   What's-their-name.

GEORGE   Who?

MARTHA   WHAT'S-THEIR-NAME!

GEORGE   Who what's-their name?

MARTHA   I don't know what their name is, George. . . . You met them tonight . . . they're new . . . he's in the math department, or something. . . .

GEORGE   Who . . . who are these people?

MARTHA   You met them tonight, George.

GEORGE   I don't remember meeting anyone tonight. . . .

MARTHA   Well you did. . . . Will you give me my drink, please. . . . He's in the math department . . . about thirty, blond, and . . .

GEORGE   . . . and good-looking. . . .

MARTHA   Yes . . . and good-looking. . . .

GEORGE   It figures.

MARTHA   . . . and his wife's a mousey little type, without any hips, or anything.

GEORGE   *(Vaguely.)* Oh.

MARTHA   You remember them now?

GEORGE   Yes, I guess so, Martha. . . . But why in God's name are they coming over here now?

MARTHA   *(In a so-there voice.)* Because Daddy said we should be nice to them, that's why.

GEORGE   *(Defeated.)* Oh, Lord.

MARTHA   May I have my drink, please? Daddy said we should be nice to them. Thank you.

GEORGE   But why now? It's after two o'clock in the morning, and . . .

MARTHA   Because Daddy said we should be nice to them!

GEORGE   Yes. But I'm sure your father didn't mean we were supposed to stay up all *night* with these people. I mean, we could have them over some Sunday or something. . . .

MARTHA   Well, never mind. . . . Besides, *it is* Sunday. Very early Sunday.

GEORGE   I mean . . . it's ridiculous. . . .

MARTHA   Well, it's done!

GEORGE   *(Resigned and exasperated.)* All right. Well . . . where are they? If we've got guests, where are they?

MARTHA   They'll be here soon.

GEORGE   What did they do . . . go home and get some sleep first, or something?

MARTHA   They'll *be* here!

GEORGE   I wish you'd *tell* me about something sometime. . . . I wish you'd stop *springing* things on me all the time.

MARTHA   I don't *spring* things on you all the time.

GEORGE   Yes, you do . . . you really do . . . you're always *springing* things on me.

MARTHA   *(Friendly patronizing.)* Oh, George!

GEORGE   Always.

MARTHA   Poor Georgie-Porgie, put-upon pie! *(As he sulks.)* Awwwwww . . . what are you doing? Are you sulking? Hunh? Let me see . . . are you sulking? Is that what you're doing?

GEORGE   *(Very quietly.)* Never mind, Martha. . . .

MARTHA   AWWWWWWWWWW!

GEORGE   Just don't bother yourself. . . .

MARTHA   AWWWWWWWWWW! *(No reaction.)* Hey! *(No reaction.)* Hey! *(George looks at her, put upon.)* Hey. *(She sings.)*

      Who's afraid of Virginia Woolf,
         Virginia Woolf,
         Virginia Woolf. . . .

Ha, ha, ha, HA! *(No reaction.)* What's the matter . . . didn't you think that was funny? Hunh? *(Defiantly.)* I thought it was a scream . . . a real scream. You didn't like it, hunh?

GEORGE   It was all right, Martha. . . .

MARTHA   You laughed your head off when you heard it at the party.

GEORGE   I smiled. I didn't laugh my head off . . . I smiled, you know? . . . it was all right.

MARTHA   *(Gazing into her drink.)* You laughed your goddamn head off.

GEORGE   It was all right. . . .

MARTHA   *(Ugly.)* It was a scream!

GEORGE   *(Patiently.)* It was very funny, yes.

MARTHA   *(After a moment's consideration.)* You make me puke!

GEORGE   What?

MARTHA   Uh . . . you make me puke!

GEORGE   *(Thinks about it . . . then . . .)* That wasn't a very nice thing to say, Martha.

MARTHA   That wasn't *what?*

GEORGE   . . . a very nice thing to say.

MARTHA   I like your anger. I think that's what I like about you most . . . your anger. You're such a . . . such a simp! You don't even have the . . . the what? . . .

GEORGE . . . guts? . . .

MARTHA PHRASEMAKER! *(Pause . . . then they both laugh.)* Hey, put some more ice in my drink, will you? You never put any ice in my drink. Why is that, hunh?

GEORGE *(Takes her drink.)* I always put ice in your drink. You eat it, that's all. It's that habit you have . . . chewing your ice cubes . . . like a cocker spaniel. You'll crack your big teeth.

MARTHA THEY'RE MY BIG TEETH!

GEORGE Some of them . . . some of them.

MARTHA I've got more teeth than you've got.

GEORGE Two more.

MARTHA Well, two more's a lot more.

GEORGE I suppose it is. I suppose it's pretty remarkable . . . considering how old you are.

MARTHA YOU CUT THAT OUT! *(Pause.)* You're not so young yourself.

GEORGE *(With boyish pleasure . . . a chant.)* I'm six years younger than you are. . . . I always have been and I always will be.

MARTHA *(Glumly.)* Well . . . you're going bald.

GEORGE So are you. *(Pause . . . they both laugh.)* Hello, honey.

MARTHA Hello. C'mon over here and give your Mommy a big sloppy kiss.

GEORGE . . . oh, now . . .

MARTHA I WANT A BIG SLOPPY KISS!

GEORGE *(Preoccupied.)* I don't *want* to kiss you, Martha. Where *are* these people? Where are these *people* you invited over?

MARTHA They stayed on to talk to Daddy. . . . They'll be here. . . . *Why* don't you want to kiss me?

GEORGE *(Too matter-of-fact.)* Well, dear, if I kissed you I'd get all excited . . . I'd get beside myself, and I'd take you, by force, right here on the living room rug, and then our little guests would walk in, and . . . well, just think what your father would say about *that.*

MARTHA You pig!

GEORGE *(Haughtily.)* Oink! Oink!

MARTHA Ha, ha, ha, HA! Make me another drink . . . lover.

GEORGE *(Taking her glass.)* My God, you can swill it down, can't you?

MARTHA *(Imitating a tiny child.)* I'm firsty.

GEORGE Jesus!

MARTHA *(Swinging around.)* Look, sweetheart, I can drink you under any goddamn table you want . . . so don't worry about me!

GEORGE Martha, I gave you the prize years ago. . . . There isn't an abomination award going that you . . .

MARTHA I swear . . . if you existed I'd divorce you. . . .

GEORGE Well, just stay on your feet, that's all. . . . These people are your guests, you know, and . . .

MARTHA I can't even see you . . . I haven't been able to see you for years. . . .

GEORGE . . . if you pass out, or throw up, or something. . . .

MARTHA . . . I mean, you're a blank, a cipher. . . .

GEORGE . . . and try to keep your clothes on, too. There aren't many more sickening sights than you with a couple of drinks in you and your skirt up over your head, you know. . . .

MARTHA . . . a zero. . . .

GEORGE . . . your *heads,* I should say . . . *(The front door bell chimes.)*

MARTHA Party! Party!

GEORGE *(Murderously.)* I'm really looking forward to this, Martha. . . .

MARTHA *(Same.)* Go answer the door.

GEORGE *(Not moving.)* You answer it.

MARTHA Get to that door, you. *(He does not move.)* I'll fix you, you . . .

GEORGE *(Fake spits.)* . . . to you . . . *(Door chime again.)*

MARTHA *(Shouting . . . to the door.)* C'MON IN! *(To George, between her teeth.)* I said, get over there!

GEORGE *(Moves a little toward the door, smiling slightly.)* All right, love . . . whatever love wants. *(Stops.)* Just don't start on the bit, that's all.

MARTHA The bit? The bit? What kind of language is that? What are you talking about?

GEORGE The bit. Just don't start in on the bit.

MARTHA You imitating one of your students, for God's sake? What are you trying to do? WHAT BIT?

GEORGE Just don't start in on the bit about the kid, that's all.

MARTHA What do you take me for?

GEORGE Much too much.

MARTHA *(Really angered.)* Yeah? Well, I'll start in on the kid if I want to.

GEORGE Just leave the kid out of this.

MARTHA *(Threatening.)* He's mine as much as he is yours. I'll talk about him if I want to.

GEORGE I'd advise against it, Martha.

MARTHA Well, good for you. *(Knock.)* C'mon in. Get over there and open the door!

GEORGE You've been advised.

MARTHA Yeah . . . sure. Get over there!

GEORGE *(Moving toward the door.)* All right, love . . . whatever love wants. Isn't it nice the way some people have manners, though, even in this day and age? Isn't it nice that some people won't just come breaking into other people's houses even if they *do* hear some sub-human monster yowling at 'em from inside . . . ?

MARTHA SCREW YOU! *(Simultaneously with Martha's last remark, George flings open the front door. Honey and Nick are framed in the entrance. There is a brief silence, then . . .)*

GEORGE *(Ostensibly a pleased recognition of Honey and Nick, but really satisfaction at having Martha's explosion overheard.)* Ahhhhhhhhh!

MARTHA *(A little too loud . . . to cover.)* HI! Hi, there . . . c'mon in!

HONEY AND NICK *(Ad lib.)* Hello, here we are . . . hi . . . *etc.*

GEORGE *(Very matter-of-factly.)* You must be our little guests.

MARTHA Ha, ha, ha, HA! Just ignore old sour-puss over there. C'mon in, kids . . . give your coats and stuff to sour-puss.

NICK *(Without expression.)* Well, now, perhaps we shouldn't have come. . . .

HONEY Yes . . . it *is* late, and . . .

MARTHA Late! Are you kidding? Throw your stuff down anywhere and c'mon in.

GEORGE *(Vaguely . . . walking away.)* Anywhere . . . furniture, floor . . . doesn't make any difference around this place.

NICK *(To Honey.)* I told you we shouldn't have come.

MARTHA *(Stentorian.)* I said c'mon in! Now c'mon!

HONEY *(Giggling a little as she and Nick advance.)* Oh, dear.

GEORGE *(Imitating Honey's giggle.)* Hee, hee, hee, hee.

MARTHA *(Swinging on George.)* Look, muckmouth . . . you cut that out!

GEORGE *(Innocence and hurt.)* Martha! *(To Honey and Nick.)* Martha's a devil with language; she really is.

MARTHA Hey, *kids* . . . sit down.

HONEY *(As she sits.)* Oh, isn't this lovely!

NICK *(Perfunctorily.)* Yes indeed . . . very handsome.

MARTHA Well, thanks.

NICK *(Indicating the abstract painting.)* Who . . . who did the . . . ?

MARTHA That? Oh, that's by . . .

GEORGE . . . some Greek with a mustache Martha attacked one night in . . .

HONEY *(To save the situation.)* Oh, ho, ho, ho, HO.

NICK It's got a . . . a . . .

GEORGE A quiet intensity?

NICK   Well, no . . . a . . .

GEORGE   Oh. *(Pause.)* Well, then, a certain noisy relaxed quality, maybe?

NICK   *(Knows what George is doing, but stays grimly, coolly polite.)* No. What I meant was . . .

GEORGE   How about . . . uh . . . a quietly noisy relaxed intensity.

HONEY   Dear! You're being joshed.

NICK   *(Cold.)* I'm aware of that. *(A brief, awkward silence.)*

GEORGE   *(Truly.)* I *am* sorry. *(Nick nods condescending forgiveness.)* What it is, actually, is it's a pictorial representation of the order of Martha's mind.

MARTHA   Ha, ha, ha, HA! Make the kids a drink, George. What do you want, kids? What do you want to drink, hunh?

NICK   Honey? What would you like?

HONEY   I don't know, dear . . . A little brandy, maybe. "Never mix — never worry." *(She giggles.)*

GEORGE   Brandy? Just brandy? Simple; simple. *(Moves to the portable bar.)* What about you . . . uh. . . .

NICK   Bourbon on the rocks, if you don't mind.

GEORGE   *(As he makes drinks.)* Mind? No, I don't mind. I don't think I mind. Martha? Rubbing alcohol for you?

MARTHA   Sure. "Never mix — never worry."

GEORGE   Martha's tastes in liquor have come down . . . simplified over the years . . . crystallized. Back when I was courting Martha — well, I don't know if that's exactly the right word for it — but back when I was courting Martha . . .

MARTHA   *(Cheerfully.)* Screw, sweetie!

GEORGE   *(Returning with Honey and Nick's drinks.)* At any rate, back when I was courting Martha, she'd order the damnedest things! You wouldn't believe it! We'd go into a bar . . . you know, a *bar* . . . a whiskey, beer, and bourbon bar . . . and what she'd do would be, she'd screw up her face, think real hard, come up with . . . brandy Alexanders, creme de cacao frappes, gimlets, flaming punch bowls . . . seven layer liqueur things.

MARTHA   They were good . . . I liked them.

GEORGE   Real lady-like little drinkies.

MARTHA   Hey, where's my rubbing alcohol?

GEORGE   *(Returning to the portable bar.)* But the years have brought to Martha a sense of essentials . . . the knowledge that cream is for coffee, lime juice for pies . . . and alcohol *(Brings Martha her drink.)* pure and simple . . . here you are, angel . . . for the pure and simple.

(*Raises his glass.*) For the mind's blind eye, the heart's ease, and the liver's craw. Down the hatch, all.

MARTHA (*To them all.*) Cheers, dears. (*They all drink.*) You have a poetic nature, George . . . a Dylan Thomas-y quality that gets me right where I live.

GEORGE Vulgar girl! With guests here!

MARTHA Ha, ha, ha, HA! (*To Honey and Nick.*) Hey; hey! (*Sings, conducts with her drink in her hand. Honey joins in toward the end.*)

Who's afraid of Virginia Woolf,
  Virginia Woolf,
  Virginia Woolf,
Who's afraid of Virginia Woolf. . . .

(*Martha and Honey laugh; Nick smiles.*)

HONEY Oh, wasn't that funny? That was so funny. . . .

NICK (*Snapping to.*) Yes . . . yes, it was.

MARTHA I thought I'd bust a gut; I really did. . . . I really thought I'd bust a gut laughing. George didn't like it. . . . George didn't think it was funny at all.

GEORGE Lord, Martha, do we have to go through this again?

MARTHA I'm trying to shame you into a sense of humor, angel, that's all.

GEORGE (*Over-patiently, to Honey and Nick.*) Martha didn't think I laughed loud enough. Martha thinks that unless . . . as she demurely puts it . . . that unless you "bust a gut" you aren't amused. You know? Unless you carry on like a hyena you aren't having any fun.

HONEY Well, I certainly had fun . . . it was a *wonderful* party.

NICK (*Attempting enthusiasm.*) Yes . . . it certainly was.

HONEY (*To Martha.*) And your father! Oh! He is so marvelous!

NICK (*As above.*) Yes . . . yes, he is.

HONEY Oh, I tell you.

MARTHA (*Genuinely proud.*) He's quite a guy, isn't he? Quite a guy.

GEORGE (*At Nick.*) And you'd better believe it!

HONEY (*Admonishing George.*) Ohhhhhhhhh! He's a wonderful man.

GEORGE I'm not trying to tear him down. He's a God, we all know that.

MARTHA You lay off my father!

GEORGE Yes, love. (*To Nick.*) All I mean is . . . when you've had as many of these faculty parties as I have . . .

NICK (*Killing the attempted rapport.*) I rather appreciated it. I mean, aside from enjoying it, I appreciated it. You know, when you're new at a place. . . . (*George eyes him suspiciously.*) Meeting everyone, getting introduced around . . . getting to know some of the men. . . . When I was teaching in Kansas . . .

HONEY   You won't believe it, but we had to make our way all by *ourselves* . . . isn't that right, dear?

NICK   Yes, it is. . . . We . . .

HONEY   . . . We had to make our own way. . . . I had to go up to wives . . . in the library, or at the supermarket . . . and say, "Hello, I'm new here . . . you must be Mrs. So-and-so, Doctor So-and-so's wife." It really wasn't very nice at all.

MARTHA   Well, *Daddy* knows how to run things.

NICK   *(Not enough enthusiasm.)* He's a remarkable man.

MARTHA   You bet your sweet life.

GEORGE   *(To Nick . . . a confidence, but not whispered.)* Let me tell you a secret, baby. There are easier things in the world, if you happen to be teaching at a university, there are easier things than being married to the daughter of the president of that university. There are easier things in this world.

MARTHA   *(Loud . . . to no one in particular.)* It *should* be an extraordinary opportunity . . . for *some* men it would be the chance of a lifetime!

GEORGE   *(To Nick . . . a solemn wink.)* There are, believe me, easier things in this world.

NICK   Well, I can understand how it might make for some . . . awkwardness, perhaps . . . conceivably, but . . .

MARTHA   *Some* men would give their right arm for the chance!

GEORGE   *(Quietly.)* Alas, Martha, in reality it works out that the sacrifice is usually of a somewhat more private portion of the anatomy.

MARTHA   *(A snarl of dismissal and contempt.)* NYYYYAAAAHHHHH!

HONEY   *(Rising quickly.)* I wonder if you could show me where the . . . *(Her voice trails off.)*

GEORGE   *(To Martha, indicating Honey.)* Martha. . . .

NICK   *(To Honey.)* Are you all right?

HONEY   Of course, dear. I want to . . . put some powder on my nose.

GEORGE   *(As Martha is not getting up.)* Martha, won't you show her where we keep the . . . euphemism?

MARTHA   Hm? What? Oh! Sure! *(Rises.)* I'm sorry, c'mon. I want to show you the house.

HONEY   I think I'd like to . . .

MARTHA   . . . wash up? Sure . . . c'mon with me. *(Takes Honey by the arm. To the men.)* You two do some men talk for a while.

HONEY   *(To Nick.)* We'll be back, dear.

MARTHA *(To George.)* Honestly, George, you burn me up!

GEORGE *(Happily.)* All right.

MARTHA You really do, George.

GEORGE O.K. Martha . . . O.K. Just . . . trot along.

MARTHA You really do.

GEORGE Just don't shoot your mouth off . . . about . . . you know what.

MARTHA *(Surprisingly vehement.)* I'll talk about any goddamn thing I want to, George!

GEORGE O.K. O.K. Vanish.

MARTHA Any goddamn thing I want to! *(Practically dragging Honey out with her.)* C'mon. . . .

GEORGE Vanish. *(The women have gone.)* So? What'll it be?

NICK Oh, I don't know . . . I'll stick to bourbon, I guess.

GEORGE *(Takes Nick's glass, goes to portable bar.)* That what you were drinking over at Parnassus?

NICK Over at . . . ?

GEORGE Parnassus.

NICK I don't understand. . . .

GEORGE Skip it. *(Hands him his drink.)* One bourbon.

NICK Thanks.

GEORGE It's just a private joke between li'l ol' Martha and me. *(They sit.)* So? *(Pause.)* So . . . you're in the math department, eh?

NICK No . . . uh, no.

GEORGE Martha said you were. I think that's what she said. *(Not too friendly.)* What made you decide to be a teacher?

NICK Oh . . . well, the same things that . . . uh . . . motivated you, I imagine.

GEORGE What were they?

NICK *(Formal.)* Pardon?

GEORGE I said, what were they? What were the things that motivated me?

NICK *(Laughing uneasily.)* Well . . . I'm sure I don't know.

GEORGE You just finished saying that the things that motivated you were the same things that motivated me.

NICK *(With a little pique.)* I said I *imagined* they were.

GEORGE Oh. *(Off-hand.)* Did you? *(Pause.)* Well. . . . *(Pause.)* You like it here?

NICK *(Looking about the room.)* Yes . . . it's . . . it's fine.

GEORGE I mean the University.

NICK Oh. . . . I thought you meant . . .

GEORGE Yes . . . I can see you did. *(Pause.)* I meant the University.

NICK   Well, I . . . I like it . . . fine. *(As George just stares at him.)* Just fine. *(Same.)* You . . . you've been here quite a long time, haven't you?

GEORGE   *(Absently, as if he had not heard.)* What? Oh . . . yes. Ever since I married . . . uh, what's-her-name . . . uh, Martha. Even before that. *(Pause.)* Forever. *(To himself.)* Dashed hopes, and good intentions. Good, better, best, bested. *(Back to Nick.)* How do you like that for a declension, young man? Eh?

NICK   Sir, I'm sorry if we . . .

GEORGE   *(With an edge in his voice.)* You didn't answer my question.

NICK   Sir?

GEORGE   Don't you condescend to me! *(Toying with him.)* I asked you how you liked that for a declension: Good; better; best; bested. Hm? Well?

NICK   *(With some distaste.)* I really don't know what to say.

GEORGE   *(Feigned incredulousness.)* You really don't know what to *say?*

NICK   *(Snapping it out.)* All right . . . what do you want me to say? Do you want me to say it's funny, so you can contradict me and say it's sad? or do you want me to say it's sad so you can turn around and say no, it's funny. You can play that damn little game any way you want to, you know!

GEORGE   *(Feigned awe.)* Very good! Very good!

NICK   *(Even angrier than before.)* And when my wife comes back, I think we'll just . . .

GEORGE   *(Sincere.)* Now, now . . . calm down, my boy. Just . . . calm . . . down. *(Pause.)* All right? *(Pause.)* You want another drink? Here, give me your glass.

NICK   I still have one. I *do* think that when my wife comes downstairs . . .

GEORGE   Here . . . I'll freshen it. Give me your glass. *(Takes it.)*

NICK   What I mean is . . . you two . . . you and your wife . . . seem to be having *some* sort of a . . .

GEORGE   Martha and I are having . . . nothing. Martha and I are merely . . . exercising . . . that's all . . . we're merely walking what's left of our wits. Don't pay any attention to it.

NICK   *(Undecided.)* Still . . .

GEORGE   *(An abrupt change of pace.)* Well, now . . . let's sit down and talk, hunh?

NICK   *(Cool again.)* It's just that I don't like to . . . become involved . . . *(An afterthought.)* uh . . . in other people's affairs.

GEORGE   *(Comforting a child.)* Well, you'll get over that . . . small college and all. Musical beds is the faculty sport around here.

NICK   Sir?

GEORGE   I said, musical beds is the faculty. . . . Never mind. I wish you wouldn't go "Sir" like that . . . not with the question mark at the end of it. You know? Sir? I know it's meant to be a sign of respect for your *(Winces.)* elders . . . but . . . uh . . . the way you do it. . . . Uh . . . Sir? . . . Madam?

NICK   *(With a small, noncommittal smile)* No disrespect intended.

GEORGE   How old *are* you?

NICK   Twenty-eight.

GEORGE   I'm forty something. *(Waits for reaction . . . gets none.)* Aren't you surprised? I mean . . . don't I look older? Doesn't this . . . *gray* quality suggest the fifties? Don't I sort of fade into backgrounds . . . get lost in the cigarette smoke? Hunh?

NICK   *(Looking around for an ash tray.)* I think you look . . . fine.

GEORGE   I've always been lean . . . I haven't put on five pounds since I was your age. I don't have a paunch, either. . . . What I've got . . . I've got this little distension just below the belt . . . but it's hard . . . It's not soft flesh. I use the handball courts. How much do you weigh?

NICK   I . . .

GEORGE   Hundred and fifty-five, sixty . . . something like that? Do you play handball?

NICK   Well, yes . . . no . . . I mean, not very well.

GEORGE   Well, then . . . we shall play some time. Martha is a hundred and eight . . . years *old.* She weighs somewhat more than that. How old is your wife?

NICK   *(A little bewildered.)* She's twenty-six.

GEORGE   Martha is a remarkable woman. I would imagine she weighs around a hundred and ten.

NICK   Your . . . wife . . . weighs . . . ?

GEORGE   No, no, my boy. Yours! *Your* wife. My wife is Martha.

NICK   Yes . . . I know.

GEORGE   If you were married to Martha you would know what it means. *(Pause.)* But then, if I were married to your wife I would know what that means, too . . . wouldn't I?

NICK   *(After a pause.)* Yes.

GEORGE   Martha says you're in the Math Department, or something.

NICK   *(As if for the hundredth time.)* No . . . I'm not.

GEORGE   Martha is seldom mistaken . . . maybe you *should* be in the Math
         Department, or something.
NICK   I'm a biologist. I'm in the Biology Department.
GEORGE   *(After a pause.)* Oh. *(Then, as if remembering something.)* OH!
NICK   Sir?
GEORGE   You're the one! You're the one's going to make all that trouble . . .
         making everyone the same, rearranging the chromozones, or what-
         ever it is. Isn't that right?
NICK   *(With that small smile.)* Not exactly: chromo*somes*.
GEORGE   I'm very mistrustful. Do you believe . . . *(Shifting in his chair.)* . . .
         do you believe that people learn nothing from history? Not that
         there is nothing to learn, mind you, but that people learn nothing?
         I am in the History Department.
NICK   Well . . .
GEORGE   I am a Doctor. A.B. . . . M.A. . . . PH.D. . . . ABMAPHID!
         Abmaphid has been variously described as a wasting disease of the
         frontal lobes, and as a wonder drug. It is actually both. I'm really
         very mistrustful. Biology, hunh? *(Nick does not answer . . . nods . . .
         looks.)* I read somewhere that science fiction is really not fiction at
         all . . . that you people are rearranging my genes, so that everyone
         will be like everyone else. Now, I won't have that! It would be a . . .
         shame. I mean . . . look at me! Is it really such a good idea . . . if
         everyone was forty something and looked fifty-five? You didn't an-
         swer my question about history.
NICK   This genetic business you're talking about. . . .
GEORGE   Oh, that. *(Dismisses it with a wave of his hand.)* That's very upset-
         ting . . . very . . . disappointing. But history is a great deal more
         . . . disappointing. I am in the History Department.
NICK   Yes . . . you told me.
GEORGE   I know I told you. . . . I shall probably tell you several more times.
         Martha tells me often, that I am *in* the History Department . . . as
         opposed to *being* the History Department . . . in the sense of *run-
         ning* the History Department. I do not run the History Depart-
         ment.
NICK   Well, I don't run the Biology Department.
GEORGE   You're twenty-one!
NICK   Twenty-eight.
GEORGE   Twenty-eight! Perhaps when you're forty something and look fifty-
         five, you will run the History Department. . . .
NICK   . . . Biology . . .

GEORGE   . . . the Biology Department. I *did* run the History Department, for four years, during the war, but that was because everybody was away. Then . . . everybody came back . . . because nobody got killed. That's New England for you. Isn't that amazing? Not one single man in this whole place got his head shot off. That's pretty irrational. *(Broods.)* Your wife *doesn't* have any hips . . . has she . . . does she?

NICK   What?

GEORGE   I don't mean to suggest that I'm hip-happy. . . . I'm not one of those thirty-six, twenty-two, seventy-eight men. Nosiree . . . not me. Everything in proportion. I was implying that your wife is . . . slim-hipped.

NICK   Yes . . . she is.

GEORGE   *(Looking at the ceiling.)* What are they *doing* up there? I assume that's where they are.

NICK   *(False heartiness.)* You know women.

GEORGE   *(Gives Nick a long stare, of feigned incredulity . . . then his attention moves.)* Not one son-of-a-bitch got killed. Of course, nobody bombed Washington. No . . . that's not fair. You have any kids?

NICK   Uh . . . no . . . not yet. *(Pause.)* You?

GEORGE   *(A kind of challenge.)* That's for me to know and you to find out.

NICK   Indeed?

GEORGE   No kids, hunh?

NICK   Not yet.

GEORGE   People do . . . uh . . . have kids. That's what I meant about history. You people are going to make them in test tubes, aren't you? You biologists. Babies. Then the rest of us . . . them as wants to . . . can screw to their heart's content. What will happen to the tax deduction? Has anyone figured that out yet? *(Nick, who can think of nothing better to do, laughs mildly.)* But you *are* going to have kids . . . anyway. In spite of history.

NICK   *(Hedging.) Yes* . . . certainly. We . . . want to wait . . . a little . . . until we're settled.

GEORGE   And this . . . *(With a handsweep taking in not only the room, the house, but the whole countryside.)* . . . this is your heart's content — Illyria . . . Penguin Island . . . Gomorrah. . . . You think you're going to be happy here in New Carthage, eh?

NICK   *(A little defensively.)* I hope we'll stay here.

GEORGE   And every definition has its boundaries, eh? Well, it isn't a bad col-

lege, I guess. I mean . . . it'll do. It isn't M.I.T. . . . . it isn't U.C.L.A.
. . . it isn't the Sorbonne . . . or Moscow U. either, for that matter.

NICK   I don't mean . . . forever.

GEORGE   Well, don't you let that get bandied about. The old man wouldn't
like it. Martha's father expects loyalty and devotion out of his . . .
staff. I was going to use another word. Martha's father expects his
. . . staff . . . to cling to the walls of this place, like the ivy . . . to
come here and grow old . . . to fall in the line of service. One man,
a professor of Latin and Elocution, actually fell in the cafeteria
line, one lunch. He was buried, as many of us have been, and as
many more of us will be, under the shrubbery around the chapel.
It is said . . . and I have no reason to doubt it . . . that we make excellent fertilizer. But the old man is not going to be buried under
the shrubbery . . . the old man is not going to die. Martha's father
has the staying power of one of those Micronesian tortoises. There
are rumors . . . which you must not breathe in front of Martha, for
she foams at the mouth . . . that the old man, her father, is over
two hundred years old. There is probably an irony involved in this,
but I am not drunk enough to figure out what it is. How many
kids you going to have?

NICK   I . . . I don't know. . . . My wife is . . .

GEORGE   Slim-hipped. *(Rises.)* Have a drink.

NICK   Yes.

GEORGE   MARTHA! *(No answer.)* DAMN IT! *(To Nick.)* You asked me if I
knew women. . . . Well, one of the things I do *not* know about
them is what they talk about while the men are talking. *(Vaguely.)*
I must find out some time.

MARTHA'S VOICE   WHADD'YA WANT?

GEORGE   *(To Nick.)* Isn't that a wonderful sound? What I mean is . . . what
do you think they really *talk* about . . . or don't you care?

NICK   Themselves, I would imagine.

MARTHA'S VOICE   GEORGE?

GEORGE   *(To Nick.)* Do you find women . . . puzzling?

NICK   Well . . . yes and no.

GEORGE   *(With a knowing nod.)* Unh-hunh. *(Moves toward the hall, almost
bumps into Honey, re-entering.)* Oh! Well, here's one of you, at
least. *(Honey moves toward Nick. George goes to the hall.)*

HONEY   *(To George.)* She'll be right down . . . *(To Nick.)* You must see this
house, dear . . . this is such a wonderful old house.

NICK   Yes, I . . .

447

GEORGE MARTHA!

MARTHA'S VOICE FOR CHRIST'S SAKE, HANG ON A MINUTE, WILL YOU?

HONEY *(To George.)* She'll be right down . . . she's changing.

GEORGE *(Incredulous.)* She's *what?* She's changing?

HONEY Yes.

GEORGE Her clothes?

HONEY Her dress.

GEORGE *(Suspicious.)* Why?

HONEY *(With a nervous little laugh.)* Why, I imagine she wants to be . . . comfortable.

GEORGE *(With a threatening took toward the hall.)* Oh she does, does she?

HONEY Well, heavens, I should think . . .

GEORGE YOU DON'T KNOW!

NICK *(As Honey starts.)* You feel all right?

HONEY *(Reassuring, but with the echo of a whine. A long practiced tone.)* Oh, yes, dear . . . perfectly fine.

GEORGE *(Fuming . . . to himself.)* So she wants to be comfortable, does she? Well, we'll see about that.

HONEY *(To George, brightly.)* I didn't know until just a minute ago that you had a son.

GEORGE *(Wheeling, as if struck from behind.)* WHAT?

HONEY A son! I hadn't known.

NICK You to know and me to find out. Well, he must be quite a big . . .

HONEY Twenty-one . . . twenty-one tomorrow . . . tomorrow's his birthday.

NICK *(A victorious smile.)* Well!

GEORGE *(To Honey.)* She told you about him?

HONEY *(Flustered.)* Well, *yes.* Well, I mean . . .

GEORGE *(Nailing it down.)* She told you about him.

HONEY *(A nervous giggle.)* Yes.

GEORGE *(Strangely.)* You say she's changing?

HONEY Yes. . . .

GEORGE And she mentioned . . . ?

HONEY *(Cheerful, but a little puzzled.)* . . . your son's birthday . . . yes.

GEORGE *(More or less to himself.)* O.K., Martha . . . O.K.

NICK You look pale, Honey. Do you want a . . . ?

HONEY Yes, dear . . . a little more brandy, maybe. Just a drop.

GEORGE O.K., Martha.

NICK May I use the . . . uh . . . bar?

GEORGE Hm? Oh, yes . . . yes . . . by all means. Drink away . . . you'll need

	it as the years go on. *(For Martha, as if she were in the room.)* You goddamn destructive . . .
HONEY	*(To cover.)* What time is it, dear?
NICK	Two-thirty.
HONEY	Oh, it's so late . . . we *should* be getting home.
GEORGE	*(Nastily, but he is so preoccupied he hardly notices his own tone.)* For what? You keeping the babysitter up, or something?
NICK	*(Almost a warning.)* I told you we didn't have children.
GEORGE	Hm? *(Realizing.)* Oh, I'm sorry. I wasn't even listening . . . or thinking . . . *(With a flick of his hand.)* . . . whichever one applies.
NICK	*(Softly, to Honey.)* We'll go in a little while.
GEORGE	*(Driving.)* Oh, no, now . . . you mustn't. Martha is changing . . . and Martha is not changing for me. Martha hasn't changed for me in years. If Martha is changing, it means we'll be here for . . . days. You are being accorded an honor, and you must not forget that Martha is the daughter of our beloved boss. She is his . . . right ball, you might say.
NICK	You might not understand this . . . but I wish you wouldn't talk that way in front of my wife.
HONEY	Oh, now . . .
GEORGE	*(Incredulous.)* Really? Well, you're quite right. We'll leave that sort of talk to Martha.
MARTHA	*(Entering.)* What sort of talk? *(Martha has changed her clothes, and she looks, now, more comfortable and . . . and this is most important . . . most voluptuous.)*
GEORGE	There you are, my pet.
NICK	*(Impressed, rising.)* Well, now . . .
GEORGE	Why, Martha . . . your Sunday chapel dress!
HONEY	*(Slightly disapproving.)* Oh, that's most attractive.
MARTHA	*(Showing off.)* You like it? Good! *(To George.)* What the hell do you mean screaming up the stairs at me like that?
GEORGE	We got lonely, darling . . . we got lonely for the soft purr of your little voice.
MARTHA	*(Deciding not to rise to it.)* Oh. Well, then, you just trot over to the barie-poo . . .
GEORGE	*(Taking the tone from her.)* . . . and make your little mommy a gweat big dwink.
MARTHA	*(Giggles.)* That's right. *(To Nick.)* Well, did you two have a nice little talk? You men solve the problems of the world, as usual?
NICK	Well, no, we . . .

GEORGE *(Quickly.)* What we did, actually, if you really want to know, what we did actually is try to figure out what you two were talking about. *(Honey giggles, Martha laughs.)*

MARTHA *(To Honey.)* Aren't they something? Aren't these . . . *(Cheerfully disdainful.)* . . . *men* the absolute end? *(To George.)* Why didn't you sneak upstairs and listen in?

GEORGE Oh, I wouldn't have *listened*, Martha. . . . I would have *peeked*. *(Honey giggles, Martha laughs.)*

NICK *(To George, with false heartiness.)* It's a conspiracy.

GEORGE And now we'll never know. Shucks!

MARTHA *(To Nick, as Honey beams.)* Hey, you must be quite a boy, getting your Masters when you were . . . what? . . . twelve? You hear that, George?

NICK Twelve-and-a-half, actually. No, nineteen really. *(To Honey.)* Honey, you needn't have mentioned that. It . . .

HONEY Ohhhh . . . I'm proud of you. . . .

GEORGE *(Seriously, if sadly.)* That's very . . . impressive.

MARTHA *(Aggressively.)* You're damned right!

GEORGE *(Between his teeth.)* I said I was impressed, Martha. I'm beside myself with jealousy. What do you want me to do, throw up? *(To Nick.)* That really is very impressive. *(To Honey.)* You should be right proud.

HONEY *(Coy.)* Oh, he's a pretty nice fella.

GEORGE *(To Nick.)* I wouldn't be surprised if you did take over the History Department one of these days.

NICK The Biology Department.

GEORGE The *Biology* Department . . . of course. I seem preoccupied with history. Oh! What a remark. *(He strikes a pose, his hand over his heart, his head raised, his voice stentorian.)* "I am preoccupied with history."

MARTHA *(As Honey and Nick chuckle.)* Ha, ha, ha, HA!

GEORGE *(With some disgust.)* I think I'll make *myself* a drink.

MARTHA George is not preoccupied with *history*. . . . George is preoccupied with the *History Department*. George is preoccupied with the History Department because . . .

GEORGE . . . because he is *not* the History Department, but is only *in* the History Department. We know, Martha . . . we went all through it while you were upstairs . . . getting up. There's no need to go through it again.

MARTHA That's right, baby . . . keep it clean. *(To the others.)* George is

450

bogged down in the History Department. He's an old bog in the History Department, that's what George is. A bog. . . . A fen. . . . A G.D. swamp, Ha, ha, ha, HA! A SWAMP! Hey, swamp! Hey, SWAMPY!

GEORGE *(With a great effort controls himself . . . then, as if she had said nothing more than "George, dear" . . .)* Yes, Martha? Can I get you something?

MARTHA *(Amused at his game.)* Well . . . uh . . . sure, you can light my cigarette, if you're of a mind to.

GEORGE *(Considers, then moves off.)* No . . . there are limits. I mean, man can put up with only so much without he descends a rung or two on the old evolutionary ladder . . . *(Now a quick aside to Nick.)* . . . which is up your line . . . *(Then back to Martha.)* . . . sinks, Martha, and it's a funny ladder . . . you can't reverse yourself . . . start back up once you're descending. *(Martha blows him an arrogant kiss.)* Now . . . I'll hold your hand when it's dark and you're afraid of the bogey man, and I'll tote your gin bottles out after midnight, so no one'll see . . . but I will not light your cigarette. And that, as they say, is that. *(Brief silence.)*

MARTHA *(Under her breath.)* Jesus! *(Then, immediately, to Nick.)* Hey, you played football, hunh?

HONEY *(As Nick seems sunk in thought.)* Dear . . .

NICK Oh! Oh, yes . . . I was a . . . quarterback . . . but I was much more . . . adept . . . at boxing, really.

MARTHA *(With great enthusiasm.)* BOXING! You hear that, George?

GEORGE *(Resignedly.)* Yes, Martha.

MARTHA *(To Nick, with peculiar intensity and enthusiasm.)* You musta been pretty good at it . . . I mean, you don't look like you got hit in the face at all.

HONEY *(Proudly.)* He was intercollegiate state middleweight champion.

NICK *(Embarrassed.)* Honey . . .

HONEY Well, you were.

MARTHA You look like you still got a pretty good body *now*, too . . . is that right? Have you?

GEORGE *(Intensely.)* Martha . . . decency forbids. . . .

MARTHA *(To George . . . still staring at Nick, though.)* SHUT UP! *(Now, back to Nick.)* Well, have you? Have you kept your body?

NICK *(Unselfconscious . . . almost encouraging her.)* It's still pretty good. I work out.

MARTHA *(With a half-smile.)* Do you!

NICK Yeah.

HONEY Oh, yes . . . he has a very . . . firm body.

MARTHA *(Still with that smile . . . a private communication with Nick.)* Have you! Oh, I think that's very nice.

NICK *(Narcissistic, but not directly for Martha.)* Well, you never know . . . *(Shrugs.)* you know . . . once you have it . . .

MARTHA . . . you never know when it's going to come in handy.

NICK I was going to say . . . why give it up until you have to.

MARTHA I couldn't agree with you more. *(They both smile . . .)* . . .

BILL COSBY

The recent court case brought against Cosby by an alleged illegitimate daughter has failed to tarnish his reputation as the epitome of the hard-working, mild-mannered, American "family man." (Indeed, his courage in the face of the recent brutal murder of one of his five children has brought him forward once more as a public exemplar of strength, dignity, and stability.) Born in Philadelphia in 1937, Cosby's childhood was filled with challenges. He grew up in poverty in a rough Philadelphia neighborhood, the son of a welder. His father, an alcoholic and fearful figure to him, abandoned the family many times. Early on he was attracted to the work of Mark Twain, which his mother read to him; and he won the hearts of America as a young standup comedian in much the same way as Twain did — with self-effacing grace, a philosophical tolerance for human frailties, and gentle satire on the human condition. Interestingly, on the way to achieving the pinnacle of success in the entertainment industry (the situation comedy show that bore his name was one of the longest running and most popular in the history of television) Cosby earned a Ph.D. in education from the University of Massachusetts.

"Your Beloved Foe," from Love and Marriage

"I was married once," says a man in *The Importance of Being Earnest.* "It was the result of a misunderstanding between myself and a young woman."

Misunderstanding does unfortunately lie at the heart of marriage, for no matter how deeply a man and woman love each other, they are often like two

UN delegates whose headphones have jammed. They are constantly finding common ground that turns out to be quicksand.

A few years ago, Camille would happily have gone into quicksand rather than into the sauna I had built for our house in Los Angeles.

"That steam room," she said right after it had been completed. "Are you planning to do your own dry cleaning?"

"It'll be dry cleaning *us*," I replied. "It's for *you* and *me*."

"Honey, *I* can't take that much heat."

"It'll be a complete rebirth for you."

"Have I complained about the first one? Bill, those saunas go up to a hundred and twenty *degrees*."

"But it's so healthful," I said, aware of my marital duty to keep educating my wife, but deciding not to educate her with the news that the temperature would not be a hundred and twenty: it would be a hundred and ninety-five.

"It's healthful to pass out?" she said.

"That's the wrong attitude. A sauna purges the body of all impurities. And it's not just your average hundred and twenty degrees; it's *dry* heat."

"Let's put it this way: it's not the heat, it's the stupidity."

"Millions of *Finns* do it. They not only do it, but they roll in the snow afterward."

"And that's why Finland never wins a war."

In spite of Camille's objection, my blend of intellect and charm was persuasive enough to lure her into trying the new sauna with me. This woman did, after all, have courage: she had passed up countless bread-winners to marry a nightclub comedian.

And so, together we took off our clothes and walked into a six-by-six wooden room that conjured up visions of a Russian prison sentence.

"Now just remember, dear," I said as the waves of heat began striking us, "that this is good for the *skin*. It gets out the dirt."

"That's what they told Joan of Arc," she said.

It was deeply moving to see what my wife was doing in the name of love. After ten minutes, the temperature was a hundred and forty-five, but luckily Camille couldn't see the thermometer because her eyes were rolling back in her head.

"Bill, I think that's enough for today," she said, falling against the door and opening it. "My dermatologist likes me medium-rare."

"But you're missing the full benefit," I told her.

"Why don't we try to get that in a picnic at Death Valley next week?"

Teaching your wife little things, like how to broil herself or brush her teeth, is a form of education that can move the student to throw something at you. And once something is thrown at you, there is liable to be a fight. The experts on marriage, most of whom are divorced, like to say that marital fighting is good because it clears the air; but it seems to me that such fighting often leaves the air quality as unacceptable as it was when your wife happened to say:

"I think you should know I'm really tired of your always saying that I'm an urban village idiot."

"No, dear," you reply, "you're not paying attention. I don't *always* say that you're an urban village idiot. I have said it only *twice:* last Tuesday evening at your mother's and last May seventeenth at church. Our relationship would be stronger if you kept better score."

"And you *always* correct me like that."

"No, again not *always:* just the few thousand times when you're wrong."

"But I'm *not* wrong. I remember *precisely* what you've said to me."

"No, you remember *imprecisely* what I've said to you. Or else precisely what some *other* husband has said."

"You never *listen* to me."

"You're nothing-for-three today. The truth is, I probably listen too much. I should be more selective."

"You know what I've decided?"

"What?"

"That you're the most irritating man in the world."

"You've got to watch those generalizations. The most irritating man in the world is Mr. Botha."

"Who's Prince Charming compared to *you.* Oh, how I wish I had tapes of our conversations to prove to you what you really said."

"*Your* half belongs on 'The Twilight Zone.' Which is where I think I'm living sometimes. Just tell me this: Did you happen to move my collection of hand grenades from my table in the den?"

"Yes, I did."

"And do you happen to remember where you put them?"

"The same way I remember everything you say. I put them in the attic."

"You doing some decorating up there?"

"Down *here* they were in the way."

"In the way of *what?* A plate of Swedish meatballs? A picture of Wilt Chamberlain? Those hand grenades were souvenirs and they were *mine.* You just can't keep on hiding my things. I walk around this house looking for my things like somebody who's lost his mind."

"Yes, that *is* your best imitation."

This kind of heartfelt give-and-take is what the matrimonial sages say will bring you two closer together. And often it does: often the combat leads to a peace conference that is sexually delicious. In building to this conference, however, you have to fight fairly, keep your obscenities polite, and remember how precious you are to each other, even though you both are thinking:

That's it! *There is no way I can continue living with this person. I want to live with something better, like a gerbil.*

If the fighting is to lead to the climax of a passionate embrace, then the man must be careful never to say the five words that launched the Women's Movement:

"Are you expecting your period?"

These are the last five words that Samson said to Delilah. They are the words that were spoken one day to a young Fall River lady named Lizzie Borden. They are the words that have moved luggage from closets to front doors all over the world.

This question *is* a very tempting weapon for the American fighting man because women are prone to irrationality just before menstruation. Men, on the other hand, have a nice evenness to their irrationality. They can be just as crazy at Easter as they are on Veterans Day.

It is, of course, not always possible for your wife to leave you during a fight because sometimes the fight has been in a car and she would find no comfort fleeing to the shoulder of I-95. For some reason, a car is the scene of matrimonial highs and lows. Early in your marriage, the two of you exchange endearing smiles when you are driving along and your wife suddenly says, "Look out for that armored column!"

"What a thoughtful and sharp-eyed sweetheart you are to take the trouble to point out all those slowly approaching tanks," you reply. "I probably would've seen them on my own and they're probably friendly and they're probably stopping at the light, but your spotting them for me still makes my heart hum like the engine of a Rolls."

Later in the marriage, however, the same helpful tip brings a different response from you at the wheel.

"Look out for that armored column!" she says.

"You think I don't *see* it?" you reply.

"I'm never sure *what* you see."

"I'm starting to see bachelorhood in a whole new light."

Moreover, your automotive rapport suffers the same decline during the years that the two of you keep trying to navigate toward unknown destinations. Early in the marriage, it is gaily romantic for the two of you to get lost together, just as it was a merry moment when Columbus told his first mate, "India, Youngstown, who *cares* as long as we're having fun!"

"Darling," your young wife says, "please understand the spirit in which I say this: I think Chicago was a *left* at that fork."

"I took a shot," you reply, "just as I did when I married you. Maybe I'll luck out again."

And she laughs and puts her befuddled head against your uncertain steering arm and says, "Getting there with you is half the fun, even if we're going nowhere."

However, later in the marriage, getting lost is less enchanting.

"You missed the turn, Magellan," she says. "Chicago was a *left* at that fork. Or are you trying to get there by way of Montreal?"

"No, it was a *right* at the fork," you reply, "but thanks anyway for the misinformation. Why don't you just concentrate on holding the change for the tolls?"

"Why don't *you* concentrate on changing from someone who always yells at me?"

"I don't *always* yell at you. You call just twenty-three times this week *always?*"

An interesting thing has happened. Two different arguments have converged: the one about your always doing something and the one about your recently taking the wrong turn. And at the convergence are the tears of your wife.

"Now, crying doesn't make you right," you say. "It just stuffs you up so you hear even less of the wisdom I keep trying to impart to you. If you'd just start *listening* to me, you'd learn — "

"I don't want to learn from you 'cause I don't want a diploma in wrong turns! You make me feel like I'm stupid when *you're* the one who doesn't know how to drive!"

"Let me ask you a question that even *you* might be able to answer: Did you ever wonder why they put all the instruments on *this* side of the car? They put them here for *me* because this is where I'm sitting. There's no copilot in these things."

"And did *you* ever wonder why you didn't pull over to the first gas station and get proper directions for Chicago instead of wandering around like Moses in the wilderness?"

"Because I know what I'm doing."

"What you're doing is getting lost and I'm not talking to you anymore."

"Is that a promise?"

"So many men I could have married and I had to pick the happy wanderer."

"All right, let's try it your way," you say, swerving into a service station. "Let's ask *him.*"

"No, not *him*," she says.

"Why?"

"Because he doesn't look as though he knows."

"But he looks as though he did well on the SATs."

"I tell you he's weak on geography."

And off you go, moving farther away from both your destination and each other.

Suddenly, you come to a sign. NOT A THROUGH STREET.

"This street looks good," you say. "That sign is just to keep out the trucks."

"If this doesn't work," she says, "you can turn into the next black hole."

A half hour later, when you reach a gas attendant whose face reveals a high IQ to your wife, you receive the right instructions, but they lack a certain value because you have listened to only every fifth word: "Hang a left . . . hang a right . . . hang yourself . . ."

"Well, what do we do *now*, Mrs. Navigator?" you ask your wife when you arrive at the Mexican border.

"How do *I* know? *You're* Mr. Iacocca. I told you: I'm not even in the car with you anymore."

"Don't tease me with my dreams."

When you finally arrive at your destination two days later, you are silent enemies. The fight will resume, of course, after your visit, unless you wisely abandon the car and come home by bus. Even in a bus, however, the battle might still flare up again and the other passengers might have to listen to endless themes and variations of the two lines that are the favorites in most marital fights:

THE HUSBAND: That's not what I'm *saying*.

THE WIFE: Then what's your *point*?

THE HUSBAND: My point is that's not what I'm *saying*.

THE WIFE: Do you think that you'll ever be saying your *point*? Or would you rather get a pencil and paper and try *drawing* it?

Camille and I once accidentally switched these two lines because we'd forgotten our parts during a long spell of peace, but I found that I didn't have my heart in asking her what was her point, and she seemed to lack a flair for telling me what she was saying. She seemed uncomfortable trying to clarify a thought that she probably wanted to keep obscure.

Reading the wrong dialogue is bad enough, but going blank is even worse. The argument I dislike most is the one in which Camille just suddenly walks away from me and I forget my next line. When she returns, I can either vamp until I remember what I was talking about or I can start a new fight about her halftime break.

"That was really lovely to just walk out that way," I once told her.

"I thought I'd do some shopping while you were trying to find your point," she said.

In my twenty-five years on the roller coaster of marriage, I have discovered that marital fights sometimes last for three or four days because the opponents aren't playing the same game: men and women fight differently. For example, at certain times in a fight a woman likes to respond by sticking her fingers in her ears, but a man does this only to catch mosquitoes.

"Now *that's* truly adult," you say. "Just tuning out . . . Did you *hear* me? I said, 'That's truly adult.'"

And then she starts to hum, but not even one of your favorite tunes, just something that *sounds* like a mosquito. She not only is hearing nothing from you, but she is also broadcasting a noise that brings to your mind the part of the marriage vow covering "for better or worse." It rarely gets much worse than this — except perhaps the night that I was reading in the den and she came in, went to the thermostat, turned up the heat, and started to leave.

"Hey there," I said. "I'm here. Perhaps you didn't see me sitting here and quietly improving my mind."

"I saw you," she replied.

"Well, perhaps you didn't know that the temperature was quite comfortable for me. In fact, I was just telling myself, 'Bill, you don't have to take a vacation because you're already in a place where the heat is just right.'"

"You don't know if a room is hot or cold."

Now this indeed was a memorable moment. My wife is surely more intelligent than I am because she knows what to tell the children to keep them from putting holes in each other, but even *my* modest IQ usually lets me know if a room is hot or cold. And so, what does a man do when his wife feels he needs a class in remedial thermostat reading?

If I were smarter, I would know.

Ever since Socrates' wife told him to go and seek the truth in another house, philosophers have debated whether a husband and wife should go to bed angry at each other. There are two sound reasons for making up at bedtime: it feels like the right moment for reconciliation and a fight is harder to sustain when one of the fighters falls asleep. In fact, there is nothing more maddening than finally finding the words you've been looking for — *That's not what I'm saying* — and then having to deliver them to an unconscious foe, who cannot ask you, *Then what's your point?* Do you wake her up to hear your words, thus taking a chance on learning what it feels like to be part of a justifiable homicide? Or do you save the words until morning, when she will have even less idea of what you're talking about?

In spite of the beauty of our love, Camille and I have had bedtimes never discussed by Mister Rogers. Like two heavyweights going for the title, we enter the downy ring and then turn away from each other and move to our corners. And now I start thinking of all the people I could have married who kept their fingers out of their ears and who would have let me try to figure out all by myself if I was cold. Denise, Artemis, Rosemary, Charlene, Lori, Millie, Sarah, Ruth . . . They may have been dumb about sports or had no taste in music or liked stolen jewelry, but all of them are suddenly looking like Whitney Houston to me.

I'm not going to touch her, I think, as the two of us lie there in stony silence. *I won't even shake hands with her lawyer. And if she touches* me, *I'll wash it off with Brillo.*

But then her heel grazes mine and this least erogenous part of her calls up a memory so sweet that it almost stops me from trying to fill her with guilt.

"If you don't want me in this bed," I quietly tell her, "just say the word."

"Don't let *me* keep you from leaving," she replies.

"Just say the word."

"If you have travel plans . . ."

"Just say the word."

"Have a good trip."

"All right, I know a hint when I hear one. I'll just sleep on the floor. I'll pretend I'm back in the Army."

"You were in the Navy."

"Whatever. Okay, I'll be hitting the deck now. That's the sound you'll be hearing."

When I finally do drop to the floor, there is a certain loss of dignity. On the other hand, I have strengthened my bargaining position for pity.

"Camille?"

"Yes, sailor?"

"You just going to leave me down here?"

"I don't vacuum till Tuesday."

"Just leave me down here like an old bear rug?"

"Bear? You know what I can't *bear?* The way you're always such a . . . such a . . . *man.* Only a *man* would think that moving to a lower level makes him right."

"Well, I just want to say one more thing that happens to *be* right: I love you."

"See? If you talk long enough, you finally make sense. And I love you."

"Well, sending me to the floor isn't the tenderest way to show it."

"Honey, you booked that trip yourself."

"Sometimes you take me for granted, you know. There are plenty of other women who'd have me and never move me to the floor."

"*Plenty* of other women? Name *one* of 'em who'd take a man who spends half the day looking for his glasses and the other half looking for his keys." She began to laugh. "And this man can find his keys only if he finds his glasses first."

"At least I have missions in life," I say, climbing back into bed and moving toward her. "A man has to — "

"Just close your mouth and kiss me and stop trying to explain men. Let a veterinarian do that."

"I'll bet Charlene is still waiting for me," I say, drawing her into an embrace that has made the whole battle worthwhile.

"Charlene . . ." says Camille after releasing my lips. "Was she the one who pretended that she liked John Coltrane? Or was she the one whose head you almost took off at the track meet?"

JOHN GOTTMAN

John Gottman, co-director of Seattle Marital and Family Institute, is Mifflin Professor of psychology at the University of Washington. His M.S. degree in mathematics-psychology was earned at M.I.T., and his doctorate at the University of Wisconsin. Gottman has written numerous scholarly articles. His proponency of a "scientifically based marital therapy" culled from watching stable married couples interact, has elicited much controversy in the psychotherapeutic community. But despite his sharp critique of the classical techniques of marital counseling, his contributions to the field of marital therapy have been widely admired and embraced. Gottman's scholarly works (such as *Meta-Emotion* and *The Marriage Clinic*) are more erudite and perhaps more important in the long run than the popular work selected here. But this work, written with the help of *Parents* magazine's editor Nan Silver, is accessible and entertaining as well as insightful.

The Seven Principles for Making Marriage Work

Emotionally Intelligent Marriages

What can make a marriage work is surprisingly simple. Happily married couples aren't smarter, richer, or more psychologically astute than others. But in their day-to-day lives, they have hit upon a dynamic that keeps their negative thoughts and feelings about each other (which all couples have) from overwhelming their positive ones. They have what I call an emotionally intelligent marriage.

Recently, emotional intelligence has become widely recognized as an important predictor of a child's success later in life. The more in touch with emotions and the better able a child is to understand and get along with others, the sunnier that child's future, whatever his or her academic IQ. The same is true for relationships between spouses. The more emotionally intelligent a couple — the better able they are to understand, honor, and respect each other and their marriage — the more likely that they will indeed live happily ever after. Just as parents can teach their children emotional intelligence, this is also a skill that a couple can be taught. As simple as it sounds, it can keep husband and wife on the positive side of the divorce odds.

Why Save Your Marriage?

Speaking of those odds, the divorce statistics remain dire. . . . Half of all divorces will occur in the first seven years. Some studies find the divorce rate for second marriages is as much as 10 percent higher than for first-timers. The chance of getting divorced remains so high that it makes sense for all married couples — including those who are currently satisfied with their relationship — to put extra effort into their marriages to keep them strong.

One of the saddest reasons a marriage dies is that neither spouse recognizes its value until it is too late. Only after the papers have been signed, the furniture divided, and separate apartments rented do the exes realize how much they really gave up when they gave up on each other. Too often a good marriage is taken for granted rather than given the nurturing and respect it deserves and desperately needs. Some people may think that getting divorced or languishing in an unhappy marriage is no big deal — they may even consider it trendy. But there's now plenty of evidence documenting just how harmful this can be for all involved.

Thanks to the work of researchers like Lois Verbrugge and James House, both of the University of Michigan, we now know that an unhappy marriage can increase your chances of getting sick by roughly 35 percent and even shorten your life by an average of four years. The flip side: People who are happily married live longer, healthier lives than either divorced people or those who are unhappily married. Scientists know for certain that these differences exist, but we are not yet sure why.

Part of the answer may simply be that in an unhappy marriage people experience chronic, diffuse physiological arousal — in other words, they feel physically stressed and usually emotionally stressed as well. This puts added wear and tear on the body and mind, which can present itself in any number of physical ailments, including high blood pressure and heart disease, and in a host of psychological ones, including anxiety, depression, suicide, violence, psychosis, homicide, and substance abuse.

Not surprisingly, happily married couples have a far lower rate of such maladies. They also tend to be more health-conscious than others. Researchers theorize that this is because spouses keep after each other to have regular check-ups, take medicine, eat nutritiously, and so on.

Recently my laboratory uncovered some exciting preliminary evidence that a good marriage may also keep you healthier by directly benefiting your immune system, which spearheads the body's defenses against illness. Researchers have known for about a decade that divorce can depress the immune system's function. Theoretically this lowering in the system's ability to fight foreign invaders could leave you open to more infectious diseases and cancers. Now we have found that the opposite may also be true. Not only do happily married people avoid this drop in immune function, but their immune systems may even be getting an extra boost.

When we tested the immune system responses of the fifty couples who stayed overnight in the Love Lab, we found a striking difference between those who were very satisfied with their marriages and those whose emotional response to each other was neutral or who were unhappy. Specifically, we used blood samples from each subject to test the response of certain of their white blood cells — the immune system's major defense weapons. In general, happily married men and women showed a greater proliferation of these white blood cells when exposed to foreign invaders than did the other subjects.

We also tested the effectiveness of other immune system warriors — the natural killer cells, which, true to their name, destroy body cells that have been damaged or altered (such as infected or cancerous ones) and are known to limit the growth of tumor cells. Again, subjects who were satisfied with their marriage had more effective natural killer cells than did the others.

It will take more study before scientists can confirm that this boost in the immune system is one of the mechanisms by which a good marriage benefits your health and longevity. But what's most important is that we know for certain that a good marriage does. In fact, I often think that if fitness buffs spent just 10 percent of their weekly workout time — say, twenty minutes a day — working on their marriage instead of their bodies, they would get three times the health benefits they derive from climbing the StairMaster! . . .

Innovative Research, Revolutionary Findings

When it comes to saving a marriage, the stakes are high for everybody in the family. And yet despite the documented importance of marital satisfaction, the amount of scientifically sound research into keeping marriages stable and happy is shockingly small. When I first began researching marriage in 1972, you could probably have held all of the "good" scientific data on marriage in one hand. By "good" I mean findings that were collected using scientific methods as rigorous as those used by medical science. For example, many studies of marital happiness were conducted solely by having husbands and wives fill out questionnaires. This approach is called the self-report method, and although it has its uses, it is also quite limited. How do you know a wife is happy just because she checks the "happy" box on some form? Women in physically abusive relationships, for example, score very high on questionnaires about marital satisfaction. Only if the woman feels safe and is interviewed one on one does she reveal her agony.

To address this paucity of good research, my colleagues and I have supplemented traditional approaches to studying marriage with many innovative, more extensive methods. We are now following seven hundred couples in seven different studies. We have not just studied newlyweds but long-term couples who were first assessed while in their forties or sixties. We have also studied couples just becoming parents and couples interacting with their babies, their preschoolers, and their teenagers.

As part of this research, I have interviewed couples about the history of their marriage, their philosophy about marriage, how they viewed their parents' marriages. I have videotaped them talking to each other about how their day went, discussing areas of continuing disagreement in their marriage, and also conversing about joyful topics. And to get a physiological read of how stressed or relaxed they were feeling, I measured their heart rate, blood flow, sweat output, blood pressure, and immune function moment by moment. In all of these studies, I'd play back the tapes to the couples and ask them for an insider's perspective of what they were thinking and feeling when, say, their heartrate and blood pressure suddenly surged during a marital discussion. And I've kept track of the couples, checking in with them at least every year to see how their relationship is faring. . . . Our data offers the first real glimpse of the inner workings — the anatomy — of marriage. . . .

What *Does* Make Marriage Work?

The advice I used to give couples earlier in my career was pretty much what you'd hear from virtually any marital therapist — the same old pointers about conflict resolution and communication skills. But after looking squarely at my own data, I had to face the harsh facts: Getting couples to disagree more "nicely" might reduce their stress levels while they argued, but frequently it wasn't enough to pump life back into their marriages.

The right course for these couples became clear only after I analyzed the interactions of couples whose marriages sailed smoothly through troubled waters. Why was it that these marriages worked so well? Were these couples more intelligent, more stable, or simply more fortunate than the others? Could whatever they had be taught to other couples?

It soon became apparent that these happy marriages were never perfect unions. Some couples who said they were very satisfied with each other still had significant differences in temperament, in interests, in family values. Conflict was not infrequent. They argued, just as the unhappy couples did, over money, jobs, kids, housekeeping, sex, and in-laws. The mystery was how they so adroitly navigated their way through these difficulties and kept their marriages happy and stable.

It took studying hundreds of couples until I finally uncovered the secrets of these emotionally intelligent marriages. No two marriages are the same, but the more closely I looked at happy marriages the clearer it became that they were alike. . . .

Friendship versus Fighting

At the heart of my program is the simple truth that happy marriages are based on a deep friendship. By this I mean a mutual respect for and enjoyment of each other's company. These couples tend to know each other intimately — they are well versed in each other's likes, dislikes, personality quirks, hopes, and dreams. They have an abiding regard for each other and express this fondness not just in the big ways but in little ways day in and day out.

Take the case of hardworking Nathaniel, who runs his own import business and works very long hours. In another marriage, his schedule might be a major liability. But he and his wife Olivia have found ways to stay connected. They talk frequently on the phone during the day. When she has a doctor's appointment, he remembers to call to see how it went. When he has a meeting with an important client, she'll check in to see how it fared. When they have chicken for dinner, she gives him both drumsticks because she knows he likes them best. When he makes blueberry pancakes for the kids Saturday morning, he'll leave the blueberries out of hers because he knows she doesn't like them. Although he's not religious, he accompanies her to church each Sunday because it's important to her. And although she's not crazy about spending a lot of time with their relatives, she has pursued a friendship with Nathaniel's mother and sisters because family matters so much to him.

If all of this sounds humdrum and unromantic, it's anything but. Through small but important ways Olivia and Nathaniel are maintaining the friendship that is the foundation of their love. As a result they have a marriage that is far more passionate than do couples who punctuate their lives together with romantic vacations and lavish anniversary gifts but have fallen out of touch in their daily lives.

Friendship fuels the flames of romance because it offers the best protection against feeling adversarial toward your spouse. Because Nathaniel and Olivia have kept their friendship strong despite the inevitable disagreements and irritations of married life, they are experiencing what is known technically as "positive sentiment override." This means that their positive thoughts about each other and their marriage are so pervasive that they tend to supersede their negative feelings. It takes a much more significant conflict for them to lose their equilibrium as a couple than it would otherwise. Their positivity causes them to feel optimistic. . . .

The Purpose of Marriage

In the strongest marriages, husband and wife share a deep sense of meaning. They don't just "get along" — they also support each other's hopes and aspirations and build a sense of purpose into their lives together. That is really what I mean when I talk about honoring and respecting each other.

Very often a marriage's failure to do this is what causes husband and wife to find themselves in endless, useless rounds of argument or to feel isolated and lonely in their marriage. After watching countless videotapes of couples fighting, I can guarantee you that most quarrels are really not about whether the toilet lid is up or down or whose turn it is to take out the trash. There are deeper, hidden issues that fuel these superficial conflicts and make them far more intense and hurtful than they would otherwise be.

Once you understand this, you will be ready to accept one of the most surprising truths about marriage: *Most marital arguments cannot be resolved.* Couples spend year after year trying to change each other's mind — but it can't be done. This is because most of their disagreements are rooted in fundamental differences of lifestyle, personality, or values. By fighting over these differences, all they succeed in doing is wasting their time and harming their marriage.

467

How I Predict Divorce

Dara and Oliver sit face to face in the Love Lab. Both in their late twenties, they have volunteered to take part in my study of newlyweds. In this extensive research, 130 couples have agreed to put their marriages not only under the microscope but in front of the camera as well. Dara and Oliver are among the fifty who were observed during an overnight stay at the Love Lab "apartment." My ability to predict divorce is based in part on my analysis of these couples and their interactions.

Dara and Oliver say their lives are hectic but happy. She attends nursing school at night, and he works long hours as a computer programmer. Like many couples, including those who remain content as well as those who eventually divorce, Dara and Oliver acknowledge that their marriage isn't perfect. But they say they love each other and are committed to staying together. They positively beam when they talk about the life they plan to build.

I ask them to spend fifteen minutes in the lab trying to resolve an ongoing disagreement they are having while I videotape them. As they speak, sensors attached to their bodies gauge their stress levels based on various measurements of their circulatory system, such as how quickly their hearts beat.

I expect that their discussion will be at least somewhat negative. After all, I have asked them to quarrel. While some couples are capable of resolving disagreements with understanding words and smiles, more often there's tension. Dara and Oliver are no exception. Dara thinks Oliver doesn't do his share of the housekeeping, and he thinks she nags him too much, which makes him less motivated to do more.

After listening to them talk about this problem, I sadly predict to my colleagues that Dara and Oliver will see their marital happiness dwindle. And sure enough, four years later they report they are on the verge of divorce. Although they still live together, they are leading lonely lives. They have become like ghosts, haunting the marriage that once made them both feel so alive.

I predict their marriage will falter not because they argue — after all, I asked them to. Anger between husband and wife doesn't itself predict marital meltdown. Other couples in the newlywed study argue far more during the fifteen minutes of videotaping than do Dara and Oliver. Yet I predict that many of these couples will remain happily married — and they do. The clues to Dara and Oliver's future breakup are in the *way* they argue.

The First Sign: Harsh Startup

The most obvious indicator that this discussion (and this marriage) is not going to go well is the way it begins. Dara immediately becomes negative and accusatory. When Oliver broaches the subject of housework, she's ready to be sarcastic. "Or lack thereof," she says. Oliver tries to lighten things up by cracking a joke: "Or the book we were talking about writing: Men are pigs." Dara sits poker-faced. They talk a bit more, trying to devise a plan to make sure Oliver does his share, and then Dara says, "I mean, I'd like to see it resolved, but it doesn't seem like it is. I mean, I've tried making up lists, and that doesn't work. And I've tried letting you do it on your own, and nothing got done for a month." Now she's blaming Oliver. In essence, she's saying the problem isn't the housekeeping, it's him.

When a discussion leads off this way — with criticism and/or sarcasm, a form of contempt — it has begun with a "harsh startup." Although Dara talks to Oliver in a very soft, quiet voice, there's a load of negative power in her words. After hearing the first minute or so of their conversation, it's no surprise to me that by the end Dara and Oliver haven't resolved their differences at all. The research shows that if your discussion begins with a harsh startup, it will inevitably end on a negative note, even if there are a lot of attempts to "make nice" in between. Statistics tell the story: 96 percent of the time you can predict the outcome of a conversation based on the *first three minutes* of the fifteen-minute interaction! A harsh startup simply dooms you to failure. So if you begin a discussion that way, you might as well pull the plug, take a breather, and start over.

The Second Sign: The Four Horsemen

Dara's harsh startup sounds the warning bell that she and Oliver may be having serious difficulty. Now, as their discussion unfolds, I continue to look out for particular types of negative interactions. Certain kinds of negativity, if allowed to run rampant, are so lethal to a relationship that I call them the Four Horsemen of the Apocalypse. Usually these four horsemen clip-clop into the heart of a marriage in the following order: criticism, contempt, defensiveness, and stonewalling.

Horseman 1: Criticism

You will always have some complaints about the person you live with. But there's a world of difference between a complaint and a criticism. A complaint only addresses the specific action at which your spouse failed. A criticism is more global — it adds on some negative words about your mate's character or personality. "I'm really angry that you didn't sweep the kitchen floor last night. We agreed that we'd take turns doing it" is a complaint. "Why are you so forgetful? I hate having to always sweep the kitchen floor when it's your turn. You just don't care" is a criticism. A complaint focuses on a specific behavior, but a criticism ups the ante by throwing in blame and general character assassination. Here's a recipe: To turn any complaint into a criticism, just add my favorite line: "What is wrong with you?"

Usually a harsh startup comes in the guise of criticism. You can see how quickly complaint turns into criticism when Dara begins to talk. Listen again to what she says:

Dara: I mean, I'd like to see it resolved, but it doesn't seem like it is. *(Simple complaint)* I mean, I've tried making up lists and that doesn't work. And I've tried letting you do it on your own, and nothing got done for a month. *(Criticism. She's implying the problem is his fault. Even if it is, blaming him will only make it worse.)* . . .

If you hear echoes of yourself or your spouse in these criticisms, you have plenty of company. The first horseman is very common in relationships. So if you find that you and your spouse are critical of each other, don't assume you're headed for divorce court. The problem with criticism is that when it becomes pervasive, it paves the way for the other, far deadlier horsemen.

Horseman 2: Contempt

Dara doesn't stop at criticizing Oliver. Soon she's literally sneering. When he suggests that they keep a list of his chores on the refrigerator to help him remember, she says, "Do you think you work really well with lists?" Next, Oliver tells her that he needs fifteen minutes to relax when he gets home before starting to do chores. "So if I leave you alone for fifteen minutes, then you think you'll be motivated to jump up and do something?" she asks him.

"Maybe. We haven't tried it, have we?" Oliver asks.

Dara has an opportunity here to soften up, but instead she comes back with sarcasm. "I think you do a pretty good job of coming home and lying around or disappearing into the bathroom," she says. And then she adds challengingly, "So you think that's the cure-all, to give you fifteen minutes?"

This sarcasm and cynicism are types of contempt. So are name-calling, eye-rolling, sneering, mockery, and hostile humor. In whatever form, contempt — the worst of the four horsemen — is poisonous to a relationship because it conveys disgust. It's virtually impossible to resolve a problem when your partner is getting the message you're disgusted with him or her. Inevitably, contempt leads to more conflict rather than to reconciliation. . . .

Horseman 3: Defensiveness

[When her husband, Peter, accuses her of wasting money paying someone to wash her car,] Cynthia defends herself. She points out that she doesn't get her car washed as often as he thinks. She explains that it's more difficult physically for her to wash her car herself than it is for him to wash his truck.

Although it's understandable that Cynthia would defend herself, research shows that this approach rarely has the desired effect. The attacking spouse does not back down or apologize. This is because defensiveness is really a way of blaming your partner. You're saying, in effect, "The problem isn't *me*, it's *you*." Defensiveness just escalates the conflict, which is why it's so deadly. When Cynthia tells Peter how hard it is for her to wash her car, he doesn't say, "Oh, now I understand." He ignores her excuse — he doesn't even acknowledge what she's said. He climbs farther up his high moral ground, telling her how well he takes care of his vehicle and implying that she's spoiled for not doing the same. Cynthia can't win — and neither can their marriage.

Criticism, Contempt, and Defensiveness don't always gallop into a home in strict order. They function more like a relay match — handing the baton off to each other over and over again, if the couple can't put a stop to it. You can see this happening as Oliver and Dara continue their discussion about cleaning their house. Although they seem to be seeking a solution, Dara becomes increasingly contemptuous — mocking Oliver in the guise of questioning him and tearing down every plan he devises. The more defensive he becomes, the more she attacks him. Her body language signals condescension. She speaks softly, her elbows resting on the table, her intertwined fingers cradling her chin. Like a law professor or a judge, she peppers him with questions just to see him squirm.

Dara: So you think that's the cure-all, to give you fifteen minutes? *(sneering)*
Oliver: No, I don't think that's the cure-all. I think, combined with writing up a

list of weekly tasks that have to get done. Why not put it on a calendar? Hey, I'll see it right then and there.

Dara: Just like when I write stuff in your Day-Timer it gets done? *(mocking him; more contempt)*

Oliver: I don't always have a chance to look at my Day-Timer during the day. *(defensive)*

Dara: So you think you'll look at a calendar, then? . . .

Horseman 4: Stonewalling

In marriages like Dara and Oliver's, where discussions begin with a harsh startup, where criticism and contempt lead to defensiveness, which leads to more contempt and more defensiveness, eventually one partner tunes out. This heralds the arrival of the fourth horseman.

Think of the husband who comes home from work, gets met with a barrage of criticism from his wife, and hides behind the newspaper. The less responsive he is, the more she yells. Eventually he gets up and leaves the room. Rather than confronting his wife, he disengages. By turning away from her, he is avoiding a fight, but he is also avoiding his marriage. He has become a stonewaller. Although both husbands and wives can be stonewallers, this behavior is far more common among men, for reasons we'll see later.

During a typical conversation between two people, the listener gives all kinds of cues to the speaker that he's paying attention. He may use eye contact, nod his head, say something like "Yeah" or "Uh-huh." But a stonewaller doesn't give you this sort of casual feedback. He tends to look away or down without uttering a sound. He sits like an impassive stone wall. The stonewaller acts as though he couldn't care less about what you're saying, if he even hears it.

Stonewalling usually arrives later in the course of a marriage than the other three horsemen. That's why it's less common among newlywed husbands such as Oliver than among couples who have been in a negative spiral for a while. It takes time for the negativity created by the first three horsemen to become overwhelming enough that stonewalling becomes an understandable "out." That's the stance that Mack takes when he and his wife Rita argue about each other's behavior at parties. She says the problem is that he drinks too much. He thinks the bigger problem is her reaction: She embarrasses him by yelling at him in front of his friends. Here they are, already in the middle of an argument:

Rita: Now I've become the problem, again. I started off with the complaint, but now I am the problem. That always seems to happen.

Mack: Yeah, I do that, I know. *(Pause.)* But your tantrums and childishness are an embarrassment to me and my friends.

Rita: If you would control your drinking at parties, puleese . . .

Mack: *(Looks down, avoids eye contact, says nothing — he's stonewalling.)*

Rita: Because I think *(laughs)* for the most part, we get along pretty well, really *(laughs)*.

Mack: *(Continues to stonewall. Remains silent, makes no eye contact, head nods, facial movements, or vocalizations.)*

Rita: Don't you think?

Mack: *(No response.)*

Rita: Mack? Hello?

The Third Sign: Flooding

It may seem to Rita that her complaints have no effect on Mack. But nothing could be further from the truth. Usually people stonewall as a protection against feeling *flooded*. Flooding means that your spouse's negativity — whether in the guise of criticism or contempt or even defensiveness — is so overwhelming, and so sudden, that it leaves you shell-shocked. You feel so defenseless against this sniper attack that you learn to do anything to avoid a replay. The more often you feel flooded by your spouse's criticism or contempt, the more hypervigilant you are for cues that your spouse is about to "blow" again. All you can think about is protecting yourself from the turbulence your spouse's onslaught causes. And the way to do that is to disengage emotionally from the relationship. No wonder Mack and Rita are now divorced.

Another husband, Paul, was quite up front about why he stonewalls when his wife, Amy, gets negative. In the following discussion he articulates what all stonewallers are feeling.

Amy. When I get mad, that's when you should step in and try to make it better. But when you just stop talking, it means, 'I no longer care about how you feel.' That just makes me feel one inch tall. Like my opinion or feelings have absolutely no bearing on you. And that's not the way a marriage should be.

Paul: What I'm saying is, if you wanna have a serious conversation, you're gonna do it without yelling and screaming all the time. You start saying things that are hurtful. . . .

Amy kept telling Paul how it made her feel when he shut down. But she did not seem to hear him tell her *why* he shuts down: He can't handle her hostility. This couple later divorced.

A marriage's meltdown can be predicted, then, by habitual harsh startup and frequent flooding brought on by the relentless presence of the four horsemen during disagreements. Although each of these factors alone can predict a divorce, they usually coexist in an unhappy marriage.

The Fourth Sign: Body Language

Even if I could not hear the conversation between Mack the stonewaller and his wife, Rita, I would be able to predict their divorce simply by looking at his physiological readings. When we monitor couples for bodily changes during a tense discussion, we can see just how physically distressing flooding is. One of the most apparent of these physical reactions is that the heart speeds up — pounding away at more than 100 beats per minute — even as high as 165. (In contrast, a typical heart rate for a man who is about 30 is 76, and for a woman the same age, 82.) Hormonal changes occur, too, including the secretion of adrenaline, which kicks in the "fight or flight response." Blood pressure also mounts. These changes are so dramatic that if one partner is frequently flooded during marital discussions, it's easy to predict that they will divorce.

Recurring episodes of flooding lead to divorce for two reasons. First, they signal that at least one partner feels severe emotional distress when dealing with the other. Second, the *physical* sensations of feeling flooded — the increased heart rate, sweating, and so on — make it virtually impossible to have a productive, problem-solving discussion. When your body goes into overdrive during an argument, it is responding to a very primitive alarm system we inherited from our prehistoric ancestors. All those distressful reactions, like a pounding heart and sweating, occur because on a fundamental level your body perceives your current situation as dangerous. Even though we live in the age of in vitro conception, organ transplants, and gene mapping, from an evolutionary standpoint not much time has passed since we were cave dwellers. So the human body has not refined its fear reactions — it responds the same way, whether you're facing a saber-toothed tiger or a contemptuous spouse demanding to know why you can never remember to put the toilet seat back down.

When a pounding heart and all the other physical stress reactions happen in the midst of a discussion with your mate, the consequences are disastrous. Your ability to process information is reduced, meaning it's harder to pay attention to what your partner is saying. Creative problem solving goes out the window. You're left with the most reflexive, least intellectually sophisticated responses in your repertoire: to fight (act critical, contemptuous, or defensive) or flee (stonewall). Any chance of resolving the issue is gone. Most likely, the discussion will just worsen the situation.

Men and Women Really Are Different

In 85 percent of marriages, the stonewaller is the husband. This is not because of some lack on the man's part. The reason lies in our evolutionary heritage. Anthropological evidence suggests that we evolved from hominids whose lives were circumscribed by very rigid gender roles, since these were advantageous to survival in a harsh environment. The females specialized in nurturing children while the males specialized in cooperative hunting.

As any nursing mother can tell you, the amount of milk you produce is affected by how relaxed you feel, which is related to the release of the hormone oxytocin in the brain. So natural selection would favor a female who could quickly soothe herself and calm down after feeling stressed. Her ability to remain composed could enhance her children's chances of survival by optimizing the amount of nutrition they received. But in the male, natural selection would reward the opposite response. For these early cooperative hunters, maintaining vigilance was a key survival skill. So males whose adrenaline kicked in quite readily and who did not calm down so easily were more likely to survive and procreate.

To this day, the male cardiovascular system remains more reactive than the female and slower to recover from stress. For example, if a man and woman suddenly hear a very loud, brief sound, like a blowout, most likely his heart will beat faster than hers and stay accelerated for longer. . . . The same goes for their blood pressure — his will become more elevated and stay higher longer. Psychologist Dolf Zillman, Ph.D., at the University of Alabama, has found that when male subjects are deliberately treated rudely and then told to relax for twenty minutes, their blood pressure surges and stays elevated until they get to retaliate. But when women face the same treatment, they are able to calm down during those twenty minutes. (Interestingly, a woman's blood pressure tends to rise again if she is pressured into retaliating!) Since marital confrontation that activates vigilance takes a greater physical toll on the male, it's no surprise that men are more likely than women to attempt to avoid it.

This gender difference in how physiologically reactive our bodies are also influences what men and women tend to think about when they experience marital stress. As part of some experiments, we ask couples to watch themselves

475

arguing on tape and then tell us what they were thinking when our sensors detected they were flooded. Their answers suggest that men have a greater tendency to have negative thoughts that maintain their distress, while women are more likely to think soothing thoughts that help them calm down and be conciliatory. Men, generally, either think about how righteous and indignant they feel ("I'm going to get even," "I don't have to take this"), which tends to lead to contempt or belligerence. Or they think about themselves as an innocent victim of their wife's wrath or complaint ("Why is she always blaming me?"), which leads to defensiveness. . . .

. . . Frequently feeling flooded leads almost inevitably to distancing yourself from your spouse. That in turn leads you to feel lonely. Without help, the couple will end up divorced or living in a dead marriage, in which they maintain separate, parallel lives in the same home. They may go through the motions of togetherness — attending their children's plays, hosting dinner parties, taking family vacations. But emotionally they no longer feel connected to each other. They have given up.

The Fifth Sign: Failed Repair Attempts

It takes time for the four horsemen and the flooding that comes in their wake to overrun a marriage. And yet divorce can so often be predicted by listening to a single conversation between newlyweds. How can this be? The answer is that by analyzing any disagreement a couple has, you get a good sense of the pattern they tend to follow. A crucial part of that pattern is whether their repair attempts succeed or fail. Repair attempts . . . are efforts the couple makes ("Let's take a break," "Wait, I need to calm down") to de-escalate the tension during a touchy discussion — to put on the brakes so flooding is prevented.

Repair attempts save marriages not just because they decrease emotional tension between spouses, but because by lowering the stress level they also prevent your heart from racing and making you feel flooded. When the four horsemen rule a couple's communication, repair attempts often don't even get noticed. Especially when you're feeling flooded, you're not able to hear a verbal white flag. . . .

That's why I can predict a divorce by hearing only one discussion between a husband and wife. The failure of repair attempts is an accurate marker for an unhappy future. The presence of the four horsemen alone predicts divorce with only an 82 percent accuracy. But when you add in the failure of repair attempts, the accuracy rate reaches into the 90s. This is because some couples who trot out the four horsemen when they argue are also successful at repairing the harm the horsemen cause. Usually in this situation — when the four horsemen are present but the couple's repair attempts are successful — the result is a stable, happy marriage. In fact, 84 percent of the newlyweds who were high on the four horsemen but repaired effectively were in stable, happy marriages six years later. But if there are no repair attempts — or if the attempts are not able to be heard — the marriage is in serious danger.

In emotionally intelligent marriages I hear a wide range of successful repair attempts. Each person has his or her own approach. Olivia and Nathaniel stick out their tongues; other couples laugh or smile or say they're sorry. Even an irritated "Hey, stop yelling at me," or "You're getting off the topic" can defuse a tense situation. All such repair attempts keep a marriage stable because they prevent the four horsemen from moving in for good.

Whether a repair succeeds or fails has very little to do with how eloquent it is and everything to do with the state of the marriage. One happily married couple who taught me this lesson were Hal and Jodie. Because of the nature of his research, Hal, a chemist, would often find out at the last minute that he wouldn't be able to get home for dinner. Although Jodie knew Hal couldn't control his hours, the dinner situation frustrated her. When they discussed the problem in our lab, she pointed out to him that the kids always refused to eat dinner till he got home, so they were often having their dinner very late, which she didn't like. So Hal suggested that she give them a snack to tide them over. Incredulous, Jodie snapped at him: "What do you think I have been doing all along?"

Hal realized that he had screwed up. He had displayed a significant lack of awareness about what went on in his own home and, worse, had insulted his wife's intelligence. In an unhappy marriage this could easily be the grounds for some major league sniping. I waited to see what would happen next. Since all other evidence suggested they were happily married, I anticipated that Hal would use some very skillfully wrought repair attempt. But Hal just gave Jodie a really goofy smile. Jodie burst out laughing, and they went on with their discussion....

I am convinced that far more marriages could be saved than currently are. Even a marriage that is about to hit bottom can be revived with the right kind of help. Sadly, most marriages at this stage get the *wrong* kind. Well-meaning therapists will deluge the couple with advice about negotiating their differences and improving their communication. At one time I would have done the same. At first, when I figured out how to predict divorce, I thought I had found the key to saving marriages. All that was necessary, I presumed, was to teach people how to argue without being overridden by the four horsemen and without getting flooded. Then their repair attempts would succeed, and they could work out their differences.

But like so many experts before me, I was wrong. I was not able to crack the code to saving marriages until I started to analyze what went *right* in happy marriages. After intensely studying happily married couples for as long as sixteen years, I now know that the key to reviving or divorce-proofing a relationship is not in how you handle disagreements but in how you are with each other when you're not fighting. . . .

9   What about Divorce?

"Mrs. Fisher, have you ever thought of divorce?"
"Of divorce, never; of murder, frequently."

— LADY FISHER,
the wife of the
Archbishop of Canterbury

Thus grief still treads upon the heels of pleasure;
Married in haste, we may repent at leisure.

— WILLIAM CONGREVE

Introduction

In this chapter, we broach the sensitive subject of divorce. While modern Americans tend to think of easy divorce as a relatively recent phenomenon, our reading in Deuteronomy demonstrates otherwise. In biblical times, a man could cast off a woman merely because he found "something obnoxious about her."

Christian doctrine on divorce represented a quite radical change from Jewish doctrine, as the reading from the Gospel of St. Matthew shows. Here, Jesus declares the Jewish doctrine "hard-hearted" and warns that "Whosoever shall put away his wife except it be for fornication, and shall marry another, committeth adultery." In the Gospel of St. Mark, Jesus proclaims this very same view of marriage, but does not even permit divorce on the grounds of adultery.

The teachings of Jesus and Paul on the indissolubility of marriage are critical to an understanding of both the Catholic Church's proscription on divorce and the evolution of its view of marriage. By the time of St. Thomas Aquinas, the idea of marriage as a sacrament had matured. Marriage was seen not only as a union of natural purposes, but also as an avenue of grace which, once opened, must forever remain open. The short reading by Aquinas included here compares the union of man and woman in marriage with the union of Christ and the Church. Thus, in forbidding divorce, the Catholic Church underlined its elevation of marriage to holy purpose, and with this elevation emphasized both the dignity of the aspiration to marriage and the critical importance of sound spousal choice. (It should be noted that the Catholic Church, in forbidding divorce, does not forbid marital dissolution, the grounds for which have traditionally been coerced marriages, fundamental misrepresentation of character or faith and, of course, wrongful failure to pay the "conjugal debt.")

The Reformation brought a very different take on divorce. Since marriage was no longer viewed as a sacrament, but rather as a divinely ordained civil estate, it might under certain circumstances be dissoluble. The prominent sixteenth-century Protestant theologian Martin Bucer's views on the subject of divorce, outlined in his work, *De Regno Christi*, are more permissive than Luther's or Calvin's, but they are deduced from the same basic principle: namely, that loving, companionate marriages are the very basis of a healthy civic life, and that where marriages cease to reflect the cooperative purposes of civic life, they threaten to undermine the entire community.

The selection from the Qur'an that follows reflects an entirely different religious perspective on divorce, a perspective that focuses on marriage as repositories of property, family distinction, and personal honor rather than as the pillar of communal life. The prophet Muhammad exhorts his followers not to divorce their wives capriciously "for God hears all and knows everything." Divorce may be revoked up to two times after being pronounced, and during the period of waiting for divorce, husbands are encouraged to reconcile with their wives. "Keep [your wives] honorably or let them go with honor," warns Muhammad. In fact, while Islamic law has traditionally been far more lenient with regard to divorce than the law of Christian countries, divorce was never very common among the followers of Islam. The Islamic tradition taught that divorce was an "abomination" to God, but a necessary concession to human weakness. Thus, Islam provided means for arbitration of a troubled marriage, and protected women from the worst socio-economic effects of divorce. It would be important to underline here that for many centuries Islamic women enjoyed greater legal privileges that their Western counterparts. They could hold and manage their property separately in marriage and could leave their marriages with that property intact. In the event they were divorced by their husbands, the Qur'an explicitly enjoined their ex-husbands not to stand in the way of remarriage. Finally, women could initiate divorce, if unhappy in marriage.

Similar protections in the event of divorce were accorded women in the Jewish tradition, as we learn from Maimonides in his twelfth-century explication of Jewish legal code. The "ketubah" (marriage contract) protected the property a woman brought into the marriage, and provided as well an agreed-upon sum to be paid to her in the event of divorce — unless, of course, she had committed adultery or publicly defied the laws of piety. For Jews the economic disadvantages of divorce were considerable enough that very few men could afford to divorce capriciously. Remarriage for both parties was encouraged, so that no lasting social stigma tended to be attached to divorce. But remarriage was delayed so as not to endanger the welfare of any unborn children of a dissolved union. Jewish women traditionally have been able to initiate divorces, but not by simply announcing their intention to divorce and showing cause. They had to request a bill of divorce from their husbands by bringing suit in court. Jewish courts were bound to compel a man to divorce his wife if he had not fulfilled his basic marital obligations — the provision of food, clothing, and conjugal rights — or if he repeatedly mistreated her, demonstrated moral depravity, or squandered her property. Women could also demand a bill of divorce if, after marriage, their husbands had become sexually repulsive for reasons of illness, or had taken to practicing certain unattractive professions. Judaism, like Islam, has never been pro-divorce, but it has always acknowledged the possibility of marital failure, has respected mutual desires for marital dissolution, and has taken pains to facilitate the ability of unhappily married men and women to seek marital fulfillment elsewhere.

In ancient China, the penal code stated that a man who cast off his wife without proving one of seven "causes" received eighty lashes. According to E. Westermarck, the seven causes were "barrenness, lasciviousness, disregard of the husband's parents, talkativeness, thievish propensities, envious and suspicious temper, and inveterate infirmity. Yet none of these seven causes," Westermarck goes on to say, could "justify a divorce if the wife has mourned three years for the husband's parents, if the family has become rich since the marriage . . . or if the wife had no parents living to receive her back again."[1] In practice, however, many Chinese women were cast off for no other reason than that they displeased their husbands. Legally, Chinese women had no right, themselves, to initiate divorce. The situation was similar in Japan until the last century, but not in India, because according to the Hindu tradition, marriage was a sacrament, and therefore indissoluble.

The selections from Chinese literature included here were composed approximately 1500 years apart. "Old Poem" was probably written in the late second century A.D.; the prologue to "The Lady Yu-Nu" belongs in a collection of tales compiled in the seventeenth century. Yet, each work retains a freshness of wisdom and insight that resonates for the modern reader. In "Old Poem," a man accidentally meets his ex-wife. When she asks him whether his "new wife" pleases him, he is forced to admit that the "old wife" was better. In the prologue to "Lady Yu-Nu" a woman impatient with living in poverty abandons her husband and marries another man. Her first husband rises to wealth and fame, but does not remarry, nor does he ever renege on his obligation to support and protect her, even though she has left him. These two very amusing works show us that divorce is not always the best answer to marital complaints. Nor does it necessarily mean a final severing of moral or emotional ties.

In Locke's *Two Treatises,* the seventeenth-century political philosopher and theologian puts forth an argument that has had enormous influence on American divorce law: that marriage should be regarded as a private contract. Although a devout Christian, Locke probably sought to make it easier for men and women who experienced no "Communion of Interest" to separate from each other. At a time when divorce was all but impossible in England, Locke asserted that society's major interest in marriage was in the procreation and the upbringing of children. Although Locke never said this directly, the implications of his argument were that childless couples and couples whose children were grown and self-supporting might be allowed to divorce if they so chose.

The negative effects of divorce on children have been a serious concern for all modern philosophers and legal thinkers on the subject of divorce. In his famous essay, *Marriage and Morals,* the British philosopher Bertrand Russell revisited the importance of "stability in marriage" for children. Writing in

485

1929, at a time when there were many public calls for the easing of restrictions on divorce in Britain, Russell warned that while divorce might well be made easier to procure, it should never be made too easy; the more divorce, the more likely growing numbers of children would suffer the consequences of fatherlessness. Russell's ruminations on divorce serve as a useful critical summary of the history of the institution of divorce in Western culture. They also offer a sharply critical, if unconventional, review of the traditional grounds for divorce. (Russell, for example, did not consider infidelity a justifiable ground for divorce.) In an age of liberal divorce laws and frequent divorce, Russell's defense of marriage as a child-rearing bond gives us pause for thought. The underlying inference of his argument — that society is better off promoting stable marriages than stressing happy marriages — has been borne out by contemporary research, which has shown the enormous costs of divorce-on-demand to child well-being.

Indeed, this is the subject of the selection that concludes our examination of divorce. Here psychologist Judith Wallerstein reflects on the tragic legacy of the modern "divorce culture" — alegacy threatening the well-being of children of divorce well into adulthood.

DEUTERONOMY

The Book of Deuteronomy, the last of the Five Books of Moses that comprise the core of the Old Testament, is composed of several parts: first, a history of the people of Israel between the Exodus and the death of Moses; second, a recapitulation of the laws of Israel; and third, the story of the death of Moses. Biblical scholars attribute the book to the seventh century B.C., and assume that it represented the first attempt to record Jewish law.

Deuteronomy 24:1-5

1 When a man hath taken a wife, and married her, and it come to pass that she find no favour in his eyes, because he hath found some uncleanness in her; then let him write her a bill of divorcement, and give it in her hand, and send her out of his house.

2 And when she is departed out of his house, she may go and be another man's wife.

3 And if the latter husband hate her, and write her a bill of divorcement, and giveth it in her hand, and sendeth her out of his house; or if the latter husband die, which took her to be his wife;

4 Her former husband, which sent her away, may not take her again to be his wife, after that she is defiled; for that is abomination before the LORD; and thou shalt not cause the land to sin, which the LORD thy God giveth thee for an inheritance.

5 When a man hath taken a new wife, he shall not go out to war, neither

shall he be charged with any business; but he shall be free at home one year, and shall cheer up his wife which he hath taken.

THE GOSPEL ACCORDING TO ST. MATTHEW;
THE GOSPEL ACCORDING TO ST. MARK

The term "Gospel" refers to the New Testament's biographies of Jesus. The Gospel of Matthew appears in the New Testament as the First Book, but is actually considered to have been written after the Gospel of St. Mark, which is the oldest source on Jesus' life and preachings. Because Matthew contains more references to the Old Testament than the other three Gospels, Matthew is considered to have been written with the conscious aim of convincing the Jews that Jesus was the promised Messiah, his new law the rightful successor to the old Mosaic Law.

Matthew 19:1-11

1 And it came to pass, that when Jesus had finished these sayings, he departed from Galilee, and came into the coasts of Judaea beyond Jordan;
2 And great multitudes followed him; and he healed them there.
3 The Pharisees also came unto him, tempting him, and saying unto him, Is it lawful for a man to put away his wife for every cause?
4 And he answered and said unto them, Have ye not read, that he which made them at the beginning made them male and female,
5 And said, For this cause shall a man leave father and mother, and shall cleave to his wife; and they twain shall be one flesh?
6 Wherefore they are no more twain, but one flesh. What therefore God hath joined together, let not man put asunder.
7 They say unto him, Why did Moses then command to give a writing of divorcement, and to put her away?

8 He saith unto them, Moses because of the hardness of your hearts suffered you to put away your wives; but from the beginning it was not so.

9 And I say unto you, Whosoever shall put away his wife, except it be for fornication, and shall marry another, committeth adultery; and whoso marrieth her which is put away doth commit adultery.

10 His disciples say unto him, If the case of the man be so with his wife, it is not good to marry.

11 But he said unto them, All men cannot receive this saying, save they to whom it is given.

Mark 10:2-12

2 And the Pharisees came to him, and asked him, Is it lawful for a man to put away his wife? tempting him.

3 And he answered and said unto them, What did Moses command you?

4 And they said, Moses suffered to write a bill of divorcement, and to put her away.

5 And Jesus answered and said unto them, For the hardness of your heart he wrote you this precept.

6 But from the beginning of the creation God made them male and female.

7 For this cause shall a man leave his father and mother, and cleave to his wife;

8 And they twain shall be one flesh; so then they are no more twain, but one flesh.

9 What therefore God hath joined together, let not man put asunder.

10 And in the house his disciples asked him again of the same matter.

11 And he saith unto them, Whosoever shall put away his wife, and marry another, committeth adultery against her.

12 And if a woman shall put away her husband, and be married to another, she committeth adultery.

ST. THOMAS AQUINAS

The *Summa contra Gentiles* is Aquinas's great apology for the Christian faith. It is directed to both Christians and non-Christians, and curiously reflects the influence of the Jewish philosopher Maimonides, who states that there are two separate spheres of knowledge accessible to us: reason and revelation. In the *Summa contra Gentiles,* Aquinas separated those elements of Christian doctrine that could be rationally argued and justified from those that must be accepted as revealed knowledge, on faith alone. Book Four of the *Summa,* entitled "Salvation," deals with the latter.

Salvation, Book Four of the Summa contra Gentiles

Chapter 78. On the Sacrament of Matrimony

[1] Now, we grant that by the sacraments men are restored to grace; nonetheless, they are not immediately restored to immortality. We have given the reason for this.[1] But things which are corruptible cannot be perpetuated except by generation. Since, then, the people of the faithful had to be perpetuated unto the end of the world, this had to be done by generation, by which, also, the human species is perpetuated.

[2] But let us consider this: When something is ordered to different ends there must be differing principles directing it to the end, for the end is proportioned to the agent. Human generation, of course, is ordered to many things; namely, to the perpetuity of the species and to the perpetuity of some political

good — the perpetuity of a people in some state for example. It is also ordered to the perpetuity of the Church, which consists in the collection of the faithful. Accordingly, generation of this kind must be subject to a diversity of directions. Therefore, so far as it is ordered to the good of nature, which is the perpetuity of the species, it is directed to the end by nature inclining to this end; thus, one calls it a duty of nature. But, so far as generation is ordered to a political good, it is subject to the ordering of civil law. Then, so far as it is ordered to the good of the Church, it must be subject to the government of the Church. But things which are dispensed to the people by the ministers of the Church are called sacraments. Matrimony, then, in that it consists in the union of a husband and wife purposing to generate and educate offspring for the worship of God, is a sacrament of the Church; hence, also, a certain blessing on those marrying is given by the ministers of the Church.

[3] And as in the other sacraments by the thing done outwardly a sign is made of a spiritual thing, so, too, in this sacrament by the union of husband and wife a sign of the union of Christ and the Church is made; in the Apostle's words: "This is a great sacrament; but I speak in Christ and in the church" (Eph. 5:32).

[4] And because the sacraments effect that of which they are made signs, one must believe that in this sacrament a grace is conferred on those marrying, and that by this grace they are included in the union of Christ and the Church, which is most especially necessary to them, that in this way in fleshly and earthly things they may purpose not to be disunited from Christ and the Church.

[5] Since, then, the union of husband and wife gives a sign of the union of Christ and the Church, that which makes the sign must correspond to that whose sign it is. Now, the union of Christ and the Church is a union of one to one to be held forever. For there is one Church, as the Canticle (6:8) says: "One is My dove, My perfect one." And Christ will never be separated from His Church, for He Himself says: "Behold I am with you always, even to the consummation of the world" (Matt. 28:20); and, further: "we shall be always with the Lord" (1 Thess. 4:16), as the Apostle says. Necessarily, then, matrimony as a sacrament of the Church is a union of one man to one woman to be held indivisibly, and this is included in the faithfulness by which the man and wife are bound to one another.

[6] Thus, then, there are three goods of matrimony as a sacrament of the Church: namely, offspring to be accepted and educated for the worship of God; fidelity by which one man is bound to one wife; and the sacrament — and, in accord with this — there is indivisibility in the marriage union, in so far as it is a sacrament of the union of Christ and the Church.

[7] Now, all the other things one ought to consider in matrimony we have dealt with in Book III.[2]

MARTIN BUCER

Martin Bucer (1491-1551) was born in Alsace and educated in Heidelberg. After reading Erasmus and meeting Luther, he left the Dominican order and married. Bucer dedicated great efforts to unify the theological principles of the different confessional groups in the early Reformation. Because he refused to accept the introduction of the Interim that restored Catholic worship in Strasbourg, he left the continent of Europe and settled in England in 1549, where he became religious advisor to Edward VI. Bucer's writings on divorce were made famous by Milton's 1644 translation of them in a pamphlet entitled *The Judgement of Martin Bucer*.

De Regno Christi

Chapter XLIII

That to grant divorce for all the causes which have bin hitherto brought, disagrees not from the words of Christ naming only the cause of adultery.

Now wee must see how these things can stand with the words of our Saviour, who seems directly to forbid all divorce[1] except it be for adultery. To the understanding wherof, wee must ever remember this: That in the words of our Saviour there can be no contrarietie. That his words and answers are not to be stretcht beyond the question propos'd. That our Saviour did not there purpose to treat of all the causes for which it might be lawfull to divorce and marry again; *for then that in the Corinthians of marrying again without guilt of adultery could not be added.*[2] That it is not good for that man to be alone who hath not the special gift from above.[3] That it is good for every such one to be married, that he may shun fornication. With regard to these principles let us see what our Lord answered to the tempting Pharises about divorce, and second mariage, and how farre his answer doth extend.

First, No man who is not very contentious, will deny that the Pharises askt our Lord whether it were lawfull to put away such a wife, as was truly, and according to Gods law, to be counted a wife; that is, such a one as would dwell with her husband, and both would & could perform the necessary duties of wedlock tolerably. But shee who will not dwell with her husband, is not put away by him, but goes of her self: and shee who denies to be a meet help, or to be so, hath made her self unfit by open misdemeanours, or through incurable impotencies cannot be able, is not by the law of God to be esteem'd a wife; as hath bin shewn both from the first institution, and other places of Scripture. Neither certainly would the Pharises propound a question concerning such an unconjugall wife; *for thir depravation of the law had brought them to that passe, as to think a man had right to put away his wife for any cause, though never so slight.*[4] Since therfore it is manifest that Christ answer'd the Pharises concerning a fit and meet wife according to the law of God, whom he forbid to divorce for any cause but fornication. Who sees not that it is a wickednes so to wrest and extend that answer of his, as if it forbad to divorce her who hath already forsak'n, or hath lost the place and dignitie of a wife by deserved infamy,[5] *or hath undertak'n to be that which she hath not naturall ability to be.*[6]

This truth is so powerfull that it hath mov'd the Papists to grant their kind of divorce for other causes besides adultery, as for ill usage, and the not performing of conjugal dutie; and to separate from bed and board for these causes, which is as much divorce, as they grant for adultery.

But some perhaps will object, that though it be yeilded, that our Lord granted divorce not only for adultery, yet it is not certain that he permitted mariage after divorce, unlesse for that only cause. I answer, first, that the sentence of divorce, and second mariage, is one and the same. So that when the right of divorce is evinc't to belong not only to the cause of fornication, the power of second mariage is also prov'd to be not limited to that cause only; and that most evidently, when as the holy Ghost, *I Cor. 7.*[7] so frees the deserted party from bondage, as that he may not only send a just divorce in case of desertion, but may seek another marriage.

Lastly, seeing God will not that any should live in danger of fornication and utter ruine for the default of another, and hath commanded the husband to send away with a bill of divorce her whom he could not love, it is impossible that the charge of adultery should belong to him who for lawfull causes divorces and marries, or to her who marries after she hath bin unjustly rejected, or to him who receavs her without all fraud to the former wedlock.[8] For this were a horrid blasphemy against God, so to interpret his words, as to make him dissent from himself;[9] for who sees not a flat contradiction in this, to enthrall blameles men and women to miseries and injuries, under a false and soothing title of mariage, and yet to declare by his Apostle that a brother or sister is not under bondage in such cases. No lesse doe these two things conflict with themselvs, to enforce the innocent and faultlcs to endure the pain and misery of anothers perversnes, or els to live in unavoidable temptation; and to affirm elswhere that he lays on no man the burden of another mans sin, nor doth constrain any man to the endangering of his soul.[10]

Chapter XLVII

The Conclusion of this Treatise.

These things, most renowned King, I have brought together, both to explain for what causes the unhappy, but somctimes most necessary help of divorce ought to be granted, according to Gods Word, by Princes and Rulers: as also to explain how the words of Christ doe consent with such a grant. I have bin large indeed both in handling those Oracles of God, and in laying down those certain principles, which he who will know what the mind of God is in this matter, must ever think on, and remember. But if wee consider what mist and obscuritie hath been powrd out by Antichrist upon this question, and how deep this pernicious contempt of wedlock, and admiration of single life, ev'n in those who are not call'd therto, hath sunk into many mens persuasions, I fear lest all that hath bin said, be hardly anough to persuade such that they would cease at length to make themselvs wiser & holier then God himself, in beeing so severe to grant lawfull mariage, and so easie to connive at all, not only whordoms, but deflowrings, and adulteries. When as among the people of God, no whordom[11] was to be tolerated.

Our Lord Jesus Christ, who came to destroy the works of Satan, send down his Spirit upon all Christians, and principally upon Christian Governours both in Church and Common-wealth (for of the cleer judgement of your royall Majesty I nothing doubt, revolving the Scripture so often as yee doe) that they may acknowledge how much they provoke the anger of God against us, when as all kind of unchastity is tolerated, fornications and adulteries winkt at: But holy and honourable wedlock is oft withheld by the meer per-suasion of Antichrist, from such as without this remedy, cannot preserve them-selves from damnation! For none who hath but a spark of honesty will deny that Princes and States ought to use diligence toward the maintaining of pure and honest life among all men, without which[12] all justice, all fear of God, and true religion decayes.

And who knows not that chastity and purenes of life, can never be restor'd, or continu'd in the Common-wealth, unlesse it be first establisht in private houses, from whence the whole breed of men[13] is to come forth. To ef-fect this, no wise man[14] can doubt that it is necessary for Princes and Magis-trates first with severity to punish whordom and adultery;[15] next to see that mariages be lawfully contracted, and in the Lord, then that they be faithfully kept; and lastly, when that unhappines urges, that they be lawfully dissolv'd,[16] and other mariage granted, according as the law of God, and of nature, and the Constitutions of pious Princes have decreed; as I have shewn both by evident autorities of Scripture, together with the writings of the ancient Fathers, and other testimonies. Only the Lord grant that we may learn to preferre his ever just and saving Word, before the Comments of Antichrist, too deeply rooted in many, and the false and blasphemous exposition of our Saviours words. *Amen.*

THE QUR'AN

The Qur'an, the sacred text of Islam, contains the often-passionate revelations of Muhammad, preacher and founder of the Islamic religion (b. 570?). The text of the Qur'an was codified in the seventh century, soon after Muhammad's death. This work, comprising 114 chapters (or "suras"), is ordered by chapter length, from the longest to the shortest. The excerpts here are from two of the longer chapters, probably revelations from late in Muhammad's life. Muhammad, who died in 632, only perceived his calling as prophet of the Arab nation at the age of 40. Moving from his native Mecca, where his preachings were rejected, to Medina, he organized a small but determined band of followers who rapidly disseminated his religious ideas, often by the use of force. Muhammad has the reputation of having collected wives somewhat acquisitively. But his first marriage, to a woman much older than himself, and to whom he was greatly devoted, was monogamous. He practiced polygamy only after his first wife's death.

The Qur'an 2:223-42; 4:35

Women are your fields: go, then, into your fields whence you please. Do good works and fear God. Bear in mind that you shall meet Him. Give good tidings to the believers.

2:224 Do not make God, when you swear by Him, a means to prevent you from dealing justly, from guarding yourselves against evil, and from making peace among men. God hears all and knows all.

225 God will not call you to account for that which is inadvertent in your oaths. But He will take you to task for that which is intended in your hearts. God is forgiving and lenient.

Those that renounce their wives on oath must wait four months. If they change their minds, God is forgiving and merciful; but if they decide to divorce them, know that God hears all and knows all.

228 Divorced women must wait, keeping themselves from men, three menstrual courses. It is unlawful for them, if they believe in God and the Last Day, to hide what God has created in their wombs: in which case their husbands would do well to take them back, should they desire reconciliation.

Women shall with justice have rights similar to those exercised against them, although men have a status above women. God is mighty and wise.

229 Divorce may be pronounced twice, and then a woman must be retained in honour or allowed to go with kindness. It is unlawful for husbands to take from them anything they have given them, unless both fear that they may not be able to keep within the bounds set by God; in which case it shall be no offence for either of them if the wife ransoms herself.

These are the bounds set by God; do not transgress them. Those that transgress the bounds of God are wrongdoers.

230 If a man divorces his wife, he shall not remarry her until she has wedded another man and been divorced by him; in which case it shall be no offence for either of them to return to the other, if they think that they can keep within the bounds set by God.

Such are the bounds of God. He makes them plain to men of knowledge.

231 When you have renounced your wives and they have reached the end of their waiting period, either retain them in honour or let them go with kindness. But you shall not retain them in order to harm them or to wrong them. Whoever does this wrongs his own soul.

Do not make game of God's revelations. Remember the favour God has bestowed upon you, and the Book and the wisdom He has revealed for your instruction. Fear God and know that God has knowledge of all things.

If a man has renounced his wife and she has reached the end of her waiting period, do not prevent her from remarrying her husband if they have come to an honourable agreement. This is enjoined on every one of you who believes in God and the Last Day; it is more honourable for you and more chaste. God knows, but you know not.

233 Mothers shall give suck to their children for two whole years if the father wishes the sucking to be completed. They must be maintained and clothed in a reasonable manner by the child's father. None should be charged with more than one can bear. A mother should not be allowed to suffer on ac-

count of her child, nor should a father on account of his child. The same duties devolve upon the father's heir. But if, after consultation, they choose by mutual consent to wean the child, they shall incur no guilt. Nor shall it be any offence for you if you prefer to have a nurse for your children, provided that you pay her what you promise, according to usage. Have fear of God and know that God is cognizant of all your actions.

234   Widows shall wait, keeping themselves apart from men, for four months and ten days after their husbands' death. When they have reached the end of their waiting period, it shall be no offence for you to let them do whatever they choose for themselves, provided that it is decent. God is cognizant of all your actions.

It shall be no offence for you openly to propose marriage to such women or to cherish them in your hearts. God knows that you will remember them. Do not arrange to meet them in secret, and, if you do, speak to them honourably. But you shall not consummate the marriage before the end of their waiting period. Know that God has knowledge of all your thoughts. Therefore take heed and bear in mind that God is forgiving and lenient.

236   It shall be no offence for you to divorce your wives before the marriage is consummated or the dowry settled. Provide for them with fairness; the rich man according to his means and the poor man according to his. This is binding on righteous men.   237   If you divorce them before the marriage is consummated, but after their dowry has been settled, give them the half of their dowry, unless they or the husband agree to waive it. But it is more proper that the husband should waive it. Do not forget to show kindness to each other. God is cognizant of all your actions.

238   Attend regularly to your prayers, including the middle prayer, and stand up with all devotion before God. When you are exposed to danger pray on foot or while riding; and when you are restored to safety remember God, as He has taught you what you did not know.

You shall bequeath your widows a year's maintenance without causing them to leave their homes; but if they leave of their own accord, no blame shall be attached to you for any course they may deem fit to pursue. God is mighty and wise.   241   Reasonable provision shall also be made for divorced women. That is incumbent on righteous men.

Thus God makes known to you His revelations that you may grow in understanding.

4:35   If you fear a breach between a man and his wife, appoint an arbiter from his people and another from hers. If they wish to be reconciled God will bring them together again. Surely God is all-knowing and wise.

MAIMONIDES

Maimonides, Rabbi Moses Ben Maimon (1135-1204), is known to many Jews as "Rambam." He is considered to be the greatest Jewish legal scholar, ethicist, and scriptural commentator of the Middle Ages; but he was also a gifted doctor, logician, and astronomer. Born in Cordova, he and his family were forced into exile during the Arab invasions. They finally settled, after ten years of wandering, in Cairo, where Maimonides became the sultan's personal physician. Maimonides' most important contribution to Jewish thought was the *Guide to the Perplexed,* which became a model for Thomas Aquinas in its reconciliation of philosophy with religion. The selection included here is from his fourteen-book commentary on the Mishna, the Jewish legal code that itself formed the core of Jewish commentary on the Five Books of Moses. It might be mentioned here that Maimonides has been considered the "liberator of Jewish women," since it is his interpretation of Jewish law that forbade once and for all the practice of polygamy among Jews.

The Code of Maimonides, Book Four: The Book of Women

Treatise I: Marriage

Chapter XXIV

1. If a man marries a barren woman and has no children by her, nor another wife by whom he might have children, then, notwithstanding that he must be

compelled to dismiss her, she has the same status as any other wife, and is entitled to her kĕtubbah[1] and to the additional stipulations attached to it. The husband too is entitled to the same rights as he would be entitled to with regard to any other wife of his.

2. If, however, a man marries a woman without being aware of any defect in her, and she is then found to be barren or forbidden to him by a negative commandment; or likewise, if he marries a woman of secondary degree of consanguinity, whether knowingly or unknowingly, she is entitled to neither the statutory kĕtubbah nor to any of the stipulations additional thereto. She is, however, entitled to the supplementary amount. She is not entitled to maintenance, even after his death. And when they are forced to separate, she is not entitled to recover from the husband for the usufruct of her property.

3. Why are these women not entitled to the statutory kĕtubbah, yet are entitled to the supplementary amount? Because the statutory kĕtubbah was instituted by the Sages in order that the husband should not think lightly of dismissing his wife; since in case he was not aware of her defect, she is not entitled to statutory kĕtubbah.

As for the supplementary amount, he himself has assumed an obligation for it so long as she is willing to stay with him, and she has in fact kept her part of the agreement and given him the benefit of her person, and is staying with him. It is the Torah that has forbidden her to him; what can she do about it? That is why she is entitled to the supplementary amount. It is not her own actions that are responsible for her becoming forbidden after the marriage; rather, she was forbidden to him before.

4. Why did the Sages, in the case of a woman of secondary degree of consanguinity, make no distinction between the husband who was aware of her defect and the one who was not aware of it, but rather ruled that she is not entitled to the statutory kĕtubbah in all circumstances? Because she is forbidden to him by Scribal law only,[2] and for this reason they reinforced this prohibition.

If, however, he marries a woman forbidden to him by a negative commandment, and is aware of her defect, or if he marries a woman forbidden to him by a positive commandment, and is or is not aware of her defect, she is entitled to her kĕtubbah. For in the case of a woman forbidden by a negative commandment, when he married her even though he was aware of her defect, he showed thereby his willingness to maintain her out of his property. As for a woman forbidden by a positive commandment, in her case the prohibition is a light one. Both of them are therefore entitled to maintenance after his death.

Similarly, if she borrows in order to provide for her maintenance, he is liable for repayment. And when he is compelled to dismiss her, she is entitled to recover from him for the usufruct of all of her property. . . .

6. A woman who has played the harlot while under her husband is not entitled to a kĕṯubbah, neither to the statutory nor to the supplementary amount, nor to any of the stipulations of the kĕṯubbah, because it is her own actions which have caused her to become forbidden to her husband.

7. What is the rule concerning these women in regard to their dowry?[3] Any woman whose dowry is still in existence, may take what is hers and go her way, even if she had played the harlot. If she is a forbidden relative of the secondary degree, or one of those prohibited by a positive commandment, whether her husband was aware of it or not; or if she is barren or forbidden by a negative commandment, and he was aware of it, she has, as far as her dowry is concerned, the same status as any other wife. In the case of iron sheep property, he is liable for it. In the case of mĕlog̱[4] property, whatever was stolen or lost, the loss is hers, and he is not liable for repayment.

8. If she is barren or forbidden by a negative commandment, and he was not aware of it, whatever was lost, or stolen, or worn out, or worn threadbare out of iron sheep property, need not be repaid by the husband, because she had given him permission to keep these with him.

As for whatever was lost or stolen out of mĕlog̱ property, he is liable for repayment, which is the reverse of the rule governing all other women; for inasmuch as there is no complete matrimony here, he did not acquire any rights to her mĕlog̱ property. . . .

10. A woman who has played the harlot while under her husband is not entitled to her kĕṯubbah, neither to the statutory nor to the supplementary amount. . . .

Not only a woman who has played the harlot, but also one who has transgressed the law of Moses or Jewish practice, or one who is dismissed because of her ill repute, has no kĕṯubbah, neither the statutory nor the supplementary amount nor any of the stipulations of the kĕṯubbah.

Each of these women may take what there is on hand of her dowry and go her way, and the husband is not liable for repayment of anything that he has caused to depreciate or has lost.

11. The following acts, if committed by a woman, render her guilty of transgressing the law of Moses: going out into the street with the hair of her head uncovered, making vows or swearing oaths and not fulfilling them, indulging in sexual intercourse during menstruation, failing to set aside her dough offering, or serving her husband prohibited food, that is, not only such food as swarming and creeping creatures or carrion, but also untithed food.

How can this become known? If, for example, she says to her husband, "So-and-so, the priest, has regularized this produce for me," or "The woman So-and-so has set aside the offering from this dough in my behalf," or "So-and-so, the Sage, has declared to me that this stain is ritually clean," and if after he eats this food, or has intercourse with her, he inquires of So-and-so, and is told "These things never did happen." The same is true if she is presumed by her neighbors to be menstruating, but tells her husband, "I am clean," and he then has intercourse with her.

12. And what constitutes Jewish practice? It is the custom of modesty as observed by the daughters of Israel, and the following acts, if indulged in by a woman, render her guilty of transgressing Jewish practice: going out into the street or into an open alley with head uncovered and without the veil worn by all women, even if her hair is covered with a kerchief; spinning in the street, with a rose or a similar ornament in front of her face, on her forehead, or on her cheeks, in the manner of brazen heathen women; spinning in the street, with her arms exposed to the public; frolicking with young men; demanding intercourse from her husband in a voice so loud that her neighbors can hear her discussing sexual matters; cursing her father-in-law in her husband's presence.

13. Ezra ordained that a woman should always wear drawers in her home for the sake of modesty. If she does not wear them, however, she is not transgressing the law of Moses, and therefore does not forfeit her kĕtubbah.

Thus also, if she goes from courtyard to courtyard within the same alley with her hair uncovered, she does not transgress the law, so long as her hair is covered with a kerchief.

14. The woman who thus transgresses the law forfeits her kĕtubbah only after due warning and on the testimony of witnesses. If she transgresses while she and her husband are alone, and he knows that she is transgressing, and warns her, but without witnesses being present, and if she then transgresses again, he thereupon claiming, "She transgressed after due warning," and she claiming, "I did not transgress at all," or "He did not warn me," the rule is as follows: If he wishes to dismiss her, he must pay her the kĕtubbah after she swears an oath that she did not transgress; for should she admit that she had transgressed after this warning, she would be entitled to nothing.

15. How is a woman to be dismissed on the ground of ill repute? For example, if witnesses testify that she has done something exceedingly unseemly, indicating that a transgression has been committed, even though there is no clear evidence of harlotry.

How so? If, for example, she is alone in the courtyard, and people seeing a spice-peddler come out, immediately at the moment of his exit enter and find her rising from the couch and putting on her trousers or tying her belt, or find moist saliva above the canopy; or if both of them come out of a dark place, or help one another to ascend from a pit, or the like; or if they see him kiss her at the opening of her chemise, or see them kiss or hug each other, or if the two of them enter a place one after the other and shut the doors, or act in a similar manner. In any case such as these, if the husband wishes to dismiss her, she may be dismissed without her kĕtubbah, and no warning is required.

16. In the case of the woman who has transgressed the Mosaic law or deviated from Jewish practice, as well as the one who has done something unseemly, the husband may not be compelled to divorce her, and if he wishes to retain her, he may do so. But even if he does not dismiss her, she is not entitled to her kĕtubbah. For the Sages have instituted the kĕtubbah in order that the husband should not think lightly of dismissing his wife; but in this they were concerned only for the virtuous daughters of Israel. As for these dissolute ones, this safeguard is not for them; on the contrary, let the husband think lightly of dismissing such a one.

17. If a man sees his wife play the harlot, or if one of his or her relatives, in whom he places credence and reliance, tells him that she has played the harlot — whether the informant is a man or a woman — once his mind is firm in the belief that the information is true, he is obligated to dismiss her, and is forbidden to have intercourse with her; he must, however, pay her her kĕtubbah.

If she admits to him that she had played the harlot, she must be dismissed without her kĕtubbah. Therefore, if only he himself had witnessed her misconduct, he must make her swear an oath, while holding a sacred object, that she had not played the harlot while under him, and only then may she claim her kĕtubbah. If, however, the witness is someone else, the husband cannot subject her to an oath, unless she is already subject to an oath for some other reason, in which case this matter may be added on to it also.

18. If a woman tells her husband that she has, while under him, played the harlot of her own free will, no attention need be paid to her statement, since she may have cast her eyes upon another man. She does, however, forfeit her kĕtubbah, both the statutory and the supplementary amount, as well as her right to worn-out garments, seeing that she has admitted harlotry.

But if he believes her, and places reliance in her words, he is obligated to divorce her. The court, however, may not compel a man to divorce his wife for any of these causes, unless two witnesses come forth to testify that his wife has indeed played the harlot in their presence, and of her own free will. Only thereafter may they compel him to divorce her.

19. If a woman has, while under her husband, played the harlot unwittingly or under duress, she is permitted to him, as it is said, *neither she be seized* (Num. 5:13), implying that if she was seized, she is permitted, whether she was raped by a heathen or by an Israelite.

Any woman subjected to duress at the beginning of intercourse is permitted to her husband, even if she finally acquiesced in it, and even if she said,

"Leave him alone, for had he not overpowered me, I would have hired him to do it." For she has no more than succumbed to impulse, and at the outset she was indeed subjected to duress.

20. Women kidnapped by robbers are regarded the same as captive women subjected to duress, and are therefore permitted to their husbands. If the robbers had let them go unmolested, and they went along with them of their own volition, they are considered guilty of willful misconduct, and are therefore forbidden to their husbands.

The same rule applies to both the woman acting unwittingly and the one acting under duress, because an unwitting act has an element of duress in it.

21. When does this apply? When her husband is an Israelite. The wife of a priest, however, who has acted unwittingly or under duress, is forbidden to her husband, because in either case she has acquired the status of a harlot, and he is forbidden to a harlot, as will be explained in the Laws Concerning Forbidden Intercourse.

22. The wife of either an Israelite or a priest, if raped, retains her kĕtubbah, the statutory as well as the supplementary amount, and does not forfeit any part of it. The priest, however, must be compelled to pay her her kĕtubbah and divorce her. . . .

Chapter XXV

1. If a man marries a woman without stipulating any conditions, and she is found to be subject to vows, she may be dismissed without her kĕtubbah, either the statutory or the supplementary amount.

What vows are meant here? Not to eat meat, or not to drink wine, or not to adorn herself with colored garments. The same applies to other ornamental objects with which it is the local custom for all women to adorn themselves. If, however, she is found to be subject to a vow other than these, she does not forfeit anything.

2. Thus also, if a man marries a woman without stipulating any conditions, and she is found to be afflicted with one of the female defects which we have already described, and if the husband was unaware of this defect, nor did he hear of it, so that he might have accepted it, she may be dismissed without her kĕtubbah, either the statutory or the supplementary amount.

How so? If there is a public bathhouse in the city, and if he has relatives, he cannot say, "I was not aware of these defects," even if these are hidden defects, because he is bound to investigate the matter through his female relatives, and the presumption is that he had heard of the defects and accepted them.

If there is no public bathhouse there, or if he has no relatives, he may put in a claim respecting concealed defects. Epilepsy recurring at definite times is classed as a concealed defect.

In case of obvious defects, however, he has no claim, inasmuch as everyone can see them and is bound to tell him. The presumption is, therefore, that he had heard of them and became reconciled to them.

Now it is obvious that this rule applies only to those places where it is the custom for women to walk about in the street with their faces uncovered, and where everybody knows them well enough to say, "This one is the daughter of So-and-so, and that one is the sister of So-and-so," as is the case in the cities of Edom at the present time.

In those places, however, where it is the custom for women not to go out in the street at all, and where a woman would go out to the public bathhouse only at night and disguised, so that no one can see her except her own female relatives, he may put in a claim respecting even obvious defects, provided that there is no public bathhouse there, and that he has no female relative to examine her.

If, however, there is a public bathhouse in that city, and it is the custom there for women not to go out with uncovered faces, he cannot protest if he has a female relative, inasmuch as everyone can see her naked in the bathhouse. If, however, it is their custom to go about disguised and to seek privacy even in the bathhouse, so that a woman would bathe only at night, or alone in a little compartment in the bathhouse, thus neither seen nor recognized, he may put in a claim respecting even obvious defects. These are matters of common sense, and not of Scriptural decree. . . .

4. How is the claim respecting defects to be put in? If the defects found in her are such as were of a certainty in her prior to her espousal — for example, an extra finger, or the like — her father must show proof that the husband was aware of them and accepted them, or that the presumption is that he was aware of them. If he cannot bring such proof, she may be dismissed without anything at all of her kĕtubbah.

If the defects are such as might have developed in her after her espousal, the rule is as follows: If they are discovered after her entrance into her husband's house, the husband must bring proof that she had them before the espousal, and that his acquisition of her was consequently based on a misapprehension. If the defects are discovered while she is still in her father's house, the father must prove that they had developed after the espousal and that it is therefore the groom's misfortune.

5. If the husband brings proof that the defects were in her before the espousal, or that she herself had admitted this fact to him, while the father brings

proof that the husband had seen them and remained silent, thus showing that he was reconciled to them, or that the presumption is that he was aware of them and was reconciled to them, the husband is liable for her kĕtubbah.

6. If after having intercourse with his wife he tarries several days, and then claims that he did not notice this defect until now, no attention need be paid to him, even if the defect is in the folds of her skin or on the sole of her foot, because the presumption is that no man would drink out of a cup without first examining it thoroughly. It is therefore presumed that he was aware of the defect and accepted it. . . .

10. The same applies to a woman who develops defects after her marriage, even if she is stricken with boils; if the husband wishes to retain her, he may do so; if he wishes to dismiss her, he must pay her her kĕtubbah.

11. If a man develops defects after his marriage, even such defects as the amputation of his arm or leg, or the blinding of his eye, and if his wife refuses to abide with him, he may not be compelled to dismiss her and pay her her kĕtubbah; rather, if she consents to abide with him, she may do so; if not, she must be dismissed without her kĕtubbah, like any other rebellious wife.

If, however, he develops bad breath or nasal odor, or if he turns to collecting canine droppings, hewing copper out of its source, or tanning hides, he must be compelled to dismiss her and pay her her kĕtubbah. But if she is willing to abide with him, she may do so.

12. If a man is stricken with boils, he must be compelled to dismiss his wife and pay her her kĕtubbah. Even if she is willing to abide with him, no attention need be paid to her, and they should be separated against their wishes, because she is bound to aggravate his condition. If, however, she says, "Let me abide with him" in the presence of witnesses, so that he would have no intercourse with her, her wish may be honored.

13. If a woman's husband is afflicted with bad breath or nasal odor, or collects canine droppings, or has a similar defect; and if he dies, and she then becomes subject to levirate marriage with his brother who is afflicted with the same defect, she may say, "From your brother I could take it, but from you I cannot," whereupon he must . . . pay her her kĕtubbah.

Treatise II: Laws Concerning Divorce

Chapter X

12. A man who divorces his wife because of her evil reputation, or because she is reckless in making vows, should be instructed, "Let her know that you are di-

vorcing her for that very reason, in order to punish her." He should be told further, "Be it known unto you that you may not take her back ever."

And why is a man who divorces such a wife forbidden to take her back ever? As a precaution, lest, having thereupon married another man, she should repent and live in chastity under him, whereat the first husband might say, "Had I known that this would happen, I would not have divorced her." This would make it appear as if he had divorced her conditionally, and the condition not having been fulfilled, the get[5] would then become null and void retroactively. He should therefore be told, "Make up your mind to divorce her irrevocably, for she will never be permitted to come back to you." Nevertheless, should he transgress and take her back before she is betrothed to another man, he need not dismiss her.

13. Similarly, one who divorces his wife because she is barren, or is habitually subject to bleeding during sexual intercourse, may never take her back, lest, having married another man, the barren woman should then give birth, or the bleeding woman become cured, whereat the first husband might say, "Had I known that this would happen, I would not have divorced her," with the result that the divorce would become null and void, and the children born of the second marriage would have the status of bastards. Nevertheless, should he transgress and take her back, he need not dismiss her.

14. An agent who conveys a get outside the Land of Israel and declares, "It was written and signed in my presence," may not himself marry the divorcée, because of apprehension that he may have cast his eyes upon her and testified in her behalf with that end in view.

Similarly, the sole witness who testifies that a woman's husband had died and thus entitles her to remarry, may not himself marry her.

So, too, a Sage who has declared a woman forbidden to her husband because of her vow, may not himself marry her.

17. If a man divorces his wife, and then, before she remarries, has intercourse with her before witnesses, the rule is that inasmuch as she was his wife, whether she was divorced after marriage or after espousal, the presumption is that he has taken her back and has had intercourse with her for the purpose of betrothal, and not for the purpose of harlotry, even if he is seen paying her money. For it is presumed that no man would make his intercourse with his wife meretricious, seeing that it is within his power to make it licit. She is therefore presumed to have been assuredly betrothed to him again, and therefore requires a second get from him.

18. If he secludes himself with her in the presence of witnesses — provided that these witnesses see it simultaneously — and if she was divorced after marriage, there is cause for apprehension that she may have had intercourse

with him, and the witnesses to their seclusion are at the same time regarded also as witnesses to their intercourse. For he who betroths a woman by way of intercourse need not perform the act itself in the presence of the witnesses, but need only seclude himself with her in their presence, and may then have intercourse with her in privacy, as we have explained.

Hence she requires a second get, out of doubt, seeing that her second betrothal is likewise doubtful.

If, however, she was divorced after espousal, there is no cause for apprehension, since he is not yet on intimate terms with her.

Chapter XI

18. A divorcée or a widow may not remarry or become betrothed without waiting ninety days, exclusive of the day of her divorce or of her husband's death, and exclusive of the day of her espousal, in order to determine whether she is or is not pregnant, and in order to distinguish between the seed of the first husband and the seed of the second.

25. The Sages have also enacted that a man should not marry another man's pregnant or nursing wife, even though it is known who had impregnated her, lest the child should be harmed during subsequent intercourse, since the child not being his, he will not take proper precautions; or, in the case of a nursing woman, lest her milk should spoil, since he will not take care to remedy the milk with such things as are helpful in such an event.

26. How long is the period of nursing? Twenty-four months, exclusive of the day of delivery and the day of the woman's subsequent espousal.

28. If a man transgresses and marries a pregnant or nursing woman within this period of time, he must dismiss her with a get, even if he is a priest.

If he is an Israelite, he may take her back upon the termination of the twenty-four months prescribed for a nursing mother. If he marries her, then flees, and some time thereafter returns and bides with her, it no longer matters.

If a man espouses a pregnant or nursing woman, he need not be compelled to dismiss her or consummate the marriage until after the period of nursing or until the child has died.

"OLD POEM"

"Old Poem" is an anonymous work of the Han dynasty, which ruled China for four hundred years, from 202 B.C. to 220 A.D. The Han dynasty established Confucianism as a state religion and made great strides in education and the arts. "Old Poem" reflects the widespread use of a form of poetry called "shih," which employs five characters, or syllables.

Old Poem

She went up the hill to pick angelica;
she came down the hill and met her former husband.
She knelt and asked her former husband,
"How do you find the new wife?"
"The new wife I would say is fine,
but she lacks the old wife's excellence.
In face and complexion they're much alike,
but quite unlike in skill of hand.
When the new wife came in the gate,
the old wife left by the side door.[1]
The new wife is good at weaving gauze,
the old wife was good at weaving plain stuff.
Weaving gauze, one does a bolt a day,
weaving plain stuff, five yards or more.[2]
And when I compare the gauze with the plain stuff,
I know the new wife can't equal the old!"

PROLOGUE TO "THE LADY YÜ-NU: A BEGGAR CHIEF'S DAUGHTER"

"The Lady Yü Nu" was first published in the late seventeenth century, during the early Manchu dynasty, in a forty-tale collection attributed to one Pao Wen Lao Jen. (The name of the story collector, which meant, "hugging the old man," was obviously an assumed one.) Like many other collections of popular stories by anonymous authors, this one began with a prologue, itself a tale, in which the major theme of the story was either complemented or contrasted. The custom seems to have been that storytellers would always open their stories with a short prelude, during which time their audience would be given a chance to settle down. The translation is by Ch'u Chai and Winberg Chai.

Prologue to "The Lady Yü Nu"

A woman's relationship to her husband is compared to that of the blossom to the bough: though the bough may be stripped of its blossom, it will bloom again in spring; the blossom once it leaves the bough, can never hope to return. So I recommend that a woman serve her husband to the best of her power, share joy and sorrow with him, and remain true to him to the end. Never scorn poverty or covet riches; never change your mind or waver in your affection only to repent too late.

Now let me tell you of a famous minister of the Han dynasty whose wife, before he had made his name, "had eyes but did not recognize Mount Tai," so that she left him. In later years, she repented in vain. What was the famous minister's name? Where did he come from? His name was Chu Mai-chen, he was

511

also known as Wong-tzu, and he was a native of Kuaichi. While yet poor and unrecognized, he shared with his wife a thatched hut in a mean lane. Every day he went to the hills to cut firewood and carry it to the market for sale. He was fond of study, and always carried a book. Even though he shouldered two loads of firewood, be would grasp a book in his hand. This he would read aloud, studying and pondering as he walked along. The market people, who were used to him, knew Mai-chen was coming with his firewood as soon they heard the sound of his reading. Out of pity for the poor scholar they all bought from him; moreover, he never haggled over the price but simply took whatever they wanted to give him, so that he sold his firewood more quickly than anyone else. But there were always gangs of shallow-brained youngsters and street-urchins who gathered round to make fun of him as be came along, reading classics with a load of firewood on his shoulders. Mai-chen simply ignored them. One day when his wife went out to draw water, she felt greatly humiliated by the sight of these children skipping after Mai-chen with his load, clapping their hands and laughing. When he had sold his firewood and returned home, she began to scold him. "If you want to study, don't sell firewood, and if you want to sell firewood, don't study. Why should you, not being a fool or a lunatic, act like that at your age and let all the children make fun of you? It's a wonder you don't die of shame!"

"I sell firewood to save us from poverty," answered Mai-chen, "and I study to become rich and famous. These two things do not interfere with each other. Let them laugh."

But his wife laughed at this and said, "If you could become rich and famous, you wouldn't be selling firewood. Who ever saw a woodcutter becoming an official? But you talk all this nonsense!"

"Wealth and poverty, fame and humbleness — each has its time," said Mai-chen. "A fortuneteller, on the basis of my eight horoscopic characters [pertaining to the year, month, day, and hour of the birth], told me that I should win fame at fifty. The proverb says: 'The sea cannot be measured with a bucket.' You should not slight me."

"That fortuneteller could see what a fool you looked," said his wife, "and deliberately made fun of you. You should not believe him. By the time you are fifty you won't be able to carry firewood. Then we shall starve to death, and you talk about becoming an official! Unless, of course, Yama of Hades wants another judge in his court and is waiting for you to fill the vacancy!"

"Ch'iang Tai-Kung was still a fisherman by the River Wei at the age of eighty," continued Mai-chen, "but when King Wen of Chou found him, he carried him off in his chariot and appointed him Grand Counselor. Kung-sun Hung, Prime Minister of the present dynasty, was still a swineherd at Tunghai when he was fifty-nine. Only when he was just turned sixty was he presented to the present Emperor, who made him a general and marquis. If I become famous at fifty . . . I shall be in front of the other two. You must have patience for a while."

"Don't quote history at me!" said his wife. "That fisherman and that swineherd were men of talent and learning. But you, with those obsolete books of yours, will still be the same even if you study till you're a hundred. What's there to hope for? I am unlucky to be your wife! When children are jeering at you, I lose my face, too. If you won't listen to me and throw your books away, I'm not going to stay with you. We had better each lead our own life, so that we will not act as a drag on each other."

"I am forty-three this year," said Mai-chen, "and in seven years I shall be fifty. The longest part is past, and you won't have much longer to wait. How can you be so heartless as to desert me? You will certainly regret it in years to come."

"The world is not short of woodcutters," rejoined his wife. "What would I have to regret? If I stay with you, I shall starve by the roadside long before the seven years are over. You had better do me a favor and let me go, so as to spare my life."

When Mai-chen saw that his wife had determined to leave him and could not be dissuaded, he said with a sigh, "Very well, then, I only hope that you will marry a better man than Chu Mai-chen."

"Whoever he is couldn't be worse," said his wife. After saying this, she curtsied to him and went joyfully away without so much as looking back.

And Mai-chen greatly grieved over this, and wrote the following four lines on the wall:

Marry a dog, follow a dog;
Marry a cock, follow a cock.
My wife has forsaken me,
But I do not desert her.

By the time Mai-chen had reached the age of fifty, Emperor Wu of the Han dynasty issued a decree calling for men of worth. Mai-chen went to the Western Capital, submitted a memorial to the throne, and declared himself eligible for an official appointment. Meanwhile he was recommended by a fellow-townsman, Yen Chu. The emperor understood that Mai-chen, a native of Kuai-chen, must know the people of his native place and their general conditions, so he appointed him governor of Kuaichi, and Mai-chen set off by post carriage to take up his position.

When the officials of Kuaichi heard that the new governor was on his way, they mobilized a large number of men to repair the roads. Among these con-scripts was the second husband of Mai-chen's former wife. This woman, bare-foot and with tousled hair, was carrying her new husband food, when, among great bustle and rustle, the governor and his suite arrived. And when she looked up from the roadside, she saw her former husband, Chu Mai-chen!

Mai-chen in his carriage also caught sight of her and recognized her. He ordered his attendants to take her along in a carriage. At the official residence, the woman did not know where to put herself for shame; she kowtowed in re-morse. Mai-chen asked to see her second husband, and in no time the man was brought in. As he knelt down on the ground, not daring to look up, Mai-chen burst out laughing and said to his former wife, "This man doesn't look better than I, Chu Mai-chen."

The woman kept on kowtowing and confessing her error. She had eyes but no pupils and had not recognized his worth, and she begged permission to return as his maid or concubine, serving him to the end of his life. Mai-chen or-dered a bucket of water to be fetched and poured out in the courtyard. Then he said to his former wife, "If spilt water can be recovered, then you can return. In memory of our childhood betrothal, I shall give you some land in my back gar-den to cultivate with your husband so you can support yourselves."

As the woman went out of the official residence with her second husband, passers-by pointed at her and said, "That's the wife of the new governor!" She then felt too ashamed to face the world, and when she reached the back garden, she jumped into the river and drowned herself.

JOHN LOCKE

John Locke's (1632-1704) most famous philosophical work was the *Essay Concerning Human Understanding,* in which he outlined his theory that all knowledge proceeds from sense experiences that are organized by the rational mind. He is thus one of the founders of the philosophy of "empiricism." Locke's *Two Treatises on Government* (1690) held that all men were equal and entitled to "life, health, liberty" and property. In order to ensure these rights for everyone, Locke believed in government by "social contract," with "checks and balances." Locke's view of human beings as basically good, along with his belief that the rational pursuit of individual contentment would inevitably benefit the general well-being of society, had enormous influence on the American founding fathers in determining principles of government.

Two Treatises on Government

Chapter VII: Of Political or Civil Society

77. God, having made man such a creature that, in His own judgment, it was not good for him to be alone, put him under strong obligations of necessity, convenience, and inclination, to drive him into society, as well as fitted him with understanding and language to continue and enjoy it. The first society was between man and wife, which gave beginning to that between parents and children, to which in time, that between master and servant came to be added. And though all these might, and commonly did, meet together and make up but one

515

family, wherein the master or mistress of it had some sort of rule proper to a family, each of these, or all together, came short of "political society," as we shall see if we consider the different ends, ties, and bounds of each of these.

78. Conjugal society is made by a voluntary compact between man and woman, and though it consist chiefly in such a communion and right in one another's bodies as is necessary to its chief end, procreation, yet it draws with it mutual support and assistance, and a communion of interests too, as necessary not only to unite their care and affection, but also necessary to their common offspring, who have a right to be nourished and maintained by them till they are able to provide for themselves.

79. For the end of conjunction between male and female being not barely procreation, but the continuation of the species, this conjunction betwixt male and female ought to last, even after procreation, so long as is necessary to the nourishment and support of the young ones, who are to be sustained by those that got them till they are able to shift and provide for themselves. This rule, which the infinite wise Maker hath set to the works of His hands, we find the inferior creatures steadily obey. In those viviparous animals which feed on grass the conjunction between male and female lasts no longer than the very act of copulation, because the teat of the dam being sufficient to nourish the young till it be able to feed on grass, the male only begets, but concerns not himself for the female or young, to whose sustenance he can contribute nothing. But in beasts of prey the conjunction lasts longer, because the dam, not being able well to subsist herself and nourish her numerous offspring by her own prey alone (a more laborious as well as more dangerous way of living than by feeding on grass), the assistance of the male is necessary to the maintenance of their com-mon family, which cannot subsist till they are able to prey for themselves, but by the joint care of male and female. The same is to be observed in all birds (ex-cept some domestic ones, where plenty of food excuses the cock from feeding and taking care of the young brood), whose young, needing food in the nest, the cock and hen continue mates till the young are able to use their wings and provide for themselves.

80. And herein, I think, lies the chief, if not the only reason, why the male and female in mankind are tied to a longer conjunction than other creatures — viz., because the female is capable of conceiving, and, *de facto*, is commonly with child again, and brings forth too a new birth, long before the former is out of a dependency for support on his parents' help and able to shift for himself, and has all the assistance is due to him from his parents, whereby the father, who is bound to take care for those he hath begot, is under an obligation to continue in conjugal society with the same woman longer than other creatures, whose young, being able to subsist of themselves before the time of procreation

returns again, the conjugal bond dissolves of itself, and they are at liberty till Hymen, at his usual anniversary season, summons them again to choose new mates. Wherein one cannot but admire the wisdom of the great Creator, who, having given to man an ability to lay up for the future as well as supply the present necessity, hath made it necessary that society in man and wife should be more lasting than of male and female amongst other creatures, that so their industry might be encouraged, and their interest better united, to make provision and lay up goods for their common issue, which uncertain mixture, or easy and frequent solutions of conjugal society, would mightily disturb.

81. But though these are ties upon mankind which make the conjugal bonds more firm and lasting in a man than the other species of animals, yet it would give one reason to inquire why this compact, where procreation and education are secured and inheritance taken care for may not be made determinable, either by consent, or at a certain time, or upon certain conditions, as well as any other voluntary compacts, there being no necessity, in the nature of the thing, nor to the ends of it, that it should always be for life — I mean, for such as are under no restraint of any positive law which ordains all such contracts to be perpetual.

82. But the husband and wife, though they have but one common concern, yet having different understandings, will unavoidably sometimes have different wills too. It therefore being necessary that the last determination (*i.e.*, the rule) should be placed somewhere, it naturally falls to the man's share as the abler and the stronger. But this, falling but to the things of their common interest and property leaves the wife in the full and true possession of what by contract is her peculiar right, and at least gives the husband no more power over her than she has over his life; the power of the husband being so far from that of an absolute monarch that the wife has, in many cases, a liberty to separate from him where natural right or their contract allows it, whether that contract be made by themselves in the state of Nature or by the customs or laws of the country they live in, and the children, upon such separation, fall to the father or mother's lot as such contract does determine.

83. For all the ends of marriage being to be obtained under politic government, as well as in the state of Nature, the civil magistrate doth not abridge the right or power of either, naturally necessary to those ends — viz., procreation and mutual support and assistance whilst they are together, but only decides any controversy that may arise between man and wife about them. If it were otherwise, and that absolute sovereignty and power of life and death naturally belonged to the husband, and were necessary to the society between man and wife, there could be no matrimony in any of these countries where the husband is allowed no such absolute authority. But the ends of matrimony requir-

ing no such power in the husband, it was not at all necessary to it. The condition of conjugal society put it not in him; but whatsoever might consist with procreation and support of the children till they could shift for themselves — mutual assistance, comfort, and maintenance — might be varied and regulated by that contract which first united them in that society, nothing being necessary to any society that is not necessary to the ends for which it is made.

84. The society betwixt parents and children, and the distinct rights and powers belonging respectively to them, I have treated of so largely in the foregoing chapter that I shall not here need to say anything of it; and I think it is plain that it is far different from a politic society.

85. Master and servant are names as old as history, but given to those of far different condition; for a free man makes himself a servant to another by selling him for a certain time the service he undertakes to do in exchange for wages he is to receive; and though this commonly puts him into the family of his master, and under the ordinary discipline thereof, yet it gives the master but a temporary power over him, and no greater than what is contained in the contract between them. But there is another sort of servants which, by a peculiar name we call slaves who being captives taken in a just war are, by the right of Nature, subjected to the absolute dominion and arbitrary power of their masters. These men having, as I say, forfeited their lives and, with it, their liberties, and lost their estates, and being in the state of slavery, not capable of any property, cannot in that state be considered as any part of civil society, the chief end whereof is the preservation of property.

86. Let us therefore consider a master of a family with all these subordinate relations of wife, children, servants and slaves, united under the domestic rule of a family, which what resemblance soever it may have in its order, offices and number too, with a little commonwealth, yet is very far from it both in its constitution, power, and end; or if it must be thought a monarchy, and the paterfamilias the absolute monarch in it, absolute monarchy will have but a very shattered and short power, when it is plain by what has been said before, that the master of the family has a very distinct and differently limited power both as to time and extent over those several persons that are in it; for excepting the slave (and the family is as much a family, and his power as paterfamilias as great, whether there be any slaves in his family or no) he has no legislative power of life and death over any of them, and none too but what a mistress of a family may have as well as he. And he certainly can have no absolute power over the whole family who has but a very limited one over every individual in it. But how a family, or any other society of men differ from that which is properly political society, we shall best see by considering wherein political society itself consists.

87. Man being born, as has been proved, with a title to perfect freedom and an uncontrolled enjoyment of all the rights and privileges of the law of Nature, equally with any other man, or number of men in the world, hath by nature a power not only to preserve his property — that is, his life, liberty, and estate against the injuries and attempts of other men, but to judge of and punish the breaches of that law in others, as he is persuaded the offence deserves, even with death itself, in crimes where the heinousness of the fact, in his opinion, requires it. But because no political society can be, nor subsist, without having in itself the power to preserve the property, and in order thereunto punish the offences of all those of that society, there, and there only, is political society where every one of the members hath quitted this natural power, resigned it up into the hands of the community in all cases that exclude him not from appealing for protection to the law established by it. And thus all private judgment of every particular member being excluded, the community comes to be umpire, and by understanding indifferent rules and men authorized by the community for their execution, decides all the differences that may happen between any members of that society concerning any matter of right, and punishes those offences which any member hath committed against the society with such penalties as the law has established; whereby it is easy to discern who are, and are not, in political society together. Those who are united into one body, and have a common established law and judicature to appeal to, with authority to decide controversies between them and punish offenders, are in civil society one with another; but those who have no such common appeal, I mean on earth, are still in the state of Nature, each being where there is no other, judge for himself and executioner; which is, as I have before showed it, the perfect state of Nature.

BERTRAND RUSSELL

Bertrand Arthur William, third Earl Russell (1872-1970), was a philosopher and mathematician, the scion of a prominent and politically influential British noble family. A prolific writer and one of the major thinkers of the twentieth century, he wrote a number of groundbreaking works in both disciplines. Russell's unconventional political and moral views were irksome to the authorities. Indeed, he never obtained a promised teaching position at the College of the City of New York because of the positions with respect to divorce and adultery that he took in *Marriage and Morals,* published in 1929. A pacifist (except during World War II, a war he found ethically defensible), he was imprisoned in England during the First World War, sacrificing his job at Cambridge and his private library for his principles. Later, at the age of 89, he again did a stint in jail for attending a protest against nuclear war. Russell was an empiricist, believing that all knowledge was the product of experience interpreted by reason. In *Why I Am Not a Christian,* he defended atheism (some charge, weakly) on the grounds that all principles motivating men must be held on the basis of reason, and reason alone. It should be noted that with his wife, Dora, Russell founded one of the first progressive schools in England.

Marriage and Morals

Chapter XVI: Divorce

Divorce as an institution has been permitted in most ages and countries for certain causes. It has never been intended to produce an alternative to the monogamic family, but merely to mitigate hardships where, for special reasons, the continuance of a marriage was felt to be intolerable. The law on the subject has been extraordinarily different in different ages and places, and varies at the present day even within the United States from the extreme of no divorce in South Carolina to the opposite extreme in Nevada.[1] In many non-Christian civilizations, divorce has been very easy for a husband to obtain, and in some it has also been easy for a wife. The Mosaic law allows a husband to give a bill of divorcement; Chinese law allowed divorce provided the property which the wife had brought into the marriage was restored. The Catholic Church, on the ground that marriage is a sacrament, does not allow divorce for any purpose whatsoever, but in practice this severity is somewhat mitigated — especially where the great ones of the earth are concerned — by the fact that there are many grounds for nullity.[2]

In Christian countries the leniency towards divorce has been proportional to the degree of Protestantism. Milton, as everyone knows, wrote in favour of it because he was very Protestant. The English Church, in the days when it considered itself Protestant, recognized divorce for adultery, though for no other cause. Nowadays the great majority of clergymen in the Church of England are opposed to all divorce. Scandinavia has easy divorce laws. So have the most Protestant parts of America. Scotland is more favourable to divorce than England. In France, anti-clericalism produces easy divorce. In the Soviet Union divorce is permitted at the request of either party, but as neither social nor legal penalties attach to either adultery or illegitimacy in Russia, marriage has there lost the importance which it has elsewhere, at any rate so far as the governing classes are concerned.

One of the most curious things about divorce is the difference which has often existed between law and custom. The easiest divorce laws by no means always produce the greatest number of divorces. In China, before the recent upheavals, divorce was almost unknown, for, in spite of the example of Confucius, it was not considered quite respectable. Sweden allows divorce by mutual consent, which is a ground not recognized in any state of America; yet I find that in 1922, the latest year for which I have comparable figures, the number of divorces per hundred thousand of the population was 24 in Sweden and 136 in the United States.[3] I think this distinction between law and custom is important, for while I favour a somewhat lenient law on the subject, there are to my mind, so long as the biparental family persists as the norm, strong reasons why custom should be against divorce, except in somewhat extreme cases. I take this view because I regard marriage not primarily as a sexual partnership, but above all as an undertaking to cooperate in the procreation and rearing of children. It is possible, and even probable, as we have seen in earlier chapters, that marriage so understood may break down under the operation of various forces of which the economic are the chief; but if this should occur, divorce also would break down, since it is an institution dependent upon the existence of marriage, within which it affords a kind of safety valve. Our present discussion, therefore, will move entirely within the framework of the biparental family considered as the rule.

Both Protestants and Catholics have, in general, viewed divorce not from the point of view of the biological purpose of the family, but the point of view of the theological conception of sin. Catholics, since they hold that marriage is indissoluble in the sight of God, necessarily maintain that when two persons have once married, neither of them can, during the lifetime of the other, have sinless intercourse with any other person, no matter what may happen in the marriage. Protestants, in so far as they have favoured divorce, have done so partly out of opposition to Catholic doctrine on the sacraments, partly also because they perceived that the indissolubility of marriage is a cause of adultery, and they believed that easier divorce would make the diminution of adultery less difficult. One finds accordingly that in those Protestant countries where marriages are easily dissolved, adultery is viewed with extreme disfavour, while in countries which do not recognize divorce, adultery, though regarded as sinful, is winked at, at any rate where men are concerned. In Tsarist Russia, where divorce was exceedingly difficult, people did not think the worse of Gorki for his private life, whatever they may have thought of his politics. In America, on the contrary, where no one objected to his politics, he was hounded out on moral grounds, and no hotel would give him a night's lodging.

Neither the Protestant nor the Catholic point of view in this matter can be upheld on rational grounds. Let us take the Catholic point of view first. Suppose that the husband or wife becomes insane after marriage; it is in this case not desirable that further children should spring from an insane stock, nor yet that any children who may already be born should be brought into contact with insanity. Complete separation of the parents, even supposing that the one who is insane has longer or shorter lucid intervals, is therefore desirable in the interests of the children. To decree that in this case the sane partner shall never be permitted any legally recognized sex relations is a wanton cruelty which serves no public purpose whatever. The sane partner is left with a very painful choice. He or she may decide in favour of continence, which is what the law and public morals expect; or in favour of surreptitious relations, presumably childless; or in favour of what is called open sin, with or without children. To each of these courses there are grave objections. Complete abstinence from sex, especially for one already accustomed to it in marriage, is very painful. It leads either a man or a woman, very often, to become prematurely old. It is not unlikely to produce nervous disorders, and in any case the effort involved tends to produce a disagreeable, grudging and ill-tempered type of character. In a man, there is always a grave danger that his self-control will suddenly give way, leading him to acts of brutality, for if he is genuinely persuaded that all intercourse outside marriage is wicked, he is likely, if he does seek such intercourse, to feel that he might as well be hanged for a sheep as for a lamb, and therefore to throw off all moral restraints.

The second alternative, namely, that of having surreptitious childless relations, is the one most commonly adopted in practice, in such a situation as we are considering. To this, also, there are grave objections. Everything surreptitious is undesirable, and sex relations which are serious cannot develop their best possibilities without children and a common life. Moreover, if a man or woman is young and vigorous, it is not in the public interest to say: "You shall have no more children." Still less is it to the public interest to say what the law does in fact say, namely, "You shall have no more children unless you choose a lunatic for their other parent."

The third alternative, namely, that of living in "open sin," is the one which is least harmful, both to the individual and to the community, where it is feasible, but for economic reasons it is impossible in most cases. A doctor or a lawyer who attempted to live in open sin would lose all his patients or clients. A man engaged in any branch of the scholastic profession would lose his post at once.[4] Even if economic circumstances do not make open sin impossible, most people will be deterred by the social penalties. Men like to belong to clubs, and women like to be respected and called on by other women. To be deprived of these pleasures is apparently considered a great hardship. Consequently open sin is difficult except for the rich, and for artists and writers and others whose profession makes it easy to live in a more or less Bohemian society.

It follows that in any country which refuses divorce for insanity, as England does, the man or woman whose wife or husband becomes insane is placed in an intolerable position, in favour of which there is no argument whatever except theological superstition. And what is true of insanity is true also of venereal disease, habitual crime and habitual drunkenness. All these are things which destroy a marriage from every point of view. They make companionship impossible, procreation undesirable, and association of the guilty parent with the child a thing to be avoided. In such cases, therefore, divorce can only be opposed on the ground that marriage is a trap by which the unwary are tricked into purification through sorrow.

Desertion, when it is genuine, should, of course, be a ground for divorce, for in that case the decree merely recognizes in law what is already the fact, namely, that the marriage is at an end. From a legal point of view, however, there is the awkwardness that desertion, if it is a ground for divorce, will be resorted to for that reason, and will be therefore far more frequent than it would be if it were not such a ground. The same kind of difficulty arises in regard to various causes which are in themselves perfectly valid. Many married couples have such a passionate desire to part that they will resort to almost any expedient allowed by the law. When, as was the case in England formerly, a man had to be guilty of cruelty as well as adultery in order to be divorced, it not infrequently happened that a husband would arrange with his wife to hit her before the servants, in order that evidence of cruelty might be forthcoming. Whether it is altogether desirable that two people who passionately desire to part should be forced to endure each other's companionship by the pressure of the law is another question. But we must in all fairness recognize that whatever grounds of divorce are allowed will be stretched to the uttermost, and that many people will purposely behave in such a manner as to make these grounds available. Let us, however, neglecting legal difficulties, continue our enquiry into the circumstances which in fact make the persistence of the marriage undesirable.

Adultery in itself should not, to my mind, be a ground of divorce. Unless people are restrained by inhibitions or strong moral scruples, it is very unlikely that they will go through life without occasionally having strong impulses to adultery. But such impulses do not by any means necessarily imply that the marriage no longer serves its purpose. There may still be ardent affection between husband and wife, and every desire that the marriage should continue. Suppose, for example, that a man has to be away from home on business for a number of months on end. If he is physically vigorous, he will find it difficult to remain continent throughout this time, however fond he may be of his wife. The same will apply to his wife, if she is not entirely convinced of the correctness of conventional morality. Infidelity in such circumstances ought to form no barrier whatever to subsequent happiness, and in fact it does not, where the husband and wife do not consider it necessary to indulge in melodramatic orgies of jealousy. We may go further, and say that each party should be able to put up with such temporary fancies as are always liable to occur, provided the underlying affection remains intact. The psychology of adultery has been falsified by conventional morals, which assume, in monogamous countries, that attraction to one person cannot coexist with a serious affection for another. Everybody knows that this is untrue, yet everybody is liable, under the influence of jealousy, to fall back upon this untrue theory, and make mountains out of molehills. Adultery, therefore, is no good ground for divorce, except when it involves a deliberate preference for another person, on the whole, to the husband or the wife as the case may be.

In saying this I am, of course, assuming that the adulterous intercourse will not be such as to lead to children. Where illegitimate children come in, the issue is much more complicated. This is especially the case if the children are those of the wife, for in that case, if the marriage persists, the husband is faced with the necessity of having another man's child brought up with his own, and (if scandal is to be avoided) even as his own. This goes against the biological basis of marriage, and will also involve an almost intolerable instinctive strain. On this ground, in the days before contraceptives, adultery perhaps deserved the importance which was attached to it, but contraceptives have made it far more possible than it formerly was to distinguish sexual intercourse as such from marriage as a procreative partnership. On this ground it is now possible to attach much less importance to adultery than is attached to it in the conventional code.

The grounds which may make divorce desirable are of two kinds. There are those due to the defects of one partner, such as insanity, dipsomania and crime; and there are those based upon the relations of the husband and wife. It may happen that, without blame to either party, it is impossible for a married couple to live together amicably, or without some very grave sacrifice. It may happen that each has important work to do, and that the work requires that they should live in different places. It may happen that one of them, without disliking the other, becomes deeply attached to some other person, so deeply as to feel the marriage an intolerable tie. In that case, if there is no legal redress, hatred is sure to spring up. Indeed, such cases, as everyone knows, are quite capable of leading to murder. Where a marriage breaks down owing to incompatibility or to an overwhelming passion on the part of one partner for some other person, there should not be, as there is at present, a determination to attach blame. For this reason, much the best ground of divorce in all such cases is mutual consent. Grounds other than mutual consent ought only to be required where the marriage has failed through some definite defect in one partner.

There is very great difficulty in framing laws as regards divorce, because whatever the laws may be, judges and juries will be governed by their passions, while husbands and wives will do whatever may be necessary to circumvent the intentions of the legislators. Although in English law a divorce cannot be obtained where there is any agreement between husband and wife, yet everybody knows that in practice there often is such an agreement. In New York State it is not uncommon to go further and hire perjured testimony to prove the statutory adultery. Cruelty is in theory a perfectly adequate ground for divorce, but it may be interpreted so as to become absurd. When the most eminent of all film stars was divorced by his wife for cruelty, one of the counts in the proof of cruelty was that he used to bring home friends who talked about Kant. I can hardly suppose that it was the intention of the California legislators to enable any woman to divorce her husband on the ground that he was sometimes guilty of intelligent conversation in her presence. The only way out of these confusions, subterfuges, and absurdities is to have divorce by mutual consent in all cases where there is not some very definite and demonstrable reason, such as insanity, to justify a one-sided desire for divorce. The parties would then have to settle all monetary adjustments out of court, and it would not be necessary for either party to hire clever men to prove the other a monster of iniquity. I should add that nullity, which is now decreed where sexual intercourse is impossible, should instead be granted on application whenever the marriage is childless. That is to say, if a husband and wife who have no children wish to part, they should be able to do so on production of a medical certificate to the effect that the wife is not pregnant. Children are the purpose of marriage, and to hold people to a childless marriage is a cruel cheat.

So much for the *law* of divorce; the *custom* is another matter. As we have already seen, it is possible for the law to make divorce easy while, nevertheless, custom makes it rare. The great frequency of divorce in America comes, I think, partly from the fact that what people seek in marriage is not what should be sought, and this in turn is due partly to the fact that adultery is not tolerated. Marriage should be a partnership intended by both parties to last at least as long as the youth of their children, and not regarded by either as at the mercy of temporary amours. If such temporary amours are not tolerated by public opinion or by the consciences of those concerned, each in its turn has to blossom into a marriage. This may easily go so far as completely to destroy the biparental family, for if a woman has a fresh husband every two years, and a fresh child by each, the children in effect are deprived of their fathers, and marriage therefore loses its *raison d'être*. We come back again to St. Paul: marriage in America, as in the First Epistle to the Corinthians, is conceived as an alternative to fornication; therefore whenever a man would fornicate if he could not get a divorce, he must have a divorce.

When marriage is conceived in relation to children, a quite different ethic comes into play. The husband and wife, if they have any love for their children, will so regulate their conduct as to give their children the best chance of a happy and healthy development. This may involve, at times, very considerable self-repression. And it certainly requires that both should realize the superiority of the claims of children to the claims of their own romantic emotions. But all this will happen of itself and quite naturally, where parental affection is genuine and a false ethic does not inflame jealousy. There are some who say that if a husband and wife no longer love each other passionately, and do not prevent each other from sexual experiences outside marriage, it is impossible for them to cooperate adequately in the education of their children. Thus Mr. Walter Lippmann says: "Mates who are not lovers will not really cooperate, as Mr.

Bertrand Russell thinks they should, in bearing children; they will be distracted, insufficient, and, worst of all, they will be merely dutiful."[5] There is here, first of all, a minor, possibly unintentional, misstatement. Of course mates who are not lovers will not cooperate in *bearing* children; but children are not done with when they are born, as Mr. Walter Lippmann seems to imply. And to cooperate in *rearing* children, even after passionate love has decayed, is by no means a superhuman task for sensible people who are capable of the natural affections. To this I can testify from a large number of cases personally known to me. To say that such parents will be "merely dutiful" is to ignore the emotion of parental affection — an emotion which, where it is genuine and strong, preserves an unbreakable tie between husband and wife long after physical passion has decayed. One must suppose that Mr. Lippmann has never heard of France, where the family is strong, and parents very dutiful, in spite of an exceptional freedom in the matter of adultery. Family feeling is extremely weak in America, and the frequency of divorce is a consequence of this fact. Where family feeling is strong, divorce will be comparatively rare, even if it is legally easy. Easy divorce, as it exists in America, must be regarded as a transitional stage on the way from the biparental to the purely maternal family. It is, however, a stage involving considerable hardship for children, since, in the world as it is, children expect to have two parents, and may become attached to their father before divorce takes place. So long as the biparental family continues to be the recognized rule, parents who divorce each other, except for grave cause, appear to me to be failing in their parental duty. I do not think that a legal compulsion to go on being married is likely to mend matters. What seems to me to be wanted is, first, a degree of mutual liberty which will make marriage more endurable, and secondly, a realization of the importance of children which has been overlaid by the emphasis on sex which we owe to St. Paul and the romantic movement.

The conclusion seems to be that, while divorce is too difficult in many countries, of which England is one, easy divorce does not afford a genuine solution of the marriage problem. If marriage is to continue, stability in marriage is important in the interests of the children, but this stability will be best sought by distinguishing between marriage and merely sexual relations, and by emphasizing the biological as opposed to the romantic aspect of married love. I do not pretend that marriage can be freed from onerous duties. In the system that I commend, men are freed, it is true, from the duty of sexual conjugal fidelity, but they have in exchange the duty of controlling jealousy. The good life cannot be lived without self-control, but it is better to control a restrictive and hostile emotion such as jealousy, rather than a generous and expansive emotion such as love. Conventional morality has erred, not in demanding self-control, but in demanding it in the wrong place.

JUDITH WALLERSTEIN

The *Unexpected Legacy of Divorce,* published in the fall of 2000, is the third of three books on the effects of divorce on children written by psychologist Judith Wallerstein. These books have followed 131 subjects over a period of thirty years since the divorce of their parents, tracing their external lives and their internal worlds. The conclusions Wallerstein draws from her longitudinal study are unambiguous. Divorce damages children in profound and long-term ways. In the conclusion to *The Unexpected Legacy,* Wallerstein offers some hard-hitting advice to parents considering divorce: If your marriage is "not so explosive or chaotic or unsafe that . . . living together" is "intolerable, . . . seriously consider staying together for the sake of your children."

The Unexpected Legacy of Divorce

Conclusions

A very important judge on the family law bench in a large state I shall not name invited me to come see him. I was eager to meet with him because I wanted to discuss some ideas I have for educating parents under court auspices that go beyond the simple advice "don't fight." After we had talked for a half an hour or so, the judge leaned back in his chair and said he'd like my opinion about something important. He had just attended several scientific lectures in which researchers argued that children are shaped more by genes than by family environment. Case in point, studies of identical twins reared separately show that in adulthood such twins often like the same foods and clothing styles, belong to the same political parties, and even bestow identical names on their dogs. The judge looked perplexed. "Do you think that could mean divorce is in the genes?" he asked in all seriousness. "And if that's so, does it matter what a court decides when parents divorce?"

I was taken aback. Here was a key figure in the lives of thousands of children asking me whether what he and his colleagues do or say on the bench makes any difference. He seemed relieved by the notion that maybe his actions are insignificant.

I told him that I personally doubt the existence of a "divorce gene." If such a biological trait had arisen in evolution, it would be of very recent vintage. But, I added, "What the court does matters enormously. You have the power to protect children from being hurt or to increase their suffering."

Now it was his turn to be taken aback. "You think we've increased children's suffering?"

"Yes, Your Honor, I do. With all respect, I have to say that the court along with the rest of society has increased the suffering of children."

"How so?" he asked.

We spent another half hour talking about how the courts, parents, attorneys, mental health workers — indeed most adults — have been reluctant to pay genuine attention to children during and after divorce. He listened respectfully to me, but I must say I left the judge's chambers that day in a state of shock that soon turned to gloom. How can we be so utterly lost and confused that a leading judge would accept the notion of a "divorce gene" to explain our predicament? If he's confused about his role, what about the rest of us? What is it about the impact of divorce on our society and our children that's so hard to understand and accept?

Having spent the last thirty years of my life traveling here and abroad talking to professional, legal, and mental health groups plus working with thousands of parents and children in divorced families, it's clear that we've created a new kind of society never before seen in human culture. Silently and unconsciously, we have created a culture of divorce. It's hard to grasp what it means when we say that first marriages stand a 45 percent chance of breaking up and that second marriages have a 60 percent chance of ending in divorce. What are the consequences for all of us when 25 percent of people today between the ages of eighteen and forty-four have parents who divorced? What does it mean to a society when people wonder aloud if the family is about to disappear? What can we do when we learn that married couples with children represent a mere 25 percent of households in the 1990s and that the most common living arrangement nowadays is a household of unmarried people with no children? These numbers are terrifying. But like all massive social change, what's happening is affecting us in ways that we have yet to understand.

For people like me who work with divorcing families all the time, these abstract numbers have real faces. When I think about people I know so well, including the "children" you've met in this book, I can relate to the millions of children and adults who suffer with loneliness and to all the teenagers who say, "I don't want a life like either of my parents." I can empathize with the countless young men and women who despair of ever finding a lasting relationship and who, with a brave toss of the head, say, "Hey, if you don't get married then you can't get divorced." It's only later, or sometimes when they think I'm not listening, that they add softly, "but I don't want to grow old alone." I am especially worried about how our divorce culture has changed childhood itself. A million new children a year are added to our march of marital failure. As they explain so eloquently, they lose the carefree play of childhood as well as the comforting arms and lap of a loving parent who is always rushing off because life in the postdivorce family is so incredibly difficult to manage. We must take very seriously the complaint of children like Karen who declare, "The day my parents divorced is the day my childhood ended."

Many years ago the psychoanalyst Erik Erikson taught us that childhood and society are vitally connected. But we have not yet come to terms with the changes ushered in by our divorce culture. Childhood is different, adolescence is different, and adulthood is different. Without our noticing, we have created a new class of young children who take care of themselves, along with a whole generation of overburdened parents who have no time to enjoy the pleasures of parenting. So much has happened so fast, we cannot hold it all in our minds. It's simply overwhelming.

But we must not forget a very important other side to all these changes. Because of our divorce culture, adults today have a greater sense of freedom: The importance of sex and play in adult life is widely accepted. We are not locked into our early mistakes and forced to stay in wretched, lifelong relationships. The change in women — their very identity and freer role in society — is part of our divorce culture. Indeed, two-thirds of divorces are initiated by women despite the high price they pay in economic and parenting burdens afterward. People want and expect a lot more out of marriage than did earlier generations. Although the divorce rate in second and third marriages is sky-high, many second marrages are much happier than the ones left behind. Children and adults are able to escape violence, abuse, and misery to create a better life. Clearly there is no road back.

The sobering truth is that we have created a new kind of society that offers greater freedom and more opportunities for many adults, but this welcome change carries a serious hidden cost. Many people, adults and children alike, are in fact not better off. We have created new kinds of families in which relationships are fragile and often unreliable. Children today receive far less nurturance, protection, and parenting than was their lot a few decades ago. Long-term marriages come apart at still surprising rates. And many in the older generation who started the divorce revolution find themselves estranged from their adult children. Is this the price we must pay for needed change? Can't we do better?

I'd like to say that we're at a crossroads, but I'm afraid I can't be that optimistic. We can choose a new route only if we agree on where we are and where we want to be in the future. The outlook is cloudy. For every person who wants to sound an alarm, there's another who says don't worry. For everyone concerned about the economic and emotional deprivations inherited by children of divorce there are those who argue that those kids were "in trouble before" and that divorce is irrelevant, no big deal. People want to feel good about their choices. Doubtless many do. In actual fact, after most divorces, one member of the former couple feels much better while the other feels no better or even worse. Yet at any dinner party you will still hear the same myths: Divorce is a temporary crisis. So many children have experienced their parents' divorce that kids nowadays don't worry so much. It's easier. They almost expect it. It's a rite of passage. If I feel better, so will my children. And so on. As always, children are voiceless or unheard.

But family scholars who have not always seen eye to eye are converging on a number of findings that fly in the face of our cherished myths. We agree that the effects of divorce are long-term. We know that the family is in trouble. We have a consensus that children raised in divorced or remarried families are less well adjusted as adults than those raised in intact families.

The life histories of this first generation to grow up in a divorce culture tell us truths we dare not ignore. Their message is poignant, clear, and contrary to what so many want to believe. They have taught me the following:

From the viewpoint of the children, and counter to what happens to their parents, divorce is a cumulative experience. Its impact increases over time and rises to a crescendo in adulthood. At each developmental stage divorce is experienced anew in different ways. In adulthood it affects personality, the ability to trust, expectations about relationships, and ability to cope with change.

The first upheaval occurs at the breakup. Children are frightened and angry, terrified of being abandoned by both parents, and they feel responsible for the divorce. Most children are taken by surprise; few are relieved. As adults, they remember with sorrow and anger how little support they got from their parents when it happened. They recall how they were expected to adjust overnight to a terrifying number of changes that confounded them. Even children who had seen or heard violence at home made no connection between that violence and the decision to divorce. The children concluded early on, silently and sadly, that family relationships are fragile and that the tie between a man and woman can break capriciously, without warning. They worried ever after that parent-child relationships are also unreliable and can break at any time. These early experiences colored their later expectations.

As the postdivorce family took shape, their world increasingly resembled what they feared most. Home was a lonely place. The household was in disarray for years. Many children were forced to move, leaving behind familiar schools, close friends, and other supports. What they remember vividly as adults is the loss of the intact family and the safety net it provided, the difficulty of having two parents in two homes, and how going back and forth cut badly into playtime and friendships. Parents were busy with work, preoccupied with rebuilding their social lives. Both moms and dads had a lot less time to spend with their children and were less responsive to their children's needs or wishes. Little children especially felt that they had lost both parents and were unable to care for themselves. Children soon learned that the divorced family has porous walls that include new lovers, live-in partners, and stepparents. Not one of these relationships was easy for anyone. The mother's parenting was often cut into by the very heavy burdens of single parenthood and then by the demands of remarriage and stepchildren.

Relationships with fathers were heavily influenced by live-in lovers or stepmothers in second and third marriages. Some second wives were interested in the children while others wanted no part of them. Some fathers were able to maintain their love and interest in their children but few had time for two or sometimes three families. In some families both parents gradually stabilized their lives within happy remarriages or well-functioning, emotionally gratifying single parenthood. But these people were never a majority in any of my work.

Meanwhile, children who were able to draw support from school, sports teams, parents, stepparents, grandparents, teachers, or their own inner strengths, interests, and talents did better than those who could not muster such resources. By necessity, many of these so-called resilient children forfeited their own childhoods as they took responsibility for themselves; their troubled, overworked parents; and their siblings. Children who needed more than minimal parenting because they were little or had special vulnerabilities and problems with change were soon overwhelmed with sorrow and anger at their parents. Years later, when contemplating having their own children, most children in this study said hotly, "I never want a child of mine to experience a childhood like I had."

As the children told us, adolescence begins early in divorced homes and, compared with that of youngsters raised in intact families, is more likely to include more early sexual experiences for girls and higher alcohol and drug use for girls and boys. Adolescence is more prolonged in divorced families and extends well into the years of early adulthood. Throughout these years children of divorce worry about following in their parents' footsteps and struggle with a sinking sense that they, too, will fail in their relationships.

But it's in adulthood that children of divorce suffer the most. The impact of divorce hits them most cruelly as they go in search of love, sexual intimacy, and commitment. Their lack of inner images of a man and a woman in a stable relationship and their memories of their parents' failure to sustain the marriage badly hobble their search, leading them to heartbreak and even despair. They cried, "No one taught me." They complain bitterly that they feel unprepared for adult relationships and that they have never seen a "man and woman on the same beam," that they have no good models on which to build their hopes. And indeed they have a very hard time formulating even simple ideas about the kind of person they're looking for. Many end up with unsuitable or very troubled partners in relationships that were doomed from the start.

The contrast between them and children from good intact homes, as both go in search of love and commitment, is striking. (As I explain in this book, children raised in extremely unhappy or violent intact homes face misery in childhood and tragic challenges in adulthood. But because their parents generally aren't interested in getting a divorce, divorce does not become part of their legacy.) Adults in their twenties from reasonably good or even moderately unhappy intact families had a fine understanding of the demands and sacrifices required in a close relationship. They had memories of how their parents struggled and overcame differences, how they cooperated in a crisis. They developed a general idea about the kind of person they wanted to marry. Most important, they did not expect to fail. The two groups differed after marriage as well. Those from intact families found the example of their parents' enduring marriage very reassuring when they inevitably ran into marital problems. But in coping with the normal stresses in a marriage, adults from divorced families were at a grave disadvantage. Anxiety about relationships was at the bedrock of their personalities and endured even in very happy marriages. Their fears of disaster and sudden loss rose when they felt content. And their fear of abandonment, betrayal, and rejection mounted when they found themselves having to disagree with someone they loved. After all, marriage is a slippery slope and their parents fell off it. All had trouble dealing with differences or even moderate conflict in their close relationships. Typically their first response was panic, often followed by flight. They had a lot to undo and a lot to learn in a very short time.

Those who had two parents who rebuilt happy lives after divorce and included children in their orbits had a much easier time as adults. Those who had committed single parents also benefited from that parent's attention and responsiveness. But the more frequent response in adulthood was continuing anger at parents, more often at fathers, whom the children regarded as having been selfish and faithless.

Others felt deep compassion and pity toward mothers or fathers who failed to rebuild their lives after divorce. The ties between daughters and their mothers were especially close but at a cost. Some young women found it very difficult to separate from their moms and to lead their own lives. With some notable exceptions, fathers in divorced families were less likely to enjoy close bonds with their adult children, especially their sons. This stood in marked contrast to fathers and sons from intact families, who tended to grow closer as the years went by.

Fortunately for many children of divorce, their fears of loss and betrayal can be conquered by the time they reach their late twenties and thirties. But what a struggle that takes, what courage and persistence. Those who succeed overcome their difficulties the hard way — by learning from their own failed relationships and gradually rejecting the models they were raised with to create what they want from a love relationship. Those lucky enough to have found a loving partner are able to interrupt their self-destructive course with a lasting love affair or marriage.

In other realms of adult life — financial and security, for instance — some children were able to overcome difficulties through unexpected help from fathers who had vanished long before. Still others benefit from the constancy of parents or grandparents. Many men and women raised in divorced families establish successful careers. Their workplace performance is largely unaffected by the divorce. But no matter what their success in the world, they retain some serious residues — fear of loss, fear of change, and fear that disaster will strike, especially when things are going well. They're still terrified by the mundane differences and inevitable conflicts found in every close relationship.

I'm heartened by the hard-won success of these adults. But at the same time, I can't forget those who've failed to straighten out their lives. I'm especially troubled by how many divorced or remained in wretched marriages. Of those who have children and who are now divorced, many, to my dismay, are not protecting their children in ways we might expect. They go on to repeat the same mistakes their own parents made, perpetuating problems that have plagued them all their lives. I'm also concerned about many who, by their mid- and late thirties, are neither married nor cohabiting and who are leading lonely lives. They're afraid of getting involved in a relationship that they think is doomed to fail. After a divorce or breakup, they're afraid to try again. And I'm struck by continuing anger at parents and flat-out statements by many of these young adults that they have no intention of helping their moms and especially their dads or stepparents in old age. This may change. But if it doesn't, we'll be facing another unanticipated consequence of our divorce culture. Who will take care of an older generation estranged from its children?

10 Will We Grow Old Together?

- From *Love and Other Infectious Diseases* by Molly Haskell

- "The Voices of Our Informants," from *Vital Involvement in Old Age,* by Erik Erikson et al.

- "Elegy for Iris" by John Bayley

- From *Love in the Time of Cholera* by Gabriel García Márquez

- Euripides, *Alcestis,* lines 747-1163

- From *Man's Search for Meaning* by Viktor Frankl

We have never interfered with each other, and strangely enough, never been jealous of each other. And now, in our advancing years, we love each other more deeply than ever. And also more agonizingly, since we see the inevitable end. It is not nice to know that one of us must die before the other.

— VITA SACKVILLE-WEST

"Ah, dear Juliet,
Why art thou still so fair? shall I believe
That unsubstantial death is amorous,
And that the lean abhorred monster keeps
Thee here in dark to be his paramour?
For feat of that, I still will stay with thee;
And never from this palace of dim night
Depart again. . . . lips, O you
The doors of breath, seal with a righteous kiss
A dateless bargain to engrossing death!"

— WILLIAM SHAKESPEARE

Introduction

How does old age and illness change a marriage? Molly Haskell's *Love and Other Infectious Diseases* is a witty and brutally honest memoir about an episode of illness that puts a marriage under severe strain. In the summer of 1983, Haskell's husband, the movie critic Andrew Sarris, was admitted to the hospital with what turned out to be a long-term, life-threatening infirmity. As Haskell traces the frightening course of his illness and his slow, fragile recovery, she reweaves the subtle fabric of their marital relationship, exploring the wonders and renewing powers of spousal love in their deepest psychological complexity.

In Erik Erikson's study, *Vital Involvement in Old Age,* the eminent psychologist allows the eloquent voices of ordinary people to be heard on the subject of love, loss, marriage, and remarriage in the sunset years. Not all married couples adjust well to the challenges of growing old together. But many of the comments contained in this excerpt are testimony to marriage at its best: here we see the endurance and resilience of conjugal love, the adaptability of the marital relationship to new conditions of life, its spiritual potential, and finally, the office of marriage as a school for service to others.

In the next reading, John Bayley, husband of the novelist Iris Murdoch, recounts her struggle with Alzheimer's disease. In this beautiful memoir, Bayley describes a metamorphosis in his marital relationship. Charged now, at the end of his life, with the custodial care of a woman who can utter only primal "mouse cries," he realizes that the claims of the outer world no longer interfere in his marriage as they once did. Every day, he asserts, "we move closer and closer together. . . . There is a certain comic irony — happily, not darkly, comic — that, after more than forty years of our taking marriage for granted, marriage has decided it is tired of this and is taking a hand in the game." The greatest promise of marriage, it turns out, comes not with the passionate sexual union of youthful romance, but in the quiet care and devotion of old age.

In the following vignette from Gabriel García Márquez's great novel, *Love in the Time of Cholera,* Fermina Daza is forced to cope with the sudden loss of her husband. So distraught is she that she is unable to sit down for a meal. She determines to assuage her grief by purging every reminder of his former presence from her surroundings. But try as she might, she cannot simply exorcise him from her life and memory. In his very absence he is ever present.

Can love be so great as to subdue even Death? Euripides' *Alcestis* tinkers with this theme. Alcestis loves her husband so deeply she offers to die that he, Admetus, might be spared his life. Now Admetus feels so intensely his grief at her passing, that he yearns for release from life. Lucky for the couple, Heracles saves the day, wresting Alcestis from the powers below, and bringing her back to life. Or does he actually bring Alcestis to life? Euripides' half-satirical play probes one of the greatest ironies of spousal loss. No sooner is the pitiful Admetus home from the funeral, having resolved never to look at another woman, than someone looking very much like his former wife catches his eye. . . . Often, men and women who feel most desolate at the loss of an "irreplaceable" spouse are the quickest to remarry. Marriage, after all, is an affirmation of life.

Viktor Frankl's work, *Man's Search for Meaning,* offers a final reflection on the spiritual component of a loving marriage. During his internment in a concentration camp, the constant thought of his wife and his love for her allowed Frankl to "retreat from . . . terrible surroundings to a life of inner riches and spiritual freedom." By the contemplation of his wife's image, Frankl found inner peace in the most horrible of circumstances. It turned out that for all the time of his imprisonment, his wife was dead, but Frankl claims that even if he had known of her demise, his "mental conversation with her would have been just as vivid and just as satisfying." "Love," he quotes, "is as strong as death."

MOLLY HASKELL

Molly Haskell was born in Charlotte, North Carolina, in 1939. Since 1969 she has been married to film critic Andrew Sarris. Her own film criticism has been published in the *Village Voice, New York* magazine, and *Vogue,* among other publications. Haskell is the author of the much-praised film study, *From Reverence to Rape: The Treatment of Women in the Movies* (1973). It is of interest because she puts forward the bold argument that Hollywood treated female characters with great dignity in the 1940s, portraying them in essentially egalitarian relationships with men. By the 60s and 70s however, despite the big social gains of feminism, the movies seemed to be peopled with female characters used and abused by males.

Love and Other Infectious Diseases

Chapter 6

After Andrew was taken up in the late morning, I went home and paced. And paced. Mother and I ate lunch, made small talk, and in trying to distract each other, distracted ourselves for at least a few minutes at a time. Then I would pace some more, panic, pray.

The need to believe survives loss of faith, survives everything, and then, it's the position you're in: once something has brought you to your knees, there is nothing to do but pray.

I made deals. I would take Andrew back on any terms. I would no longer nag him about reading newspapers all day, or shush him when his voice rose in restaurants. I would cherish his oft-told tales, his doomsday economic theories, the fingerprints he left on walls and surfaces, the burned teakettles, his absent-minded-professorisms, his driving.

I rationalized that Andrew was more precious to God than I was, and that it was his life I was praying for. But this was not quite true. I was praying for my life when I prayed for him. I could no more imagine eating, breathing, walking the face of the earth without him than I could imagine hanging upside down from a tree branch, or living underwater.

As the minutes and hours dragged by, I tried to picture what they might be doing to his poor belly, what demon they would find there. . . . I knew, from what I could remember of my own drug-hazed experience, that the surgical chamber was a disappointingly small room, more like a dentist's office, with bright lights and high-tech machinery, than the great amphitheater of early movies, or the one pictured in Thomas Eakins's majestic nineteenth-century painting *The Gross Clinic*. Speaking of medical pornography, that's the one in which the master surgeon — a stand-in for the artist in Eakins's view — is cutting up the leg of an unanesthetized young man while the distraught mother leaps forward in horror. The medical students stand by, interested but detached. With whom are we to identify? Andrew would be the star patient that day, but thanks to twentieth-century progress, he would be happily unconscious, while I sat at home, alternating between both "onlooker" viewpoints: surges of emotional panic and the more fear-numbing and voyeuristic view of the medical students.

I was suspended in a time warp, a sort of sensory-deprivation chamber, in which there were only two possibilities: Andrew would live; Andrew would die. It was like a dividing line in the middle of my life: everything that had come before was now rounded off and given an ending, but I was in blind ignorance about the future.

Finally, at 4:00 P.M., Dr. Gaines called with great news: the operation had been a success. He had performed a colostomy, which he hoped would be temporary, and I should notice "a marked improvement in a couple of days." I cried out to Mother. A marked *improvement* in only a couple of days? This seemed hard to believe, but I would believe anything.

The phone rang again. "Hold on there," said Sam, puncturing my euphoria when I told him what Gaines had said. He was shocked at Gaines's words. "Surgeons see things a little differently. No, what we have is a very scary situation. Andrew's blood pressure has gone down to 50, he's in shock, and he has a major-league infection."

But how could — ? How could there be such diametrically different versions? I had a sudden insight into the bizarre yet strangely logical thinking of surgeons and specialists in general (scientists, even artists: Eakins was right in implying an analogy). He had done his job and done it magnificently: he had attacked the problem, perhaps saved Andrew's life, found the solution, and he wasn't concerned with the aftermath and the problems that might arise. They belonged to somebody else.

Sam hadn't told me the whole of it, only what he felt he needed to tell me at the time, and even that was a good deal worse than I imagined. I didn't know (or choose to consider) what the drop in blood pressure signaled (a heart attack or ongoing septicemia, with possible mental damage, was most likely). So while Andrew's life hung by a thread, while I waited by the phone, both hoping and dreading someone would call, I focused on the one aspect of the whole thing that was least dangerous, but — and? — most vivid and easily imagined — the colostomy. In a colostomy, a section of the colon is removed, and then the end is brought through the surface of the stomach wall and enclosed in a waste bag. Some of these are temporary, others permanent. Although thousands of people live with colostomies gracefully, uncomplainingly, and often unbeknownst to most of their friends, I couldn't imagine Andrew being one of them. I could more easily imagine him without an arm or a leg. So instead of praying he wouldn't die, I prayed he wouldn't have a sloshy little shit bag attached to his belly for life.

The next morning Sam called to report that Andrew was still alive.

"I got him into the surgical ICU on the eleventh floor, one of the two best in the hospital," he said proudly. These days a major criterion of a good doctor is one with the clout to get his patients onto the best floors, into the best units, in touch with the best specialists. I wasn't complaining, only when I finally got in to see Andrew, I wished Sam could have spent a minute or two preparing me.

The ICU was itself an otherworldly experience. I was the only visitor — they'd agreed to let me in for a few minutes before regular hours. It was an antiseptic enclosure cut off from the rest of the hospital and the flow of life by its restricted visiting hours (11:00 to 11:45 in the morning, 5:00 to 5:45 in the evening). It was like an airship, suspended in space, sterile because there were none of the ordinary signs or sounds of life, only the whirring and clicking of machines surrounding mummylike patients, each click signaling that death had been forestalled by another moment. I walked along the small passageway, between two glass panes, where the patients, four on the right, two on the left, were lined up side by side, with tubes of the most expensive lifesaving machinery in the world reaching like tentacles into every orifice, and with their faces, peering out from oxygen masks, unrecognizable as to sex and age. They weren't humans but cyborgs, half man–half machine, new arrivals on display from the planet of near-death.

Andrew was pointed out to me: he was in the room on the left, the last patient. He was swollen to twice his normal size, three times what he'd been the day before. He'd gained this astounding amount of weight from water that had been pumped into him to bring up the blood pressure and treat vascular collapse. His whole right side was a purplish blue due to a blood transfusion that had missed the vein and gone subcutaneous. There were six or seven tubes coming out of his body — a catheter into the heart, a drainage tube, the Foley tube, peripheral lines in various veins. And a respirator the size of a vacuum-cleaner tube was in his mouth, which was taped over completely. His hands were tied down. And his eyes, dazed in his man-in-the-moon face, told me nothing. Did he recognize me? What was going on in his head? He was grotesque, unknowable.

That night I dreamed of a Frankenstein monster guarding the gates of Hell. Only Hell was Heaven, a cartoon-blue heaven, with white puffy clouds.

The next day Andrew had swollen even more, gaining over sixty pounds from the thirty liters of fluid he was being given daily. The fluid was to replace what had been lost from the vascular system. One of the problems with sepsis is that fluid leaks out of the small vessels, the capillaries, leaving the brain, heart, lungs, and kidneys deprived. Mentally he was the same except a little more alert, the anesthesia having worn off. His eyes moved, he could shake and nod his head. When I asked him if he recognized me, he nodded. But when I asked if he loved me, he shook his head, a vehement negative.

When I told the doctors how shocked I was over his appearance, I realized they didn't "see" him as I did. Looking bad or good to them didn't mean puffy or purple or crazy-eyed; it meant what was going on "inside" — the fever and the status of his organs. Even his mental state didn't interest them now, because it couldn't be distinguished from the disorientation produced by the surroundings.

"Everybody goes crazy in intensive care," Sam said. It has to do with the weird atmosphere: the fact that, due to the twenty-four-hour fluorescent lighting, there is no distinction between day and night; with the click-clicking of the machines, the gurgling of liquids, the constant blaring and bleating of the radio that the nurses keep on for their own sanity — late-night talk, early-morning talk, the same pop tunes (Lionel Richie singing "Truly," over and over again); what keeps the nurses sane drives the patients crazy even in their semiconscious state.

The doctors were elated that Andrew had gotten this far without dying or, at the very least, his heart or kidneys failing.

"There are a thousand things that can go wrong," Sam said. One was that if the liquid filled the vascular system beyond its capacity, fluid would seep over into the lungs and drown the patient. Another worry was adult respiratory distress syndrome, when the lungs fill with water — the large concentration of oxygen required to ventilate the patient with adult respiratory disease syndrome damages the lungs even further — they tighten up and fill with water, and nothing can be done. To me, he had never seemed so alien and unreachable. His appearance and hostility were so distressing that I thought I might take a day off. I asked Sam if he thought I could.

"No," he said. "It's important for you to come in. On some level he knows you're here and needs you."

I was almost relieved by diversion that came in the form of the two-week marathon viewing of films, by the selection committee, for the New York Film Festival. At the end of July and the beginning of August, the five of us who were on the committee gathered in a screening room and, from ten in the morning until five or six in the evening, watched the offerings that had poured in since Cannes — the grim, the ghastly, and the tedious, the minimalist, the folkloric, the earnest, and the occasional, very occasional gem that supposedly justifies all the time and expense. My colleagues that year were the late Richard Roud (he who virtually invented the festival and was unceremoniously dumped in 1987), Richard Corliss, Jim Hoberman, and David Thomson, and they were what made these two weeks in the dark worthwhile. This was a hip group of moviemanes and, under the directorship of Roud, a group that endured long hours and a very modest fee as much for the pleasure of each other's company as for the films themselves. Richard, slipping back and forth between London, Paris, and New York, elusive yet incandescently *there,* was the magnetic center of the group. He was one of the world's most charming and impossible people, and his running commentary on the generally mediocre films was the art form that held us all spellbound. He was the mischievous ringleader, but none of us was above taking a few pot shots.

It was a sort of game: who would be the first to sneer, to risk showing dislike for a movie someone else might be watching in impressed silence; or, conversely (and more courageously), who would have the nerve to defend a movie once it had elicited a snicker or a chuckle.

As if my nerves weren't already on edge, keeping up with this bunch of wiseacres was like being on a quiz show when you never knew what subject they were going to throw at you. The new film critics are an awesomely knowledgeable breed, smarter than most of the movies they review and the audiences who read their reviews, and they love to show off for each other, tossing off figures and gossip from the latest trade papers along with the minutiae and esoterica of film history, and there was a subtle atmosphere of male preening. Being with them, I felt like a peahen among the peacocks or a woman trapped in the press section of a sporting event, where the guys — in their egghead version of the macho men slogging it out on the field or the court — are reciting batting averages and recalling strategies and plays from great and obscure games of the past. It's a form of bonding and competing at the same time, a holdover from the time when boys separated themselves from girls through the numbers and lists, those male obsessions that seem to give them a handle on the world, to impose Reason and Order as a defense against death, birth, the unruly world of the emotions.

This summer, Andrew's demise and/or my emotional breakdown were an ever-present possibility, and their "facts" and *bons mots* and gossip and showy *aperçus* were a blanket of comfort — their way of distracting me. When I came in each morning, they would look at me awkwardly, then look away, with a barely audible sigh of relief: if I was there, Andrew wasn't dead yet. None of us mentioned Andrew, but I felt their unfailing compassion.

I could sense them slumping in their seats at certain scenes — death scenes and hospitals were very big that year — worried as to how they would affect me. Actually, these didn't bother me at all; on the contrary, they enthralled me: it was boring scenes and the tedium of bad films that threw me back on myself and my misery.

They shared the tension with me, and no doubt wondered, as they looked at my haggard, distraught face, how long I could go without collapsing under the strain. I felt their awkward, silent sympathy in all its complicated forms, the tension of all of us keeping up a front, so that it was almost a relief when, one day, I finally did break down.

Strangely — or not so strangely — it was over Mother, not Andrew. It came, seemingly, out of nowhere. The committee and I were having lunch at our hangout, Wolff's Delicatessen on Broadway, now gone, like Richard. I'd left home early that day, without seeing Mother, and having tried to get her on the telephone all morning, I went down to the pay phone to call her once again. When the phone rang and rang and she still didn't answer, I became upset, grew overwrought, then hysterical. I had visions of her lying in ashes, one of her cursed cigarettes having smoldered all night and finally set the bed on fire. That and emphysema were the two terminal fates my brother and I had always imagined for Mother, and now, as I displaced my anxiety for Andrew onto her, it seemed more than possible, it seemed absolutely *certain* that she had died in the night.

The two Richards took turns coming down to the phone booth with me, reassuring me as best they could.

"She's out doing errands," said Richard Roud sensibly, but I would hear none of it.

"She's probably still asleep," offered Richard Corliss, a late-show night owl and workaholic, who never got to bed until 3:00 A.M.

I reached Gabor, our superintendent, a gentle, sexy, and efficient Hungarian on whom every woman in our building had a secret crush, mechanical competence being the real turn-on to us cave-dwelling wives of urban klutzes. I asked him to go up and check to see if Mother was in the apartment, and gave him the number of the pay phone. Moments later, the phone rang and his reassuring, accented voice reported that the apartment was intact, but no sign of my mother. My anxiety refused to be quieted, ran in other directions: she'd been run over, she was lying in a gutter. Call the police.

Eventually she turned up: she had, indeed, been out doing errands. I talked to her, was finally calmed, and went back to the screening room for the afternoon. That evening, when I told her how upset I'd been, she was astonished.

"I didn't know you cared about me so much," she said, pleased. It was my turn to be astonished. How could she not have known how much I loved and needed her, that I couldn't have gotten along without her these last weeks? Because we didn't discuss such things. Because — such was the early imprinting I had had at her hands — I couldn't tell her so. This was the central irony in the complicated pact between us. In fostering my self-reliance, she had created a child who believed that the best way of getting her love was not to ask for it, not to behave like a child, not to *need* like a child. I had so suppressed such needs, had so little experience in finding words for them, that I had misplaced them altogether. Was it possible that on some level I really didn't know, or hadn't accepted, how much I needed Mother, and how great was my fear of being abandoned?

Something like this had happened earlier, back when Andrew was on the neurology floor, when I "lost" Mother one day at the hospital. We were to meet in the solarium, but through some misunderstanding, she was in one, I in another. I asked the nurses; everyone thought they had seen her go home. Annie and Jeffrey took me home, hysterical, plied me with Valium, and at my insistence called the police. They went through the motions, asked at the 96th Precinct if a Southern lady in her seventies had turned up, were told no. Finally Mother appeared, having of course been waiting for me at the *other* solarium. The relief in each case was so overwhelming that it was almost as if I had constructed the disappearance — the false "death" — in order to reverse it. I had "lost" a loved one — Mother as herself and as Andrew — in order to find them again in a happy ending that would portend Andrew's survival.

549

People tried to distract me — Mother with television, friends with detective stories — and I had all sorts of books piled up as usual beside my bed. But nothing worked. Death, in even the most stylized detective stories, seemed real: those refined British corpses gave off a stench. Any movie, whether bad or good, provoked thoughts of what it would have been like seeing it with Andrew and was thus tainted by a connection with him. Even the things I enjoyed *apart from him* — music, philosophy, more and different books, the occasional flirtatious lunch with another man — were things, I suddenly realized, that I enjoyed precisely because they *were* apart from him, a defense against his swallowing me up completely. My life was connected to his even by the interruptions in the chain and the disruptions of the harmony.

Andrew had been in the hospital five weeks, and gradually the sense of what life was like before was slipping away. I could barely remember what reading and discussing the paper in the morning was like, or listening to each other's boring dreams, laughing over each other's jokes. I thought of the byplay between us, those routines and alter egos we'd developed, as couples do, doppelgängers with squeaky voices, animal personae, sweet and sour versions of ourselves.

More and more I felt a sense of amputation. One of the worst things was, simply, the bedroom: waking up in it each morning, returning to it each night, feeling his absence everywhere, in the sheets, the smell of the pillow, the worn place in the rug between the bed and the closet, the filing cabinet with more papers on top than in. And especially the closet, that quintessence of Andrew. Before, Andrew's mess had driven me crazy, the dozens of mismatching tennis shoes, the scuffed loafers, ties fallen from the tie rack, the hangers tumbling out, the socks stuffed into the shoes (one black, one brown), all reminders of his inveterate sloppiness. But, in that curiously transfiguring way that absence has, these mementos had taken on a holy glow, had become the still-warm relics of a saint.

And finally it came to me with the force of a revelation, clear and painful and shocking. I was dependent on Andrew, wholly and utterly. Far from being independent, an "equal" partner in a marriage of equals, I was almost wholly supported by him, emotionally, financially, and intellectually. The idea of life without him, though my mind could hold it only for a flash, was pitch black, literally impossible to imagine. How was it possible, and how had I come to this? I was a clinging vine, not in the obvious ways, oh, no! On the surface, and to everyone including myself, I was self-defining, confident, but my heart was embedded in him, my lungs got their oxygen from his. I realized that I was crazier than Andrew, that my love for him was a kind of madness more insidious for being hidden, undiagnosed.

As someone who had always prided herself on looking life straight in the eye, this came as a shock. My rather pathetic solution to my own evasion was to play a sort of game in which I exorcised the fear of death by confronting it directly, or pretending to.

"Oh, death, where is thy sting?" said I, in effect. I made plans: "Okay, so die — now, while I'm still relatively young. I'll get remarried. Die, and I'll get rid of all those books, call Columbia and get them to send a truck down for all the papers, spilling out of filing cabinets and closets. And I'll have space!"

Space? Yes, but where? In some walk-up in Brooklyn or a nice two-room in Hoboken? Until this moment, nothing had come to ruffle the vision of myself as a bona fide liberated woman, a writer slash feminist with a book under her belt, a marriage-of-equals partner. But when it came to the nuts and bolts of finances, there was nothing equal about our marriage. I now had to face the unpleasant fact that without Andrew I was anything but independent, and without Andrew's income I was anything but self-supporting. In purely practical New York terms, I would be destitute. So far, it appeared that both *The Village Voice* and Columbia, in their quite surprising munificence, would continue Andrew's salary during his illness, but if he died I became a statistic in the feminization of poverty.

And what about the image I'd always cherished of myself as a loner, treasuring those evenings when Andrew went out of town, or when I went on trips. Like most women, I was delirious when sprung from domesticity, obedience to schedule; I would go anywhere for which a free ticket was supplied. Yet the solitude that I loved was hardly the solitude of the single woman, the divorcee, the widow. It was always circumscribed by Andrew; he was the music that always played in my head, the symphonies, the operas, the show melodies, against which I lived my life.

As a test to my hypothetical widow, I resurrected from mothballs my old Village-bohemian fantasy to see how it played, and it didn't. Living in poetic disarray in a basement apartment on Perry Street was out of the question now — too expensive; I was too old, too afraid of cancer, and too much of an insomniac to drink espresso and smoke Gitanes. Village coffee houses had been replaced by fast-food outlets, intellectuals were outnumbered by scruffy outerborough types, there were no places to hang out and discuss Mallarmé (reading and finally penetrating Mallarmé in the original was part of my Village fantasy).

And what were our finances anyway? . . .

. . . For the moment, I thought we were all right, assuming the hospital and doctors' bills were going to be covered by either Blue Cross or Major Medical, of which Andrew had two policies. But for how long? He had a $250,000 lifetime ceiling on his plan at Columbia, but it was now only August 6, and obviously nowhere near the end of the illness: Sam predicted this was going to be one of the most expensive illnesses on record. There was not only the astronomical cost of the ICU and all its technology, but because of the length of the illness and continuing bafflement, the need for more tests, more specialists. Columbia was pressing to know whether Andrew would be able to return for the fall term; unable to face the obvious — that even if Andrew didn't die, he would hardly be up to teaching anytime in the near future, I put them off.

What terrified me most was also the most shaming. It was my intellectual dependence on Andrew. He was a walking reference book, a live-in fund of insights and erudition, and a sounding board for my ideas. I rarely wrote an article without discussing it with him, calling upon his sweeping sense of the past, his instinct for spotting and defining social phenomena. Our lives and our work merged and cross-fertilized, a long-running talk show in which we stimulated and inspired each other. My reliance on him was a secret canker. How could I know if I could get along without him since I had never tried? And whom would I write for? Andrew was my reader, his the eyes I wanted to see light up with pleasure, not mine.

Strangely enough, I suspected that most of our friends would have been startled at this glimpse of our marriage, would have thought that if one of us were to die, it would be my death that would devastate Andrew. But I knew now it wasn't so. As crazy about me as Andrew was, as theatrically devoted — an anxious look if he lost sight of me at a party, a hangdog voice on the phone if I was away — it was I who was more deeply in need of him. If I had died, Andrew would have crawled back into his hole, contented himself with movies, with thinking, with his own solitary form of being: he had never quite believed his good fortune in getting me to begin with. Whereas I . . . I felt that if Andrew died, I would die, too. Not by suicide, but just automatically, as bees die when they are detached from the hive. . . .

. . . Then, finally one night he was off the respirator, with only an oxygen mask to assist his breathing. He was making those beautiful respiratory sounds on his own, a soft, just audible hissing. He didn't say anything for a long time, but at last he reached out — his hands had been temporarily untied — and took mine in his and grasped them tight. Then said, "I love you so much."

I felt such a rush of happiness, a physical sense of life coming back into me. Just as his lungs had finally begun to push air through his body, just as his organs were beginning to tremble with life, so some frozen-over pool of sane emotion had thawed. I fell over him, leaned gently across his bandaged body, listened to the miraculous sound of his breathing, and as I did so it was as if we had found each other in some place that was neither life nor death, sanity nor madness, some hole in the universe where we were joined each to each, and through each other to the dead. It may be that Andrew had come halfway back from death and I had gone the rest of the way to meet him. It may be that Andrew had a stronger hold on life than I did, and was pulling us both back from the brink.

A few days later, Andrew was still breathing well but he was in full, flaming paranoia. He begged me to get an ambulance and take him to the D.A.'s office where our friend Bob Morgenthau would issue a writ to get him out. Moments later, he asked for a gun. I asked him why.

"I want to shoot myself, because" — and here came that absurd understatement that had become his trope — "I'm fed up." So I tried to distract him — "Andrew, you've always been an advocate of gun control" — but he just kept asking for the gun.

Now, some of the 720 things that could go wrong were going wrong. Michael said he would have to be kept in Intensive Care longer because the infected incision wasn't healing. Despite the scraping away of dead skin to encourage the cells to start regenerating, Andrew's weakness and anemia were delaying their growth. The morphine he needed during the scraping process slowed down his body functions and depressed the activity of the lungs and bowels. His hematocrit had now fallen from 32 to 28 (normal is 40 to 47) so they were transfusing him and increasing the hyperalimentation he was being given intravenously. According to the hematologist, the drop could be attributed to any one of a number of things: a loss of white blood cells, which could be a reaction to the drugs (they had stopped administering the possibly offending antibiotic vancomycin); an underlying disease, whatever it might be; or the infection. The decrease in red and white cells could mean bone-marrow suppression. Yet, as Sam put it, the disease was so ominous and multifaceted, if some of these things weren't going wrong, something would be wrong — with their perceptions. Andrew's wasn't an isolated infection, but a multiple one, its ramifications showing just how interdependent all the systems in the body were.

Now the thing that I had been dreading was upon us — the August exodus. Sam would be going to Martha's Vineyard Friday, and on Thursday, when all of this was happening, he was preparing me for his departure. We were standing in the small hallway of the ICU going over the details. Medically, Andrew would be in the best hands: all the specialists who were already dealing with him would continue and a new man, a Dr. Davis, would take over for Sam and act as coordinator. My fear expressed itself in a sudden anxiety over financial details. . . .

As Sam went over details I began to feel spasms of self-pity and aggravation rise in me. Sam was standing there in his white coat and a blue shirt, leaning against the paneled wall, that boyish shock of hair falling over his forehead, guiding me impeccably through what might be expected to occur in his absence, when in the midst of it I let out a sigh. A sigh! I was ready to collapse, fall to the floor, sob, throw myself in Sam's arms for comfort, rage at him for deserting me, but I did none of these. What I did was sigh. A poor, pitiful — but socially acceptable — sigh.

And how did Sam react? He shook his head reprovingly. "None of that now," he said.

I was cut to the quick. He wasn't just saying "Buck up" — that I could have taken; he was rebuking me, he was saying that my sigh was excessive, my implied complaint out of place. I felt breathless with embarrassment. Had I been troublesome? Called him night and day? Asked for emotional support? Painted myself a martyr? No, none of the above. On the contrary, I'd been a model of restraint, I'd even thought to get points for my stoicism, perhaps unconsciously hoped for a little praise ("You're doing great, Molly, keep it up!"), and instead I stood there with egg on my face, humiliated. . . .

Andrew was now alternating between periods of hallucination and a proximate lucidity, i.e., he had developed some vague sense of his predicament, but still saw it as something that had been inflicted on him by his enemies, or by friends who were now deserting him. One of the most consistent symptoms of his madness was that he never knew where he was, a peculiarity that seems to be generally true of people with delusions or brain disease, as if to admit to where they are would concede important ground to the opposition. Actually, I think the simplest explanation would be that their wandering minds literally are elsewhere, back in the town where they were born, on the high seas, anywhere but here. Andrew could answer questions of a historical nature: the name of a movie, the year of a war, who killed Jack Kennedy. But to the question of where he was (i.e., recent memory; awareness of surroundings) he never gave the same answer. Now he thought he was in Nebraska and asked the nurses why nobody came to see him. He threatened to kill himself again. He was in his bitter sardonic mood one day when Mother came in, the first time she'd seen him since surgery nine days earlier.

She came out after a brief visit and told me she felt he looked better. When I went in later, Andrew said, "Your mother looked worried."

"But no," I said. "She told me she thinks you look better."

To which Andrew, without a trace of irony in his voice, replied, "Maybe that's why she looks worried." He mumbled something bitterly about the cream of the jest, and the next day, when I came in, he said he'd had a "bad fantasy."

"Your mother prefers a statue of me to the real thing." He paused. "Also, she wanted to cut off my head."

There was a marvelous and uncanny appositeness to this fantasy, intertwining the fear of castration at the hands of the "enemy" mother, with Mother's abstract art, her style of painting figures without faces, without features.

Next to Andrew was a woman in her sixties who'd also had a colostomy — one of those hair-raising horror stories in which a doctor had given her a barium enema, sent her home, and then, when she reported, and continued to report, bleeding and pain, he kept ignoring the symptoms and telling her to lie down and rest. By the time she came in she had a perforated colon, and now peritonitis.

Her visitors — a husband, children, nieces — provided rich material for Andrew's fantasies. Her husband had stolen her pocketbook, Andrew reported, and was pawning her eyeglasses. He also thought they had stuck an umbrella down his throat, and insisted that I look at his bottom to see if it had come out the other end. In fact, though I didn't know it at the time, he was developing bedsores on his rump, which may have provoked this striking image.

He had gotten numerous letters and get-well cards from friends and fans. Most of them he ignored, but his face lit up over one of them, a card with a stunning photograph of Garbo on the front. He was even more pleased at the message, affectionate words from a fan who missed his column. I taped it to the wall so that he could see it from his bed, but he frowned.

"That doesn't count for anything here," he said morosely, referring both to the glorious Garbo and to his own status as a Garbo-worshiping critic reduced to the status of a nobody. His attitude toward me was less one of rage or fury than the exasperation of someone who has lost all hope of persuading the other of the reality of his world. The classical Hitchcock hero/victim whose own mother and/or wife refuse to believe him.

"I love you," he said sadly at one point, "but you and I are talking at cross-purposes."

And another time, he said, "I have a selfish suggestion. Could you be the one to suffer ninety percent of this torture?"

He was being given transfusions and the white cells were down, nothing of major significance, but it always seemed to me he just wasn't getting any better. On August 12 his spinal fluid showed a rise in white cells. Dr. Davis, the covering doctor, said the fever wasn't high, that it could indicate either an infection of the wound or a slight case of pneumonia, both of which would resolve themselves as Andrew improved.

Then, out of left field, came a blow of surreal proportions. On Tuesday,

August 14, they discovered that Andrew couldn't move his legs. "Flaccid paralysis," they called it, and planned to do X-rays. Wouldn't that just be the normal atrophying of the muscles? I asked, but Dr. Ramir thought it was more than weakness. He speculated it might be something called porphyria, a metabolic problem in which, because of the body's abnormal ability to break down hemoglobin (which makes up a good portion of the body's blood), abnormal products build up. But Andrew didn't fit the diagnosis neatly, so it could be some aspect of this carried to an extreme . . . or something else altogether. The abnormality, according to Ramir, was not in the spinal cord itself, but in the nerves leaving the spinal cord. It was unbelievable, yet it wasn't. A paralysis of the legs? Andrew, if he survived, might never walk again? I mean, after all, why not? And walking seemed small potatoes compared to living.

At 4:00 P.M. Ramir called. Tests showed that nerves were disconnected from the muscles. There might be a small abscess within the spinal column. The next day they would do a myelogram — a spinal tap in which the patient is placed at an angle and injected with a dye that's heavier than spinal fluid. Jeffrey, who'd been away for two weeks, saw Andrew two days in a row, then called to confirm the paralysis and say that his legs were worse the second day. I had kept hoping it might be some kind of temporary immobility, but Jeffrey assured me that it was a real paralysis. It could be any of a number of things (Jeffrey doubted it was porphyria), one of which was Guillain-Barré syndrome. This, of course, was a familiar term to me now, and, as far as Andrew was concerned, a dreaded one. There was no way, it seemed to me, that anyone in his condition could survive a paralysis that traveled upward from the legs to the hips, the chest, the lungs, all those organs that had been living daily under siege.

It was at this time that I began to dread going to see him. The craziness, the weakness, those wretched moods, never a moment of lightness or hope, of normal discourse — it was more than I could bear. I told Jeffrey I didn't think I could go in one more day, and he agreed saying he didn't know how I'd been able to keep it up until now. The strength that enabled me to trudge down there twice a day, day after day, only to see that blighted body and familiarly unfamiliar face began to seem a mixed blessing. I longed to break down, have an excuse for not coming in. I dreaded it, yet something — morbid fascination, perhaps — kept me going. I *had* to see him, see what twists and turns he had taken that day, that hour.

The results of the myelogram were to come in on Friday, August 17. On Friday evening, still not having heard, I sat through a screening of Milos Forman's *Amadeus,* trying to get with the antic playfulness of Tom Hulce's Mozart and hiss at the mordant envy of Salieri, but feeling, even in the divine Mozartian score, only tragedy. Jeffrey called me that night with the results —

negative — but he pointed out that this was not so good: it could mean a Guillain-Barré-type "ascending paralysis," which would develop within a week.

The plan was to move Andrew from the ICU on Monday to a private room on F7, supposedly the best nursing floor in the hospital. In addition, he would have to have round-the-clock registered nurses to dress the wound, which was still dangerously infected — dangerous to Andrew and dangerous to those around him. On Saturday and Sunday he was extremely tired, and weak, and thin, but he seemed to be more interested in the outside world. When I told him about the DeLorean acquittal and Reagan's gaffe over bombing the Russians, he wanted to know if the election was over.

"How long do you think you've been here?" I asked him.

"Six months," he said. (It wasn't yet two.) Nor could he tell me where he was when I asked him. When I came in Sunday evening, he was still hallucinating. He looked at me with surprise. "I thought you'd had an operation," he said. I explained that that was several years ago. Then I mentioned his mother, and he looked even more shocked.

"But she's dead," he said. I argued back and forth with him for half an hour before I could convince him otherwise. That night, prior to the move, he was very confused, insisting that he was in Auschwitz, and he slept with his eyes wide open, the pupils rolling back in his head while he murmured and mumbled. When I told him he wouldn't remember any of this, he said, "I remember all too clearly through a hole in my stomach."

His mind had hatched yet another striking image to integrate and organize the horrors he experienced into a poetically apt metaphor. He was like those lunatics who believe they are receiving position papers from God or messages from outer space through their belly-buttons, only he really had a hole, a giant crater of a receiving dish — a womb, or a missile launching pad? — for his transmissions.

There is always an undercurrent of anxiety and suspense before a move, and Sunday, the day before Andrew's, was fraught with both. The woman in the bed beside him, the woman who'd also had a perforated colon, died. I couldn't tell if Andrew quite took it in, but it was a blow to the rest of us. She had never really come back, yet here was Andrew, talking gibberish, seeming far sicker in many ways, but apparently determined to elude the Grim Reaper.

The evening before Andrew's move, I said good-bye to the staff of the ICU with emotion. He would have his own nurses, and the regular nursing staff but we'd be more on our own now. A small miracle had taken place here and I didn't want to leave those responsible. Michael, my favorite, had hoped to come down with us as night nurse, but Andrew's stay in the ICU had been longer than expected, and he had to return to school. Finally, I shook hands with the intern who'd seen him over the last two weeks.

He was standing by Andrew's bed, looking first at him, then at me. "You know," he said, "he came as close to death as a person can come without actually dying."

I looked over at Andrew, still in some twilight zone of his own. Why hadn't he died and what was it in him that had brought him this far? His darting eyes and baleful mutterings weren't going to tell me. And certainly the doctors, who still didn't know what he had, couldn't tell me. Through some phenomenal combination of medical technology, first-class nursing, and his own incredible constitution, Andrew had — so far — survived. But it wasn't over yet, as the doctors and nurses assured me.

I left the room and, glancing briefly at the patients on the left, surreal, isolated, and unrecognizable (were they the same ones I'd seen nineteen days ago? no way of knowing), I walked along the corridor, and out the door of the surgical Intensive Care Unit and I never looked back.

ERIK ERIKSON

Erik Erikson (1902-1994) was born in Frankfurt, Germany. He studied during the 1920s at Freud's Vienna Psychoanalytic Institute. In 1933 he immigrated to the United States, where he taught at Harvard and then at Yale. Erikson's major contribution to the field of individual psychology lay in his theories of child development, which posited the adolescent "identity crisis" as fundamental to healthy adult personality formation in modern society. (See *Childhood and Society,* 1950.) He was also a gifted psycho-biographer, the author of the Pulitzer Prize winning *Gandhi's Truth,* and the acclaimed *Young Man Luther.* In *Vital Involvement in Old Age* Erikson extends to older adults his investigation of the impact of culture and society on personality development. The work was written in 1986 in collaboration with Helen Q. Kivnick, and Erikson's wife of then fifty-six years, Joan Mowat Serson Erikson.

"The Voices of Our Informants," from Vital Involvement in Old Age

Our informants include long-married couples, individuals who are widowed and divorced, and ones who are now remarried. (Throughout this chapter we shall use the word *widow* as a generic term, to refer to a man or a woman whose marital partner has died.) Regardless of their current marital status, however, they fondly recall the courtship experiences of their teens and twenties — experiences that marked the beginning of long-term marriages in which they have experienced the intimacy that has dominated their adult lives.

For some, very specific memories seem to evoke an immediate, sensual reinvolvement in their earliest adulthood commitments to intimacy. One woman met her husband through his family, and she says, eyes twinkling, "I was crazy about him. We went out together for three months, but he never touched me. Finally I told him, 'Something better happen tonight or else.' I wouldn't explain any more. So he kissed me that night, and he kissed me until the day he died." This woman has now been widowed for many years. She has filled her life with children and grandchildren, and with friends and activities. Because of her lively sense of humor and essential good-heartedness, she is regarded as a welcome companion. But for her no current companion can replace her husband. The love she shares with these others cannot replace the love she shared with him. Perhaps her telling anecdotes about her life together with him continues to evoke in her that particular, special love that she has not shared with anyone since he died.

In the past few years, this woman has become nearly blind and increasingly deaf. Having lost one leg to a diabetes-related disease, she is confined to a wheelchair. Hugs and touches of affection are increasingly important, as they convey several critical messages. Most obviously, they tell her that she is loved, and they allow her to express her love in return. In addition, they supplement the dubiously reliable information provided by her eyes, in letting her know that she is not alone in a room. Finally, this kind of touching conveys, quite physically, the message that although she is old and although she is ill, she is still part of the world of living people, where individuals reach out to one another in body as well as in spirit. Sadly, for this woman as for many similarly disabled elders, fragility tends to keep at bay the spontaneous, affectionate physical contact that is so much a part of old loving. It is primarily with grandchildren that she, like many others, is able to enjoy the loving reassurance of physical contact. Reminiscing about the sensuality of early love enables her to view with life-span perspective the unwelcome extent to which she now remains largely apart. Perhaps, in eliciting the feelings of an earlier time, it also helps fill this current void.

As the sexual quality of long-intimate relationships undergoes age-related changes, and as now-unmarried individuals live in often unchosen celibacy, reminiscing allows elders to reintegrate qualities of earlier-life tenderness, affection, and sexuality. However shyly or awkwardly, many of our subjects describe having chosen their partners on the basis of a measure of sexual attraction. A few people speak openly about early feelings of love and fondness. An extremely conservative man of few words blushes as he recalls that after high school he and his girlfriend (later to become his wife) attended different colleges but "kept on liking each other pretty good." Another man chuckles as he explains, "I met my wife at one of them kissing parties." For these individuals, as for many others, the recalling of earlier sensuality seems to serve as a source of happiness, as it brings to life intimate experience that has been missed for many years. . . .

Most of the people in our study recall, or at least describe, marriages of lifelong mutual affection, supportiveness, understanding, companionship, and ever-increasing appreciation. A thoughtful man, married in his teens and comfortable today after decades of grappling with poverty and setbacks, notes with real tenderness, "The fondness we had for each other has always eased all other pains." Other informants cite numerous aspects of consistent mutuality and gratification in their long married lives: "We have always shared all our activities and made all decisions together." "We enjoy our own company." "We tried hard to please each other." "We grew closer over time." "We always enjoyed each other so darned much." "We have a better understanding as we get older as a family." "I need him for some things and he needs me. We're complementary." "We were always happy being together and doing things together." All of these recollections are integral to the fondness, devotion, and passion of love in old age.

We find quite striking the consistency and uniformity of these descriptions of marital intimacy, particularly in view of various suggestions, in the files of such informants as the woman discussed at length above, of earlier-life marital difficulties and dissatisfactions. Such discrepancies between today's descriptions and those given forty years ago seem to indicate an important psychological process. They suggest that for some elders, after decades in which the balance between intimacy and isolation was often precarious, integrating a sense of love across the whole life cycle may involve the reevaluating and recasting of earlier experiences to such an extent that these experiences become unrecognizable to the outsider.

Even those of our informants for whom, according to the historical data, difficulties and separateness seemed to outweigh intimate mutuality for decades — even they are reluctant to mention marital difficulties of any sort, past or present, in their conversations with us. On the whole, they prefer to report gratifying marriages of affection and complementarity. The cases of two individuals are particularly illustrative. A woman, a rather recent widow whom, in earlier life, the Guidance Study had advised against the divorce she repeatedly threatened, now describes her marriage as having been "devoted from the very beginning. We were sweethearts to the day he died." For this woman it seems that, throughout the period of childrearing, marriage meant gratifying intimacy in chaotic imbalance with frustrating isolation. This imbalance lessened when the children left home, and for more than the last twenty years of their life together, she and her husband shared an intimacy that was perhaps especially gratifying in its contrast to the unhappiness of the preceding decades. This woman is both pleased with and proud of the mutual devotion of the latter half of her marriage. In her old age, this immediately preceding period clearly dominates her sense of marital intimacy, and it is the one she most wants to remember.

Historical records indicate that throughout her thirties and forties, a second woman reported to the Guidance Study that she had nothing in common with her husband, that they quarreled incessantly, that he was offering little either to her or to their three sons, that she was responsible for him as for an additional child, and that she wanted very much to be out of what she experienced as an oppressive and unrewarding marriage. Today she asserts, "The fact that we think so much alike is one of the strongest ties that has held us together. We have always done everything together. Always helped one another. For sixty-one years." Today, indeed, this couple do seem to do everything together. In a manner often characteristic of people who have known each other very well, for a long, long time, they participate in a gentle, playful teasing, interspersed with matter-of-fact observations about each other's strengths and idiosyncrasies. They figure in almost every sentence of each other's conversation, and they are clearly and inextricably part of each other's lives. The fact of this old-age intimacy has certainly transcended the painful marital differences of forty years ago. Still, the disparity between these two views of this marriage remains striking. Perhaps this woman would feel disloyal at mentioning shortcomings perceived earlier in the partner to whom she has been so close for so long. Or perhaps years of mutual devotion have colored her memories, so that she remembers the early decades of marriage as a time not of argument with each other but, instead, of mutual struggle against the outside world.

Many of the women in our study came of age in an era of Victorian prudishness that frequently led to ignorance about sexuality. One exclaims, "Can you imagine, six older brothers and I didn't even know where babies come from until a month before I was married!" Another recalls ruefully, "I didn't know anything about sex until I was grown and almost married. When I found out I was just sick." Typical of partners in Victorian marriages, many of our subjects seem to have experienced difficult marital adjustments and serious early sexual problems, often characterized by frigidity in women and resigned good humor in men. For most couples, sincere affection and good-natured patience often made possible marriages that weathered their stormy beginnings and proved, ultimately, to be mutually satisfying and enduring. As they seek to reintegrate qualities of fondness, affection, and sexuality into a lifelong sense of love, the elders in our study are able to pass over short-lived early difficulties and to focus, instead, on a long lifetime of marital satisfaction.

Only a very few of our aged informants are explicitly critical of or disappointed in their spouses or their lifelong marriage. One woman, now widowed, looks back on her husband as having been incapable of affection. She recalls, "I looked to my children for intimacy." This woman does not speak of her feelings toward her husband during the long years of their marriage. Historical data indicate that in addition to being incapable of affection he was also unable to earn a living, leaving to his wife the responsibility of supporting the family. She met this responsibility and blossomed with it. However, while she developed certain dimensions of generativity and industriousness to a greater extent than she might have if her family and work situations had been more traditional, she developed dimensions of intimacy to a lesser extent than most women in more traditional circumstances. Particularly since her husband's death, this woman has developed a valuable mutuality in relations with her children. Today she looks back with resigned acceptance on the absence of closeness with her husband, and she quickly moves on to consider the more immediate, more gratifying intimacy she has been able to share with the children. Somehow, she has been able to balance the isolation in her marital past with an overall sense of intimacy that exists into the present.

In contrast, the following man cannot put behind him the sense of isolation he felt in his marriage. Divorced for approximately twenty years, he complains that his wife felt superior to him from the very beginning: "I often wonder why I married that woman. And to think that I stayed with her for thirty-two years!" This man has been single since his divorce, and his bitterness against his ex-wife still pervades his conversation. He blames her for turning the children against him. Although she died several years ago, it continues to rankle that she remarried shortly after leaving him, while he has remained alone. In comparison with the woman discussed immediately above, this man does not seem to have maximized other psychosocial strengths to compensate for the enduring lack of intimacy in his marriage. Neither has he found subsequent intimacy with children or friends. Thus, in old age he looks back on a marriage that failed more than two decades ago, as his primary experience in an intimate relationship. From that temporally distant marriage, feelings of bitter isolation persist with a degree of affect usually associated with events of the present. It is as if he has not been able to relegate his ex-wife or his failed marriage to the past, and so they, and the feelings they engender, remain very much a part of his present.

Among the very few elders who acknowledge disharmony in their present-day relationships are a long-married couple whose current life painfully illustrates several issues that may arise as deteriorating aged partners seek to reintegrate the lifelong themes of intimacy and isolation. This couple present a rosy view of their history together. Theirs seems to have been a rather traditional, highly complementary marriage. On a severely restricted budget, the wife showed enormous energy and ingenuity in raising five children, nurturing their intellectual and artistic talents, and maintaining an interesting and visually attractive home. The husband worked long, hard hours to provide the family's income. Both parents enjoyed their particular family-related tasks. With respect to the world outside the home, the wife remained perpetually in the background. She facilitated and applauded her husband's achievements. She laughed at his jokes. He always relied on and appreciated her support.

Now the husband observes, "We've been a good balance to each other in the past. But there's not a good balance now." The wife's arthritis forced this couple to move to a bland, ordinary apartment, away from the lovely home into which they had put so much effort, and in which they had planned to live out their days. Her condition has continued to deteriorate, forcing a more recent move into a two-room unit in a facility that serves meals and provides medical and therapeutic care. She dozes off in the middle of conversations, meals, and movies.

Instead of being well cared for by a clever, energetic, appreciative partner for whom he could enjoy striving to excel, the husband is now required to provide care for an often unappreciative invalid. Yet, as hard as he may try, he knows that he cannot provide all of the care she needs. He must arrange for her to receive supplementary professional assistance. He resents being forced to learn the kinds of domestic activities that have never been part of his repertoire. He resents the loss of his cheering section at a time when his own confidence requires boosting. He is angry at her abandoning him with so little notice. He sadly misses his companion of many decades, and he is truly concerned about her deteriorating condition. Searching for other sources of mutuality, he has developed an active friendship network within their building, and he often flees his apartment for companionship.

The wife is resentful of his impatience with her, and she becomes increasingly determined to rely on him for everything. She will not accept assistance from workers who are paid to provide such services as bathing or physical therapy; she will accept assistance only from her husband. After years of running a household, she is frustrated and embarrassed at being helpless. She is frightened and furious at the perception that when, for the first time in their life together, she has had to be dependent on her husband, he does not reciprocate her years of devotion himself, but, instead, passes the buck by enlisting assistance. Afraid of being without him, she ties him to her with a very short rope. She asserts that she has no interest in being friends with any of the people in the building, but when her husband is visiting with a neighbor, she will phone, insist that he come fetch her, and then somehow be unable to remain in the neighbor's home for more than a few minutes.

This couple represents a poignant extreme in the kinds of adjustments old age and its deteriorations can force long-term partners to make in their expectations of and behaviors toward one another. These people's long-established, complementary patterns of intimacy are no longer effective, and thus far they have been unable to adapt to their perpetually changing circumstances. Each of them feels wronged, isolated, and abandoned, Each feels so angry and frightened that neither seems able to make the gestures that might strengthen them both — gestures toward meaningful intimacy, toward caring cooperation. After nearly sixty-five years of marriage, their intimate, loving satisfaction now derives almost entirely from their past. And this past they describe in terms so mutually consistent, so rigidly unchanging, that the description takes on the quality of a mantra. Perhaps the strength of this consensual, frequently reevoked image of appropriate intimacy will somehow either soothe or outweigh the sense of separateness that now threatens to overwhelm each one of them.

Perhaps this couple's old-age situation will stabilize in such a way that they will be able to accommodate, to establish a new, workable balance between current intimacy and current individual isolation. Whatever progress they are able to make for the future, today's present difficulties will be part of the past on which they will look back in ten years, as they seek to integrate mutuality and separation across their old age.

Even couples whose physical health does not precipitate such sudden, severe alterations in lifelong patterns must adapt to changes in daily routine, imposed by diminished energy, by professional retirement, and by new interests and activities. They must adapt to changes in individual trust, autonomy, initiative, industriousness, and identity — in themselves and in each other. And with such adaptation must come the establishment of a new equilibrium between feeling close and feeling alone.

The wife of a new retiree observes, "We get on each other's nerves a little bit. We're not used to being together all the time." This couple face the challenge of developing satisfying patterns of individual independence in a context of physical proximity and emotional closeness. The wife can no longer count on her husband to leave her alone each day and to return home with salary in hand, full of interesting, entertaining stories about his day's adventures as a photojournalist. Throughout most of their marriage, she has devoted her energies to making their home a place where he can relax and "refuel" between workdays. Her vicarious pleasure in the excitement and glamour of his career has long rewarded her for the housework she might otherwise have found boring and repetitive. Now that his career has come to an end, she must look to the past for those rewards on which she has relied, for meeting the household responsibilities that have not terminated along with her husband's employment. . . .

The mourning process seems to provide the opportunity to experience currents of sadness, guilt, passion, resentment, delight, fear, and the many other conflicting emotions that were part of a lifetime of marital love. One man who had come to take his wife's companionship for granted finds himself vividly recalling details of their long life together, every time he looks at the chair in which she used to sit and in which she recently died. A woman speaks of her angry frustration at her husband's leaving her with so little notice or time for preparation, perhaps reflecting other resentments that historical data have documented in this marriage. Expressions of resentment soon give way, however, to memories of the intimate devotion and mutual delight that seem to have predominated in the half century of this couple's love for one another.

Among our informants, widows of long-intimate marriages never really finish with the reexperiencing that is so much a part of mourning. Rather, they seem to reach a point at which these feelings no longer dominate every minute of every day. At this juncture, they find themselves able to begin to build upon the lifelong strength of marital love, in developing new kinds of mutuality with relatives and friends who are still alive. Still, even those individuals who successfully organize their lives in such a way that they spend time with loving friends and family, engage in activities of interest, and participate in programs that provide various kinds of assistance to others — even they often find themselves missing their partners profoundly, after many years of widowhood. They try to be optimistic about this feeling of isolation. A woman explains, "I like to be alone in a way, and I don't really feel lonely. But it is hardest getting along without him because we were so close. I miss his companionship so much." In grappling with this ongoing emptiness, aged widows must continually reconcile the extent to which the lifelong sense of marital intimacy is an inextricable part of old-age identity. These individuals cannot feel like themselves in old age without considering the partners who were part of their lives for so long. In the absence of these partners, a measure of isolation seems to be a necessary dimension of widowhood identity.

Of those widows who have remained alone, most speak quite explicitly about being uninterested in marrying again. A woman laughs and says, "When my friends ask if I don't want a husband I always say, 'Of course! I need three — one to manage the finances, one to maintain the house, and one to keep me company.'" She adds, "When you get old everybody can kiss you, and you're not a threat to anybody." Her humor and perceptive observation hint at the strength of the intimate bond she still has with her husband. Although he is dead, she remains married to him; marriage to someone new would be tantamount to bigamy. This woman does appreciate male company, and she is often grateful to have a man escort her to a nighttime event she would otherwise not attend. She would, quite possibly, be grateful to a man who offered to manage her finances or her household. But although all of these functions are part of the everyday balance of responsibilities making up a marriage, in themselves they concern shared maintenance activities and not the mutuality of marital love. For some women, remarrying may represent a breach of loyalty to their husbands. For others, it may represent an impossible abandonment of a part of themselves. For still others, its challenges may seem to require more energy than they can muster — to face, anew, issues of sexual and emotional intimacy. Although many of these women may wish for assistance in meeting maintenance responsibilities, most seem to view a search for a new marriage partner as all but unthinkable.

Also among the widows in our study are some who are either currently remarried or widowed for the second time. These individuals provide interesting insights into an old-age integration of successive marital intimacy. One man was widowed in his early fifties, when his wife died of cancer. Now in his early nineties, he has been married to his second wife for considerably longer than the twenty-three years he spent with his first. He explains, "I compare the two marriages, but not too much. I never bring up my first wife in conversation. This wife is attentive. She loves me, and I know she does, and I love her. But you can love two people, you know. For a long time, I didn't think about my first wife, and now as I get older I am starting to think more about her." He goes on to speak of his belief that when he dies he will be reunited with his first wife and will spend eternity with her: "I know other people who feel this way, too. One fellow, he really loved his second wife. But when he was dying, it was the first one he called for. No matter how it may seem betweentimes, the first love is the one that lasts forever."

A remarried woman feels much the same way about first and second marriages, although her circumstances are quite different. Her first husband died after a long, serious illness, and she says, "I was a widow months before he died, completely, in my mind." They had married young, and she had enthusiastically devoted her life to being the appropriate wife for a man in his constantly rising corporate position. At the time of his death, they had achieved considerable financial and social status. Her second husband is of a different social and economic stratum. They are relatively recently married, and their relationship rests on mutual enjoyment and affection rather than on shared social or professional achievement. She explains, "When I die I know I'll be reunited with my first husband. We belong together. And my dear second husband will be reunited with his first wife. He loved her far too much ever to spend eternity with anyone else."

In the minds of our remarried subjects, marriage in youth and marriage in later life seem to represent two different kinds of intimacy. Marriage in youth appears to imply the fusion of individual identities in mutual intimacy, and these people view this fusion as permanent, regardless of the interventions of death or remarriage. In contrast, marriage in later life seems to represent a commitment to companionship. Although that commitment involves intimacy, sacrifice, compromise, and reciprocity, although it may be expected to last for the rest of life, it nonetheless remains separate from the early, intimate fusion that seems to transcend death and time.

Another indication of the sense that real marital intimacy is not interrupted by death is the acknowledgment by several widows that they have been visited by their departed spouses. They all differentiate these visits from dreams of visits, which they also describe having had. The first person to mention such visits says simply, "My wife still comes to see me. I write it down in this astronomy diary we used to keep together, alongside what stars I see each night." He goes on to explain, "I wasn't asleep. And it wasn't a dream. Her body was real and substantial, and when I held her she was real. And when she left, it wasn't that I just woke up — because I wasn't asleep. She told me good-bye, and she left my arms, and then, as she moved across the room, she slowly began to fade away. I was awake the whole time. It meant so much to me to see her and to hold her those few times." This man recalls having met his wife in a high school game of spin the bottle, and his early sensual involvement with her has clearly endured.

No other subjects volunteered information about such visits, but when explicitly asked, a number of them seemed quite relieved and eager to describe their experiences. One woman recalls, "A few days after my husband passed away, I was awake in the morning and I was crying. And I looked up and I saw him at the foot of the bed, just as plain as anything, just as he often stood after coming in from his early-morning chores. And he said, 'It's all right Mom.'" Another explains, "Sometimes you feel his presence. Not like a ghost appearing, but you know that as long as you don't turn around he'll be there right behind you. You can feel him almost touching you, comfortable and reassuring as always."

Among the individuals who acknowledge having been visited are those who respond to questions along these lines with suddenly tearful exclamations: "I wish he would come to visit me like that!" "I have prayed for so long that he would come to see me. And if other people have come back, then I still have cause for hope." "I wish I had had some visits. O God, how I wish for a visit like that!" These people seem to regard the notion of being visited by a departed spouse as a meaningful part of old age's sense of lifelong intimacy. Whether or not they themselves have received such visits, none of them disregard or disdain these experiences in their peers. . . .

Widows often emerge from the loss of a spouse in newly intimate relationships with children, siblings, and other relatives and age-mates. One woman recalls that her children were very attentive to her at the time of her husband's death, and she observes that since then "they have taken very good care of [her], in ways they didn't used to." They are concerned that her car be maintained in problem-free running condition. They support her rejecting of new obligations that she feels she should take on but that would, realistically, be far too burdensome for her to discharge at this time. This woman has always been close to her children, has always been concerned for their welfare, and has always provided assistance at critical points in their lives. But it is only since the death of her husband that she has begun to accept from her children the kind of concerned caring that she has always offered to them. The individual ways in which this mother and her children experienced isolation at the death of her husband, their father, and the ways in which they have empathized with one another's isolation have all brought a new mutuality to their closeness.

Many elders devote more and more energy to appreciating and assisting the children who have stepped in to try to mitigate losses imposed by death, disease, and distance. One woman has lived with her daughter's family since immediately after she was widowed. Before this move, she and her husband had gone to great lengths not to play favorites among their many children. Now, however, she asserts, "Doing things for my daughter and her children is my total livelihood right now. They are so wonderful to me. They let me cook for them, read to them, tell stories with them. I don't think they could do anything I might want to criticize." While this woman's husband was alive, her paramount concern was with his happiness. He was the source of her delight, and she tried to delight him in return. Now that he is gone, she demonstrates a similar attitude toward the daughter and family with whom she lives. The members of this family are now her major source of caring and vitality. She appreciates them more than she can express, and she "would give them the world if it was [hers]."

JOHN BAYLEY

John Bayley was born in 1925, in India, the son of a British army officer. He was educated at Eton and Oxford. An Oxford professor, a prolific literary critic, and a member of the Booker Prize Committee, he is most well known for his work *Tolstoy and the Novel*, 1966. In 1956 he married Iris Murdoch, the prominent British novelist/philosopher who was the inspiration for the 1998 work excerpted here.

Elegy for Iris

Scenes from an indomitable marriage

We trail slowly over the long field toward the river. The heat seems worse than ever, although the sun, overcast, does not beat down as fiercely as it did earlier in the day. The hay was carried some time before, and the brownish surface of the field is baked hard and covered with molehills. A pair of crows flaps lazily away as we approach the riverbank. Crows are said to live a long time, and I wonder idly if they are the same birds we saw here on our bathing visits, many years past.

The little nook where we usually entered the river is empty, as usual. Once, we would have shed our clothes as soon as possible and slid silently into the water. Now I have quite a struggle getting Iris's clothes off: I managed to put her bathing dress on at home, before we started. Her instinct nowadays seems to be to take her clothes off as little as possible. Even in this horribly hot weather, it is hard to persuade her to remove trousers and jersey before getting into bed.

She protests, gently though vigorously, as I lever off the outer layers. In her shabby old swimsuit, a two-piece, with a skirt and separate tunic top, she is an awkward and anxious figure, her socks trailing round her ankles. She is obstinate about not taking them off, and I give up the struggle. A pleasure barge chugs slowly past, an elegant girl in a bikini sunning herself on the deck, a young man in white shorts at the steering wheel. Both turn to look at us with an air of disbelief. I should not be surprised if they burst into guffaws of ill-mannered laughter, for we must present a comic spectacle — an elderly man struggling to remove the garments from an old lady, with white skin and incongruously fair hair.

Iris suffers — as her mother did before her — from Alzheimer's. Its victims are not always gentle: I know that. But Iris remains her old self in many ways. The power of concentration has gone, along with the ability to form coherent sentences, and to remember where she is or has been. She does not know that she has written twenty-six remarkable novels, as well as her books on philosophy; received honorary doctorates from major universities; become a Dame of the British Empire. If an admirer or a friend asks her to sign a copy of one of her novels, she looks at it with pleasure and surprise before laboriously writing her name and, if she can, that person's: "For Georgina Smith." "For Dear Reggie." It takes her some time, but the letters are still formed with care, and they resemble, in a surreal way, her old handwriting. She is always eager to oblige. And the old gentleness remains.

Once in the water, Iris cheers up a bit. It is almost too warm, hardly refreshing. But the river's old brown slow-flowing deliciousness remains, and we smile happily at each other as we paddle quietly to and fro. Water-lily leaves, with an occasional fat yellow flower, rock gently at the passage of a pleasure boat. Small, bright-blue dragonflies hover motionless above them. The water is deep, and cooler as we move out from the bank, but we do not go out far. Looking down, I can see Iris's muddy feet, still in their socks, moving in the brown depths.

Once, if there had been little river traffic about, we would have swum straightaway the hundred yards or so across the river and back. Now it is too much trouble, and a possible producer of that omnipresent anxiety of Alzheimer's which speaks to the one who looks after the Alzheimer's sufferer. Not that it would be dangerous; Iris still swims as naturally as a fish. Since we first entered the water here together, forty-four years ago, we have swum in the sea, in lakes and rivers, in pools and ponds, whenever we could and wherever we happened to be.

Iris was never keen on swimming, as such. She never swam fast and noisily or did fancy strokes. It was being in the water that she loved. Twice she came quite close to drowning. I think of those times, with the anxiety that has now invaded both our lives, as we approach the river's bank again, to scramble out. This has always been a more difficult and inelegant operation than slipping into the river, but it has never bothered us in the past. The river is as deep near the bank as in midstream, the bank itself undercut by the water's flow. I pull myself out first and turn to help Iris. As she takes my hands, her face contracts into that look of childlike dread which so often comes over it now, filling me, too, with worry and fear. Suppose her arm muscles fail her and she slips back into deep water, forgetting how to swim, and letting water pour into her mouth as she opens it in a soundless appeal to me? I know on the spot that we must never come to bathe here again. . . .

A woman I sometimes meet, whose husband is, like Iris, an Alzheimer's sufferer, once cheerfully remarked, "Like being chained to a corpse, isn't it?" Then she amended the remark, giving me a slightly roguish glance: "Oh, a much loved corpse, naturally."

I was repelled by the suggestion that Iris's affliction could have anything in common with that of this jolly woman's husband. It's not an unusual reaction, I've come to realize, among Alzheimer partners. One needs very much to feel that the unique individuality of one's spouse has not been lost in the common symptoms of a clinical condition.

But the woman's image of the corpse and the chain did not lose its power to haunt me. There is a story by Thomas Hardy called "On the Western Circuit," in which a young barrister meets a country girl while accompanying the rounds of the circuit judge. They fall in love and he makes her pregnant. Because she is illiterate, she implores the sympathetic married woman in whose house she works as a maid to write letters for her to the young man. Her mistress does so, and as a result of their correspondence begins to fall for the young man herself. He, instead of escaping from his predicament, as he had first intended, becomes so charmed by the girl's sensible and loving little letters that he determines to marry her. The marriage takes place in London, and the sole meeting between the young man and the girl's employer, before she returns to her own lonely and barren married life in Wessex, reveals to him their involuntary intimacy. The love letters she has written have made him love her — not the girl — and he is left to face the future fettered to an unchosen partner, like a slave chained to another in a galley.

I remembered the story while the woman was speaking. Our situations were not the same as that of the young man and the girl. Fate had not deceived us. We had known our partners as equals over many years, told and listened and communed together, until communication had dwindled and faltered and all but ceased. No more letters, no more words. An Alzheimer's sufferer begins many sentences, usually with an anxious repetitive query, but they remain unfinished, the want unexpressed. Usually it is predictable and easily satisfied, but Iris produces every day many such queries, involving "You know, that person," or, simply, "that . . . ," which take time and effort to unravel. Often they remain totally enigmatic, related to some unidentifiable man or woman in the past who has swum up to the surface of her mind, as if encountered yesterday. At such times, I feel my own mind and memory faltering; it is as if they'd been required to perform a function too far outside their own beat and practice.

The continuity of joking can very often rescue such moments. A burst of laughter, snatches of doggerel, song, teasing nonsense rituals once lovingly exchanged awake an abruptly happy response, and a sudden beaming smile that must resemble those moments in the past between explorers and savages, when some sort of clowning pantomime on the part of the former seems to have evoked instant comprehension and amusement on the part of the latter. At cheerful moments, over drinks or in the car, Iris sometimes twitters away incomprehensibly but self-confidently, happily convinced that an animated exchange is taking place. This prompts me to produce my own stream of consciousness, silly sentences, or mashed-up quotations. "The tyrant of the Chersonese was freedom's best and bravest friend," I assure her, giving her a solemnly meaningful look. At which she nods her head gravely, and seems to act out a conspiring smile, as if the ringing confidence of Byron's lines mean a lot to her, too.

Our mode of communication seems like underwater sonar, each of us bouncing pulsations off the other and listening for an echo. The baffling moments when I cannot understand what she is saying, or about whom or what — moments that can produce in Iris tears and anxieties, though never, thank goodness, the raging frustration typical of many Alzheimer's sufferers — can sometimes be dispelled by my embarking on a jokey parody of helplessness, and trying to make it mutual: both of us at a loss for words.

At happy moments, Iris seems to find words more easily than I do — like the swallows when we lived in the country. Sitting on the telephone wire outside our bedroom window, a row of swallows would converse animatedly with one another, always, it seemed, signing off each burst of twittering speech with a word that sounded like "Weatherby," delivered on a rising note. Now I tease Iris by saying, "You're just like a Weatherby, chattering away." She loves to be teased, but when I make the tease a tender one by adding, "I love listening to you," her face clouds over. She can always tell the difference between the irresponsibility of a joke or a straight tease and the note of "caring" or of "loving care" — which, however earnest and true, always sounds inauthentic.

Most days are, for her, a sort of despair, although despair suggests a conscious and positive state whereas what she feels is a vacancy that frightens her by its lack of dimension. She mutters "I'm a fool" or "Why didn't I?" or "I must," and I try to seem to explain the trouble while rapidly suggesting that we must post a letter, walk around the block, go shopping in the car. Something urgent, practical, giving the illusion of sense and routine. The Reverend Sydney Smith, a benevolent clergyman of Jane Austen's time, urged a parishioner in the grip of depression to take "short views of human life — not further than dinner or tea." I used to quote this to Iris, when her troubles began, as if I were recommending a real policy, which could intelligibly be followed. Now I repeat it sometimes as an incantation or a joke, which can raise a laugh if it is accompanied by some horsing around, a live pantomime of "short views" being taken.

Smiling transforms Iris's face, bringing it back to what it used to be like, and with an added glow that can seem almost supernatural. The Alzheimer's face has been clinically described as the "lion face" — an apparently odd comparison but in fact a very apt one. The features settle into a leonine impassivity that does remind one of the king of beasts and the way his broad, expressionless mask is represented in painting and sculpture. The Alzheimer's face is neither tragic nor comic, as a face can appear in other forms of dementia, suggesting human emotion in its most distorted guises. The Alzheimer's face indicates only an absence. It is, in the most literal sense, a mask.

That is why the sudden appearance of a smile is so extraordinary. Then the lion face becomes the face of the Virgin Mary, with a gravity that gives such a smile, in paintings and sculpture, its deepest meaning. Only a joke survives — the last thing to find its way into consciousness when the brain is atrophied. After all, the Virgin Mary presides over the greatest joke of the lot, the wonderful fable made up, elaborated, repeated all over the world. No wonder she is smiling.

My ancient Greek is virtually nonexistent; and Iris's — which once was extensive — has gone completely. I used to try reading the "Agamemnon" and other Greek plays to her in translation, but it was not a success. Nor was any other attempt at reading aloud. It all seemed and felt unnatural. I did several chapters of *The Lord of the Rings* and *The Tale of Genji*, two of Iris's old favorites, before I realized this. For someone who was accustomed not so much to read books as to slip into their world as effortlessly as she slipped into a river or the sea, this laborious procession of words clumping into her consciousness must have seemed a tedious irrelevance, although she recognized the people and events described. But the relation of such recognition to true memory is clearly a painful one. Tolkien and Lady Murasaki had been inhabitants of her mind, as native to its world as were the people and events who so mysteriously came to her in her process of creation. To meet them again in this way was an embarrassment.

I think that the attempt at reading and being read to was also a reminder to Iris of the loss of identity — although "reminder" is hardly the word for what she must be feeling, for an Alzheimer's patient is not usually conscious, in any definable way, of what has happened. Some sufferers do remain conscious of their state, paradoxical as this seems. The torment of knowing that you cannot speak or think what you want must be intolerable, and I have met patients in whom such a torment is clearly visible. But when Iris speaks to me the result seems normal to her and to me surprisingly fluent, provided I do not listen to what is being said but apprehend it in a matrimonial way, as the voice of familiarity, and thus of recognition.

Time constitutes an anxiety because its conventional shape and progression have gone, leaving only a perpetual query. There are some days when "When are we leaving?" never stops, though the question is repeated without agitation. Indeed, there can seem something quite peaceful about it, as if it hardly mattered when we went, or where, and to stay at home might in any case be preferable. In Faulkner's novel *Soldier's Pay,* the blinded airman says to his friend, "When am I going to get out?" This makes one flinch: the writer has contrived, unerringly, to put the reader in the blind man's place. Iris's query does not, in itself, suggest desire for change or release into a former state of being; nor does she want to know when we are getting in the car and going out to lunch. The journey on which we are leaving may for her mean the final one; or, if that sounds too portentous, simply some sort of disappearance from the daily life that, without her work, must have lost all sense and identity.

Iris once told me that the question of identity had always puzzled her. In fact, she thought that she herself hardly possessed such a thing, whatever it was. I replied that she must know what it was like to be oneself, even to revel in the consciousness of oneself, as a secret and separate person — a person unknown to any other. She smiled, was amused, and looked uncomprehending. It was not something she bothered about. "Then you live in your work? Like Keats and Shakespeare and all that?" I said. She disclaimed any such comparison; and she did not seem particularly interested when I went on to speak of the well-known Romantic distinction between the great egocentric writers, like Wordsworth or Milton, whose sense of self was so overpowering that it included everything else, and those identity-free spirits, like Shakespeare and Keats, for whom being is not what they are but the world they live in and reveal. As a philosopher, she, I suspect, found all such distinctions crude. Perhaps one has to be very much aware of oneself as a person in order to find them at all meaningful or interesting. Nobody less narcissistic than Iris can be imagined.

Conceivably, it is the persons who hug their identity most closely to themselves for whom the condition of Alzheimer's is most dreadful. Iris's own lack of a sense of identity seemed to float her more gently into the Alzheimer's world of preoccupied emptiness. Placidly, every night, she insists on laying out quantities of her clothing on my side of the bed, and when I quietly remove them back they come again. She wants to look after me — is that it? It may be a simpler sort of confusion, for when we go to bed she often asks me which side she should be on. Or is it something deeper and fuller, less conscious and less "caring" than that far too self-conscious adjective suggests? She has never wanted to look after me in the past, thank goodness; indeed, one of the pleasures of living with Iris was her serenely benevolent unawareness of one's daily welfare. So restful. She never needed to tell herself to look after me. But when I broke my leg once in the snow at Christmas, and had to lie up for a few days in Banbury hospital, a dozen miles off, she came and stayed in a bed-and-breakfast hotel outside the hospital gate. I besought her to remain at home and work, instead of wasting her time. There was nothing she could do. But no. She stayed there until I was fit enough to come home with her. . . .

About her greatness as a novelist, I have no doubts at all, although she has never needed, possessed, or tried to cultivate the charisma that is the most vital element to the success of a sage or mage. Her books create a new world, which is also, in an inspired sense, an ordinary one. They have no axe to grind; they are devoid of intellectual pretension, or the need to be different. They are not part of a personality that fascinates and mesmerizes its admirers. Although any of her readers might say or feel that a person or an event in her fiction could occur only in a Murdoch novel, this does not mean that the personality of the writer herself is, in any obvious sense, remarkable.

Where Iris is concerned, my memory, like a snug-fitting garment, seems to have zipped itself up to the present second. As I work in bed early in the morning, typing on my old portable with Iris asleep beside me, her presence seems as it always was, and as it always should be. I know she must once have been different, but I have no true memory of a different person.

Waking up for a peaceful second or two, she looks vaguely at the Olivetti lying on my knees, cushioned by one of her jerseys. Not long ago, when I asked if it disturbed her, she said that she liked to hear that funny noise in the morning. She must be used to it, although a couple of years ago she would have been getting up herself at this time — seven o'clock — and preparing to start her own day. Nowadays, she lies quietly asleep, sometimes giving a little grunt or murmur, and often sleeping well past nine, when I rouse and dress her. This ability to sleep like a cat, at all hours of the day and night, must be one of the rare blessings that sometimes go with Alzheimer's, the converse of the anxiety state that comes on in wakefulness.

Most days, dressing is a reasonably happy and comic business. I am still far from sure which way round her underpants are supposed to go: we usually decide between us that it doesn't matter. Trousers are simpler: hers have a grubby white label on the inside at the back. I ought to give her a bath, or at least a wash of some sort, since baths are tricky, but I tend to postpone it from day to day. For some reason, it is easier to do the job in cold blood, as it were, at an idle moment later in the day. Iris never objects to this; she seems in a curious way to accept it as both quite normal and wholly exceptional, as if the two concepts had merged for her. Perhaps this is why she seems to accept her daily state as if no other had ever existed: assuming, too, that no one else would find her changed in any way; just as my memory works with her only as she is now, and — so my memory seems to assume — must always have been.

At the same time, Iris's social reflexes are, in a weird way, still very much in place. If someone comes to the door — the postman, the man to read the gas meter — she receives him with her social smile, and calls for me in those unhurried, slightly gracious tones that married couples automatically use on each other in the presence of a stranger: "Oh, I think it is the man who has come to read the meter, darling." In the same way, she deals instinctively with more complex social situations, seeming to follow the conversation, prepared to bridge a silence by asking a question. It's usually "Where do you come from?" or "What are you doing now?" — questions that get repeated many times in the course of a social event. Other people, visitors or friends, adjust themselves well to these repetitions as soon as they grasp what is happening.

In the old days of our marriage, I would sometimes produce what in childhood used to be called "a tantrum" if something had gone wrong or not been done properly, something for which, rightly or wrongly, I held Iris responsible. She would then become calm, reassuring, almost maternal, not as if deliberately but with some deep, unconscious, female response that normally had no need to come to the surface. Iris, in general, was never "female" at all — a fact for which I sometimes remembered to be grateful. Now I have learned to make, on occasions, a deliberate use of tantrums. If she has been following me all day, interrupting tiresome business or letter writing (very often letters to her fans), I erupt in what can seem even to me an uncontrolled fit of exasperation, stamping on the floor and throwing the papers and letters on it, waving my hands in the air. It always works. Iris says "Sorry . . . sorry," and pats me before going quietly away. She will be back soon, but that doesn't matter. My tantrum has reassured her as no amount of caring, or calming efforts to reply to her rationally, could have done.

The lady who told me in her deliberately jolly way that living with an Alzheimer's patient was like being chained to a corpse went on to an even greater access of desperate facetiousness. "And, as you and I know, it's a corpse that complains all the time." I don't know it. In spite of her anxious and perpetual queries, Iris seems not to know how to complain. She never has. Alzheimer's, which can accentuate personality traits to the point of demonic parody, seems only to exaggerate the natural goodness in her.

On a good day, her need for a loving presence, mutual pattings and murmurs, has something angelic about it; she seems to become the presence found in an icon. It is more important for her still on the days of silent tears, when her grief is unconscious of that mysterious world of creation she has lost and yet is aware that something is missing.

December 25, 1997. London is uncannily silent on Christmas morning. If there are churchgoers and church bells, we see none, hear none. The silence and the emptiness seem all the better.

We walk to Kensington Gardens, up the deserted street, between the tall stucco façades falling into Edwardian decay but still handsome. Henry James lived on the left here; Browning farther up, on the right. We pass their blue plaques, set in the white walls. A few yards back, we passed the great gloomy red brick mansions where T. S. Eliot had a flat for many years. His widow must be in church now.

Our route on Christmas morning is always the same — we have been doing this for years. As we pass the spectral houses, I utter a little bit of patter like a guide. Henry James, Robert Browning, T. S. Eliot. We used to gaze up at their windows, talk a bit about them, on mornings like these. Now I just mention the names. Does Iris remember them? She smiles a little. They are still familiar, those names, as familiar as this unique morning silence. Just for this morning, those writers have laid their pens down, as Iris herself has done, and are taking a well-earned rest, looking forward to their dinners. Thackeray, the gourmet, whose house is just around the corner, would have looked forward to his with special keenness.

Now we can see the park, and beyond it the handsome Williamite façade of Kensington Palace. A few dogs here, unimpressed by Christmas but seeming merrier than usual, in contrast with the silence. There is one bell now, tolling somewhere on a sweet high note. Up in the sky, the jet trails move serenely on, their murmur fainter when it comes.

The Round Pond. Canada geese stand meditatively, for once making no demands. The same path as usual, downward, to the Serpentine. Nobody around the Peter Pan statue. Not even a Japanese couple with a camera. Young Pan himself, bronze fingers delicately crooked, his double pipe to his lips, has the sublimely sinister indifference of childhood. Captain Hook, his great enemy, was always made nervous by that pose. He considered Peter to have "good form" without knowing it, which is, of course, the best form of all. Poor Hook was in despair about this. It made Iris laugh when I told her all this, before we were married. I read a bit of the book to her. Iris, I recall, was so amused that she later put the good-form business into one of her novels.

As we walk around and admire, I tell Iris that my mother assured me that if I looked hard enough over the railings, into the private dells where the bluebells and daffodils come up in spring, I might see fairies, perhaps even Peter Pan himself. I believed her. I could almost believe her now, with the tranquil sunshine in the park making a midwinter spring, full of the illusion of flowers and fairies as well as real birdsong.

Iris is listening, which she rarely does, and smiling, too. There have been no anxious pleas this morning, no tears, none of those broken sentences whose only meaning is the dread in her voice and the demand for reassurance. Something or someone this morning has reassured her, given her, for an hour or two, what the prayer book calls "that peace which the world cannot give."

Perhaps it is the Christmas ritual. We shall return to my brother, who has attended Matins this morning at Chelsea Old Church, where Sir Thomas More used once to worship. We shall eat sardines and sausages and scrambled eggs together, with a bottle or two of the Bulgarian red wine that goes with everything. I shall do the eggs and sausages, with Iris standing beside me, and we shall bring the wine.

A snooze then. Iris sleeps deeply. Later, we listen to carols and Christmas music. And I have the illusion, which fortunate Alzheimer's partners must feel at such times, that life is just the same, has never changed. I cannot imagine Iris any different. Her loss of memory becomes, in a sense, my own. In a muzzy way — the Bulgarian wine, no doubt — I find myself thinking of the Christmas birth, and also of Wittgenstein's comment that death is not "an event in life." We are born to live only from day to day. "Short views of human life — not further than dinner or tea." The Reverend Sydney Smith's advice is most easily taken during these ritualized days: the ancient saving routine of Christmas, which for us today has been twice blessed.

Life is no longer bringing the pair of us "closer and closer apart," in A. D. Hope's tenderly ambiguous words. Every day, we move closer and closer together. We could not do otherwise. There is a certain comic irony — happily, not darkly, comic — that, after more than forty years of our taking marriage for granted, marriage has decided it is tired of this and is taking a hand in the game. Purposefully, persistently, involuntarily, our marriage is now getting somewhere. It is giving us no choice, and I am glad of that.

Every day, we are physically closer; and Iris's little "mouse cry," as I think of it, signifying loneliness in the next room, the wish to be back beside me, seems less and less forlorn, more simple, more natural. She is not sailing into the dark: The voyage is over, and under the dark escort of Alzheimer's she has arrived somewhere. So have I.

GABRIEL GARCÍA MÁRQUEZ

Born in Colombia in 1928, Gabriel García Márquez began his literary career as an editor and journalist. His passionate and colorful novels of provincial Colombian life are among the best loved of any Latin American writer of this century, his most famous work being *One Hundred Years of Solitude* (1967). García Márquez spent many years of his life in self-imposed exile from his native Colombia because of his political opposition to the right-wing regime there. In 1982 he won the Nobel Peace Prize. And in the mid-80s he returned to his country to arbitrate between leftist rebels and the Colombian government.

Love in the Time of Cholera

When she awoke on her first morning as a widow, she turned over in bed without opening her eyes, searching for a more comfortable position so that she could continue sleeping, and that was the moment when he died for her. For only then did it become clear that he had spent the night away from home for the first time in years. The other place where this struck her was at the table, not because she felt alone, which in fact she was, but because of her strange belief that she was eating with someone who no longer existed. It was not until her daughter Ofelia came from New Orleans with her husband and the three girls that she sat at a table again to eat, but instead of the usual one, she ordered a smaller, improvised table set up in the corridor. Until then she did not take a regular meal. She would walk through the kitchen at any hour, whenever she was hungry, and put her fork in the pots and eat a little of everything without placing anything on a plate, standing in front of the stove, talking to the serving women, who were the only ones with whom she felt comfortable, the ones she got along with best. Still, no matter how hard she tried, she could not elude the presence of her dead husband: wherever she went, wherever she turned, no matter what she was doing, she would come across something of his that would remind her of him. For even though it seemed only decent and right to grieve for him, she also wanted to do everything possible not to wallow in her grief. And so she made the drastic decision to empty the house of everything that would remind her of her dead husband, which was the only way she could think of to go on living without him.

It was a ritual of eradication. Her son agreed to take his library so that she could replace his office with the sewing room she had never had when she was married. And her daughter would take some furniture and countless objects that she thought were just right for the antique auctions in New Orleans. All of this was a relief for Fermina Daza, although she was not at all amused to learn that the things she had bought on her honeymoon were now relics for antiquarians. To the silent stupefaction of the servants, the neighbors, the women friends who came to visit her during that time, she had a bonfire built in a vacant lot behind the house, and there she burned everything that reminded her of her husband: the most expensive and elegant clothes seen in the city since the last century, the finest shoes, the hats that resembled him more than his portraits, the siesta rocking chair from which he had arisen for the last time to die, innumerable objects so tied to her life that by now they formed part of her identity. She did it without the shadow of a doubt, in the full certainty that her husband would have approved, and not only for reasons of hygiene. For he had often expressed his desire to be cremated and not shut away in the seamless dark of a cedar box. His religion would not permit it, of course: he had dared to broach the subject with the Archbishop, just in case, and his answer had been a categorical no. It was pure illusion, because the Church did not permit the existence of crematoriums in our cemeteries, not even for the use of religions other than Catholic, and the advantage of building them would not have occurred to anyone but Juvenal Urbino. Fermina Daza did not forget her husband's terror, and even in the confusion of the first hours she remembered to order the carpenter to leave a chink where light could come into the coffin as a consolation to him.

In any event, the holocaust was in vain. In a very short while Fermina Daza realized that the memory of her dead husband was as resistant to the fire as it seemed to be to the passage of time. Even worse: after the incineration of his clothing, she continued to miss not only the many things she had loved in him but also what had most annoyed her: the noises he made on arising. That memory helped her to escape the mangrove swamps of grief. Above all else, she made the firm decision to go on with her life, remembering her husband as if he had not died. She knew that waking each morning would continue to be difficult, but it would become less and less so.

EURIPIDES

Alcestis is the oldest of the extant works of Euripides. Its comic tone derives from its position as the final in a tetralogy of plays; the custom of ancient Greek theater was that a comedy always followed the performance of three related tragedies. *Alcestis* is an excellent example of what Moses Hadas calls Euripides' "critical deflation of the heroic outlook," his sly "parody" on the narratives of old. It should probably be mentioned that Heracles, the hero of this tale, is perhaps better-known by his Roman name: Hercules.

Alcestis

lines 747-1163

BUTLER   Many strangers who came to Admetus' house from all sorts of places have I known and waited on at table, but never have I received at this hearth a worse rascal than today's guest. In the first place, though he saw Master in mourning he came in and crossed the threshold without a scruple. Secondly, he had not the decency to accept whatever fare we happened to have, realizing our trouble, but if there was something we did not serve he hurried us on to serve it. He took in his hands the ivy cup and swilled the neat juice of the dark grape until the wine's fire wrapped him about and heated him. He crowned his head with branches of myrtle and howled discordant tunes. Two strains could be heard: he kept sing-

ing, caring nothing for Admetus' troubles, and we servants be-
wailed our mistress. But we did not let the guest see that our eyes
were wet, for so had Admetus bidden us. Now here I am at home,
feasting this stranger, some rascally thief or highwayman, but she is
gone forth from the house, and I did not follow the funeral or
stretch my hand out to lament my mistress, who was a mother to
me and to all the servants. She saved us from a thousand difficulties
by mollifying her husband's anger. Am I not right in loathing this
stranger who has intruded on our troubles?

[*Enter Heracles, garlanded, goblet in hand, drunk.*]

HERACLES You there, why that sober and anxious look? A servant ought not to
glower at a guest, but receive him affably. You see a man here who is
your master's comrade, and you receive him with a morose and
frowning look, making much of a trouble not your own. Come here
and learn a thing or two. Do you understand the nature of morality? I suppose you don't: how should you? But listen to me. All men
have to pay the debt of death, and there is not a mortal who knows
whether he is going to be alive on the morrow. The outcome of
things that depend on fortune cannot be foreseen; they can neither
be learnt nor discovered by any art. Hearken to this and learn of me,
cheer up, drink, reckon the days yours as you live them; the rest belong to fortune. Pay honor too to Cypris, most sweetest of goddesses to men; she is a gracious deity. Let these other things go, and
heed my words — if I seem to you to be talking sense; I think I am.
Won't you then get rid of this inordinate grief? Come away from the
door there, bind your head with garlands, and drink with me. I
know well enough that the splash of the wine in the cup will shift
you from this dour, tight, moodiness. We are only human, and our
thoughts ought to be human. Life for all you sober and frowning
folk, if you take my opinion, is not really life but a calamity.

BUTLER I know all this. But our situation doesn't call for revelry and mirth.

HERACLES The woman who died was a stranger. Don't grieve over-much. The
masters of the house are alive.

BUTLER What, alive? Don't you know the trouble of this house?

HERACLES If your master didn't lie to me.

BUTLER He is much too hospitable, much.

HERACLES Ought I to suffer just because some stranger woman is dead?

BUTLER A stranger she was, yes indeed, too much so!

HERACLES There wasn't some trouble of which he didn't tell me?

BUTLER Go in peace. *We* are involved in our masters' misfortune.

HERACLES This talk does not sound like a stranger's woes!

BUTLER   Otherwise I should not have been annoyed when I saw you hilarious.

HERACLES Have I been tricked by my host?

BUTLER   You did not come at a suitable time to be received in this house. We have been bereaved. You see that our clothing is deep mourning and that our hair is shorn.

HERACLES Who has died? Is it one of the children — his old father?

BUTLER   The wife of Admetus has died, stranger.

HERACLES What is it you say? And did he then entertain me?

BUTLER   He was ashamed to turn you away from his house.

HERACLES Poor man, what a wife you have lost!

BUTLER   We are all ruined, not she alone.

HERACLES I did notice something. I saw that his tears were flowing and his hair shorn and the look of his face; but he persuaded me, saying he was taking a stranger's corpse to its burial. Against my better feeling I entered these gates, and I was drinking in the house of a hospitable man while he was in such a state! And am I yet reveling with garlands on my head? [*Tears off garland, throws goblet down.*] And you — a calamity like this in the house, and you didn't tell me! Where is he burying her? Where shall I go to find him?

BUTLER   Straight along the road that leads to Larissa. Outside the city you will see a hewn tomb.

HERACLES Heart much-enduring and hand of mine, show now the sort of son that Tirynthian Alcmena, Electryon's daughter, bore to Zeus. I must save the woman that is newly dead. I must establish Alcestis in this house again. I must render this gratitude to Admetus. I shall go and watch for Death, the gloomy-garbed lord of the dead; methinks I shall find him drinking the libations of the dead hard by the tomb. If I rush upon him from ambush and seize him and pin him with the hoops of my arms, however much his sides heave, none can deliver him from my bone-crushing hold until he surrenders this woman to me. But if I miss this quarry and he come not to the bloody offering, I will betake me to the sunless mansions of Cora and her lord below, and I will make my request. I am certain I shall bring Alcestis up and place her in the hands of my host, who received me into his house and thrust me not away though he was smitten with a grievous calamity; noble as he is, he concealed it, and showed regard for me. Who of the Thessalians is more hospitable than this man? Who that dwells in Hellas? He shall not say it was a base man he showed kindness to, himself so noble.

> [*Exit: the funeral procession with Admetus returns.*]

ADMETUS Ah, hateful is this homecoming, hateful the sight of these widowed halls. Alas for me, alas! Woe! Woe! Whither shall I go? Where stand? What shall I say? What not? Would I might perish! To a heavy doom did my mother bring me forth. I envy the dead, I yearn for them, in their houses I crave to dwell. I take no joy in looking upon the sunlight, or in treading the ground underfoot. Such a hostage has Death robbed me of and delivered to Hades!

SOME OF CHORUS *Go forward! Go forward! Step into the house!*

ADMETUS Alas! Alas!

OTHERS Worthy of groans are your sufferings.

ADMETUS Ah! Ah!

OTHERS Through tortures have you passed, I know it well.

ADMETUS Alack! Alack!

OTHERS You are in no way helping her below.

ADMETUS Woe is me! Woe is me!

OTHERS Bitter it is never again to behold the face of your beloved wife.

ADMETUS You have mentioned that which has bruised my soul. What greater evil can befall a man than to lose his faithful wife? Would I had never married, never lived with her in this house! I envy those mortals who do not marry, who have no children; their life is single, and its grief a burden within measure. But to have to look upon the sicknesses of children, or bridal beds devastated by death, is unendurable when it is possible to go through life childless and unwed.

SOME OF CHORUS *Fate, fate hard to wrestle against, has come upon you.*

ADMETUS Alas! Alas!

OTHERS No bound have you set to your griefs.

ADMETUS Ah! Ah!

OTHERS Heavy are they to bear, and yet —

ADMETUS Alack! Alack!

OTHERS Bear up! You are not the first to lose —

ADMETUS Woe is me. Woe is me!

OTHERS A wife. Calamity has various faces and smites various mortals.

ADMETUS Ah, the long sorrow and the grief for friends that are under the earth! Why did you prevent me from flinging myself into her hollowed grave, from lying dead with her who was so far the best? Then would Hades have had instead of one soul two, the most faithful that ever crossed the infernal lake together.

CHORUS   *I have a certain kinsman whose only son, a young man worthy of lamentation, was taken from his house. Nevertheless he endured his misfortune with moderation, childless though he was, though his hair was turning hoary and he was far advanced in life.*

ADMETUS   [*pauses at the doors of the palace*]. Ah, my fine house! How can I enter you? How live in you, with my changed fortune? Ah me! Great is the change. Then with Pelian torches and with bridal songs did I enter in, holding the hand of my beloved wife. There followed a merry, shouting crowd, congratulating her that is dead and me, and acclaiming the union of gentle folk, both of noble descent. But now with wailing instead of hymeneals and with deep mourning instead of bright garments I am ushered into my deserted couch.

CHORUS   *Your life was happy, you did not know what sorrow was, and then came this blow. But you have saved your life. Your wife has died, has left her love behind. Is this so strange? Many men has death separated from their wives.*

ADMETUS   Friends, I regard my wife's fate as happier than my own, though it might not seem to be so. Her no pain will ever touch again; she has surcease of many toils, and with glory. I, on the other hand, who ought not to have lived, have escaped destiny, but shall drag out a bitter life. Too late I realize it.

How can I bear to enter this house? Whom should I speak to, by whom should I be addressed, that I may find joy in going out? Whither shall I turn? The loneliness within will drive me out when I see my wife's bed empty, and the seats upon which she used to sit, and the floor all through the house unswept. The children will fall about my knees and weep for their mother, and the servants lament the gentle mistress they have lost.

Such are the things that will happen in the house. Abroad, marriages of Thessalians will drive me away, and their gatherings crowded with women. I shall not bear to look at the young women who were my wife's companions. Any man that happens to be unfriendly to me will say: "Look at the fellow who keeps alive so shamefully; he had not the courage to die, but gave in exchange the woman he married, in his cowardice, and escaped Hades. Do you call that a man? He hates his parents, though he himself was not willing to die." Such is the reputation I shall have, beside my other troubles. What have I to gain by living, friends, with a wretched reputation *and* a wretched life?

CHORUS   *I have surveyed the Muses and the heavens on high; of many doctrines* have I laid hold, but I have found nothing mightier than Necessity. For it there is no remedy in the Thracian tablets which the word of Orpheus prescribed, nor among the drugs which Phoebus gave to the Asclepiads, dispensing medicines to suffering mortals.

This goddess alone has no altars or image to approach; she heeds no sacrifices. Reverend goddess, come not upon me more mightily than in time past. Your aid even Zeus must have to work his will. The iron of the Chalybes is less strong than you; in your rugged spirit is no respect of persons.

You, Admetus, this goddess has gripped in the inescapable bond of her arms. But be brave; never can you bring the dead up from below by weeping. Even the gods' offspring go down to the darkness of death. Dear was she when she was among us, dear will she be though dead. The noblest wife of them all did you join to your bed.

Not as a mound over the dead that have perished shall the tomb of your wife be accounted, but it shall be honored like the shrines of the divinities, an object of reverence for passers by. The traveler shall go up the winding path and say, "This woman once died for her husband; now she is a blessed divinity. Hail, lady revered, and grant us blessing!" Such are the salutations that shall greet her.

LEADER But here as it seems, Admetus, is Alcmena's son; he is coming toward your hearth.

[Enter Heracles leading a veiled woman.]

HERACLES To a friend a man should speak freely, Admetus, and not keep reproaches in his bosom in silence. I thought that when I arrived in your hour of sorrow I should be accounted a friend. But you did not tell me that the body which you had to bury was your wife's. You entertained me in your house as if your mourning were for some stranger's grief. And I crowned my head and poured libations to the gods in this house of yours while it was in sorrow. I blame you, yes, I blame you for this treatment. But I do not wish to trouble you in your misfortune.

I shall tell you why I turned and came here again. Take this woman and keep her for me until I kill the king of the Bistones and come back with the Thracian horses. If I fare as I hope I shan't — I pray I do come home again — I give this woman to serve in your house. She came into my hands as the result of hard work. I found certain men had arranged a public contest, a proper toil for athletes. From there I bring this woman, whom I received as a prize of victory. Those who won the lighter contests had horses to lead off;

those who won the heavy events, boxing and wrestling, had cattle, and with them went a woman. It was shameful for me to neglect this honorable prize when I had happened on it. But now, as I said, you must take care of this woman. She is not stolen, but won by labor. Perhaps in time you too will thank me.

ADMETUS   Not because I misjudged you, not because I was ashamed, did I keep my poor wife's fate hidden. But it would have been sorrow added to sorrow if you had gone on to the house of some other host: I had enough trouble to weep for, as it was.

I beg of you, my lord, if it is at all possible, bid this woman stay with some other Thessalian who has not suffered as I have; you have many friends among the Pheraeans. Do not remind me of my sorrow. I should not be able to see her in my house without weeping. Do not add a disease to my sickness — I am weighed down enough with my calamity.

Where could a young woman be cared for in my house? She is young, as her dress and ornaments indicate. Shall she live under the same roof with men? How can she remain pure if she will be in the company of young men? It is not easy, Heracles, to restrain a young man in his prime. I am thinking of your interests. Shall I bring her into the chamber of her that is dead and keep her there? How can I bring this woman into *her* bed? I fear a twofold reproach: some citizen may charge me with betraying my benefactress and falling upon the bed of another young woman; and she that is dead would not like it. She has deserved my respect, and I must be very prudent.

Know you, lady, whoever you are, that you have the same stature as Alcestis, and you resemble her in figure. Ah me! 'Fore the gods, take this woman out of my sight; do not press on my weakness! When I look at her I seem to be looking at my own wife. It confuses my heart; springs of tears gush forth from my eyes. Ah, wretch that I am, at last I have begun to taste the bitterness of my loss.

LEADER   I cannot call your lot happy, but the dispensation of heaven, however it strikes us, we must accept with fortitude.

HERACLES   Would I had the power to bring your wife from the abodes of the dead into the light, and bestow this kindness upon you!

ADMETUS   Well I know you have the will. But how can this be? It is not possible that the dead should come into the light.

HERACLES   Don't overdo it; bear your trouble decently.

ADMETUS It is easier to advise someone else than to be firm when you are suffering.

HERACLES What would be your advantage if you determine to keep groaning forever?

ADMETUS I know that myself, but a sort of passion drives me frantic.

HERACLES Loving a person that is dead makes for tears.

ADMETUS She has ruined me, more than I can say.

HERACLES You have lost a splendid wife; who will deny it?

ADMETUS So splendid that I can no longer enjoy life.

HERACLES Time will soften your trouble; now it is still fresh.

ADMETUS Time will, if by time you mean death.

HERACLES A woman, the desire for a new union, will put an end to your sorrow.

ADMETUS Hush! What a thing to say! I did not expect that of you!

HERACLES Why? Won't you marry? Will you keep a widowed bed?

ADMETUS The woman who will lie with me does not exist.

HERACLES You don't expect you are helping her that is dead in any way?

ADMETUS Her I must honor wherever she is.

HERACLES Splendid! Splendid! But you are liable to be called foolish.

ADMETUS But know you will never call me bridegroom.

HERACLES I admire your faithful love to your wife.

ADMETUS May I die if I betray her, even if she is dead.

HERACLES Receive this woman now into your noble house.

ADMETUS Nay, I beseech you, by Zeus who begot you!

HERACLES You will be making a mistake if you don't do this thing.

ADMETUS And if I do my heart will be gnawed with sorrow.

HERACLES Trust me; this favor may turn out to your advantage.

ADMETUS Ah, would you had never won her in that contest!

HERACLES But I did win, and now you share in my winning.

ADMETUS I appreciate it; but let the woman leave this place!

HERACLES She will go away if she must, but first consider whether she must.

ADMETUS She must, unless it will make you angry with me.

HERACLES I know what I am about; that is why I insist.

ADMETUS Have it your way, then, but I am not pleased with what you are doing.

HERACLES The time will come when you will thank me; only trust me.

ADMETUS [*to attendants*]. Bring this woman in, if she must be received in my house.

HERACLES I would not hand this woman over to servants.

ADMETUS Then do you yourself lead her into the house if you will.

HERACLES I shall put her into *your* hands.

ADMETUS I won't touch her. There's the house; she may enter.

HERACLES To your right hand alone will I entrust her.

ADMETUS My lord, you are forcing me to do this against my will.

HERACLES Venture to put out your hand and touch the stranger.

ADMETUS [*stretching his hand, with head averted*]. I am putting it out — as if I were beheading the Gorgon.

HERACLES Have you got her?

ADMETUS I have, yes.

HERACLES Keep her, then, and one day you will say that Zeus' son is a noble guest. [*Approaches Woman and raises her veil.*] Look at her and see whether she has any resemblance to your wife. Be happy and leave off your grief.

ADMETUS Gods! What shall I say? A marvel beyond hope! Is this my wife I see? Really mine? Or is some mockery of delight from a god distracting me?

HERACLES No; this is your own wife that you see.

ADMETUS See that this isn't some phantom from the shades!

HERACLES Don't make your guest out a necromancer.

ADMETUS But am I looking at my own wife that I buried?

HERACLES You are indeed. I don't wonder you distrust your luck.

ADMETUS May I touch her, may I speak to her as my living wife?

HERACLES Speak to her. You have all that you desired.

ADMETUS Dearly beloved wife! Dear face and form! Beyond all hope I possess you. I thought I should never see you again.

HERACLES You do possess her. May none of the gods be jealous.

ADMETUS Noble son of greatest Zeus, be ever blessed! May the Father that begot you preserve you. You alone have raised my state. How did you restore her to the light from the shades?

HERACLES I joined battle with the power that has charge of such matters.

ADMETUS You say you fought this fight with death? Where?

HERACLES At the tomb. I seized him from ambush with my hands.

ADMETUS But why does she stand here speechless?

HERACLES It is not permitted for you to hear her voice until her consecration to the powers below be removed and the third day come. But take her into the house. And in future, Admetus, show respect for guests, as is right. Farewell; I go to perform the labor that is before me for the king, the son of Sthenelus.

ADMETUS Stay with us, and share our hearth.

HERACLES I will, another time; now I must be getting on.

ADMETUS   Good luck go with you then, and a happy return.

[Exit Heracles.]

To all the citizens of my realm I ordain that dances be instituted for these happy events and that the altars be made to steam with atoning sacrifices of cattle. We have changed our state of life from its former condition for the better. I shall not deny that I am fortunate.

[Exit to palace, holding Alcestis.]

CHORUS   *Many are the forms of divine intervention; many things beyond expectation do the gods fulfil. That which was expected has not been accomplished; for that which was unexpected has god found the way. Such was the end of this story.*

[Exeunt.]

VIKTOR FRANKL

Austrian neurologist and psychiatrist Viktor Frankl (1905-1997) was the founder of "logotherapy," a theory of psychology that held that mental health depended on the ability of the individual to derive a transcendent sense of meaning in life. *Man's Search for Meaning: An Introduction to Logotherapy* represented his attempt to elucidate the development of his theories for a general audience. The work has been translated into several languages, and has been enormously popular, selling more than one and a half million copies. The reader may be interested to know that Frankl remarried after the war and fathered a child.

"Experiences in a Concentration Camp," from Man's Search for Meaning

In spite of all the enforced physical and mental primitiveness of the life in a concentration camp, it was possible for spiritual life to deepen. Sensitive people who were used to rich intellectual life may have suffered much pain (they were often of a delicate constitution), but the damage to their inner selves was less. They were able to retreat from their terrible surroundings to a life of inner riches and spiritual freedom. Only in this way can one explain the apparent paradox that some prisoners of a less hardy make-up often seemed to survive camp life better than did those of a robust nature. In order to make myself clear, I am forced to fall back on personal experience. Let me tell what happened on those early mornings when we had to march to our work site.

There were shouted commands: "Detachment, forward march! Left-2-3-

4! Left-2-3-4! First man about, left and left and left and left! Caps off!" These words sound in my ears even now. At the order "Caps off!" we passed the gate of the camp, and searchlights were trained upon us. Whoever did not march smartly got a kick. And worse off was the man who, because of the cold, had pulled his cap back over his ears before permission was given.

We stumbled on in the darkness over big stones and through large puddles, along the one road leading from the camp. The accompanying guards kept shouting at us and driving us with the butts of their rifles. Anyone with very sore feet supported himself on his neighbor's arm. Hardly a word was spoken; the icy wind did not encourage talk. Hiding his mouth behind his upturned collar, the man marching next to me whispered suddenly: "If our wives could see us now! I do hope they are better off in their camps and don't know what is happening to us."

That brought thoughts of my own wife to mind. And as we stumbled on for miles, slipping on icy spots, supporting each other time and again, dragging one another up and onward, nothing was said, but we both knew; each of us was thinking of his wife. Occasionally I looked at the sky, where the stars were fading and the pink light of the morning was beginning to spread behind a dark bank of clouds. But my mind clung to my wife's image, imagining it with an uncanny acuteness. I heard her answering me, saw her smile, her frank and encouraging look. Real or not, her look was then more luminous than the sun which was beginning to rise.

A thought transfixed me: for the first time in my life I saw the truth as it is set into song by so many poets, proclaimed as the final wisdom by so many thinkers. The truth — that love is the ultimate and the highest goal to which man can aspire. Then I grasped the meaning of the greatest secret that human poetry and human thought and belief have to impart: *The salvation of man is through love and in love.* I understood how a man who has nothing left in this world still may know bliss, be it only for a brief moment, in the contemplation of his beloved. In a position of utter desolation, when man cannot express himself in positive action, when his only achievement may consist in enduring his sufferings in the right way — an honorable way — in such a position man can, through loving contemplation of the image he carries of his beloved, achieve fulfillment. For the first time in my life I was able to understand the meaning of the words, *"The angels are lost in perpetual contemplation of an infinite glory."*

In front of me a man stumbled and those following him fell on top of him. The guard rushed over and used his whip on them all. Thus my thoughts were interrupted for a few minutes. But soon my soul found its way back from the prisoner's existence to another world, and I resumed talk with my loved one: I asked her questions, and she answered; she questioned me in return, and I answered.

"Stop!" We had arrived at our work site. Everybody rushed into the dark hut in the hope of getting a fairly decent tool. Each prisoner got a spade or a pickax.

"Can't you hurry up, you pigs?!" Soon we had resumed the previous day's positions in the ditch. The frozen ground cracked under the point of the pickaxes, and sparks flew. The men were silent, their brains numb.

My mind still clung to the image of my wife. A thought crossed my mind: I didn't even know if she were still alive. I knew only one thing — which I have learned well by now: Love goes very far beyond the physical person of the beloved. It finds its deepest meaning in his spiritual being, his inner self. Whether or not he is actually present, whether or not he is still alive at all ceases somehow to be of importance.

I did not know whether my wife was alive, and I had no means of finding out (during all my prison life there was no outgoing or incoming mail); but at that moment it ceased to matter. There was no need for me to know; nothing could touch the strength of my love, my thoughts, and the image of my beloved. Had I known then that my wife was dead, I think that I would still have given myself, undisturbed by that knowledge, to the contemplation of her image, and that my mental conversation with her would have been just as vivid and just as satisfying. *"Set me like a seal upon thy heart, love is as strong as death."*

A Word about Translations

In compiling an anthology that includes many translations of ancient works, it was not always easy to choose which translations to use. Does one go with a modern translation of the Bible or an older one? The classic seventeenth-century King James Old Testament, for example, or the Jewish Publication Society's delightfully antique-sounding 1916 version, or even the elegant Revised English Bible of 1989? For certain of the ancient sources included here in *The Book of Marriage* — notably, the Bible, Homer, and Euripides — there was a plethora of English translation choices. And there were distinct advantages to each translation. How to decide?

On the principle that consistency has its virtues, and that a somewhat antiquated English usage also has its charm, we decided to use the old King James Version of the Bible everywhere in this collection. The translation is plenty accurate for our purposes here, and the splendor of the language irresistible — full of liveliness and color. Added to these advantages, the King James Bible is no longer under copyright protection, which enabled the editors to avoid securing reproduction rights.

Now to Homer and Euripides. The reader will, we hope, indulge us for some inconsistency here. We have used the newest translation of Homer, that of Robert Fagles, yet an older translation of Euripides, by Moses Hadas. The Homer selection is verse, the Euripides selections prose. Why? Simply because these are the translations that spoke to us most directly. With Homer, we want to hear the bard singing his epic poem of Odysseus. That is, we want to hear the music of verse. Whereas *Medea,* in our opinion, may be quite effectively rendered in prose; her setting is more properly drama than poetry. Of course, these things are matters of taste. Our choice may not be the reader's favorite. But hopefully the reader will understand that in choosing every translation included in this volume, we have endeavored to give due measure to considerations of accessibility, mood, and beauty of language.

One more note to the reader with regard to the East Asian selections: the names of Asian authors, translators, and characters have been kept in East Asian order — that is, surname first. The only exceptions have been in the rare case in which an author or translator has a Western given name.

Notes

INTRODUCTION

1. Leading books in the marriage communication field are John Gottman, *Why Marriages Succeed or Fail* (New York: Simon and Schuster, 1994); H. Markman, S. Stanley, and S. Blumberg, *Fighting for Your Marriage* (San Francisco: Jossey-Bass, 1994); S. Stanley, D. Trathen, S. McCain, M. Bryan, *A Lasting Promise* (San Francisco: Jossey-Bass, 1998).

2. Linda Waite, "Does Marriage Matter?" *Demography* 32, no. 4 (November 1995): 483-504.

3. For a similar list, see "Marriage in America" (New York: Institute for American Values, 1995), pp. 10-11; also see John Witte, *From Sacrament to Contract: Marriage, Religion, and Law in the Western Tradition* (Louisville: Westminster/John Knox, 1997), p. 2.

4. Aristotle, "Politics," in *The Basic Works of Aristotle,* ed. Richard McKeon (New York: Random House, 1941), bk. I, ch. 2.

5. Aristotle, "Politics," bk. I, ch. 2.

6. For a discussion of how Aristotelian naturalism is contextualized within Jewish-Christian doctrines of creation, see Don Browning, Bonnie Miller McLemore, Pam Couture, Bernie Lyon, and Robert Franklin, *From Culture Wars to Common Ground: Religion and the American Family Debate* (Louisville: Westminster/John Knox, 1997), pp. 113-24.

7. For the idea of the classic, see Hans-Georg Gadamer, *Truth and Method* (New York: Crossroad, 1982), pp. 253-58; also see Paul Ricoeur, *Hermeneutics and the Human Sciences* (Cambridge: Cambridge University Press, 1981), pp. 59-61, 62-100.

8. For Leo XIII's version of the argument, see his "Rerum Novarum," in *Proclaiming Justice and Peace: Papal Documents* (Mystic, Conn.: Twenty-Third Publications).

9. Thomas Aquinas, *The Summa Contra Gentiles,* bk. III, ii, ch. 122 (London: Burns, Oates & Washbourne).

10. John Locke, "Second Treatise," *Two Treatises of Government,* ed. Peter Laslett (Cambridge: Cambridge University Press, 1991), ch. 7, para. 80.

11. Goody believes this is true in landholding agricultural societies in both Europe

and Asia but not true in sub-Sahara Africa where dowry and bride price came under the exclusive control of clan patriarchs rather than held in reserve for the bride, thus marking one of the fundamental differences between the family systems of these different parts of the world. See Jack Goody, *Production and Reproduction: Comparative Study of the Domestic Domain* (Cambridge: Cambridge University Press, 1976), and *The East and the West* (Cambridge: Cambridge University Press, 1996).

12. Witte, *From Sacrament to Contract,* pp. 36-38; James Brundage, *Law, Sex, and Christian Society in Medieval Europe* (Chicago: University of Chicago Press, 1987), pp. 325-416.

13. Witte, *From Sacrament to Contract,* pp. 189-91; Steven Ozment, *When Fathers Ruled* (Cambridge, Mass.: Harvard University Press, 1983), pp. 25-31.

14. Lawrence Stone, *Road to Divorce: England 1530-1987* (Oxford: Oxford University Press, 1990), pp. 96-120.

15. Anthony Giddens, *The Transformation of Intimacy: Sex, Love, and Eroticism in Modern Societies* (Stanford: Stanford University Press, 1992).

16. Aristotle, "Politics," bk. II, ch. 4.

17. Witte, *From Sacrament to Contract,* pp. 2, 48-53.

18. Witte, *From Sacrament to Contract,* pp. 130-34.

19. John Stuart Mill, *The Subjection of Women* (Indianapolis: Hackett Publishing, 1988).

20. *Supporting Families* (Home Office, 1998).

21. *To have and to hold* (Canberra: House of Representatives Standing Committee on Legal and Constitutional Affairs, 1998).

22. Leo Perdue, Joseph Blenkinsopp, John Collins, and Carol Meyers, *Families in Ancient Israel* (Louisville: Westminster/John Knox Press, 1997), pp. 239-44.

23. Thomas Aquinas, *Summa Theologica,* III, "Supplement," Q. 42 (New York: Benziger Brothers, 1948).

24. For an interpretation of this view of Aquinas, see Browning et al., *From Culture Wars to Common Ground,* pp. 120-24.

25. Augustine, "The Good of Marriage," *The Fathers of the Church* (New York: Fathers of the Church, Inc., 1955), p. 12; Aquinas, *Summa Theologica,* III, "Supplement," Q. 41.

26. Aristotle, "Nichomachean Ethics," *The Basic Works of Aristotle* (New York: Random House, 1941), bk. VIII, ch. 11.

27. Carolyn Osiek and David Balch, *Families in the New Testament World* (Louisville: Westminster/John Knox, 1997), p. 115.

28. For a balance of the unitive and procreative in Pope John Paul II, see his "Letter to Families," *Origins* 23, no. 37 (March 3, 1994).

29. For a philosophical elaboration of the Golden Rule, see Immanuel Kant, *Foundations of the Metaphysics of Morals* (Indianapolis: Bobbs-Merrill, 1959), p. 47.

CHAPTER 1

The Future of Marriage in Western Civilization by Edward Westermarck

1. W. Schäffner, *Geschichte der Rechtsverfassung Frankreichs,* iii. (Frankfurt a. M., 1850), p. 186.

2. D. M. Kauschansky, 'Die persönliche und wirtschaftliche Lage der Frau in der Ehe nach europäischem Recht', in *Zeitschrift für Sexualwissenschaft und Sexualpolitik,* xviii. (Berlin & Köln, 1932), pp. 379, 484.

3. V. H. R. Rivers, *The History of Melanesian Society,* ii. (Cambridge, 1914), p. 145.

4. See my *Three Essays on Sex and Marriage* (London, 1934), p. 171 *sqq.*

5. W. Volz, *Nord-Sumatra,* ii. (Berlin, 1912), p. 364.

6. W. Munnecke, *Mit Hagenbeck im Dschungel* (Berlin, 1931), p. 77 *sqq.*

7. Cf. R. M. and Ada W. Yerkes, *The Great Apes* (New Haven & London, 1929), p. 541.

8. *Cf. ibid.* p. 541.

9. *Three Essays on Sex and Marriage,* p. 181 *sqq.*

10. S. Zuckerman, *The Social Life of Monkeys and Apes* (London, 1932), pp. 147, 212, 213, 314 *sq.;* F. Doflein, *Das Tier als Glied des Naturganzen* (Leipzig & Berlin, 1914), pp. 692, 694.

11. R. M. and Ada W. Yerkes, *op. cit.* p. 543.

12. E. Reichenow, 'Biologische Beobachtungen an Gorilla und Schimpanse', in *Sitzungsbericht der Gesellschaft Naturforschender Freunde zu Berlin,* no. 1, 1920 (Berlin), p. 15 *sqq.*

13. E. Westermarck, *The History of Human Marriage,* i. (London, 1921), p. 68.

14. *Idem, The Origin and Development of the Moral Ideas,* i. (London, 1912), pp. 118-22, 135-37, 139 *sqq.* For the characteristics and origin of moral disapproval, see *ibid.* vol. i. ch. ii. p. 21 *sqq.*

15. *The History of Human Marriage,* i. 46 *sqq.*

16. *Ibid.* i. 49 *sqq.*

17. *Ibid.* i. 72 *sqq.*

18. A. E. Brehm, *Thierleben,* i. (Leipzig, 1877), p. 97.

19. *Ibid.* xiii. (Leipzig, 1920), p. 661.

20. The Duke Adolphus Frederick of Mecklenburg, *In the Heart of Africa* (London, 1910), p. 139.

21. H. O. Forbes, *A Hand-book to the Primates,* ii. (London, 1894), p. 197.

22. D. Livingstone, *The Last Journals of, in Central Africa,* ii. (London, 1874), p. 55.

23. Forbes, *op. cit.* p. 193; H. von Koppenfels, 'Meine Jagden auf Gorillas', in *Die Gartenlaube,* 1877 (Leipzig), p. 418.

24. Forbes, *op. cit.* ii. 193.

25. Von Koppenfels, *loc. cit.* p. 418 *sq.*

26. B. Burbridge, *Gorilla* (London, 1928), p. 238.

27. A. E. Jenks, 'Bulu Knowledge of the Gorilla and Chimpanzee', in *The American Anthropologist,* N.S, xiii. (Lancaster, 1911), p. 58.

28. Brehm, *op. cit.* xiii. 48, 571, 581.

29. I. Bloch, *The Sexual Life of Our Time* (London, 1908), p. 188 *sqq.*

30. *The History of Human Marriage,* vol. i. ch. iii.

31. *Ibid.* vol. i. chs. iv.-viii.

32. C. Darwin, *The Descent of Man,* ii. (London, 1888), p. 394 *sq.* Before Darwin J. J. Virey (*De la femme* [Paris, 1823], p. 148) argued that promiscuity would have caused perpetual fighting between the men.

33. *The History of Human Marriage,* i. 54 *sqq.*

34. B. Malinowski, 'Kinship', in *Encyclopaedia Britannica,* xiii. (London, 1929), pp. 404, 405, 408.

35. A. Bebel, *Woman in the Past, Present, and Future* (London, 1885), p. 9; F. Engels, *Der Ursprung der Familie, des Privateigenthums und des Staats* (Hottingen-Zürich, 1884), p. 17. See also J. Loewenthal's reference to Krishe's book, *Das Rätsel der Mutterrechts- gesellschaft* (München, 1927), in *Zeitschrift für Sexualwissenschaft,* xiv. (Berlin & Köln, 1927), p. 27 *sq.*

36. R. Briffault, 'Introduction' to V. F. Calverton's book, *The Bankruptcy of Marriage* (London, 1931), p. 7.

37. V. F. Calverton, 'The Compulsive Basis of Social Thought', in *American Journal of Sociology,* xxxvi. (Chicago, 1931), pp. 700, 702.

38. E. Westermarck, *The History of Human Marriage,* ii. (London, 1921), p. 31 *sq.*

39. *Ibid.* i. 160.

40. *The History of Human Marriage,* iii. 290.

41. *Ibid.* i. 362.

42. *Ibid.* i. 375.

43. T. K. Cheyne, 'Harlot', in Cheyne and J. S. Black, *Encyclopaedia Biblica,* ii. (London, 1901), p. 1964.

44. See *Psalms,* cxxvii. 4.

45. Jebamoth, fol. 63 b, quoted by H. Vorwahl, 'Die Sexualität im Alten Testament', in *Zeitschrift für Sexualwissenschaft und Sexualpolitik,* xv. (Berlin & Köln, 1928), p. 127.

46. E. Brauer, 'Die Frau bei den südarabischen Juden', *ibid.* xviii. (Berlin & Köln, 1931), p. 158.

47. N. D. Fustel de Coulanges, *La Cité antique* (Paris, 1864), p. 54 *sq.*

48. H. Risley, *The People of India* (London, 1915), p. 154.

49. *Vendîdâd,* iv. 47 (*The Sacred Books of the East,* vol. iv. [Oxford, 1880]).

50. J. Darmesteter, in *The Sacred Books of the East,* iv. p. lxii.

51. Plato, *Leges,* vi. 773.

52. Isaeus, *Oratio de Apollodori hereditate,* 30, p. 66.

53. *Oratio in Neæram,* in Demosthenes, *Opera* (Parisiis, 1843), p. 1386.

54. *1 Corinthians,* vii. 1 *sq.*

55. Athenagoras, *Legatio pro Christianis,* 33 (J. P. Migne, *Patrologia cursus completus,* Ser. Graeca, vi. [Parisiis, 1857], col. 966).

56. F. E. Traumann, 'Das Rundschreiben des Papstes Pius XI über die christliche Ehe und die Sexualreform', in *Zeitschrift für Sexualwissenschaft und Sexualpolitik,* xviii. (Berlin & Köln, 1931), p. 124.

57. Katharine B. Davis, *Factors in the Sex Life of Twenty-two Hundred Women* (New York & London, 1929), p. 355 *sqq.*

58. G. V. Hamilton, *A Research in Marriage* (New York, 1929), p. 382.

59. Davis, *op. cit.* 372 *sqq.*

60. H. Harmsen, *Bevölkerungspolitik Frankreichs* (Berlin, 1927), reviewed in *Zeitschrift für Sexualwissenschaft und Sexualpolitik,* xv. (Berlin & Köln, 1929), p. 588.

61. Havelock Ellis, *More Essays of Love and Virtue* (London, 1931), p. 16 n. 1.

62. A. W. Thomas, 'The Decline in the Birth Rate', in *British Medical Journal*, 1906, vol. ii. (London), p. 1066.

63. See Havelock Ellis, *Studies in the Psychology of Sex*, vi. (Philadelphia, 1923), p. 589.

64. L. D. Pesl, 'Fruchtabtreibung und Findelhaus', in *Zeitschrift für Sexualwissenschaft und Sexualpolitik*, xv. (Berlin & Köln, 1928), p. 260.

65. A. Moll, 'Der "reaktionäre" Kongress für Sexualforschung', *ibid.* xiii. (Bonn, 1927), p. 330; F. Burgdörfer, *Der Geburtenrückgang und die Zukunft des deutschen Volkes* (Berlin, 1928), quoted *ibid.* xvi. (Berlin & Köln, 1929), p. 67. See also A. V. Knack, 'Die Wegbereitung einer vernunftgemässen Bevölkerungspolitik', in A. Weil, *Sexualreform und Sexualwissenschaft* (Stuttgart, 1922), p. 203.

66. Davis, *op. cit.* p. 14.

67. Hamilton, *op. cit.* p. 134.

68. S. Ranulf, 'Die moralische Reaktion gegen neomalthusianische Propaganda in Dänemark', in *Zeitschrift für Sexualwissenschaft und Sexualpolitik*, xvi. (Berlin & Köln, 1929), p. 47 *sqq.*

69. Havelock Ellis, *Views and Reviews* (London, 1932), p. 82.

70. *Idem, Studies in the Psychology of Sex*, 'Analysis of the Sexual Instinct, etc.' (1903), p. 16.

71. Th. H. van de Velde, *Sex Hostility in Marriage* (London, 1931), pp. 70, 76, 78.

72. B. Russell, *Marriage and Morals* (London, 1929), p. 170.

73. *Ibid.* p. 159.

74. P. Popenoe, *Modern Marriage* (New York, 1927), p. 4.

75. E. H. Kisch, *Die sexuelle Untreue der Frau*, ii. (Bonn, 1918), p. 122.

76. *The History of Human Marriage*, ii. 24 *sq.*

77. *Ibid.* ii. 25 *sqq.*

78. *The Indo-Chinese Gleaner*, i. (Malacca, 1818), p. 164.

79. A. Kaegi, *The Rigveda* (Boston, 1886), p. 15.

80. J. A. Dubois, *A Description of the Character, Manners, and Customs of the People of India* (Madras, 1862), p. 109.

81. J. L. Burckhardt, *Notes on the Bedouins and Wahábys* (London, 1830), p. 155.

82. Cf. G. Lowes Dickinson, *The Greek View of Life* (London, 1896), p. 159.

83. Plato, *Symposium*, p. 181.

84. See my book, *Wit and Wisdom in Morocco* (London, 1930), p. 80.

85. Ellis, *Studies in the Psychology of Sex*, vi. p. 133.

86. G. C. Beale, *Wise Wedlock* (London, 1922), p. 57 *sq.*

87. Russell, *op. cit.* pp. 99, 224.

88. Margaret Sanger, *Happiness in Marriage* (London, 1927), p. 140.

89. Marie Stopes, *Married Love* (London, 1926), p. 94.

90. L. Loewenfeld, *On Conjugal Happiness* (London, 1912), p. 164 *sqq.*

91. Cf. E. Spranger, *Psychologie des Jugendalters* (Leipzig, 1924), p. 81 *sqq.;* R. Lagerborg, *Kärleksruset* (Helsingfors, 1925), p. 31 *sqq.;* Th. H. van de Velde, *Ideal Marriage* (London, 1928), p. 11 *sq.;* R. Müller-Freienfels, 'Zur Psychologie der erotischen Selektion', in *Zeitschrift für Sexualwissenschaft und Sexualpolitik*, xv. (Berlin & Köln, 1928), p. 86.

92. See E. Westermarck, *The Origin and Development of the Moral Ideas,* i. (London, 1912), p. 635 *sq.*

93. D. V. Glass, 'Divorce in England and Wales', in *The Sociological Review,* xxvi. (London, 1934), p. 306.

94. A. Cahen, *Statistical Analysis of American Divorce* (New York, 1932), p. 115. *Cf.* W. F. Willcox, *The Divorce Problem* (New York, 1891), p. 34.

95. E. Glasson, *Le Mariage et le divorce* (Paris, 1880), p. 470.

"The Man with No Family to Take Leave Of" by Tu Fu

1. The defeat of the T'ang forces at Hsiang-chou in 759.
2. The drum used in battle to signal troop movements.

CHAPTER 2

"The Good of Marriage" by St. Augustine

1. Cf. Gen. 2:21.
2. Gen. 1:28.
3. Cf. *De civ. Dei* 1.14.
4. Cf. Ps. 137:3.
5. Cf. Wisd. 2:24.
6. 1 Thess. 4:17.
7. Cf. Gen. 2:17.
8. Cf. Deut. 29:5.
9. Cf. Matt. 19:9.
10. Cf. John 2.
11. 1 Cor. 7:4.
12. 1 Tim. 1:5.
13. 1 Cor. 7:7.
14. 1 Cor. 7:29-34.
15. 1 Cor. 7:9.
16. Cf. Phil. 1:23.

17. Cf. *Retractationes* 2:22: 'This was said since the good and proper use of passion is not a passion. Just as it is wicked to use good things wrongly, it is good to use wicked things rightly. I argued more carefully about this matter on another occasion, especially against the new Pelagian heretics.'

18. 1 Cor. 7:9.
19. Cf. Luke 19:3.
20. Cf. 1 Kings 17:4.

21. Cf. *Retractationes* 2:22: 'What I said concerning Abraham . . . I do not entirely approve. It ought to be thought that he believed that his son, if he had been killed, must soon be returned to him by a resurrection from the dead, as it is read in the Epistle to the Hebrews' [11:19].

22. Gen. 21:12.

23. Apoc. 14:4.
24. 1 Tim. 5:14.
25. 1 Cor. 7:4.
26. 1 Cor. 7:10.
27. Cf. 1 Cor. 7:32.
28. Cf. 2 Cor. 10:12.
29. Eccli. 3:20.
30. Cf. Matt. 8:11.

From the *Summa Theologica* by St. Thomas Aquinas

1. *Hom.* i in the *Opus Imperfectum,* falsely ascribed to St. John Chrysostom.
2. Cf. P. III, Q. 61, A. 1; Q. 65, A. 1.
3. Cf. P. III, Q. 66, A. 1.
4. Peter Lombard, iv, *Sent.* D. 2.
5. St. Albertus Magnus, iv, *Sent.* D. 26.
6. St. Bonaventure, iv, *Sent.* D. 26.
7. Cf. P. III, Q. 66, A. 3 *ad* 4.
8. St. Augustine, *Tract.* lxxx, *in Joan.*
9. Cf. Q. 18, A. 1, where St. Thomas uses the same expression; and Editor's notes at the beginning of the Supplement and on that *Article.*

On Modern Marriage and Other Observations by Isak Dinesen

1. The day of the storming of the Bastille, the seminal event of the French Revolution.

CHAPTER 3

"The Great Rooted Bed," Book 23 in *The Odyssey* by Homer

1. Editors' note: Odysseus had left home to fight at Troy.

"Izutsu" by Zeami Motokiyo

1. Critical remarks on these poets (Abbot Henjō, Ono-no-Komachi, Bun'ya-no-Yasuhide, Ōtomo-no-Kuronushi, Monk Kisen, and Ariwara-no-Narihira) appear in the preface of the *Kokinshū.*
2. Editors' note: The sources of this play are a tale attributed to Narihara and the poems exchanged by Narihara and the daughter of Ki-no-Aritsune, his wife. The latter are foun in volume 15 of the *Kokinshū.*
3. The temples referred to are: Tōdai-ji, Kōfuku-ji, Gangō-ji, Daian-ji, Yakushi-ji, Saidai-ji, and Hōryū-ji. Some are situated in the city itself, others in the neighbourhood.

4. Situated in Yamato Province and famous for the Hase-dera Temple dating from the eighth century.

5. Pass crossing a hill of the same name in the mountain range between Yamato and Kawachi Provinces. The Tatsuta Shrine, one of the most ancient Shinto temples, situated on the eastern slope of Tatsuta Hill south of Mt. Shigi, was erected in the seventh century by Imperial order and dedicated to the wind-god. The river flowing east of the hill is also called Tatsuta and has been much celebrated in ancient literature on account of the autumn tints of the maples which line its banks.

6. Or a small wooden bucket with a spray of leaves representing flowers.

7. In Jōdo-kyō except for the Shin sect, it was customary for a dying person to hold in the left hand one end of a thread attached to a hand of the image of Amida Buddha in order that he should fix his mind on His saving power.

8. The metaphor seems analogous to that found in the third chapter of *St. John,* except that here the changeableness of wind is used to symbolize the uncertainty of human life.

9. Each chapter of the *Ise Monogatari* begins with the words: "In ancient times there was a man." Since the anonymous hero is understood to be Narihira, the author of the present play pretends that Narihira was called the 'Ancient' in his life-time.

10. Situated at the foot of a mountain of the same name in Naka-Kawachi County of that province.

11, 12. Quoted from the *Ise Monogatari,* ch. xxii.

13. It was an ancient custom for lovers to sleep with their kimono turned inside out so that they might dream of their beloved, as mentioned in a poem by Ono-no-Komachi in the *Kokinshū:*

> When overwhelmed
> By the yearning for the one I love,
> I go to bed,
> Wearing my garment inside out.

14. Quoted from the *Ise Monogatari,* ch. xvi, as attributed to the hero of the work, i.e., Narihira. The poem is also found in the *Kokinshū* where the author's name is not mentioned.

15. Quoted from the *Ise Monogatari,* ch. iv.

The Mystery of Love and Marriage by Derrick Sherwin Bailey

1. *I and Thou,* p. 46.

2. Buber, *op. cit.,* p. 76.

3. Buber's terminology will be used without further comment; it is now familiar and is indispensable. For an exposition of his theory of relation the reader is referred to *I and Thou.*

4. *Op. cit.,* p. 33.

5. All that is said here, from the man's point of view, of woman as *She,* is of course equally true from the woman's, of man as *He.*

6. *Op. cit.,* p. 17; cf. p. 99: 'Love itself cannot persist in the immediacy of relation. . . .

Every *Thou* in the world is enjoined by its nature . . . to re-enter continually the condition of things.'

7. *Ibid.,* p. 33.

8. *Ibid.,* p. 105.

9. See especially: *He came down from Heaven,* ch. 5; *Religion and Love in Dante;* and *The Figure of Beatrice.* I am glad to be able to acknowledge Mr. Williams's influence, and his kindness in permitting me to make full use of his works.

10. *The Figure of Beatrice,* p. 20.

11. *The Figure of Beatrice,* pp. 63-64; cf. p. 35.

12. *He came down from Heaven,* pp. 96-97.

13. Denis de Rougement, *Passion and Society,* p. 314.

14. Buber, *op. cit.,* p. 75.

15. *Ibid.,* p. 106.

16. *Ibid.,* p. 100.

17. *He came down from Heaven,* pp. 92-93.

18. Buber, *op. cit.,* p. 8.

19. *He came down from Heaven,* p. 93.

20. *He came down from Heaven,* pp. 93 and 94.

21. *Ibid.,* p. 97; cf. *Religion and Love in Dante,* p. 11; *The Figure of Beatrice,* pp. 21-22.

22. Cf. C. S. Lewis, *The Allegory of Love,* pp. 34ff.

23. Brunner's remark in this connexion is apposite: 'The love which is supposed to "come of itself where true Christians marry" belongs to the sphere of Christian legend'; see *The Divine Imperative,* p. 360.

24. For a suggestive expansion of this point, see *The Figure of Beatrice,* pp. 15-16 and 63.

25. Brunner, *Divine Imperative,* p. 347.

26. In this connexion see the important remarks by Dr. J. R. Oliver in *Psychiatry and Mental Health,* pp. 203ff.

27. Buber, *op. cit.,* p. 15.

CHAPTER 4

Introduction

1. Editors' note: For a revealing look at the relative instability of interreligious marriages in the Christian community, see Michael J. Lawler et al., *Ministry to Interchurch Marriages: A National Study,* published by Creighton University Center for Marriage and Family, 1999. Besides noting several previous studies which have shown a significantly "higher rate of instability in religiously heterogamous marriage," this study goes on to pinpoint specific reasons why religious intermarriages pose greater risks to marital stability, chief among them being the tendency of interreligious couples to enjoy fewer religious activities together, to have greater differences with regard to religious beliefs, and to be more conflicted about the religious upbringing of their children.

Medea by Euripides

1. Editors' note: The children of foreign women were not entitled to any privileges of citizenship in ancient Athens. Thus, Jason would have had some justification to argue that his marriage to a Greek princess would advance Medea's children.

The Book of Ruth

1. Editors' note: From the Hebrew word for "bitter."
2. This passage refers to the practice of levirate marriage, the custom of marrying a widow to her late husband's brother in cases where the first marriage had not produced an heir.

CHAPTER 5

Introduction

1. For a comprehensive discussion of the economic benefits of stable marriage to the individual, see Linda J. Waite and Maggie Gallagher, *The Case for Marriage* (New York: Doubleday, 2000), chapter 8.

"Beginning of Spring — A Stroll with My Wife" by Hsü Chün Ch'ien

1. Wine on which blossoms have been floated.

Paradise Lost by John Milton

1. **grateful** pleasing, and expressing gratitude.
2. **diffident** distrustful.
3. **Access** accession.
4. **still** always.
5. **event** outcome.
6. **still erect** always alert (and with "God-like erect" contrasted with the Fall).
7. **mind** remind.
8. **securer** too confident.
9. **Oread or Dryad** wood- or mountain-nymph.
10. **Delia** Diana, goddess of hunting.
11. **Guiltless of** without experience of (but fire is associated with guilt in the story of Prometheus — see IV 715-19 — and "Guiltless" is prophetic here).
12. **Pales** goddess of pastures.
13. **Pomona** goddess of fruit.
14. **Vertumnus** god of the seasons and of gardens.
15. **Ceres** goddess of agriculture; see IV 268-72.

"Marriage" by Bronislaw Malinowski

1. See Bronislaw Malinowski, "Anthropology," *Encyclopaedia Britannica*, 1936, first suppl. ed., p. 132.

CHAPTER 6

On the Subjection of Women **by John Stuart Mill**

1. Editors' note: Divorces at the time were extremely difficult to obtain in England.

Getting Married **by George Bernard Shaw**

1. Editors' note: At the time, legal separation was possible, but seldom divorce.

CHAPTER 7

"The Forbidden Wife" by Ts'ao Chih

1. Chao-yao is the first star in the handle of the Big Dipper; when the handle points west-southwest, it signals the beginning of autumn.

"The Estate of Marriage" by Martin Luther

1. This story, referred to frequently by Luther, is from the *Attic Nights of Giulus Gellius*, 1. Vi. 1-6. Metellus Numidieus was a Roman censor in 102 B.C.

2. *Des melhs, wie die mauss nu satt sind.* Luther's variation of the old proverb about the sated mouse may be paraphrased in English, "To a full belly all meat is bad." See Wander (ed.), *Sprichwörter-Lexikon*, III, 541-542, "*Maus*," Nos. 177, 195.

3. *Eyn kurtze freud und lange unlust.* Cf. Wander (ed.), *Sprichwörter-Lexikon*, I, 1166, 1168, "*Freude*," Nos. 40, 92.

4. For centuries Margaret of Pisidian Antioch was widely venerated as the patron saint of pregnant women. According to tradition, she suffered torture and martyrdom for refusing to renounce her faith and marry the Roman prefect, Olybrius. Her dates are uncertain though she may have died about the time of the Diocletian persecution (*ca.* 303-305). Among the legends of her martyrdom is the story of her prayer, just before being beheaded, that "whenever a woman in labor should call upon her name, the child might be brought forth without harm."

5. Cyprian, Bishop of Carthage, martyred in A.D. 258, was the author of numerous letters, to one of which Luther is referring. In his letter to Fidus on the baptizing of infants (Ep. LXIV, 4) Cyprian writes, "In the kiss of an infant, each of us should, for very piety, think of the recent Hands of God, which we in a manner kiss, in the lately formed and recently born man, when we embrace that which God has made." *The Epistles of St. Cyprian*

("A Library of Fathers of the Holy Catholic Church Anterior to the Division of the East and West" [Oxford: Parker, 1844]), p. 197.

6. *Unrhedlich. CL* 2, 355, n. 23, suggests the meaning *verschwenderische* [i.e., wasteful].

7. Editors' note: Interestingly, recent research indicates that cohabiting couples are three times more prone to violent arguments than married people. They are also less inclined to report themselves happy. See Linda J. Waite and Maggie Gallagher, *The Case for Marriage* (New York: Doubleday, 2000), esp. pp. 67-68, 155-56.

8. See Wander (ed.), *Sprichwörter-Lexikon*, I, 166, *"Aufstehen,"* No. 16, cf. V, 842, No. 65.

9. Syphilis was widespread in Luther's day. Its sudden upsurge late in the fifteenth century gave rise to the legend that it was brought from the New World by the sailors of Columbus. See Preserved Smith, *The Age of the Reformation* (New York: Holt, 1920), p. 512. An early treatise on the disease by Nicolaus Leonicenus was published in 1497. Cf. also Luther's reference to the Turkish menace in *LW* 35, 300, 404, 406-407, and in *PE* 5 (77), 79-123.

10. *Mehr eyngebubet denn aussgebubet.* Luther's play on words depends on the close similarity between the German words for "boy" *(Bube)* and "fornicate" *(buben). Ausbuben* in relation to *Bube* meant to put away childhood, grow up, reach maturity, and in this connection also to have one's fling or sow one's wild oats. However, in relation to *buben*, the term also meant more literally to put away the unclean life, abandon immorality. Luther frequently used the term *hineinbuben* to express the very opposite. Both words thus carried overtones referring to age as well as to morality. See Grimm, *Deutsches Wörterbuch*, II, 457-462; I, 840; IV^2 1416.

11. Wander (ed.), *Sprichwörter-Lexikon*, III, 936, *"Narren,"* No. 3.

12. See Wander (ed.), *Sprichwörter-Lexikon*, III, 936, *"Narren,"* No. 3; cf. also II, 1048-1050, *"Jugend,"* Nos. 190, 141, 166, 176, 193.

13. Wander (ed.), *Sprichwörter-Lexikon*, I, 820, *"Engel,"* No. 7.

14. Luther frequently cited this line from the Roman comic poet Terence (*ca.* 190-*ca.* 159 B.C.), "It is no crime, believe me, that a youth wenches" (*The Brothers*, I, ii, 21-22). See, e.g., *LW* 1, 166.

15. Wander (ed.), *Sprichwörter-Lexikon*, I, 1634, *"Gesund,"* No. 6.

CHAPTER 8

The Theology of Marriage by Joseph E. Kerns

1. Mt. 19,10.

2. *De Virginitate*, c. 27, PG 48, 552-53. Cf. Gregory of Nyssa, *De Virg.*, c. 3, PG 46, 331-35.

3. *De Virg.*, c. 6, PL 16, 287.

4. *Exhort. Virg.*, c. 4, PL 16, 358. Cf. *De Vid.*, c. 11, PL 16, 268.

5. Cf. Jerome, *Epist.*, 123, n. 5, PL 22, 1048-49; Augustine, *Serm.*, 37, c. 6, PL 38, 225.

6. Abelard, *Prob. Hel.*, 14, PL 178, 701. Cf. Fulgentius, *Epist.* 2, c. 6, PL 65, 314; Sedulius Scotus, *In 1 Cor.* 7, PL 102, 142; Hatto of Vercelli, *Expos. in Ep. Pauli* 1 Cor., PL 134, 357; Peter Damian, *Epist.* 14, PL 144, 452.

7. *Summa De Arte Pr.*, c. 46, PL 210, 194.

8. *In Tob.* 3, a. 3, *Works* 5, 97. Cf. *In Matt.* 19, a. 33, *Works* 11, 213; *De Laud. Vita Conj.*, a. 3, *Works* 38, 61.

9. *Summa S. Th.*, III, tit. 1, c. 25.

10. Cajetan, *In Gen.* 2, 23; cf. Soto *In 4 Sent.*, d. 31, q. 1, a. 1; Buys, *op. cit.*, p. 224; Canisius, *Summa Doct. Christ.*, I, P. 1, c. 4, n. 7, q. 207; II, *ibid.*, q. 213; Sanchez, *De Sac. Mat.*, lib. 2, disp. 29, q. 1.

11. *Serm.*, 2e dim. Epiph., *Works* 2, 375-77.

12. *Hom. 62 in Matt.*, PG 58, 599.

13. *Adv. Jov.*, lib. 1, n. 28, PL 23, 261.

14. *Ibid.*, n. 47, PL 23, 289-90.

15. *Report.*, lib. 4, d. 28, q. 1, schol. 2. Cf. Hildebert of Mans, *Epist.*, lib. 1, ep. 21, PL 171, 193-94; Lothair Segni (Innocent III), *De Contemptu Mundi*, lib. 1, c. 18, PL 217, 710; Vincent of Beauvais, *op. cit.*, cc. 37-38, 47.

16. *Report.*, lib. 4, d. 28, q. 1, schol. 2.

17. *Pars* 2, c. 10.

18. *Laud. Vita Conj.*, a. 3, *Works* 28, 61. Cf. *In Matt.* 19, a. 33, *Works* II, 214; St. Antoninus, *Summa S. T.*, III, tit. 1, c. 1.

19. Cf. Soto, *In 4 Sent.*, d. 31, q. 1, a. 1; Alvarez de Paz, *De Exterm. Mali*, lib. 5, pars 2, c. 5, *Works* 4, 577-78.

20. *De Bono Status Cast.*, c. 5, *Opusc.*, p. 884-85. Cf. *De Jure et Jus.*, lib. 4, c. 2, dub. 15.

21. *Serm. sur les oblig. de l'état rel.*, *Works* (Besançon: Outhenim-Chalandre Fils, 1840), 6, 537.

22. *Divers Sentiments*, c. 50.

23. *Serm.*, 2e dim. Epiph., *Works* 2, 375. Cf. De la Columbère, *Réfl. Chrét.*, du mariage, *Works*, 5, 180.

24. *Serm. de Virg.*, Works 6, 24.

25. *Adv. Oppugnatores Vitae Monast.*, lib. 3, n. 15, PB 47, 375-76. Cf. Gregory Nazianzen, *Carm.*, lib. 1, sect. 2, n. 6. 1. 6, PG 37, 643; Gregory of Nyssa, *De Virg.*, c. 3, PG 46, 331-35.

26. *De Vid.*, c. 11, PL 16, 268. Cf. Jerome *Adv. Jov.*, lib. 1, n. 28, PL 23, 261.

27 *Moralia*, lib. 26, PL 76, 374. Cf. Isidore of Seville, *De Eccl. Off.*, lib. 2, c. 20, PL 83, 810; Tajon, *Lib. Sent.*, lib. 3, c. 7, PL 80, 857.

28. St. Paschasius Radbert, *In Matt.*, lib. 10, c. 19, PL 120, 651. Cf. Sedulius Scotus, *In 1 Cor. 7*, PL 102, 142.

29. *Sermones de Diversis*, Serm. 35, PL 183, 634.

30. Cf. Scotus, *Report.*, lib. 4, d. 28, q. 1, schol. 2.

31. *Opusc.* 10, Vitis Myst., Add. 4, c. 30, n. 106, Quar. 8, 210. Cf. Aquinas, *In 4 Sent.*, d. 39, a. 4 ad 1; *S.T.* I II, q. 108, a. 4; II II, q. 184, a. 3; *Contra Gent.*, lib. 3, cc. 131-39.

32. *Laud. Vita Conj.*, a. 3, *Works* 38, 61.

33. *Op. cit.*, vol. 5, tr. 9, p. 49.

34. *Lett.* 664, *Works* 3, 550.

35. *Réfl. Chrét.*, mariage, *Works*, 5, 179-80.

36. *Ibid.*

37. *Serm.*, 2e dim. Epiph., *Works* 2, 382.

38. *Ibid.*, p. 378.

"On Questions of Marriage and Sex: To Stephen Roth" by Martin Luther

1. The reference is to assuming the form of a servant, mentioned below.
2. For this proverb, see Ernst Thiele, *Luthers Sprichwörtersammlung* (Weimar, 1900), pp. 295, 296.
3. Cf. 1 Corinthians 11:7.
4. Cf. Philippians 2:7.

CHAPTER 9

Introduction

1. See E. Westermarck, "Divorce," *Encyclopedia Britannica*, 1948, vol. 7, p. 453.

"Salvation," Book Four of the *Summa Contra Gentiles* by St. Thomas Aquinas

1. See above, ch. 55.
2. SCG, III, ch. 122-126.

De Regno Christi by Martin Bucer

1. Divorce: *cf. Scripta* (1577), p. 125: "uxorem . . . dimittere, & alteram ducere" (to dismiss a wife and take another).
2. Matter in italics added by Milton.
3. Who . . . above: *cf. Scripta* (1577), p. 125: "qui castrationem propter regnum coelorum non capiunt, ac ideo in periculo versantur fornicationis" (who do not receive the castration for the kingdom of heaven, and are therefore put in danger of fornication).
4. Matter in italics added by Milton.
5. Here Milton has considerably condensed Bucer, omitting a passage (*Scripta*, 1577, p. 125) in which Bucer tries to prove that Christ was speaking only of a "fit and meet wife," and preserving the summary.
6. Material in italics added by Milton, who omits a paragraph (*Scripta*, 1577, pp. 125-26) in which Bucer argues that 1 Corinthians 7 proves that the causes of divorce are not restricted to adultery.
7. Reference added by Milton.
8. Milton omits a passage (*Scripta*, 1577, p. 126) developing the danger of fornication to a man compelled to live with an intolerable wife.
9. Milton has considerably compressed the expression here, omitting several clauses that substantially summarize the preceding argument.
10. Milton omits two paragraphs (*Scripta*, 1577, p. 127) consisting of repetition and summary of the foregoing arguments against restricting divorce to adultery.
11. No whordom: *cf. Scripta* (1577), p. 133: "Nullus omnino scortator, nullumque scortum debeat tolerari" (No whoremonger at all and no whoredom ought to be tolerated).

12. Without which: *qua neglecta* (by the neglect of which).

13. Whole breed of men: *cives* (citizens).

14. No wise man: *cf. Scripta* (1577), p. 133: "nemo unquam sapientum, & honestae vitae amantium" (no wise man and lover of honest life).

15. Whordom and adultery: *cf. Scripta* (1577), p. 133: "non stupra tantùm, & adulteria, sed etiam omnes vagas libidines, omnes illegitimas marium & foeminarum conjunctiones" (not only whoredoms and adulteries, but also all loose passions, all lawless conjunctions of men and women).

16. Lawfully dissolv'd: *cf. Scripta* (1577), p. 133: "sed non nisi legitimè, disolvantur" (dissolved, but not otherwise than lawfully).

The Code of Maimonides

1. Editors' note: Here and elsewhere Maimonides refers to the "ikkar ketubah," the most important part of the ketubah, or marriage contract, which provides a specific cash gift to the bride set aside for her in the event of divorce or the husband's death. (Traditionally, this sum, which was called the "mohar," was set at 200 silver coins.) It should be mentioned here that where Maimonides refers to the "supplementary" amount, he is probably referring to the "tosefet ketubah," an additional sum the husband could voluntarily set aside for his wife in case of his death or divorce. Traditionally, this sum was 100 silver coins.

2. Editors' note: This is a reference to rabbinic as opposed to biblical law. It was characteristic of the rabbis to interpret rabbinic law more strictly than biblical.

3. Editors' note: Traditionally, Jewish women were required to bring dowries into their marriages. The dowry, or "naddan," was that part of the bride's inheritance from her father which was "leased" to her husband as long as they remained married, and included not only cash but clothes, furniture, and household objects. Fathers were required to provide their daughters with at least enough of a dowry to enable them to purchase clothes for a year.

4. Editors' note: The "nikhsei melog" is that property given to the bride which belongs to her alone, and which she is entitled to manage. Because her husband is entitled only to the usufruct of that property, the "nikhsei melog" is not mentioned in the ketubah.

5. Editors' note: The word *get* is Hebrew and refers to the divorce document.

"Old Poem"

1. Some commentators take these two lines as the words of the wife, questioning her husband's sincerity by reminding him of how he treated her. I [the editor, Burton Watson] take them as an indirect admission by the husband that he acted badly.

2. One bolt or *p'i* is equivalent to four yards or *chang*.

Marriage and Morals by Bertrand Russell

1. In Nevada, the grounds are wilful desertion, conviction of felony or infamous crime, habitual gross drunkenness, impotency at the time of marriage continuing to the

time of the divorce, extreme cruelty, neglect to provide for one year, insanity for two years. See "Sex in Civilization," ed. by V. F. Calverton and S. D. Schmalhausen, 1929, p. 224.

2. It will be remembered that in the case of the Duke and Duchess of Marlborough it was held that the marriage was null because she had been forced into it, and this ground was considered valid in spite of the fact that they had lived together for years and had children.

3. Since then the total number of divorces and nullities in Sweden increased from 1531 in 1923 to 1966 in 1927, while the rate per 100 marriages increased in U.S.A. from 13.4 to 15.

4. Unless he happens to teach at one of the older universities and to be closely related to a peer who has been a Cabinet minister

5. "Preface to Morals," 1929, p. 308.

Permissions List

The editors and publisher gratefully acknowledge permission to include material from the following sources:

Chapter 1

Edward Westermarck, *The Future of Marriage in Western Civilization,* 1970, Books for Libraries Press. Reprinted by permission of Ayer Company Publishers.

Tu Fu, "The Man with No Family to Take Leave Of," from *The Columbia Book of Chinese Poetry: From Early Times to the Thirteenth Century,* trans. Burton Watson. © 1984 Columbia University Press. Reprinted by permission of the publisher.

The Seven Benedictions of Jewish Marriage, from Maurice Lamm, *The Jewish Way in Love and Marriage,* 1980, Jonathan David Publishers, www.jdbooks.com. Reprinted by permission.

Giovanni Boccaccio, *The Decameron,* trans. G. H. McWilliam (Penguin Classics 1972, Revised edition 1995), © G. H. McWilliam, 1972, 1995, pp. 431-437. Reproduced by permission of Penguin Books Ltd.

Franz Kafka, "The Judgment," from the collection published in the U.S. under the title *Franz Kafka: The Complete Stories,* edited by Nahum N. Glatzer, translated by Willa and Edwin Muir, © 1946, 1947, 1948, 1949, 1954, 1958, 1971 by Schocken Books. Used by permission of Schocken Books, a division of Random House, Inc. Published by Seckerm & Warburg in the UK under the title *The Complete Stories and Parables* by Franz Kafka. Used by permission of the Random House Group Limited.

Chapter 2

St. Augustine, "The Good of Marriage," from *Fathers of the Church Vol. #27: St. Augustine: Treatises on Marriage and Other Subjects,* trans. Charles T. Wilcox et al., © 1955 The Catholic University Press of America. Reprinted by permission.

St. Thomas Aquinas, *Summa Theologica,* complete English edition in five volumes, trans. by Fathers of the English Dominican Province (Westminster, Md.: Christian Classics, 1948).

Desiderius Erasmus, "Marriage," from *The Colloquies of Erasmus,* trans. Craig R. Thompson (Chicago: University of Chicago Press, 1965).

"An Iron Net," from the *Mahabharata,* introduced by B. A. van Nooten, illustrated by Shirley Triest, © 1973 The Regents of the University of California, published by the University of California Press. Reprinted by permission.

Isak Dinesen, from *On Modern Marriage and Other Observations,* © 1986 The Rungstedlund Foundation. Reprinted by permission of St. Martin's Press, LLC.

Chapter 3

"Book 23: The Great Rooted Bed," from *The Odyssey* by Homer, translated by Robert Fagles, © 1996 by Robert Fagles. Used by permission of Viking Penguin, a division of Penguin Putnam Inc.

Apuleius, "Cupid and Psyche," from *The Stories of the Greeks,* adapted by Rex Warner, 1967, Farrar, Straus & Giroux. Used by permission of Michigan State University Press.

Zeami Motokiyo, "Izutsu," from *The Noh Dramas,* 1955, Charles E. Tuttle Co. Used by permission of Nippon Gakujutsu Shinkokai.

William Shakespeare, *Othello,* from *The Works of Shakespeare,* ed. C. H. Herford (London: MacMillan, 1904).

Pages 9, 10-24 from *The Mystery of Love and Marriage* by Derrick Sherwin Bailey, © 1952 by Harper & Brothers. Reprinted by permission of HarperCollins Publishers, Inc., and SCM Press.

From *The Good Marriage.* © 1995 by Judith S. Wallerstein and Sandra Blakeslee.

Reprinted by permission of Ticknor & Fields/Houghton Mifflin Co. and the Carol Mann Agency. All rights reserved.

Chapter 4

Euripides, from *Medea*, in *Euripedes: Ten Plays*, ed. Moses Hadas, 1960, Bantam. Used by permission of the Estate of Moses Hadas.

"The Thirteenth Night," from *In the Shade of Spring Leaves: The Life of Higuchi Ichiyo With Nine of Her Best Short Stories* by Higuchi Ichiyo, translated by Robert Lyons Danley. © 1981 by Robert Lyons Danley. Used by permission of W. W. Norton & Company, Inc.

Elizabeth von Arnim, from *Love*, 1988, Washington Square Press. Used by permission of Little Brown, UK.

"A Jew Discovered," from *The Color of Water* by James McBride, © 1996 by James McBride. Used by permission of Riverhead Books, a division of Penguin Putnam, Inc.

Chapter 5

Aristotle, from *Politics*, trans. Carnes Lord, 1984, The University of Chicago Press. Used by permission.

Hsü Chün Ch'ien, "Beginning of Spring — A Stroll with My Wife," from *The Columbia Book of Chinese Poetry: From Early Times to the Thirteenth Century*, trans. Burton Watson. © 1984 Columbia University Press. Reprinted by permission of the publisher.

Jane Austen, *Pride and Prejudice* (New York: The Modern Library, 1995).

John Milton, *Paradise Lost*, ed. Christopher Ricks (New York: The Signet Classic Poetry Series, 1968).

Bronislaw Malinowski, "Marriage." Reprinted with permission from the Encyclopædia Britannica, 14th Edition, © 1948 by Encyclopædia Britannica, Inc.

Chapter 6

Geoffrey Chaucer, "The Wife of Bath," in *Canterbury Tales*, ed. A. Kent Hieatt and Constance Hieatt (New York: Bantam, 1964).

"The Man Makes and the Woman Takes," pages 49-54 from *Mules and Men* by

Zora Neale Hurston. © 1935 by Zora Neale Hurston. Copyright renewed 1963 by John C. Hurston and Joel Hurston. Reprinted by permission of HarperCollins Publishers, Inc.

William Shakespeare, *The Taming of the Shrew*, ed. C. H. Herford (London: MacMillan, 1904).

J. S. Mill, *On the Subjection of Women* (Greenwich, Conn.: Fawcett Publications, 1971).

George Bernard Shaw, from *Getting Married*, ed. Dan H. Laurence, 1986, Penguin Books. Used by permission of The Society of Authors, on behalf of the Bernard Shaw Estate.

Francesca M. Cancian, "Gender Politics: Love and Power in the Private and Public Spheres." Reprinted with permission from Alice S. Rossi, editor, *Gender and the Life Course* (New York: Aldine de Gruyter). © 1985 American Sociological Association.

Chapter 7

Ts'ao Chih, "The Forsaken Wife," from *The Columbia Book of Chinese Poetry: From Early Times to the Thirteenth Century*, trans. Burton Watson. © 1984 Columbia University Press. Reprinted by permission of the publisher.

Martin Luther, "The Estate of Marriage." Reprinted from *Luther's Works Vol. 45*, edited by Walther L. Brandt, © 1962 Fortress Press. Used by permission of Augsburg Fortress.

From *Anna Karenina* by Leo Tolstoy, translated by David Magarshack, © 1961, renewed 1989 by David Magarshack. Used by permission of Dutton Signet, a division of Penguin Putnam Inc.

Excerpts from *To the Lighthouse* by Virginia Woolf, © 1927 by Harcourt, Inc. and renewed 1954 by Leonard Woolf, reprinted by permission of Harcourt, Inc. and The Society of Authors as the Literary Representative of the Estate of Virginia Woolf.

Chapter 8

Joseph E. Kerns, "For Better, for Worse," from *The Theology of Marriage*, 1964, Sheed & Ward. Reprinted by permission of Sheed & Ward, an Apostolate of the Priests of the Sacred Heart, 7373 South Lover's Lane Road, Franklin, WI 53132.

Martin Luther, "On Questions of Marriage and Sex: To Stephen Roth," from *Let-*

ters of Spiritual Counsel, ed. Theodore G. Tappert. Philadelphia: Westminster/John Knox Press, 1955. Used by permission.

George Eliot, *Daniel Deronda* (Harmondsworth: Penguin, 1995).

Excerpt from *Who's Afraid of Virginia Woolf?* by Edward Albee. © 1962 Edward Albee, reprinted with the permission of Scribner, a Division of Simon & Schuster, and William Morris Agency.

"Your Beloved Foe," from *Love and Marriage* by Bill Cosby, © 1989 by Bill Cosby. Used by permission of Doubleday, a division of Random House, Inc.

From *The Seven Principles for Making Marriage Work* by John M. Gottman and Nan Silver. © 1999 by John Mordechai Gottman and Nan Silver. Reprinted by permission of Crown Publishers, a division of Random House, Inc., and Weidenfeld & Nicolson.

Chapter 9

From *Summa contra Gentiles, Book Four: Salvation* by St. Thomas Aquinas, translated by Charles J. O'Neill. Translation © 1957 by Charles O'Neill. Used by permission of Doubleday, a division of Random House, Inc.

Martin Bucer, *De Regno Christi,* as translated by John Milton in "The Judgement of Martin Bucer," *Complete Prose Works of John Milton, Volume II: 1643-1648* (New Haven: Yale University Press, 1959).

From *The Koran,* translated by N. J. Dawood (Penguin Classics 1956, Fifth Revised Edition, 1990) © N. J. Dawood, 1956, 1959, 1966, 1968, 1974, 1990, 1993, 1994, 1995. Used by permission.

From *The Code of Maimonides Book Four — The Book of Women,* 1972, Yale University Press. Used by permission of the publisher.

"Old Poem," from *The Columbia Book of Chinese Poetry: From Early Times to the Thirteenth Century,* trans. Burton Watson, © 1984 Columbia University Press. Reprinted by permission of the publisher.

Prologue to the "Lady Yu-Nu: A Beggar Chief's Daughter," from *A Treasury of Chinese Literature,* tr./ed. Ch'u Chai & Winberg Chai, 1965, Appleton-Century. Used by permission of Winberg Chai.

John Locke, *Two Treatises on Government,* Book 2 (London: George Routledge and Sons, 1884).

From *Marriage and Morals* by Bertrand Russell. © 1929 by Horace Liveright, Inc., renewed 1957 by Bertrand Russell. Used by permission of Liveright Publishing Corporation, Routledge, and The Bertrand Russell Peace Foundation.

From *The Unexpected Legacy of Divorce: A 25 Year Landmark Study,* by Judith

Wallerstein, Julia M. Lewis and Sandra Blakeslee. © 2000 by Judith Wallerstein, Julia M. Lewis and Sandra Blakeslee. Reprinted by permission of the Carol Mann Agency and Hyperion.

Chapter 10

Love and Other Infectious Diseases, by Molly Haskell. © 1990 by Molly Haskell. Reprinted by permission of Georges Borchardt, Inc., for the author.

From *Vital Involvement in Old Age: The Experience of Old Age in Our Time* by Erik H. Erikson, Joan M. Erikson, and Helen Q. Kivnick. © 1986 by Joan M. Erikson, Erik H. Erikson, and Helen Q. Kivnick. Used by permission of W. W. Norton & Company, Inc.

From *Elegy for Iris* by John Bayley, © 1999 by John Bayley. Originally published in *The New Yorker.* Reprinted by permission of St. Martin's Press, LLC, and Gerald Duckworth & Co. Ltd.

From *Love in the Time of Cholera* by Gabriel García Márquez, trans. Edith Grossman, © 1988 Alfred A. Knopf Inc. Reprinted by permission of Alfred A. Knopf, a Division of Random House Inc.

Euripides, from *Alcestis,* in *Euripides: Ten Plays,* ed. Moses Hadas, 1960, Bantam. Used by permission of the Estate of Moses Hadas.

From *Man's Search for Meaning* by Viktor E. Frankl, © 1959, 1962, 1984, 1992 by Viktor E. Frankl. Reprinted by permission of Beacon Press, Boston.